JOHN SKYLI[TZES]

A synopsis [of histories]

John Skylitzes' extraordinary Middle Byzantine chronicle covers the reigns of the Byzantine emperors from the death of Nicephorus I in 811 to the deposition of Michael VI in 1057, and provides the only surviving continuous narrative of the late tenth and early eleventh centuries. A high official living in the late eleventh century, Skylitzes used a number of existing Greek histories (some of them no longer extant) to create a digest of the previous three centuries. It is without question the major historical source for the period, cited constantly in modern scholarship, and has never before been available in English. This edition features introductions by Jean-Claude Cheynet and Bernard Flusin, along with extensive notes by Cheynet. It will be an essential and exciting addition to the libraries of all historians of the Byzantine age.

JOHN WORTLEY is Professor of History Emeritus at the University of Manitoba. He has published widely on the Byzantine era, and completed several translations to date, including *Les Récits édifiants de Paul, évêque de Monembasie, et d'autres auteurs* (1987), *The 'Spiritual Meadow' of John Moschos, including the additional tales edited by Nissen and Mioni* (1992), *The spiritually beneficial tales of Paul, Bishop of Monembasia and of other authors* (1996) and *John Skylitzes: A Synopsis of Histories (AD 811–1057)*, a provisional translation published in 2000.

JOHN SKYLITZES
A Synopsis of Byzantine History, 811–1057

INTRODUCTION, TEXT AND NOTES
TRANSLATED BY
JOHN WORTLEY

CAMBRIDGE
UNIVERSITY PRESS

CAMBRIDGE UNIVERSITY PRESS
Cambridge, New York, Melbourne, Madrid, Cape Town,
Singapore, São Paulo, Delhi, Tokyo, Mexico City

Cambridge University Press
The Edinburgh Building, Cambridge CB2 8RU, UK

Published in the United States of America by Cambridge University Press, New York

www.cambridge.org
Information on this title: www.cambridge.org/9781107404748

© John Wortley 2010

This publication is in copyright. Subject to statutory exception
and to the provisions of relevant collective licensing agreements,
no reproduction of any part may take place without the written
permission of Cambridge University Press.

First published 2010
3rd printing 2011
First paperback edition 2011

A catalogue record for this publication is available from the British Library

Library of Congress Cataloguing in Publication Data
Scylitzes, John, fl. 1081.
[Synopsis historiarum. English]
A synopsis of Byzantine history, 811–1057 / John Skylitzes ;
translated by John Wortley.
p. cm.
Includes bibliographical references and index.
ISBN 978-0-521-76705-7 (hbk.)
1. Byzantine Empire–History–527–1081–Early works to 1800. I. Title.
DF553.S36 2010
949.5′02–dc22
2010007557

ISBN 978-0-521-76705-7 Hardback
ISBN 978-1-107-40474-8 Paperback

Cambridge University Press has no responsibility for the persistence or
accuracy of URLs for external or third-party internet websites referred to in
this publication, and does not guarantee that any content on such websites is,
or will remain, accurate or appropriate.

Contents

The English translator's Preface		*page* vii
Introduction: John Skylitzes, the author and his family by *Jean-Claude Cheynet*		ix
Re-writing history: John Skylitzes' *Synopsis historion* by *Bernard Flusin*		xii

John Skylitzes, *Synopsis*
Foreword 1

1.	Michael I Rangabe, the Kouropalates [811–813]	4
2.	Leo V the Armenian [813–820]	15
3.	Michael II the Stammerer [820–829]	27
4.	Theophilos [829–842]	51
5.	Michael III, the son of Theophilos [842–867], and his mother Theodora [842–862]	82
6.	Basil I Kephalas, the Macedonian [867–886]	116
7.	Leo VI the Philosopher (the Wise) [886–912]	165
8.	Alexander [912–913]	188
9.	Constantine VII, Porphyrogennetos [913–959]	191
10.	Romanos I Lekapenos [919–944]	206
11.	Constantine VII [944–959]	225
12.	Romanos II the Younger [959–963]	239
13.	Basil II Bulgaroktonos and Constantine VIII [976–1025]	245

14.	Nikephoros II Phokas [963–969]	250
15.	John I Tzimiskes [969–976]	271
16.	Basil II and Constantine VIII *bis* [976–1025]	298
17.	Constantine VIII [1025–1028]	349
18.	Romanos III Argyros [1028–1034]	354
19.	Michael IV the Paphlagonian [1034–1041]	370
20.	Michael V Kalaphates [1041–1042]	391
21.	Constantine IX Monomachos [1042–1055]	397
22.	Theodora [1055–1056]	447
23.	Michael VI the Elder/Stratiotikos [1056–1057]	449

Glossary 466
Bibliography 475
Index 484

The English translator's Preface

It would be unfortunate if the extraordinary process by which this translation came into being were not noted. A critical edition of Skylitzes' text appeared in 1973, a German translation of the first half of the text shortly after (the second half seems never to have seen the light of day), both the work of Hans Thurn. Thus, since not everybody can read German and even fewer the rather convoluted kind of Greek found in the *Synopsis,* Skylitzes' has literally remained a closed book for many readers. This is unfortunate for, although it is far from being an original work (in fact it consists almost entirely of other men's words), it not only preserves extracts from some sources which have survived in no other form; it also constitutes the unique source for some periods of the Byzantine experience. It was therefore particularly regrettable that this text remained virtually inaccessible to many readers. When therefore the present writer learnt that his Parisian colleagues Bernard Flusin and Jean-Claude Cheynet were proposing to make the work available in French, he suggested to them (and they agreed) that it should be published in English too. A cooperative plan was evolved: it was proposed that Wortley and Flusin should each translate into his own language, then exchange versions, chapter by chapter, so that each could use the other's work to control his own. Meanwhile Cheynet was to produce footnotes for the French edition which would in due course be translated by Wortley for the English publication. Nineteen years after the original agreement was made, all this has finally been accomplished. Since the French translation appeared (in 2003) other works have been published; these have been duly noted by M. Cheynet in the revised footnotes and bibliography that accompany this volume.

The English translator wishes gratefully to acknowledge the unfailing courtesy and kindness of Bernard Flusin and Jean-Claude Cheynet, without whose splendid efforts and patience this work could never have been realised. He also wishes to acknowledge and thank others who from time to time have generously offered helping hands, most especially: Margaret Mullett, Catherine McColgan and Robert Jordan in Belfast, Catherine Holmes in Oxford, Rory Egan in Manitoba.

One pondered long and carefully about what to call this book. John Skylitzes described his work simply as 'a synopsis of histories'. By this he meant a digest of a number of historical writings he had to hand (see his *Proimion*, page 1 below) but it seemed that 'a synopsis of histories' would be very puzzling to many a modern reader. Therefore, after much deliberation, *A Synopsis of Byzantine History, 811–1057* was finally selected as an adequate title. It was chosen because it has the triple advantage of being totally comprehensible to the modern reader and of accurately describing the contents of the book, while retaining at least an echo of the original title by retaining the word *synopsis*.

The numbers in square brackets in the text indicate the pages in Thurn's Greek text.

Introduction: John Skylitzes, the author and his family

Jean-Claude Cheynet

What little information exists concerning the author of the *Synopsis historion* is all found either in the manuscripts of that work itself or in a few archival documents.[1] He was known by two names: Skylitzes and Thrakesios. There is no doubt that these refer to the same person because the twelfth-century historian John Zonaras, narrating the abdication of Isaac Komnenos (AD 1059) in his *Epitome historion*, makes reference to a passage in which John Thrakesios describes the awesome vision which persuaded that emperor to step down.[2] His near contemporary George Kedrenos also makes reference to the earlier synopsist in his own *Synopsis* (in which he slavishly follows Skylitzes' account), calling him the protovestiarios John Thrakesios. This name is clearly a reference to the place from which he (or his parents) came: the Thrakesion theme in western Asia Minor.[3]

John Skylitzes is mentioned in certain legal documents dated 1090 and 1092 as droungarios of the watch (*tes biglas*), a title which at that time designated the principal magistrate of the main judicial tribunal of Constantinople. In 1091[4] Skylitzes petitioned Alexios Komnenos for elucidation of the *novel* (new law) concerning betrothals, to which he received a reply from the emperor in the following year.[5] In addition to his appointment as grand droungarios, John also held the post of eparch of Constantinople with the title of proedros. Werner Seibt thinks this was too lowly a title for

---

[1] There is a short study of this person by W. Seibt, 'Ioannes Skylitzes. Zur Person des Chronisten', *JÖB*, 25 (1976), 81–5.

[2] John Zonaras III, *Ioannis Zonorae epitomae historiarum*, ed. M. Pinder (CSHB, Bonn, 1897), 18.6.5, 673:4–18.

[3] His contemporary, Michael Attaleiates, also bore the name of his place of origin: the city of Attaleia, now Antalya. Had either of them hailed from Thrace (rather than the Thrakesion theme) the appropriate epithet would have been *Thrax* (Thracian), not Thrakesios.

[4] The date of this act has been commented on at length. It was finally established by P. Wirth: *Regesten der Kaiserkunden des oströmischen Reiches*, II, *Regesten von 1025–1204*, ed. F. Dölger and P. Wirth (Munich, 1995), 1162a.

[5] A. E. Laiou, *Mariage, amour et parenté à Byzance aux XIe–XIIIe siècles* (Paris, 1992), 36.

such a senior officer at that time. Assuming that a scribe had mistakenly omitted a syllable,[6] he proposes to amend it to read protoproedros, and in fact two years later we find John addressed as kouropalates when he received from Alexios Komnenos the solution [*lysis*] to a problem he had raised some months earlier concerning the impediments to marriage.[7] As Seibt has convincingly demonstrated, Skylitzes could not have exercised the office of protovestiarios; this is probably a misreading of an abbreviated form indicating the rank of protovestes, even of protovestarches.[8]

Briefly: it appears that John Skylitzes (born before 1050) followed a career in the judiciary which led to the highest positions under Alexios Komnenos. He may have survived into the first decade of the twelfth century, or even a little later. It is possible that he was also the author of the work known as *Skylitzes Continuatus* of John Skylitzes.[9] Nothing is known of his social background; he appears to be the first person bearing that surname to have risen so high in the civil service. As in the case of Michael Psellos and Michael Attaleiates before him, a good education was probably what brought about his social advancement, which it was certainly capable of doing in the eleventh century. John's contemporary, Basil Skylitzes, attained the by no means insignificant dignity of proedros. But it was in the following century that the Skylitzes family fortunes achieved their apogee. That was when members of the clan acquired numerous civil and ecclesiastical appointments in the way that was usual at that time for men of learning. We can reconstruct the career of Stephen Skylitzes, metropolitan of Trebizond (who reorganised the church there in the time of John II) from a lament by Prodromos.[10] Stephen's brother was the director of St Paul's school. George Skylitzes, who was the next generation after Stephen, first served under Manuel Komnenos, participating in the synod of 1166 as protokouropalates and grammatikos (secretary) to the emperor.[11] Subsequently, under Andronikos Komnenos, he became protoasekretes,[12]

---

[6] Seibt, 'Ioannes Skylitzes', 82. The scribe would have simplified the already abbreviated form of the title by reducing *(proto)(pro)edros* to *(pro)edros*.
[7] Dölger and Wirth, *Regesten*, 1167; see the comments of Laiou, *Mariage*, 30.
[8] Seibt, 'Ioannes Skylitzes', 83–4.
[9] *He synecheia tes chronographias tou Ioannou Skylitze*, ed. E. T. Tsolakes (Thessalonike, 1968), 76–99. Tsolakes believes this to be the work of Skylitzes, others disagree.
[10] R. Browning, 'The Patriarchal School at Constantinople in the twelfth century', *B*, 32 (1962), 175–6, repr. R. Browning, *Studies in Byzantine history, literature and education* (London, 1977), x.
[11] *PG*, 140, 253.
[12] J. A. van Dieten, *Nicetae Choniatae Orationes et Epistulae* (CFHB, 3, Berlin and New York, 1972), 335. Many of his seals of have survived, one of which has the rare distinction of portraying St George on horseback: Fogg Art 5 Museum no. 573. Another seal reveals that George became *sebastos*: *SBS*, 3 207.

head of chancellery. A man of great learning, George was the author of poems, theological works, canons and of a *Life of John of Rila*, the Bulgar saint.[13] His wife, Anna Eugeniotissa, also pertained to the highest ranks of the civil service.[14] The Skylitzai did not disappear after the turmoil of 1204, for a Theodore Skylitzes was an officer of the treasury at Mourmounta (the region of Miletos) in 1263, in the service of the panhypersebastos George Zagarommates.[15] The last members of the family known in the time of the Palaiologoi did not play any role of great importance.[16]

[13] *ODB* II, 913–14.
[14] S. Lampros, 'Ho Markianos kodix 524', *Neon Hellenomnemon*, 8 (1911), 249.
[15] *PLP*, ed. E. Trapp and H.-V. Beyer (Vienna, 1976–96), no. 26234
[16] *PLP*, ed. Trapp and Beyer, nos 26232–26236

Re-writing history: John Skylitzes' Synopsis historion

Bernard Flusin

John Skylitzes' *Synopsis historion* was written during the reign of Alexios Komnenos (1081–1118), almost certainly towards the end of the eleventh century.[1] It purports to cover the years 811 to 1057: from the death of Nikephoros I to the abdication of Michael VI. From the mid-tenth century onwards it provides a source of major importance for some periods of Byzantine history, an outstanding example being the long reign of Basil II.[2] It also constitutes an important element in the historiography of Byzantium. Its title reveals the nature of the work: *Synopsis of histories*, meaning a comprehensive digest of historical works already in existence. The author makes no claim to be dealing for the first time with hitherto neglected material, nor does he endeavour to rework in his own way the research which others have already conducted. His task is rather to rewrite the works of his predecessors, combining, harmonising and abridging them. The *Synopsis* is a second-hand work, the work of an author who views history as a literary genre, and of a historian who creates a text on the basis of other histories. The prooimion to the *Synopsis* contains valuable

---

[1] The first edition of the *Synopsis historion* appeared in 1973: *Ioannis Scylitzae Synopsis historion*, editio princeps, ed. I. Thurn (CFHB, 5, Berlin and New York, 1973). See the comments of G. Fatouros, 'Textkritische Beobachtungen zu Ioannes Skylitzes', *JÖB*, 24 (1975), 91–4. Prior to 1973 Skylitzes' text could be read in the George Kedrenos, *Compendium historiarum*, ed. I. Bekker, 2 vols. (CSHB, Bonn, 1838), of which it forms an integral part. On the continuation of Skylitzes covering the years 1057–79 (almost certainly the work of Skylitzes himself) see below, p. 23. For a general study of the author and his work: G. Moravcsik, *Byzantinoturcica*, I, *Die byzantinischen Quellen der Geschichte der Türkvölker* (Berlin, 1958), 335–40; H. Hunger, *Die hochsprachliche profane Literatur der Byzantiner* (Munich, 1978), I, 389–93 (Greek tr. Athens, 1992), 210–16. Contrary to the opinion of this author, we do not think Skylitzes addressed himself to a wide audience: 'Skylitzes could only partially fulfil the promises made in his prologue. This can be excused if we bear in mind that, in common with the other chroniclers, he was writing for a wide public, hence he could not escape the general trend in less serious literature', Hunger, *Literatur der Byzantiner*, 212 in the Greek translation. Neither the continuators of Theophanes nor Skylitzes are in the business of writing popular literature and their work is not to be included under the heading of 'less serious literature'. It is intended for court circles and the upper echelons of the administration, the circles in which those authors lived and moved.

[2] See C. Holmes, *Basil II and the Gouvernance of Empire (976–1025)* (Oxford, 2005).

indications of how we are to understand the nature of this undertaking; these must be investigated wherever it is possible to check them by studying the ways in which Skylitzes handled his sources.

THE PROLOGUE (PROOIMION)

The prooimion of the *Synopsis historion*[3] is a statement of capital importance in Byzantine historical literature; it has frequently been discussed because it contains the names of certain historians whose works have not survived.[4] Its importance for us here lies in the fact that in this statement Skylitzes defines the project he is undertaking. First he defines it in a very positive fashion by placing it under the patronage of two authors whose sanctity and excellence he reveres: George the synkellos and Theophanes. Then he defines it in a somewhat negative way by identifying certain historical works of which he is critical. Hence the genre in which Skylitzes intends to operate is not history in the strict sense of the word, but historical digest (*epitome historias*), the genre of George and Theophanes (themselves following in the steps of some older writers of whom our author says nothing, but whom he must not pass over in silence). The works of his two model writers are extant.[5] They represent, to quote Cyril Mango, 'the most ambitious effort ever made by Byzantine historiography to provide a systematic account of what has befallen humanity'.[6] As Skylitzes says, one of them covers the period from the creation of the world to the accession of Diocletian; the other from then to the coronation of Leo V (not merely 'until the death of Nikephoros the former genikos'). Thus both the *Synopsis* and Theophanes' narrative (of which the former is the continuation) record the reign of Michael I Rangabe.[7] The affinity between the

---

[3] Skylitzes, *Synopsis historion*, ed. Thurn, 3–4.
[4] See (esp.) *Théodore Daphnopatès. Correspondence*, ed. J. Darrouzès and L. G. Westerink (Paris, 1978), 6–7; I Grigoriadis, 'A study of the prooimion of Zonaras' chronicle in relation to the other twelfth-century prooimia', *BZ*, 91 (1998), 327–44, at 338–9; A. Markopoulos, 'Byzantine history writing at the end of the first millennium', *Byzantium in the year 1000*, ed. P. Magdalino (The Medieval Mediterranean, 45, Leiden and Boston, 2003), 192–3.
[5] *Georgii Syncelli Ecloga Chronographica*, ed. A. A. Mosshammer (Leipzig, 1984), tr. W. Adler and P. Tuffin, *The Chronography of George Synkellos: a Byzantine chronicle of universal history from the creation* (Oxford, 2002); Theophanes, *Chronographia*, ed. C. de Boor, 2 vols. (Leipzig, 1883–5), tr. C. Mango and R. Scott, *The Chronicle of Theophanes Confessor, Byzantine and Near Eastern History ad 284–813* (Oxford, 1997).
[6] *Chronicle of Theophanes Confessor*, ed. Mango and Scott, lii.
[7] The discrepancy between the true ending of Theophanes' *Chronographia* and the ending alleged by Skylitzes may simply mean that the latter was speaking in general terms. Another possibility is that, because Theophanes wrote before Leo V openly declared himself in favour of iconoclasm, he portrayed that emperor in more favourable colours than Skylitzes was prepared to endorse.

Chronographia of Theophanes Confessor and the *Ekloge chronographias* of George the synkellos is very close because, when he was dying in 810, George requested Theophanes to continue the work that he was leaving unfinished, bequeathing the material he had collected to his friend.[8] Although Theophanes' *Chronographia* (completed before 814)[9] was the sequel to George's work, there are clearly discernible differences between the two. While chronology occupies an important position in both of them, the computation of George the synkellos (derived from a tradition which goes back to Eusebius of Caesarea) is the more scholarly. Yet throughout his *Chronographia* Theophanes, for his part, regularly sets down the year of creation (*anno mundi*), the year of the incarnation (*anno domini*), the indiction, the regnal years of the emperor and of the Sassanid ruler (of the caliph later on), to which he adds the pontifical year of the patriarchs. There is, however, little trace of this chronological aspect of the work of his predecessors in Skylitzes. Sometimes he states the indiction or the year of creation, but there is nothing systematic about the way he does it. This is an important difference, but it is not an innovation on Skylitzes' part. Already in the ninth century Byzantine historiography had left behind the chronological apparatus found in some late antique writers. Indeed from this point of view George the synkellos was already a man of the past.[10] There are, however, other indications that Skylitzes stood in succession to Theophanes, above all the way in which he worked, rifling the available historical texts with the intention of providing a digest of them. Theophanes declares that, in addition to the material bequeathed to him by George the synkellos, he has worked through the history books and made a selection of what they had to offer.[11] In the past, when George the synkellos claimed that he had made an abridgement of his sources, he also employed the same term (*synopsis*)[12] that Skylitzes was to use to

---

Genesios likewise began his *History of the Reigns* with the second year of Michael I: *Iosephi Genesii Regnum libri quattuor*, ed. A. Lesmüller-Werner and J. Thurn (CFHB, 14, Berlin and New York, 1978), 3.

[8] *Chronicle of Theophanes Confessor*, ed. Mango and Scott, lv.
[9] *Chronicle of Theophanes Confessor*, ed. Mango and Scott, lvii.
[10] *Chronicle of Theophanes Confessor*, ed. Mango and Scott, lii. Neither Joseph Genesios nor the continuators of Theophanes in the tenth century made any effort to establish a systematic chronology.
[11] Theophanes, *Chronographia*, ed. de Boor, 1:4; tr. *Chronicle of Theophanes Confessor*, ed. Mango and Scott, 2
[12] 'I have noted this in brief [ἐν συντόμῳ] in the so-called *Life of Adam* ... on the basis of other *Origins*, of the Scriptures inspired by God and of the best known historical records which succeeded them. It is from those sources that I have gleaned most of the events described (with the exception of a few events that have taken place in our own times), events of which I will attempt to make a *synopsis*', George Synkellos, ed. Mosshammer, 5–6.

describe his own work. There is the matter of style too: 'simple, unaffected language, touching exclusively on the substance of the events which had taken place', meaning narrative written so that it might be clearly understood. On this point 'chronography' is to be distinguished from sophisticated history, whose rhetorical pretensions march off in a different direction. Of course Skylitzes is not content merely to follow the examples of George and Theophanes. While he continues their work, it is clear that in his own eyes the *Synopsis* he is compiling is no more than a section of a chronography which others had begun; a chronography that started with the creation of the world and that others in turn will carry forward.

The idea of continuing the work of Theophanes was not a new one in the eleventh century nor was it the exclusive property of Skylitzes. He was well aware that during the period covering almost three centuries between the reign of Leo V and his own time there were those who had preceded him. He knew of them, but considered them unsatisfactory. We can follow in his footsteps by dividing these predecessors into two groups, the first of which would include 'Sikeleiotes grammatikos' (meaning Theognostos),[13] Psellos and 'some others', who remain anonymous. Now the two names just mentioned are not names one would have expected. Theognostos' work, dating probably from 820–30, is lost to us. We only know of it because the so-called 'continuators of Theophanes'[14] made use of it to report an event which occurred in Sicily (the passage is found in Skylitzes too).[15] It is even more surprising to find Michael Psellos in this context. The *Chronographia*, so brilliant and personal, which we owe to this author, has none of the dryness for which he is reproved.[16] The solution could be that it is to another work of Psellos that reference is made here, his *Historia syntomos* (Short History), which better fits the description

---

[13] For Markopoulos, 'Byzantine history writing', 193, 'Sikeliotes *didaskalos* is surely a phantom', yet it appears that he can now be definitively identified. On Theognostos, author of a treaty on orthography and also of a history (now lost) that was a source used by the continuators of Theophanes: Hunger, *Literatur der Byzantiner*, I, 340, Greek tr., II, 144.

[14] *Scriptores post Theophanem*, ed. I Bekker (CSHB, Bonn, 1838), 1–1481. See Hunger, *Literatur der Byzantiner*, I, 339–43, Greek tr., II, 143–8.

[15] The event is the attempted usurpation of Euphemios in Sicily in the reign of Michael II: *Theophanes Continuatus*, ed. I. Bekker (CSHB, Bonn, 1838), 81–3 (Theognostos is identified as the source of this information, 82, lines 17–20); Skylitzes, *Synopsis historion*, ed. Thurn, Michael II, ch. 20, 45–6. On this episode, its date and the account of Theognostos, see M. Nichanian,V. Prigent, "Les stratèges de Sicile. De la naissance du thème au règne de Léon V", *REB* 61 (2003) 97–141, especially 129–30 and note 229.

[16] Michel Psellos, *Chronographie ou histoire d'un siècle de Byzance (976–1077)*, ed. tr. E. Renauld, 2 vols. (Paris, 1920); *Fourteen Byzantine rulers: the Chronographia of Michael Psellus*, tr. E. R. A. Sewter (London and Newhaven, CT, 1953); *Michele Psello. Imperatori di Bisanzio (Cronografia)*, ed. S. Impellizzeri, U. Criscuolo, tr. S. Ronchey, 2 vols., (Fondazione Valla, 1984)

given of it in Skylitzes' prologue.[17] So far as Skylitzes is concerned, these bumbling continuators of Theophanes have done little more than set out lists of emperors, either omitting the most important events or distorting those they include. Brutal criticism! Nor is the second group of authors – ten in all – spared, though we are in no position to appreciate the validity of the charges made by Skylitzes against them as six of the ten are scarcely more than names for us today.[18] The works of two of those writers are still extant. *Reigns* (*Peri basileion*), composed by Joseph Genesios at the command of Constantine VII Porphyrogennetos,[19] can indeed be considered as a continuation of Theophanes as far as it goes, for it commences where Theophanes left off. The *History* (*Historia*) of Leo the Deacon (or Leo of Asia, as Skylitzes calls him) was written at the end of the tenth century. It covers the reigns of Nikephoros Phokas and John Tzimiskes.[20] The two remaining names are problematic. Theodore Daphnopates is a known writer of the reign of Constantine VII, but we possess no historical writing under his name. It is possible that a part of the sixth book of *Theophanes Continuatus* is to be attributed to him: this matter is still under discussion.[21] A similar problem arises in the case of Niketas the Paphlagonian,

---

[17] The specialists, however, are still discussing this point. J. N. Ljubarskij, *Mihail Psell. Lichnosti'tvortchestyo* (Moscow, 1978), 177, sees the then unedited *Historia syntomos* of Psellos as the work of that author which Skylitzes criticises, and his opinion is shared by K. Snipes, 'A newly discovered history of the Roman emperors by Michael Psellos', *XVI. Internat. Byzantinistenkongress. Akten* II/3, = *JÖB*, 32/33 (1982), 53–61, esp. 55. The first editor of the work in question, W. J. Aerts, challenges this opinion. For him the criticisms of Skylitzes are inappropriate to Psellos and in any case it is by no means certain that Psellos is the author of the *Historia syntomos*; Aerts even tries to attribute it to the other writer mentioned by Skylitzes in this passage of the prooimion, the 'schoolmaster of Sicily': *Michaelis Pselli Historia Syntomos. Editio princeps*, ed. tr. and commentary W. J. Aerts (CFHB, 30, Berlin and New York, 1990), X–XIII. While Aerts' arguments are less than convincing, he has nevertheless cast serious doubts on the attribution of the *Historia syntomos* to Psellos.

[18] These are: Manuel of Byzantium, the author of a work dealing with John Kourkouas; a Phrygian known as Nikephoros the Deacon; three bishops, Theodore of Side, Theodore of Sebastaea and Demetrios of Kyzikos, and the monk John the Lydian, not to be confused with the sixth-century writer of that name. See below on Theodore of Sabastaea.

[19] In his prologue, Genesios, ed. Lesmüller-Werner and Thurn, 3, Genesios claims to have written at the command of Constantine VII: 'It was from the emperor Constantine who by nature and by choice loves that which is good, the most learned of emperors who ever existed, son of the most wise Leo, that sovereign of eternal memory, that I received the command to secure in writing the events that had taken place in and since the reign of Leo [V] the Amalekite (whose godlessness sated his soul), and that had not yet been collected into a history book.'

[20] Leo the Deacon, *Leonis Diaconi Caloënsis historiae libri decem*, ed. C. B. Hase (CSHB, Bonn, 1828)

[21] Hunger, *Literatur der Byzantiner*, I, 343, Greek tr., II, 147, endorses the opinion of A. Kazhdan, *Iz istorii vizantijskoj hronografii*, Xv, 19, (1961), 91–6, who thinks that the attribution of a portion of Book VI of *Theophanes Continuatus* to Daphnopates is not without foundation. The opposite opinion is expressed by A. Markopoulos, 'Théodore Daphnopates et la continuation de Théophane',

a somewhat verbose writer of the end of the ninth and the beginning of the tenth centuries: none of the writings by him which have survived is of a historical nature.[22] Some scholars have proposed to recognise as the work of Niketas mentioned in Skylitzes' prologue a *Life of the patriarch Ignatios* written at the end of the ninth century.[23] This (they say) is what he is referring to when he mentions 'a pamphlet directed against a patriarch' [*psogos patriarchou*], for it contains some violent attacks on the patriarch Photios.[24] It seems more likely though that the Prologue refers to some historical work by Niketas of which there is some evidence, and which A. Markopoulos has even suggested might be an anonymous ecclesiastical history mentioned in Codex Baroccianus graec. 142.[25]

Skylitzes levels a variety of charges against these authors, all of which boil down to their having moved too far from the spirit of George the synkellos and of Theophanes. They have concerned themselves with their own times or with the recent past (he alleges). Rather than producing the kind of 'historical digest' beloved of Skylitzes, they have played the historian and, allowing their prejudices to sway their judgement, written what from a classical point of view should be carefully differentiated: commendation [*epainos*], eulogy [*enkomion*] and censure [*psogos*]. The reader is thus plunged into confusion; not only are these historical discourses too heavy but also, given the prejudices of the writers, the facts are unreliable.

Judging by the works which have survived, Skylitzes' allegations are sometimes valid. Genesios' *Reigns* is not particularly at fault (or scarcely more so than the *Synopsis*), but the first part of the *Historia* of Leo the Deacon is frankly a eulogy for the emperor Nikephoros Phokas. This is precisely what Skylitzes wants to avoid. He wants to get back to the digest, the *synopsis*, pure and simple, along the lines laid down by George the synkellos and Theophanes the Confessor, in the true spirit of Byzantium;

JÖB, 35 (1985), 171–82. The matter is fully aired in *Théodore Daphnopatès. Correspondence*, ed. J. Darrouzès and L. G. Westerink (Paris, 1978), 6–10, where the attribution of all or part of *Theophanes Continuatus* to Daphnopates is rejected.

[22] S. A. Paschalides, Νικέτας Δαβὶδ Παφλάγων, τὸ πρόσωπο καὶ τὸ ἔργο του (Thessalonike, 1999).

[23] BHG 817, PG 105:488–574

[24] This is the opinion of R. J. H. Jenkins, 'A note on Nicetas David Paphlago and the *Vita Ignatii*', *DOP*, 19 (1965), 241–7. The text of the *Vita Ignatii (BHG 817)* is in *PG*, 105, 488–574. An unpublished dissertation by A. Smithies, 'Nicetas David Paphlago's Life of Ignatius, a critical edition and translation' (Washington, DC, 1987), proved inaccessible.

[25] A. Markopoulos, 'He chronographia tou Pseudosymeon kai hoi peges tes' (dissertation) University of Joannina, 1978, 132 and n. 48. See the contrary opinion of F. Winkelmann, 'Hat Niketas David Paphlagon ein umfassendes Geschichtswerk verfasst?', *JÖB*, 37 (1987), 137–52. The matter is all laid out in Paschalides, *Niketas Dabid Paphlagon*, 253–8.

the kind of work to which (for example) the name of Constantine Porphyrogennetos is attached[26] and of which the reader can easily grasp the meaning. But he also wants to handle his sources critically, in order to present a clearer picture of the facts; that is, by discarding anything which might have been generated by the writer's emotions and everything that smacks of the miraculous.

The modest claims made for his work by Skylitzes need not, however, be taken too seriously. For if the history is a simple digest, a mere manual to prepare the reader for more serious works, an aide-mémoire, it is also a remedy for all the pernicious elements in historiography. Skylitzes does not merely make use of the work of his predecessors: he claims to correct it.

THE SOURCES

Skylitzes names fourteen sources in his prologue; this, however, does not necessarily mean that he used all of them or that he used *only* those sources. No systematic investigation has yet been conducted into the sources of the *Synopsis*; the matter is complicated by the fact that many of the texts which were available at the end of the eleventh century have since been lost.[27] Here is a summary of what is generally admitted, with some personal remarks interspersed.

At the beginning of the *Synopsis*, for the reigns of Michael I Rangabe and Leo V the Armenian, Skylitzes used an unidentified source[28] at first (for Michael I), then he made free use of the work Joseph Genesios wrote at the command of the emperor Constantine VII Porphyrogennetos (944–59), *Reigns* (*Peri Basileion*), each of the five chapters of which is devoted to a separate emperor: Leo V, Michael II, Theophilos, Michael III and Basil I. Skylitzes was still using this source when he described the beginning of the reign of Michael III.[29]

Very soon, however, in fact from the reign of Leo V, he makes use of another source, the so-called *Theophanes Continuatus,* which rapidly gains

---

[26] In the preface to each chapter of the Constantinian *Excerpta* the compilers (who were following the instructions of Constantine VII) complain of the excessive bulk of the historical works, a defect which it was their function to correct. There is a French translation of this prologue in P. Lemerle, *Le premier humanisme byzantin* (Paris, 1971), 281–2. The editors of the *Excerpta* dealt with the overwhelming mass of their sources by extracting passages from it and arranging them in a systematic order.

[27] The remarks of F. Hirsch, *Byzantinische Studien* (Leipzig, 1876), 356–75, are basic to this question; see also Holmes, *Basil II*.

[28] See Hirsch, *Byzantinische Studien*, 362–4.

[29] On Genesios see notes and above. For Skylitzes, *Synopsis historion*, ed. Thurn, Michael III, ch. 1, 81 (107 below), the source is not the equivalent passage in *Theophanes Continuatus,* but the one

precedence to the extent that the *Synopsis* often looks like an abridgement of it. *Theophanes Continuatus* is another work composed at the instigation of Constantine VII by his collaborators, and in the case of Book V (the *Life of Basil I/Vita Basilii*) by that emperor himself using material that he had assembled.[30] *Theophanes Continuatus* consists of six books, five of which deal each with a single emperor (as in the case of Genesios), from Leo V to Basil I, while Book VI (a later composition) deals with several reigns: Leo VI, Alexander, Constantine VII with Romanos I Lekapenos, followed by the personal reigns of Constantine VII and Romanos II until 961.

The fifth book of *Theophanes Continuatus* is of particular importance, for it is a *Life of Basil* [I] written by (or – as its title suggests – composed from material assembled by) Constantine VII. Its object is to bring the character of the founder of the Macedonian dynasty, Constantine's own grandfather, to the notice of the public. Skylitzes makes massive use of *Theophanes Continuatus* right down to the end of the first part of Book VI, to the conclusion of the reign of Romanos Lekapenos. It is truly surprising that he apparently failed to mention this source, to which he owes so much, in his prologue; a source that the *Synopsis* he is writing (it too a continuation of Theophanes) so closely resembles. It is this failure that leads one to think that Theodore Daphnopates – whom Skylitzes *does* mention – could have been the author of a portion of *Theophanes Continuatus*.[31] Yet even in the part of his work under consideration it is noticeable that Skylitzes has drawn on sources other than his principal one. As noted above, the influence of Genesios can still be detected at the beginning of the reign of Michael III; after the siege of Amorion in the

---

in Genesios, which has been somewhat rewritten. Skylitzes, *Synopsis historion*, Michael III, ch. 2, 81–4, contains at least one piece of information mentioned only by him (John the Grammarian marking his backside with lead to give the impression that he had suffered a beating). In *Theophanes Continuatus* he cuts the veins of his belly; nothing resembling this is to be found in Genesios. For ch. 3, Skylitzes, *Synopsis historion*, ed. Thurn, 84–6, the same thing applies as for ch. 1. For ch. 4, Skylitzes, *Synopsis historion*, ed. Thurn, 86–8, the *Synopsis* is far removed from the text of *Theophanes Continuatus*; less remote from Genesios perhaps, but certainly re-written. It is only from ch. 5 that Skylitzes seems to rely exclusively on the continuators of Theophanes, and there are still points at which questions arise, e.g. the end of ch. 9, Skylitzes, *Synopsis historion*, ed. Thurn, 96, or in ch. 16, Skylitzes, *Synopsis historion*, ed. Thurn, 105, giving the list of professors appointed to the Magnaura by Caesar Bardas.

[30] *Theophanes Continuatus*, ed. I. Bekker (CSHB, Bonn, 1838). On the question of the authorship of the *Vita Basilii* and the doubts sometimes expressed: I. Ševčenko, 'Storia Letteraria', *La Civiltà Bizantina dal IX all'XI secolo. Aspetti e problemi* (Corsi di Studi 11, 1977, Bari, 1978), 99–101.

[31] This matter is not yet decided (cf. n. 37): see P. Frei, 'Das Geschichtswerk des Theodoros Daphnopates als Quelle der *Synopsis Historiarum* des Johannes Skylitzes' in E. Ploickinger (ed.), *Lebendige Altertumswissenschaft: Festgabe zur Vollendung des 70. Lebensjahres von Herman Vetters*, Vienna 1985, 348–53, who tries to show that the historical work of Daphnopates used by Skylitzes in not *Theophanes Continuatus*, VI.

reign of Theophilos, he seems to be using some text independent both of *Theophanes Continuatus* and of Genesios, unless (as F. Hirsch suggests) he has thoroughly re-worked those sources.[32] Then there are several events described in the reign of Romanos Lekapenos which have no parallel in the work of the other continuators (such as the stratagem by which the patriarch Tryphon was obliged to abdicate).[33] It is events such as these that made Hirsch think that Skylitzes was using some source(s) in addition to *Theophanes Continuatus*.[34]

For the personal reigns of Constantine VII and Romanos II, Skylitzes abandons the continuators of Theophanes, possibly because their work smacked too much of encomium for his liking.[35] He turns now to another source, one that is very difficult to identify. This source is critical of Constantine VII and is possibly the 'source A' which we are about to discuss. For the great warrior emperors Nikephoros Phokas and John Tzimiskes, the narrative runs more or less parallel (certainly for the reign of Phokas) to the ten books of the *Historia* which Leo the Deacon wrote before 992, covering the period from the death of Constantine VII in 959 to the death of Tzimiskes in 976. Since Skylitzes mentions Leo the Deacon (calling him 'Leo of Asia') in his prologue and since several pages of the *Synopsis* run parallel to Leo's *Historia,* the temptation is to conclude that one used the other. The work of Sjuzjumov, taken up and completed by Alexander Kazhdan, shows, however, that the situation is much more complicated than that.[36] An analysis of the *Synopsis* reveals that the author has used two different sources here, the first of which [A] is a text which is hostile to the Phokas family. Its presence can already be detected in the reign of Constantine VII, who is presented in a very inauspicious light. He is severely censured for failing to appoint adequate persons to senior posts in the government. There are criticisms of Nikephoros Phokas too, but John Tzimiskes gets off more lightly. The person whom the author of source A most favours is not an emperor at all; it is the patriarch Polyeuktos. Kazhdan thinks that this source was composed shortly before AD 1000 by somebody who had lived through the events he narrates,

---

[32] Hirsch, *Byzantinische Studien*, 369.
[33] Reign of Romanos Lakapenos, c. 26. Skylitzes, *Synopsis historion*, ed. Thurn, 226–7.
[34] Hirsch, *Byzantinische Studien*, 372–3.
[35] It is possible that Skylitzes simply did not know the second part of *Theophanes Continuatus*, VI, which was written later than the first part.
[36] A. P. Sjuszjumov, 'Ob istochnikah L'va Djakona i Skilicy', *Visantijskoe obozrenie*, 2 (1916), 106–66; A. P. Kazhdan, 'Iz istorii visantijskoj hronógrafii X. v. Istochniki l'va Diakona i Skilicy dlja istorii tret'ej chestverti X stoletija', *VV*, 20 (1961), 106–28. C. Zuckerman is warmly thanked for translating this article into French.

sometimes recording his own memories, sometimes what others were saying. The second source [B] is a very different matter. It is favourable not only to the emperor Nikephoros II, but to the entire Phokas family, from which the detailed information on Italo-Byzantine relations must have come. Source B was used by Leo the Deacon too, which explains the parallels that can be found between his work and Skylitzes'. These come to an end with the death of Nikephoros Phokas, for Skylitzes abandons source B and uses source A for the reign of John Tzimiskes. Szuzjumov (who first drew attention to the existence of source B) thought that this would have been written during the reign of Basil II, subsequent to the fall of Basil Lekapenos, the parakoimomenos; but Kazhdan thinks it should be dated prior to the assassination of Phokas in 969 since Tzimiskes, who was one of the murderers, is presented in a favourable light. J. Shepard has suggested that he also used a war journal[37] for the reign of Tzimiskes, but it is difficult to know whether this was a direct or an indirect source.

The question of the sources of the *Synopsis historion* takes on a different aspect with the beginning of the personal reign of Basil II.[38] Sometimes Skylitzes' text is unique (which gives it a special value); sometimes it runs parallel to pre-existing texts such as the *Chronographia* of Michael Psellos. But if Skylitzes knew these works, he did not make use of them and his sources are lost. Indeed, his reign of Basil II (for which he is a witness of prime importance) seems to have been inspired by a work of the Theodore of Sebasteia mentioned in the prologue, now lost.[39] As for what comes after, Jonathan Shepard has emphasised the quality of the information which Skylitzes has at his disposal on the person of Katakalon Kekaumenos, beginning in the reign of Michael IV the Paphlagonian.[40] This could indicate that he was using some work, maybe autobiographical, maybe not, which was centred on that great man. Skylitzes was able to use it right to the end of the *Synopsis*, until his narrative of the revolt of the military chiefs that terminated the reign of Michael VI the elder. As for the concluding passages of his work, the possibility should not be excluded of Skylitzes having had recourse to oral witnesses, as he says in his prologue.

---

[37] Holmes, *Basil II*, 95 and note 63.   [38] *Ibid.*, 120–70.
[39] See Hunger, *Literatur der Byzantiner*, I, 391, Greek tr., 11, 213, referring to B. Prokić, *Die Zusätze in der Handschrift des Johannes Skylitzes codex Vindobensis hist. Gr. LXXIV. Ein Beitrag zur Geschichte des sog. Wesbulgarischen Rieches* (Munich, 1906), 23. In a 12th-cent. *Traité des transferts* there is a reference to Theodore of Sabastaea 'who composed the *chronikon biblion* of Sire Basil Porphyrogenitos': J. Darrouzès, 'Le traité des transferts', *REB* 42 (1984) 181.
[40] J. Shepard, 'A suspected source of Skylitzes' *Synopsis Historion*: the great Catacalon Cecaumenos', *BGMS*, 16 (1992), 171–81; J. shepard, 'Scylitzes on Armenia in the 1040s, and the Role of Catacalon Cecaumenos', *RÉArm.*, n.s. 11 (1975–6), 269–311.

In its entirety, Skylitzes' *Synopsis* is thus dependent upon the very small number of written works which he had to hand. For the most part (insofar as it is possible to tell) he uses a main source, sometimes only a single source, such as the *Vita Basilii* or one of the other books of *Theophanes Continuatus*, so that the source text runs parallel with his and sometimes the rewriting is very slight indeed.[41] His is no 'metaphrastic version', whose author has felt obliged systematically to revise the vocabulary of the original text. Entire phrases are reproduced with some slight change in the order of words, which earned him the rather severe condemnation of Hans Thurn:

> For a long time we have made the mistake of over-estimating Skylitzes. There are long sections in which he does nothing more than paraphrase a single source; and, when he does offer some supplementary information, there is good reason to be cautious because it is by no means certain that he is making use of other sources in such places. Often all he offers is embellishment (e.g. in the description of battles) or even imagination. In this respect I totally agree with the conclusions of D. I. Polemis.[42]

This judgment is not inaccurate so far as the first part of the *Synopsis* is concerned – that is, the part which depends on the continuators of Theophanes – but it should not be applied to the complete work too hastily. There are passages in which the editing process is thorough enough to make one hesitate and ask: did Skylitzes not have some other sources at his disposal? As we have seen, at the beginning of the *Synopsis* and then, more especially, in the reign of Nikephoros Phokas, when he is using 'source A' and 'source B', he is not (or at least not always) content to base his narrative on a single source. He is not able to make simultaneous use of two sources tending in opposite directions without a certain lack of coordination. Kazhdan has succeeded in noting a number of doublets, contradictions, and even some references that appear to go nowhere.

---

[41] On the literary aspects of Skylitzes' work, see C. Holmes, 'The rhetorical structures of John Skylitzes' *Synopsis Historion*', *Rhetoric in Byzantium*, ed. E. Jeffreys (SPBS, 11, Aldershot, 2003), 187–99.
[42] H. Thurn, p. xxxiii, referring to D. I. Polemis, 'Some cases of erroneous identification in the chronicle of Skylitzes', *BS*, 26 (1965), 74–81, that examines an interesting phenomenon: in the earlier part of the *Synopsis*, down to 948, where Skylitzes is using the sources that have survived (*Theophanes Continuatus*, Genesios and 'a recension of Symeon the Logothete') there are places where he provides additional information (such as Christian names) that is not found in the texts he is using. Polemis' hypothesis is that Skylitzes is not dependent on other sources for this information, but that he has gone in search of it himself (and sometimes has got it wrong). Without examining the soundness of this hypothesis, one can say that the idea of Skylitzes having made a personal effort to complete his sources is attractive. C. Holmes (*Basil II*) tends to assign him 'an active authorial role' (p.130) but for the sections where Skylitzes' sources are lost it is always difficult to know whether one is reading a source or his own composition.

It is very difficult to tell whether Skylitzes' modifications follow a set pattern. At times there seems to be some system or a definite direction in the selections he makes from the source he is using. Thus, in the reign of Romanos Lekapenos, he has omitted the erudite digressions found in Book VI of *Theophanes Continuatus*: passages that certainly had no place in the kind of abridged history that he had in mind.[43] He has also avoided the eulogistic element that is so often to the fore in his source for this reign. Many details favourable to Kourkouas, to Theophanes the parakoimomenos and even to Romanos I himself are passed over in silence. In the reign of Basil I (where he follows the *Vita Basilii* very closely, abridging it as he goes along) there are certain omissions that also seem to be according to some plan. A number of advances made under Constantine VII are omitted, presumably because they smacked too much of eulogy.[44] So too are some other passages, possibly because they were considered too implausible, for instance the effects of the emperor's vows on the war against the Manichees.[45] Thus Skylitzes seems to have remained faithful to the principles set out in his prologue[46] and certainly not to have used his sources uncritically.

THE HISTORICAL NARRATIVE

It is not only the content of his narrative that Skylitzes borrows from his predecessors; he found a connecting thread in them (or, at least in some of them) by which the *Synopsis* is held together: it is not difficult to spot what it is. The title that Joseph Genesios set at the head of his work exactly describes what Skylitzes also wrote: a *History of the Reigns*. It begins (as the title and the opening words claim) immediately after the death of one emperor (Nikephoros I) and ends with the deposition of another one (Michael VI). At least in outward appearance it is divided into reigns of different lengths, ranging from a few pages (e.g. Michael I, Romanos II or Michael V, not to mention one of the only two empresses who ruled in their

---

[43] For an analysis of Skylitzes' treatment of the reign of Romanos I: Holmes, *Basil II*, 125–52.
[44] e.g. Basil I, chs. 29 and 38, Skylitzes, *Synopsis historion*, ed. Thurn, 151–2 and 160, *Vita Basilii*, chs. 59 and 72, where passages in praise of Basil have been omitted. On the other hand, in Basil I, ch. 26, Skylitzes, *Synopsis historion*, ed. Thurn, 145–7, Skylitzes has omitted the insulting epithets applied to Michael III in *Vita Basilii*, ch. 55.
[45] The story in the *Vita Basilii*, chs. 41–3 (CSHB), 271–6, portrays the emperor's vows as an essential cause of the imperial victory over the Manichees. It ends with the striking figure of Basil letting fly three arrows at the detached head of Chrysocheir which has been sent to him; there is nothing of this in Skylitzes: Basil I, chs. 18–19, Skylitzes, *Synopsis historion*, ed. Thurn, 135–40.
[46] For a contrary opinion, see Hirsch, *Byzantinische Studien*, 374.

own right, Theodora) to as much as forty pages: Basil II Bulgaroktonos and Constantine IX Monomachos. In this way the reigns of the emperors provide an outer framework for the *Synopsis* that actually becomes less rigid at times, for example, when a prince 'born in the purple' but too young to rule is supplanted by a successful usurper. Thus Constantine VII, who held the title of *autokrator* on the death of his father, Leo VI, was kept in the background for many years by Romanos I Lekapenos until he seized control of the government and then exercised his personal authority for some years, 944–59. The same is true of the brothers Basil II and Constantine VIII, both emperor in name, but abandoning the supreme position in the empire first to Nikephoros Phokas, then to John Tzimiskes, before reigning (theoretically) together until Constantine VIII became sole emperor on the death of his brother in 1025. The division into reigns does not interrupt the narrative; it comes as no surprise (for instance) to find the portrait of Romanos II at the beginning of the reign of Basil and Constantine.[47]

There is yet another reason for seeing the *Synopsis* as a 'history of the reigns': as the narrative proceeds, everything is organised around the ruling emperor, the *autokrator*. There is nothing, or at least hardly anything, said here about the many events which took place in detachment from the sovereign. Even natural occurrences such as comets, earthquakes, famines, the appearance of conjoined twins and so forth are interpreted as signs of divine approval or censure of this or that emperor. And because his work is organised around the emperor, Skylitzes limits himself to those parts where the emperor's writ ran. For him time is defined by the reigns, space by the extent of the empire.

Because it is divided into reigns and focused on the emperor, in common with several other Byzantine historical works, Skylitzes' *Synopsis* bears some resemblance to another literary genre well defined in rhetoric, the *basilikos logos*, 'in praise of the sovereign'. This is especially true of the *Vita Basilii* which Skylitzes did little more than abridge. But while it is appropriate to observe this resemblance to the rhetorical eulogy, it must be pointed out that at the time when Skylitzes was writing, the genres of the 'history of reigns' and of the *chronographia* were already defined; those to whom the *Synopsis* was addressed knew what to expect. It is well known that, when commanded to do so by Constantine VII, the compilers who were working at court rifled the extant corpus of historical writing to obtain selections which they then organised under fifty-two heads according

---

[47] Reign of Basil and Constantine, ch. 2, Skylitzes, *Synopsis historion*, ed. Thurn, 254.

to topic (*hypothesis*).⁴⁸ The titles of those heads are partially known; they are of interest, given the extent to which they show what categories the Romans of the tenth century devised for the various matters which they expected historians to write about. The Constantinian *Excerpta* started out with a section devoted to the proclamation of emperors, and this is indeed the first event narrated by a whole series of Byzantine historians whose attention is focused on the imperial power. Skylitzes is no exception; the beginning of the *Synopsis* is devoted to the process which brought Leo V to power rather than to the reign of Michael I; Leo's is the first reign he really deals with, from accession to death, the latter accompanied by a final assessment. And, just like the death of Michael I, the death of Leo V is at once an end and a new beginning: his assassin, Michael II, mounts his throne. Such are the events which confer on the *Synopsis* its measured pace and provide its cyclic procession: accession, first measures taken, reign, death (or, more rarely, deposition), length of the reign.

Skylitzes pays special attention to a discrete category of events to which the editors of the Constantinian *Excerpta* had also devoted a chapter (now lost) called *epiboulai*,⁴⁹ meaning attempts on the emperor's life, attempted *coups d'état* and usurpations, both abortive and successful. Thus more than half the reign of Michael II is taken up with the revolt of Thomas the Slav while the attempted usurpation of Euphemios is mentioned more than once. The entire reign of Michael VI Stratiotikos is concerned with the revolt of the eastern commanders and the rise to power of Isaac Komnenos.

After the accession comes the exercise of power. The events which Skylitzes chooses to mention fall into two categories: internal matters and foreign affairs, which in effect means Constantinople in the one case, war in the other. On the home front the question is whether an emperor was devout, just, benevolent. As the ancient opposition between church history and secular history no longer applied in the middle Byzantine period, religious affairs are included too, more frequently in the case of the iconoclastic emperors or of Michael III, but in a rather conventional way once orthodoxy was re-established. Apart from the appointment of patriarchs, foundations and bequests to the church, not much is reported. Pride of place is given to the justice, the good (or bad) administration and the

---

⁴⁸ See Lemerle, *Premier humanisme*, 283–4; B. Flusin, 'Les *Excerpta* constantiniens: logique d'une anti-histoire', *Fragments d'historiens grecs. Autour de Denys d'Halicarnasse*, ed. S. Pittia (Collection de l'Ecole française de Rome, 298, Rome, 2002), 553–8.
⁴⁹ *Peri epiboulon kata basileon gegonuion*, 'About the attempts on emperors' lives which have taken place', see Flusin, 'Les *Excerpta* constantiniens', 555.

personal behaviour of a sovereign (especially up to the reign of Romanos II); and these contribute to both the equilibrium and the interest of the *Synopsis*. In certain cases Skylitzes follows his sources in noting the buildings of an emperor, but the only emperor for whom this traditional chapter of the imperial eulogy is filled out in detail is Basil I.[50] A special place is reserved for cultural history; the author is pleased to report how a major figure such as Caesar Bardas or a sovereign like Constantine VII was able to revive learning.[51]

For Skylitzes (as for his sources) the beginnings of a reign and the appointments that went with it are an object of especial attention, indicating that this was something of great interest for Byzantine historians and their public. The end of a reign will often provide our author with the opportunity of devoting rather more attention to internal events. Yet in many of the reigns it is war (civil or foreign) that occupies centre stage.[52] Of the long reign of Basil II (for instance), the first half is taken up with the revolts of Bardas Skleros and Bardas Phokas, the second by the Bulgar campaigns. Other events are distributed between these subjects and dealt with briefly as though they were incidental. This is true whether they are struggles for power (e.g. the disgrace of the parakoimomenos Basil Lekapenos), other revolts, church affairs (the death of the patriarch Anthony and the accession of Nicholas Chrysoberges), internal matters (the introduction of the *allelengyon*), natural phenomena, rare diplomatic developments (Basil and Venice) or other campaigns (e.g. the submission of Khazaria). In the case of John Tzimiskes even more weight is given to his campaigns against the Russians and the Bulgars. The theatre of operations shifts around the total extent of the empire, from Italy in the west to the eastern frontiers, and sometimes the chronology of the narrative is slightly dislocated. The kinds of events described often remain the same: sieges, battles, defeats and victories or (the Constantinian *Excerpta* has a special chapter on this topic)[53] recoveries in the state of affairs. Sometimes there is simply a list of places conquered, including naval successes; sometimes, but less often, an ethnographic digression to introduce a new enemy.[54] It is noticeable

---

[50] Skylitzes, *Synopsis historion*, ed. Thurn, 161–4. The passages in *Theophanes Continuatus* (139–48) describing the building activity of Theophilos are not reproduced in the *Synopsis*.

[51] Skylitzes, *Synopsis historion*, ed. Thurn, 101, 237–8.

[52] This is also how Skylitzes' methods of abbreviation can lead to some unfortunate distortions: Holmes, *Basil II* 99–109.

[53] In the *Excerpta* there are separate heads for battles, leading armies, victories, defeats and defeats turned into victories, see Flusin, 'Les *Excerpta* constantiniens', 555.

[54] e.g. Reign of Constantine IX, ch. 9, Skylitzes, *Synopsis historion*, ed. Thurn, 442–5 and ch. 16, Skylitzes, *Synopsis historion*, ed. Thurn, 455–7, on the Turks and the Patzinaks.

that the exploits of a given person can hold an important place in the war stories; this advances to centre stage a character who has an important part to play (a Kekaumenos or a Maniakes), and who is often an eminent member of the Byzantine aristocracy too. This is very different from anything one might find in Theophanes, and it very probably says something about new ways of fighting. It is also symptomatic of the great interest of Skylitzes and his readers in the great families and their members.[55]

The *Synopsis historion* is not merely a linear succession of reigns; a wider, more general plan can be detected. Here too Skylitzes borrowed (for the period down to the mid-tenth century) from some of his sources: Genesios and especially *Theophanes Continuatus*. That was where he found the prophecy of the monk of Philomilion,[56] which provides the structure for the beginning of the *Synopsis* by throwing three key characters together in a dramatic encounter and proclaiming their fate: the two emperors Leo V and Michael II together with the usurper Thomas the Slav. After that, the revived iconoclasm of Leo V provides another linking element until the re-establishment of orthodoxy under Michael III, thus offering a unifying factor for several reigns. But it is above all from *Theophanes Continuatus* and the ideology which it reflects that Skylitzes borrows a huge project, the sole object of which is to enhance the dynasty of the 'Macedonian' emperors while denigrating the Amorians. There is a striking similarity between these dynasties: the one founded by Michael II and occupying the imperial throne until the death of Michael III, the other the dynasty of Basil I and his successors. Both were instituted by an assassination: Michael II killed Leo V and thus rose to power; Basil I did the same to Michael III. This similarity, however, is carefully concealed; under the orders of Constantine VII (who was only following his family's tradition), *Theophanes Continuatus* presents a totally different aspect. In a powerful narrative[57] the murder of Leo V is projected (with a wealth of attendant detail) in such a way as to emphasise the sacrilege involved ('They have slain the Lord's anointed within the sanctuary!'). The justice of Theophilos (partly hypocritical)[58] cannot wash away the indelible stain on the succession of Michael of Amorion. It is a different matter at the death of Michael III, where Basil is carefully absolved.[59] This murder is

---

[55] Sometimes Skylitzes gives new information (compared with his sources) on the names and titles of the people of whom he speaks, but caution is called for: Holmes, *Basil II*, 131ff.
[56] Skylitzes, *Synopsis historion*, ed. Thurn, 27–8.
[57] Skylitzes, *Synopsis historion*, ed. Thurn, 19–23, *Theophanes Continuatus*, ed. Bekker, 33–40.
[58] Skylitzes, *Synopsis historion*, ed Thurn, 49–50.
[59] *Theophanes Continuatus*, ed. Bekker, 254. After a long and violent indictment of Michael III, Constantine lays the murder of that prince at the door of the principal dignitaries of the Senate.

made to look like a simple blow for public safety and an act of legitimate defence. In a wider sense the entire reign of Michael III 'the drunkard' is contrived to show that emperor as a godless and unworthy prince, while the *Vita Basilii* creates an image of the ideal sovereign. Those things, moreover, which in the case of Michael II are presented as lamentable defects (the lowliness of his origins, aggravated by heresy, his rudeness and illiteracy) in Basil's case become matters for praise. Thus his modest birth is a sure indication that he will be benevolent to his people; nevertheless it is compensated for by a fictitious genealogy and by a wealth of portents indicating that he is the emperor chosen by God. Even if he soft-pedals certain details, Skylitzes faithfully reproduces his sources on all these points.[60]

After the end of the reign of Basil I the plan of the *Synopsis* is perhaps less clear, but a favourable attitude towards the Macedonians (some of whom are censured) is still perceptible even if it is only in the fact that the author seems to have intended his narrative to conclude with the end of that dynasty, Michael VI being the last emperor raised up by a Macedonian princess. More qualified approval is accorded the great warrior-emperors Nikephoros Phokas (especially) and John Tzimiskes, but the pride which Skylitzes feels in the Byzantine achievement probably reaches its apogee in the reign of Basil II, who was both the legitimate heir to the throne and sovereign warrior. Once that high point is past we have to wait until the reign of Constantine IX Monomachos to find an overall assessment of the period under review. It is alleged, possibly on the authority of a lost source, that it was with that ruler that decadence set in:

there is one thing which has to be mentioned and I will say it: that it was from the time of this emperor and on account of his prodigality and pretentiousness, that the fortunes of the Roman empire began to waste away. From that time until now it has regressed into an all-encompassing debility.[61]

The general organisation and unity of the *Synopsis* derive from this overall plan and from its unwavering commitment to the centrality of the emperor. But it is at a less elevated level that the true literary value of the work is to be found and where it really succeeds. I am referring to the many stories that are included in each reign, discrete stories of one or more episodes

---

Skylitzes says that Basil murdered Michael, but he accompanies the murder with all kinds of extenuating circumstances; Skylitzes, *Synopsis historion*, ed. Thurn, 113–14 and 131.

[60] There are some portents announcing the reign of Basil that he leaves aside, but others he retains. As for the murder of Michael, see the previous note.

[61] Reign of Constantine IX, ch. 29, Skylitzes, *Synopsis historion*, ed. Thurn, 476.

which render the work of Skylitzes so immediately appealing.[62] There is (for instance) the tragi-comic story of the assassination of Leo V on Christmas Eve, prepared for well ahead of time by the apparently irrelevant comment on his inferior musicianship.[63] Then too, interrupting the monotonous catalogue of the campaigns of Basil II, there is the tale of the confrontation of Daphnomeles and Ibatzes the Bulgar.[64] Skylitzes, however, wins very little credit as a storyteller for he does little more than reproduce what he found in those who had written before him. This probably accounts for variations in style that hardly seem to have troubled our author.[65] In the earlier reigns, down to Theophilos, the style is somewhat archaic; ecclesiastical affairs loom large and are treated in some detail. With the reign of Basil I we enter the domain of imperial legend.

After that it is not so much the style in the strict sense of the word as the nature of the stories that varies, depending on the sources which Skylitzes has at his disposal: more military in character for Tzimiskes or Basil II, more balanced in the case of Romanos III or Constantine IX. In this last reign, when he describes the campaigns against the Patzinaks and especially in the fine digression on the Turks, Skylitzes' horizons suddenly open out way beyond the limits of the Roman empire. It is possible that the vigour of the earlier stories has been somewhat attenuated by their abbreviation. On the last night of the life of Leo V (for instance), one cannot understand why the emperor – visiting the quarters of the *papias* – was recognised by his red buskins. But Genesios and *Theophanes Continuatus* inform us that the servant who noticed the footwear was lying flat on his stomach under the bed of the future Michael II, hence all he could see of him was the feet.[66] Nevertheless Skylitzes has on the whole managed to retain the attraction and the interest of the originals. And even though the terms he found in his sources sometimes show through in the text he has written, Skylitzes has performed his task of compiler in such a way as to produce a unity of style and voice, presenting his readers with refined and objective narratives of the events he reports, be they heroic or tragic, horrible or amusing.

---

[62] See Holmes, *Basil II*, 110, where Skylitzes' penchant for discreet episodes is noted (following J. Shepard).
[63] Leo the Armenian, chs. 6 and 11, Skylitzes, *Synopsis historion*, ed. Thurn, 18 and 22. It is the *troparion* that Leo sings (badly) that is the signal for the assassins to strike him down.
[64] Basil II, ch. 42, Skylitzes, *Synopsis historion*, ed. Thurn, 360–3.
[65] Zonaras seems to have been very sensitive to differences in the style of the sources he used; he apologises (and congratulates himself) for having respected them: Zonaras, *Praef.*, ch. 2, 8–9.
[66] Leo the Armenian, ch. 11, Skylitzes, *Synopsis historion*, ed. Thurn, 22; Genesios, ed. Lesmüller-Werner and Thurn, 17; *Theophanes Continuatus*, ed. Bekker, 38.

THE TEXT AND ITS HISTORY

Simple though it may be, Skylitzes' work enjoyed great success at Constantinople; this is clear from the transmission of the text and from other Byzantine writers who made use of it. In order to make his edition, Hans Thurn had access to nine manuscripts of the entire text of the *Synopsis* dating from the twelfth to the fourteenth centuries. In addition to other manuscripts containing only extracts from the work, there is the *Chronographia* of George Kedrenos which includes the entire text of the *Synopsis* of Skylitzes almost unchanged. Considering how many Byzantine historical works are only known in a single medieval copy (*Theophanes Continuatus* is a case in point), the *Synopsis*, without being among those works which are best attested, nevertheless occupies an honourable place in comparison with them.

Among the extant manuscripts of this work, the 'Madrid Skylitzes' must be mentioned, Codex Matrit. Bibl.nat.Vitr.26.2. Thurn dates this codex to the thirteenth or fourteenth century, but N. G. Wilson has now shown that it dates from the end of the twelfth century.[67] With its 574 miniatures the *Matritensis* is one of the most remarkable monuments of Byzantine art.[68] It is also the only surviving example of an illustrated chronicle from the Greek milieu.

For a work of which there are many witnesses, the text of Skylitzes is distinguished by having been interpolated at an early date. Thurn was of the opinion that there stood between the original and all the other surviving medieval manuscripts of the work a manuscript (now lost) which had already been enriched with marginal notes by an attentive reader who was quite familiar with the history and topography of Bulgaria; notes that were subsequently incorporated into the text of several manuscripts.[69] Other interpolations would have other origins. Special mention must, however, be made of the many interpolations which are found in the fourteenth-century manuscript U in the edition of Thurn, Codex Vind. Nationalbibl., hist.gr.74. These are particularly rich and interesting for the history of Bulgaria and are the work of a known person: Michael of Diabolis.[70]

---

[67] N. G. Wilson, 'The Madrid Scylitzes', *Scrittura e civiltà* 2 (Turin, 1978), 209–19.
[68] *L'Illustriation du manuscrit de Scylites de la Bibliothèque nationale de Madrid*, ed. A. Grabar and M. Manoussacas (Venice, 1979); most recently, V. Tsamakda, *The illustrated chronicle of Ioannes Skylitzes in Madrid* (Leiden, 2002).
[69] On the question of the interpolations, see Skylitzes, *Synopsis historion*, Thurn's preface, xxix–xxxiv (and the stemma on xxxv) on what he calls 'Skylitzes interpolatus'.
[70] This person was identified by B. Prokić, *Die Zusätze* ...; see J. Ferluga, 'John Skylitzes and Michael of Devol', *ZRVI*, 10 (1967), 163–70.

The *Synopsis* is found in two forms in the medieval manuscripts: a shorter one which ends with the deposition of Michael VI the elder in 1057, and a longer one using Michael Attaleiates as its principal (if not its unique) source. The longer version continues to 1079, embracing the reigns of Isaac Komnenos, Constantine X Doukas, Romanos IV Diogenes, Michael VII Doukas and the beginning of the reign of Nikephoros III Botaneiates. Several questions arise from the existence of these two forms, not the least of which is the question of which one is the original form of the work. It is unanimously agreed that the shorter form is the earlier one; that is, the one in which the narrative concludes with the deposition of Michael VI and the proclamation of Isaac Komnenos in 1057, as indeed the title of the work as it is found in Thurn's manuscripts V and M says it will. But if what comes after 1057 is a continuation, then the question arises whether this too was written by Skylitzes or by an anonymous continuator. In spite of what C. de Boor and G. Moravcsik think, there are many arguments in favour of the first answer.[71] In the manuscripts in which it is found, the continuation follows on without interruption under the same title, *Synopsis*; hence this too is attributed to Skylitzes.[72] Already in the twelfth century Zonaras cites it as a work of this author.[73] Even though the influence of Attaleiates is perceptible in the *Continuatio*, E. Tsolakis was able to assemble a small dossier of reasons for thinking that it was composed by the same author as the *Synopsis*. The general opinion nowadays is that Skylitzes first published his chronography in its shorter form and then later extended it under the influence of Attaleiates, whose work had recently appeared.[74] According to this likely hypothesis, Skylitzes must have written the *Synopsis* in the 1080s, the continuation some years (or even decades) later. One can imagine that, as he was writing in the time of Alexios I Komnenos, his first intention was to end his work before dealing with the reign of the uncle of the reigning emperor and that he *later* decided to pursue his project down to the time of that emperor's predecessor.

In due course Skylitzes' work provided material for other Byzantine historians. Thus Nikephoros Bryennios, the husband of Anna Komnena,

---

[71] C. de Boor, 'Weiteres zur Chronik des Skylitzes, *BZ*, 14 (1905), 409–67; Moravcsik, *Byzantinoturcica*, 340.

[72] Manuscripts A (Vindob. Hist. gr. 35, twelfth century) and O (Achrid 79, twelfth century) proclaim that the *Synopsis* goes until the reign of Nikephoros Botaneiates (O) or to the proclamation of Alexios I Komnenos (A).

[73] See note 4.

[74] For the *Historia* of Michael Attaleiates (dedicated to the emperor Nikephoros II Botaneiates), see *Miguel Ataliates, Historia*, ed. I. Perez Martin (Madrid, 2002); Hunger, *Literatur der Byzantiner*, 1, 382–9.

reproduced the digression on the Turks in the *Synopsis* almost word for word in his *Historical material* (*Hyle historias*), the first part of which was written before the death of Alexios I Komnenos in 1118.[75] Then at the end of the eleventh century and the beginning of the twelfth George Kedrenos (unknown in any other context) incorporated the entire work of Skylitzes almost unchanged in his own chronography, a work that goes from the creation of the world to the end of the reign of Michael VI and also bears the title *Synopsis historion*.[76] Around the year 1150 Constantine Manasses[77] made use of Skylitzes for his *Chronike synopsis*, a chronography written in verse (a rarity in the Byzantine world) at the command of Eirene Komnena, wife of the sebastokrator Andronikos Komnenos.[78] It was probably at the beginning of the second half of the twelfth century that John Zonaras, after a career in which he rose to be chief of the imperial chancery, withdrew to the monastery of St Glykeria on the Propontis and there composed his chronography, beginning at the creation of the world and ending with the death of Alexios I Komnenos.[79] 'The Thracian' (*alias* Skylitzes) figures among the sources of Zonaras' *Epitome historion* ('abridged history') that was very successful at Byzantium; the same is true of the *Biblos chronike* ('chronicle') that Michael Glykas, a former imperial secretary, composed shortly after Zonaras wrote.[80] Ephraim in the fourteenth century and Theodore Gaza in the fifteenth were still using the *Synopsis*.[81] Thus Skylitzes' work was neither without influence nor isolated. It may not be one of the most original historical works of the eleventh and

---

[75] Nikephoros Bryennios, *Hylē historias, Nicephori Bryennii historiarum libri quattuor*, ed. P. Gautier (CFHB, 9, Brussels, 1975), 88–9; Skylitzes, Reign of Constantine IX, ch. 9, ed. Thurn, 442–5. It is by no means certain that Bryennios did not simply use the same (to us unknown) source as Skylitzes.

[76] ed. I Bekker, 23 vols. (Bonn, 1838–9); Hunger, *Literatur der Byzantiner*, I, 393, Greek tr., II, 216–17.

[77] ed. O. Lampsidis, *Constantini Manassis Breviarum Chronicum*, CFHB 36, 1–2, Athens 1992; *cf* Hunger, *Literatur der Byzantiner*, 1:419–22 (trad. Gr. II:216–17).

[78] *Breviarium historiae metricum*, ed. I Bekker, Bonn 1837

[79] ed. M. Pinder and T. Büttner-Wobst, 3 vols. (Bonn, 1841–97); see Hunger, *Literatur der Byzantiner*, I, 416–19, Greek tr., II, 246–50. On Zonaras' use of Skylitzes: Hirsch, *Byzantinische Studien*, 379–83. The fact that the witness of 'The Thracesian' is invoked for the reign of Isaac Komnenos (Zonaras 18.7.5, ed. Hirsch, 673⁴) shows that Zonaras knew the *Synopsis* together with its continuation and that he attributes the latter to Skylitzes.

[80] ed I. Bekker, Bonn 1836; see Hunger *Literatur der Byzantiner*, I, 422–6, Greek tr., II, 255–61.

[81] See Hunger, *Literatur der Byzantiner*, I, 478–80, Greek tr., II, 329–32. E. Pinto, *Teodoro Gaza. Epistole* (Naples, 1975). Theodore frequently refers to Skylitzes, calling him *Skylax*. He mentions him by name in his ninth letter, *de Origine Turcarum*, ed. Pinto, 100: 'Skylax, who wrote the great deeds of the emperors from Nikephoros the *genikos* to Isaac Komnenos (under whom he lived), a man of no mean intelligence, but whose style is unsophisticated (*idiotes*).'

twelfth centuries, but it does occupy an honourable place in the genre of chronography.

ON THE TRANSLATION

This translation is based on the edition of Hans Thurn.[82] On the rare occasions when it diverges from the edition there is a note to say so. Two solutions have been adopted for showing the interpolations that Thurn displays in smaller type within the body of the text. Where possible, these have been included in the text of the translation enclosed with brackets. Where they would have disturbed the text, they appear in the notes. In each case it is intimated in which manuscript(s) the interpolation in question is found by using the letters Thurn assigned to them. Where it has been necessary to add words not found in the Greek text in order to make the meaning clear, those words have been place in square brackets. Some technical words and terms have been left unchanged (*autokrator, parakoimomenos*) while for others the modern equivalent has been used (emperor, commander, etc.). Proper nouns present a difficult problem; where a modern equivalent exists (Michael, Constantinople), that has been used; otherwise the word as it stands in the text has been transliterated, using ê for eta, y for upsilon and ô for omega.

[82] See note 1. above.

A SYNOPSIS OF HISTORIES BEGINNING WITH THE DEATH OF THE EMPEROR NIKEPHOROS, THE EX-MINISTER OF FINANCE AND EXTENDING TO THE REIGN OF ISAAC KOMNENOS, COMPOSED BY JOHN SKYLITZES, THE KOUROPALATES WHO SERVED AS COMMANDER-IN-CHIEF OF THE WATCH

Foreword

After the ancient writers, the best compendium of history was written, first by George the monk,[1] synkellos to the most holy patriarch Tarasios,[2] then by Theophanes the confessor, hegoumenos of the monastery of Agros.[3] These men carefully read through the history books, making a précis of them in simple, unaffected language, touching exclusively on the substance of the events which had taken place. George began with the creation of the world and continued to [the time of] the tyrants, Maximian and Maximinos, his son.[4] Theophanes took the other's conclusion as his starting point and brought his work to an end with the death of the emperor Nikephoros, the ex-minister of finance. After [Theophanes] nobody continued their effort. There were those who attempted to do so, such as the Sicilian schoolmaster[5] and, in our own time, the supremely honourable consul of the philosophers, [Michael] Psellos.[6] There were others too but, because they took their task too lightly, they all failed to write

---

[1] George the monk died after 810; he composed a chronicle from creation to AD 284, English translation by W. Adler, *The chronography of George Synkellos. A Byzantine chronicle of universal history from creation* (Oxford, 2002).

[2] Patriarch of Constantinople, 784–806.

[3] Born in 760, Theophanes was the scion of a military family. A fervent devotee of the icons, he became hegoumenos of the Bythinian monastery of Agros; he died on 12 March 817 (*PmbZ* 8107 = *PBE* Theophanes 18). He is the author of a *Chronographia* which covers the years 280–815, a continuation of the work of George Synkellos. English translation by C. Mango and R. Scott, with G. Greatrex, *The Chronicle of Theophanes Confessor: Byzantine and near eastern history ad 284–813* (Oxford, 1997).

[4] The son of Maximian, one of the Tetrarchs, was in fact Maxentius who was killed by Constantine at the battle of the Milvian Bridge, 28 October 312.

[5] Theognostos: *ODB*, III, 2055.

[6] Michael Psellos (mentioned by Skylitzes in his account of the reign of Michael VI) is the author of a *Chronographia* in which he describes the reigns of the emperors Basil II to Michael VII Doukas, who was his pupil; English translation by E. R. A. Sewter, *Fourteen Byzantine emperors*

with the requisite degree of accuracy. Many important events they omitted altogether and their works are of little value to posterity. They are little more than calculations of the duration of each reign and reports on who held the sceptre after whom – no more. Even when they appear to mention certain events, these writers do their readers a disservice and no good because they fail to write about them accurately. Theodore Daphnopates,[7] Niketas the Paphlagonian,[8] Joseph Genesios[9] and Manuel,[10] these two of Constantinople, Nikephoros the deacon from Phrygia,[11] Leo from Asia,[12] Theodore, bishop of Side[13] and his nephew of the same name who presided over the church of Sebasteia,[14] Demetrios, bishop of Kyzikos[15] and the monk John the Lydian[16] – these all set themselves their own goals: maybe the glorification of an emperor, the censure of a patriarch, or to extol a friend – each attains his own ends under the guise of writing history and every one of them falls far short of the mentality of those godly men of whom we spoke. For in composing a rambling account of his own times (and a little before) as though he was writing history, one of them writes a favourable account, another a critical one, while a third writes whatever he pleases and a fourth sets down what he is ordered to write. Each composes his own 'history' and they differ so much from each other in describing the same events that they plunge their audience into dizziness and confusion. For my own part, I took great pleasure in reading the work of the men [first] mentioned above and I hope that [a continuation of their]

(London, 1953). But Skylitzes probably used Psellos' *Historia syntomos*, edited and translated into English by W. J. Aerts (Berlin and New York, 1990).

[7] Theodore Daphnopates was a senior civil servant who rose to be eparch under Romanus III. There survive letters, homilies and saints' lives written by him and he may have responsible for the later parts of *Theophanes Continuatus*.

[8] Niketas David the Paphlagonian was the disciple of Arethas of Caesarea (the bitter opponent of Leo VI in the Tetragamy controversy). Niketas edited numerous works in praise of various saints, a *Commentary on the Psalms* and, most notably, a *Life of Ignatios* in which his profound antipathy to Photios is apparent.

[9] An anonymous *History of the Reigns* has been attributed to Genesios on the sole authority of a marginal comment in the one remaining manuscript of the work. Skylitzes alone gives the man's Christian name. There is reason to doubt this attribution, even the very existence of a 'Joseph Genesius', although a family of that name is well attested from the tenth century onward.

[10] Manuel, Judge and Protospatharios, had apparently composed a work in eight volumes dealing with the exploits of John Kourkouas.

[11] No other mention of an author of this name is known.

[12] This is Leo the deacon, who was born *c*. 950 at Kaloe of Tmolos (Asia Minor). His *History* is very favourable to the family of the Phokai, especially to the emperor Nikephoros II

[13] Author of another lost work.

[14] Possibly the editor of a biography of Basil II.

[15] Nothing remains of the work of this author who lived in the earlier part of the eleventh century and wrote mainly theological works.

[16] An unknown writer who must not be confused with the sixth-century writer of the same name.

summary will be of no small benefit to those who love history, especially to those who prefer that which is easily accessible to what has to be striven for; a summary, that is, which will provide them with a brief overview of what has taken place at various times and thus free them of the need to consult massive tomes of memoirs. I read the histories of the above-mentioned writers with great care. I conjured away from them all comments of a subjective or fanciful nature. I left aside the writers' differences and contradictions. I excised whatever I found there which tended toward fantasy; but I garnered whatever seemed likely and not beyond the bounds of credibility and, to this, I added whatever I learnt from the mouths of sage old men. All of this I put together in summary form and this I now bequeath to future generations as an easily digestible nourishment, 'finely ground up' as the proverb has it. Those who have already read the books of the above-mentioned historians will have in this little book a reminder of their reading which they will be able to take along with them and consult as a handbook. Reading provokes recollection; recollection nourishes and expands memory, just as, quite the contrary, negligence and laziness provoke forgetfulness which darkens and confuses the memory of what has happened in the past. Those who have not yet encountered the histories will find a guide in this compendium and, when they go in search of the more fulsome writings, they will gain a more comprehensive impression of the course of events. And now it is time to begin.

CHAPTER I

Michael I Rangabe, the Kouropalates [811–813]

1. [5] After the emperor Nikephoros was slain in Bulgaria, his son Staurakios, having survived mortally wounded in the capital, relinquished both his life and his throne only two months later.[1] The emperor's brother-in-law (who went by the name of Rangabe)[2] found himself holding the Roman sceptre at the behest of the senate and people. He would have refused the office, alleging that he was not competent to sustain the burden of such great responsibilities. He was in fact prepared to relinquish the power in favour of the patrician Leo the Armenian. This Leo gave the impression of being a choleric and vigorous type of man. He was serving as commanding officer of the Anatolikon army[3] at that time and he had no desire to accept it should it be offered to him. He protested his unworthiness of the imperial throne; it was in fact he who persuaded Michael that it was fitting for him to assume the power. Leo took it upon himself to be [Michael's] most faithful and vigorous servant and adjutant for as long as he lived; these promises he confirmed with most terrifying oaths.[4]

---

[1] According to Theophanes, Staurakios refused to abdicate even though he was seriously wounded (*PmbZ* 6890 = *PBE* Staurakios 2). It was his brother-in-law who usurped the throne with the support of the principal officers who had survived the disaster in Bulgaria. Staurakios professed himself a monk with the name of Symeon on 2 October 811, but only lived until 11 January of the next year: P. Grierson, 'The tombs and obits of the Byzantine Emperors (337–1042) with an additional note by C. Mango and I. Ševčenko', *DOP*, 16 (1962), 3–63, at 55. His widow, Theophano (*PmbZ* 8163 = *PBE* Theophano 2), a relative of the empress Eirene the Athenian, was given a palace (Ta Hebraïka) which she transformed into a monastery dedicated to the Holy Trinity (location unknown: R. Janin, *La géographie ecclésiastique de l'empire byzantin*, I, *Le siège de Constantinople et le patriarcat œcuménique*, III, *Les églises et les monastères de L' empire byzantin*, 2nd edn (Paris, 1969), 470–1). On Staurakios' marriage see P. Speck, 'Eine Brautschau für Staurakios', *JÖB*, 49 (1999), 25–30.

[2] On this reign see W. Treadgold, *The Byzantine revival, 782–842* (Stanford, CA, 1988), 177–89; also *PmbZ* 4989 = *PBE* Michael 7.

[3] The strategos of the Anatolikon theme commanded the largest of the thematic armies (15,000 men in theory). He was the most senior of the army officers, outranking even the domestic of the scholai. Thus D. Turner, 'The origins and accession of Leo V (813–820)', *JÖB*, 40 (1990), 171–203; also *PmbZ* 4244 = *PBE* Leo 15.

[4] Genesios (1.2) says that Michael I preserved the text of these oaths in writing. On this practice see N. Svoronos, 'Le serment de fidélité à l'empereur byzantin et sa signification constitutionelle', *REB*, 9 (1951), 106–42.

2. Once Michael had thus, somewhat against his own intention, come into possession of the reins of the empire,[5] Krum, the ruler[6] of the Bulgars, puffed up by his previous successes, together with his subjects (now become presumptuous on account of their victories) burnt and devastated the western regions.[7] So Michael decided to mount a campaign against them, to do the best he could to restrain and throw back the Bulgar foraging parties. He therefore quickly sent out orders in all directions and troops [6] were hastily assembled. When Krum heard of the emperor's mobilisation, he recalled his own men from foraging and concentrated them in one place. He established a heavily fortified camp there and awaited the arrival of the emperor. When [Michael] arrived, he encamped over against Krum, who was sitting near to Adrianople.[8] There were frequent skirmishes and battles within archery range and, in all these encounters, the Romans seemed to have the upper hand. This went to the soldiers' heads; they urged and yearned for hand-to-hand fighting and a general engagement. Either out of cowardice (as they said in the ranks) or because he was looking for the opportune moment, the emperor delayed and held back. The host became mutinous and shouted at the emperor, to his face, threatening that, if he did not lead them out, they would break down the palisade themselves and fall upon the enemy. Overwhelmed by this argument, the emperor opened the gates of the encampment and drew up his battle line.[9] Krum did likewise: he got his men into line and stood them over against the emperor. Each [ruler] harangued his army at length; each spoke words of encouragement and praise, words capable of inciting men to prowess in arms. Finally, they gave the signal with the trumpets for battle to commence and each [side] charged the other. The Romans now withstood the enemy with such heroism and fought so bravely that the Bulgar forces were worn down. The enemy would even have considered a general retreat, for Krum himself was already growing weary, riding in all directions and taking in hand those [units] of the army which were being sorely pressed. And then Leo, the strategos of the Anatolikon theme (who wanted to be emperor), and, with him, the troops under his command (whom he had

---

[5] Michael was proclaimed on 2 October 811: *Theophanis Chronographia*, I and II, ed. C. de Boor (Leipzig, 1883–5), 493.
[6] *Archon*, which means the chief of a nation when applied to foreigners.
[7] i.e. the themes of Thrace and Macedonia.
[8] The exact location of this place is not known, but its name is Versinikeia. See P. Soustal, *Thrakien (Thrake, Rodope und Haiminontos)* (TIB, 6, Vienna, 1991), 205.
[9] The battle of Versinikeia was fought on 22 June 813, Soustal, *Thrakien*.

corrupted) broke ranks and took themselves off in flight, for no reason whatsoever. The remainder of the army was astounded at this sight; the men's courage began to wither away. The Bulgars, on the other hand, regained their courage and came howling at the Romans as though the thought of retreat had never crossed their minds; and theirs now became the winning side. The spirit of the Romans was broken by what had happened. They did not wait for the Bulgars' assault, but immediately turned and fled.[10] Many of the soldiers were killed; not a few of the commanders also fell.[11] The emperor only just managed to find refuge in Adrianople, together with a portion of the army still intact. From there he proceeded to the capital, leaving the above-mentioned [7] Leo and his entourage in Thrace. They were to stand their ground against the plundering of the Bulgars and interrupt their onslaughts. Once he was alone, Leo brought out into the open the defection which he had been secretly nurturing within. He shared it with his fellow enthusiasts, telling them the time was ripe to accomplish what they intended. By the mouths of these people he spread the word throughout the whole army that it was on account of the emperor's incompetence and his lack of training in military studies that the Roman forces had been reduced [to flight] and that the former glory and renown of the Romans had departed. Thus too he corrupted the soldiers who, having been dispersed in the rout, came back on foot, devoid of arms and equipment, to join the army that was with him; and thus he persuaded them to accept the possibility of revolt. Suddenly they flocked around his tent, hurling improper and shameless words against the emperor, calling him an unmanly coward who had destroyed the Roman forces and besmirched the distinction and glory of the empire by his incompetence. On the other hand, they openly acclaimed Leo and declared him to be emperor of the Romans. When he made light of it and would have rejected the [supreme] command,

---

[10] Skylitzes is following a lost work of the patriarch Nikephoros when he accuses Leo of treason. Turner, 'Leo V', 89–193, challenges this widely held view, basing himself on Genesios (who gives two contradictory accounts of Leo's behaviour) and on Theophanes, a contemporary of the events in question, both of whom were well disposed towards Leo. Skylitzes' narrative is inconsistent, claiming that Michael I left Leo behind to defend Thrace. This he would surely not have done had Leo been responsible for the recent disaster.

[11] MSS AC add: 'one of whom was the magister Michael Lachanodrakes/Lachanodrakon' but there must be some confusion here for the surly partisan of Constantine V would have been of a great age by now, and in any case that Michael is known to have fallen in a previous defeat at the hand of the Bulgars, near Marcellai, in 792: Theophanes, ed. de Boor, 468; *PmbZ* 5027 = *PBE* Michael 5. One who did fall in this action was the patrician John Aplakes, commander of Macedonia: *PmbZ* 3197 = *PBE* John 19; *Scriptor incertus*, intro. E. Pinto; text, Italian tr. and notes, F. Iadevaia (Messina, 1987), 338.

Michael of Amorion,[12] 'the stammerer',[13] himself a commander of a unit of the Roman army, drew his sword. He invited others who were party to the affair to do likewise and then he threatened to execute Leo if he did not of his own free will accept the [supreme] command. It was thus that the diadem was set on the brow of this man and thus that he was proclaimed emperor of the Romans.

3. Prior to this, as the emperor Michael was returning after the army had been put to flight, he was met by John Exaboulios[14] as he approached the capital. He encouraged the emperor to endure the unfortunate occurrence in a noble and magnanimous way; then he sought to know whom he had left in command of the army. The emperor replied that he had left Leo, the Commander of the Anatolikon theme, a very intelligent fellow and devoted to the empire. When Exaboulios heard this, he said: 'Oh, emperor, it seems to me that you are very much mistaken insofar as the intentions of this person are concerned.' That is what he said, and even before the emperor arrived at the palace, the public proclamation of Leo was reported. The sovereign was deeply disturbed by that report. He was trying to decide what action to take when some of his entourage urged him to do everything in his power to hold on to the supreme command and to resist the usurper [8] to the full extent of his capability. But he was a man of peace, with no wish to involve himself in an affair the outcome of which was unpredictable. So he ordered those who were saying such things not to incite him to engage in a murderous civil war. And he sent off to Leo one of those close to him, bearing the imperial insignia: the diadem, the purple robe and the scarlet buskins.[15] He undertook to cede the throne to Leo, for he judged it better to pass from his own life than to see the shedding of a single drop of Christian blood. Leo should set aside all fear and uncertainty; let him come and take possession of the palace [said the emperor]. The empress Procopia, however, was opposed to what

---

[12] Amorion was the seat of the strategos of the Anatolikon theme, the most important of the eastern themes. The ruins of the fortress which housed a significant garrison are presently being excavated: C. S. Lightfoot, Y. Mergen, B. Y. Olcay, and J. Witte-Orr, 'The Amorium project: research and excavation in 2000', *DOP*, 57 (2003), 279–92.

[13] This is the future emperor Michael II (820–9), founder of the 'Amorian' dynasty.

[14] John Exaboulios (*PmbZ* 3196 = *PBE* John 81) was then count of the walls. Later he was logothete of the drome under Leo V and counsellor to Michael II, from whom he received the title of patrician. According to Genesios (1.3), Exaboulios was the name of a *genos* but no other person is known by this name. Other Exaboulitai are mentioned in the eleventh century but there is no indication that these were related to the above John.

[15] On the imperial vestments and insignia: P. Grierson, *Catalogue of the Byzantine coins in the Dumbarton Oaks Collection and in the Whittemore Collection*, II–III (Washington, DC, 1968–1973), III, 107–45.

was being done. She said the empire was a fine winding sheet,[16] and when she failed to convince [the emperor], in order to have the last word, she said it would be strange, indeed even more than merely strange, if the upstart's wife were to deck herself out in the imperial diadem.[17] She made fun of her alluding to her name, calling her 'Barka'.[18] Then she began to think about her own situation. And that is what was going on around the emperor.

The usurper, on the other hand, entered [the capital] by the Golden Gate,[19] acclaimed by the army, the senate and the people. He proceeded to the [monastery-] church of the Forerunner at Stoudios,[20] and from there, accompanied by a guard of honour, he arrived at the palace. As he was about to offer to God a prayer on his return in the Chrysotriklinos,[21] he took off the over-garment he happened to be wearing and handed it to Michael, the head groom,[22] who promptly put it on himself. To those who saw it, this seemed to be an omen that he would mount the imperial throne after Leo. The emperor then put on another garment and set out for the church in the palace. Michael was walking behind him without paying attention to where he was going. In this way he recklessly stepped

---

[16] The famous words of the empress Theodora (quoting Isocrates) at the time of the Nika revolt. See J. B. Bury, *History of the Later Roman empire from the death of Theodosius I to the death of Justinian*, 2 vols. (London, 1923), II, 45 and note 4.

[17] The *modiolos* was a crown used at the coronation; it has been the subject of various studies, from P. Charanis, 'The imperial crown and its constitutional significance', *B*, 12 (1937), 189–95, to A. P. Kazhdan, 'The crown Modiolus once more', *JÖB*, 38 (1988), 339–40, and C. Morrisson, 'Le modiolos: couronne impériale ou couronne pour l'empereur', *Mélanges Gilbert Dagron*, ed. V. Déroche, D. Feissel, C. Morrisson, C. Zuckerman, *TM*, 14 (2002), 499–510.

[18] Clearly an insult, but the exact meaning is unclear. It has sometimes been taken to be a proper name, which led Treadgold, *Byzantine revival*, 198–9, to think that Leo had divorced his first wife (Theodosia).

[19] By this gate the Egnatian Way entered the city, close to the sea of Marmara. The main gate only admitted emperors and victorious generals (R. Janin, *Constantinople byzantine* (*AOC*, 4 A, Paris, 1964), 115–17). *Theophanis Chronographia*, ed. de Boor, 501, says Leo entered by the Gate of Charisios, which is far more likely for one coming from Adrianople, by which name that gate was also known. This triumphal entry took place on 11 July 813 and was followed by the coronation the day after.

[20] If Leo entered by the Golden Gate, a station would be expected at this, the most illustrious of the Constantinopolitan monasteries, then under the direction of Theodore of Stoudios. Following the tenth-century historians: Genesios 1.4, *Theophanes Continuatus*, ed. I. Bekker (Bonn, 1838), 18; Skylitzes here describes the traditional route of a triumphal procession.

[21] This was one of the state rooms in the sixth-century Great Palace reserved for imperial receptions and banquets: Janin, *Constantinople byzantine*, 115–17. According to *Theophanes Continuatus*, ed. Bekker, 19; it was in the Chalke that Leo prayed on entering the palace.

[22] Michael (*PmbZ* 4990, 5047 = *PBE* Michael 10) had just been appointed *protostrator* by Leo. It was a great honour to be handed something the emperor had been wearing. Genesios (1.4) says the vestment in question was a *kolobion*, a tunic decorated with the eagle motif.

on the hem of the imperial vestment. Leo took this to be a bad omen and he began to suspect that an insurrection would originate with that man.

That is how the usurper entered the palace and came into possession of the throne which could have been his without a struggle. Instead, he took it with considerable trouble and disturbance.

The emperor Michael, his wife Prokopia and their children[23] now took refuge in the church of the Mother of God known as the church of the Lighthouse,[24] where they sought sanctuary. The usurper expelled them from there and separated them from each other. Michael he exiled to the monastery on the island of Prote,[25] where his layman's hair was tonsured and where he spent the remaining portion of his life. Theophylact, the [9] oldest of Michael's sons, he castrated and sent him into exile, together with his mother and brothers.[26]

4. That is what happened; and here it is worthwhile recalling the prophecy of the monk installed near Philomelion.[27] There was a person, one of the most distinguished of people, whose name was Bardanios Tourkos.[28] He was one of the principal members of the senate, a patrician in rank and, at that time, domestic of the scholai for the east.[29] He was always contemplating the possibility of attempted usurpation and, if it could be, of seizing control of the empire, but he was tossed by conflicting emotions. He burned with longing for the throne, but he trembled and feared at the

---

[23] Michael had many children. The names of three sons and two daughters (Gorgo and Theophano) are known: *PmbZ* 2290; *PBE* Georgo 1; *PmbZ* 8164 = *PBE* Theophano 1. The eldest son (Staurakios) was dead already (*PmbZ* 6890 = *PBE* Stavrakios 12). The second, Theophylact (named after his paternal grandfather), became a monk with the name of Eustratios and died in January 849, aged fifty-six (*PmbZ* 8336 = *PBE* Theophylaktos 9). His younger brother, Niketas, took the monastic name of Ignatios; this is the future patriarch: Treadgold, *Byzantine revival*, 405, n. 163.

[24] *Tou Pharou*, allegedly built by Constantine V; this is the church which housed the greater part of the imperial relic collection (Janin, *Eglises et monastères*, 232–4), situated (as the name implies) by the lighthouse on the Marmara coast. The earliest mention of this edifice is in connection with the marriage of Leo IV with the Chazar princess in 768: Theophanes, ed. de Boor, 444.

[25] Now Kinali island in the sea of Marmara, a traditional place of exile. Bardanios Tourkos was sent there after the failure of his uprising in 803: R. Janin, *Les églises et les monastères des grands centres byzantins* (Paris, 1975), 70–2.

[26] The harsh treatment meted out to Michael's sons rather suggests that the transfer of power was not effected quite so smoothly as the chroniclers suggest.

[27] A town in the Anatolikon theme, now Akşehir, see K. Belke and N. Mersich, *Phrygien und Pisidien* (TIB, 7, Vienna, 1990), 359–60.

[28] The name Tourkos (the Turk) might indicate that he had Khazar blood; he was domestic of the scholai then strategos of the Anatolikon theme under Eirene and Nikephoros. His career is described in E. Kountoura-Galake, 'He epanastase tou Bardane Tourkou', *Symmeikta*, 5 (1983), 203–15. See also *PmbZ*, 759, 760, 762, 771 and *PBE*, Bardanes 3.

[29] An anachronism, for this title is unknown prior to the reign of Romanos II: N. Oikonomides, *Les listes de préséance byzantines des IXe et Xe siècles* (Le monde byzantin, Paris, 1972), 329. Bardanios was monostrategos, 'sole commander', of all the eastern themes, meaning that he was temporarily in command of all the eastern armies, no doubt to coordinate resistance to the Moslems.

uncertainty of the outcome. Then he heard that at Philomelion there was a monk; a solitary who had attained the acme of virtue, of whom it was said that he could foretell the future. [Bardanios] knew that he simply had to share his plans with this man and obtain his judgement. Since this is what he thought, he devised a hunting party. He took Leo with him, a good-looking, fine figure of a man with sound judgement in political matters, who served him as equerry-in-chief. He also took with him the above-mentioned Michael of Amorion, 'the stammerer', and, in addition to these two, a fellow named Thomas,[30] an Armenian by race, who had his home on lake Gazouro.[31] At a certain point, he told the large company of men that was with him to stay where they were while he and the men just mentioned went to the monk's cave. [Bardanios] went in alone to the solitary and told him what he had on his mind. When these things reached his ears, the monk immediately discouraged him from what was proposed. He asserted that if Bardanios did not obey him and desist from his plan, he would both lose the sight of his eyes and be deprived of his fortune. The commander lost heart at these words and was very close to losing his mind. However, when the customary prayer had been said and the commander was about to leave, his horse was brought forward and he mounted it. Holding the bridle was Michael; it was Thomas who steadied the right stirrup and Leo who gave the commander a leg-up into the saddle as he mounted the horse. At that point, the monk leaned out of his window, peered down at the men and told Bardanios to come back again, [10] a recall which the latter received with gladness. In less time than it takes to tell, he leapt from the saddle and ran in to the monk, expecting to hear something to his liking. Getting him to come and stand close beside him again, the monk said: 'Commander, yet again I advise and counsel you in no way whatsoever to have anything more to do with what you have in mind. Otherwise, make no mistake about it! It will cost you the crippling of your eyes and the confiscation of your goods. But, of the three men who brought up your horse, the one who gave you a leg-up when you were about to mount, he will be the first to gain possession of the throne, and, secondly, the one who held the bridle. As for the third man, the one who held the stirrup for your right foot, he will be proclaimed emperor but never reign. Furthermore, he will lose his life by a most pitiful death.' When Bardanios heard this, he brushed aside what had been

---

[30] This is Thomas 'the Slav', who raised a serious revolt against Michael II.
[31] Lake Karalis to the ancients, Pougouse or Scleros in the Middle Ages, this is now Beysehir Golie, one of the largest lakes in Turkey, lying between Galatia and Lykaonia: K. Belke (mit Beiträgen von M. Restle) *Galatien und Lykaonien* (TIB, 4, Vienna, 1984), 218.

said as though it were a laughing matter and reversed his opinion of the monk. Now he railed against him as a sorcerer, incapable of foreseeing any forthcoming event, rather than as a seer and one who had foreknowledge of what was about to happen. All he did was to take stock of this or that person from his appearance and, as such people usually do, proceed to bring prophecy into disrepute. [Thus he could claim that] a man of patrician rank, occupying the position of domestic, a man of distinguished birth and family, entrusted with ultimate authority, would fail to obtain his object, while persons of no distinction, hired hands incapable of saying from whom they were descended, were to be raised to the summit of imperial authority![32]

Jesting and sneering like that at what had been said, he made his way back to his own command. And there, once he had spoken to his fellow conspirators, he raised his hand against the emperor. (It was Nikephoros, the ex-minister of finance, who was holding the reins of the empire at that time.) Bardanios assembled the largest force he could, had himself proclaimed emperor and established his camp in Bithynia.[33] As soon as the emperor heard of Bardanios' movements, he sent a substantial body of men against him. At the very moment when the armies were about to fall on each other, however, Bardanios asked for a pardon for himself and amnesty for his misdeeds. This Nikephoros granted him on the strength of an oath, and sent him into exile on an estate of his on the island of Prote.[34] Shortly afterwards, some soldiers arrived from Lykaonia, whether of their own accord or at the secret instigation of the emperor, who knows? They attacked the estate and blinded Bardanios; then they took refuge in the Great Church of God.[35] Leo, Michael and Thomas, the attendants of Bardanios (as we said), [11] ranged themselves on the side of the emperor Nikephoros once the rebellion was declared. Of these three, Leo was appointed colonel of the corps of the foederati[36] and Michael the Stammerer was entrusted with the authority of the

---

[32] These persons were probably not obscure, e.g. Leo may have been the son of a strategos of the Armeniakon theme named Bardas: Turner, 'Leo V', 172–3; *PmbZ* 784 = *PBE* Bardas 4.

[33] At Malagina, where armies traditionally assembled before marching east (Theophanes, ed. de Boor, 479).

[34] The revolt of Bardanios lasted from 18 July to 8 September 803: W. Kaegi, *Byzantine military unrest 471–843: an interpretation* (Amsterdam, 1981), 245–6.

[35] The *tagma* of the Lykaonians supported their follow countryman, Nikephoros, who was from Pisidia. He brought it to Constantinople to assure his safety: Theophanes, ed. de Boor, 480.

[36] The foederati were a *corps d'élite* first raised by Tiberius II. Having survived the reverses of the seventh century, they were now stationed permanently as a unit in the Anatolikon theme: J. F. Haldon, *Byzantine praetorians* (Bonn, 1984), 246–9.

count of the tent[37] while Thomas remained faithful to his own master right to the end.[38]

A Saracen attack on Roman territory took place at that time. Leo (who was then a subaltern of the commander of the Anatolikon theme) confronted the Hagarenes[39] with the forces under his command and triumphed gloriously.[40] This gained him a reputation which reached the ears of the emperor Michael (Nikephoros had already been killed) who conferred upon him the rank of patrician. That is how these matters came about.

5. It might not be impertinent to record here too the manner in which it was revealed to the emperor Michael how he would lose his throne. Michael had a maidservant working in his immediate household; she used to be afflicted with mental derangement at the time of the new moon. When she was prey to this disorder, she would come to the place where the ox and the lion stand sculpted in stone, for which reason that place is customarily known as the Boukoleon.[41] There she would cry out to the emperor in a resounding voice: 'Come down, come down! Get away from what belongs to others.' When this had occurred several times, the emperor became alarmed and it caused him no small anxiety. So he shared his concern about the matter with one of his customary and familiar associates, Theodotos, the son of the patrician Michael Melissenos,[42] also known as Kassiteras,[43] urging him to look closely into the things she said. [Theodotos] gave the following advice: when the maid was prey to the madness, she was to be apprehended and asked to whom the residence in

---

[37] Michael became count of the tent (chief of staff) for the Anatolikon theme.
[38] Skylitzes' text must be disrupted here. It has to be understood that of Bardanios' three followers, two (Leo and Michael) have abandoned him and only Thomas remains faithful.
[39] i.e. Moslems; also known as Ishmaelites and Saracens; see Genesis 21 & 25 where Hagar, the Egyptian servant of Sarah, bears a child to Abraham named Ishmael, thought to be the ancestor of the Arabs.
[40] According to Theophanes, ed. de Boor, 490–1, Leo had just succeeded Romanos (who had fallen fighting the Bulgars in 811) as strategos of the Anatolikon theme when he conquered Thabit bin Nasr, killing 2,000 men and taking a great deal of booty. Hence there is a chronological discrepancy, since Skylitzes credits Leo with this victory while he was still colonel of the foederati.
[41] This statue of a lion bringing down a bull stood near the imperial gate to the south of the Great Palace, giving its name to another palace nearby. It was thrown down by an earthquake in 1532 (Janin, *Constantinople*, 101).
[42] In 765–6 Michael Melissenos was appointed strategos of the Anatolikon theme by Constantine V, whose third wife was the sister of Michael's wife. Five years later he suffered a severe defeat at the hands of the Arabs: Theophanes, ed. de Boor, 440, 445; *PmbZ* 5028 = *PBE* Michael 4. Theodotos became patriarch under Leo V: *PmbZ* 7954 = *PBE* Theodotos 2.
[43] On this surname: F. Winkelmann, *Quellenstudien zur herrschenden Klasse von Byzanz im 8. und 9. Jahrhundert* (Berlin, 1987), 2:152, 160, 182; also A. P. Kazhdan, 'The formation of Byzantine family names in the ninth and tenth centuries', *BS*, 56 (1997), 99.

the palace belonged and by what marks this person could be identified. Which is what they did, with Theodotos managing the affair. When the woman was apprehended while she was in the grips of madness and asked the question, she revealed the name of Leo, his physical features and form. She went on to say that if one were to go to the Acropolis, one would meet two men there. Of these two, the one riding a mule would surely mount the imperial throne. She said her say and Theodotos for his part, paying very close attention, went to the place she had mentioned. [12] There he recognised the man from the indications she had given; then he knew that the woman had said nothing false. However, he repeated not a word of what he had learnt to the emperor. He said the woman's words were mere idle talking, sheer nonsense without a word of truth in them. But he took Leo by the hand and went into the church of Paul the Apostle by the Orphanage.[44] When they had given each other their word, he revealed what had been indicated but he withheld the whole truth. He said that it had been made known by divine revelation that Leo would certainly take over as commander-in-chief of the Romans. He asked that, as the bringer of this good news, he might not go unrewarded once it was fulfilled. Leo undertook that Theodotos would not be disappointed in his request if what he said was borne out by subsequent events.

6. That is how these things fitted together. It so happened that the war between the Romans and the Bulgars mentioned above now broke out; this for a variety of reasons, not the least of which is the one about to be related. There were some Bulgars who had left the accustomed dwelling place of their forefathers and come into Roman territory, together with their families. They were received by the emperor Michael and were settled in various areas. There were also some Romans who had been taken prisoner in the wars of which we spoke, who now 'broke their bonds asunder'[45] and returned to their fatherland. Krum, the ruler of the Bulgars, demanded the return of all these men. There were advantages in effecting this return, according to some of the Romans.[46] The emperor and some

---

[44] The orphanage (under the supervision of the orphanotrophos) was one of the principal charitable institutions of the capital; it was situated on the Acropolis, where the Seraglio now stands. The orphanage of St Paul was founded by Justin II and the empress Sophia in the sixth century: T. Miller, 'The Orphanotropheion of Constantinople', *Through the eye of a needle: Judaeo-Christian roots of social welfare*, ed. E. Hanawalt and C. Lindberg (Kirksville, MO, 1994), 83–103. A school was added to the orphanage in the eleventh century by Alexios Komnenos: S. Mergiali-Falangas, 'L'école Saint-Paul de l'orphelinat à Constantinople. Bref aperçu sur son statut et son histoire', *REB*, 49 (1991), 237–46. A further study is: J. Nesbitt, 'The Orphanotrophos: some observations on the history of the office in light of seals', *SBS*, 8 (2005), 51–62.

[45] See Ps. 2:3.

[46] Theophanes, ed. de Boor, 498–9, also mentions this imperial council. The patriarch Nikephoros (*PmbZ* 5301 = *PBE* Nikephoros 2) and the metropolitan bishops were in favour of peace but

monks worthy of consideration[47] subscribed to this opinion, thinking that by returning the refugees, they would prevent the barbarian from laying the land waste. There were others who were of the contrary opinion, led by the patriarch Nikephoros, the magister Theoktistos[48] (the leading man of his time in virtue and intelligence) and by no means a few others. They said it was better to commit personal interests to God and not, by the surrender of the fugitives, to set aside the all-powerful aid of the Deity merely to propitiate the false pretensions of the barbarian. As there was no agreement whatsoever on this vexed question, the above-mentioned war with Krum broke out: which brought about the defeat of the Romans and the destruction of many of them. It would appear that God, in his providence, was directing affairs otherwise.

Theodore of Stoudios was opposed to the idea of surrendering the renegades. Skylitzes (no doubt wrongly) numbers Nikephoros among those who were in favour of war.

[47] Although he is not named, this is almost certainly a reference to Theodore of Stoudios, on whom see (most recently) T. Pratsch, *Theodoros Studites (759–826) zwischen Dogma und Pragma: der Abt des Studiosklosters in Konstantinopel im Spannungsfeld von Patriarch, Kaiser und eigenem Anspruch* (Berlin, 1998); also R. Cholij, *Theodore the Stoudite: the ordering of holiness* (Oxford, 2002), and *PmbZ* 7574 = *PBE* Theodoros 15.

[48] Theoktistos, patrician and quaestor (*PmbZ* 8046 = *PBE* Theoktistos 2), was involved in the overthrow of Eirene on 31 October 802 (Theophanes, ed. de Boor, 476). He was made magister by Nikephoros, whose close adviser he remained throughout the reign. He also played a leading role in the transfer of power to both Staurakios and to Michael Rangabe.

CHAPTER 2

Leo V the Armenian [813–820]

1. [13] Meanwhile, having assumed the office of emperor, Leo[1] appointed Thomas ['the Slav'] colonel of the corps[2] of the foederati. This was one of the three men who, as our narrative recorded, accompanied Bardanios when he visited the monk at Philomelion; a young, impetuous man. The emperor made Michael the Stammerer who was godfather to his son and also one of the three, patrician and count of the regiment of the Exkoubitores. As for the other affairs of state, [Leo] disposed of them as he pleased.

Puffed up even more by the recent defeat of the Romans, the Bulgars overran Thrace, laying waste and devastating wherever their foot trod.[3] The emperor decided to send an embassy to initiate peace negotiations, but when the Bulgar rejected the peace proposal with an angry snort, he had no choice but to fight.[4] Accordingly, once the armies were assembled, a violent battle ensued and, again, the Roman forces got the worst of it. The Bulgars fell to pursuing them and the emperor, standing on an elevated site with his retinue, saw what was happening. He realised that, in pursuing the fleeing troops, the Bulgars were not following any plan and that they had completely broken ranks. He therefore rallied the men accompanying him, exhorting them to be of good courage and not to let the reputation of the Romans waste away to nothing. Then he made a lightning assault on the enemy, a move so unexpected that he was able to

---

[1] On this reign see (most recently) T. K. Korres, *Leo V the Armenian and his age: a crucial decade for Byzantium (811–820)* (in Greek) (Thessalonike, 1996).
[2] *Tourmarch* of the *tagma*.
[3] Skylitzes has passed over some very serious events. In July 813 Leo tried to surprise Krum and kill him while negotiations were in progress. This so enraged the khan that he ravaged Thrace as far as Ganos, burning and devastating Selymbria, Rhaidestos and Apros. Meanwhile Krum's brother seized Adrianople and numerous prisoners were taken back to Bulgaria. Krum died suddenly on 13 April 814 while attacking Constantinople yet again. The uncertainties of the Bulgar succession led to the lifting of the siege: W. Treadgold, *The Byzantine revival, 782–842* (Stanford, CA, 1988), 201–7.
[4] By the beginning of 816 Omurtag, son of Krum, had established himself as Khan of the Bulgars.

turn back those whom he encountered and to throw the rest of the Bulgar forces into confusion by this unexpected attack. They were so filled with terror and dismay that nobody gave a thought to valour. Many were those who fell in this attack, including the commander-in-chief, although he was quickly placed in the saddle of a very fast horse by his close associates and was able to save his life by running away. Many more were taken prisoner than fell in the field.[5] This action humbled the high-minded Bulgars while giving new courage to the Romans, whose hopes had been flagging and falling low. [14] Re-entering the capital with illustrious trophies and much booty,[6] the emperor applied himself to the affairs of state.

2. It was at this point that the emperor recalled to mind the matter of the monk of Philomelion; he resolved to reward him with gifts and offerings for the prophecy concerning himself. So he sent one of the men in whom he had the most confidence, entrusting him with offerings: furnishings, vessels of silver and gold and sweet-smelling goods such as are sent to us from India. But it emerged that the monk in question was dead and that another monk was installed in his cell as his successor. This monk's name was Sabbatios, one who was filled with the godless heresy of those who oppose the icons.[7] When the man sent by the emperor arrived in the presence of this monk, he urged him to accept the gifts which the emperor had sent for his master – and to reward the sender with a letter and his prayers. But the monk, unwilling to receive what was sent, urged the bearer to retrace his footsteps. The emperor was unworthy of the purple (he said), because he was addicted to the idols and, moreover, he put his trust in what had been said by the empress Eirene and the patriarch Tarasios. Of these,

---

[5] The sources differ in their accounts of the battle. *Scriptor incertus*, intro. E. Pinto; text, Italian trs. and notes, F. Iadevaia (Messina, 1987), claims that Leo took the enemy camp by surprise, at night. All agree, however, that the emperor scored a great victory (April 816).

[6] After the defeat of 816 the Bulgars agreed to a peace treaty at the end of that year. It was to be valid for three-quarters of a century, and it provided for the restoration of Thrace and Macedonia which had been gravely damaged in the recent wars: W. Treadgold, 'The Bulgars' treaty with the Byzantines in 816', *Rivista di Studi Bizantini e Slavi*, 4 (1984), 213–20.

[7] The iconoclastic controversy broke out in the reign of Leo III the Isaurian and was exacerbated under his son, Constantine V Kopronymos, who made iconoclasm the official teaching of the empire at the council of Hiereia in 754. With the support mainly of the monks the empress Eirene re-established the cult of images at the council of 787, but significant opposition to their use still smouldered among both clergy and laity. The confrontation was acrimonious, iconoclasts calling their adversaries idolaters while these charged those with impiety. Of the many writings on iconoclasm, see G. Dagron, *Histoire du christianisme*, IV: *Evêques, moines et empereurs (610–1054)*, ed. G. Dagron, P. Riché and A. Vauchez (Paris, 1993), 93–105. On the sources for this period: L. Brubaker and J. Haldon, *Byzantium in the Iconoclast Era (ca 680–850): the sources; An annotated survey with a section on the architecture of Iconoclasm: the buildings* by R. Ousterhout, Birmingham Byzantine and Ottoman monographs 7, Aldershot 2001.

he called Eirene 'panther'[8] and 'folly', while this evil man renamed that ever-memorable patriarch 'taraxios' [trouble maker]. He threatened that the emperor would soon fall from his imperial rank and lose his life unless he were quickly convinced by the monk's arguments and overturned the divine images. When the sovereign received the letter and learnt from the messenger what he had heard the monk say with his own ears, he was deeply troubled. He sent for Theodotos Melissenos and discussed with him what should be done concerning this matter. Now Theodotos had been in the clutches of this [iconoclastic] heresy for some time and was only waiting for the right moment to speak openly of such impiety. Some such advice as this he gave to the emperor: there was a monk living in Dagisthe[9] (he said) who performed extraordinary deeds. 'The matter must be entrusted to him,' he said, 'and whatever he prescribes, that is what must be done' – that is what he said to the emperor. Then he came out quickly and went to the monk in question and said to him: [15] 'Tomorrow night the emperor will come to you in ordinary clothing, to ask about the faith and other pressing matters. For your part, you are to remember to threaten him with the imminent loss of his life and his fall from the throne, unless he choose of his own free will to embrace the dogma of the emperor Leo the Isaurian and to cast out the idols' – that is what he called the holy icons – 'from the churches of God. Nor must you forget to promise him that, if he adopts the way of life you suggest, he will enjoy a long life and a fortunate reign of many years.' Having given the monk his instructions and coached him in what he ought to say to the emperor, he went his way. Shortly after, taking the emperor with him dressed in ordinary clothing, he came to the monk by night. When the conversation was under way, the monk, standing right next to the emperor, said to him (as though it had just been revealed to him by divine inspiration that this man was of imperial rank): 'What you are doing is not sensible, O emperor, deceiving us with private citizens' clothes and concealing the emperor hidden within them. Do what you will, the grace of the divine Spirit has not allowed us to be outsmarted by you any longer.' The emperor was taken aback when he heard this and realised that he had not succeeded in concealing his imperial rank beneath a simple costume, but this is hardly surprising in one who did not know the mischief that was being practised on him.

[8] *Pardo* in Greek, possibly a reference to her father whose name might have been Leo Pardos.
[9] Dagisthe took its name from the palace (no doubt built by Justinian's general Dagisthe) and baths of that name lying between the forums of Constantine and Theodosius. The palace in question belonged to Leo; he had received it from the emperor Nikephoros: R. Janin, *Constantinople byzantine* (*AOC*, 4A, Paris, 1964), 331–3.

Taking the monk to be a godly man, he obediently undertook speedily to execute what he proposed; he accordingly decreed the taking-down of the sacred icons.

First of all, he made a secret enquiry whether it was possible for him to accomplish what he had in mind without stirring up a storm in church circles. Then he brought the dogma out into the open and the leading citizens and churchmen bowed to his command, some willingly, some against their will. Even the great patriarch Nikephoros of eternal memory was being coerced to set his signature to the document ordering the holy icons to be taken down. And, when he refused to be coerced, this patriarch Nikephoros (who had observed some time beforehand the sinister intentions of Leo and how he would harm and disturb church affairs) was exiled by the emperor to Prokonnesos.[10] Indeed, when the blessed Nikephoros was setting the diadem on Leo's head, it had seemed to him as though his hands were being pierced by prickles and thorns – which he set down as a symbol and omen of the evils which ensued.

[16] When the great patriarch was being taken into exile,[11] Theophanes Confessor, hegoumenos of the monastery of Agros,[12] was staying on an estate [of that monastery]. Perceiving the other's approach by divine inspiration, he accompanied him with incense and lights as he went by in a ship. As for the patriarch, he received this salutation with profound acts of obeisance, greeting Theophanes in return by stretching out his hands in blessings. Neither man saw, nor was seen by, the other; but, beholding each other with the eyes of the spirit, each one offered the other the customary reverence. One of those who travelled with him asked the patriarch: 'Lord-and-master, whom were you greeting with your hands raised on high?' 'The most holy confessor, Theophanes, hegoumenos of the Agros monastery, who accompanies us with incense and lights,' he replied. Not long afterwards, the patriarch's prediction was borne out by the event for, before long, Theophanes (along with many others) was banished from the church. After being subject to many and unlimited woes, he received the confessor's crown, never again being permitted to set eyes

---

[10] A large island in the sea of Marmara, famous for its marble quarries which furnished the material for many of the buildings erected in the earlier Byzantine period.
[11] 13 March 815.
[12] Born into a military family in 760, Theophanes became hegoumenos of the Agros monastery in Bithynia. He is the author of the chronicle (*Chronographia*) which concludes with the accession of Leo V (Skylitzes mentions him in his prooimion). On the Agros monastery see C. Mango and I. Ševčenko, 'Some churches and monasteries on the southern shore of the sea of Marmara', *DOP*, 27 (1973), 259ff; on Theophanes as chronicler, see A. Kazhdan, in collaboration with L. F. Sherry and C. Angelidi, *A history of Byzantine literature (650–850)* (Athens, 1999), 205–34.

on the patriarch, so that not even in this particular did his prediction fail to come true.[13]

Once the patriarch had been sent into exile, as we reported, on the very day of the resurrection of the Lord, Theodotos Melissenos (also known as Kassiteras, as our narrative said) unworthily acceded to the patriarchal throne. Once he had mounted the throne, having the cooperation of the imperial authority, he proclaimed the heresy of those who were opposed to the icons, no longer in secret and in corners, but openly and boldly.[14]

3. Puffed up by the above-mentioned victory against the Bulgars, Leo had also recently achieved some success against the Arabs. He was now unbearable in his attitude, inclined to be harsh and very cruel. He became implacable in his anger and excessively severe in punishing faults. To those who wished to plead with him, he had nothing to say and was very hard to deal with. For small offences he awarded heavy punishments. For some, he cut off a hand, for others a foot or, in other cases, [17] some other vital member. The pieces which he had ordered to be amputated he now caused to be hung up along the main thoroughfare, no doubt to strike consternation and fear into those who beheld them. Thus he earned the hatred of all his subjects.

4. Subsequent events increased that hatred yet further, for it was not only against men of equally distinguished origin that he raged and stormed; he was also filled with frenzy against the sacred faith itself and against God. As his efficient agent for this business he employed a man well known for villainy, the master of the order of palatine choristers. Outwardly he seemed to be worthy and god-fearing but within, as though beneath a thick fleece, he was really a wolf lying in wait. This wicked man[15] found a suitable occasion to strike; it was when – as custom dictated – one read aloud in church the prophecy of that most eloquent of the prophets, Isaiah, the one which says: 'To whom will ye liken the Lord? Or with what will ye compare

---

[13] Convicted of revering the icons, Theophanes was banished to Samothrace where he died in March 817. His *Life* can be read in *Theophanis Chronographia*, ed. C. de Boor, 2 vols. (Leipzig 1883–5), II, 3–30.
[14] Before reintroducing the acts of the iconoclast council of Hiereia, Leo V did in fact discuss the matter with the most eminent churchmen, including the patriarch Nikephoros and Theodore, hegoumenos of Stoudios' monastery, both of whom were in favour of the icons. He overrode their opposition and re-enacted iconoclasm just after Easter 815 – without encountering a great deal of opposition from the secular church (Dagron, *Histoire du Christianisme*, IV, 139–42).
[15] According to the *Scriptor incertus* (349–52), John the Grammarian, subsequently synkellos and patriarch under Theophilos (*PmbZ* 3199 = *PBE* Ioannes 5), was ordered to peruse the works of ancient authors in the libraries looking for arguments to support the condemnation of the cult of images. It is by no means certain that this is the man to whom Skylitzes is referring since there is no confirmation of John ever having been the palace choirmaster.

him? Was it not the carpenter who made the image, the goldsmith who melted gold and gilded it, and made a likeness of himself' … and the rest of the prophecy.[16] Then he approached the emperor and whispered in his ear: 'Give understanding to what is said [here], oh emperor, and do not let the truth elude you. Embrace the pattern of devotion which the prophet proposes for you.' And, so saying, he implanted yet more of the poison of the heresy in Leo's mind. The result was that the manner of worship which, formerly, he was at pains to proclaim sparingly and with hesitation, he now proclaimed brazenly and shamelessly. Or, to speak more plainly, he compelled people to follow the heresy by threats and affliction. From that day, all those who chose the softer path and betrayed the truth were safe and sound; but those who disobeyed his most sacrilegious command were handed over to irremediable tortures and afflictions.

5. In spite of such impiety and criminality, he was extremely vigilant in his handling of affairs of state, to the point that [18] nothing necessary or useful was left unattended to. They say too that, after his death, the patriarch Nikephoros opined that, although the Roman state had indeed lost an irreligious ruler in Leo, he was, nevertheless, a great one. And, in addition to his diligent and attentive administration of public business, he was the implacable foe of those who acted unjustly. Thus, one day as he was leaving the palace, a man came up to him and complained that a member of the senate had taken his wife away. 'I complained to the prefect of the city about this, but received no satisfaction.' Having heard what the man said, the emperor immediately ordered the accused senator and the prefect to appear before him when he returned. Immediately, when he was home again, the aggrieved man who sought justice, the one who had committed the alleged deed and the prefect himself appeared before him. When the emperor commanded the plaintiff to relate what had befallen him, the man explained the matter from beginning to end. As for the one accused of the offence, since he was unable to escape from the accusation and could see that he was hemmed in on every side by the allegations against him, he confessed his transgression. When the emperor asked the prefect why he had not awarded a fitting punishment for this crime, he was struck dumb and incapable of offering any excuse, so the emperor dismissed him from his office. He handed the adulterer over to suffer the punishments prescribed by law. For most of the time, the emperor used to sit in the Lausiac hall appointing commanders, generals and governors,

---

[16] Isa. 40:18–20, read at the morning office (orthros) on Tuesday of the fifth week of Lent.

choosing them from among the most worthy and incorruptible of men, being disdainful of money and very parsimonious himself.[17]

6. He was very proud of his voice and aspired to be something of a musician, but his natural gifts were not commensurate with this aspiration.[18] He could not keep time and he had little talent for singing in tune either. Nevertheless, he was accustomed to lead the worship in the psalm-singing, and especially so when the canons of the feast were being sung on the day of Christ's nativity. He would intone the odes with his strident but untrained voice and when he intoned the verse of the seventh ode [for Christmas] which begins: 'For love of the Sovereign supreme they poured contempt …'[19] he opened himself up to be laughed to scorn by those who heard him, he who had 'poured contempt' upon the fear of God and thrown in his lot with the demons by denying the all-sacred icons. So much for the emperor in these matters.

7. [19] Michael of Amorion, ever attempting to advance and to rise to higher things,[20] was accused of high treason. Having albeit with difficulty cleared himself of this charge, he was sent by the emperor to drill the troops under his command. Now Michael was prone to all the other vices, but he was especially incapable of disciplining his tongue, the very member which is capable of divulging the secrets one hides within the heart. He spoke all his thoughts openly and even uttered some unseemly remarks against the emperor himself, threatening to deprive him of the throne and to take his wife in an unholy union. When the emperor heard about these things he first attempted resourcefully, without revealing the nature of this knowledge, to turn Michael aside from his imprudent loquacity and evil counsels, for he knew that the man suffered from the terrible affliction of an unbridled tongue. But when he had taken resource, to the extent practicable, to threats and exhortations, he discovered that Michael not only denied saying the things that were said but also, once he had again gained the courage, did not distance himself from what he intended to do. He secretly sent out spies and eavesdroppers against him, who frequently encountered him at banquets and drinking parties when, detached from his wits by wine, he quite enthusiastically added to his former statements. They duly reported this to the emperor and their testimony was endorsed

---

[17] It is surprising to read this frank praise of an iconoclast emperor. Theophilos receives similar approval for his sense of justice.
[18] The other sources credit Leo with a fine voice and praise his musicianship.
[19] Hirmos of the seventh ode of the iambic canon sung during the morning office (orthros) on 25 December.
[20] Michael was by now a patrician and domestic of the Exkoubitai.

by Hexaboulios,[21] a man of good sense and a frequent companion of the emperor, not unknown to Michael. He often tried to turn Michael aside from talking indiscreetly. He counselled him to be silent and not to speak out so inopportunely, attracting such obvious danger to himself. But, since he would not heed the warnings, the man made a clean breast of everything concerning Michael to the emperor. So, on Christmas Eve,[22] being in possession of these allegations, the emperor presided over a court of inquiry in the chamber of the principal secretaries, discharging the role of a diligent examiner of the charges that had been laid. Michael was now convicted of attempted usurpation; indeed, he was obliged to admit it himself, such was the weight of the evidence against him. He was condemned to death by fire. They were to throw him into the furnace of the palace bathhouse and the emperor was going to witness the execution. He was led away, a prisoner condemned to death, the emperor following after, eager to see what was going to happen next.

8. [20] As they made their way to the bathhouse, the empress Theodosia (Arsaber's[23] daughter) heard what was going to take place. She came flying out of her boudoir, burning with rage and fury. Approaching the emperor, she told him that he was an offence to heaven and an enemy of God if he failed to exercise forbearance on this sacred day in which he was going to receive the communion of the divine body. And she blunted his determination, for he was afraid of offending God. So he straightaway reversed his judgement and granted Michael a reprieve. But he put him in leg-irons and kept the key himself, giving the keeper of the palace[24] charge of the prisoner. Then he turned to his wife and said: 'Woman, thanks to your ravings, I have done as you required. But before long, you and my offspring will see what bad fortune is in store for us, even though you have delivered me from sinning this day.' Thus he, who was by no stretch of the imagination a prophet, accurately predicted the future.

---

[21] The same name occurs above in the form of Exaboulios. Leo V had promoted him to patrician and appointed him logothete of the drome. This is why he was given the responsibility of keeping an eye on Michael. Among other departments, the logothete of the drome directed the intelligence services.

[22] 24 December 820.

[23] Arsaber, patrician and quaestor of Armenian origin, rebelled against Nikephoros I in 808 (*ODB*, 1, 156 and *PmbZ* 600 = *PBE* Arsaber 1). Theodosia had already crossed her husband on the question of the icons, the patriarch Nikephoros having asked her to intervene to prevent him from condemning them.

[24] The *papias* was the keeper of the keys of the palace, superintendent of its buildings and chief warder of its prison. No other mention of this office is known prior to the reign of Leo VI: N. Oikonomides, *Les listes de préséance byzantines des IXe et Xe siècles* (Le monde byzantin, Paris, 1972), 306.

9. It is said that an oracle had been delivered to him some time earlier which said that he was destined to be deprived both of the imperial dignity and also of his very life itself on the day of the birth and incarnation of Christ our God. It was a Sibylline oracle, written in a certain book in the imperial library which contained not only oracles, but also pictures and the features of those who had been emperors, depicted in colours.[25] Now there was a ferocious lion portrayed in that book. Above its spine and going down to its belly was the letter X. There was a man running after the beast and striking it a mortal blow with his lance, right in the centre of the X. On account of the obscurity of the oracle, only the then quaestor could make sense of its meaning: that an emperor named Leo was going to be delivered to a bitter death on the day of Christ's nativity. The emperor was no less dismayed and frightened by his own mother's vision. It seemed to her (who was a frequent visitor at the holy church of the Mother of God at Blachernae) that she met a maiden there carrying a lance, escorted by two men dressed in white. But she also saw that sacred church filled with blood; and the maiden in the vision ordered one of those dressed in white to fill a vessel with blood and give it to Leo's mother to drink. She protested that throughout her long widowhood she had eaten neither meat nor anything else containing blood, and this was her excuse for not touching the vessel. 'Then why,' the maiden angrily exclaimed, 'does your son not refrain from filling me with blood and from angering my son and God?' From then on, she used to intercede with her son to desist from the heresy of the iconoclasts, recounting the vision in tragic tones. And there was yet another vision which troubled him more than a little. In his dreams he saw the patriarch Tarasios of blessed memory, long since passed from this life. He seemed to call upon the name of a certain Michael, inciting him against Leo, to deal him a death blow. The prediction of the monk at Philomelion disturbed him too, as well as the exchange of garments which Michael had affected, which we related above in the course of the narrative. Frightened by all these things, the emperor fell prey to fear. His soul was tossed hither and thither; hence, he was frequently awake all night long.

10. Wiser counsels prevailing (or, at least, an attitude more becoming of an emperor), Leo forced the door leading to the palace keeper's quarters

---

[25] The compilation of imperial oracles (as opposed to Sybillines) is only attested in rather late MS but there is good reason to suppose that such texts were being made prior to the seventh century: *ODB*, 1890–1. On the uses of prophecies in general: P. Magdalino, 'The history of the future and its uses: prophecy, policy and propaganda', *The making of Byzantine history: studies dedicated to Donald M. Nicol*, ed. R. Beaton and C. Roueché (London, 1993), 3–34.

and looked in to see what was happening. As he entered a room, a sight met his eyes which left him dumbfounded. He beheld the condemned man lying gloriously ensconced in a high bed, while the palace keeper lay on the bare floor. He approached and looked more carefully at Michael. Did he have the shallow and troubled sleep of those whom destiny tosses around and whose life is a gamble? Or did he, on the contrary, enjoy a calm, untroubled rest? When he found him sleeping calmly (he couldn't waken him even when he touched him) his anger became yet more inflamed at this unexpected revelation. He went off at a deliberate pace, inveighing not only against Michael, but against the palace keeper too.

11. So much for the emperor. This [visit], however, did not pass unknown to the palace keeper's staff, for one of Michael's chamberlains recognised the purple buskins[26] [22] and reported everything in detail. Greatly perturbed and almost beside themselves at what they had heard, the palace keeper's staff puzzled their brains how to escape from danger. Day was breaking when Michael came up with this insidious plan: there were certain grave sins on his conscience which he wanted to confess to a godly father, using as intermediary Theoktistos, whom he later promoted to be prefect of the inkpot.[27] The emperor gave his approval and Michael, having summoned up his courage, said to Theoktistos: 'Now is the hour, Theoktistos. Threaten the conspirators that unless they make haste to get me out of danger, I am going to reveal the whole business to the emperor.' When Theoktistos had done as he was bidden, those who were privy to the plot encountered an unfortunate difficulty. They cast around in their minds how to save themselves and how to rescue Michael, who was now in even greater danger of death than before. They devised a plan to deliver themselves which would not only save Michael's life, but gain him the office of emperor. In those days it was not the custom (as it is now, and has been since the time of which we are speaking) for the clerks who sing in the palatine church to live in the palace, but each in his own home. About the third watch of the night they would assemble at the Elephantine Gate[28] and proceed from there to the church where they would sing the dawn

---

[26] The other sources say this person was sleeping *under* Michael's bed, hence he would only see the feet of the visitor.
[27] This Theoktistos, a eunuch not to be confused with the magister of the same name mentioned above, must have been very young at the time. He served the Amorion dynasty faithfully until he was assassinated by Caesar Bardas: *ODB*, III, 2056, *PmbZ* 8050 = *PBE* Theoktistos 3.
[28] Located within the Great Palace, the Elephantine (or Ivory) Gate provided access to the galleries on the upper floor of the palace of Daphne; this is where the prison of the Great Palace was located: R. Guilland, *Études de topographie de Constantinople Byzantine*, 2 vols. (Amsterdam, 1969), I, 170.

service. The conspirators mingled discreetly with the clerks, their daggers hidden in their cloaks, and went in with them. They then assembled in a dark corner of the church, awaiting the prearranged signal. As the hymn was being sung, the emperor – who was already there – led off the singing, as was his custom: 'For love of the sovereign supreme they poured contempt …'[29] (As we remarked, he had a strident voice.) It was then that the conspirators struck, en masse. Their first attack went awry because they mistook the master of the clerks for the emperor, perhaps because he bore a certain physical resemblance to him; or because he was wearing the same kind of headgear. For it was a cold winter night, so everybody was in heavy clothing and each man had covered his head with a closely fitting pointed felt hat. The master of the clerks averted the danger by removing the cap from his head and accomplished his survival with his baldness. When the emperor realised that he was being attacked, he went into the sanctuary and seized the thurible by its chains (some say it was the sacred cross) [23] with which to ward off the blows of his attackers. But the conspirators attacked all together, not one at a time. One struck him on the head, another in the belly, each wounding a different part of his body. He was able to resist for some time by parrying the sword thrusts with the sacred cross, but then he was set upon from all sides, like a wild beast. He was already beginning to flag from his wounds when, finally, seeing a giant of a man about to deal him a blow, he invoked the grace which inhabited the church with an oath and begged to be spared. This good fellow was one of the Krambonitai family.[30] 'This is not the time for swearing oaths, but for killing,' he declared – and dealt [Leo] a blow that cut the arm right through, not only severing it from the collar-bone but also sundering a branch of the cross. Someone also cut off his head, which was already damaged by wounds and hanging down.

Such was the end of Leo's life, in the month of December, about the tenth hour of the night, when he had reigned for seven years and five months. He was the most cruel man who ever lived, more sacrilegious

---

[29] Menaion for 25 December, the seventh ode at orthros.
[30] Great though the Krambonitai may have been at the time of the assassination, this family does not appear to have known any further distinction. One Constantine Krambonites, spatharios and koubikoularios, possessed the eleventh-century Cod. Vatic. gr. 1615: F. Evangelatou-Notara, *Sêmeiômata*: a Greek codex as a source for the study of the economic and social life of Byzantium from the ninth century to the year 1204 (in Greek, Athens 1982), 107–8. Several seals of members of this family have survived: M. Popovic, 'Der Familienname Krambonites und ähnliche Formen aud Siegeln sowie in anderen Quellen' in *Akten des 8. Internationalen Symposion für Byzantinische Sigilographische*, ed. Cl. Ludwig, Berliner Byzantinische Studien 7, Frankfurt–Berlin 2005, 123–9.

than all his predecessors, which rather detracts from both the care with which he conducted affairs of state and his excellence in war. It is said that a voice from heaven immediately resounded, announcing the good news of his demise to many people. Among those who heard it were some sailors who noted the time and the [hour of] the night. Later, when it was all over, [the announcement] was found to have been quite correct.

CHAPTER 3

Michael II the Stammerer [820–829]

1. [24] After Leo was put to death, his assassins callously dragged his corpse through the Skyla gate[1] and brought it into the Hippodrome, fearing nothing because the imperial palace was guarded at all points by their own forces. His wife was hauled off from the palace together with her four children, Symbatios (whose name was changed to Constantine after his proclamation as co-emperor), Basil, Gregory and Theodosios.[2] They were thrust into a skiff and brought to the island of Prote[3] where all four were castrated. Theodosios succumbed and went to share his own father's grave.

As for Michael, he was now released from the prison of the *papias*, his feet still restrained by fetters[4] because the key to the irons was kept in Leo's bosom. It was thus that he now sat on the imperial throne, fetters and all; that is how he was when all those then holding palatine appointments acclaimed him and fell down before him. Then, towards midday, when the rumour had spread in all directions (by now his fetters had been struck off with a hammer),[5] without even washing his hands, with no fear of God in his heart nor with any thought of what else ought to be done, off he went to the Great Church of the [holy] Wisdom, anxious to be crowned by the hand of the patriarch and to be publicly acclaimed. He trusted nobody

---

[1] This gate provided communication between the *triklinos* of Justinian II in the Great Palace and the Hippodrome: R. Guilland, *Études de topographie de Constantinople byzantine* (Amsterdam, 1969), I, 518.
[2] Pseudo-Symeon Logothetes (619) says that all four of them became monks. Symbatios-Constantine (*PmbZ* 3925 = *PBE* Constantine 29) is mentioned below: the miracle of his voice recovered and his faith in the icons. Nothing more is heard of him. Basil (*PmbZ* 927 = *PBE* Basil 54) and Gregory (*PmbZ* 2474 = *PBE* Gregory 70) became iconophiles like their elder brother and supported the elevation of Methodios to the patriarchate in 847: Genesios 4.18.
[3] One of the Princes' islands where there were several monasteries in which deposed emperors and their heirs were interned from time to time: R. Janin, *Les églises et les monastères des grands centres byzantins* (Paris, 1975), II, 70–2.
[4] A reference to Ps. 104:18?
[5] According to Genesios (2.1), John Exaboulios revealed that the keys were still on Leo's corpse; that is how they freed him from his chains.

other than his fellow conspirators who had carried out the assassination. At this point one might well wonder at these two emperors' lack of judgement: the outgoing one who had no one to help him among such a large and varied rout of flatterers, all of whom took refuge in their holes like snakes; and the disorderly, shameless nature of the one after him who went into church, not like some murderer or executioner with bloodied hands, but rather as a victorious athlete and conqueror, [25] exulting over what had happened – he who had just shed the blood of a fellow countryman, not in any common place, but in God's sanctuary where the Lord's blood is daily poured out for the forgiveness of our sins.

2. This Michael[6] was from a city named Amorion in upper Phrygia. In former times numerous Jews,[7] Athinganoi and other impious people took up residence there.[8] Out of their contact and constant communication with each other there emerged a sect of a novel kind, one with absurd doctrines. Following in the religious tradition of his family, Michael was a member of this sect. It permitted its adepts to partake of the godly and salvific [rite of] baptism but otherwise reverently observed the Mosaic law – except for circumcision. Michael had living with him a Jew (or maybe a Jewess) as his teacher and almost his governor, by whom he was inducted into the sect. This person not only gave him spiritual instruction, but also dictated how his household was to be run. Under this tutor he retained nothing that was pure but, rather, an agglomeration of disbeliefs; for he debased Christian doctrines, counterfeited Jewish beliefs and corrupted all the rest. From a religious point of view he was as diverse and varied as those African beasts which (they say), impelled by thirst, gather together at the rare watering holes and all mate with each other. Once he acceded to imperial power, he solemnly maintained and gloried in these doctrines, more so than in the diadem and the purple. As for literature and education (which could have modified his beliefs and taught him better

---

[6] Arab sources say his father's name was Leo, his grandfather George (A. A. Vasiliev, *Byzance et les Arabes*, I: *La dynastie d'Amorium, 820–867* (Brussels, 1935); II: *Les relations politiques de Byzance et des arabes à l'époque de la dynastie macédonienne*, ed. M. Canard (CBHB, 2.1, Brussels, 1968), 1, 311, the translation of Tabari).

[7] There is no confirmation of this elsewhere.

[8] On these see J. Starr, 'An eastern Christian sect: the Athinganoi', *Harvard Theological Review*, 29 (1936), 93–106; also I. Rochow, 'Die Häresie des Athinganer in 8. und 9. Jahrhundert und die Frage ihres Fortlebens', *Studien zum 8. und 9. Jahrhundert in Byzanz*, ed. H. Köpstein and F. Winckelmann, 163ff. Lastly: P. Speck, 'Die vermeintliche Häresie der Athinganoi', *JÖB*, 47 (1997), 37–50. The Athinganoi were banished from Constantinople to Phrygia by Michael I. The future Leo V (then strategos of the Anatolikon theme) carried out the operation: *Theophanis Chronographia*, ed. C. de Boor (Leipzig, 1883–5), 497. The Phrygians were notoriously receptive to heresies ever since the arrival of the Montanists; see J. Gouillard, 'L'hérésie dans l'Empire byzantin des origines au xiie siècle,' *TM*, 1 (1965), 299–324.

things), these he rejected and scorned,[9] eminently favouring those skills in which he excelled. These consisted of such abilities as being able to predict which of a litter of newborn pigs would fare well and not fail to develop large bodies, which would fall prey to adversity; standing close to kicking horses; having the knack of restraining kicking asses from far away. He was an excellent judge of mules, able to tell which would serve best as beasts of burden, which would be serviceable mounts and not be suddenly affrighted into throwing the rider and breaking his neck. He could even tell just by looking at horses which would have speed and stamina on the road, which would serve their riders valiantly in battle. As for sheep and cattle, [26] he could tell to which it had befallen by nature to produce fine young or an abundance of milk; he could discern by which mothers newly born animals had been born, and just from their appearance. Such then were the skills in which he gloried, not only in his youth but, it must be said, towards the end of his life too.

3. By the time he achieved manhood, persistent poverty was his lot – but he left no stone unturned in his attempts to remedy this situation. One day when he was accompanying his commander,[10] the latter noted that he stammered when reporting to him. One of the Athinganoi, a man with whom the commander was acquainted, disclosed to him that this Michael and another person would soon become famous and attain the imperial throne before long. This so impressed the commander that, thinking he was seeing the future in a mirror, he was loath to postpone an opportunity which might not easily be recaptured. So he immediately prepared a feast and invited the two men to dine, to the exclusion of all others, even of those who were of superior birth and rank. When the wine was flowing freely, he introduced his daughters and gave them to his guests, announcing that they were to be his sons-in-law.[11] At first the two were quite overcome by the strange and puzzling nature of the proceedings, but they accepted the offer and gave their undertakings, thinking that such a thing had to be the work of God, not of man. That is how it was.

Having accepted the pronouncement of the aforementioned adherent of the Athinganoi as a divine prediction, Michael took the second pronouncement of the monk of Philomelion (we have already spoken of this) as a prophecy too. Then he was more eager and determined than

---

[9] These harsh words are occasioned by Michael's alleged iconoclasm, even though he never committed himself to it. All the iconoclast emperors were accused of being under the influence of enemies of the faith, especially of Jews.
[10] Bardanios Tourkos.
[11] Michael's first wife, Thekla, was the daughter of Bardanios Tourkos: D. Turner, 'The origins and accession of Leo V (813–20)', *JÖB*, 40, (1990), 171–203, at 202.

ever to assassinate Leo. Having showed himself treacherous towards his former benefactor (the man named Bardanios), he would now do even worse to his second, meaning Leo, who was the godfather of his own son.[12] Nevertheless, having brought about the atrocious murder of Leo, he did stipulate that a portion of Leo's confiscated possessions be set aside for the maintenance of his children [27] and of their mother. Also, some of his own servants were seconded to wait upon them. Leo's spouse he ordered to be confined in the monastery known as Despotai,[13] the male children on the island of Prote (as we said), where Theodosios died after they had all been castrated.[14] Constantine (whose name had been changed to Basil) was struck dumb after the castration. He prayed God to release his voice and prayed also to Gregory,[15] famous among theologians, of whom there was an image there. The saint received his prayer and [his] sacred image appeared to Constantine proclaiming: 'Take this candle and, at the dawn service this morning, read.' Trusting in what was said, he entered [the church] and read [the prayer] 'Yet again, O my Jesus'[16] with a clear, pure voice. Once he had regained his voice, he held the hereditary madness [of iconoclasm] as anathema and converted to the right attitude towards the sacred icons. But that was later.

4. Once Michael had arrogated the imperial power and was doing with it what he would, Nikephoros, the patriarch of eternal memory, sent him a letter imploring him to re-establish reverence for the sacred icons and to restore godliness. Michael replied that he was not come to do any mischief to the established religious practices nor in any way to attack or damage the received traditions: 'Let each one do what seems right and desirable to him, free of punishment and knowing no affliction.' But he, who was no true Christian at the beginning, certainly did not maintain this attitude

---

[12] Theophilos.
[13] This may have been at Constantinople, possibly to be identified with the monastery of the Despoinai founded by Mary, the wife of Constantine VI: R. Janin, *La géographie ecclésiastique de l'empire byzantin*, I, *Le siège de Constantinople et le patriarcat œcuménique*, III, *Les églises et les monastères* (Paris, 1969), 88.
[14] Thus Leo's children suffered the fate he had inflicted on the children of Michael I. Leo's eldest son, Symbatios, had been associated with his father under the name of Constantine (cf. Leo III and Constantine V, father and son who co-ruled for some years). The other sons were Basil, Gregory and Theodosius (Turner, 'Leo V', 202).
[15] Gregory of Nazianzos, *c.* 329 to *c.* 390, patriarch of Constantinople, 380–1, famed for his opposition to heresy expressed in letters and homilies. There are several *vitae* of this saint, one written in the seventh century by Gregory the Priest: *ODB*, 880–2. It is impossible to say in which church this icon of Gregory Theologos was located; Janin knows of no shrine dedicated in his name either on Prote or Halke (where Basil later stayed with his mother): Janin, *Grands centres*, II, 70–2 and 72–6.
[16] From the *troparion* sung at Vespers on 2 January, a poem by Andrew of Crete.

Michael II the Stammerer

to the end. As his hold on the empire became more firmly established, so did he (with his extremely crude and diabolically malignant nature) renew the war [28] against the Christians, his fellow countrymen. Now he would assault the monks, afflicting them with a variety of terrors and devising one punishment after another; now he would throw others of the faithful into gaol or send them into exile. Methodios,[17] who a little later was thought worthy of the patriarchal throne, and Euthymios, then bishop of Sardis, withstood him, refusing to renounce the practice of revering the sacred icons; these he expelled from the capital city for their pains. He imprisoned the sacred Methodios on the island of Akritas[18] and put the blessed Euthymios to death by a merciless flogging with bull's sinews at the hand of Theophilos, his [Michael's] own son.[19] In the same measure by which he thus afflicted Christ's heritage, he also relieved the Jews of taxes and restraints; for these he loved and cherished most dearly above all other men. As a pattern and model for imitation in his own life he took the life of Kopronymos[20] and made every effort to be like him. Thus he attained the very acme and meridian of godlessness, now ordering fasting on Saturdays, now sharpening his tongue against the sacred prophets; now denying the resurrection to come and decrying the good things promised in the next world. He would affirm that there was no such thing as the devil because there was no mention of him in the Mosaic [law]. He embraced *porneia*,[21] stipulated that swearing should always be by God and, with his unbridled tongue, located Judas among the saved. He ridiculed the feast of salvation-bringing Easter for being celebrated badly and out of season, portraying it as a pagan tradition. He was so alienated from our own sacred teaching that he would not even allow the young

---

[17] Hailing from Syracuse, Methodios studied at Constantinople, became a monk in one of the Bithynian monasteries and some time after 815 was sent to Rome to plead the cause of the deposed patriarch Nikephoros. He returned in 821 but was expelled by Michael II: *ODB*, 1355, *PmbZ* 4977 = *PBE* Methodios 1.

[18] This island (today Tuzla) lies in the mouth of the Bosporos. Janin *Grands centres*, II, 53–4, says Methodios would have been kept in the monastery of St Andrew.

[19] Until his death in 831, Euthymios of Sardis was one of the most outstanding proponents of the icons. He became a bishop towards 790 but was sent into exile by Nikephoros for political reasons and kept there by Leo V for religious ones. Contrary to what Skylitzes says, Michael II allowed him to return. Theophilos accused him of plotting and flogged him so hard he died. His *Life* was composed by Methodios: ed. J. Gouillard, 'La vie d'Euthyme de Sardes (*ob* 831)', *TM*, 10 (1987), 1–101; *PmbZ* 1838 = *PBE* Euthymius 1.

[20] The emperor Constantine V Kopronymos (741–75), the notorious iconoclast who was nevertheless victorious against both Arabs and Bulgars. His detractors claim that he defiled the font at his baptism.

[21] A difficult word to translate; it denotes every form of illicit sexual activity, in thought, word or deed.

to be educated, this so that nobody would be able to withstand and condemn his mindlessness; nor any man whose eye had been sharpened and his speech quickened by education get the better of him. He was so slow in construing his letters and reading syllables that it was easier for one to read a [whole] book than for this slow-minded fellow to decipher the letters of his own name. But I should leave aside this matter which has been sufficiently dealt with elsewhere and get on with the history.

5. [29] A civil war broke out in the east at that time which filled the inhabited world with all kinds of evil; there was great loss of life and, consequently, depopulation. Thomas was the originator of this uprising, of whom they tell two different stories. One says he was the child of insignificant, poor parents of barbaric origin. After living in poverty for a long time, gaining the necessities of life by manual labour, even as a hired hand sometimes, he left his native land and came to this great city. Here he entered the service of a senator but became so undisciplined and arrogant that he even dared to insult his master's marriage bed. Caught in the act, he could not bear the reproach and he was terrified of the kind of punishments reserved for such crimes, so he fled to the Hagarenes. He gained their confidence by performing appropriate deeds and by confirming the deeds with constancy – for his stay with them lasted twenty-five years; also by forswearing the holy religion of the Christians and embracing that of the cursed Mohammed. He was designated chief of a war band and dispatched against the Christians, for he had undertaken to deliver the empire of the Romans into their hands. To ensure that his difference of race and religion provide no obstacle to his reception by the Romans, he gave it out that he was Constantine [VI] the son of Eirene. (On account of his evilmindedness, his disgusting manners and his odious habits, she deprived her son of both his throne and of his eyes; subsequently he lost his life.)[22]

So huge was the undertaking and so powerful the aspirations which ruled [Thomas] that a colleague was necessary to cope with the situation. He could not possibly have dealt with it alone, having undertaken to wage war both by land and by sea. He adopted as his son a man the mere

---

[22] Constantine VI was too young to reign at the death of his father (Leo IV the Khazar), hence he had to endure the regency of his mother, Eirene, who, moreover, imposed an odious marriage on him. He put away his wife in favour of a relative of Theodore the Stoudite, thus provoking the so-called moechian scandal. When he finally achieved the throne, his foreign policy was such a failure and his relations with his supporters so inept that his mother was able to regain power, whereupon she blinded her son, thus provoking his death. Skylitzes takes a favourable view of Eirene because she permitted the first restoration of the icons. W. Treadgold, *The Byzantine revival, 782–842* (Stanford, CA, 1988), 96–110.

physical appearance [30] of whom declared the vacuity of his soul. He committed a sufficient force to this man (whom he renamed Konstantios) and despatched him to one region with orders to devastate Roman territory.[23] As for himself, he went off to a another region, wasting and ravaging everything in his path. Leo [V] the Armenian (who was holding the reins of the empire at that time) sent out an inadequate force against him which suffered a total defeat, thus rendering Thomas yet more bold and impetuous. Such is the first story of this uprising and it is widely believed.[24]

According to the second story, Thomas was the man who was formerly with Bardanios and concerning whom that monk uttered his prediction at Philomelion. He had already been put in command of the regiment of the foederati by the emperor Leo when he learnt that Leo had been assassinated by Michael. So, under pretence of avenging his benefactor but also to serve his own interests (for he and Michael had been rivals since their youth) he raised a hand against [the emperor], the fear inspired by what the monk had prophesied of him at Philomelion notwithstanding. His revolt began in the Anatolikon theme where he was stationed;[25] there he assembled a force by no means weak and small but weighty and courageous. Every man capable of bearing arms of any kind he obliged to follow him, some by force, others for the sake of their friendship towards him; some by the prospect of the booty they might seize, others because of the hatred they had for Michael. He was indeed so widely hated for being so crude, for adhering to the sect of the Athinganoi, for his stammering and on account of his baseness and indolence, that everybody agreed to fight with

---

[23] This first adoptive son may have been called Konstantios (Genesios 2.4), recalling Constantine the Great whose son and successor was Konstantios. It is also possible that Thomas did not claim to *be* Constantine VI (he was too well known to the eastern armies) but that he was defending the legal rights of that prince; a difficult task since everybody knew he had been blinded, which would have extinguished any rights to the throne.

[24] The revolt of Thomas the Slav (*PmbZ* 8459 = *PMB*: Thomas 7) has been studied in depth by Paul Lemerle, 'Thomas le Slave', *TM*, 1 (1965), 255–97, whose conclusions are followed in these notes. The first tradition reported by Skylitzes is inconsistent; it aims to exonerate Michael II of the first defeats by attributing them to the armies of Leo V. It is unlikely that Thomas would have rebelled against Leo, whose faithful companion he was, rather than against Michael who was his adversary. This tradition depends upon an official version of the events of which the oldest known account is a letter sent to Louis the Pious by Theophilos in 824. It is possible, however, that the two traditions are less contradictory than Lemerle thought; see H. Köpstein, 'Zur Erhebung des Thomas', *Berliner byzantinischen Arbeiten*, 51 (1983), 61–87. Recently it has been argued that the revolt of Thomas began under Leo V, as George the Monk and the *Vita* of Euthymios of Sardis testify, which would indicate that Skylitzes' first version of the story may be an old one, but not necessarily that it is correct: D. Afinogenov, 'The date of *Georgios Monachos* reconsidered', *BZ*, 92 (1999), 446–7.

[25] He was still *tourmarch* of the foederati, a unit pertaining to the Anatolikon theme.

the upstart.[26] But as for Thomas himself, even though he was disabled in one foot and the descendant of barbarians,[27] he was of venerable appearance with his grey locks[28] and he spoke well, in a civilised manner. These are all things which the soldier admires and, in addition to these, he was second to none in the nobility of his physical appearance.

This Thomas now gained control of the entire east and brought the collectors of the public taxes under his thumb. By his magnanimity and outstanding liberality he went from small to great, from weakness to strength.[29] There were those whom he brought over by persuasion and friendship, the sort of people who were enamoured of *coups d'état* [31] and acquiring wealth. There were others whose obedience he gained by coercion and violence, those who held civil disturbance in horror. Then, when the civil war broke out, it was like the cataracts of a river – not of water, but of blood – which inundated the earth. Asia in its entirety was overrun and laid waste, suffering a fate worse than death.[30] Some of the cities there submitted to Thomas out of fear; some kept faith with the emperor until they were sacked and their citizens led into captivity. The whole of Asia fell to the rebel, except for the Opsikion theme, whose governor, Katakylas,[31] remained faithful to the emperor to the end, and for the Armeniakon theme where Olbianos[32] was governor, who [also] remained faithful to the emperor. As a reward, the emperor settled upon them the income accruing to the imperial treasury from the public tax which is usually called the hearth tax.[33]

6. The Hagarenes rejoiced and were glad at the news of the civil war, seizing the opportunity of freely invading every island and territory.[34]

---

[26] As Michael was a person of no distinction, his hold on the throne was not very secure.
[27] This is an allusion to his Slavic origins; he may well have descended from a family established in Asia Minor on one of the many occasions when populations were transferred there over the course of the two preceding centuries.
[28] He and Michael would both have been about fifty years old by now.
[29] His appropriation of the fiscal resources of the east was an important factor in the measure of success his revolt achieved: J.-C. Cheynet, *Pouvoir et contestations à Byzance (963–1210)* (Paris, 1990), 163–5.
[30] This may be an exaggeration for such was the strength of Thomas that very few actions were fought in Asia Minor.
[31] The patrician Katakylas (*PmbZ* 3639 = *PBE* Katakylas 1), a cousin of Michael II (Genesios 2.3), had just replaced Gregory Pterotos, a nephew of Leo V, as strategos.
[32] The antecedents of this man are unknown (*PmbZ* 5646 = *PBE* Olbianos 3). There is a seal (*DOSeals* 1.43.31) which suggests that he may have been strategos of Macedonia. One of his ancestors may be known by a lead seal: G. Zacos and A. Veglery, *Byzantine lead seals*, I (Basle, 1972), no. 3041.
[33] *Kapnikon* which, as the name suggests, was based on the hearth: N. Oikonomides, *Fiscalité et exemption fiscale à Byzance, IXe–XIe siècles* (Athens, 1996), 30–1.
[34] The caliph Al-Ma'moun, son of Harun al-Raschid, was now installed at Baghdad, having himself come to power amid civil wars launched against him by his brother. Victim of several dissident movements the most important of which was led by Babek, he was disposed to negotiate with the

Michael II the Stammerer

Thomas began to fear that his followers might abandon him and go back home for fear of the onslaught of the Hagarenes for, as we said, they seized everything they could get their hands on and took captive every one they came across. He realised that he would have to withstand their attack by making a personal appearance. He would dismay them by the size of his superior forces and craftily bring them to sue for peace. And that is what happened. While the Saracens were ravaging the east, he frightened them by a sudden appearance. Talks ensued at which he promised to deliver the Roman lands into their hands and to place these under their authority.[35] Once relieved of fear of [the Hagarenes] he proclaimed himself emperor, placed a diadem on his head and had himself recognised as sovereign at Antioch by Job who was at that time [chief] pastor of the church there.[36] He assembled a great company of men [32] and received others from the Hagarenes, not only from our neighbouring peoples, but from those afar off: Egyptians, Indians, Persians, Assyrians, Armenians, Chaldeans, Iberians, Zechs and Kabirs.[37] When he had strengthened and defended himself with all these troops, he thought it best to take a colleague and co-ruler, someone whose name he would change and whom he would adopt as his son.[38]

7. He then set out, ravaging and laying waste all of Anatolia; when the emperor heard of this he made preparations to resist the upstart. He sent an army and a commander against him, neither of them fit for battle. Thomas descended on the army in force, destroyed it, killing one half of it

---

Romans. Traditionally the loss of Crete has been connected with the revolt of Thomas, it being alleged that both Thomas and the emperor had withdrawn the naval forces protecting the Aegean Sea. The truth of the matter is that the conquest of the island happened some years after the end of Thomas' revolt: D. Tsougarakis, *Byzantine Crete: from the fifth century to the Venetian conquest* (Athens, 1988), 33–40.

[35] Far from delivering the empire into the hands of the Saracens, Thomas maintained the peace by a demonstration of strength.

[36] Thomas was unwilling to wait until he had conquered Constantinople to receive religious sanction. Job (*PmbZ* 3397 = *PBE* Job 1), the Melkite patriarch of Antioch (before 821–43), crowned him in his see-city. As this was under Arab domination, it is possible that the caliph recognised Thomas as emperor.

[37] This long list of foreigners, all of them from the east, serving in Thomas' army should not lead us astray. The greater part of his army consisted of soldiers from Asia Minor. The other chroniclers give different lists, which suggests that not all the people listed supplied troops to the rebel. The Persians lived in Iran, the Assyrians in upper Mesopotamia; the Chaldees in Pontos, around Trebizond (the theme of Chaldia). The Kabirs were, generally speaking, the inhabitants of Kabeira, the ancient name of Neocaesarea in Pontos. The Iberians were Georgians living along the border with the empire; the Zechs lived on the north shore of the Black Sea between the Caucasus and the Straits of Kertch. Genesios (2.2) adds to this list Slavs, Huns, Vandals, Getes, Manichees, Lazes and Alans.

[38] This refers to Konstantios.

and putting the other half to flight.[39] Being now free to move as he wished, he sought to strengthen his position by equipping warships and other vessels to carry supplies and horses. He made himself master of the imperial navy and mustered the entire fleet off Lesbos.[40] He himself marched off to Abydos[41] at the head of eighty thousand men,[42] intending to cross [the Hellespont] there. He overran all the places on the way there and reduced them to ashes, not just humble and defenceless ones, but even the most important [ones], very difficult to take.

There was one burgh that remained faithful to the emperor, against which he sent his own [adoptive] son. Under the impression that there were no forces opposed to them in the place, [the young man] rashly led a disorganised cavalry attack on it – and fell into an ambush set by Olbianos who cut off his head as a lesson to him not to be rash.[43] He sent that wretch's head to the emperor who, in turn, sent it to Thomas, the man's father, as he advanced in insolence and boasting all the way. [Thomas] received it but made no change in his plans; he passed through Thrace as far as the township they call Horkosion[44] where he crossed [the straits] at the new moon. This had already been a matter of concern for Michael before it happened, for he anticipated such a crossing. [33] He had personally confirmed the loyalty of the towns, reinforced their garrisons and fortified the weaker places. But none of this was to any avail for, as soon as he returned to the capital and Thomas crossed over, they all broke faith with him and rallied to the apostate, anxious to campaign against the capital with him.

8. The emperor concentrated what troops he could and raised an army which had the appearance of being sufficient for the task. He appointed the aforementioned Katakylas and Olbianos to be its commanders and sent them into action against the upstart. He also gave his attention to the navy, so far as possible. But sweeping down like a spring flood from the high mountains, the upstart came and scattered the [imperial] forces by land and by sea, putting such fear into the emperor that he stretched

---

[39] A reference perhaps to a defeat suffered by Olbianos who, nevertheless, preserved most of his troops.
[40] But Michael still controlled a portion of the imperial fleet that was based on Constantinople. Lesbos, the largest of the Aegean islands, was an important naval base and the one nearest to the capital.
[41] Abydos was a fortress controlling the Dardanelles, hence the crossing from Asia to Europe. It was the residence of a count, a *commerciarius* and of a *paraphylax*.
[42] This number must not be taken too seriously. It merely indicates that Thomas' army seemed very large to his contemporaries and was more numerous than the emperor's force.
[43] The young man had remained in Asia to protect Thomas' rear; that is how he came to be surprised by the strategos of the Armeniakon theme.
[44] Probably Horkos, a village between Parion and Lampsaka.

an iron chain from the Acropolis to the opposite township, rendering the inner sea inaccessible.[45]

There was a former commander [named Gregory][46] living in exile on Skyros, a nephew of the emperor Leo [V]. After [Leo's] assassination, he frequently spoke out boldly and accused Michael of murder to his face; that is why he had been sent into exile. Thomas had taken him as a companion and set him in command of a land force of about ten thousand men. He prepared the fleet for action and set another person over that; then he dispatched these two forces as vanguard against the capital under the impression that it would be advantageous to launch the attack both by land and by sea. So it was; the naval and land forces appeared together in the gulf before Blachernae,[47] for the iron chain, stretched [34] out the way I said, was totally incapable of withstanding [them]; a general assault on the walls ensued. Thomas arrived soon after and the siege was vigorously pursued on all sides; but nothing worthy of note was accomplished because those within made a spirited defence and repulsed the siege engines. Thomas thought that he had only to appear before the capital and the citizens would open wide the gates to him out of hatred for Michael. That is why he sent Gregory ahead (as we said), himself following with all his forces and with Anastasios,[48] his adoptive son, who had recently abandoned the monastic life and returned to lay status. When none of his hopes was fulfilled, rather was he reviled and derided by the besieged, he set up a fortified encampment in Paulinos' quarter[49] – where the church of the wonder-working *Anargyroi* stands. Troops were sent out as far as the Euxine Bridge and the so-called Hieron[50] to sound out whether the townships would join him and to ensure there was no enemy at his back.

---

[45] Michael wanted to deny Thomas access to the Golden Horn where his ships could have found shelter and from which he could have launched an attack against the least well defended part of the city.

[46] Surnamed Pterotos according to *Theophanes Continuatus*, ed. I. Bekker (Bonn, 1838), 57: *PmbZ* 2477 = *PBE* Gregorios 71.

[47] Thus Thomas' fleet sailed into the Golden Horn and made contact with his land forces near the port of Blachernae, to the north-west of the capital.

[48] Anastasios (*PmbZ* 317 = *PBE* Anastasios 23) is unanimously discredited by the Byzantine chroniclers. The choice of this man by Thomas and the missions which were assigned to him suggest that he had previous military experience.

[49] *Ta Paulinou*, also known as *Kosmidion*, just outside the walls on the Golden Horn, a short distance beyond Blachernae. Here was located a famous sanctuary dedicated to saints Kosmas and Damian, the healing saints who 'take no silver' (*an-argyroi*): R. Janin, *Constantinople byzantine* (*AOC*, 4A, Paris, 1964), 461–2. On the location of the church: C. Mango, 'On the cult of the saints Cosmas and Damian at Constantinople', *Thymiama stē mnēmē tēs Laskarinas Mpoura* (Athens, 1994), 189–92.

[50] The fortress of Hieron at the entry into the Bosporos from the Black Sea served the same purpose as Abydos on the Hellespont/Dardanelles. It was the duty of the count of the Hieron to control

He took these precautions and gave himself a few days for preparations then, from a high place, he observed that Michael had set up his war banner on the roof of the church of the Mother-of-God at Blachernae and that, from that location, he was issuing orders and taking command of his forces against the enemy. Meanwhile Theophilos, his son, together with the patriarch and his retinue, was processing around the entire ramparts of the city carrying the life-giving Wood of the Cross together with the raiment of the all-pure Mother-of-God.[51] Now Thomas began to despair of the undertaking and to be of two minds. Not knowing what on earth to do but trusting in his superior manpower, he thought that all would be decided by a battle. Accordingly, next day at first light he signalled for the onslaught to begin and led out his men. He committed the attack on the land walls to his son while he himself, with the greater forces, powerful siege-engines and machines, assaulted the towers of Blachernae. Ladders as long as the walls were high were brought up against them; in some place there was an attack by *testudo*, in others by battering ram. Using archery and catapults, he thought that a show of such force would frighten the citizens and deliver the city into his hands. He blockaded the rest [35] of the wall with his naval force, terrifying [the citizens] with fire and arrows.

But great though this show of strength was, it accomplished nothing for him that might be advantageous. A contrary wind suddenly blew up and dispersed the fleet, causing the ships to scatter in all directions, for the storm was of considerable violence. On land the citizens fought bravely and disabled his siege-engines. Short of all supplies, he withdrew. The besieged citizens took new heart and pursued the supporters of the apostate more boldly than ever. Some of those within even opened the apertures in the city gates, sallied forth and engaged the enemy. On account of the severity of the winter in Thrace, the apostate decided to go into winter quarters elsewhere; he left with his host for milder climes.

9. Having done this, once spring began to shine, he decided to attack the city of Constantine again by land and sea. But he found that Michael, unlike the first time, had now assembled a businesslike army and had put

---

the passage of ships and to levy the customs duty (see *DOSeals*, 3.81 for earlier references and some seals of these counts).

[51] The relic of the True Cross came to Constantinople in the time of Herakleios and was conserved in the palace church of the Lighthouse (*Tou Pharou*). The vestment of the Theotokos could have been either her *skepe* (shawl) kept at Blachernae or her *zone* (girdle) from Chalkoprateia. Processions of this kind are well attested from the time of the first siege (by the Avars) in 626 to the Russian onslaught in 860.

to sea another fleet.[52] Thomas gathered his strength and attacked the same part [of the fortifications] as before, the gulf at Blachernae. Once the signal to attack was given, he brought up his siege-engines and attempted to breach the walls. Meanwhile Michael engaged some of the apostate's comrades in discussion; he promised them an amnesty for their offences and plenty of fine rewards if they would change sides and stop staining their hands with the blood of their fellow countrymen. Nothing was accomplished; rather the opposite, for he rendered those to whom he addressed his offer even more bold, while freeing them of the fear which had paralysed them and of confirming their loyalty to the apostate. So he abandoned that project; he spoke to his companions at length, urging them to be good men and true and not to throw away their liberty on an execrable upstart. Then [his men] suddenly and unexpectedly rushed out from several posterns and attacked the enemy. By the element of surprise [the emperor] was able to throw his fear-stricken foes into disarray (many of whom he slaughtered), and to gain a significant [36] victory. The fleet of the apostate also fared badly. Just as the imperial ships put to sea and were about to engage it, the enemy fleet was assailed by panic and disorder. The [enemy ships] turned tail and were driven aground. Some of the sailors threw in their lot with the emperor while others took refuge in the camp of their land army. Thus was the upstart's navy effortlessly brought to naught.

10. It was then that Gregory, nephew of the emperor Leo, realised that Thomas was not a very dangerous adversary and suspected that he would become even less dangerous with the passage of time. He made contact with the emperor through a monk of Stoudios' monastery and conceived the idea of seceding, together with a portion of the company he commanded,[53] and of attacking the upstart from the rear. This was partly to strike fear in Thomas, partly to reconcile himself with the emperor and partly to ensure the safety of his wife and children; for they had been in custody since he threw in his lot with Thomas. But before the emperor heard of this, Thomas, fearing that Gregory might suddenly increase in importance and wishing to inspire his own men with fear, without moving his encampment before the city (for fear of being pursued from the rear) took just so many experienced soldiers as he needed to engage

---

[52] Constantinople was not blockaded during the winter; hence Michael had been able to receive reinforcements from the Asiatic themes which remained faithful to him; also to raise some mercenary forces paid by the treasury.

[53] Defections usually followed when a rebel was checked in his advance, this being the most propitious moment at which to go over to the emperor: Cheynet, *Pouvoir*, 169–73.

Gregory and went out to meet him. Gregory was overthrown in battle, taken in flight and executed. [Thomas] returned in haste to his forces besieging the city and sent out letters everywhere boasting that he had won a victory, which was not the case. He ordered the fleet that he was keeping in the Helladikon theme[54] to approach with all haste, once again to contend for mastery of the sea. Making a direct voyage, the fleet came quickly and anchored off a place called Berydes,[55] three hundred and fifty warships and supply vessels in all. When the commanders of the imperial fleet learned of their arrival, they attacked by night while the enemy ships were riding at anchor. [37] So sudden was the attack that they were able to capture several panic-stricken vessels, crews and all, and to burn other ships with Greek fire. A few escaped from the disaster altogether and hastened to gain the gulf at Blachernae where they could join the land army, which they succeeded in doing.

11. Such was the state of affairs at sea. On land it was continuous skirmishing; first Michael then Theophilos his son would sally forth against the rebels, together with Olbianos and Katakylas. Sometimes the emperor's men prevailed, sometimes [Thomas] the apostate's. But there was no sustained and significant battle waged in a brave and orderly way because the imperial forces were inferior in numbers and unable to withstand the strength of the upstart.

12. Meanwhile, the word having gone out through the whole world that the Roman emperor lay besieged and confined within his own walls, Mortagon, king[56] of the Bulgars, sent him a secret message announcing that he would send help of his own free will and conclude a treaty with him. Either because he really did have pity on his fellow country men or because he resented the expense (he was the most parsimonious emperor there ever was), Michael thanked the Bulgar for his intentions but refused the proferred aid. Mortagon, however, delighted in war and was very fond of acquiring the spoils of it. Seeking to revitalise and strengthen the thirty-year treaty made with Leo [V],[57] the previous emperor, he raised an army

---

[54] One of the oldest European themes, created before 695: N. Oikonomides, *Les listes de préséance byzantines des IXe et Xe siècles: introduction, text, French translation and commentary* (Le monde byzantin, Paris, 1972), 351.

[55] Location uncertain.

[56] *Basileus*. Omurtag, son of Krum, had been Khan of the Bulgars since 815: Treadgold, *Byzantine revival*, 214–15.

[57] It was Michael who summoned the Bulgar to his aid, no doubt promising renewal of the treaty of 816 (a thirty-year treaty but which had to be confirmed every ten years), possibly suggesting there was booty to be had in Thrace. This account of the matter (Skylitzes is here following *Theophanes Continuatus* and/or Genesios) is somewhat unlikely. George the Monk (797) says – which is more easily believed – that Michael asked the Bulgar for help (Lemerle, 'Thomas le slave', 279–80).

against the upstart and, once he was inside the Roman border, encamped near the place called Kedouktos.[58]

The matter became known and the apostate could not be unaware of it. He was shaken without a doubt and deeply moved in his inner being, but when he had regained his composure he armed his own forces. [38] It seemed to him that if he divided his forces he would be greatly weakened and easily overcome (for it needs no small force to besiege the capital; rather, a numerous and significant army). The emperor had now assembled a formidable host, well able to withstand the enemy face to face. No small company would have sufficed to withstand the army of the Bulgars; it required a large and above average army to succeed. Thomas now withdrew from the city to avoid rendering himself easy to defeat by dividing his forces. Under the impression that he was a worthy opponent for the Bulgar, he drew up his forces in battle order at the place just mentioned. An engagement ensued in which the upstart was worsted and many of his people slain.[59] The survivors saved their lives by taking to their heels and reassembled in an inaccessible location where they waited to see what would happen. The Bulgar chieftain took the prisoners of war and the great amount of booty he had captured and returned to his own land, exulting in and boasting of his victory. The fleet [of Thomas] which was still left blockading the city went over to the emperor in its entirety when news of the upstart's reverse arrived. The apostate was brought to such a pitch of madness by the demons which (it seemed) were fighting on his side that he continued to dream of seizing the imperial throne. Harassed on all sides and reduced to a mere shadow of his former strength, he still carried on the siege. When he finally came to the conclusion that this was wasted effort, off he went with his entire army to the plain known as Diabasis,[60] some furlongs from the city, a place rich in pasture and flowing streams. There he set up camp from which he made forays to pillage the splendour of the city's suburbs. But the people of the city saw no more of him, unlike the way it was before.

When Michael perceived this, he assembled a considerable force, appointing Katakylas and Olbianos to command it. Taking the two corps of palace guards, the Scholae and the Hetairiae, under his own command,

---

[58] Near Herakleia in Thrace; the name is derived from the Latin *aquaeductus*.
[59] November 822. This information can hardly be correct; Thomas, even if victorious, must at least not have suffered too severe losses or how could he have thought of continuing the siege? On the other hand, the fact that he did not blockade the city right away suggests that he had suffered more than a minor reverse.
[60] A plain 50 km from the city, from which he could easily pillage the estates (*proasteia*) of the rich citizens of Constantinople.

he marched out against the upstart, wishing to have the matter decided by a formal battle. The upstart awaited the emperor in a firmly established position, intending to get the better of his adversaries by a feint, once battle was joined. He ordered his men [39] to turn and run away when the adversary charged; but when [Michael's men] came in pursuit, his own were suddenly to turn on them and rout them by this unexpected manoeuvre.[61] Such were his orders, but it was not to turn out as he intended. The soldiers of his company had been deprived of their wives and children for a long time on his account. They had stained their hands with the blood of their fellow countrymen and they were distressed by how long it had gone on. For they had now spent three years in serving the ambition and aspirations of one man – with nothing to show for it. Thus his orders were an opportunity not to be missed for these men. When the trumpet signalled 'to arms' and the ranks engaged in hand-to-hand combat, these made no *pretence* of running away (as they were ordered to do) but simply broke ranks in a disorderly, undisciplined manner and scattered in all directions. At first a few, then many more of them went over to the emperor. Thomas found refuge with a few others of his men in Adrianople.[62] His illegitimate and bastard son, Anastasios, fled to the fortified town of Bizyes and occupied it.[63]

13. Following on their heels, the emperor decided first to besiege Thomas, so he set up a blockade around him. He was, however, in no haste to reduce him with siege engines and war machines, partly to spare his fellow countrymen a civil war, partly because of the Scyths living around Adrianople: he did not want them to acquire the ability to reduce cities by the use of machines. So he sought to reduce the adversary by famine and by depriving him of the necessities of life. Thus he invested Adrianople, encompassing it with ditch and stockade. Thomas expelled all the people who were unfit for service and every useless animal from the city. Then, when the famine became intense and there was no hope of relief, some of his company secretly let themselves out through the apertures in the gates while [40] others slid down from the walls by night. These then went and surrendered themselves to the emperor while others fled to the apostate's bastard son, Anastasios, in the town of Bizyes. The besieged were now seriously in need of the necessities of life and were reduced to eating some

---

[61] This was a traditional subterfuge of nomadic peoples, often practised to their own cost by the Byzantines.
[62] The headquarters of Thomas were at Arkadioupolis.
[63] A Thracian stronghold north of the Adrianople-Constantinople road. Anastasios is said to be his *adoptive* son in c. 5, above.

strange dishes, forced by necessity even into partaking of boiled hides and boot-soles, with which they were perforce nourished. They entered into secret negotiations with Michael, asking pardon for their misdeeds – which they received. Then they laid hands on Thomas and brought him bound before his enemy.[64] First performing a deed which was customary for the emperors of old time but which is no longer in use,[65] [Michael] placed his foot on [the apostate's] neck as he lay sprawled on the ground. Then he cut off his hands and feet, set him on an ass and made a spectacle of him around the camp – him crying out nothing other but: 'Be merciful to me, you who are truly the emperor!'

Then the emperor asked [Thomas] whether any of his [the emperor's] own friends might be supporters of Thomas, at which the apostate might have named several of them, had not the patrician John Hexaboulios objected: 'My Lord emperor, it is improper and quite insane to believe one's enemies [testifying] against one's friends.' With this protest he delivered some unfortunate citizens and friends from the punishment which would otherwise have been unleashed against them.[66]

In his agony, the apostate died a slow death, yielding up his soul in mid October.[67] At first he had seemed to be a bold fellow, capable of great things: one who achieved what he set out to accomplish. But the further he went, it became clear that there was much less to him than he himself believed, and than what others expected of him. The men in the fortress of Bizyes quickly changed their minds when they became aware of the fate which awaited them. For once they heard of the fate which had befallen Thomas, fearing a similar one for themselves, they laid hands on Anastasios, bound him hand and foot and brought him to the emperor. This one suffered more or less as his father had suffered and died a violent death. Even after the upstarts had been executed, Panion and Herakleia, coastal cities of Thrace, still persisted in maintaining the rebellion out of hatred [41] of Michael and for his refusal to restore the sacred icons. Panion was reduced after an earthquake had thrown down its fortifications while Herakleia[68] was taken by a naval assault.

---

[64] This in October 823.
[65] This procedure marking the triumph of an emperor was known as *calcatio* (the double amputation was superfluous). It did not on this occasion take place at Constantinople but before the rebel army.
[66] The number of Michael's sometime adversaries was so great that he was obliged to grant a general amnesty.
[67] Genesios (2.8) and George the Monk (788) say he was impaled at the end.
[68] Herakleia, ancient Perinthos, fell without loss of blood.

14. Such was the end of the revolt of Thomas. The emperor returned from the Thracian cities swathed in triumph and chose to take no further action against those who had risen with Thomas, now his prisoners of war, than to parade them mounted on asses when the Hippodrome was full and to send them into exile.

15. The fortified towns of Kabala and Saniana[69] were still hotbeds of insurrection, the one held by Choireas, the other by Gazarenos.[70] From these towns they set out to rob and plunder. Before they had yet received the imperial letter[71] granting them amnesty and promotion (in fact the emperor made each of them magister), they went out as usual to forage. But on their return, they found the gates of the fortresses closed in their faces, the men within having been bribed to shut them out.[72] They fled to Syria but the governors of the frontier regions arrested and impaled them.[73]

16. That is how the uprising was completely extinguished and stamped out; but the sequence of disasters was not going to end there. For after the two land masses (I mean Asia and Europe, like the head and tail of the same body) underwent the wrath of the Lord (even though not conscious of it), afflicted by killings, burnings, earthquake, brigandage, civil war, hopeless dislocation of cities, portents in the sky, portents in the air; then it was the wretched islands, located as it were in the middle, that disasters struck in order to afflict the entire body. But there was no correcting those who refused to revere [42] the likeness of the God-man.[74]

The revolt of Thomas had scarcely begun but word of it was going out into all lands. The Hagarenes inhabiting the western gulf of Iberia facing onto the [Atlantic] ocean, the ones called Spaniards, had become too numerous. They realised that the land they occupied was poor stuff, incapable of sustaining them. So they went to Abu Hafs, their leader

---

[69] Kabala was a fortified town of Lykaonia, to the north of Iconium, while Saniana in Galatia was on the western bank of the Halys, not far from Ancyra (*TIB*, 4:182–3 and 222).

[70] Gazarenos (*PmbZ* 1941 = *PBE* Gazarenos 1), originally from Koloneia (*Theophanes Continuatus*, ed. Bekker, 71), and Choireas were both commanders under Thomas.

[71] The Greek expression *basilike syllabe* was not used in the imperial chancellery. It is not found in the index of F. Dölger and J. Karayannopoulos, *Byzantinische Urkundenlehre: Erste Abschnitt die Kaiserkunden* (Munich, 1968). *Theophanes Continuatus*, ed. Bekker, 72, speaks of a chrysobul, the normal document for the conferring of such high dignities.

[72] At Saniana it was the oikonomos of a church who, bribed with a promise of the metropolitan see of Neocaesarea, shut the gates: *Theophanes Continuatus*, ed. Bekker, 72.

[73] A very strict watch was kept on the Arab–Byzantine border by persons whose task it was to report enemy incursions: G. Dagron and H. Mihàescu, *Le traité sur la guérilla de l'empereur Nicéphore Phocas* (Paris, 1986), 228–9.

[74] *Ten theanthropon ... morphen*, i.e. the icon of Jesus. The implication is that all the foregoing woes were incurred by the iconoclasts.

(called *amermoumnes*[75] in the language of those parts) and asked him if he could settle them elsewhere and give them a change of land, for they were oppressed by their numbers and bereft of the necessities of life. He gave their request a ready welcome; warships were immediately prepared and manned by a force recruited from among those people. The purpose of the exercise was kept secret while this fleet was permitted to ravage the eastern isles which are ours. Thus he was able to assuage the hunger of his subjects by filling them with others' bread, while spying out whether there was one of the islands suitable for them to colonise.[76] He sailed out in springtime and attacked several islands without finding anybody to oppose him. The islands were all destitute of help as the fleet which usually defended them was away fighting with Thomas. Thus he was able to reap much gain from every island he attacked. One day he came to Crete, overran it and took as many prisoners as possible. When he perceived the excellence and pleasant nature of that island, this is what he said to his subjects: 'Behold, a land flowing with milk and honey.' That was all he said at that time but, having charged his fleet with all manner of good things, he thought about it on the way home. When winter was over and spring began to shine,[77] he filled forty ships with fighting men then, chancing on a favourable wind, set sail for Crete, more or less bypassing the other isles. When he got to Crete he anchored off the promontory called Charax. As there was [43] no military resistance, neither to his arrival nor to his disembarkation, he set up a fortified encampment and sent out capable men to forage, himself remaining with the others. Then a wind began to get up, and when the foragers were more than ten or fifteen furlongs away he put fire to the ships and burnt them all; not one of them did he save. The army returned at once, terrified and amazed by the unexpected nature of this occurrence. They demanded to know the reason for it and began to utter mutinous threats. What they heard was something they had long yearned to hear: 'You yourselves are the cause of these events, for you sought to settle elsewhere and in a good land. As I could think of no land better than this, I chose this way of granting

---

[75] Apochaps in the text. Abu Hafs was not caliph (*amermoumnes* in Greek, from the Arabic *amir al-mu'minin* means 'emir of believers' or 'ruler of the faithful') but a mere emir. On the conquest of Crete see V. Christides, *The conquest of Crete by the Andalousian Muslims* (Athens, 1984); Tsougarakis, *Crete*, 30–4; Treadgold, *Byzantine revival*, 248–57.

[76] The reality is somewhat different. Abu Hafs had seized Alexandria in Egypt and was then himself besieged in that city by a general of the Abassid caliph Al Ma'moun in 827. Negotiations took place as a result of which Abu Hafs was allowed to withdraw on condition that he installed his people on imperial territory.

[77] There has been much discussion of the year in which the Arabs arrived in Crete. If Abu Hafs was in Alexandria in 827, then 828 is the earliest possible date, already five years after the end of the revolt of Thomas the Slav.

you your heart's desire and ridding myself of your objections.' When they brought to his mind their wives and children, Abu Hafs said: 'You take these prisoners here for wives and soon enough they will give you children.' They were reduced to silence by these words for they felt that what had been said was an adequate explanation. They excavated a deep ditch and fortified it with a stockade,[78] from which the place took the name by which it is still designated: Chandax. There they passed the nights.

Before very long the emperor was made aware of what had happened;[79] he delegated everything concerning Crete to the protospatharios Photeinos,[80] commander of the Anatolikon theme. He went there, learned all about it and reported the matter to the emperor, requesting that forces be sent sufficient to frighten the enemy away. The emperor now despatched the protospatharius Damian, a count of the imperial stables, with a large, well-equipped force,[81] to assist Photeinos the commander. Once their forces met up with each other they prepared to attack the Hagarenes but, in the end, achieved nothing worthwhile. Damian himself was mortally wounded in the first encounter; his death provoked a reversal of fortunes for all the rest. Photeinos got away in a fast ship by the skin of his teeth and himself reported to the emperor what had happened. As he always stood high in the emperor's favour, he was now transferred to govern Sicily instead of Crete. The Saracens for their part were still leading a troubled and worried existence [44] when a monk came down from the mountains of the island and told them they were making a mistake if they thought they could live in security if they established themselves in that place. Saying this to them, he pointed out Chandax,[82] a favourable spot with abundant crops of all kinds. They founded a city there which was like an acropolis for the whole island. Setting out from that base they conquered that entire island and others too. They enslaved the indigenous population

---

[78] *Charax* in Greek; in Arabic *chandaq* means a ditch. In the west it was known as Candie; today, Heraklion.
[79] The chronology of the first Cretan expeditions is somewhat confused. Skylitzes (following *Theophanes Continuatus*) would have us understand that the campaigns of Photeinos, Krateros and Ooryphas (*PmbZ* 5654 = *PBE* Ooryphas 2) took place in Michael's reign, i.e. in the space of less than two years, which seems impossible. The second and third campaigns would have taken place under Theophilos.
[80] This Photeinos (*PmbZ* 6241 = *PBE*, Photeinos 9) is the great-grandfather of Zoe Carbonopsina, the fourth wife of Leo VI: *Theophanes Continuatus*, ed. Bekker, 76.
[81] The emperor added a section of the central army to the thematic forces. This was the usual procedure when armies were sent to combat the Arabs in Crete.
[82] This passage is inconsistent with the previous statement that the Arabs had already established their camp at Chandax when they disembarked. The author has probably used two different accounts of the founding of Chandax and not noticed the contradiction.

and took [all] the cities of Crete except one.[83] It was at that time that Cyril, bishop of Gortyn, achieved the martyr's crown rather than deny Christ.[84] That was how Crete was conquered.

17. Once he was delivered from the civil war, the emperor Michael did not ascribe this victory to God, but to his own cunning and tactics. Hence, puffed up with pride, he could not master his own impulses. After his wife died, he pretended to lead a bachelor life, but he secretly sent notes to leading senators urging them to beseech him to marry another wife and to threaten him with violence if he refused. They were to offer the elegant argument that it was unbecoming for them to be subject to an emperor while their wives were deprived of a Sovereign Lady and empress. At some length he was finally convinced by their artificial arguments. First he demanded of his subjects a handwritten statement of loyalty, stating that after his death they would most certainly honour her who was to be his wife and the children born of her; that they would accept one of these to be the next emperor and her as Sovereign Lady. Thus he believed he had made provision, not only for his own generation, but for the next one too. Then, won over by the specious requests of the Senate, he took to wife a woman who had formerly been betrothed to Christ, having espoused the monastic profession and lived as a nun in the Prinkipo monastery since she was a child. She was called Euphrosyne and her father was said to have been the emperor Constantine [VI] whom his mother, Eirene, justly blinded for his disorderly conduct.[85] So much for the story thus far.

18. [45] Michael sent another fleet against the Saracens in Crete, under the command of Krateros, commander of the Kibyrrhaiote theme.[86] This man took the seventy ships already under his command plus all

---

[83] If this information is correct, the town in question may have been Eleutherna: Tsougarakis, *Crete*, 34. According to *Theophanes Continuatus*, ed. Bekker, 77, this town negotiated with the invader and was allowed to remain Christian.

[84] No other source, other than the one on which Genesios, *Theophanes Continuatus* and Skylitzes drew, says that the Arabs executed martyrs. There may be confusion here with the martyrdom of Cyril of Gortyn in 304: Tsougarakis, *Crete*, 209 and note 58.

[85] In this way Michael laid claim to a connection with the glorious dynasty of the Isaurians, which he greatly admired and of which Constantine VI was the last representative. Euphrosyne (*PmbZ* 1705 = *PBE* Euphrosyne 1) was the daughter of Constantine VI and Mary of Amnia, who was the granddaughter of Philaretos the Merciful: J. Herrin, *Women in purple: rulers of medieval Byzantium* (London, 2001), 130–4.

[86] This attack took place in the reign of Theophilos. The Kibyrrhaiote theme provided the greater part of the thematic navy. This may be the same Krateros who, as strategos of the Anatolikon theme, escorted Theodore the Stoudite into exile (*PmbZ* 4159, 4158 = *PBE* Krateros 2, 1). The role of this family (which first appeared in the entourage of Leo V and preserved its high rank into the tenth century) has not been sufficiently emphasised: J.-C. Cheynet, 'Une famille méconnue: les Kratéroi', *REB*, 59 (2001), 225–38 = Cheynet, *Société*, 583–98.

[he could muster] from the other isles and arrived in Crete in great pomp. He did not find the Hagarenes bowing to his authority, but rather boldly withstanding the danger. They locked horns just as the sun was illuminating the mountain ridges and until midday neither side gave an inch, each persisting in a determined resistance. But, as the day began to wane, the weakened Cretans took to their heels. Many of them died in action; more threw down their arms and were taken prisoner. The city might have been taken the same day if night had not fallen – and completely changed the situation. The Romans were now as if they were already conquerors, expecting to make very short work of the little that was left of the enemy next day. They proceeded to indulge themselves in drink and other pleasures as though they were at home and not stationed in a foreign country. They gave no thought to posting sentries or to any other safety precautions. They could think of nothing other than sleep, repose and relaxation – which can so easily undo everything. Thus, around midnight, the Cretans (who were wide awake and deeply worried) learned from their own sentries that the men in the Roman encampment had fallen prey to sleep and wine. They promptly attacked with loud shouting and, finding [the Romans] overcome with wine, slew them to a man, leaving 'not even a messenger' (as the proverb says) to tell the tale. Only the commander managed to save his life – by embarking on a merchant vessel. The Saracen commander mounted an intensive search for him, first among the fallen, then among the prisoners, but in vain. Then, learning of his flight, he sent men in pursuit of him. They caught up with him in the island of Kos where they executed him by crucifixion.

19. [46] Then, at the emperor's command, a warrior by no means lacking in intelligence and shrewdness whose name was Ooryphas,[87] assembled an army called 'the fortiers' – because each man received forty pieces of gold.[88] He went against the other islands, killing the Hagarenes caught foraging, either in ambush or in open combat. He turned back the Cretans and withstood their massive and irresistible onslaught.

20. That is what happened so far. About the same time a man named Euphemios who was in charge of a unit in Sicily[89] fell in love with a maiden

[87] The first mention of this person who is to be identified with the droungarios of the watch under Theophilos, probably the father of the famous admiral Niketas Ooryphas who distinguished himself in the service of Basil I.
[88] This was 3.3 times the most an experienced thematic soldier could hope to earn each year, twelve pieces of gold (W. Treadgold, *Byzantium and its army, 284–1081* (Stanford, CA, 1995), 119–23).
[89] Euphemios (*PmbZ* 1701 = *PBE* Euphemius 1) was a *tourmarch* whom the commander of the Island, Constantine Soudes (*PmbZ* 3928 = *PBE* Konstantinos 231), had put in charge of the

who had lived the monastic life since childhood. He made many efforts to satisfy his desires with no respect for the law whatsoever. He looked to the emperor who had dared to do the same thing as his sole exemplar. He snatched the maiden from her monastery and took her home with him against her will. Her brothers went and reported the matter to Michael; he ordered the commander [of the theme] to cut off bold Euphemios' nose if he found the charge were true. When Euphemios learnt of this, he bound those under his command to him with oaths and also some of his fellow officers. He drove off the commander who came to execute the emperor's order and fled to the ruler of Africa.[90] To him he promised to put the whole of Sicily in subjection and to pay much tribute if he would proclaim [Euphemios] emperor of the Romans. Agreeing to this offer, the emir proclaimed him emperor of the Romans and furnished him with a sizeable body of troops.[91] Thus [the emir] became master of Sicily, which was delivered into his hands by this man. But Euphemios was not able to enjoy his imperial status for long, [47] because his head was cut off in retribution for his apostasy and misdeeds. The way in which he was eliminated is worth reporting. As he was going around Sicily in imperial regalia, being proclaimed, he arrived before Syracuse.[92] Drawing ahead of his company and bodyguard, he came to within a bowshot of the city and addressed the citizens, endeavouring to conciliate them with his words. Two Syracusan brothers, however, noted that he was isolated. They put their heads together and came to an agreement. With one mind they approached him in a dissembling way (but scornfully), going through the motions of offering him the reverence due to an emperor. Totally unaware of their pretence, Euphemios readily accepted their acknowledgement and greeting; then he amicably invited them to approach him so he could embrace them himself. But as he bowed his head and brought his mouth near to the mouth of one of the brothers, this one seized him firmly by the

---

fleet: Treadgold, *Byzantine revival*, 248–9); V. Prigent, 'La carrière du tourmarque Euphèmios, basileus des Romains', *Actes du XXe Congrès International d'Etudes Byzantines* (Paris, 2001).

[90] Present-day Tunisia corresponds more or less to the ancient Roman province of Africa. It was then governed by the dynasty of the Aghlabids (800–909), technically (and decreasingly) subservient to the Abbasids. The rebellion of Euphemios started in 826 and lasted two years (Treadgold, *Byzantine revival*, 250–4).

[91] Ten thousand infantry (?) and seven hundred cavalry. For details of the operation reported by the Arab sources see Vasiliev and Canard, I, 66–8.

[92] Syracuse was the other main city of Sicily besides Palermo. It was well fortified and possessed a fine harbour from which it derived its importance. The assassination actually took place near to Henna/Castrogiovanni, one of the principal fortified positions on the island: M. Amari, *Bibliotheca Arabo-Sicula* (Leipzig, 1857), I, 367. Now see E. Kislinger, *Regionalgeschichte als Quelleproblem. Die Chronik von Monemvasia und das sizilianische Demenna. Eine historich-topographische Studie* (Vienna, 2001).

hair while the other brother cut off his head. Thus Euphemios paid the just price for his folly.

21. From then on the Hagarenes became masters, not only of Sicily,[93] but of Calabria and of the greater part of Italy – where they overran and ravaged everything.

22. When Michael had ruled the empire for nine years and eight months he fell ill with dysentery and died.[94] He had brought upon the Roman state all the evils we mentioned as the narrative progressed, through his disrespect for God and his ineptitude in state affairs. The whole of [48] Dalmatia[95] rebelled in his reign too. There was an ancient oracle referring to him which went like this:

> The reign of evil will afflict the earth
> When Babylon is by a dragon ruled,
> A stammerer with too much love of gold.

His corpse was buried in the great mausoleum of Justinian at [the church of the] Holy Apostles in a sarcophagus of green marble from Thessaly.[96]

---

[93] After an initial setback, the army and fleet sent by Michael II at the end of 828 under the command of Theodotos recovered almost the entire island. But the African Arabs returned to the attack and for three-quarters of a century endeavoured to conquer the whole of Sicily.

[94] 2 October 829.

[95] Byzantine Dalmatia was reduced to little more than a coastal strip, including the towns of Dubrovnik and Zadar. Its status in the earlier tenth century is unsure. According to the *Taktikon Uspensky* (842/843) it was theoretically under the command of an *archon*, but it may have been elevated to the rank of a theme commanded by a strategos for a time: J. Ferluga, *L'amministrazione bizantina in Dalmazia* (Venice, 1978) and Oikonomides, *Listes*, 353.

[96] P. Grierson, 'The tombs and obits of the Byzantine emperors (337–1042), with an additional note by C. Mango and I. Ševčenko', *DOP*, 16 (1962), 3–63, at 56.

CHAPTER 4

Theophilos [829–842]

1. [49] After the death of Michael [II], his son, Theophilos (who was already of age), succeeded to his father's throne in the month of October, in the eighth year of the indiction.[1] According to what he said, he wanted to acquire a reputation for being a zealous devotee of justice and a diligent observer of the laws of the state, but the truth of the matter is that he made this pretence in order to distance himself from the conspirators, thus ensuring that nobody make a desperate move against him.

So, from the outset, he resolved to bring ruin and destruction on all those who had taken part with his father in the death of Leo [V]. To this end, he issued a command that everybody who enjoyed imperial titles and all who had benefited from imperial munificence in any way whatsoever were to assemble in the Magnaura;[2] that is, at the Pentapyrgion. When that was accomplished and everybody was gathered together as he had commanded, keeping the ferocity of his soul concealed, he spoke to the assembled company in a modest and gentle voice: 'O my people and my inheritance; it was the will and desire of my late father to bestow many titles, benefits and other honours upon those who supported and defended his rule. Events overtook him and it is to me, the successor to his throne, that he has left this undischarged debt, in order that he not appear ungrateful to his supporters. So, let each one of those men step forward from the crowd and show himself to us plainly; so that, knowing which

---

[1] Theophilos (*PmbZ* 8167 = *PBE* Theophilos 5), born at Amorion in 813, was crowed co-emperor in 821. He was sixteen when his father died and he became sole emperor – 2 October 829; Grierson, 'The tombs and obits of the Byzantine emperors (337–1042), with an additional note by C. Mango and I. Ševčenko', *DOP*, 16 (1962), 3–63, at 56. Unlike his predecessors, he had received an excellent education (supervised by John the Grammarian) to prepare him for the throne: A. Markopoulos, 'The rehabilitation of the emperor Theophilos', *Byzantium in the ninth century: dead or alive?*, ed. L. Brubaker (SPBS, 5, Ashgate, 1998), 37–49, reproduced in Markopoulos, *History*, no. xx.

[2] Built by Constantine the Great, the Magnaura was a basilica in the Great Palace with three naves, used characteristically for the formal reception of foreign ambassadors. The pentapyrgium was a display cabinet where various precious objects could be seen to advantage: R. Janin, *Constantinople byzantine* (AOC, 4A, Paris, 1964), 115.

of you are friends, we may reward you as you deserve.' All those wretches who had participated in the slaying of Leo [V] were deceived and had their heads turned by these words, with the result that each one showed himself. Having thus netted his prey, Theophilos immediately ordered the eparch[3] to apply [50] the laws of the state to them, saying: 'Go to it, eparch; you have authority from God and from our own Serenity to pass judgement on these persons and to reward them according to their deeds: not only for having stained their hands with human blood, but also because they slew the Lord's anointed within the sanctuary.'[4] Having made this pronouncement, he dissolved his first and truly amazing general assembly [*syllogos*]. The wretched fellows in question were arrested by the eparch and each of them underwent the punishment for murder.[5]

2. Theophilos also drove his stepmother from the palace and obliged her to enter the monastery in which she was originally tonsured. Thus the oaths which the senate had sworn to Michael were of no avail.[6]

3. This was how Theophilos started out, but what came afterwards is not unworthy of praise. Dedicating himself to the cause of justice, he inspired terror in every malefactor, but admiration in the righteous; in these because he showed himself to be a just man who hated evil, in those because of his rigour and severity towards them. He cannot, however, be acquitted of all evil; for while he kept faith with God, he kept faith *a fortiori* with the abominable heresy (inherited from his father) of those who opposed the icons. Thus, throughout his reign he relentlessly afflicted the pious and allholy people, allowing them not a moment of calm throughout his reign.[7]

[3] The eparch of the City was effectively the governor of Constantinople: *ODB*, I, 704.
[4] *Ho christos tou Kyriou*, term found in 1 Sam. 16:6; 24:6, 10; 26:9,16, etc.
[5] Not all Michael's co-conspirators appear to have suffered the same fate. One of them, the eunuch Theoktistos, was promoted prefect of the inkpot by Michael and pursued a successful career under both Theophilos and Michael III.
[6] This refers to the previous passage on the remarriage of Michael II. Theophilos was assisted by his stepmother, Euphrosyne (as Michael II intended) until his marriage in 830 when, a new empress having come on the scene (Theodora), she withdrew either to her monastery of Prinkipo (Skylitzes) or, which is less likely, to the Constantinopolitan monastery of Gastria, as others relate: R. Janin, *La géographie ecclésiastique de l'empire byzantin*, I, *Le siège de Constantinople et le patriarcat œcuménique*, III, *Les églises et les monastères* (Paris, 1969), 67–8. The date of 830 for the marriage of Theophilos is problematic since it requires the children of that marriage to have been born remarkably close to each other and also contradicts the statement that Alexios Mosele was given the title of caesar on the occasion of his engagement to Maria around 835, whereas he seems already to have been caesar when the triumph of 831 was celebrated at Constantinople: C. Mango, 'On re-reading the *Life* of St Gregory the Decapolite', *Byzantina*, 13 (1985), 640–3.
[7] Theophilos had been educated by John the Grammarian, the proponent of the second phase of iconoclasm. This may explain why, unlike his father, the new emperor was a determined opponent of the icons and why, during his reign, persecution of the iconodoules began again, of which the most famous example is the maltreatment of the brothers known as *Graptoi*, 'written on' (see below).

That is why he was never successful in war but was always worsted; and that is why he never came home [in triumph] as an emperor should.[8]

In his devotion to justice and to what he believed to be faith in and zeal for Christ and his Mother, each week he would ride out on horseback together with his bodyguard along the thoroughfare leading to the sacred church of the Mother of God at Blachernae. In this way he rendered himself accessible to all, especially to those who had suffered injustice, giving them a chance to rehearse their woes, free of any hindrance by the perpetrators of the injustice in their fear of being punished by the emperor.[9]

It was also his pleasure to inspect the wares as he passed though the marketplace. [51] He would enquire of the tradesmen when he was in the market how much they sold each item for. This was no casual enquiry, merely referring to one commodity, but to all the foodstuffs, beverages, the fuel and clothing and, in short, everything that you find in a market.[10] In everything he showed great care and concern for the common good, sometimes in the courts, sometimes (as we said) in his weekly excursions.

4. Once when he was looking down, out to sea, from the palace wall for the sake of diversion, he saw a merchant vessel of large tonnage, running before the wind in full sail, a ship of unrivalled size and unsurpassable beauty – at the sight of which he was very much taken aback. He enquired whose this merchantman might be and what kind of cargo it was carrying. On learning that it belonged to the augousta [Theodora],[11] he kept his counsel for the time being and bided his time until the day on which he was accustomed to go to the sacred church at Blachernae. When Sunday came round and he knew where the ship had docked (he had requested that information from somebody), he took the route which passed that way. He approached the vessel and stationed himself at the prow. Then he asked those present several times of what part of the cargo they stood

---

[8] The writer here is reacting to propaganda in favour of Theophilos. Unlike his father, Theophilos the determined iconoclast, following in the paths of the Isaurians, would have it that victory over the Arabs was a sure sign of divine approval for his religious policies. In spite of the severe reverse of 838, Theophilos' record in the field does not merit this degree of censure; yet again a ruler's alleged impiety is said to be responsible for his setbacks.

[9] The emperor was not normally accessible to anybody other than his relations and close associates, even though he was the final judge of appeal. Theophilos was being very innovative in opening himself up to people in this way (Harun al Rashid is said to have done likewise, but incognito). It was a 6 km ride from the Great Palace to Blachernae, which gave many people the opportunity of approaching him, many more of seeing him.

[10] It was a matter of great importance that the capital had a reliable supply of the necessities of life at stable prices, to avoid civil unrest. There is nothing here to suggest that the prices were controlled. The eparch of the city and his lieutenant (*symponos*) were responsible for order in the marketplaces: N. Oikonomides, *Listes*, 320 and note 189.

[11] *PmbZ* 7286 = *PBE* Theodora 2; J. Herrin, *Women in purple: rulers of medieval Byzantium* (London, 2001), 185–239.

in need: grain, wine or some other commodity. After he had asked many times, they finished by replying, somewhat reluctantly: 'Those who are under the protection of your rule and reign lack nothing.' 'But are you not aware,' said the emperor, 'that while, at God's behest, I have become emperor, my augousta and wife is turning me into a merchant shipping magnate?' Then he added bitterly: 'Who ever saw a Roman emperor or his spouse indulging in commerce?' With these words, he gave orders that at that very hour, merely allowing time for the crew to disembark, the ship was to be given to the flames, together with all its rigging and everything she was carrying. As for the Sovereign Lady, he assailed her with reproaches and threatened to take her life if she was ever detected doing any such thing again.

5. [52] The empress Theodora originated from Paphlagonia and she could boast of having as parents Marinos, a man of no mean distinction, and Theoktiste Phlorina. Both had been raised in piety and neither had renounced their devotion to the holy icons (as everybody was doing at that time), but rather embraced them and clasped them to their breasts with zeal. When Theodora was crowned with the diadem,[12] her mother, Theoktiste, was also promoted to the rank of girdled patrician.[13] This Theoktiste[14] had her own house close by the monastery of Gastria[15] and there she would receive Theodora's children, of which there were five: Thekla, Anna, Anastasia, Pulcheria and Maria.[16] She gave them

---

[12] Theodora received the golden apple from Theophilos in a beauty competition organised by the empress Euphrosyne. Among the copious literature on this topic see W. Treadgold, 'The brideshows of the Byzantine emperors', *B*, 49 (1979), 395–413; D. Afinogenov, 'The bride-show of Theophilos: some notes on the sources', *Eranos*, 95 (1997), 10–18; I. Sorlin, 'La plus belle ou la meilleure? Notes sur les concours de beauté à Byzance et dans la Russie muscovite des XVIe–XVIIe siècles', *Mélanges Hélène Ahrweiler* (Paris, 1998), 635–50. Bride-shows, long considered a mere literary invention, are now being taken seriously again: M. Vinson, 'The life of Theodora and the rhetoric of the Byzantine bride-show', *JÖB*, 49 (1999), 31–60. Theophilos rejected the candidature of the poetess Kassia in this competition because he thought she was too impertinent. On Kassia see I. Rochow, *Studien zu der Person, den Werken und dem Nachleben der Dichterin Kassia* (Berlin, 1967). Theophilos was perhaps married on 5 June 830: W. Treadgold, 'The problem of the marriage of the emperor Theophilos', *GRBS*, 16 (1975), 325–41.

[13] *Zoste*. This is confirmed by a seal of Theoktiste (*PmbZ = PBE* Theoktiste), where this dignity is displayed with a note that she is the mother of an empress (G. Zacos, *Byzantine lead seals*, compiled by J. W. Nesbitt (Berne, 1985), no. 1083). Marinos, Theodora's father, was a self-made soldier who reached the rank of *tourmarch*. He had probably died before the wedding took place for there is no mention of him receiving any honour. Theodora had many brothers and sisters all of whom did well in life or made fine marriages.

[14] Skylitzes (here following *Theophanes Continuatus*) is doubtless wrong in attributing this attitude to Theoktiste rather than to Euphrosyne, Michael's second wife.

[15] This appears to have been a family foundation; Theodora's close relatives were buried there.

[16] Thekla (*PmbZ* 7261 = *PBE* Thekla 1) the eldest was associated as empress with her brother, Michael III, during the regency of Theodora. She was the mistress of the future emperor Basil I for a while,

various gifts which are attractive to the female sex. Then, taking them aside, she would earnestly entreat them not to be feeble nor to remain the women they were, but to play the man and to think the kind of thoughts which were worthy of and appropriate to their mother's breast. They were to hold in abomination their father's heresy and to do homage to the outward forms of the holy icons. Whereupon she would thrust some of the icons (which she kept in a chest) into their hands, setting them against their faces and lips, to sanctify the girls and to stir up in them a devotion to the icons. Now it did not escape Theophilos' attention that she was habitually behaving in this manner, nor that she was kindling a favourable attitude to the sacred icons in her grandchildren. For he enquired what they had received by way of gifts from their grandmother and what she had done that had pleased them. The daughters whose intellects were already mature neatly sidestepped their father's inquiries as though they were statements made to be refuted. But Pulcheria, who was still a little child, spoke of the kindnesses, the quantity of fruits, and then she went on to mention the revering of the sacred icons, saying (her words reflected the simplicity of her mind) that her grandmother had many dolls in the chest, 'And she puts them to our heads and to our faces after kissing them.' This put the emperor [53] into a rage, but such was the respect and devotion he had for his wife that he was restrained from dealing very severely with his mother-in-law, even more so on account of the freedom of speech with which Theoktiste addressed him. For she used to rebuke him openly and remonstrate with him about the daily persecution of the [iconodule] confessors and on the subject of the heresy already mentioned. She was almost alone in openly declaring the hatred which everybody had for him. All he did was to prevent his daughters from visiting Theoktiste.

A similar occurrence also befell the empress Theodora herself. There was a pitiful fellow living at the palace, a eunuch named Denderis, not unlike Homer's Thersites. He said such odd things that people laughed at him; he was maintained in the palace to entertain people. Now one day he burst into the empress' boudoir and surprised her kissing the sacred icons. When the fool saw them he asked what they were, and he came nearer to find out. Speaking like a peasant, the empress said: 'These are my pretty dolls and I love them very much.'

but finally he confiscated her belongings; she ended her days at Blachernae. Anna (*PmbZ* 460 = *PBE* Anna 2) and her sisters Anastasia (*PmbZ* 231 = *PBE* Anastasia 2) and Pulcheria (*PmbZ* 6384 = *PBE* Poulcheria 1) were tonsured and sent to the family monastery *Ta Gastria* by Michael III when he became sole ruler. Theophilos' favourite daughter, Maria (*PmbZ* 4735 = *PBE* Maria 4), was given in marriage to Alexios Mosele (see below).

The emperor, who was at table when this deformed young man came to him, asked him where he had been. The eunuch replied that he had been with 'mama', for that is what he called Theodora; also that he had seen her taking pretty dolls from under her pillow in her chamber. The emperor took the point: in great wrath he left the table and went to her immediately. He hurled verbal abuse at her, calling her (with his unbridled tongue), among other things, idolatress, repeating as he did so what the deformed one had said. The empress, meanwhile, placating the [54] emperor's wrath, said: 'O, emperor, you have misunderstood; the truth is not as you perceive it. I was looking at myself in the mirror, attended by my handmaids. Denderis saw the faces reflected in it and, from that, he witlessly came and reported to you what you said.' With these words, she assuaged the emperor's wrath. She condemned Denderis to a suitable punishment, convincing him never again to say anything about the dolls to anybody. So that once when Theophilos was infuriated with the Sovereign Lady, and asked Denderis whether 'mama' was still kissing her pretty dolls, setting his hand to his lips, the fellow replied: 'Hush emperor, hush! Not a word about the dolls!' That is how this matter went.[17]

6. There was a brave soldier who had a high-spirited and well-trained horse. The commander under whom he served passionately coveted that horse for it had many times brought the soldier safely from the battlefield. The commander attempted to gain possession of it, offering a great price, and when the man refused he tried coercion. Since the soldier was still not persuaded to hand over his horse, the governor brought a charge of cowardice against him before the emperor and had him expelled from the regiment in which he served. At that time, Theophilos was in search of an outstanding horse. Orders were sent out in all directions for such a beast to be found and to be sent to him. Seizing the opportunity, the commander confiscated the man's horse (very much against its owner's will) and sent it to the emperor as though it were his own property. Then war broke out and there was a need of more soldiers. The emperor directed that absolutely every man capable of bearing arms was to be enlisted; thus the soldier mentioned above re-entered the ranks. Then a rout occurred in which he lost his life, for he had no horse capable of saving him.[18] He fell leaving a wife

---

[17] W. Treadgold, *The Byzantine revival, 782–842* (Stanford, CA, 1988), 446–7, has noted, following Grégoire, that the Theodora anecdote is a doublet of the foregoing one. It is intended to show Theodora as a fervent devotee of the icons. Theophilos' reaction could hardly be called severe since he clearly allowed those nearest to him to honour the icons if they were discreet about it.

[18] This sounds as though it could be Theophilos' campaign of 838 in which the Roman army suffered some serious defeats.

and children. Hearing of the emperor's love of justice, the wife, inflamed by devotion to her husband and no longer able to provide for the needs of her children, went up to the capital. She saw Theophilos on the day when it was his custom to go to the sacred church at Blachernae – saw him in fact mounted upon her husband's horse! With a great burst of speed she seized the beast by the bridle, saying it was hers and that it was none other but [55] the emperor himself who was responsible for her husband's death. This greatly surprised the emperor; he ordered her to wait until he came back to the palace. As soon as he returned, he had her brought before him, whereupon he questioned her to discover more precisely the substance in what she had said. Taking up the story from the beginning, the woman told it to the end for the emperor's benefit. The commander was immediately ordered to appear and a rigorous enquiry ensued concerning the horse – during which, at the emperor's command, the woman remained out of sight. When the governor insisted that the horse was his own property and not something he had acquired by confiscation, the emperor suddenly produced the woman from behind a curtain, an infallible witness, contradicting what the governor said. When the accused saw her, he was thunderstruck and stood there, speechless, for some time. Then he just managed to regain enough of his composure to embrace the emperor's feet in tears and become a humble petitioner, having made a clean breast of all his misdeeds. And what did the emperor do? He declared that the woman and her children were to be brothers and sister to the commander, of equal rank with him and co-heirs of his fortune. He relieved the culprit of his command and sent him into perpetual exile.[19] That was how implacably opposed he was to those who seized others' goods and those who sought to enrich themselves by unjust means.

7. The same emperor was also involved in building and he took particularly great care of the city walls. He tore down the lower ones and built them higher, making them insurmountable by the enemy. They stand to this day, bearing his title inscribed upon them.[20] In addition to that, he drove the prostitutes from certain dwellings and, having cleared all that

---

[19] In those days the horse was not provided by the state; it was the personal property of the soldier, which is why the commander was charged with theft. Commanders had complete authority, including judicial authority, over their subordinates: *Le traité sur la guérilla de L'empereur Nicéphore phocas*, ed. G. Dagron and H. Mihàescu (Le monde byzantin, Paris, 1986), 269–72. Subordinates had little chance of satisfaction if they were wronged by their superiors. Here the commander suffers a double punishment: exile (with the loss of his pay) and the partial confiscation of his property, which has to be shared with the woman and her children. This would be an exemplary story meant to restrain greedy senior officers from acting unjustly.

[20] One such inscription (now lost) used to be visible at the Pege gate near the Golden Horn. Others were placed along the wall bordering the sea of Marmara (Janin, *Constantinople*, 290, 294–5).

quarter, he built a very large and beautiful hostelry there which bears his name.[21]

8. That is what he did to counteract sexual immorality, and yet it is said of him that he once fell prey to the beauty of a handmaid who served the empress [56] and that he slept with her; this at a time when his life was not so well disciplined. When he realised what he had done and that Theodora, fully aware of his fall, was very depressed, they say that he held his hands up to God and declared on oath that this was the only time he had fallen; and that he begged forgiveness of his own wife.

He built a palace for his daughters in the district called *Ta Karianou*, traces of the ruins of which can be seen in our own times.[22]

9. Wishing to render the power of the empire abundantly clear to the Saracens, either to make them fully aware of his munificence or to render himself fearful to them, he sent his former teacher, John the synkellos,[23] to the ruler of the Syrians. Loyal to the emperor and of the same heresy as him, [John] was experienced in affairs of state and highly skilled in debating.[24] In addition to forty *kentenaria* of gold, he was entrusted with many things which are the wonder of the Roman empire and the astonishment of other people. The other goods were sent as gifts for the *amermoumnes*; the gold was provided so that John could be lavish and generous in his munificence. For if an ambassador scattered gold at will, as though it were sand, he who sent him would so much the more gain the admiration which he deserved. In addition to this, the emperor also gave him two golden vessels set about with precious stones, commonly called *cherniboxestra*.[25] In this way he made every effort to promote and enhance his ambassador.[26]

---

[21] Apart from maintenance of the walls and the construction of the Eleuthere palace, imperial building had virtually ceased since the time of Heraklios; hence Theophilos' buildings suggest an economic revival: Treadgold, *Byzantine revival*, 265; Janin, *Constantinople*, 108, 114, 132, 434, etc. The hospice in question replaced a convent which was falling down, the nuns having been transferred elsewhere.

[22] Janin, *Constantinople*, 132, says this palace – close to Blachernae – must be distinguished from the building of the similar name (Karianos) erected by Theophilos within the Great Palace. For the evidence of the *Patria*: A. Berger, *Untersuchungen zu den Patria Konstantinupoleos* (Poikila Byzantina, 8, Bonn, 1988), 476–7.

[23] John the Grammarian of the Armenian family of the Morocharzanioi was appointed by Michael II to educate his son. He was appointed [proto-] synkellos, which in those days meant he would succeed the sitting patriarch in due course: P. Lemerle, *Le premier humanisme byzantin* (Paris, 1971), 154–68; *ODB*, II, 1052.

[24] When he was superior of the monastery of SS Sergios and Bacchos, John was appointed by Leo V to head a commission whose task was to prepare for the return of iconoclasm.

[25] These ewers are sometimes mentioned in wills, e.g. of Eustathios Boilas and of Kale Pakouriane: P. Lemerle, *Cinq études sur le XIe siècle byzantin* (Le monde byzantin, Paris, 1977), 37; *Actes d'Iviron*, II: *Du milieu du XIe siècle à 1204*, ed. J. Lefort, N. Oikonomidès, and D. Papachryssanthou (Archives de l'Athos, 16, Paris, 1990) Act 47, line 27.

[26] The Byzantine embassy led by John set out shortly after the accession of Theophilos, probably in the autumn of 829. The ruler of Syria in that case would be the Abbassid caliph al Ma'mún

As he approached Babylon (now known as Baghdad),[27] John greatly distinguished himself by the words which smoothly flowed from his lips; greatly also by the wealth which proliferated about him. Nor were they small gifts which he gave to those who were sent to him or came to visit him, but large ones, as befits the emperor of the Romans. The ambassador gained the wonder and respect of the Saracens from the moment he crossed the frontier of the barbarians. When he had reached [57] the ruler and given him the emperor's message, he withdrew to his place of residence. It was there that he demonstrated his magnanimity and his kindly skill in all things. In order to exalt and magnify the Roman state, to every person who, for whatever reason, great or small, came or was sent to him, he presented a silver vessel filled with gold pieces. On one occasion when he was banqueting with the barbarian, he told his servants to make one of those rich vessels mentioned above disappear without a trace. There was no small outcry at the disappearance of this object. The barbarians, who were deeply impressed by the beauty of it, were sick at heart and undertook a great search and enquiry to find the stolen object. John then ordered the other vessel to be produced and the one that was lost to be written off, at which the search was to be called off. This led the Saracens to wonder greatly.

Responding in kind to this munificence and not wishing to be left in second place, the ruler of the Arabs showered the ambassador with gifts – in which he took no interest, but which he rejected before the ruler's face, as though they were dust. So the ruler gave him a hundred prisoners newly released from prison, whom he had stripped of the mournful garb of imprisonment and dressed in fine clothing. John praised the generosity of the giver but, even so, he would not accept them. He said they should remain in comfort and at liberty with the Arabs until a fitting compensation were arranged and an equal number of Saracen prisoners, now languishing in Roman gaols, be given in exchange. In these ways he reduced the Saracen [ruler] to amazement. He no longer treated John as a foreigner, but as a familiar friend whom he frequently invited to his home, showing

---

(813–33), the son of Harun al Rashid. The object of displaying all that wealth was to discourage him from leading raids into Roman territory under the pretence of jihad. Skylitzes says nothing of a second objective: to negotiate with Manuel, the former commander of the Asiatic themes who had taken refuge in Baghdad from a false charge of conspiracy. Treadgold, *Byzantine revival*, 268 and 431.

[27] Baghdad was founded by the caliph Mansur in 762. It was located near to Ctesiphon, capital city of the Seleucids, itself the heir to Babylon. Babylon was also the name given to the fortress in Egypt near to which the Arabs founded Fustat; from this some confusion has arisen.

him his personal treasure and the beauty of his palaces. He honoured him in various ways until the day he went back to the Romans.[28]

When John left Syria and returned to Theophilos, he described how things were there and also persuaded the emperor to build the *Bryas* palace based on the Saracens' [58] way of building palaces, deviating from their model in no detail of plan nor in the diversity of its decoration. He proposed to oversee the project himself and to be the architect of the building. He convinced the emperor and the task was accomplished along the lines John described, except for the addition of one item: a church erected in the name of the Mother of God within the imperial residence itself. In the forecourt of this palace a church with three apses was built. It far exceeded all other churches both in size and in beauty. The central apse was dedicated in the name of Michael the arch-commander: the apses to either side in the names of holy women martyrs.[29]

10. In suchlike matters [Theophilos]] seemed (and was thought) to be magnificent and wonderful, but to those who revered the divine and pure icons he was very harsh and severe, striving to outdo all the tyrants who had preceded him in cruelty. Those predecessors were: Leo [V] and his own father, Michael [II] the Stammerer. The latter directed that on no painted icon (if any such paintings there were anywhere) was the word holy [= saint] to be written, because such a word was appropriate only to God – in which his reasoning was not very shrewd. For God applied the word 'god' to men,[30] which is higher than the epithet 'saint', for 'saint' is a much more lowly title – so He would not have denied it to men. Nevertheless, that is what Michael [II] decreed; and the emperor before him [Leo V] completely forbade the veneration of icons. For his part, Theophilos ruled that there was to be no painting of icons. It was ignoble (he said) to be impressed with such objects; one should look only upon what is real and true. Whereupon all the sacred figures in the churches were removed.

[28] The embassy was really a failure for it did not succeed in averting the caliph's victorious campaign of 830. Manuel remained with the caliph, serving as counsellor to his son, given the task of putting an end to the rebellion of Babek in Chorassan (*ODB*, II, 1289).

[29] The palace of Bryas (the foundations of which can still be seen today) was built on the Asiatic shore of the Bosporos (*ODB*, I, 328), not on the return of John but after the emperor returned victorious from his campaign against Sozopetra and Melitene in 837. It is possible that the prisoners of war included some masons familiar with Muslim building techniques. The names of the other saints to whom the church of St Michael was consecrated are not known. Treadgold, *Byzantine revival*, 294–5, thinks these may have been Thekla, Anna and Anastasia, the same as Theophilos' first three eldest daughters, while Janin (*Constantinople*, 146) opts for Menodora, Metrodora and Nymphodora, the objects of particular veneration in Bithynia. See most recently A. Ricci, 'The road from Baghdad to Byzantium and the case of the Bryas palace in Istanbul', *Byzantium in the ninth century: dead or alive?*, ed. L. Brubaker (SPBS, 5, Aldershot, 1998), 131–49.

[30] Ps. 81/82:6, 'I have said you are gods'.

Depictions of wild beasts and birds were set up in their stead, [59] which showed the beastly and slavish nature of that emperor's mentality.[31] Then the holy and sacred objects were thrown into the marketplace by sacrilegious hands and treated abominably. Then the prisons which were intended to hold evil-doers were filled with those who honoured the sacred pictures: monks, bishops, layfolk and icon-painters. Full too then were the mountains and caves; full of those who were being put to death by hunger and thirst, as though they were evil-doers.[32] For the emperor decreed that the cities be out of bounds to the monks; he ordered them to be kept at a distance by all available means. They should not even dare to show themselves in the countryside.[33] By these means he transformed the monasteries and places of retreat into glorious tombs, for the holy men were unwilling to betray virtue and their sacred habit, preferring rather to lose their lives by hunger and affliction. But there were some who held their cloth in low esteem and, on that score, went down to destruction. Many of those who lived in an easy-going way took up a yet more dissolute and relaxed lifestyle, setting aside not only divine hymns and songs, but even the wearing of the habit. For the tyrant did not even allow them to hold the assemblies [*syllogoi*] that often are alone capable of restraining (like a kind of bridle) those who abandon themselves to their passions in a disorderly manner.

However, not even then did all men refrain from speaking their minds freely and boldly. Many of the more zealous, several of them as individuals,[34] some in groups (such as the monks from the monastery of the Abramites),[35] appeared boldly before him and, making a reasoned case from the sayings of the holy fathers (Dionysios the Great, Hierotheos and Irenaeus), demonstrated that it was not yesterday nor in recent times that the monastic way of life had been invented and established, but that it was something ancient, going back to the beginnings. They also pointed out that the figures of the sacred icons were something familiar to the apostles,

---

[31] On painting in the iconoclastic period: J. Lafontaine-Dosogne, 'Pour une problématique de la peinture d'église à l'époque iconoclaste', *DOP*, 41 (1987), 321–37; A. Cutler and J.-M. Spieser, *Byzance médiévale 700–1204* (Paris, 1996), 9–47; N. Thierry, *La Cappadoce de l'antiquité au moyen age* (Turnhout, 2002), 135–42.

[32] Oblique reference to Heb. 11:36–8. While Theophilos was undoubtedly the most determined antagonist of the second wave of iconoclasm, his repression does not seem to have fallen on any famous victims other than Euthymios of Sardis. He was content to keep the leading proponents of the icons in exile, where a number of outstanding figures died during his reign: Joseph the brother of Theodore the Stoudite, archbishop of Thessalonike, John of Kathara, Peter of Atroa and so forth.

[33] Probably a reference to the decree of 833 ordering the arrest of known iconodules.

[34] Certain Bithynian monks in particular, e.g. John of Kathara and Macarios of Pelekete.

[35] A celebrated monastery at Constantinople possibly dating back to the sixth century: Janin, *Églises et monastères*, I, 4–6.

since Luke, the sacred apostle, portrayed the figure of the Mother of God. And Christ, our Lord and God, left his own figure imprinted on a piece of linen without the intervention of hands.[36]

So, then, these godly men who exposed the tyrant's mindlessness and provoked his brutality by speaking far too freely [60] were exiled from the city after suffering much torture and many blows. They reached the sacred church of the Forerunner [John the Baptist] known as Phoberos (on the Euxine sea)[37] and there, completely overwhelmed by their whip-inflicted wounds, they were deemed worthy of their eternal rest. Their venerable bodies were left lying on the ground, where they remained intact for some considerable time, until some pious souls took them up and buried them. These accorded them honours similar to those that are rendered to the martyrs who died for Christ who is God.

Exploits comparable with and of the same kind as these were performed by another monk who had recently attained the priesthood. Filled with divine zeal, he withstood the tyrant to his face and, among many other things, he cited that dictum of Paul the Apostle which says: 'If any man preach unto you any other gospel than that which you received, let him be anathema.'[38] [The emperor] had him severely flogged and then, when he realised that the man stood even firmer in his convictions, he sent him to Jannes,[39] who had been the tyrant's master and teacher and whom he besought to convince the man by argument. But this noble athlete reduced [Jannes] to the dumbness of fish, not by sophistical and syllogistic demonstrations, but by the words of the apostles and of the gospels. He promptly received another good beating and was sent into exile. Later on he took refuge with Ignatios the Great, with whom he stayed for some time. He made some pronouncements about the emperors who were yet to come, for he had been found worthy to receive the gift of prophecy, and then he went to the Lord.

In his hatred of the godly icons, the tyrant forced every likeness-painter either to quit the society of men or, if he chose to live, to spit on the icons

---

[36] The famous *mandylion* of Edessa, the most celebrated of the *acheiropoietos* – images ('not made with hands') brought to Constantinople in 944 (see below). This and the icon of the Theotokos allegedly painted by St Luke are often cited by the iconodules in their polemic, e.g. in the *Life of Stephen the Younger*, ch. 9.

[37] This monastery was located at the north of the Bosporos; it was sufficiently isolated to serve as a prison for obdurate iconodules: Janin, *Grands centres byzantins*, II, 7–8.

[38] Gal. 1:9.

[39] This is a deliberate attempt to distort the name of John the Grammarian (Ioannes), the future patriarch. Jannes is a biblical character, a magician who opposed Moses: 2 Tim. 3:6–8, possibly referring to Ex. 7 and 8; see S. Gero, 'Jannes and Jambres in the *Vita Stephani Iunioris*, BHG 1666', *AnalBoll*, 113 (1995), 287–8. The monk who disputed with John remains unidentified (*PBE*, Anonymous, 194).

and to tread them under foot on the ground, as an abomination. Lazaros the monk was arrested along with the others; in those days, he was a celebrated practitioner of the art of the likeness-painter.[40] The enemy of God first tried flattery to bring him into line but, perceiving him to be beyond the reach of any kind of fawning, he resorted to violence, his natural ally. He tortured him [61] so severely that it was thought unlikely that he would survive. Grievously broken in body, he was confined in a prison. When [the emperor] learned, however, that he was no sooner restored to health than he started setting up the sacred pictures[41] again, he ordered iron plates to be heated in the coals and to be applied to the palms of his hands. The fire devoured his flesh to the point at which the athlete lost consciousness and lay half-dead. But the grace of God must have determined that he survive to be a spark [to ignite] those who would come after. For when the tyrant learnt that this saintly man was at his last breath, bowing to the entreaties of the empress and of others close to him, he released him from prison and concealed him in the church of the Forerunner known as Phoberos. There, in spite of his wounds, the man painted an icon of the Forerunner. It was kept there for a long time and it accomplished healings. This is what happened at that time; after the death of the tyrant and the restoration of orthodoxy it was Lazaros who set up the icon of Jesus Christ, God and man, in the Chalke with his own hands.[42] He was invited by the extraordinary empress Theodora to grant pardon to her husband and to intercede for him. 'O empress,' he replied, God is not so unjust as to forget our love and our labour on his behalf while holding in higher honour the hatred and the presumptuous folly of that man.' But this comes later.

The blood-stained tyrant, knowing that Theophanes the confessor and Theodore his brother were quite different from the many others so far as learning is concerned, summoned them to the banqueting hall of Lausiakos[43] to engage in a public debate concerning matters of faith. 'Come on then, you accursed ones,' he said, 'by what sayings of scripture are you persuaded to worship the idols' – for that is how he spoke of the

---

[40] This monk of Khazar origins was employed to transport the gifts sent by Michael III to the Roman pope Benedict III (*PmbZ* 4234 = *PBE* Lazaros 2). See C. Mango, 'Documentary evidence in the apse mosaics of St Sophia', *BZ*, 47 (1954), 395–402.
[41] *Morphai*.
[42] According to the chronicler Theophanes, it was the taking down of this very icon which instigated the iconoclast controversy in 726.
[43] Built by Justinian II to the north of the Chrysotriklinos, this chamber was decorated by Theophilos with mosaics on a field of gold: R. Guilland, *Études de topographie de Constantinople byzantine* (Amsterdam, 1969), 154–60.

holy icons in his unbridled thought and speech – 'and to persuade the innocent common people to do likewise?' To this he added some other discordant blasphemies against the icon of Christ our God, with a mouth that knew no shame. The blessed ones declared: 'Let the mouth be dumb which speaks iniquity against God.'[44] For his part, he concealed the lion for the time being and played the part of the fox, asking what might be the pronouncements of the prophets and [62] the testimonies which enjoined the veneration of the icons. When one of the brothers, the blessed Theophanes, advanced something taken from the prophecy of Isaiah, Theophilos objected that the quotation was incorrect. Leafing through his own book, he showed them the alleged correct wording. The saint protested that he had tampered with not only that book, but also every other book which had come into his hands. He proposed that someone should bring him the book which lay in such-and-such a place in the patriarchal library at Thomaites[45] to confirm what he was alleging. Someone was sent and, quicker than it takes to tell, brought the book. Quite deliberately, the emperor missed the passage in question as he leafed through it and quite shamelessly jumped over the statement they were looking for as he went in search of one passage or another. The blessed Theophanes indicated this to him and, pointing with his finger, he said: 'Turn three leaves and you will find the passage we are looking for.' The emperor could not tolerate being so boldly told he was wrong, especially when he knew there was truth in what the other said. He cast aside his mask of patience, revealing the beast within. 'An emperor ought not to be subject to the insults of men like you,' he said. He ordered them to be taken to the inner garden of the Lausiakos and to be beaten. They were to receive two hundred blows with the heaviest rods, and on the foreheads were to be inscribed by barbaric tattooing some worthless iambic lines he had written. Here they are:

> When all the world went running to that town
> Where the all-holy feet of God the Word
> Once stood t'ensure the safety of the world,
> In that most pious place these did appear
> Who are an evil vessel of superstitious error.
> Which superstitious men, achieving there
> With impious mind the deeds of unbelief
> Most horrid, were expelled as apostates
> And exiles. Thence they fled, sad refugees, [63]

---

[44] Pss. 30:19 and 106:42.
[45] R. Guilland, 'Le Thomaites et le Patriarcat', *JÖB*, 5 (1956), 27–40, repr. *Topographie*, II, 14–27.

Unto the capital and seat of government –
But did not leave aside their foolishness
Hence, indicted and condemned, an evil perpetrator of the image,
They are banished once again.

This was quickly accomplished and, for their part, [the brothers] acquired the confessors' and martyrs' crowns. But, as for that violent and most wretched of all wretches, it was revealed to everybody that he was a blasphemer, a persecutor and the most false believer of all the false believers who might ever exist.[46] He also took Michael,[47] synkellos of the church of the Holy City, with many other ascetics and shut them up in prison – in the hope that prolonged affliction would bring them into subjection. Such was his outrageous aggression against the saints, and that is how he despitefully insulted both the Man who appeared on earth for us who is truly God and also that Man's genuine servants. And this was not for a short time or a limited period; his whole lifetime long he was maltreating them and subjecting them to irremediable afflictions.

11. He prided himself on being something of a poet/musician;[48] thus he composed some hymns and set some verses to music, ordering them to be sung. Among other things, he transposed 'Bless ye the Lord' of the fourth ode along the lines of 'Give ear, O Virgin' of the eighth ode, endowing it with a different rhythm. This he ordered to be sung publicly in the church of God. There is also a story that he was so enamoured of music that he did not consider it beneath his dignity to conduct [the singing] with his own hand on high festival days at the Great Church – for which he gave the clergy one hundred pounds of gold. They say that the Palm Sunday anthem, 'Go out ye people, go forth O Gentiles', is the fruit of his intellect.

12. [64] His hair was very thin by nature; in fact he was bald on the forehead. So he published an edict[49] that everywhere men should cut their hair close to the skin and that no Roman should be permitted to wear his hair below the neck. He who disobeyed this decree was to be given a sound whipping. Thus the emperor prided himself on restoring the virtue of the ancient Romans.

---

[46] There is some discussion about when the *Graptoi* ('written on') brothers (*PmbZ* 7526 = *PBE* Theodoros 68; *PmbZ* 8093 = *PBE* Theophanes 6), originally from Jerusalem, suffered. It was probably in 839 at the latest. See (most recently) S. Efthymiadis, 'Notes on the correspondence of Theodore the Studite', *REB*, 53 (1995), 141–4.

[47] On this person (*PmbZ* 5059 = *PBE* Michael 51): M. Cunningham, *The Life of Michael the Synkellos* (BBTT, 1, Belfast, 1991).

[48] *Melodos* has both meanings, as the context makes clear.

[49] *Theophanes Continuatus*, ed. I. Bekker (CSHB, Bonn, 1838), 107; F. Dölger, *Regesten der Kaiserurkunden des oströmischen Reiches von 565–1453*. I. Teil. *Regesten von 565–1025* (Munich and Berlin, 1924) no. 445.

13. Being the father of five daughters (as we said before) but no male heir,[50] he thought he should find a husband for his youngest daughter, Maria,[51] who was most especially dear to him. The bridegroom he selected was a member of the Krinitai family, from the land of the Armenians. He was called Alexios, and Mosele was his surname. He was handsome and in the flower of manhood.[52] First the emperor honoured him with the titles of patrician and proconsul, then of magister and, finally, caesar.[53] He gave him a considerable army and sent him to Longobardia to deal with a pressing problem.[54] Alexios acquitted himself well in his commission and did as the emperor expected, whereupon his popularity increased. But so too did the envy of men; some gave it out that he was aiming at the throne, because sooner or later, *alpha* must take precedence over *theta*.[55] When the caesar heard of this, he appeared to shrug off the slander, but he urgently entreated the emperor to permit him to renounce the world in favour of the monastic life. This the emperor refused to permit for he would not have his daughter left a widow; so the caesar went on quietly managing the affairs of state. Meanwhile Michael[56] was born to the emperor, and Maria, the caesar's wife, departed this life. So greatly did [her father] revere her that her corpse was laid in a casket covered with silver and the right of sanctuary was accorded to her tomb for men taking refuge there, no matter of what [65] they might be accused. As for Alexios, he secretly renounced the world and took the monastic habit. It was only when he could not be prevailed upon to reverse his decision that the emperor reluctantly gave his permission, granting him the imperial monastery at Chrysopolis for a residence, followed by Byrsis' monastery and the one at Elaias.[57] While

---

[50] At that time Theophilos had five daughters (Thekla, Anna, Anastasia, Maria and Pulcheria) and one son, to whom he had given the imperial name of Constantine but who had died in childhood in 835, accidentally drowned in a cistern of the Great Palace.
[51] Maria was not the youngest; Pulcheria was, but maybe she was born after the marriage.
[52] The first Mosele known to us (also Alexios) was strategos of the Armeniakon theme under Eirene (*PmbZ* 193 = *PBE* Alexios 1); he rebelled in 790: Treadgold, *Byzantine revival*, 289; Maria's husband (*PmbZ* 195 = *PBE* Alexios 2) may have been his grandson.
[53] Since the title of caesar was reserved for members of the imperial family, Theophilos (who at this point had no male heir) may have been indicating that he was designating Alexios his successor.
[54] In 836 Alexios Mosele reconquered the coast between the rivers Nestos and Strymon, thus restoring to the empire control of the Via Egnatia from Constantinople to Thessalonike. He scored numerous successes in Sicily but came short of expelling the Arabs from the Island: Treadgold, *Byzantine revival*, 292, 305–6.
[55] The initials of Alexios and Theophilos.
[56] Michael was born 9 January 840: C. Mango, 'When was Michael III born?', *DOP*, 21 (1967), 253–8, repr. *Byzantium and its image* (London, 1984), no. XIV.
[57] The monastery at Chrysopolis may well be the Philippikos (see below); Byrsis is otherwise unknown but there was an Elaias monastery on the Asiatic shore of the Bosporos: Janin,

Alexios was residing at Chrysopolis, one day when he felt the need to take a walk, he found himself in the place called Anthemios. He decided to buy the place and, procuring an imperial decree,[58] he built a magnificent monastery[59] there, in which he spent his last years. When he departed this life, it was in that monastery that he was buried (together with his brother, Theodosios the patrician), leaving considerable evidence behind him there of his virtuous way of life.

14. When Imbrael, ruler of the Arabs, campaigned against the Romans, not to be outdone Theophilos also went forth, setting all fear aside.[60] He would have achieved great things indeed, had he possessed the experience in war and the nobility of those who were with him: Theophobos and Manuel. Manuel was known for his boldness even to the enemy, for he had commanded the army of the Anatolikon theme under Leo and was head groom (what they call *protostrator*) under Michael, Leo's predecessor.[61]

15. This narrative will now show how and under what circumstances Theophobos, being of Persian descent, became acquainted with the emperor and received his sister in marriage. Some time ago a member of the Persian royal family arrived in the city of Constantine on an embassy. He begot [Theophobos] while he was there, not in licit wedlock, but secretly and in hiding; then he returned to his own people. Now the Persians have an immutable law that no person who is not of the royal family may take command and rule over them. But, on account of frequent wars against the Hagarenes, the royal family had died out. There was a persistent rumour in Persia that there lived a [member of that family] by the name of Theophobos at Byzantium; it was spread around by the father who had engendered him. The Persian council of elders thought it would be a good idea to send some people secretly to search out the man they were looking for. They reached our city and, after a great deal of enquiry, found him with his mother in the Oxeia. He was made known to and recognised by them not only by his features but also by the characteristics

---

Constantinople, 28. There is a gentle irony here, that one could renounce the world – and receive three monasteries. It gives a whole new meaning to *aktemosyne* (voluntary poverty).

[58] Dölger, *Regesten*, no. 440.

[59] The Asian suburb known as Ta Anthemiou probably owed its name to the western emperor Anthemios. The monastery which Alexios Mosele built here in 840 should be distinguished from another monastery of the same name, lying in Constantinople, founded by another Mosele: a contemporary of Romanos Lekapenos.

[60] After a long period of preparation Ma'mun invaded Roman territory in July 830.

[61] Manuel (*PmbZ* 4707 = *PBE* Manuel 1) was related to the empress Theodora, her uncle according to *Theophanes Continuatus*, 148. He was already an important person under Michael I (protostrator) and under Leo V he went on to be strategos of the Armeniakon theme. He fled to the Arabs after being accused of treason in 829.

of his body and soul. And one of the neighbours attested to the woman's former liaison with the Persian (for there is no secret which is not common knowledge with the masses). The ambassadors now identified themselves to the emperor and explained the object of their mission. They promised peace, a treaty and the submission of the entire nation if he would agree to hand Theophobos over to them. The promises were pleasing to the emperor so, once he was convinced that they were telling the truth, he received the man into the palace, where he had him brought up as a gentleman and given a liberal education.

According to another story, it was not by an ambassador that Theophobos was engendered, but (due to the changes and chances of war) by the ruler, or one very closely related to the ruler, who had fled from Persia and come to the imperial city. Here he lived in penury, working for a woman who kept a tavern. He fell in love with her and Theophobos was born [to her] in legal wedlock. After the father passed from the land of the living the Persians learnt of his son by astronomy and divination (they say that these arts flourish in Persia). They learnt that he was of the royal line and living in Byzantium, whereupon they arrived in haste at the city of Constantine, looking for him whom they hoped to find; in this way he came to the notice of the emperor.[62] When his distinction was made known to all the Persians by the returning ambassadors, everybody thought it would be a good idea to rise up in revolt against the Hagarenes and to side with the Roman empire, in order to [67] reap the good fortune of having a commander of royal blood. And besides all this, it transpired that it was now the fifth year since the Persian commander, Babek, had rebelled against the Hagarenes with seven thousand men.[63] Motivated by devotion to Theophobos and fear of the Hagarenes, he advanced into Roman territory. He came to the city of Sinope and there he placed himself and all his men under the emperor's command.[64] This led Theophilos

---

[62] The two stories of the birth of Theophobos (*PmbZ* 8237 = *PBE* Theophobos 1) are of course legends. The identification of Nasr with Theophobos is, however, not contested. See M. Rekaya, 'Mise au point sur Théophobe et l'alliance de Bâbek avec Théophile (833/34–839/40)', *Byzantion* (1974), 43–67; also *PmbZ* 729 = *PBE* Babak 1.

[63] With the support of nationalist Iranian elements Babek rebelled against the Abassid Caliphate of Baghdad in 816 and held Azerbaijan for some time, causing disturbances as far away as Kurdistan. Around 833 another revolt against the Caliphate arose in Iran, in the province of Hamahan, around Nasr the Khurramite.

[64] It was not Babek, but Nasr (who was not directly related to Babek) who entered Roman territory. As the consequence of a severe defeat he took refuge in the empire in 834 with the majority of the survivors. Both he and his men converted to Christianity and took Roman wives. Now Nasr, become Theophobos ('he who fears God'), entered the imperial family. His soldiers stayed together, forming a new unit in the central army. Babek was defeated in 837 and executed in January of the following year.

to advance Theophobos to the rank of patrician and to give him his own sister in marriage,[65] enjoining each of the Persians (many of them he distinguished with imperial honours) to bind himself to the Romans with bonds of marriage. He also ordered what he chose to call 'the Persian brigade' to be entered in the military registers and to be numbered with the Romans who were campaigning against the Hagarenes.

16. Putting his trust in these two men, Manuel and Theophobos, Theophilos went off to war against the Hagarenes. When the armies made contact, he held a council. Manuel said it was not befitting for the Roman emperor to do battle with the *amermoumnes*. One of the generals, taking a portion of the army, should meet the enemy face to face. But Theophobos wanted the emperor to be in the battle line. He advised a night attack on the enemy by the infantry, with the cavalry being brought in as and when needed. The emperor could not be convinced, it being the case that many were saying Theophobos was trying to appropriate for himself the glory of the Romans; that was why he was counselling them to fight by night. The general opinion was that they should give battle at daybreak.

Either out of haughtiness or for fear of the emperor, Imbrael, the *amermoumnes*,[66] took a portion of the army and withdrew, sending out one of his generals, Abouzachar,[67] with eighty thousand men, to carry on the war against the emperor. The armies approached each other and there was an engagement in which many fell on either side. Finally the regiment of the scholai under its domestic [68] wavered and fell back in retreat. The emperor with the imperial infantry and two thousand Persians (including Theophobos) took his stand on a hillock and was surrounded by Saracens. There was heavy fighting around the hillock until evening, those on one side hoping to take the emperor prisoner, those on the other warding off their attacks and holding on to prevent the emperor from being taken. When night had fallen, Theophobos deceived the Saracens with a trick; he ordered the soldiers to clap and shout, to play their stringed and brass instruments, as though some relief column had arrived for them. This is indeed what the Saracens imagined; they retreated six miles for fear of being encircled. Taking advantage of the brief respite which this afforded, the emperor and those with him took to their heels and contrived to find safety with that portion of the army which had fled the field. The emperor limited himself to scolding the army which had abandoned him; he did nothing else unpleasant. But he awarded gifts and various honours to those who were with Theophobos. Thus Theophobos

---

[65] In fact Theophobos married one of the empress' sisters, probably Eirene.
[66] The caliph al-Mu'talim, 833–42.
[67] al-Afsin Haidar ibn Káwús (*PmbZ* 110 = *PBE* Abuchazar 1).

became increasingly popular with the Persians; they requested that it should be only they, under his command, who should wage the war against the Hagarenes. This, they strongly maintained, the emperor should allow. The emperor was so won over by their arguments that he willed no other person but Theophobos to command them.[68]

The following year the emperor set out again with the forces and joined battle with the Hagarenes near Charsianon, where he put them to flight and captured not a few of them. He took twenty-five thousand prisoners and returned to the capital in great triumph.[69]

17. One of the Hagarenes taken prisoner was bold in action and renowned for his extraordinary physical powers. He was known to the domestic of the scholai, who testified that he was an accomplished horseman; from the saddle he could effectively manipulate two lances at once for striking down the enemy. Since it was the duty of the domestic to direct the victory celebrations at the Hippodrome, this captive led [69] the parade. When the emperor saw him, beguiled by his glowing reputation, he ordered him to mount and to be given two lances, so that his excellence and skill might be demonstrated to the entire city. The exhibition took place, to the delight of the less sophisticated. But standing near to the emperor was Theodore Krateros,[70] who shortly afterwards became a commander of the corps of the holy Forty-two Martyrs. He scoffed at the Hagarene, saying that he had demonstrated nothing particularly brave or astonishing. The emperor took exception to this: 'Could you do anything like that, you effeminate gelding?' 'Having never learnt to operate two lances, emperor, I cannot,' Krateros replied; 'nor is there any need of such foolishness in war. But I have firm trust in God that I could unseat that fellow and knock him down from his horse using only one lance.' This made the emperor really angry. He said – and he swore an oath on his own head to this effect – that he would put the saint[-ly man] to death unless he confirmed his words by deeds. Theodore leapt into the saddle, took a lance

---

[68] The incident concerns the battle of Dazimon where Theophilos was in danger of being taken by the Arabs, see below, chs. 18 and 23. Skylitzes has failed to distinguish the two actions, which throws his chronology into disarray.

[69] In spring 831 Theophilos and Manuel (meanwhile returned from Baghdad and pardoned) surprised and crushed a large body of Arabs in the Armeniakon theme. The reception of the victorious emperor (said to have taken 20,000 prisoners of war) is described in some detail by Constantine Porphyrogennetos, *Constantine Porphyrogenitus: three treatises on imperial military expeditions: introduction, edition, translation and commentary*, ed. J. F. Haldon (CFHB, 28, Vienna, 1990), 146–50.

[70] The Krateroi have already appeared in Skylitzes' narrative (Reign of Michael II, c. 18). The commander of the Kibyrrhaiote theme who failed to take Crete was so named. Yet Theodore, as a eunuch, may not have been a member of the family but rather one of its servants.

and engaged the Saracen whom, before very long, he had thrown down from his horse. The emperor was chagrined to see the Saracen thrown down by a man who was a eunuch. Nevertheless, to please the populace, he congratulated him, giving him robes and raiment, thus acknowledging the man's sterling qualities.[71]

As spring was now arriving, Theophilos assembled an army again and went out against the Saracens. He took the holy Methodios with him, as was his custom when he went to war – either for the sake of his learning and his ability to solve problems which baffled most men by the wisdom he possessed, or to ward off the possibility of an uprising under Methodios' leadership on account of the war being waged against the godly and venerable icons. For the man was held in considerable veneration by a select and God-fearing element of the populace. This is why the emperor thought it disadvantageous to leave him behind.[72]

18. Eventually the two armies fell on each other and the Ishmaelites got the upper hand for the time being. The emperor found himself surrounded and [70] in a very vulnerable position, about to be taken prisoner. When Manuel (who was in command of the army) learnt of this, he spurred on his men and boldly charged into the midst of danger, for he counted it a terrible thing for a Roman emperor to be taken in battle. He found the emperor in a perilous situation, despairing of getting out alive and declaring that he did not want to abandon his men by taking to his heels. 'Come now, emperor,' he said; 'follow me as I go ahead and find the way for you.' Manuel set off, but the emperor was too afraid and did not follow, so he was obliged to turn back again. When the emperor missed his chance again, he came back a third time and threatened him with death if he did not follow. It was thus that, very late in the day and with great difficulty, the emperor was saved. For this, the emperor caused him to receive honours commensurate with his service, showering him with gifts and addressing him as 'benefactor' and 'saviour'.[73]

19. Jealousy, however, began to develop towards such a man as this and he was maliciously charged with high treason.[74] He realised that he was

---

[71] This could be the first mounted joust recorded in the Middle Ages. See M. McCormick, *Eternal victory: triumphal rulership in late antiquity Byzantium, and the early medieval west* (Cambridge, MA, 1986), 148–9. On this occasion Theophilos issued a follis on the reverse of which was inscribed: 'O emperor Theophilos, you are conqueror'.

[72] The charge against Methodios was that he had announced the death of the emperor in a pamphlet, which was certainly a political move. He and other iconodoules were arrested and confined in a monastery. This persecution occasioned the death of Euthymios of Sardis.

[73] This story refers to a later campaign, the one in 838.

[74] At the beginning of Theophilos' reign Manuel was accused of conspiracy by Myron (*PmbZ* 5214 = *PBE* Myron 2) who, as logothete of the drome, was responsible for the intelligence service. Skylitzes'

standing in very great danger and he was informed that they were going to blind him. This intelligence came from a man who was utterly devoted to him, a former servant of his, now Theophilos' wine-pourer. It caused him to throw off the imperial yoke and to go over to the Hagarenes. They, to whom he seemed to be of great importance, awarded him highest honours. He was entrusted with a large army and sent out against some hostile neighbours known as the Kormates.[75] It was his will that he should have no followers other than the imprisoned Romans to campaign with him. He achieved great and glorious victories and even took by storm a place called Khorossan. It was not merely the superior boldness [of his force] which confused the enemy, but the difference in language, the change in uniform and the amazingly unconventional method of giving battle which reduced [71] the adversary to unwonted timidity.

It was not only against the enemy that he displayed his boldness; he was courageous [in killing] the wild beasts which were ravaging the countryside. Because he was the author of great benefits for the people, he was greatly beloved by the ruler of the Saracens and his council of elders. When Theophilos learnt of all this, naturally he was not pleased. He left no stone unturned in his efforts to recall the man. By the hand of a mendicant monk, he sent him a cross and a chrysobull, inviting him to return and granting him a complete amnesty for his misdeeds by these means.[76] Conveying the things he had received, the monk secretly delivered them into the hands of Manuel, whose heart burned within him after receiving them. Trading on the confidence his former accomplishments had inspired, he let the Saracen ruler know that he cherished a desire of campaigning against the Romans and of revenging himself on those who had slandered him before the emperor, dwellers of Cappadocia.[77] He asked that the ruler's son be sent along with him, to add credence to his proposal. Ishmael acceded to his requests and gave him permission to depart on campaign. When Manuel approached the Roman border, he let the commander of the Cappadocian theme know who he was and that he was

---

sources (Symeon Magister, 220–1; Leo the Grammarian, 218; *Georgios monachos continuatus*, 796) do not imply any causal connection with the previous episode in the narrative as Sktlitzes does.

[75] The Khurramites of Babek. Accompanied by Al'Abbas, the son of Ma'mûn, Manuel had a certain measure of success against them but he was unable to free Khorassan (the region to the north of Iran) of them.

[76] A chrysobull bearing the emperor's autograph signature and the cross constituted the most solemn guarantee of clemency a rebel could receive. Manuel was appointed domestic of the scholai when he returned.

[77] Returning via the pass of Adata, Manuel entered the empire in the theme of Cappadocia.

Theophilos

about to return to the Romans. He also intimated that the commander should set a detachment in such and such a place to lie in ambush, 'So that, when I come that way,' he said, 'I can send off the Saracen vanguard to some other place while I run across to the Roman side.' And that is what happened. As they were approaching the appointed place, the one agreed upon, he warmly embraced the son of Ishmael, saying: 'Go safely away to your father, child, for I am going to my lord and emperor.' He got away from there safely, reached the capital and encountered the emperor at the church of the Mother of God at Blachernae. He was honoured with the title of magister by him and was thenceforth treated as his kinsman.[78] That is what is known of Manuel.

20. [72] When Theodotos Melissenos (also known as Kassiteras, as the narrative revealed above) was released from this life after occupying the patriarchal throne of Constantinople for some considerable time, Jannes, the mentor of Theophilos, succeeded him on the throne. He received the high priesthood as a reward for impiety and unbelief.[79]

21. Theophilos was then seeking most diligently to know about those who would rule after him. A woman captured among the Hagarenes in one of the foregoing wars who was talented for this kind of foretelling came before the emperor. He asked what he wished, directing her to proclaim in which family there would be a long succession of emperors. Moved either by a divine frenzy or by demonic force, she said: 'O emperor, [your] successor will be [your] son together with his mother; but after them, the family of the Martinakioi will rule the empire for a long time.'[80] No sooner were the words out of her mouth than he tonsured Martinakios – even though he delighted in his company – and turned that man's house into a dwelling place for monks.[81] This is not the only prediction of the woman in question, for she foretold many other things that were about to happen. She predicted the fall of Jannes from the patriarchal throne; also that

---

[78] On adoption: R. J. Macrides, 'Kinship by arrangement: the case of adoption', *DOP*, 44 (1990), 109–18, repr. *Kinship and justice in Byzantium, 11th–15th centuries*, ed. R. J. Macrides (Aldershot, 1999), no. 11.

[79] When Melissenos died in 821 he was in fact succeeded by Antony Kassimates (*PmbZ* 550 = *PBE* Antonios 3), formerly bishop of Sylaion in Pamphylia. It was only on *his* death in 838 that John Morocharzanes (held to be too young in 821) became patriarch. On John see, among others, S. Gero, 'John the Grammarian, the last iconoclastic patriarch of Constantinople', *Byzantina*, 3/4 (1974–5), 25–35.

[80] The founder of the Macedonian dynasty, Basil I, was married to Eudocia Ingerina, a relative of the Martinakioi, a family which appears to have owed its ascent to the accession of Leo V. The first known Martinakios is a certain Anastasios who served under that emperor (see *The Life of Theodore the Stoudite*, PG 99: 292, 300).

[81] On this monastery, situated near the Sophian port: Janin, *Églises et monastères*, I, 328.

the sacred icons would receive the honour and reverence which was their due. Theophilos was so disturbed at this that he frequently summoned the empress and Theoktistos, the logothete of the drome, and bound them with terrible oaths neither to deprive Jannes of the patriarchate nor to see the restoration of the cult of idols (as he called the sacred icons) after his death. The woman was not the only one to foretell these things, for Jannes, acting as a dish-diviner,[82] clearly showed him who was going to succeed to the office of ruler. Nor did the woman only answer the emperor's queries; she also indicated to Constantine (who at that time was the most powerful man among the [73] Triphyllioi)[83] what was going to happen to him. She said that he and his sons[84] would be deprived of their property and be clothed in clerical attire, which indeed happened later on, when Basil had taken over as ruler. To George, [logothete of] the stratiotikon,[85] she predicted how he would come to his end in the U-turn[86] of the Hippodrome: it was there that he was later beheaded, in the reign of Basil, having come to grief on a charge of rebellion.

22. When spring began to lighten the sky the Hagarenes and Theophilos sallied forth against each other but, as each was exceedingly cautious of the other, they returned with nothing accomplished. On his return, Theophilos received an embassy from the Chagan of the Khazars, requesting that the fortress known as Sarkel be built. This seemed to be a sure fortification, protecting them from the onslaught of the Patzinaks in the region of the river Tanais.[87] The emperor acceded to the request and sent out a man named Petronas to accomplish it. When this man came back, he gave the emperor his opinion that the only way he could safely rule Cherson was by appointing somebody there to be its commander. Until that time, none of our own people had been sent to command there; one of the local people, known as the *proteuon*,[88] used to attend to

---

[82] *dia lekano-manteias*; this was practised by throwing precious stones and metals into a basin full of water and observing their formation when they reached the bottom.
[83] Sisinnios Triphyllios (*PmbZ* 6795 = *PBE* Sisinnios 1) and Nicetas Triphyllios (*PmbZ* 5426 = *PBE* Niketas 1) were already influential in the time of Nikephoros I; the first of these two lost his life in 811 at the same time as the emperor.
[84] Genesios, ed. Lesmueller-Werner and Thurn, 3.15, says Constantine (*PmbZ* 3950 = *PBE* Konstantinos 42) had received honours for his services as an ambassador. His son Niketas (*PmbZ* 7261 = *PBE* Niketas 157) was in charge of an important section of the treasury, the *eidikon*.
[85] George (*PmbZ* 2268 = *PBE* Georgios 230) was logothete of the *stratiotikon*. According to what Genesios says (which is less than clear), he was a brother of Niketas Triphyllios.
[86] *Sphendone*, the 'hairpin bend' of the Hippodrome, a frequent place of execution.
[87] The river Don.
[88] Literally, 'the first'. The city of Cherson long maintained its ancient municipal institutions which included a 'father of the city', an *ekdikos* and some curiales known as *proteuontes*: N. A. Alekseenko, 'Newly found seals of the representatives of the city administration of Chersonesos',

municipal affairs. The emperor accepted his advice; the person he sent out to command the district was none other than this same Petronas. He sent an ordinance to the *proteuon* and to the other indigenous potentates commanding them to give unswerving obedience [to the commander]. From that time, it was the practice to send commanders to Cherson.[89]

23. The following year, at the inception of spring, Theophilos went out against the Hagarenes in great force and with many troops.[90] He advanced [74] deep into Syria, stripping the land bare, pillaging and laying waste everything he came across. He took two cities by the rules of war and led their citizens captive. He even took by storm the city called Sozopetra,[91] the homeland of the *amermoumnes* – who sent many letters pleading on its behalf. But though he pleaded for his homeland to be spared, the emperor paid no attention to his letters.[92] When he had settled things there, Theophilos returned to the capital leaving Theophobos behind. His orders were to make satisfactory arrangements for the army and then to come to the emperor in all haste. But the Persians were exasperated by delays in their pay. So they detained him at Sinope and proclaimed him emperor, against his will. Indeed, he prayed and besought them to abandon this initiative, warning them that on account of this uprising they were exposing themselves to harsher sufferings than ever.[93] As they paid no attention to him but were heart and soul completely dedicated to the undertaking, he secretly let the emperor know what had happened. He gave his assurance with an oath that it was not himself but the Persians

---

MAIET, 5 (1996), 155–70 (in Russian); N. A. Alekseenko, 'Les sceaux des *proteuontés* de Kherson au Xe siècle', *SBS*, 7 (2002), 79–86.

[89] This whole incident is recorded by Constantine Porphyrogennetos (*Constantine Porphyrogenitus, De administrando*, ed. G. Moravcsik and tr. R. H. J. Jenkins (CFHB, 1, Washington DC, 1967), 183–5). Established on the plains to the north of the Black Sea, the Khazars maintained a long tradition of friendship with Byzantium, to whom they offered a reciprocal alliance against the Moslems of Armenia. Petronas, the first *Kamateros* of whom we know, received orders to proceed to the Khazar land with vessels of both the imperial fleet and the Paphlagonian fleet, to build Sarkel at the mouth of the Don. The theme of Cherson, formerly known as the theme of Klimata, was created in 841; C. Zuckerman, 'Two notes on the early history of the thema of Cherson', *BMGS*, 21 (1997), 210–22.

[90] In spring 837 Theophilos took advantage of the fact that the bulk of the Moslem forces were engaged against Babek.

[91] A fortress 56 km to the south-west of Melitene: F. Hild and M. Restle, *Kappadokia (Kappadokia, Charsianon, Sebasteia und Lykandos)* (TIB, 2, Vienna, 1981), 286–7.

[92] Al Mu'tasim had succeeded his brother in 833; there is no indication that he was born at Sôzopetra. This legend would have been devised to make the loss of Amorion (home city of the reigning dynasty) less excruciating to the Romans by creating the impression that the adversaries dealt each other blow for blow.

[93] The revolt of the Persian soldiers is attested by other sources but the chronology is wrong here. It actually took place after the defeat at Dazimon when the Persians had every reason to be afraid, given their equivocal role in that defeat: J.-C. Cheynet, 'Théophile, Théophobe et les Perses', *Byzantine Asia Minor, 6th–10th centuries* (Athens, 1998), 39–50.

who were responsible for the uprising. The emperor accepted his version of the story and summoned him to the palace, restoring his former privileges. He also granted a pardon for all the Persians and an amnesty for their misdeeds.[94] The Persians believed his promises and evacuated Sinope; the emperor knew he would have to disperse them and not let so large a multitude stay together. Since the entire host of the Persians amounted to thirty thousand men, after careful thought he transferred two thousand of them to each theme, with instructions that they were to be under the orders of the commanders.[95] This is because he no longer trusted the Persians and why he put Theophobos to death a little later. But there was another reason for this, which will be revealed in due course.

The *amermoumnes* was so wounded in heart by the capture of his beloved homeland that he sent out a general decree that men of all ages from Babylon, Phoenicia, Palestine, Coelo-Syria and even [75] distant Libya were to be assembled, and that every fighting man was to inscribe on his own shield the word: 'Amorion', signifying the forthcoming attack on that city.[96] The entire army was concentrated around him at Tarsus.[97] Then Theophilos also advanced; he came to Dorylaion, three days' journey from Amorion. Many were they whose advice was that the troops stationed at Amorion be withdrawn and that the Romans retreat before the irresistible advance of the Saracens. Theophilos, however, thought this to be inglorious and unmanly. He thought a better and more valiant way would be further to fortify the city and to preserve it by committing it to the discretion of a noble commander. So he despatched the patrician Aetios,[98] commander of the Anatolikon theme, with a sufficient force to repulse the enemy. He also gave him as army commanders those who would shortly die the death of martyrs: Theodore Krateros, Theophilos, Baboutzikos and

---

[94] Theophobos had nothing to hope for from such an undertaking; he could not even look for Moslem support, given the nature of his origin.

[95] There are precedents for this practice of dispersing foreigners of dubious loyalty among the themes. Slav prisoners were transferred into the themes of Asia Minor, especially under Justinian II: H. Ditten, *Ethnische Verschiebungen zwischen der Balkanhalbinsel und Kleinasien vom Ende des 6. bus zur zweiten Hälfte des 9. Jahrhunderts* (Berlin, 1993), 217–19. The numbers given by Skylitzes and found in his sources are too high. In spite of what W. Treadgold says (*Army*, 69), it is unlikely that such a dispersion took place because it is known that Theophobos fell at the head of his troops some years later.

[96] After spending some years pacifying his empire and once Babek was executed, Al Mu'tasim addressed himself to the great offensive against the infidel, as was the duty of a caliph. The expedition of 838 was the last one to be led by a caliph in person.

[97] Tarsus, chief fortress of Cilicia and seat of an emir, was (together with Melitene) the traditional base from which Arab raids into Roman territory were launched: F. Hild and H. Hellenkemper, *Kilikien und Isaurien* (TIB, 5, Vienna, 1990), 428–39.

[98] *PmbZ* 108 = *PBE* Aetios 2.

Theophilos 77

the others.[99] These were not only commanders of that expeditionary force, but also of the corps of the Forty-two Martyrs.

When the Saracen ruler found himself with all his hosts at Tarsus, having consulted with his colleagues and taken the auspices, he judged it inexpedient to go directly to Amorion, but better first to test the emperor's strength by sending out his son with a portion of the army.[100] His thinking was that if the son got the better of the emperor, victory would surely follow for the father. If the son failed, it were better to stay where he was. Having considered that advice and come to this decision, he despatched his son, who took with him Amr, the then emir of Melitene,[101] ten thousand Turks, the entire army of the Armenians and their commander-in-chief.[102] He pitched camp when he came to a place called Dazimon.[103] Theophilos advanced to meet him, leading a valiant army consisting of Persians, westerners and easterners. When he reached a place called Anzes, he wanted to spy upon the gathered host of the enemy to judge its strength before the battle and the attack. Manuel, the domestic of the scholai, [76] brought him to a high point from which he observed the enemy host and concluded that the Saracen forces were superior to his own. 'Look not upon the number of the men, O emperor,' said Manuel, 'but notice how the lances of each side bristle like reeds.'[104] But since the adversaries seemed to constitute the stronger army, it was his advice

---

[99] Treadgold, *Byzantine revival*, 298, thinks Theodore Krateros (the eunuch who distinguished himself before Theophilos by unhorsing the Hagarene of two lances, c. 17 above) was commanding the Hikanatoi whereas Vasiliev says he was strategos of the Boukellarioi. Skylitzes says he commanded the corps of the Forty-two Martyrs at one time but it really is not known what his command was now. Treadgold, *Byzantine revival*, 298, suggests that this Theophilos was commanding the imperial unit known as the Exkoubitai. The Baboutzikoi were related to the emperor Theophilos: note Constantine Baboutzikos (below) who was married to Sophia, sister of the empress Theodora.

[100] The story of this campaign and the strategy adopted is reported by a number of Arab sources, Tabari among them: A. A. Vasiliev, *Byzance et les Arabes*, II *Les relations politiques de Byzance et des Arabes à L'époque de la dynastie macédonienne*, ed. M. Canard (CBHB, 2, 1, Brussels 1968) 1, 137–43 and Treadgold, *Byzantine revival*, 297–305.

[101] 'Umar, emir of Melitene (*PmbZ* 8552 = *PBE* Amr 3) was the most formidable of the empire's foes until his death in 863.

[102] *Archon ton archonton*, literally 'chief of chiefs': this is the first mention of this title given to the leading Armenian Christian by the Moslems (still masters of Armenia) who thus recognised his pre-eminence over his equals and made him responsible for leading his fellow countrymen into battle.

[103] Dazimon was one of the *aplekta*, camps where troops assembled when the emperor was setting out on campaign. In the list given in *De Caeerimoniis*, Dazimon in the Armeniakon theme comes sixth after Malagina, Dorylaeon, Kaborkin, Colonea and Caesarea: J. F. Haldon, *Constantine Porphyrogenitus, three treatises in imperial military expeditions* (CFHB, 28, Vienna, 1990), 81.

[104] Manuel was trying to use an objective criterion to estimate the strength of the armies: the distance separating the individual lances in each battle line, assuming that one lance meant one soldier.

that an attack should be launched using trickery. Manuel, together with Theophobos, was in favour of a night attack but the rest of the commanders thought the attack should take place in daytime; the emperor came round to their way of thinking.

Since this was then the prevailing opinion, fierce fighting broke out at daybreak. The imperial units fought so vigorously that the Ishmaelites wavered and took to their heels. But by incessant use of their bows, the Turks deterred the Romans from pursuing them, which caused the battle to take on a different character.[105] Unable to withstand the continuous hail of Turkish arrows, the Romans did an about-turn and abandoned the emperor. But neither the officers of the units nor the Persians permitted themselves such behaviour: they rallied around the emperor and made vigorous efforts to save him. They would all have been destroyed too, but as night fell a light rain began to fall from the sky, causing the enemies' bowstrings to slacken. This gave the Romans a respite from the arrows and a chance to get away.

During the night, while Manuel was inspecting the guard posts, he heard the Persians, speaking in the Saracen tongue, making an agreement with the Saracens to betray the Roman encampment and to return to their native land. This information he immediately communicated to the emperor, urging him to flee to safety with a body of picked men, not waiting to be taken captive. 'How can I do that,' the emperor replied, 'when those who remain on my account will be destroyed?' Manuel insisted: 'To you alone [77] it is granted by God, O emperor, to reach safety; those will surely look to their own interests.' So, late in the night, towards morning, the emperor fled and reached safety at a place called Chiliokomon;[106] there he was met by the deserters, declaring that they were unfit to live for having abandoned the emperor in the battle, whereupon each man offered to surrender his sword. The sight of this pierced the emperor to the heart. 'Since, by the grace of God I got safely away, do you also go your way in safety,' he declared. The collusion of the Persians with the Sons of Hagar gave the enemies of Theophobos (who had chosen to bring about his death) a second reason and an excellent opportunity for denouncing him.

When the *amermoumnes* heard of the victory, he concluded that he should advance on Amorion without delay. Having gathered his own

---

[105] The battle was fought on 22 July 838 (A. A. Vasiliev *Byzance et les Arabes*, 1: *La dynastie d'Amorium, 820–867*, ed. M. Canard (Brussels, 1935), 156) and the turnaround is confirmed by other sources.
[106] A plain lying to the north of Amasea.

army together and indicated to his son that he should do likewise, forth he went.[107] When the armies were met together they set up a strong line of fortification. The city was surrounded with a deep ditch then subjected to a vigorous and energetic siege. The Turks made constant use of their bows; the Saracens brought their siege-engines right up to the walls. Yet the beleaguered Romans within put up a determined and heroic struggle, easily beating back the engines.

While the unrelenting and incessant siege of the city was being prosecuted without interruption, Theophilos (who only just managed to get away from the disaster) arrived in Dorylaeon. There he stayed, waiting to see what the outcome would be. He tried the temper of the mind of the *amermoumnes* to see whether he could dissuade him from continuing the siege. Ambassadors were sent to intercede with him; off they went loaded with rich gifts and empowered to give serious undertakings. They reached the Saracen encampment, came before the ruler and declared what messages the emperor had entrusted to them. But the ruler had fallen into a blind rage because of the capture of his homeland. He heaped insults on the emperor for his cowardice; he belittled and derided the embassy and clapped the ambassadors in irons, waiting to see what the outcome of the matter would be. Now he intensified the siege: [78] he divided the army into several companies so they could attack in relays. The intent was that those within the walls, weary from the regularity and the intensity of the alternating attacks and the endless effort required of them, would eventually surrender. But the beleaguered ones continued to ward off the attacks and all the efforts of the besiegers achieved nothing. The city would have escaped capture too had not one of those within betrayed and handed over his homeland on account of some quarrel or other. This man (his name was Boiditzes) had been corrupted with gifts and had abjured the Christian faith. Being in secret communication with the Saracens, he showed them a place in the wall where they would find easy access when launching their attacks; and that is how the city came to be captured. Since it was taken under the rules of war, what account could suffice to declare the multitude of the slain and of the prisoners? The Saracens were beside themselves with anger because so many of their illustrious soldiers had lost their lives during the siege; hence, they showed no mercy to those whom they encountered. The men were slain, the women were led away captive together with their children and youths; the finest of the buildings were

---

[107] The Arabs took Ankyra on their way (Vasiliev and Canard, 1, 159). This was the usual residence of the strategos of the Boukellarioi theme but it was abandoned by its inhabitants.

put to the flames.[108] In a very short time that most distinguished of eastern cities had taken on the appearance of a deserted ruin. Also taken alive were the officers of the army corps: the patricians Kallistos,[109] Constantine and Theodore Krateros and many other illustrious commanders,[110] distinguished by the highest honours.

When the city was safely in his hands, the Saracen ruler forced each of the ambassadors to inspect what had been done there, as though he revelled and delighted in those deeds. Then he sent them back so they could themselves announce the disaster to the emperor. For his part, he promptly returned them to the *amermoumnes* with a request that the persons of note taken captive in the siege be handed over to him, together with his relatives and all the other prisoners. He promised to pay twenty-four *kentenaria* in ransom money for them.[111] [79] The *amermoumnes* received the embassy and again he sent the ambassadors packing, heaping insults on them. Would it not be senseless if he, who had disbursed a thousand *kentenaria* to assemble his own army,[112] were to hand back the prisoners for so small a sum?

24. When the ambassadors returned empty-handed, Theophilos was dumbfounded by the overwhelming magnitude of the disaster. He rejected all food and drink and almost took no nourishment, except water squeezed out from snow; then he fell sick with dysentery. Even when he fell into that pitiful state he did not calm down, nor was he able to take the catastrophe of Amorion with equinanimity. He sought for an occasion and manner of revenging himself on his enemy. Thus, he sent the patrician Theodosios, a member of the Baboutizikoi family, to the king of the Franks[113] to ask for some aid to be sent to him; also for a fighting

---

[108] The siege lasted from 1 to 12 August 838; the *Life of Theodora* (BHG 1731, ed. A. Markopoulos, *Symmeikta*, 5 (Athens, 1983), 249–85), reproduced in Markopoulos, *History*, no. V, and George the Monk, 797, give 15 August as the day on which the fortress fell.

[109] This man (*PmbZ* 3606 = *PBE* Kallistos 2) belonged to the illustrious family of the Melissenoi. He was not captured at Amorion but in a separate action, he being then strategos of Koloneia.

[110] These are numbered among the forty-two martyrs of Amorion who were executed on 6 March 845. Euodios the monk wrote the narrative of this collective martyrdom shortly after the event (the last of its kind). Euodios also narrates the siege and capture of Amorion: see A. Kazhdan, 'Hagiographical notes', *Byzantion*, 56 (1986), 150–60; A. Kolia-Demirtzaki, 'The execution of the forty-two martyrs of Amorion: proposing an interpretation, *Al Masāq*, 14/2 (2002), 141–62, gives all the recent bibliography; suggests the tardiness of the execution can be explained by the internal situation of the caliphate.

[111] Other sources say two hundred *kentenaria*.

[112] The sum of 7.2 million pieces of gold is surely excessive. Treadgold, *Army*, 189, demonstrates that at that time a campaign would cost about 0.2 million pieces of gold. What is certain is that the Abassid caliphate, then at the apogee of its fortunes, could raise more money and men than the empire was capable of raising.

[113] Lothair, son of Louis the Pious who had died in 840.

force to be despatched to ravage certain parts of Africa belonging to the *amermoumnes*. But this embassy achieved nothing, for Theodosios died on the journey. Disappointed in this hope and more severely oppressed by his illness, Theophilos had himself brought on a stretcher into the Magnaura, where he had assembled the senate and the rest of the eminent citizenry. In doleful tones he recited and lamented his woes, beseeching the assembled company graciously to honour his memory by keeping faith and dealing kindly with his wife and son, preserving the throne for them, unassailed by any conspiracy. The assembly was deeply touched by the emperor's pathetic words; groaning and wailing arose on all sides. Everybody interceded with the Deity, praying for the emperor's health and life. And if he should [80] die (which they certainly did not wish to happen), they undertook to surrender their lives if necessary for his lady wife their empress and the children, to keep the throne secure for them. That is what they promised; shortly afterwards, completely consumed by his illness, the emperor paid the debt which all must pay, having governed the empire for twelve years and three months.[114]

25. As the narrative related, Theophobos' accusers acquired grounds on which to proceed against him in the way mentioned above. When Theophilos realised that his end was near, he cast [Theophobos] into the darkest of dungeons, at the Boukoleon. Then, when he was about to die, he ordered them to cut off the man's head and bring it to him. When he received it, he seized it by the hair with his hands and uttered his last words: 'From this moment, I am no longer Theophilos and you are no longer Theophobos.'[115] There are those who accuse Ooryphas, then droungarios of the watch, of slaying Theophobos; they say that he received no orders, but acted on his own authority.[116]

---

[114] Theophilos died of dysentery on 20 January 842.

[115] This is probably a legend but there is nevertheless a certain logic in it: aware that there is about to be a regency, the dying emperor removed those influential people of whose loyalty he was less than sure. According to the Moslem historians, however, Theophobos-Nasr had already fallen in 838–9 at the head of a troop of Khorramites under his command (Vasiliev and Canard, I, 175–6).

[116] MS E adds: The emperor Theophilos reigned for twelve years and twenty days. He came to power on 2 October and died on the 22nd of the same month. He was buried in the church of the Holy Apostles in the *Heroon* of Justinian, in a green sarcophagus. (Others gave the same incorrect date elsewhere.)

CHAPTER 5

Michael III, the son of Theophilos [842–867], and his mother Theodora [842–862]

1. [81] After Theophilos[1] had departed this life it was his son, Michael, who, together with his mother, Theodora, succeeded to the sceptre of the empire. He had the magister Manuel[2] (then domestic of the scholai) and Theoktistos the patrician (logothete of the drome) as his guardians and tutors, just as his father had stipulated in his will.[3] Immediately after the death of Theophilos, these two got themselves away to the Hippodrome where they assembled the people and delivered speeches recalling to their minds the benevolence of the late emperor towards them. By using encouraging and flattering words, they were able to elicit the goodwill of the audience, the people promising to pour out their own blood for the safety of the emperor and confirming this promise with oaths there and then.[4]

2. Once Theodora was in control of the empire (together with her son),[5] immediately and first of all, at the suggestion of some God-fearing men, she

---

[1] Manuscript E adds 'said to be the drunkard'.
[2] According to one tradition Manuel died of his wounds five days after the battle of Dazimon; according to another (Genesios, *Theophanes Continuatus*) he survived nearly twenty years. H. Grégoire has shown that the second tradition was published in the tenth century by monks of the monastery founded by Manuel who did not want their founder to be considered one of the pillars of iconoclasm: H. Grégoire, 'Manuel et Théophobe, ou la concurrence de deux monastères', *B*, 9 (1934), 198–204. In fact the second powerful figure in the regency was the magister Sergios Niketiates (*PmbZ* 6664 = *PBE* Sergios 57), a relative of Theodora, maybe her maternal uncle. This list is incomplete because a little later Skylitzes mentions Theodora's brother Bardas as one of the *epitropoi* of Michael III.
[3] Michael (*PmbZ* 4991 = *PBE* Michael 11) was too young to reign, born on 19 January 840. Theophilos provided for a regency council during his minority with the empress presiding. Contrary to normal procedure, there seems to have been no provision made for the participation of the patriarch, the faithful John the Grammarian ('Jannes' *pace* Skylitzes).
[4] Although oaths were forbidden by the church, emperors did demand them when they were unsure of the loyalty of their subjects: N. Svoronos, 'Le serment de fidélité à l'empereur byzantin et sa signification constitutionelle', *REB*, 9 (1951), 106–42.
[5] Skylitzes fails to mention that Thekla, the eldest of Michael's sisters, shared the purple at least until 845. She appears on both gold and silver coins (*DOC*, III/1: 461–2). Her presence could be explained by Theodora's concern to ensure the survival of the dynasty which now depended on a two-year-old child.

closely examined the matter of the heresy of the enemies of the icons. This was widespread among the Romans from the reign of Leo the Armenian until the death of Theophilos. Theoktistos was in favour of its suppression but Manuel held back for some time; nobody dared to speak out boldly and make a speech expressly calling for the abolition of this heresy[6] because the greater part of both the senate and the synod (including the patriarch himself) remained faithful to it. Manuel alone, prompted by divine [82] intervention, was bold enough to make the move. As we said above, he hesitated at first on the question of devotion to the most sacred icons, but he subsequently proclaimed himself in favour of it: here is the reason why.[7]

He had fallen dangerously ill to the point that his life was despaired of; the doctors' skills had been exhausted. Hearing that he was already dead, some pious monks of Stoudios' monastery[8] came to him. As they approached his bed, they realised that he was still alive and breathing. Whereupon, they promised him his life, a recovery and the restoration of his former health. He was incredulous at first, but the men of God insisted that he should have no doubt about the divine power which had revealed the matter to them. His illness had abated a little and he said to them with a weak and feeble breath: 'And how can this be for me, godly fathers? My mental forces are all gone, my body is wasted away and emaciated. Here I lie, devoid of flesh, a mere skeleton; there is no difference between me and a corpse, except that I am breathing. What hope is there, what reason to believe in my recovery and a return to my former health?' The holy men took up the argument and said to him: 'With God, all things are possible and there is nothing that is impossible. We proclaim the good news that you will live, provided that you endeavour to extinguish the conflagration the enemies of the icons have ignited when you recover your strength, and that you restore the sacred icons to the status they enjoyed in the time of our forefathers.' Thus they spoke, then went their way. Amazingly, and contrary to all expectation, for Manuel the illness now abated; the natural forces were restored unimpaired and, in a short time, he recovered completely from his sickness.

Happily released from illness, he immediately went (on horseback) to the palace. Coming into the presence of the empress, he tried every means

---

[6] The synod had been purged of its iconodule elements under Theophilos, while in the senate, consisting as it did for the most part of senior civil servants appointed by the emperor, iconoclasts were in the majority.

[7] This episode is crucial to the fabrication of the legend of Manuel since it transforms the domestic of the scholai into a fervant iconodule.

[8] The choice of Stoudios is not unintentional. The monks of this monastery had followed the advice of Theodore, their hegoumenos, and were once again at the point of going to battle for the icons.

to persuade her (she was already casting about for a pretext to do so) to restore the sacred icons. She was constantly being incited to do this by her own mother and also by her maternal uncles, the patricians.[9] Nevertheless, Theodora resisted Manuel's arguments, either out of respect for the oaths she had sworn to her late husband, or because, as we said, she feared the multitude of those who firmly adhered to the heresy. When Manuel persisted, [83] Theodora replied: 'O magister, my late husband, the emperor, a stickler for precision, never did a thing in all his life without careful examination of the matter. If this practice [of revering the icons] were not forbidden in the sacred laws and the holy scriptures, he would not have expelled it from the church.' When she had said this, he lost no time in threatening her with the loss of her life and of the throne (her and her son too) unless she restore the godly decoration of the sacred icons to the churches. Terrified by these words (or, in our opinion, following her own desires), the empress now gave her full support to the matter. She directed that all those who were distinguished by intelligence and learning, members of senate or synod, were to assemble in the palace of Theoktistos to discuss and debate the question of orthodoxy. Everybody (so to speak) gathered there; a great number of speeches were made, a multiplicity of attestations from the holy scriptures was produced and the party of godliness carried the day. A decree went out for the immediate restoration of the sacred icons.[10] Of those bishops, monks and senators who had subscribed to the former disorder, the majority chose the better part and changed their opinions in favour of the truth.[11] As for those who were so deeply dyed with the tincture of godlessness that they could not change, they were driven from the city and sent into exile. The impious patriarch was deposed and expelled from the patriarchate by a contingent of high-ranking men charged with the security of the palace.

At first he refused their demands that he get out, assuring them that he would never willingly leave that church. They returned to the empress who had sent them and reported his disobedience. Then the patrician Bardas, the empress' brother, was sent, to find out why, since he was not of the orthodox faith, he would not abandon the patriarchate. [84] But Jannes

---

[9] Theoktiste, the mother of Theodora, was an avowed iconodule.
[10] The re-establishment of orthodoxy took place between 4 and 11 March 843. The synod reinstated the canons of the Seventh Ecumenical Council (Nicaea II): J. Gouillard, 'Le Synodikon de l'Orthodoxie: edition et commentaire,' *TM*, 2 (1967), 120ff.
[11] Such toleration on the part of the patriarch was justified by the number of former iconoclasts and the need to re-establish the unity of the church. G. Dagron, *Histoire du christianisme*, IV, *Evêques, moines et empereurs (610–1054)*, under the direction of G. Dagron, P. Riché and A. Vauchez (Paris, 1993), 159–62.

was a knavish fellow, cunning both in writing and in devising deceits if anyone ever was. He marked his front, his back and his backside all over with lead, as though some people had been whipping him. Then he cried out that it was at the hands of those sent [to expel him] that he had suffered; that they had laid it on with barbarous cruelty and that the worst offender was Constantine, droungarios of the watch.[12] He asked to be allowed a little time for his marks to disappear, as a consolation. So much for Jannes;[13] but Bardas[14] had tumbled to his mischievous device and he became very angry. He simply drove [Jannes] from the patriarchate, willy-nilly. Once he was deposed, in his stead the empress gave the church the sacred and godly Methodios as patriarch, a man who still bore in his flesh the marks of having been a confessor and martyr.[15] All the pious clergy, laity and monks, those too who led the ascetic life in the mountains,[16] they all applauded his elevation with great rejoicing. They congregated in the capital and with one voice condemned the heresy with an eternal anathema. Such then were the reforms which were effected at the beginning of the reign by the ever-memorable Theodora and her son.

3. As for the unholy Jannes, he was shut up in a monastery and somewhere there he saw an icon set up; it showed Christ our God, the Mother of God and the Archangels. He ordered his personal deacon to climb up and put out the eyes of the sacred pictures, for (he said) they did not have the faculty of sight.[17] When the devout and Sovereign Lady heard of this, burning with godly zeal, she ordered *his* eyes to be put out. This did not happen because certain kindly disposed persons interceded for him, but she dispatched some guards to punish him with two hundred lashes.

Jannes was a product of this great city which takes precedence over all others, a scion of the Morocharzianoi family. [85] He was already somewhat advanced in years when the monastery of the victorious martyrs, Sergios and Bacchus,[18] got him as hegoumenos (like a serpent lurking in

---

[12] Constantine was of Armenian origin and, according to Leo the Grammarian (236), was called Maniaces (*PmbZ* 3962 = *PBE* Bardas 5). He had been sent to Theophilos as a hostage. He became droungarios of the watch under Michael III whom he protected during the troubles consequent upon the murder of the caesar Bardas. According to Genesios (4.3), who claimed to be a descendant of this man, he was by then commanding the corps of the Exkoubitae.
[13] John the Grammarian.
[14] In fact Bardas (*PmbZ* 791 = *PBE* Bardas 5) played a minor role during his sister's regency.
[15] Methodios who, together with Euthymios of Sardis, his spiritual father, had suffered grave mistreatment under Michael II and Theophilos, acceded to the patriarchal throne on 4 March 843: Dagron, *Histoire du christianisme*, 157–8 and note 282.
[16] An oblique reference to Heb. 11:38.
[17] Ps. 113:13, Septuagint.
[18] This monastery, founded by Justinian, the church of which still exists, was in the suburb of Hormisdas: Janin, *Églises et monastères* I, 451–4. John became hegoumenos there in the time of

the church!). This firm adherent of the godless heresy of the enemies of the icons had ascended the ecclesiastical ladder rather quickly. A lifelong adept in wizardry and dish-divining,[19] he was held in high esteem by Michael the Stammerer, the father of Theophilos. Either because they shared the same heretical opinions or on account of the great reputation he had for learning, Jannes became tutor to Theophilos. When the son took the reins of power into his own hands, he promoted him to be protosynkellos and, subsequently, patriarch of Constantinople. This was because, by dish-divining and wizardry, he had been able to foretell some things.

There was a time when an unbelieving and barbarous people led by three commanders were invading Roman lands.[20] Not surprisingly, Theophilos was distressed, but Jannes exhorted him to put away his faint heart and to be filled with gladness – he need only pay heed to [the patriarch's] advice. This is what he advised: among the bronze statues set up on the Euripos[21] of the Hippodrome there was one standing there (he said) representing [a figure with] three heads.[22] Jannes now ordered an equal number of bronze hammers to be cast. These were to be taken in hand by three robust men who were to accompany him to the aforesaid statue by night. At his command, they were to strike the heads mighty blows with their hammers until the heads fell to the ground, as though they had been dealt a blow at one and the same time. Finding this proposal acceptable, the emperor ordered it to be carried out. When the men came with Jannes to that place at the darkest time of night (Jannes was in lay-clothing to escape recognition), he uttered the magic words designed to remove the innate power from statues of that kind; then he ordered the men to strike with youthful vigour. [86] Two of them, striking more forceful blows, succeeded in removing two of the statue's heads, but the third, striking less forcefully, made the head hang down a little, but did not sever it completely from the body. What happened to the leaders of the barbarians was similar to this. A great uprising took place among that invading people followed by civil war, in the course of which two of the leaders fell and the third was

---

Leo V as a reward for his support for the emperor's iconoclastic policy. Thus it was in his youth, not in his old age, that he presided over this monastery.

[19] *Lecanomancy* was practised by throwing precious stones and objects of gold and silver into a basin filled with water then observing the pattern formed when they sank to the bottom.

[20] Possibly the campaign of 838.

[21] According to *De Cer*, this was the line which marked the outer limit of the course: R. Guilland, *Études de topographie de Constantinople byzantine* (Amsterdam, 1969), 1, 445–7.

[22] This could be the celebrated serpentine column which came from the temple of Apollo at Delphi where it had been erected after the victories of Salamis and Plataea. This mutilation on the order of John is, however, very dubious because Peter Gylles claimed to have seen that monument intact in 1540: R. Janin, *Constantinople byzantine* (*AOC*, 4A, Paris, 1964), 191.

wounded; not mortally, but enough to invalidate him. Thus crippled, that people went back home. So much for wizardry.

4. This wizard had a uterine brother of patrician rank whose name was Arsaber.[23] He possessed an estate on the left bank of the straits (close to the monastery of St Phokas) built in a luxurious style with arcades, bath-houses and other charming pavilions. The wizard was a frequent resident there and there he constructed an underground dwelling similar to the cave of Trophonios.[24] To the rear he made a doorway affording access to those who would enter; it was in that workshop of iniquity that he received those who were willing. Sometimes nuns were kept there to be coupled with, or other women distinguished by their beauty in whose ruin he participated; sometimes heptoscopy,[25] dish-divining, magic and necromancy were practised there, by which (with the cooperation of demons) he was often able to foretell some of the things that were going to happen. This property later came into the hands of the chamberlain,[26] who razed it to the ground and transformed it into a monastery bearing the name of the great martyr Phokas.[27]

As we said, [Jannes] and his partisans were cast out and deposed but even then they did not keep quiet; they still raged against the holy icons and sought to do some mischief to the devout. They pieced together a false accusation against Methodios in an attempt to bring that blameless man into disrepute and thus to [87] demoralise the multitude of the orthodox. They corrupted a woman with a large amount of gold and promises if she would fall in with their plans; she was in fact the mother of Metrophanes,[28] who subsequently became bishop of Smyrna. They persuaded her to denounce the holy man before the empress and the emperor's tutors, saying that he had consorted with her.[29] An awesome

---

[23] As Skylitzes reports below (c. 11) Arsaber (*PmbZ* 602 = *PBE* Arsaber 5) owed his high rank of patrician to his marriage with Maria, the empress' sister (*PmbZ* 4738 = *PBE* Kalomaria 1). He adds that the man was eventually promoted magister, adding an acknowledgement of his bravery.

[24] An underground sanctuary in Boeotia, frequented by those in search of oracles into Roman times. Trophonios is alleged to have been the architect of the temple of Apollo at Delphi. Together with his brother he attempted to steal some treasure, which resulted in them being swallowed up by the ground.

[25] Literally, 'inspecting livers'.

[26] *Parakoimomenos*, the future emperor Basil I: *Theophanes Continuatus*, ed. Bekker, 157.

[27] On the European bank of the Bosporos, today Ortaköy: Janin, *Églises et monastères*, 1, 498.

[28] Metrophanes (*PmbZ* 4986 = *PBE* Metrophanes 1) was among the most belligerent supporters of Ignatios, playing a distinguished role in the synod which deposed Photios in 869: Dagron, *Histoire du christianisme*, 170, 178, 181.

[29] The opposition to Methodios came not only from unrepentant iconoclasts, but also from rigorists who resented his conciliatory attitude to those who had abandoned iconoclasm. The anecdote of the woman's accusation does not even appear in the *Vita Methodii*, BHG 1278.

tribunal was immediately constituted, of laymen and clerics. The devout were in evidence, cast down in grief and sorrow – while the impious, far from absenting themselves, were there in force, thinking that, as a consequence of the affair, the church of the orthodox was about to be plunged into unusual and severe disgrace. The false accusers were very confident, with broad grins on their faces, as though they had the means of making sure the accusation would be upheld. They led the woman into the midst [of the assembly], where she spoke the words she had been taught to say before the judges. The members of the court gave black looks, the magister Manuel most of all, at the prospect of the entire orthodox community being in danger of becoming the laughing stock of its enemies on one man's account. The holy Methodios was aware of all this. Wishing to frustrate the hopes of the godless, to relieve the devout of the burden of shame and to ensure that he not be a stone of stumbling[30] to the church, without paying any attention to the crowd he shook off his garments, and this man who was worthy of all respect and honour exposed his private parts to the gaze of all the onlookers. It was now revealed to everybody that [his genitals] were atrophied by some disease and totally incapable of performing their natural function. This greatly dismayed those who rejoiced in iniquity and the false accusers, but it filled the devout with gladness of heart and rejoicing. They rushed upon him with uncontainable glee, embracing and hugging him; they simply were unable to control their excessive joy. One of his closer friends came up to him and quietly questioned the patriarch, wishing to know how it came about that his genitals were withered away. In reply, the latter explained the matter from the very beginning: 'I had been sent to the pope in Rome in connection with the proceedings which had been instituted against Nikephoros, that most holy patriarch.[31] While I was staying there, I was harassed by the demon of [88] fleshly desire. Night and day, day after day, it never stopped titillating me and inciting me to the desire for sexual congress. I was so inflamed that I knew it was nearly all over for me, so I entrusted myself to Peter, the chief apostle, begging him to relieve me of that fleshly appetite. Coming to me by night, he burned my genitals by applying his right hand to them, assuring me that henceforth I would no longer be troubled by the appetite for carnal delight. Awakening in considerable pain, I found myself in the condition which you have witnessed.'

---

[30] 1 Pet. 2:8.
[31] Methodios came to Rome after Leo V proclaimed iconoclasm to be the official doctrine of the church. It would appear that the patriarch Nikephoros, forced to resign and exiled in 815, appealed to the pope, protesting against this replacement.

Manuel would not believe what the patriarch had said; suspecting a conspiracy, he handed the woman over for examination to get to the bottom of the crafty scheme. They immediately brandished a sword in her face and brought out the barbed rods while experienced torturers were to hand. Terrified by all this, the wretched creature let the truth be known. She explained how the machination had been contrived; how she had herself been corrupted with a gift of gold and many promises; who the active agents were and, in short, the complete knavery of the affair. She added that if somebody went to her house, he would find the gold in a pouch in a chest filled with grain. One of the bodyguards was immediately dispatched; he returned with the gold and thus the entire affair stood revealed. The false accusers would have been handed over to be punished accordingly, but the patriarch, imitating his own Lord, had the forbearance to request that the charges be stayed. He asked that their only retribution and punishment should be that, each year, at the feast of orthodoxy, they should process with lights from the church of the all-pure [Mother of God] at Blachernae to the sacred church of the Holy Wisdom, there to hear the anathema with their own ears; this procedure was maintained for the rest of their lives.

5. Such was the way in which the heresy of the enemies of the icons was terminated while the church of the orthodox resumed its proper embellishment with the restoration of the sacred icons.[32] Once when she was celebrating this feast of orthodoxy, [89] that blessed empress gave a banquet for all the clergy in the palace at the place called Ta Karianou.[33] Present among the guests were Theophanes and his brother, Theodore, the *graptoi*.[34] As the banquet was drawing to a close and the desserts were being set out, cakes and pastries, the empress repeatedly glanced at the faces of [those two] fathers, examining the writing that was inscribed on their foreheads, all the while uttering sighs and shedding tears. Noticing this, one of the fathers asked her why she was looking at them so often. She said: 'I am amazed at your steadfastness in enduring the inscribing of so many letters on your foreheads; the cruelty of him who did this to you deeply disturbs me.' 'It is on account of this writing,' rejoined the blessed Theophanes, 'that we will take issue with your husband, the emperor, before the implacable

---

[32] For a narration of the imperial procession on the day of the restoration of the images: D. Afinogenov, 'Imperial repentance: the solemn procession in Constantinople on March 11, 843', *Eranos*, 97 (1999), 1–10.
[33] The court celebrated the re-establishment of orthodoxy in the palace built by Theophilos on the first Sunday of Lent. The Karianos was so called because it was built of marble from Caria.
[34] The two brothers from Palestine who had been 'inscribed' (or tattooed) under Theophilos for their adhesion to the cause of the icons. See the reign of Theophilos, c. 10.

judgement seat of God.' These words pierced the Sovereign Lady to the heart. With tears in her eyes she said to the saint: 'Do I not have your affirmation to this effect and your written statement, that you not only grant [my late husband] forgiveness, but also decline to drag him into court and summon him to trial?'[35] The patriarch and the rest of the throng of bishops calmed her down and soothed her distress. Then they rose up from table and declared: 'Imperial majesty, our statements and contracts are immutable and undeviating; as for the small-mindedness of this fellow, we should not exaggerate it.' Thus was the empress' pain alleviated.

6. It was at this time that Zilician heresy arose, but it died out and disappeared together with its leader, Zilix,[36] who filled the office of asekretis. For he and his followers converted to godliness; they were anointed with the sacred chrism and baptised. So much for the affairs of the city.

7. [90] When Bogoris,[37] the ruler of the Bulgars, heard that it was a woman, together with a tender child, who was ruling the Romans, he became insolent. He sent messengers to the imperial city threatening to break the treaties and to attack the Romans' territory. There was nothing ignoble or womanly about the reply of the empress: 'You will have to reckon with me fighting against you and, if it be God's will, getting the better of you. And even if it is you who gets the upper hand (which is by no means impossible), the victory will still be mine since it will be a woman, not a man, whom you will have overcome.' These words took the wind out of the barbarian's sails; he fell silent and renewed the former treaties.

Then the empress and the ruler resumed diplomatic contact with each other: she, for her part, on account of one Theodore, surnamed Koupharas,[38] a person of distinction who was very useful to the state, but who was a prisoner in Bulgaria. As for Bogoris, he was concerned about his own sister; captured in a raid, she had lived in the imperial palace (where she was held prisoner) for a long time. During her captivity she had been initiated into the Christian faith and had also learnt to read. Subsequently released, her unbounded praise for the Christian faith was ever in her brother's

---

[35] A reference to the negotiations between Theodora and the clergy when the cult of icons was reintroduced. The clergy undertook to bring no accusations against the deceased emperor – this in order to safeguard the dynasty. This anecdote reveals that there were divisions within the ranks of the clergy.

[36] On the heresy of Zilix or Lizix (*PmbZ* 8642 = *PBE* Zeli 1): J. Gouillard, 'Deux figures mal connues du second iconoclasme', *B*, 31 (1961), 371–387 repr. *La vie religieuse à Byzance* (London, 1981), no. VI. Zilix was anointed but he was not re-baptised, which rather suggests that the heresy was not considered to deviate too far from orthodoxy.

[37] Boris (*PmbZ* 1035 = *PBE* Boris 1) was not ruling Bulgaria at this date; he succeeded his father, Persianos, when the latter died in a battle with the Serbs in 852.

[38] The name of this monk (*PmbZ* 7723 = *PBE* Theodoros 76) is not found anywhere else.

ears; in this way she sowed the seeds of faith in his heart. He had already been apprised of the divine mysteries by Koupharas. After the exchange had been effected, the woman having been delivered to her brother and Koupharas given in return to the Sovereign Lady, the Bulgar ruler kept faith with his erroneous beliefs, clinging to his own religion even though he had been instructed in and informed all about the divine mysteries. Then a severe famine afflicted the land of the Bulgars, and when all other help failed the ruler called upon the God of the Christians for aid, the God whose lore Theodore and his own sister had communicated to him, charging the entire [91] nation to do likewise. The famine abated; thus they all converted to the worship of God. Boris, being counted worthy of baptism, took the name of the emperor of the Romans, Michael, when he received holy baptism at the hands of the bishop who had been sent to him for that purpose.

Something else happened which led the ruler to the right religion and confirmed him in it. He had an insatiable appetite for hunting and he wanted to satisfy it, not only out on the chase but also when he was relaxing at home – by looking at pictures of hunting scenes. Having just built himself a new house, he now engaged a painter, a Roman monk named Methodios. He told this monk to fill the dwelling with pictures but (as though he were under the guidance of divine inspiration) he did not specify in so many words which and what kind of wild animals were to be portrayed. He told the monk to depict whatever he liked, so long as his scenes were sufficiently impressive to inspire consternation and terror in the beholder. Now the monk knew of nothing that was more awe-inspiring than the second coming of Christ, so that is what he painted there. When the project was finished, the ruler looked upon the choir of the righteous with their crowns at this side, then upon the cohort of sinners being punished over there. When the artist had explained to him what the scene portrayed, he immediately renounced his own religion, received instruction in the holy mysteries (as we said) from a godly bishop and was baptised in the middle of the night.[39]

When the rulers of the people and the common folk learned of his change of religion, they rebelled against their leader and sought to kill

---

[39] Boris-Michael was baptised in 864. Michael was not really his godfather for he was not present to receive the Bulgar from the font. Skylitzes says nothing of the way Boris had blackmailed Constantinople by threatening to place the infant church under the authority of the pope – this in order to gain greater autonomy for it. On the baptism of the Bulgars (most recently): J. Kloczowski, 'Les nouvelles chrétientés du monde occidental: la christianisation des Slaves, des Scandinaves et des Hongrois entre le IXe et le XIe siècle', *Histoire du christianisme*, IV: *Evêques, moines et empereurs (610–1054)*, ed. G. Dagron, P. Riché and A. Vauchez (Paris, 1993), IV, 921–7.

him. But with the few men who were with him and the sign of the cross going on before them, he was able to put the insurgents to flight. So amazed were they at this unexpected reverse that he was able to make them Christians.[40] When the entire nation had been converted to the worship of God, he wrote to the Sovereign Lady asking to be given land because his subjects were in dire straits. In return, he promised to unite the [two] nations and bring about an eternal and irrevocable peace. The empress received this request with great gladness and she gave him the land (it was deserted in those days) which stretches from the place called Sidera – which was then the border between the Bulgars and the Romans – as far as Debeltos, [92] which the Bulgars call Zagora.[41] So that is how the whole of Bulgaria was converted to the worship of God and the west enjoyed profound peace.

8. The western regions now lived under cloudless skies and in stable piety. The empress rejoiced and was glad in this state of affairs; with the intention of improving it yet further, she addressed herself to the task of bringing back to true religion those Manichees in the east, commonly called Paulicians after the founders of the heresy. Alternatively, if she failed to convert them, she would completely obliterate them from among mankind,[42] a decision which filled the world with many woes. For, far from discharging their commission with moderation, those who were sent to prosecute the campaign (Leo son of Argyros, Andronikos son of Doukas[43] and Soudales) acted with great savagery. Some [of the Manichees] they hung on gallows, some they put to the sword, while others were despatched with various kinds of afflictions and by diverse

---

[40] This uprising of the Boyards took place in 856 or 866. Boris, qua new Constantine, conquers by the sign of the cross like Constantine I at the Milvian Bridge.

[41] Skylitzes' narrative is incoherent; it is most unlikely that the empress would have abandoned land to the Bulgars just because they were in dire straits. Skylitzes may have been confused by his source, *Theophanes Continuatus*, which gives two versions of the same event side by side. Boris' conversion took place the year following the great victory of the Romans over the emir of Melitene, without any known coercion by Constantinople. Most recently: C. Zuckerman, 'Deux étapes de la formation de l'ancien état russe', *Les centres proto-urbains russes entre Scandinavie, Byzance et Orient*, ed. M. Kazanski, A. Nersessian and C. Zuckermann (Réalités byzantines, 7, Paris, 2000), 95–120, Appendix, 'Sur les circonstances de la conversion des Russes', 118–20.

[42] The chronology here is completely wrong in placing the move against the Paulicians shortly after the baptism of Boris-Michael. Theodora moved against them at the very beginning of her regency, possibly to conciliate the church: P. Lemerle, 'L'histoire des Pauliciens d'Asie Mineure d'après les sources grecques', *TM*, 5 (1973), 1–144, at 89.

[43] This is the first appearance of the names of two of the most important families of the military aristocracy, Leo Argyros (*PmbZ* 4506 = *PBE* Leo 109) and Andronikos Doukas (*PmbZ* 436 = *PBE* Andronikos 3). On the Argyroi see J. F. Vannier, *Familles byzantines: les Argyroi, IXe – XIIe siècles* (ByzSorb, 1, Paris, 1975); on the Doukai, D. I. Polemis, *The Doukai: a contribution to Byzantine prosopography* (London, 1968).

and multiform methods of torture, until ten times ten thousand men had been destroyed, their possessions appropriated by the state. In this way the remaining Manichees were brought to a state of insurrection; this is how they were provoked to revolt.

Theodotos Melissenos was functioning as commander of the Anatolikon [theme] and serving him in the office of protomandator was a man named Karbeas,[44] an adherent of the faith of the Manichees. When he heard that they had impaled his own father, he was outraged by this atrocity beyond sufferance and deserted to Amr, the emir of Melitene, together with five thousand of his co-religionists. From him the deserters went to the *amermoumnes* and were received by him with great honour. Pledges of loyalty were exchanged, and [93] before long these same men marched out to attack Roman territory. They undertook the building of towns, Argaoun[45] and Amara. Then, since they had grown to the point of overpopulation because there was a steady stream of Manichees arriving whom fear had driven into hiding, a third town was added; this one they called Tephrike.[46] Setting out from these towns they joined forces with Amr, emir of Melitene, and with Aleim, emir of Tarsus; then they made no end of ruthlessly invading and devastating Roman territory. Aleim, however, went off with his army into a country of the Armenians, where he lost both his life and the entire army that was following him,[47] while Amr fell foul of an uprising among his own people at the instigation of his co-ruler, said to be the son of Skleros.[48] His attention was entirely occupied with his own problems and he did not have time to fight others until he was at

---

[44] Karbeas (*PmbZ* 3625 = *PBE* Karbeas 1) was chief of the couriers, hence a member of the entourage of the strategos. Theodotos Melissenos (*PmbZ* 7962 = *PBE* Theodotos 16) must be distinguished from the patriarch of the same name who died in 821.

[45] The town of Argaoun (to the north of Melitene) was already in existence before the advent of Karbeas.

[46] Tephrike, founded by Karbeas prior to 856 on the border of the empire, succeeded in evading the control of both the emperor and of the emir of Melitene. It has succeeded in keeping its name all through the centuries: the Turks now call it Devrigi.

[47] He was appointed to a new post in Armenia, probably in 863, and met his death the following year in an encounter with the Romans near Mayyafariqin: A. A. Vasiliev, *Byzance et les Arabes*, I: *La dynastie d'Amorium, 820–867* (Brussels, 1935); II: *Les relations politiques de Byzance et des arabes à l'époque de la dynastie macédonienne*, ed. M. Canard (CBHB 2, 1, Brussels, 1968), 277.

[48] This Skleros (*PmbZ* 6822 = *PBE* Skleros 2) must be a member of the family of that name, already distinguished at Byzantium. The curious mention of a civil war in which he was on the opposite side to the emir of Melitene can be understood when one bears in mind that Armenia, in subjection to the Abbassids, would be obliged to furnish the caliph with troops. A quarrel must have broken out between Skleros the Armenian chief and his immediate superior: W. Seibt, *Die Skleroi. Eine prosopographisch-sigillographische Studie* (Byzantina Vindobonensia, 9, Vienna, 1976), 21–3.

liberty after successfully opposing his antagonist.[49] Once that matter was attended to he took advantage of the cessation of hostilities and, incapable of remaining at peace, joined up with Karbeas and went out in full force against the Romans.

He was opposed by Petronas, brother of the empress, serving as domestic of the scholai. Strictly speaking, this command pertained to Bardas, his older brother, but it was he who in fact exercised it, not because the other was dilatory but because his attention was fully engaged in his task as guardian of the young emperor. In his present office of commander of the Thracesian theme,[50] Petronas campaigned against Amr and Karbeas; in due course this history will reveal how he engaged them and what he accomplished.

9. Now that the emperor Michael was emerging from childhood and approaching manhood,[51] he was anxious to take the administration of state affairs into his own hands. In this he was encouraged by Bardas, his guardian and uncle, the empress' brother, who, for his part, was possessed by a burning desire to lay his own hands on the imperial office. He busied himself with nothing but that which might help him to attain [94] what he was aiming for. However, to make the situation clearer to the reader, let us take up the story a little earlier. The two [original] guardians to the emperor living in the palace, Manuel and the logothete Theoktistos, were so much at loggerheads with each other that a charge of high treason was brought against Manuel. He was alarmed by this and, fearing the other's jealousy, came to the conclusion that it would be better for him to be out of the palace; also to refrain from participating in regular [council-] meetings and matters of state. So he moved back into his own house located near the cistern of Aspar. (He subsequently transformed it into a monastery and it was there that his remains were laid.)[52] He would arrive from there and take part in state affairs occasionally. Having effectively rid himself of Manuel (not by his own efforts, but by the intervention of Theoktistos), Bardas was now on the lookout for an opportunity to achieve his ends. Fully aware that Theoktistos was standing in his way,

---

[49] The Arab sources appear to know nothing of this conflict. There were Skleroi living in the empire already, the first known one being a strategos of the Peloponnese under Nikephoros I: Seibt, *Skleroi*, 19–20.

[50] Thus all the commanders of Asia Minor were under the orders of Petronas (*PmbZ* 5929 = *PBE* Petronas 5), who also commanded the corps of the scholai. A similar joint command is mentioned again in 1057: Theodore in the reign of Michael VI (see below).

[51] He was in his sixteenth year.

[52] This monastery was subsequently rebuilt by Photios after an earthquake; he was eventually buried there: Janin, *Églises et monastères*, I, 320–2.

Michael III and Theodora

he turned his attention to getting rid of *him*; all the more so because [the logothete] frequently reprimanded him for his clandestine affair with his own daughter-in-law.[53] But this is what initiated the process by which he achieved his ends. The emperor Michael's schoolmaster was an ill-bred and worthless fellow whose pupil wished to promote him yet higher in the ranks of the imperial officers. The son begged his mother and Theoktistos to appoint the man to a greater honour, but Theoktistos would have none of it: 'The business of the empire must be conducted in a befitting manner, not inappropriately,' he declared. Bardas now seized upon this worthless schoolmaster as the instrument of his will, using him constantly to sow seeds of discontent in the emperor's mind against Theoktistos. One moment he would say [the logothete] was not running the government properly; at another time, that he wanted to marry [Michael's] mother or one of his sisters to some man, put out [the emperor's] eyes and remove him from the throne.[54] Frequently harping on this theme, he added that prudent and immediate advice was now called for. [Uncle and nephew] frequently exchanged opinions concerning the situation, searching for a remedy, and finally they came to the conclusion that they would have to get rid of Theoktistos. That is the decision they came to in the end and this is the plan they adopted to achieve their ends. [95] Just as Theoktistos was about to leave for the Lausiakon[55] at the end of a reports session, the emperor would accompany him a short distance and merely cry out 'Seize him!' As Theoktistos was emerging on his way out, he recognised the agreed signal when it was given; he thought he could get himself out of danger by fleeing, going towards the Hippodrome by way of the chancellery (for that is where the offices of the secretaries used to be).[56] But, being one man surrounded by many, he was forced to remain where he was. And there stood

---

[53] As usual the sources contain two stories of the death of Theoktistos, the different versions of the *Chronicle of the Logothete* on the one hand and of *Theophanes Continuatus* and Genesius on the other: P. Karlin-Hayter, 'Etudes sur les deux histoires du règne de Michel III', *B*, 41 (1971), 496–542. The ambitious Bardas was in fact in exile at the time, desirous of returning to the palace. In addition to Michael's desire to assume power (which was, after all, a legitimate desire) the logothete's performance in foreign affairs had been less than brilliant. In 843 he had failed to gain a foothold on Crete and the following year did not prevent Amr from penetrating as far as Malagina in Bithynia. In 845 the Roman chiefs captured at Amorion were executed; it was not until 855 that the empire went onto the offensive, against Anazarbos.

[54] Thekla was associated with the purple, but when Michael became sole ruler he suppressed the coins on which his sister was portrayed (*DOC*, III, 1:454). The young emperor might well have been troubled by the precedent of Eirene and Constantine VI.

[55] This was a magnificent hall, decorated with golden mosaics by Theophilos: Guilland, *Topographie*, 154–60. A guard was provided specifically for this location: Oikonomides, *Listes*, 299.

[56] This comment on the location of the offices is present in Skylitzes' source (*Theophanes Continuatus*, 170) which indicates that the offices were moved between the ninth and tenth centuries.

Bardas with a naked sword, threatening to wound anybody who stood in his way or tried to come to the other's aid. Theoktistos was taken to the Skyla[57] and thrown into a cell until the case against him was formulated. But in the end they decided it was not advantageous to let him live (for fear of the Augousta), so they sent a member of the Hetaireiai to brandish a naked sword at him. When he saw the man approaching, weapon in hand, he protected himself with a bench to escape being injured, but he was mortally wounded in the belly; his guts spilled out and he died. That is the way in which Theoktistos was eliminated.[58] When Manuel heard of the murder he came immediately to the palace where he is said to have addressed these words, as one inspired, to Bardas:

> To slay Theoktistos you bared the sword;
> Prepare yourself for slaughter day by day.

After the slaughter of Theoktistos, Bardas himself assumed the office of prefect of the inkstand. When the empress Theodora learned what had happened, she ran around with her hair down and filled the palace with lamentation, hurling reproaches and curses at both her son and her brother, calling down a similar death upon them. Finding her reproaches intolerable (and Bardas not deviating in the least from his goal) they decided to rid themselves of her too, so that in future they could do whatever without let or hindrance. This she perceived (for she was well able to observe and to conjecture) but she did not think [96] she should take any counter measures, because she had a horror of killing and bloodshed. But she did decide to reveal to the Senate the wealth which was deposited in the palace, in order to restrict the prodigal expenditure of the son and to make known her prudent stewardship. She convened the Senate and rose to address it, rendering her account in words like these: 'Fathers, lying in the imperial treasury there are nineteen hundred *kentenaria* of gold and about three thousand of silver[59] which my husband acquired, or which I was able to accumulate after his death, in addition to many other assets of various kinds. I am communicating this information to you, so that if my son, your emperor, should claim after I have departed from the palace that I

---

[57] On the Skyla prison see Guilland, *Topographie*, 151–64. The Skyla gate provided a covered way from the Great Palace to the Hippodrome.

[58] George the Monk and the versions which depend on his text omit the imprisonment of Theoktistos. The date of his death, 20 November 855, is supplied by the *Synaxarion*: F. Halkin, 'Trois dates historiques précisées grâce au synaxaire', *B*, 24 (1954), 11–14.

[59] The extraordinary amount of silver in proportion to the gold may be of some importance: N. Oikonomides, 'The role of the Byzantine state in the economy', *EHB*, 1016–17 and C. Morrisson, 'Byzantine money; its production and circulation', *EHB*, table 6 and p. 941.

left it destitute of riches, you will not readily believe him.' When she had said this, she summoned the persons in charge of the imperial treasury who confirmed what she had said. The empress bid the senate farewell, renounced all power and decision-making authority, then departed from the palace.[60]

10. Such were the extent and diversity of the imperial assets; but they did not in the least suffice for the insanity of Michael. He delighted more than any other man in horse races; nor did he consider it beneath his dignity to drive a chariot himself. Acting as godfather to the children of his fellow sportsmen, racegoers and charioteers, he would pour out the imperial assets, presenting a hundred, eighty or at least fifty pounds of gold to each one of them. He presented a gift of one hundred pounds of gold to a disreputable wastrel whom he honoured by promoting him to patrician rank, a fellow named Himerios by antithesis, for he had a savage-looking face.[61] He exceeded the Himerios in the days of Tiberius for flattery. Looking to his own advantage, he would speak in a ribald and disgraceful way at table and shamelessly break wind in the hearing of the emperor and his fellow diners; break wind (what is more) with sufficient force to blow out a candle. To this man the emperor gave one hundred pounds of gold.[62] And when he stood godfather for the son of his fellow charioteer, Cheilas,[63] him too he presented with one hundred pounds of gold.

Thus he did not draw on the public purse or expend money on any of the things he ought to have done; within a short time he had distributed so much wealth by this kind of inappropriate behaviour that when came the time for the distribution of imperial bonuses and salaries there was no money available. So he melted down that famous golden plane tree, the two golden lions and the two griffins (which were also of beaten gold); the solid gold organ and other works of art for which the Roman empire was cause of admiration, weighing no less than two hundred *kentenaria*.[64] All these he melted them down and gave [the gold] to be minted in the imperial treasury. He did likewise with the imperial vestments of which some were

---

[60] Two years actually elapsed between the death of Theoktistos and Theodora's departure (858).

[61] Himerios means something like 'longed for'. In *Theophanes Continuatus*, ed. Bekker, 172, the appearance and no doubt the behaviour of this man gained him the nickname of *choiros*, 'pig'.

[62] By comparison, the strategos of the Anatolikon theme received an annual salary of forty pounds of gold (= 2,880 pieces of gold), while a soldier received on average nine pieces of gold. On officers' and soldiers' incomes see W. Treadgold, *Byzantium and its army, 284–1081* (Stanford, CA, 1995), 119–41.

[63] Cheilas (*PmbZ* 1069 = *PBE* Cheilas 1).

[64] Equals 60 kg, which, as Treadgold notes (*Army*, 128), probably corresponds to the amount which would be due to the army at Easter 868.

of solid gold, others embroidered with gold. These he gave to the *eidikos*[65] to melt down too, but they did not get melted down before he departed from the world of men, whereupon Basil became ruler and he recalled [the vestments]. Of all that wealth Basil found no more than three *kentenaria* of gold and nine bags of small change. This he expropriated to the public purse and complained to the Senate about the deficit, asking from where he was going to find the money to discharge his public obligations.[66]

11. The empress Theodora was in the habit of going to the sacred church of the Mother of God at Blachernae both to worship and to bathe with her daughters.[67] On one occasion when the emperor and Bardas, his nephew, knew that she was visiting there, they sent Petronas (who, as the narrative mentioned above, was her brother) to subject her and her daughters to monastic tonsure.[68] For the time being they banished them to the palace known as Ta Karianou, confiscating all the wealth they possessed and stipulating that henceforth they were to live as private citizens, not in imperial style. But Theodora departed this life not long after that; the emperor Basil subsequently sent her body and her daughters to remain in the Mamme [98] monastery which was renamed the Gastria.[69] This empress [Theodora] had two brothers (the crafty, contriving Bardas and Petronas) and three sisters: Sophia, Maria and Eirene, of whom Sophia was married to the magister Constantine Baboutzikos, Eirene to the patrician Sergios, brother of Photios who later acceded to the patriarchal throne,[70] Maria to the magister

---

[65] The *eidikos* was the officer in charge of the treasury where they concentrated the coin needed for the soldiers' pay. He was also responsible for the imperial workshops where vestments were woven in silk and gold thread: *ODB*, 1, 681.

[66] The alleged melting-down of the lions and the plane tree is dubious because Liutprand of Cremona (*Antapodosis* 6.5, p. 147) claims to have seen them standing near the throne a century later. Either this anecdote is a further attempt to blacken the memory of Michael or he died before the orders were executed (as with the vestments).

[67] Leo I constructed a bathhouse adjacent to the church which was used by the court: Janin, *Eglises et monastères*, 1, 162. P. Magdalino, 'The bath of Leo the Wise and the "Macedonian Renaissance" revisited: topography, iconography, ceremonial, ideology', *DOP*, 42 (1988), 97–118.

[68] Theodora was deposed on 15 March 856 but remained in the palace until 858, when she retired to the convent of Gastria where her family tombs lay. According to George the Monk, 823, she was accompanied by her favourite daughter, Pulcheria, while the other three, Thekla, Anastasia and Anna, were sent to Ta Karianou.

[69] Theodora, three of her daughters and her brother Petronas were buried there: *De Cerimoniis aulae byzantinae Libriduo*, ed. J. J. Reiske (CHSB, Bonn, 1829–30), 647–8.

[70] Other sources (*Theophanes Continuatus*, ed. Bekker, 175) indicate that Photios was the son of Eirene, sister-in-law of Maria. The question is complex but this is probably the preferable explanation. Skylitzes may have confused two Eirenes: the sister of Theodora who was married to (?) Theophobos and the mother of Photios who was the sister of the magister Arsaber, himself the brother-in-law of Theodora as he was married to Maria, another sister of hers. On the family of Photios, see (most recently) Ch. Settipani, *Continuité des élites à Byzance durant les siècles obscur* (Paris, 2006), 175–82.

Arsaber,[71] a person of nobility and courage, outstanding among his contemporaries. All [these women] were beautiful and good-looking, falling only a little short of the apogee of virtue. Such were the relatives which Theodora left behind her when she died. However, the entire administration of public business now devolved upon Bardas alone, for he was held in higher esteem than all others by the emperor. Hence he received the dignity of kouropalates – as though this were a reward for deposing his own sister.

12. [Bardas] decided to campaign with the emperor (who had just attained manhood and left puberty behind) against the Ishmaelites and against Amr, emir of Melitene. When they arrived in enemy territory, they came before Samosata.[72] Samosata is a city on the banks of the Euphrates bristling with power and strength; this they proceeded to besiege. Feigning cowardice, the Saracens shut themselves within. As not one of them set foot outside of the walls, ostensibly for fear of the imperial army, the Romans left much to be desired in their security arrangements. On the third day of the siege (it was the Lord's Day, the first day of the week), while the bloodless sacrifice[73] was being offered and they were just about to partake of the divine mysteries, the Saracens threw open the gates and charged out, fully armed, attacking the Romans on all sides. Thrown into confusion by the unexpected nature of this assault, the latter made a determined effort to flee. The emperor Michael was only just able to mount a horse and (with great difficulty) to get away; [99] but all the baggage of the emperor and of the soldiers was captured by the enemy. Karbeas, the commander of the Manichees, was clearly superior in courage to the others. He not only put to death many of the common soldiers; he also took several of the distinguished ones alive, no fewer than a hundred commanders and lesser officers. Most of these were set free on payment of a ransom;[74] the exception was the commander of Seon,[75] who expired in prison.

---

[71] The brother of John the Grammarian (see above).
[72] This expedition of 859 is attested by the Arab sources. Michael III was now nineteen; Bardas seems to have had some success. Possibly to withstand future reprisals, Michael restored the walls of Ankyra, inserting five inscriptions (one dated June 859) which have been found: A. A. Vasiliev, *Byzance et les Arabes*, 1: *La dynastie d'Amorium, 820–867*, ed. M. Canard (Brussels, 1935), 235–6.
[73] i.e. the holy eucharist.
[74] Skylitzes' source has blended several campaigns into one. The Arab sources say the grand expedition of Amr took place in 860 (the same year as the Russian attack on Constantinople), not 861, and they make no mention of the emperor's participation: Vasiliev *Byzance et les Arabes*, 1, 245–6.
[75] According to *Theophanes Continuatus*, ed. Bekker, 177, Seon (*PmbZ* 6528 = *PBE* Seon 1) was *palatinos*. This term traditionally designates any person who served at the palace, but there is no mention of it in the *taktika* of the ninth century as a position or a dignity. There was a family in the eleventh century named Palatinos; it supplied a *katepan* to Italy: V. von Falkenhausen, *La dominazione bizantina nell' Italia meridionale dal IX all' XI secolo* (Bari, 1978), 204.

Two years went by and then Amr, leading an army of no fewer than 30,000 men, campaigned against the Romans again. Wishing to make good the former reverse, Michael raised an army of about forty thousand men from Thrace and Macedonia, then went out to meet him. When Amr heard of this, taking a short cut through difficult terrain he advanced and fell on the unsuspecting emperor, turning him back with great might and forcing him to resort to flight. He would have been taken prisoner too, had not Manuel, domestic of the scholai, cut a way through the enemy lines for him and saved him. All the others were scattered and it was each man for himself.[76]

13. In the second year after this war, Amr marched out again with forty thousand men and attacked Roman territory. He ravaged and laid waste the Armeniakon theme and also the coastal regions;[77] and then (they say) he was afflicted with a similar delusion to Xerxes for he ordered the sea to be chastised with whips for not allowing him to advance any further. Michael was grieved by these developments but he did not dare set out again himself against [Amr]. So he put his mother's brother, Petronas, governor of the Thracesian theme, in command of the Roman forces with orders to move against [the enemy] in full strength. Petronas was then near Ephesos; [100] plunged into great anguish on receipt of his orders, he immediately leapt into the saddle and rode off to visit John the monk at Mount Latros.[78] It was there that this man, famed for his virtue, was leading the life of an ascetic at that time. Petronas diligently enquired of the monk concerning the matter. The latter did not hesitate in the least at the question: 'Go forth against the Saracens, my son,' he said; 'You will have God for your vanguard.' Armed with [the monk's] prayers, he went to a place called Lalakaon which is in an area locally known as Gyres. He set up an ambush in every direction and then provoked Amr to an engagement.

---

[76] *Theophanes Continuatus*, ed. Bekker, 178, paraphrased here by Skylitzes, says that it was at Anzes that this conflict took place and from which Michael was saved by Manuel. Hence the story is the same as that of the defeat of Theophilos in 838. Grégoire was suspicious of this coincidence; he saw the Michael III version as a measure to demonstrate the 'survival' of Manuel while emphasising the incompetence of Michael: Grégoire, 'Manuel et Théophobe' 183–204.

[77] In 863 Amr reached the Black Sea port of Aminsos and took it (*Theophanes Continuatus*, 179; Genesios 4.15). George the Monk (824) and Pseudo-Symeon (665) say he reached Sinope.

[78] Latros was located to the north-east of ancient Miletus, in the Thracesian theme; several monasteries had been founded there since the eighth century if not earlier: T. Wiegand, *Der Latmos* (Berlin, 1913) and R. Janin, *Les églises et les monastères des grands centres byzantins* (Paris, 1975), II, 218. It was normal for an emperor or a strategos setting out on campaign to ask a distinguished holy man for his prayers and advice.

Amr was closed in on every side, like a wild beast, and he was extremely apprehensive concerning the outcome of the situation. He sent for one of the Roman prisoners and enquired what the name of that region might be and of the place where he had encamped – also of the river which flowed by. When he heard that the region was called Lalakaon, the place Ptoson[79] and the river Gyres, he took this to be an evil omen for himself. The names signified disaster and destruction for his host. 'It is inevitable that we will be turned back by the Romans,' he declared. 'However, there must be no wavering,' he said to those who were with him. 'We must rise up and acquit ourselves courageously in tomorrow's battle.'

When day broke, knowing that he was closed in on every side and that any attempt to break out would be in vain, he decided it would be in his best interests to move against the position which he could see that Petronas was defending. He charged the enemy with loud noises and commotion. Realising that he was attempting the impossible, he fell back a little and then attacked again in force with a sudden rush, trying to create an escape route for himself. Failing again, he undertook the same stratagem a third time, and was then at his wits' end what to do next. He could see the Romans appearing in all directions, ready to attack both from the south and from the north at the same time; his fate appeared to be inescapable. He despaired of his life and threw himself upon those immediately in front of him with great violence. Thus he fell, mortally wounded, and not one of those who were with him survived. His son had been sent out foraging with a portion of the army. When he heard of the defeat, he hastily fell back on Melitene, but he was pursued by the kleisourarch of the [101] Charsianon theme[80] and taken prisoner, he and his army. They were all handed over to Petronas, the commander-in-chief. Petronas came to the capital after achieving such a remarkable victory against Amr. He brought along the monk who had foretold the victory, singing the praises of his virtue. He praised and magnified him before both the emperor and his own

---

[79] Usually Poson; *Theophanes Continuatus*, 182, gives the origin of the form, Ptoson, and explains why it was so called: an Arab prisoner gives the place usually called Poson that name because he was foretelling the fall (*ptosis*) of Amr. This decisive battle took place on 3 September 863. The precise location is unknown, but it was towards the border of the Armeniakon theme, near the river Halys: A. A. Vasiliev, *Byzance et les Arabes*, 11: *Les relations politiques de Byzance et des Arabes à l'époque de la dynastie macedonienne*, ed. M. Canard (CBHB 2, 1, Brussels, 1968), 252–6. Its consequences are important, for the emirate of Melitene never fully recovered from this blow; which meant that one of the two pillars of Moslem defence (the other being Tarsus) was significantly diminished. This permitted the Romans to seize the initiative in the east once the Paulicians had been subdued.

[80] This kleisourarch or merarch was named Machairas: Genesios 4.15 (*PmbZ* 4656 = *PBE* Machairas 1).

brother, Bardas. [Petronas] was raised to the position of domestic of the scholai, but he died a short time later.[81]

14. Manuel also died before him, carried off by some disease. Left alone, Bardas directed and carried the responsibility for all matters of state, continually receiving imperial honours in exchange. He also aspired to the rank and honour of caesar,[82] for Michael cared nothing for affairs of state, only for theatre festivals and horse races. The worst of it was that he was not content with being a spectator; he would personally drive a chariot, making himself the plaything and laughing stock of all. This is how he occupied himself, while Bardas dealt with affairs of state, contemplating the imperial office with a view to succeeding to it when the time was ripe.

Bardas was, however, also a devotee of secular learning, the pursuit of which had, over a period of many years, become seriously dilapidated, shrinking away almost to nothing (thanks to the boorishness and ignorance of those in power).[83] He assigned a location for each discipline – whatever was available for most subjects, but for philosophy (this being superior to all the other disciplines) a place was designated within the palace itself, at the Magnaura.[84] It was from this action that the disciplines began to be rejuvenated. However, excellent and famous though this action might be, it is not strong enough to wipe the slate clean of Bardas' other deeds.

15. To Leo, that great man and philosopher, was allotted the chair in philosophy. He was the nephew of the patriarch John. He had been appointed to the see of Thessalonike but he too was deposed when the enemies of the icons were thrown out.[85] He was holding no appointment when he was promoted to this academic post. This is how he first came to the notice of the emperor Theophilos.

Leo had mastered all the academic disciplines more thoroughly than any other man knew even one of them. Yet it was in a poverty-stricken dwelling that he lived and taught those who wished to be taught whatever they wanted to learn. [102] Time went by and many students made good progress in learning. There was one young man who had progressed to the highest degree in the discipline of geometry; he went on to be secretary to a commander. The commander went forth to war and the young man

---

[81] The date of his death (11 November 865) is known from the *Life of St Anthony the Younger*: F. Halkin, 'Saint Antoine le Jeune et Pétronas le vainqueur des Arabes en 863 (d'après un texte inédit)', *AnalBoll*, 62 (1944), 196–7.
[82] 22 April 862 (*PmbZ* 791); 12 April 864 according to Grierson and Mango.
[83] Presumably with the exception of Theophilos.
[84] On this school: P. Lemerle, *Premier humanisme*, 148–76.
[85] Leo (*PmbZ* 4440 = *PBE* Leo 19) was Archbishop of Thessalonike 840–3: Lemerle, *Premier humanisme*, 48–176.

followed him. There was a reverse and the young man was taken prisoner of war.[86] He was handed over to be the slave of one of the nobility. Now the ruler of the Ishmaelites at that time, Mamoun, took an interest in Hellenic learning and was especially devoted to geometry. One day the young man's master was talking to him about the scholarly interests of the *amermoumnes*[87] and about his passion for geometry. 'I would like to hear him and his teachers,' said the young man; 'I would like to know what kind of geometrical knowledge they have.' This came to the ears of Mamoun; he gladly summoned the youth, and when he arrived enquired whether he understood such-and-such a procedure. The barbarian was incredulous when the other assured him that he did, for he pretended that in those days there was nobody other than his own teachers who was knowledgeable in geometry. When the young man declared that he would like to put their teaching to the test, there they were, quicker than it takes to tell. They devised triangular and four-sided figures, demonstrating the principles of the *Elements*[88] and teaching him that this figure has such-and-such a name while another one has that name. But they gave no explanation of how or why they were so called. When the young man saw them priding themselves and thinking they were so clever at designating figures, he said to them: 'Oh, gentlemen: with respect to every account and fact, the reason *why* is of paramount importance. You seem to me to miss the mark completely. You merely note the *existence* of a thing as you run off your comments, apparently unaware of the most important thing of all.' This threw them into confusion; they asked him to analyse and declare why each figure was so named. He examined and explained the reason [for each name], showing *why* this or another thing is given such-and-such a name, both in speech and in writing. As their minds were opened and they came to understand what was being said, they were astonished, asking him whether there were any others like him at Byzantium. He replied that [103] there were many there and that he himself was the best of the students but not of the teachers. They questioned him again about this teacher; who was he, and was he still alive? He told them who it was and assured them that he was still alive, although he lived a life of poverty, paying no attention to anything other than the pursuit of learning. Mamoun immediately

---

[86] At the sack of Amorion. The name of the young man was Manikophanes or Manikophagos (*PmbZ* 4692 = *PBE* Manikiphagos 1).

[87] This information is correct; al-Ma'mún had founded a House of Wisdom (bayt al-Hikma) in which he assembled scholars capable of translating the works of antiquity from Greek or Syriac: M.-G. Balty-Guesdon, 'Le bayt al-Hikma de Bagdad', *Arabica*, 39 (1992), 131–50.

[88] i.e. Euclid.

had a letter drawn up for Leo; it went something like this: 'The tree is known by its fruit and it is by the student that we know the teacher. Since you, who are so advanced in the study of the nature of things, remain virtually unknown to your fellow citizens, reaping no advantage from your knowledge and wisdom, do not disdain to come to us and to share your wisdom with us. The entire race of the Saracens will bow before you when you arrive and you will be deemed worthy of riches and gifts such as no other man was ever held sufficient to be accorded.' He gave this letter to the young man, demonstrated his good will to him with gifts and sent him to his teacher. He arrived safe and sound back in the capital and, finding the philosopher still alive, gave him the letter. [Leo] thought it might be dangerous to receive a written communication from the enemy without the knowledge of the emperor, so he went to the logothete of the drome. This was Theoktistos, who was later put to death by Bardas. To him [Leo] declared how the prisoner, his former student, had returned and delivered the letter of the *amermoumnes* to him. So saying, he took out the letter and delivered it into the logothete's hands. That is how Leo the Philosopher came to the knowledge of the emperor and into his favour. The student of whom we spoke publicly proclaimed the wisdom of Leo, which until then had remained unknown. The emperor summoned Leo to his presence without delay, enriched him and urged him to give public instruction. He designated a residence for him at the sacred church of the Forty Glorious Martyrs.[89] When Mamoun despaired of Leo ever coming, he set out some problems in geometry, astronomy and some other studies, asking for a clear explanation of the solution of each of them. Leo not only provided fitting resolutions; in order to amaze [the ruler], he also sent him some indications of what was about to happen. When the *amermoumnes* received the communication, [104] smitten with affection for him, he cried out in wonder at the wisdom of that outstanding man. He sent off an immediate embassy to Theophilos bearing a letter which went something like this: 'I would have liked to come to you in person, as a true friend, but this was denied me by the burden of empire which God has laid upon me and the great number of people who are under my power and authority. So I beseech you to send me – for a short time – that renowned man of yours, distinguished in philosophy and the other disciplines, to share his learning with me. For I am consumed by a raging passion for his learning. Let our differences of race and religion be no obstacle; but rather, given the rank of

---

[89] Janin lists eight churches of this dedication at Constantinople; he thinks Leo would have taught in the one on the Mese (central avenue): Janin, *Eglises et monastères*, I, 483–4.

him who asks, let his request attain its goal at the hands of reasonable and gentle friends. In grateful recognition of this kindness, you will receive one hundred *kentenaria*[90] in gold and an unlimited peace treaty.' When Theophilos received the letter, he came to the conclusion that it would be inappropriate if he were to hand out to the Gentiles that knowledge of the nature of things which distinguished the Roman race; so he refused the request. But Leo he held in yet greater esteem and promoted him to be archbishop of Thessalonike, having prevailed upon the patriarch John to consecrate him. (As we said above, Leo and John were related.)[91] After his consecration, the people of Thessalonike held him in the highest honour for his innate wisdom and his acumen in all branches of learning; but they were amazed at him above all for the following reason. The land was sterile and bore no fruit in those days; famine was strangling the inhabitants of Thessalonike and the surrounding region. Every man thought that he had to choose between becoming a refugee from his fatherland or being destroyed by famine and a lack of the necessities of life. While he brought them some relief in their affliction, Leo also declared to them a season which the rising and indication of the stars established for him, a season at which he enjoined them to cast the seed on the ground. This brought about such a harvest that it sufficed for many years for the peasants who reaped the crops.[92]

Leo used to say that he had been taught grammar and [105] poetry in the capital but rhetoric, philosophy, the knowledge of numbers and access to the other disciplines he had acquired when he was on the island of Andros.[93] It was there that he made the acquaintance of an excellent man, Michael Psellos,[94] from whom he acquired only the rudiments, some theories and a few starting points. Not finding as much as he wished, he began going around the monasteries, searching out the books which were in them. In this way he provided and studiously prepared himself for the ascent to the most advanced stage of this kind of knowledge. When he

---

[90] *Theophanes Continuatus*, 190, says twenty *kentenaria*.
[91] The version of Skylitzes and *Theophanes Continuatus* presents a difficulty of chronology in relating Ma'moun's praise of Leo (who died in 833) with his elevation to the see of Thessalonike (840). There can be no causal relationship between these two occurrences (Lemerle, *Premier humanisme*, 150–4).
[92] This veritable miracle is ascribed to Leo's learning, not to magic or wizardry. In this he is distinguished from some other iconoclasts.
[93] It is a mystery why the young Leo would have gone to Andros. See C. Angelidi, 'Le séjour de Léon le Mathématicien à Andros: réalité ou confusion?', *Mélanges offerts à Hélène Ahrweiler* (Paris, 1999), 1–7.
[94] Surely an interpolation of the name of this renowned eleventh-century scholar? On Psellos as a source for Skylitzes, see Introduction, p. xv.

had satisfied his thirst for knowledge, he returned to the capital and there he sowed the seed of the disciplines in the minds of those who were willing to receive them.

16. That is what happened at first. Then, when the heresy of the enemies of the icons had been overthrown, its supporters were deposed. These included the patriarch John [the Grammarian], and Leo too was deposed at the same time, this man whom Bardas appointed president of the philosophy school, as we said already. A certain Sergios who had been his student and was the father of the young man mentioned above [was appointed] to teach geometry while Theodegios, another associate of Leo, [was named] for arithmetic and astronomy. Generous living allowances were provided for them all.[95] Prompted by his passion for learning, [Bardas] would often visit [the school] to encourage the zeal of the students, with the result that, little by little, he brought about a florescence of scholarship. Previously it had been completely snuffed out with neither trace nor ember to be seen.

17. When the same Bardas became caesar he constantly visited the court rooms of the Hippodrome and caused the laws to be put back in force, the passage of time having led to their precise meaning being lost. However, [106] great and diverse though the benefits were which accrued from Bardas' good deeds, these were stained and cancelled out by his love of being first, which was like an innate deformity and blemish of which he could not be rid. And there was the disturbance which he created in the church, stirring it up and troubling it. This is why, instead of acquiring a truly glorious reputation, he received the opposite. When the thrice-blessed Methodios departed this life after occupying the Constantinopolitan throne for four brief years, Ignatios was enthroned as patriarch.[96] He was the grandson of the emperor Nikephoros [I] on his mother's side and the son of the emperor Michael [I] who fell from power. After he fell from power he was castrated and thus excluded from the succession; he became a monk, then hegoumenos of the monastery of Satyros.[97] Promoted to the patriarchal throne, he debarred Bardas from church for having put his wife away without cause and cohabiting with his mistress in contempt of canon

---

[95] The list of professors provided by *Theophanes Continuatus*, 192, followed by Genesios (4.17) differs somewhat: Theodegios (*PmbZ* 7277 = *PBE* Theodegios 1) taught astronomy, Theodore (*PmbZ* 7693 = *PBE* Theodoros 162) geometry, Kometas (*PmbZ* 3667 = *PBE* Kometas 4) grammar, while Leo restricted himself to philosophy.
[96] Ignatios held the patriarchal throne 847–58 and from 867 until his death in 877.
[97] The monastery of St Michael at Satyros, located on the Asian shore facing the Princes' Islands, was probably founded by Ignatios shortly before he died there in 873–4: Janin, *Grands centres*, 11, 42–3.

law.⁹⁸ Though Bardas begged and pleaded, he was unable to obtain absolution; so losing all hope of doing so, he went onto the offensive. He threw Ignatios out of the church, subjected him to a host of unbearable sufferings and finally locked him up in the tomb of [Constantine V] Kopronymos with the crudest of ferocious guards to watch over him.⁹⁹ That holiest of men would have died from grievous mistreatment had it not been for a godly soul who took advantage of the absence of the guards for some reason or other to bring [Ignatios] out of the tomb and to minister to his needs in an appropriate manner. Then [Bardas], inflicting the maximum amount of discomfort, exiled him to Mytilene. Many other bishops suffered similar and even worse treatment for failing to acquiesce in what was happening and declaring that, whatever happened, they would accept no other patriarch. Still, they eventually gave way to Bardas' will, some coerced by threats, some beguiled with promises, abandoning virtue and glory for the love of riches and breaking ranks. Now Bardas chose Photios to be patriarch, a man famed for his wisdom, who was at that time head of the chancery.¹⁰⁰ There being present at that time representatives of the pope of Rome who had been sent against the enemies of the icons, [Bardas and Photios] persuaded them to be of their mind. So [107] a synod was assembled in the church of the sacred Apostles at which they demoted Ignatios (recalled from exile) by public proclamation.¹⁰¹ Such were the wanton deeds engendered by Bardas' love of the top position.

18. The Russian fleet was ravaging and overrunning what lies within the Black Sea and all its coastline.¹⁰² The Russians are a merciless and

---

⁹⁸ Here Skylitzes' source, *Theophanes Continuatus*, is drawing on texts favourable to Ignatios, possibly edited by his fervent admirer Niketas the Paphlagon. According to Genesios (4.18) Ignatios was promoted over the heads of Basil and Gregory, both men of integrity and they too sons of a deposed emperor (Leo V), but the heresy of the father may have rendered the sons unacceptable.

⁹⁹ The tomb of Constantine V had been empty since his remains were thrown out at some time (which can no longer be accurately identified) after the restoration of the icons by Theodora. The names of the jailers are given by *Theophanes Continuatus* and other sources: John Gorgonites, Nicholas Skouteloptes and Theodore the Mad (*moros*).

¹⁰⁰ *Protoasekretis* since 858, Photios was a very senior civil servant of astounding learning who, among other duties, had been on an embassy to the caliph. Like Tarasios (his relative) and Nicephoros before him, he went from layman to patriarch in five days. He was the scion of one of the leading families of the capital which had suffered in the second wave of iconclasm: H. Ahrweiler, 'Sur la carrière de Photios avant son patriarcat', *BZ* 58 (1965) 348–63. See also W. Treadgold, *The nature of the bibliotheca of Photius* (DOS, 18, Washington, DC, 1980).

¹⁰¹ A reference to the synod held at the Holy Apostles' church during the winter of 860-1. The legates of pope Nicholas I, Rodald de Porto and Zachariah d'Anani, accepted the deposition of Ignatios (hence, the elevation of Photios) but the pope disavowed their acceptance when they returned to Rome: Dagron, *Histoire de christianisme*, 169–72.

¹⁰² This first attack of the Russians (Scandinavian Varangians) took Constantinople by surprise when two hundred of their vessels surrounded the city on 18 June 860. But according to the *Annals of Saint Bertin* in 839 a Byzantine embassy at the court of Louis the Pious brought with

savage race of Scyths living to the north of the Taurus mountains. They presented a severe danger to the very capital, but before long they experienced the wrath of God themselves and went back home.[103] Then they sent a delegation of their people to the capital begging to partake of sacred baptism – which they did. Another fleet, this one from Crete, ravaged first the Cyclades, then the coastline as far as the Prokonnesos.[104] There were also severe earthquakes. The worst of them shook the earth the day the Lord's ascension was being celebrated.[105] The wall by the Hexakionion was thrown to the ground. [The earthquake] dislocated some fine churches, illustrious dwellings, the Victory located at the Golden Gate of the city and the statues standing close by St Anne's [church] in the Second District.[106] Leo the Philosopher openly declared that the fall of [the Victory] foretold the overthrow of him who would hold power after the then emperor.[107] Rivers and springs ran dry and there were other calamities in every land. Although he took note of all this, the emperor's whole attention was given to the horse races by the church of St Mamas the Martyr which lies close to the Stenon.

19. The following story deserves not to be omitted for it is eloquent both of this emperor's stupidity and of the diligence of his predecessors. Wishing to have the Saracens' incursions on Roman territory clearly signalled (so they could not launch surprise attacks, seizing land and taking prisoner the

---

it some 'Russians' who were in fact Swedes, as the Frankish emperor and his counsellors perceived: J. Shepard, 'The Rhos guests of Louis the Pious: whence and wherefore?', *Early Medieval Europe*, 4 (1995), 41–60. These people could not get back home as their path was barred by a very savage nation (Hungarians no doubt). The first Russian 'state' was located in the north of today's Russia, centred on Staraia Ladoga, close to the Baltic Sea: S. Franklin and J. Shepard, *The emergence of Rus, 750–1200* (London, 1996), 3–70.

[103] The circumstances of the attack and withdrawal of the Russians are set out in two homilies of Photios pronounced while the events were happening: C. Mango, *The homilies of Photios patriarch of Constantinople, English translation, introduction and commentary* (Cambridge, MA, 1958), 74–110. There is no question of a miraculous storm: the Russians withdrew of their own free will, possibly on account of the speedy return of Michael III. They may have run into a storm on the return journey. Photios claims that they were converted shortly after this attack. This is not a reference to the mission of Cyril and Methodios, sent to Cherson to convert the Khazars. Of this Skylitzes says not a word, nor of their subsequent mission to Moravia.

[104] *Theophanes Continuatus*, 196, says the Cretan fleet was about thirty vessels. Nothing more is known of these raids which appear to be contemporary with the Russian attack. Maybe the reference is to the Arab onslaught which reached Athos after ravaging Mytilene, dated by Vasiliev to 862: Vasiliev and Canard, 1, 258.

[105] 16 May 865.

[106] Built by Justinian: Janin, *Églises et monastères*, 1, 35–7. The word rendered here as 'statues' (*pagias*) is not attested in this sense, but there are comparable passages to support it. DuCange translates it so, but with this unique reference.

[107] Meaning caesar Bardas. Leo probably argued that the earthquake which had shaken the 'second district' (the space between the Constantinian and the Anthemian walls) presaged the fall of the second person of the empire.

inhabitants of village and countryside), [108] the former emperors built a fort on a strategic eminence at the Cilician Gates. The name of the fort was Loulon.[108] As soon as the garrison in that fort got wind of an attack, they would light a fire. When those who were stationed on Mount Argaion[109] saw it, they would light another fire and then those on Mount Isamon likewise.[110] Seeing this, the men on Mount Aigilon[111] would light up and likewise those at the place called Mamas.[112] Then Kyrizos would follow suit, followed by Mokilos, then Mount St Auxentios[113] would report the attack to those on duty in the Great Palace.[114] This is how, by a succession of fires, the news was quickly delivered to the emperor.[115] When those who lived in the countryside got the news, they would take refuge in walled fortresses and escape from the raids. Such was the procedure which was followed when, one day, just as Michael was getting ready to run a chariot race near the church of St Mamas the Martyr, the fire at the lighthouse was lit. On seeing this, he was consumed with apprehension as great as any other man might experience when in danger of his soul – fearing that his own chariot race might lack for spectators because of that signal of ill omen! That was how shamelessly he made a spectacle of himself. So to ensure that no news of disasters occurring should cool the ardour of the spectators, he ordered that the fires nearer to the Queen of Cities were not to be activated.[116] On another occasion (the perversity of the man must be most clearly exposed) he was standing in his chariot and the starting gate was about to be raised. He was wearing the colours of the blues; Constantine, the logothete of the drome,[117] was [driving] for the greens, Cheilas for the whites and Krasas

---

[108] This fortress controlled the passage from Cilicia into Cappadocia; hence the Arabs and Romans disputed it for many centuries: Hild and Restle, *Kappadokien*, II, 223–4.

[109] Location uncertain. It could hardly be the Argion near to Caesarea in Cappadocia, a high mountain that can be seen from afar, because this would require a significant deviation from the direct route between Loulon and Constantinople. A better candidate would be what today is called Hasan dagi, close to Mokissos: Hild and Restle, *Kappadokien*, 149.

[110] Location unknown; probably near to lake Karanli in Lycaonia: K. Belke mit Beiträgen von M. Restle, *Galatien und Lykaonien* (TIB, 4, Vienna, 1984), 180.

[111] Location uncertain; possibly in the region of Sivrihisar daglari, to the south-west of Dorylaeon: Belke and Restle, *Galatien und Lykaonien*, 118.

[112] Possibly a peak in the Olympos range.

[113] This hill was on the Asiatic coast almost opposite to Constantinople, famous for the monastery in which St Stephen the Younger lived for a time: Janin, *Grands centres*, II, 43–4.

[114] In the imperial palaces (Daphne, the Magnaura) the *diaiterioi* (ushers, attendants) were under the orders of the *papias*: Oikonomides, *Listes*, 130 and note 89.

[115] This system, invented by Leo of Thessalonike (Pseudo-Symeon, 681–2) permitted the report of an Arab attack and its magnitude to be sent to the emperor by simple signals in about one hour: P. Pattenden, 'The Byzantine early warning system,' *B*, 53 (1983), 258–99; C. Zuckerman, 'Chapitres peu connus de l'apparatus bellicus,' *TM*, 12 (1994), 361–6.

[116] It was, however, still functioning in the mid-tenth century.

[117] Constantine Maniakes; he was also droungarios of the watch.

for the reds. Then news arrived that Amr, the emir of Melitene, was grievously pillaging Asia; that he was already approaching Malagina,[118] whose citizens were anticipating even worse disasters than ever before. When the *protonotarios* learnt of this he went to report it to the emperor, in great distress. He had the letter of the domestic of the scholai in his hands and gave it to [the emperor]. 'You silly head,' said he, throwing him an ugly look not unworthy of a Titan, 'how dare you [109] speak to me of things like that at the time of this crucial race? Only one thing concerns me [right now]: to see the centre [chariot] not run to the left;[119] that is the sum total of what I am striving to achieve.' That is how deluded he was and how deranged in his reason. Nor was he so in thrall to this desire and passion that he was kept apart from other passions even more unseemly, for he even pursued moderation immoderately, so that his behaviour fell short of what is appropriate to and worthy of the imperial dignity.

20. One day he met a woman on her way back from the baths, pitcher in hand; it transpired that he had stood godfather for her child at the sacred font. He got down from his horse, sent all the senators who were keeping him company to the palace which was close by and, taking with him some useless, debauched specimens of humanity whom he knew and maintained, went off with the woman. He took the pitcher from her hands and said: 'Come on, woman; receive me as your guest without fear; I need some rye bread and white cheese.' There she stood, rooted to the spot by what he had said, fully aware that she had nothing with which to entertain him, but in less time than it takes to tell, Michael took the towel the woman was bringing back from the baths, still damp, and spread it out on the ground as though it were a tablecloth. Assuming the role of the woman, he himself was host, emperor, cook, waiter and guest all in one. When he had dined with the woman, off he went to the palace, walking – on foot! – and complaining about the excessive foolishness and affectation of the former emperors (who, in fact, behaved quite appropriately).

21. This all conspired to render the man hateful, and the wrath of everybody rose up – quite justly – against him. Worst of all was the crew of catamites who followed him around, ready for any shameless deed. These

---

[118] Malagina in Bithynia was where troops assembled for campaigns in Asia; the imperial stables were located there. The Arab sources say nothing of Amr of Melitene having prosecuted such a raid. On Malagina see Cl. Foss, 'Byzantine Malagina and the Lower Sangarius,' *Anatolian Studies*, 40 (1990), 161–83; also Cl. Foss, *Fortresses and Villages of Byzantine Asia Minor* (Variorum Reprints), Aldershot, 1996, no. VII.

[119] He was concerned not to be overtaken in the privileged position, the left-hand (inside) track: Guilland, *Topographie*, 1, 4.

he held in honour and respect. To make a burlesque of the sacred mysteries [110] and profane them, he dressed these fellows up in priestly robes woven with golden thread and in stoles. Then he obliged them to celebrate the divine and most holy mysteries in a sacrilegious, indecent manner. Their leader, a fellow named Gryllos,[120] he called patriarch; the other eleven, metropolitans. The emperor himself played the role of one of the concelebrants, calling himself bishop of Koloneia. When they had to sing in celebrating the mysteries, they performed their songs to the accompaniment of guitars. Sometimes they sang softly and melodiously, sometimes stridently, just as priests make proclamations in the sacred liturgy. They had golden vessels set with [precious] stones which they filled with vinegar and mustard; this they administered to the communicants in mockery of the immaculate mysteries. On one occasion this defiled rabble encountered the blessed patriarch Ignatios in the street, walking in procession with the priestly hierarchy. When Gryllos saw him, recklessly and shamelessly refusing to give way he lifted up his chasuble, and together with the 'concelebrants' who accompanied him made yet more vigorous use of the stringed instruments, casting insults and obscene remarks at those chaste persons. Another time, when his mother was still residing in the imperial palace, this most disgusting emperor sent for her, allegedly to receive the blessing of the 'patriarch': Gryllos, pretending to be the blessed Ignatios. That most correct lady devoutly came forth [from her apartments] and prostrated herself on the ground, requesting a prayer. She did not yet in the least suspect anything, for the disgusting Gryllos had kept his beard hidden thus far.[121] Then he stood up, broke wind and spoke some words which were just what might be expected of his mouth. She protested vigorously against what had happened, hurling curses at her son and uttering a prophecy that, before very long, he would fall out of the good graces of God.

22. But incorrigible is he who has once deviated from the path of righteousness; thus he was very quickly overwhelmed by catastrophe, preceded [111] by Bardas who in turn was preceded by Theoktistos the prefect of the inkstand, two men who gratified [Michael's] desires rather than try to detach him from those most unedifying displays – which, being his guardians, is what they should have done. This narrative has already told how Theoktistos met his end; now there were signs which presaged the fall

---

[120] The real name of this companion of Michael III was Theophilos and he enjoyed the dignity of protospatharios (*PmbZ* 8222 = *PBE* Theophilos 8).
[121] Ignatios, being a eunuch, would have little or no beard.

of Bardas: comets appearing and portentous visions in dreams. While he was asleep, [Bardas] seemed to be going to the Great Church with Michael as though it were some important festival. When they arrived and were entering the sacred church, he seemed to behold some persons dressed in white who went ahead of them and brought him to the sanctuary railing. The only thing he noticed was an old man sitting by the patriarchal throne; he thought it was Peter, prince of the apostles. At the feet of this figure there grovelled the blessed Ignatios, imploring vengeance for the wrongs he had suffered. [The aged one] seemed to deliver a sword to one of those who stood by, saying: 'The man who has angered God' – that is how he designated the caesar – 'set him among those who are standing in the area on the left and then cut him in pieces. As for the impious youth' – by this expression he was clearly indicating the emperor – 'count him with those on the right[122] but tell him that the same punishment is in store for him.' Such was the dream; the narrative will show whether what was seen in the vision came to pass.

Bardas had been arming himself for an expedition against Crete with Michael and the whole army, and paying a visit to the church of the Mother of God Hodegetria,[123] he entered with lights to perform the rites of departure.[124] As he was approaching the inner sanctuary, his mantle suddenly slipped from his shoulders; this brought him the realisation that terrible things lay ahead of him. Moreover, the day before he was about to leave the city, either of his own volition or driven by what was to come, he assembled his friends in one place, treated them to a banquet and besought them to be mindful of his friendship and the bequests he had made – as though he had already departed this life. When they had set out on campaign against Crete and were arrived at a place called Choros in the Thracesian theme, [112] his attendants went ahead and pitched the tents with great vigour and enthusiasm. Thus it came about, either by design or through ignorance, that they set up the emperor's pavilion on a plain while the caesar's shelter stood higher, on a small eminence. Michael's partisans saw this as a godsend and exploited it to the caesar's disadvantage, fanning the smouldering plots against him into flames. The superior strength of the caesar disturbed them and weakened their enthusiasm for the enterprise. It

---

[122] The left and right appear to refer to Matt. 25:33ff., but the significance is less than clear.
[123] *Hodegetria* (guide of travellers) was the name of a very famous icon of the Theotokos hanging in an equally famous Constantinopolitan monastery of the same name located near the Great Palace, close by the sea wall: Janin, *Églises et monastères*, 199–207.
[124] Or, 'to pronounce [or hear?] the farewell discourse', *ton syntaktêrion [logon] ekpleron*: M. E. Mullett, 'In peril on the sea: travel genres and the unexpected', *Travel in the Byzantine world*, ed. R. Macrides (Aldershot, 2002), 259–84, at 260.

was his son, Antigonus,[125] who was in command as domestic of the scholai, and the rest of the generals respected his authority. [Bardas'] son-in-law (the husband of his daughter) Symbatios,[126] the logothete of the drome, was believed to be incontrovertibly on his side but in fact the emperor had secretly corrupted him. He it was and none other who contrived the assassination of his father-in-law by devising the agreed signal. He had just come out from reading the reports when he gave the sign for the assassination by tracing the sign of the cross on his forehead. The conspirators still hung back at the sight of the caesar's bodyguard standing there.[127] Alarmed now that [Bardas] might catch him *in flagrante delicto* and turn his sword against the emperor, Michael sent someone he trusted to put heart into his men with promises. The conspirators were so paralysed and afflicted by fear that the caesar would have escaped the danger and parried [the blow] if Basil, the future emperor (who was then chamberlain)[128] had not risen to the occasion. It was he who prevailed upon the conspirators to cast off their fear and to get on with the deed. Bardas recognised death as soon as he saw the men entering sword in hand.[129] He flung himself at the emperor's feet but they dragged him away and hewed him limb from limb. Then they hung his genital organs on a spear and made a show of them. A great disturbance broke out which put the emperor in danger, but Constantine, the droungarios of the watch, suddenly appeared with a considerable force in the midst of the disturbance and broke it up. He had the emperor acclaimed, affirming that Bardas' death was what justice demanded.[130]

23. [113] Thus Bardas quitted this life and thus the Cretan expedition was abandoned, the emperor returning to Byzantium. This was the occasion for Basil to achieve the height of imperial power. Devoid of offspring

---

[125] Antigonus (*PmbZ* 503 = *PBE* Antigonos 1) was then twelve or thirteen years old for he was already domestic of the scholai (at the age of nine or ten) in the victorious campaign against Amr: *Theophanes Continuatus*, 180.

[126] As the name suggests, Symbatios was of Armenian origin. According to another tradition it was Basil who won over Symbatios by claiming that Bardas was the obstacle to his own promotion to caesar (*PmbZ* 7169 = *PBE* Symbatios 1).

[127] Under the command of one of the Argyroi (George the Monk, 830), possibly Eustathios (Theodosios of Melitene, 171): Vannier, *Argyroi*, 21.

[128] Parakoimomenos. This is the founder of the Macedonian dynasty who seized power in 867.

[129] A list of the conspirators exists, with some variation: Marianos (*PmbZ* 4768 = *PBE* Marianos 4) and Symbatios (*PmbZ* 7168 = *PBE* Symbatios 2), brothers of Basil; Asylaion (*PmbZ* 4511 = *PBE* Leo 23) cousin of the same, Peter the Bulgar (*PmbZ* 6091 = *PBE* Petros 32), John Chaldos (*PmbZ* 3320 = *PBE* Ioannes 89) and Constantine Toxaras (*PmbZ* 4011 = *PBE* Konstantinos 39): *Georgius Monachus Continuatus*, 830; Leo the Grammarian, 244; *pseudo*-Symeon the Logothete, 678. These must have been members of Basil's retinue for they were involved in the murder of Michael III in 867.

[130] Bardas was killed on 21 April of the fourth indiction, 866: *Theophanes Continuatus*, 206. Skylitzes retells this story in the chapter on Basil I.

and incapable of running the affairs of state, Michael adopted Basil as his son and honoured him with the dignity of magister. A little later he set a diadem on his brow in the Great Church.[131] Once [Basil] was firmly in command he endeavoured to draw the emperor as far away as possible from the heinous deeds for which he was infamous, unaware that by doing so he was arousing resentment against himself. Michael could not tolerate the reprimands and took it into his head to get rid of Basil, who was preventing him from getting his own way. He brought in one Basilikinos, an oarsman of the imperial barge, dressed him in purple and set a diadem on his brow. He then led him out before the senate, holding him by the hand. As he was leading him out, he uttered words something like this: 'O friends, I should already have promoted this man rather than Basil to the illustrious rank of emperor. I regret what I did; the rank is to be given to this man for

> First, he has the appearance of a ruler
> Secondly he is a fitting candidate for the crown
> And everything about him qualifies him for that distinction.

24. It was this deed and speech which were the origin and cause of his undoing, but he added something else to them. Michael would become intoxicated from drinking unwatered wine, then, when he was drunk, command some very irregular things to be done: one man to have his ears cut off, another his nose and the head of a third. Basil prevented these things from happening, not only for the benefit of others, but also because he feared for his own person. Once Michael realised [114] that Basil was opposing him he devised a monstrous plot against him; it was this. He got somebody to throw a lance as though he were aiming at a wild beast, but in truth at Basil. This came to light because the man who was told to do it made a clean breast of it when he was at the point of death. He flung his javelin but it went wide of the mark and Basil was saved. Once he was saved, he determined to take action rather than to be the victim of it; Michael was slain in the palace of St Mamas in AM 6376, at the third hour

---

[131] Basil was crowned on 26 May 866. He does not appear on coins issued in the reign of Michael III, but the term *megas basileus* (great emperor) does feature on certain rare coins (*miliaresia*) of Michael dating from 866–7, indicating Michael's superior rank in comparison to his colleague (*DOC*, III 1:455). There is no agreement as to why Michael adopted Basil and made him co-emperor. C. Mango suggests it was a way to ensure an imperial title for the (as yet unborn) future Leo VI, fathered – as some believed – not by Basil, but by Michael. This ingenious hypothesis is somewhat weakened by the existence of Basil's older son, Constantine, who was the obvious heir apparent. For discussion of this matter and of the relations between Michael, Eudokia and Basil, see S. Tougher, *The reign of Leo VI (886–912), politics and people* (Leiden, 1997). There is information on the imperial galleon and who could sail in it in *DAI*, c. 51.

of the night. He had reigned fourteen years with his mother then eleven years alone. And although he had lived in such an unbridled and irregular manner, he was not completely devoid of praiseworthy deeds. He donated a chalice and paten to the Great Church and also a new chandelier far superior to the old one.

{The emperor Michael reigned, first with his mother then alone, for twenty-four years and eleven months. He acceded on 21 October and was killed on 24 September.[132] His body was laid beside the emperor Leo who is there[133] at the church of the Holy Apostles in the heroon of Constantine the Great, in a green marble sarcophagus which was of Justinian the Great [-'s time ?] His wife was Eudokia.}[134]

---

[132] He acceded on the death of his father, 20 January 842, and was killed on 24 September 867, so he reigned twenty-five years and nine months. He was buried in the monastery of Philippikos at Chrysopolis: P. Grierson, 'The tombs and obits of the Byzantine emperors (337–1042) with an additional note by C. Mango and I. Ševčenko', *DOP*, 16 (1962), 3–63, at 57.

[133] The text is unsure here.

[134] {...}Addition of MS E only. Michael's wife was Eudokia Dekapolitissa, whom Theodora chose for him and obliged him to marry: *PmbZ* 1631.

CHAPTER 6

Basil I Kephalas, the Macedonian [867–886]

1. [115] Once Michael was eliminated as we indicated, Basil[1] secured sole rule for himself.[2] Continuing from where it left off, the narrative will now clearly indicate who this man was, where he came from and the reasons why he, who emerged from a humble and obscure background, was able to rise up to be the supreme commander of the empire. He was born in Macedonia but he was an Armenian by race, a scion of the distinguished line of the Arsacids which possessed the exclusive right by law of ruling over Parthians, Medes and Armenians. They had obtained this right by virtue of the fame acquired by the first Arsaces for retrieving for the Parthians their right to autonomy that the Persians had arrogated to themselves.[3] The descendants of Arsaces ruled over the aforementioned peoples for a long time. The last was Artaban who, when he was expelled from his hereditary kingdom, took refuge in Byzantium together with his brother, Cleienes. Leo the Great[4] was ruling the Roman empire at the time; he received them

---

[1] There is an abundant bibliography on Basil I (*PmbZ* 832 = *PBE* Basileios 7), Holmes' *Basil II and the governance of empire (976–1025)* (Oxford Studies in Byzantium, Oxford, 2005) being the first comprehensive monograph since A. Vogt, *Basile 1er empereur de Byzance (867–886)* (Paris, 1908); however, there is an unpublished thesis: N. Tobias, 'Basil I (867–86), the founder of the Macedonian dynasty' (Rutgers University, 1969). There are several articles, not always as critical of the sources as one would wish, e.g. N. Adontz, 'L'âge et l'origine de l'empereur Basile Ier (867–86)', *B*, 8 (1933), 475–500; and 9 (1934), 223–60, repr. N. Adontz, *Etudes arméno-byzantines* (Lisbon, 1965). Among more recent work one should mention I. Ševčenko, *La biographie de Basil 1er* (Bari, 1987), 91–127; and V. N. Vlyssidiou, *Politique étrangère et réactions intérieures sous le règne de Basil Ier: recherches pour l'identification des tendances oppositionelles pendant l'époque 867–886* (Athens, 1991), in Greek with French abstract. The notice in *PmbZ* (no. 832) contains much detail. On the origins of Basil see G. Moravcsik, 'Sagen und Legenden über Kaiser Basileios I', *DOP*, 15 (1961), 61–126; and A. Schminck, 'The beginnings and origins of the "Macedonian" dynasty', *Byzantine Macedonia: identity, image and history, papers from the Melbourne Conference, July 1995*, ed. J. Burke and R. Scott (Melbourne, 2000), 61–8.
[2] Skylitzes passes over the introduction in *Theophanes Continuatus*, ed. Bekker, 211–12, which portrays Basil as a role model for his descendants and successors.
[3] The Arsacids were really a branch of the Parthian dynasty. They governed Armenia until the beginning of the fifth century. A family of the same name is known at Constantinople but much later: in the eleventh century, relatives of Gregory Magistros. There is an inventory of them prepared by W. Seibt, 'Arsakuni-armenische Aristokraten in byzantinischen Diensten', *JÖB*, 44 (1994), 349–59.
[4] Leo I Makelles, 457–74.

Basil I the Macedonian

with fitting honour, assigning them a residence in the capital commensurate with their rank. When the Persian king heard of this he sent a letter inviting them back and promising to restore them to their ancestral throne. They received the letter and, while they were discussing what to do about it, one of their attendants revealed all its contents to the emperor, who promptly confiscated it. Now the matter had become known to the emperor and he realised that the wandering foreigners were men of extremely high standing, he housed them, together with their women and children, in a fortified town of Macedonia named Nicaea.[5] Later on, when the Persian royalty had been destroyed by the Saracens, [116] the reigning *amermoumnes* did something similar: he sent a letter inviting the descendants of the Arsacides living in Macedonia to come back home. This communication was detected by the emperor Heraclius.[6] Knowing that the invitation was by no means issued out of goodwill towards the people in question, but rather, through them, to bring the race of Armenians and Parthians into subjection, he transferred the strangers to Philippi, another city of Macedonia, and from there to Adrianople. They found that place to their liking and multiplied while still preserving their national identity.

2. Time went by, and when Constantine[7] was reigning together with Eirene, his mother, a man named Maiktes,[8] a member of the Arsacid tribe, came into the capital for some reason or other. There he chanced to encounter a fellow tribesman called Leo. They became acquainted with each other and ended up being fast friends. When Leo realised that the other also had the blood of the Arsacides in his veins and was living in Adrianople, he held the stranger's land in higher esteem than his own because of the virtue of the man – and bound himself to him in a marriage alliance by marrying one of his daughters. From this marriage was born the father of our hero, a man distinguished by his vigour and the rest of his physical appearance.[9] A noble lady, said to be descended from Constantine the Great, made him her son-in-law by marrying him to her own daughter, an extremely fine-looking girl.[10] She eventually gave birth

---

[5] This is 'little' Nicaea to the south-west of Adrianople where Havsa is today – not to be confused with Nicaea opposite Constantinople where the ecumenical councils took place: P. Soustal, *Thrakien (Thrake, Rodope und Haiminontos)* (TIB, 6, Vienna, 1991), 374–5.

[6] Reigned 610–41.

[7] Constantine VI, 780–97.

[8] This Armenian name, Hmayek, is characteristic of the family of the Mamikonian: Adontz, 'L'âge et l'origine de l'empereur Basile Ier', 475–92.

[9] No source offers a name for Basil's father.

[10] This might be an allusion to the name of Basil's mother, Pankalo – which is known from an inscription on her tomb in the church of St Euphemia in the Petrion: Constantines Porphyrogenitus, *De cerimoniis aulae Byzantinae libri duo*, ed. J. J. Reiske (CHSB, Bonn, 1829–30), 648.

to Basil, but not before he had given many signs of his imperial future.[11] Given such parents, Basil was brought up with all the advantages of a leisured citizen. But Krum, the ruler of the Bulgars, was puffed up by his victories against the Romans; he collected a large army and laid siege to Adrianople. Nobody dared to lift a hand against him because, by virtue of his former good fortune in war, he seemed to be irresistible.[12] After a siege of some length, he reduced the city to the point of surrender for want of the necessities of life then deported all its inhabitants to Bulgaria as the terms [of surrender] stipulated, including [117] Manuel, bishop of the city. In this way the parents of Basil were led away into the land of the Bulgars, carrying the infant who was still at the breast.[13] When they got there, the renowned bishop, the parents of Basil and the people accompanying the bishop preserved their Christian faith. They converted several Bulgars to the orthodox faith even before the Bulgar nation had been brought to godliness. All over the Bulgar lands they sowed the seed of Christian teaching.

Krum now came to the end of his life and his successor was Murtagon, a man who greatly surpassed the late ruler in ferocity. He was fully aware of what was going on and it filled him with wrath that the Bulgar race was being quietly converted to Christianity. He angrily summoned Manuel, the sacred chief pastor, to appear before him together with the leading members of his community. First he tried to persuade them in a gentle way, [speaking] man to man, to abjure the orthodox and spotless faith of the Christians. But when he realised they were impervious to threats and promises he severely tortured them and put them to a martyr's death.

[11] This origin attributed to Basil is patently fictitious, intended to connect him with an ancient Armenian ruling family. He was undoubtedly of Armenian stock, but of modest status. The reference to a new David in an anonymous eulogy addressed to Basil confirms his humble origins: A. Markopoulos, 'An anonymous laudatory poem in honour of Basil I', *DOP*, 46 (1992), 225–32, repr. in Markopoulos, *History*, no. xiv. Nevertheless it has sometimes been maintained that Basil was the great-grandson of Leo V: Adontz and more recently C. Settipani, *Nos ancêtres de l'antiquité* (Paris, 1991), 185–6, which also contains some important notes on the families of the empress Theodora and of the patriarch Photios (who may have been the one who forged the Armenian descent of Basil, Pseudo-Symeon, 689). On the Constantinian origin of Basil: A. Markopoulos, 'Constantine the Great in Macedonian historiography: models and approaches', *New Constantines: the rhythm of imperial renewal in Byzantium, fourth to thirteenth centuries*, ed. P. Magdalino (SPBS, 2, Aldershot, 1994), 159–70.
[12] Skylitzes has gone back in time: he has already mentioned Krum's advance in 813 when he took Adrianople (reign of Michael I, cc. 2 and 6), the part played by Murtagon in the revolt of Thomas the Slav (reign of Michael II, c. 12) and even the conversion of the Bulgars, which took place after Basil's return to the Empire (reign of Michael III, c. 7).
[13] This information implies that Basil was born around 811, which contradicts the rest of the story according to which he is said still to be a child twenty years later – when his parents were liberated. See E. Kislinger, 'Der junge Basileios I und die Bulgaren', *JÖB*, 30 (1981), 37–150.

Thus did Manuel, the renowned chief pastor, together with the more distinguished members of his company, come to a martyr's end and affirm [the quality of] his life. Many other people related by blood [to Basil][14] were also found worthy of the martyr's crown.[15]

Then it came time for the remaining prisoners to be sent home (God in his heaven having striven to obtain their exodus). The Bulgar ruler had suffered a number of defeats; he could no longer resist the Roman forces, so he made peace instead of war – releasing the people from their captivity. When the prisoners were assembling prior to returning to their ancestral homes, the ruler came to inspect them and, seeing the young Basil (who was now leaving childhood behind and entering adolescence), [118] called him to his side. He had observed the boy's noble glances, his gracious smile and gestures. It pleased him to take the boy in his arms and embrace him as he stood before him – then to give him an apple of outstanding size. The boy received this gift without guile, confidently leaning against the ruler's knees, thus showing his nobility by his unaffected and natural manners. The ruler was quite amazed at this, but his subjects were secretly angered that a young man of such quality should be allowed to return home.[16]

3. Nevertheless, by the grace of God, those of the captive Romans who had survived were now released and sent home. The parents of Basil went off with them, taking along their beloved child. They say that many signs happened regarding him, indicating that he would be promoted to the summit of imperial authority. The other [portents] must be omitted from this discourse or it will be spun out too long, but it would be unforgivable

---

[14] Here the translation follows MS B, which makes more sense. The point is that the future emperor's family had provided martyrs, by way of additional distinction. Thurn's text says it was members of Manuel's family who suffered martyrdom.

[15] The martyrdom of Manuel and his companions is found in *SynaxCP* (cols. 414–16) with a slightly different chronology. Manuel was executed together with 370 other victims who included George, archbishop of Debeltos, Leon, bishop of Little Nicaea, a bishop named Peter, a priest named Pardos and the two strategoi Leo and John. The khan is Ditzevg, who succeeded Krum in 815 but was killed when he became blind and was replaced by Omurtag. The story of this persecution of Christians by Bulgars has, however, recently been called into question: M. Whittow, *The making of orthodox Byzantium, 600–1025* (London, 1996), 281.

[16] Skylitzes follows *Theophanes Continuatus* in describing a peaceful return of the Armenians to the empire; the report of the *Chronicle of the Logothete* is quite different (*Symeonis magistri*, 236–7). The Roman colony has been concentrated by the khan north of the Danube. The exiles decide to return, choosing as their chiefs Skordyles (son of Bardas) and Tzantzes. With the aid of the imperial fleet sailing up the Danube they are able to force a crossing during operations in which Tzantzes distinguishes himself, for which he is rewarded by Theophilos and appointed strategos of the Macedonian theme. The logothete does not give a date but there is good reason to think this must have happened before the renewal of the treaty with the Bulgars in 836: W. Treadgold, *The Byzantine revival, 782–842* (Stanford, CA, 1988), 219.

to pass over in silence the one I am about to relate. It was the height of summer; the child's parents went out to their own field to urge on the harvesters in their work. While they were with the workers, they tied some sheaves together to make a shelter in which the child could sleep, protected from the burning of the sun's rays. In this way they contrived for him to be unhurt by the burning heat of the sun and also for his sleep to be unbroken by anything going on outside. Thus, having improvised a nest with what came to hand and put the child to bed in it, they went to work. But the sun [came round and] shone its rays on the child, causing him some considerable discomfort; then an eagle flew down and shaded the child with outstretched wings. Those who saw it raised a shout, for fear the baby might be hurt by the animal. Immediately the mother ran to the child and found him sleeping peacefully. [119] But when she saw the eagle keeping the child in the shadow of its wings (which, far from being in the least disturbed by her arrival, seemed to expect some reward from her), she did not immediately realise the significance of the prophecy but rather picked up a stone from the ground and chased the eagle away. It flew off a short distance, but once the woman had returned to her husband, back it came and took up the same stance as before, shading the child with outstretched wings. Again a great cry went up from those who saw it; again the mother came to the child, scared the eagle away with a stone and went back to the workers. After this had happened three or more times, she was finally just able to perceive the meaning of this sign from God and to see in what was happening an indication of what was to come. The child was now reared with greatest care by none other but his own parents.

4. When Basil reached the age of a young man,[17] his father departed this life, leaving the mother a widow and this young man an orphan; distress and affliction followed. A swarm of concerns engulfed him; for the maintenance of the house and provision for his mother and brothers now became his responsibilities. Agriculture, it seemed to him, could be but little succour and help to him as a livelihood, so he was of a mind to go to the capital and there to make adequate provision for the needs of himself and of his loved ones. The desire of going to the capital possessed him, but his mother opposed him and held him back. She refused to allow him to do what he wanted to do, begging him to remain and care for her in her old age. Once she was dead [she said] and he had accompanied her in person to the grave, then he could undertake the journey his heart

---

[17] Skylitzes writes *neaniskos*, youth; *Theophanes Continuatus* has *meirakion*, one whose beard is just beginning to show, fifteen to sixteen years old.

desired. Yet even though she was so opposed to a separation, concerns about providing the necessities of life [120] caused her to relent and let him go. Leaving Macedonia, he set out for the capital. Having travelled the intervening distance he came to its Golden Gate, through which he passed towards evening. Worn out, he listlessly threw himself down to rest just where he was, which happened to be by the steps in the forecourt going up to the main entrance of the monastery of St Diomedes.[18] Subsequently, in the first watch of the night, Diomedes the Martyr appeared in a dream to the hegoumenos of the monastery[19] commanding him to go out to the main entrance of the monastery, call Basil by name and bring back the one who responded into the monastery to be cared for. This was because the man in question had been anointed[20] emperor by God and was to restore and enlarge that monastery. Reckoning that what he had seen was no more than a dream, the hegoumenos attached no importance whatsoever to the vision and went back to sleep. Again he saw the same thing, a second time; again he paid no attention to it, being slow of understanding and drugged with sleep. Then he saw the Martyr a third time, no longer issuing his command quietly and humbly, but uttering terrible threats of what would ensue if his message was not promptly attended to and (or so it seemed) brandishing a whip. The hegoumenos awoke in terror and, casting hesitation aside, went to the main entrance, calling out 'Basil,' in accordance with the sacred command. 'Here I am, sir; what orders have you for your servant?'[21] Basil immediately replied. The hegoumenos led him into the monastery and offered him all he needed by way of care and attention, entertaining him with warmest hospitality. When the hegoumenos was assured of Basil's discretion and that he would not reveal it to anybody, after charging him to keep the secret to himself he revealed the Martyr's prophecy to him, entreating him to bear the hegoumenos and the monastery in mind once things turned out as foretold. Basil put the matter out of his mind, thinking it beyond him. What he did do was to ask the hegoumenos to introduce him to one of the nobles to whom he could be of service, to which request the

---

[18] Legend said this monastery went back to Constantine the Great but there is no certain evidence of its existence prior to the sixth century: R. Janin, *La géographie ecclésiastique de l'empire byzantin*, I: *Le siège de Constantinople et le patriarcat œcuménique*, III: *Les églises et les monastères* (Paris, 1969), 95–7.

[19] This man was of the Androsalitai family. The hospitality he accorded Basil certainly brought success to his relatives: Nikolas became oekonomos and synkellos, Paul *epi tou sakelliou* (responsible for the state treasury), Constantine logothete of the genikon, John droungarios of the watch, while another brother became a physician.

[20] *Kechrismenos*, a reference to 1 Kings/1 Sam. 10 *passim*.

[21] See 1 Kings/1 Sam. 3:9–11.

hegoumenos addressed himself enthusiastically. He presented Basil to a frequent visitor of that monastery, a kinsman of the emperor Michael and of the caesar Bardas, named Theophilos – but whom they called by the nickname Theophilitzes[22] [121] on account of his small stature. It was this man's concern to surround himself with vigorous, handsome servants, well known for their bravery.[23] When he engaged such persons, he immediately dressed them in silk clothing and rendered them magnificently splendid with their other accoutrements. Basil was enlisted among them, and he seemed to surpass the others so far in physical endurance and mental courage that he was promoted chief groom.[24] Ever advancing, day by day he became dearer to Theophilos and an object of wonder, by virtue of his own superior qualities. His arm was strong, he was valorous in spirit; moreover, he carried out every order promptly and correctly.

5. That is how it was for Basil; meanwhile his mother was dying to know what sort of a journey he had had and whether he had discovered any relief from his adversity. Depressed and distressed though she was, in her sleep she saw a huge tree like a cypress, standing in her atrium with an abundance of golden leaves on golden branches and trunk; her son, Basil, was seated at the top of it. When she awoke, she recounted the vision to one of those pious women, who encouraged her to rejoice on her son's account for, interpreting the dream, she declared that he would become emperor of the Romans. Adding this [revelation] to the previous ones, from then on the mother was no longer anxious for him, but full of joy, nourishing optimistic hopes for him.

6. At that time it happened that Theophilos,[25] Basil's master, was sent to the Peloponnese on government business. Basil went with him, discharging the office which had been committed to him. When they came to Achaia,[26] Theophilos went to pray in the church of [St] Andrew, the Apostle who was the first to be called.[27] Basil did not go in with him,

---

[22] Also known (*pace Theophanes Continuatus*) as *paideumenos*, 'educated'.
[23] According to *George the Monk, Theophanes Continuatus*, ed. I. Bekker (CSHB, Bonn, 1838), 820, Nikolas had a brother who was a physician in the service of Theophylitzes and it was *he* who had the idea of presenting Basil to his master, who was just then looking for somebody to take care of his horses.
[24] *Protostrator*. The highest persons in the imperial hierarchy (Theophylitzes was related to the emperor) maintained courts modelled on the emperor's court, giving their servants titles similar to those held by the officers of the imperial court.
[25] Theophilos (*PmbZ* 8221 = *PBE* Theophilos 7) was related to Michael III and to caesar Bardas. He was count of the walls for some time and also domestic of the Noumera, a prison in the palace.
[26] Here meaning the Peloponnese.
[27] Mark 1:16, etc. Andrew was the chosen protector of Patras; he had protected it against the attacks of the Slavs established nearby in the ninth century: N. Oikonomides, 'St Andrew, Joseph the Hymnographer and the Slavs of Patras', *Leimôn: studies presented to Lennart Rydén on his*

apparently detained by his responsibilities. Later on, however, wishing to pay the usual homage to the Apostle, he seized the opportunity [122] of going into the church – alone. Now in the sacred church of the Apostle there lived a monk who had cultivated virtue all his life. When Theophilos came in with such a retinue the monk neither received him nor stood up to greet him nor even held him worth a few words. But later, when Basil came in alone (as we said), he rose up respectfully as if for one of the high and mighty ones and uttered an acclamation usually reserved for emperors. When some of the people who were present saw this, they reported it to the lady who ranked first in that region, by both her way of life and her high-birth, a lady named Danielis,[28] after her husband. Since she knew the monk was clairvoyant and possessed the gift of foretelling the future, she did not ignore what was told to her. As soon as she heard it, she summoned the monk and spoke to him reproachfully: 'All the time that you have known me, spiritual father, and have known that I outdistance all the people of this region in every way, never once have you risen respectfully on seeing me nor offered an invocation for me. You have accorded neither my son nor my grandson a similar compliment. How is it then that, just now, when you saw a man of no account, a penniless stranger earning his livelihood, you rose respectfully and greeted him like an emperor?' 'I did not see this man just as any other man,' the monk replied, 'but as one pre-ordained by Christ to be emperor of the Romans at God's behest, so I rose and offered him an acclamation; for man must surely honour those who are honoured by God.'

When he had discharged his commission, Theophilos took the road back to the capital while Basil remained in that same place, suffering from a physical illness. He received the treatment appropriate to his condition and then prepared for the return journey. The aforementioned Danielis summoned him to her presence, where she showered him with gifts and considerable favours. All she sought in return was [123] that he would bind himself to her son with the bond of spiritual brotherhood. Aware only of his own insignificance and the distinction of the woman,

---

sixty-fifth birthday, ed. J. O. Rosenqvist (Uppsala, 1996), 71–8; E. Kislinger, *Regionalgeschichte als Quellenproblem. Die Chronik von Monembasia und das sizilianische Demenna. Eine historisch-topographische Studie* (Vienna, 2001), 41–5.

[28] According to I. Ševčenko, 'Re-reading Constantine Porphyrogenitus', *Byzantine Diplomacy*, ed. J. Shepard and S. Franklin (SPBS, 1, Aldershot, 1992), 192–3, Danielis (i.e. "wife of Daniel") would have been an *archontissa* of the Peloponnese, meaning ruler of one of the autonomous enclaves created at the time of the Slav invasion, now peacefully reintegrated with the empire. Note that the text does not say she was a widow, yet she takes all the decisions, even for her son, which rather suggests that Daniel was no more.

he declined her request on the grounds that she outranked him. But he acceded to her more persistent requests and, when she had obtained what she desired, she decided not to conceal the will of God from him, but rather to reveal and make plain His mighty acts, foretold and revealed in ways of which she was well aware. Taking Basil aside privately, she said to him: 'You should know, young man, that God is going to set you up on high and appoint you master of the whole earth. I ask nothing more of you but that you be loving and merciful to me and to my descendants when my prophecy comes to pass.' He promised that, if God were to allow her prophecy to be fulfilled, he would, if it were possible, appoint her mistress of all that area. He took his leave of the woman and went off to join his own master at the capital. With the money accruing to him from this affair he purchased enough land in Macedonia to ensure a generous livelihood for all his relations,[29] but he remained in attendance on his master.

7. One day, Antigonos, commander of the scholai and the son of caesar Bardas, prepared a sumptuous feast. His father, who was to be the principal guest, came to the banquet bringing many other kinsmen, friends and acquaintances. There also came with him some Bulgars, acquaintances and friends, who happened to be staying in the capital.[30] Theophilos, the master of Basil, was also a guest at this lavish feast, for he was a relative of the caesar. When the wine was flowing freely and the banquet was in full swing, the Bulgars began to make preposterous statements and to brag about an athlete who was with them, celebrated for his physical strength. [124] They boasted that nobody could stand up to him in wrestling. Theophilos said to the caesar and before the assembled company: 'If it please your highness, there is one of my servants who could do battle with this famous Bulgar. It would be a great dishonour for the Romans if this fellow were to return to Bulgaria unchallenged.' The caesar approved his proposition and ordered the young man

---

[29] Here is one of the reasons why the fictitious story of Danielis is included. The entourage of Michael III was held to be corrupt and this accusation played an important role in the pro-Macedonian propaganda against Michael. Now Basil, the sometime close friend of Michael, became very rich prior to 866. The donation of Danielis was a convenient explanation of how this came about: S. Runciman, 'The widow Danielis', Etudes dédiées à la mémoire d'André M. Andréades, ed. K. Varvaressos (Athens, 1940), 425–30.

[30] It is not surprising that there were Bulgars at the court of Bardas, who was then ruling the empire. De cerimoniis speaks of Bulgar 'friends' participating in imperial banquets: N. Oikonomides, Les listes de préséance byzantines des IXe et Xe siècles: introduction, text, French translation and commentary (Le monde byzantin, Paris, 1972), 163.

to be brought before them. At this point the patrician Constantine,[31] the father of Thomas the logothete, a close friend of Basil because they were both of Armenian stock, noting that the place where the wrestlers were to contend was wet, scattered ashes and saw-dust on the floor to prevent them from slipping on the damp surface. When this was done, Basil came to grips with the Bulgar, grasping and strangling him like a newborn child. He lifted him up as easily as though he were a truss of hay or a fleece of wool and threw him on the table. This pleased the Romans no end, while it filled the Bulgars with shame. From that day the fame of Basil spread throughout the capital and his newly acquired distinction was on everybody's lips.

8. Then something happened which brought him even higher honours. The emperor Michael had a stiff-necked and refractory horse which exceeded every other horse that had ever been admired in size, comeliness, speed and beauty of appearance. But if it were let off the rope or otherwise set free, then it was very difficult indeed to bring back to hand, giving the grooms much trouble to get it under control. [125] One day the emperor went out hunting mounted on this horse. He managed to strike a hare with his staff, then leapt from the saddle to kill the hare. Left unattended, the horse galloped and bounded away. A host of grooms, officials and others of the emperor's retinue gave chase but nobody was able to catch the horse. In his anger the emperor ordered that, if the horse were taken, it was to be hamstrung. The caesar interceded with the emperor, begging him not to destroy such a magnificent steed in vain, for only one fault. While this discussion was taking place, Basil ran to his master and said: 'If I were to overtake the emperor's horse and, leaping from my own horse, were able to get astride of that one, would the emperor be angry with me for [sitting in] the imperial saddle and [handling] the purple bit and bridle?' [Theophilos] whispered this in the emperor's ear and *he* commanded it to be done. Basil skilfully spurred on his own horse in a direction parallel to the emperor's then suddenly leapt up and transferred himself to the imperial horse, to the immense amazement of those who were present and witnessed the deed. The emperor was astonished at [Basil's] competence and ability, not to mention his courage; he immediately relieved Theophilitzes of him and

---

[31] This is the logothete of the drome (previously droungarios of the watch, says *Theophanes Continuatus*, ed. Bekker, 150) mentioned above as the driver for the Greens in the races organised by Michael III. His son Thomas was, in his turn, logothete of the drome under Leo VI and during the minority of Constantine VII. Thomas was the father of the historian Genesios: A. Kaldellis, *Introduction to the translation of Genesios* (Canberra, 1998), xv–xvi.

enrolled him in his own corps of grooms. He took great delight in him and, very shortly, promoted him to be head groom.[32]

9. Another time, the emperor went out hunting near Philopation and his head groom rode before him bearing the emperor's flail[33] on his belt, at his side. When the company made a disturbance and let out a shout, an exceedingly large wolf leapt out of the bush. Basil raced after it and let fly a blow at it with the emperor's flail. [126] As luck would have it, he struck the beast in the middle of the head, splitting it in two. Following the emperor in the usual manner, the caesar, when he saw what had happened, privately remarked to one of his associates: 'My friend, I do believe that this man will be the complete ruin of our dynasty.' It is said that Leo the Philosopher prophesied this too. He called [Basil] by name and drew attention to some signs by pointing them out with his finger, foretelling: 'This one will be the ruin of your entire dynasty.'

10. Much as the caesar was trying to ensnare [Basil], he accomplished nothing, for it is exceedingly difficult to reverse something once it has been approved of by Providence. On another occasion, the emperor had crossed [the water] to go hunting at Armamenton;[34] after the hunt, he sat down to a banquet together with his mother, Theodora, some relatives and friends. At the emperor's command, the head groom was also invited. Fastening her eyes upon him, the empress examined and inspected everything about him. Recognising a certain portent and sign on him, she immediately suffered an attack of vertigo and fell down in a fainting fit. The emperor and his entourage were deeply disturbed; water and fragrant myrrh were brought immediately and, by sprinkling her with these, they brought the Sovereign Lady back from her calamity. As soon as she had regained her senses and emerged from the shades, the emperor, her son, asked her what had brought this sickness upon her. Scarcely herself again, she replied to her son in these words: 'O child, this fellow you call Basil will bring about the disappearance of our dynasty, for I saw in him a sign of which I was made aware and forewarned some time ago by your father. [127] At the sight of it my head spun and I fell to the ground.' But the emperor succeeded in assuaging his mother's fear, now using arguments to the contrary, now supplying information reinforced with oaths. Thus he was

---

[32] *Protostrator*; this was an official title and it placed Basil among the inner circle of Michael's associates. However, the title did not yet have the importance which it later acquired with the development of the cavalry.

[33] *Bardoukion*, a spiked ball on a chain attached to the end of a staff.

[34] The *armamenton* or arsenal was where ships were built for the imperial navy, possibly close to the Magnaura: R. Janin, *Constantinople byzantine* (*AOC*, 4A, Paris, 1964), 314. This does not, however, accord with our text as the emperor has to cross the straits to get to it.

able to bring her back to her former state and to comfort her, saying: 'My Sovereign Lady and mother, you should know that this is a generous man, of irresistible strength and with a spirit of incomparable nobility. He is faithful and devoted to us and bears us no grudge whatsoever.' And thus Basil escaped from that bad turn of fortune.

11. Damian the Chamberlain was a eunuch and Scythian holding the rank of patrician. He was very reproachful of the emperor's conduct because it was not of the standard required. He was especially reproachful of the conduct of [the emperor's] uncle, the caesar Bardas. Even the emperor (who was very dull and sluggish in the discharge of government affairs) was brought to the point of opposing the caesar and disallowed some of his acts, meaning to improve on them. This the caesar would not tolerate; he secretly conspired against Damian. He brought many accusations against him before the emperor and, since he managed to give them an air of credibility, he succeeded in diminishing the emperor's high esteem of Damian and getting him relieved of his office. With him dismissed, the office of chamberlain stood vacant for some time. The caesar and his clientele proposed first this candidate then another but divine Providence, which determines all things according to His will, rendered every endeavour and all devising of no avail. Some time later the emperor appointed Basil to be chamberlain, promoted him to the rank of patrician and married him to a woman who exceeded all other women of her age in physical elegance, beauty and sobriety. She was the daughter of Inger, renowned for his astuteness and nobility, [128] a scion of the house of the Martiniakioi.[35] When this happened, the caesar, raging with resentment, saw it as yet a further increase in the love which the emperor had for Basil; he feared for what was to come. He would often say to those who had prevailed upon him to get rid of Damian: 'Thanks to your bad advice, I chased out the fox and let in the lion – who will now gobble up the lot of us in one bite.'

12. By the time the emperor Michael set out against Crete together with his uncle, the caesar Bardas, this man was annoying the emperor a little more every day by his increasingly heavy hand in affairs of state. In this way he also gave the emperor's companions a pretext for intriguing against

---

[35] The prophecy of Theophilos' time is fulfilled (see Theophilos, c. 21 above). Eudokia (*PmbZ* 1632) seems to have had a somewhat varied romantic life, in spite of Skylitzes' assertion of her chastity. She was at this time the mistress of Michael III. See (principally) C. Mango, 'Eudocia Ingerina, the Normans and the Macedonian dynasty,' ZRVI, xiv–xv (1973), 17–27, repr. *Byzantium and its image* (London, 1984), xv, and E. Kislinger, 'Eudocie Ingerina, Basileios I und Michael III', *JÖB*, 33 (1983), 119–36. It is difficult to determine the precise date of the marriage but, as Skylitzes says, it was after Basil was promoted chamberlain to replace Damian in 864.

him. There is a place on the coast just where the river Meander discharges its waters into the sea that is called The Gardens. It was here that plotting and planning by the emperor's friends took place. They were in a hurry to eliminate Bardas as soon as possible so that *they* would not be overtaken [by him] and suffer worse than they might inflict. [He was slaughtered] clinging to the emperor's feet, as the narrative expressly stated (above); it was the first day of April, fourteenth year of the indiction.[36] As soon as Bardas was killed the emperor dispersed the army and turned his thoughts to returning home to the capital. When he arrived at Byzantium, since he had no heir of his own, he adopted Basil and raised him to the rank of magister.

13. This was intolerable to the malicious Symbatios, logothete of the drome and son-in-law of the [late] caesar Bardas. Claiming that he could no longer live in the capital, he petitioned to be made commander of the Thrakesion theme – which [129] appointment he received. A short time went by during which the administration of the empire was severely mismanaged, because the emperor's mind was on anything other than the execution of state business. Also, the death of Bardas had laid bare his utter incompetence and simplicity. As [Michael's] associate, Bardas had watched carefully over affairs of state and the administration in such a way that the emperor's ineptitude was concealed. But once Bardas was slain and the entire responsibility for the empire fell on the one emperor, then his incompetence and his lack of natural capability for state affairs stood out, clearly condemned. The common people started and continued to complain about the emperor. Neither the Senate nor the body politic as a whole was pleased with the way things were being done; even the army was troubled and disturbed. When the emperor was rendered cognisant of all this by those nearest to him, he realised that he was incapable of dealing with worldly undertakings and feared there might be an uprising. So he decided to take an associate with whom to share the power and the administration. As we said above, he had recently adopted Basil and he knew him to be distinguished above many others by his courage and intelligence; also that he was capable of compensating for [Michael's] own deficiency in piloting the ship of state. Since, moreover, he was prompted to do this by the Supreme Deity, he conferred upon Basil the distinction of imperial honour, renown and anointing on the holy day of Pentecost in the illustrious Church of the Wisdom of God. A public procession took place, then he placed the imperial crown on Basil's head; this was on the

---

[36] Actually 21 April 866.

twenty-sixth of May, fourteenth year of the indiction. When Symbatios heard of this [130] he did not take kindly to it; in association with the patrician Peganes, then commander of the Opsikion theme, he prepared to rebel.[37] They acclaimed the emperor Michael in order to win over the people and to avoid the appearance of raising their hands against the *autokrator*, but they insulted Basil, heaping insolence upon him; this was in the summer.[38] Then the arrival of winter dispersed their support and the leaders of this madness fled for their lives, Symbatios to the strong and easily defensible fortress of Plateia Petra[39] in Asia, Peganes to Kotyaeon.[40] Nevertheless, shortly afterwards they were successfully assailed and brought before the emperor himself as prisoners. Their eyes were put out, Symbatios' right hand was cut off, Peganes' nose was slit and then they were sent off into exile.

14. All the subjects of the Roman empire rejoiced at the proclamation of Basil [as emperor] for they yearned to see sitting at the helm of the empire a man who well knew from his own experience how the simple people were afflicted by the rich and powerful. Michael's regime was pain and grief to them; all softness and luxury with nothing else to do but indulge in 'rioting and drunkenness',[41] point-to-point horse racing, playing the fool and other worn-out old tricks. All this, as I stated above briefly in passing, emptied the imperial treasury prodigiously on catamites, harpists, dancers and a host of other licentious folk. From this [extravagance] the business of the Roman government came into a parlous state and so did the emperor, for want of funds. At a loss [131] what to do, he devised some unjust taxes to supply his need. He laid unholy hands on things which it was altogether prohibited for him to touch. He and a pack of defiled and licentious transvestites even went so far as to ridicule the Godhead! There was nothing unmentionable which was not committed in word or deed by him and the like-minded consorts who bore him company. Basil wished to turn him aside from this inappropriate behaviour and tried many times

---

[37] Symbatios was *strategos* of the Thrakesion theme, hence it was in the western part of Asia Minor that the rebellion broke out. On George Peganes: *PmbZ* 2263 = *PBE* Georgios 57.
[38] Summer 866. This revolt has recently been studied by A. Dapergolas, 'La révolte du stratège Symbatios et de George Peganes dans l'été 866', *14e Congrès panhellénique* (Thessalonike, 1994), 13–25. The author opines that Basil was much less popular with the troops of Asia Minor than Bardas, who had several times led them to victory. Yet neither the chronology of this uprising nor the motives of the insurgents are clearly understood.
[39] The location of this fortress is unsure, but it was on the border between the Opsikion and Thrakesion themes.
[40] A fortress of considerable importance, today Kutahya: K. Belke and N. Mersich, *Phrygien und Pisidien* (TIB, 7, Vienna, 1990), 312–16.
[41] Rom. 13:13.

to do so; he not only failed, but rather provoked the emperor to anger and to devise sinister and monstrous intrigues against him, as we said above.

15. Alarmed by the incessant plotting and scheming against him, Basil endeavoured to take the initiative before he fell victim himself. He provided himself with some associates, relations and soldiers who were guards of the imperial bedchamber and then slew Michael in the palace of St Mamas, the Great Martyr. Thus Michael came to the end of a life of undisciplined extravagance. Basil was immediately proclaimed sole ruler: first by the conspirators, then by the Senate, the imperial regiments, the entire army and the people of the City.[42] Immediately on acceding to the supreme command he convened the Senate and the ranking dignitaries and had the imperial treasury opened. Where there had once been so much wealth, now there was nothing more to be found (as we said above) than three mere *kentenaria*. The emperor sought the record of expenditures and found it in the care of an old eunuch.[43] Once he could see where the money had gone, he put the matter before a meeting of those of high standing. They gave [132] their unanimous decision that those who had received [funds] illegally were to return them to the treasury. Basil, however, very generously ordered that a half of what each one had received was to be returned to the imperial paymaster.[44] Thus there accrued to the public purse from those people three hundred *kentenaria* of gold.[45] The emperor then went in public procession to the Great Church of the Wisdom of the Word of God and on the way back he scattered a considerable amount of money to the crowd, money not from the public treasury but from his own purse.[46] There also accrued to him a large amount of unexpected money, from treasure coming to light that had been hidden in the ground.[47] There was also found in the private apartments no small amount of gold which the former emperor, Michael, had collected when he had that renowned plane tree melted down, the two golden griffins, the two lions of beaten gold, the solid gold organ, various pieces of gold work

---

[42] *The Chronicle of the Logothete*, (*Symeonis magistri*, 257–9) gives a fuller account of the taking of the palace. After the assassination Basil and his companions cross the Golden Horn, stop at the house of Eulogios the Persian and then, with the cooperation of Artavasdes, commander of the guard, they get into the outer precinct of the palace, seize the keys from the Papias and open the door.
[43] Basil the protospatharios.
[44] A usurper must show moderation in his confiscations.
[45] 2.176 million pieces of gold, equal to 9,900 kgs at 4.55 g to the nomisma.
[46] Another excellent move on the part of a usurper who must show his interest in the common good. John Tzimiskes did likewise: reign of John Tzimiskes, c. 3.
[47] On the legislation concerning treasure trove, see C. Morrisson, 'La découverte des trésors à l'époque byzantine: théorie et pratique', *TM*, 8 (1981), 321–43, repr. *Monnaie et finances à Byzance: analyses, techniques* (Aldershot, 1994), VII. Under Basil all treasure trove went to the public purse.

for use at table and even the robes for emperors and their ladies.[48] He was going to use all that to satisfy his desires, but fate determined otherwise and it passed to Basil; more about that, however, later.

16. As soon as Basil came to power, first of all he chose and appointed to the leading positions men who could not be corrupted and who had the reputation of keeping their hands clean from all bribe-taking.[49] Then he turned his attention to justice, instituting equity among his subjects and striving to prevent the rich from lording it over the poor. He promulgated regulations prescribing the total elimination of [133] injustice; he appointed judges, providing them with living allowances and all kinds of emoluments. He ordered that they were to be in court every day, settling the differences between litigants.[50] He also provided suitable locations for them, the Magnaura, the [building] called the Hippodrome[51] and the [Gate] known as Chalke, dilapidated by the passage of time and now more in danger of falling down than ever, so he refurbished and renovated it. He stipulated a living allowance for the poorer litigants so that they would not be obliged by want to withdraw from their cases.[52] When he was free from military affairs and from receiving the embassies which came from all parts, he too would devote himself to the hearing of cases. He would go down to what they call the genikon to examine those who were under investigation by the treasury, to see whether anybody was being investigated unjustly; in this way he used to come to the assistance of those who were suffering undeservedly. They say that once when he went down to perform the task just mentioned there was nobody before the tribunal. Suspecting that somebody was preventing the needy from coming before him, he sent gendarmes into many parts of the city to seek for anybody who was in need. When they returned saying that they had not been able to find any person whomsoever, [the emperor] shed tears of joy and gave

---

[48] This accusation has already be levelled: reign of Michael III, c. 10. Michael could not have destroyed all his father's treasures because some of the wonders were still in operation in the next century when Liutprand of Cremona saw them: *ODB*, 1, 235.

[49] The *Vita Basilii* says nothing of any hostile reactions to Basil, yet Niketas Ooryphas, droungarios of the fleet, was prepared to avenge the dead emperor when he heard of the death of Michael III. Basil succeeded in winning him over sometime later though: pseudo-Symeon the Logothete, 687. Ooryphas took part in the recapture of Bari, see c. 26 below.

[50] Judges were paid by the litigants on both sides; thus every reform aimed at providing a sufficient salary from the state with the intention of reducing the judges' demands for money on those who appealed to them. Andronikos I Komnenos (1183–5) attempted a similar reform.

[51] This is the *covered* Hippodrome: R. Guilland, *Études de topographie de Constantinople byzantine* (Amsterdam, 1969), 1, 199. It is from this central court that the expression 'Hippodrome judge' arises. These could be commissioned to serve as provincial judges on occasion too.

[52] Basil wants to follow in the footsteps of Theophilos, justice being one of the prime virtues in a ruler.

thanks to God. He did, however, notice that there was some opportunity for wicked men to act unjustly in the method of expressing fractions (half, sixth, twelfth and so forth) when the scribes used the old shorthand signs; he decided to suppress this opportunity of cheating completely. So he stipulated that henceforth [fractions] were to be expressed by simple letters of the alphabet which could be easily read by the peasants.[53] He also took it upon himself to pay the cost of the parchment and writing [materials] plus the scribes' fees. He also changed the direction of ecclesiastical affairs by expelling from his archbishopric [134] Photios the usurper, at a meeting of the Synod. He was ordered into retirement until God should remove his legitimate predecessor from this life. [Basil] reinstated Ignatios who had been wickedly and uncanonically removed by Bardas. Thus he conferred calm on the churches of God.[54] Seeing, moreover, that the civil law was far from clear and in a state of confusion, he made haste to reform it in an appropriate manner. He deleted some laws because they were obsolete and reduced the number of the laws still in force. Death intervened too soon, so this undertaking was completed by Leo, his son and successor.[55]

17. In the first year of Basil's reign there was a conspiracy against him instigated by the patricians George and Symbatios.[56] When the crime was detected and damning evidence came to light, they had their eyes put out for being the initiators of the plot; the entire company of the rest of the conspirators was paraded before the public and sent into exile. To cut short the machinations of other would-be emperors, he crowned Constantine and Leo, his own sons, and in the third year of his sole reign he proclaimed

---

[53] This means that fractions were to be written out as words, which probably exaggerates the ability of peasants to read. Yet this reform may have produced some results.

[54] In fact Basil had participated (in his role of co-emperor) in the synod of summer 867 and had signed its Acts. That synod which took place before the murder of Michael was Photios' moment of triumph. The acts of that synod were later destroyed on Basil's orders. There is now only one contemporary account of it, Photios' eighteenth homily: C. Mango, *The Homilies of Photius, patriarch of Constantinople: English translation, introduction and commentary* (Cambridge, MA, 1958), 297–315. Basil immediately deposed Photios when he became sole emperor, using the permanent synod, *endemousa*: J. Hajjar, *Le synod permanent (Sunodos endemousa) dans l'Eglise byzantine au XIe siècle* (Rome, 1962). Ignatios was solemnly reinstalled on 23 November 867: G. Dagron, *Histoire du christianisme*, IV, *Evêques, moines et empereurs (610–1054)*, ed. G. Dagron, P. Riché and A. Vauchez (Paris, 1993), 176–7.

[55] Basil undertook to reclassify the judicial material in the *Corpus iuris civilis*. The sixty books of the new law code, called the 'imperial laws' (*basilika*), were eventually completed under Leo VI by Christmas 888: A. Schminck, *Subseciva Groningana*, 3 (1989), 90–3.

[56] Skylitzes' presentation is a bit clumsy from a chronological point of view. This is the revolt of Symbatios, strategos of the Thrakesion theme and of Peganes, count of the Opsikion theme already mentioned above. This revolt took place after Basil's coronation but before his sole rule began.

[emperor] his third son, Alexander.[57] Stephen, the youngest of all his sons, he dedicated to and enrolled in the church of God. As he also had four daughters; these he dedicated to the sacred monastery of the universally praised martyr Euphemia.[58]

18. [1345] When he had settled the affairs of state to his satisfaction, he hastened to make war on the forces which were hostile to the Roman state.[59] The strength of the army had been diminished under Michael, the former ruler, by the reduction of pay and provisions. Basil now filled up the ranks by the recruitment of young men and marched out against the barbarians. First he marched to Tephrike, which was in the hands of Chrysocheir,[60] a man who, seeming to excel in boldness and cunning, frequently made inroads on Roman territory and pillaged it. The emperor directed his attack against this man and that city; the enemy, unable to withstand him, took refuge within the walls. The emperor overran and pillaged all the land under Chrysocheir and set up camp against the wall of Tephrike, thinking that he would take the fortification by a protracted siege. But when he realised that it was strongly fortified at all points and that it was hopeless to reduce it by siege, and also that they were running short of everything that might be taken from the land, he lifted the siege after sacking the fortified towns near Tephrike: Abara, Koptos, Spathe[61]

[57] Constantine, Basil's first and favourite son, was the child of his first marriage but S. Tougher, *The reign of Leo VI (886–912): politics and people* (Leiden, 1997), 42–67, and P. Grierson (*DOC*, III, 474) think he (as well as Leo) was borne by Eudokia Ingerina. This view has the support of sources hostile to Basil which portray Constantine as a son of Michael when they speak of his demise: e.g. *George the Monk, Theophanes Continuatus*, ed. I. Bekker (CSHB, Bonn, 1838), 844. However, it looks as though Constantine was considerably older than his brothers. He was associated with the purple between November 867 and February 868; Leo was not associated until 6 January 870 and Alexander not until after the death of Constantine, between September and November 879: *DOC*, III, 1:473–5.

[58] Basil may have been concerned that no family gain undue importance by supplying him with a son-in-law. The church in question is St Euphemia of Petrion, which became a family monastery where many relatives of Basil were interred: R. Janin, *La géographie ecclésiastique de l'empire byzantin*, I: *La siège de Constantinople et le patriarcat œcuménique*, III: *Les églises et les monastères de l'empire byzantin* (Paris, 1969), 127–9.

[59] The campaign of 871 follows the audacious raids of Chrysocheir who thrust as far as Nikomedia and Ephesos, following the collapse of negotiations with Peter of Sicily the year before. The report of that embassy is the only major source extant on the Paulicians: P. Lemerle, 'L'histoire des Pauliciens d'Asie Mineure d'après les sources grecques', *TM*, 5 (1973), 1–144, at 103. For the text see 'L'Histoire de Pierre de Sicile', ed. P. Lemerle *TM*, chs. 4 and 5, p. 8 (translation) and p. 9 (Greek text).

[60] Karbeas (already mentioned, reign of Michael II, c. 8) who had founded the Paulician army died in 863 (this had nothing to do with the defeat and death of his ally Amr, emir of Melitene). Karbeas was succeeded without difficulty by Chrysocheir, his nephew and son-in-law: Lemerle, *Pauliciens*, 95–6.

[61] Abara was a fortress on the road to Sebasteia, south of Tephrike: E. Honigmann, *Die Ostgrenze des byzantinischen Reiches von 363–1071 nach griechischen, arabischen, syrischen und armenischen*

and many others. He gathered up the army and came back from there with glorious trophies and much booty. While the territory surrounding Tephrike was being laid waste and sacked, its neighbouring town, called Taras,[62] which was in the hands of the Ishmaelites and had a defensive alliance and joint enterprise with [136] Tephrike, apprehensive of the danger it was in, sent a delegation to sue for peace and asking to be enlisted as confederates, fighting with the Romans. The emperor gave the delegation a mild reception and the request was granted. Then there was Kourtikios,[63] an Armenian by race, master of Lokana,[64] who frequently sacked and devastated the Roman border regions; he delivered himself, his city and the people under him into the emperor's hands. Meanwhile the emperor sent a body of choice warriors against the [town] called Zapetra and they took Samosata[65] too, by falling on it in a sudden attack after passing through a narrow defile. The city was taken by surprise; many of the people were slain and an innumerable host was led into captivity while [some] Roman prisoners were freed of the fetters they had worn for a long time. This expeditionary force put the adjacent territory to the flames and sacked Samosata. In the same forward thrust they crossed the Euphrates, took all the people on the further bank captive, collected a great quantity of prisoners and booty, then returned safe and sound to the emperor who was now encamped on the river Atzarnouk. Then the emperor broke camp and travelled the road to Melitene with the whole army. When he reached the Euphrates, he found it in full summer flood and quite impassable, so he had a bridge built by which he crossed over. Much of the countryside was sacked and laid waste; a fortified town named Rhapsakion was taken, then a portion of the army was detached with orders to overrun the territory between Arsinos and the Euphrates. They rushed through it with remarkable rapidity, sacking a town [137] called Karkikion, then Chachon,[66] Aman, Mourex and Abdela.[67] The emperor himself pressed on to Melitene, well populated at that time and illustrious for its multitude

---

Quellen (CBHB, 3, Brussels, 1935), 56. Koptos, perhaps the present Koubdin, was also to the south of Tephrike, halfway to Abra. According to the Escorial *taktikon*, Koptos was the seat of a strategos a century later: Oikonomides, *Listes*, 359. Of Spathe nothing is known.

[62] Taras is the present Derende, the Byzantine Taranta, situated three days' march west of Melitene. It was the seat of a strategos: Oikonomides, *Listes*, 359.

[63] Ancestor of the Kourtikioi who provided so many officers for the empire: A. P. Kazhdan, *Armjane v sostave gospodstvujuščego klassa vizantijskoj imperii v XI–XII vv.* (Erivan, 1975), 14–17.

[64] Location uncertain.

[65] The insertion of Samosata at this point confuses the sense of the passage; might it be an interpolation?

[66] Elsewhere written as Chlascon, Glaschon, Glachon.

[67] For possible identification of these places: Honigmann, *Ostgrenze*, 59–60.

of barbarians. When he approached the walls, he encountered some columns of barbarian infantry which attacked, snorting and yelling at him. The emperor engaged them boldly, himself at the head of his troops, and threw them back, while the other troops pursued the rest of them right to the city, killing so many of them that the intervening space was strewn and filled with corpses. More than a few were captured alive: the rest shut themselves up ingloriously within the walls. The emperor wished to take the place with siege engines, but then he realised how well the city was provided with towers and with what defending forces the walls bristled. When he learnt from deserters that they had an abundance of the necessities of life and feared nothing from a protracted siege, he struck camp and marched against the land of the Manichees. Everything wherever they went was reduced to ashes; the fortified towns called Argaouth, Koutakios, Stephanos and Arachach[68] went up in flames. He then gathered up his army and made his way to the capital. He honoured the most distinguished of the soldiers and dismissed them while he himself went on to the capital, passing through Thrace. He went in a solemn public procession from Hebdomon and through the Golden Gate, celebrating the most magnificent of triumphs, all the people acclaiming him with songs of victory and rousing cheers. He proceeded to the Church of the personified Wisdom of God;[69] there he offered hymns of thanksgiving to God and was adorned with crowns of victory by Ignatios, the patriarch. Then he returned to the palace where, [138] after a brief respite with his wife and children, he occupied himself again with matters of state.

19. In the following year Chrysocheir, the chieftain of the Manichees, invaded Roman territory with a powerful army and devastated it.[70] The emperor sent the officer commanding the scholai[71] as usual. He took with him the entire Roman army but, since he was afraid to risk the whole enterprise on one formal battle, he followed [Chrysocheir] at a certain distance for the time being, putting a stop to some inroads and not allowing them to rampage through the countryside with impunity. Having met with some success and some reverses, the barbarian was thinking of going

---

[68] The form Argaouth is found too, both in Skylitzes and in *Theophanes Continuatus*. It should be Argaoun. *Theophanes Continuatus* calls the place Rachat.
[69] On Basil's triumph (which was meant to rival the triumphs celebrated by the Amorion dynasty): M. McCormick, *Eternal victory: triumphal rulership in late antiquity, Byzantium, and the early medieval west* (Cambridge, MA, 1986), 152–7.
[70] He penetrated as far as Ankyra: Lemerle, *Paulicians*, 103.
[71] Christopher, *gambros* to the emperor (the husband of a daughter or, more probably, a sister of Basil who, as we saw, had shut his daughters away in a convent), had succeeded Marianos, the emperor's brother.

back home and set off with a great deal of booty. The domestic of the scholai detailed two of the commanders, those of the Charsianon[72] and the Armeniakon themes, and their forces to go along with Chrysocheir as far as the place named Bathyrryax.[73] If he were to send his troops against the Roman border lands (said the emperor), then they had to let him know about it; but if [the enemy] made to go directly home, they were to let them be and return to the main body of the army. Evening came and the barbarian army was at Bathyrryax, encamped at the foot of the mountain. While the commanders mentioned above (who occupied a more elevated position) were waiting to see what the future would bring, a contention and rivalry arose between the two thematic armies concerning the matter of seniority. Those of the Charsianon held that to them belonged the primacy for courage while the men of the Armeniakon theme claimed it for themselves. The rivalry was becoming increasingly intense as each company gave free rein to its boasting when (so they say) this was said by somebody from the Armeniakon side: 'Fellow soldiers, why this unseemly and pointless boasting [139] when we can prove our worth beyond all doubt by deeds? The enemy is at hand; it is possible for the better men to be revealed in action.' The commanders bore these words in mind and took note of the men's desire to show their courage. They were also aware of their advantageous position, in that they were about to attack from high ground an enemy lying in a hollow. They divided their forces into two, of which one, consisting of about six hundred picked men[74] led by the commanders themselves, was to attack the barbarian army. The remainder, the greater portion of the Roman army, was stationed on the heights in such a way as to appear even more numerous than it really was. It was agreed that when the smaller group attacked the enemy, the larger one was to raise a frightening pandemonium with loud shouts and braying of trumpets (to which the mountains would give echo). The [smaller portion] approached the enemy camp under cover of night, unseen. The sun had not yet caressed the mountain tops when the agreed signal was given and a great paean of shouting broke out with cries of 'the Cross

---

[72] This is the first mention of a strategos of Charsianon, previously a mere *kleisoura*.

[73] Meaning 'deep stream'. This was the usual base camp (*aplekton*) when a campaign against the Paulicians was being conducted: *Constantine Porphyrogenitus: three treatises on imperial military expeditions: introduction, edition, translation and commentary*, ed. J. F. Haldon (CFHB, 28, Vienna, 1990), 80.

[74] This number gives some idea of the size of the forces on either side: surely no more than a few thousand men. On the strengths of the Byzantine army: J.-C. Cheynet, 'Les effectifs de l'armée byzantine (Xe–XIIe)', *Cahiers de Civilisation Médiévale*, 38/4 (1995), 319–35 = Cheynet, *Aristocracy*, no. XII.

has conquered!' as they attacked the enemy, while the rest of the troops up in the mountains joined in raising the battle-cry. The barbarians were immediately dismayed by the hopelessness of the situation; they did not take time to get themselves organised or to estimate the strength of the opposing forces. Unable on the spur of the moment to devise any plan to save themselves, they began to retreat. The pursuing Romans called upon the absent commanders and units plus the officer commanding the scholai, according to orders. The fugitives became ever more afraid and troubled as they were pursued to a distance of thirty miles, the intervening countryside being strewn with innumerable corpses. It was then that the ruthless Chrysocheir (who was running away with a few of his followers) recognised the Roman who was pursuing him as a man named Poulades whom he had once held prisoner at Tephrike and with whom he had associated and thus become acquainted because he was so cultured and charming. Having seen and recognised him, he turned round and said: 'What harm have I done you, wretched Poulades, that you pursue me insanely like this, anxious to do away with me?' The other snapped back: 'I have full confidence [140] in God, sir, that this very day I am to deliver you the reward of your good deeds.' [Chrysocheir] rode on like somebody whose wits had been deranged by a stroke of lightning while the other pursued [him] with the recklessness of youth. Just as the fugitive found himself facing a deep ditch over which he could not let his horse jump, he was struck from behind by Poulades who had caught up to him, a blow in the side with a javelin. His head spun from the pain and he fell from the saddle. One of his company, whose name was Diakonitzes,[75] leapt from his horse to tend the fallen man, laying his head on his own knees and lamenting what had happened. Meanwhile Poulades was joined by others, who dismounted and cut off the head of Chrysocheir who was already in his death throes and giving up the ghost. They bound Diakonitzes and set him among the other prisoners. Reports were immediately sent to the emperor and the head of Chrysocheir with them. With the fall of Chrysocheir the flourishing manhood of Tephrike withered away. Such was the conclusion of the Tephrike affair; in one hour the great multitude of the Manichaeans, lifted up to the very pinnacle of glory, was dissipated like smoke.[76]

20. Ignatios departed this present life, and the emperor immediately handed back the church to Photios.[77]

---

[75] This Paulician would live to fight magnificently in southern Italy under the command of Nikephorus Phokas the elder: see below, c. 38.
[76] Ps. 67:3, LXX. [77] Ignatios died on 23 October 877.

138   *John Skylitzes: a synopsis of Byzantine history*

21. Then a plot was revealed to the emperor by one of the conspirators; the patrician Romanos Kourkouas was at the head of it.[78] When the conspirators had been arrested, Kourkouas was blinded while the others were beaten, tonsured and sent into exile.

22. [141] The emperor himself repossessed the fortress of Loulon which the Saracens had captured.[79] To this he added [the fortress] of Melouos,[80] which acknowledged the authority of the emperor. He also personally ravaged Kama,[81] the Manichaeans' capital.

23. When the light of spring began to shine, he set out on campaign against Syria taking his oldest son, Constantine, with him.[82] He reached Caesarea close to Argeon, the first [city] of Cappadocia, and there pitched his camp. He set the greater part of the army to work at military exercises but sent a detachment out to reconnoitre, himself following in their train.[83] The scouts and forerunners quickly traversed the desert regions, destroying the fortress called Psilokastron and the one called Phyrokastron[84] and taking their occupants prisoner. The occupants of the fortress of Phalakros[85] were so alarmed that they voluntarily surrendered themselves to the Romans. Apabdele, son of Ambron,[86] emir of Anabarzos,[87] boldly played the barbarian as long as the emperor was a long way off; but when he drew near, he joined the fleeing garrison of Melitene, seeking safety in flight like them. The emperor destroyed Kasarma, Karva, Ardala and Eremosykea.[88] It was then that the renowned Semas, son of Tael,[89] who held the unapproachable fastnesses of the Taurus from which he had been

---

[78] The conspiracy of John Kourkouas took place at the end of Basil's reign, see below.
[79] This was in 877; it opened up a new route by which the Romans could attack Tarsus, via the Podandos pass. Loulon was a link in the chain of fire signals: reign of Michael III, c. 19.
[80] Milvan Kale today, 18 km south-east of Podandos: F. Hild and M. Restle, *Kappadokien (Kappadokia, Charsianon, Sebasteia und Lykandos)* (TIB, 2, Vienna, 1981), 82.
[81] The name is deformed: *Theophanes Continuatus*, ed. Bekker, 278, gives Katavatala. This cannot be the Kama, 80 km south-west of Erzican: Hild and Restle *Kappadokien*, 82, n. 209.
[82] Since Constantine was still alive, this campaign has to be dated 878.
[83] This type of operation (which meant sending detachments out some distance from the main army) is well described for Muslim expeditionary forces in the *Traité sur la guerre de course* edited in the tenth century: *Traité*, ed. Dagron and Mihàescu, c. x.
[84] One of these two strongholds on the road from Caesarea to Melitene might be identified with Mehkiran Kalesi: Hild and Restle, *Kappadokien*, 237.
[85] Agiloren today, to the south of Mount Argeon: Hild and Restle, *Kappadokien*, 257–8.
[86] Abd'Allah, the son of Amr.
[87] The usual form of the name is Anazarbos. It is one of the main strongholds of Cilicia, protecting the capital of the emirate at Tarsus : F. Hild and H. Hellenkemper, *Kilikien und Isaurien* (TIB, 5, Vienna, 1990), 178–85.
[88] This list of fortlets of no great importance is included to inflate the magnitude of Basil's success.
[89] Símá al-Twawíl, emir of Tarsus : A. A. Vasiliev, *Byzance et les Arabes*, I: *La dynastie d'Amorium, 820–867* (Brussels, 1935); II: *Les relations politiques de Byzance et des arabes à l'époque de la dynastie macédonienne*, ed. M. Canard (CBHB 2, 1, Brussels, 1968), 11/1:87.

Basil I the Macedonian

wasting the Romans' border lands, fled to the emperor for refuge. Then the emperor crossed the river Onopniktes, the Saros too,[90] and came to Koukousos[91] with his army. He cleaned out the brush that was there, turned the pathless waste [142] into a serviceable road and captured the hideouts that were there. When he got to Kalipolis and Padasia, finding very bad and hilly roads, he himself went at the head of the army, walking on foot to encourage his men. When he had passed through the passes of the Taurus he attacked Germanicaea.[92] The opposing forces had all barricaded themselves within the walls and nobody ventured to confront [the Romans]. So the [emperor] set fire to and destroyed the desirable properties outside the city then moved on to the city of Adata.[93] Here too the inhabitants would not fight in the open but hid within the walls, so the emperor laid waste and reduced to ashes all that was outside the walls. He then invested the small town called Geron; he let his soldiers pillage then attacked the walls of the city, bringing up all kinds of machines. The siege was conducted with vigour because he had good hopes of taking the city, given the size of his forces. But he found that those within were putting up stiff resistance and were bearing their afflictions boldly, so he declared a truce and asked the defenders the reason for their confidence and why they obviously considered him with so little regard, even though their city was about to be taken. One of the elders replied that they were informed that their city would not be taken by him; fate dictated that it would be taken by somebody else of the same race whose name was Constantine. This was why they were not dismayed by their afflictions. The emperor showed them his son and told them his name was Constantine, to which the informant replied that it was not this Constantine who would overturn their city but another, some time later, one of [Basil's] descendants.[94] These words angered the emperor; now he intensified the siege, intending to condemn the prophecy as false by his deeds. But in spite of everybody's valiant effort, he could see that no progress was being made; also the weather turned bitterly cold, to the intense discomfort of men out in the open air, so he raised

---

[90] The Tzamantî su and the Seyan.
[91] Present Goksun, halfway between Caesarea and Germanicaea. Basil installed himself in the heart of the Taurus mountains.
[92] Today, Marash in the Anti-taurus, on the edge of the Mesopotamian plain, controlling one of the main routes into Syria. Germanicaea was the birthplace of Nestorius and of Leo III the Isaurian; it was much fought over by Romans and Arabs in the eighth and ninth centuries: *ODB*, II, 845.
[93] Today Seraykoy, north-east of Germanicaea, commanding one of the passes into Cappadocia: G. Dagron and H. Mihàescu, *Le traité sur la guérilla de l'empereur Nicéphore Phocas* (Paris, 1986), 125.
[94] Obviously a reference to Basil's grandson, Constantine VII, under whom (in 957) Adata was permanently conquered and then became the centre of a small theme: Oikonomides, *Listes*, 359.

the siege. As they were about to turn back, he disencumbered himself by commanding most of the prisoners who were impeding his progress to be put to the sword, then he took the road to the capital, leaving the sons of Hagar greatly afraid. [143] In anticipation of attack, he set up ambushes in the passes at suitable points and captured many who had been lying in wait hoping to surprise him. For that reason the resistance of the local chief, Abdelomeler,[95] collapsed and he sent a delegation suing for security and peace. The emperor acceded to his request and from then on had him as a willing ally against his own people. Passing through Argeon he came to Caesaraea, where he received news of victory from Koloneia and Mesopotamia. He also took delivery of much booty and of many captive Kurds[96] and Saracens, whom he had put to the sword, every one, because the army was already encumbered with much booty and many prisoners from Syria and Tephrike and he did not want to take along the additional burden, an impediment to further action. When he came to Medaeion[97] and had distributed awards to those who had distinguished themselves, he sent them into winter quarters and himself, lightly armed, went towards the capital. He received the customary crown of victory from the patriarch and triumphal songs from the multitude.[98]

24. With Tephrike going into decline the vigour of Tarsus began to blossom and flourish and, once again, the borders of Roman territory began to suffer severely. The general Andrew, a Scyth in origin, frequently went boldly against them, killing and taking prisoner many of those who came a-raiding. The emperor honoured him with the title of patrician and promoted him to the command of the scholai.[99] Now that he enjoyed higher authority and disposed of greater forces, Andrew attacked and frequently defeated the people of Melitene and Tarsus in illustrious battles. There came a time when the emir of Tarsus sent a letter (full of blasphemy) to Andrew which said: 'I will see whether the son of Mary or she who bore him will help you in any way when [144] I march out against you with my forces.' When Andrew received this abusive letter he hung it on the icon of

---

[95] There is no mention of this name in the Arab sources.
[96] Skylitzes here departs from the text of the *Vita Basilii*, *Theophanes Continuatus*, 283, where it is stated that Basil had received intelligence from Koloneia and from Loulon and that the mass of captives consisted of people from Tarsus and of Manichees: Lemerle, *Pauliciens*, 106–7.
[97] Located not too far from the great military camp at Dorylaion: Belke and Mersich, *Phrygien und Pisidien*, 341–2.
[98] For a description of this triumph, *Constantine Porphyrogenitus,* Haldon, commentary: McCormick, *Eternal victory*, 212–22.
[99] Andrew had previously been count of the Opsikion theme: W. Seibt, *Die byzantinischen Bleisiegel in Österreich*, I, *Kaiserhof* (Vienna, 1978), 242.

Basil I the Macedonian 141

the Mother of God, declaring: 'Behold, mother of the Word and of God; and do you, her son and God, behold; behold how this insulting barbarian disparages and abuses both you and the people who are special to you.'[100] Having said these words, he assembled the Roman forces and marched out against Tarsus. He advanced to Podandos[101] and there joined battle with the enemy. The barbarian host was put to flight with great loss of life, the emir himself taking an early fall. Only a few, and they with great difficulty, found refuge in Tarsus. [Andrew] buried his own people, then his opponents in a single mass grave, and had a great column erected on it as a memorial for later generations, after which he returned to his base with plenty of booty and prisoners. He wrote to the emperor reporting the victory.

25. But just as usually happens where envy is at work, evil men maligned him before the emperor saying that just when it would have been easy for him to have taken Tarsus he had failed to grasp the opportune moment through sloth and negligence. This was said so often that the emperor came to believe it and relieved the man of his command, appointing a man named Stypeiotes[102] in his stead. This man promised (among many other impossible feats) that he would take Tarsus. He assembled the forces without delay and marched them off against Tarsus with no plan of campaign in mind whatsoever, indeed with no clear intention. When he got near to Tarsus he stopped for the night at a place called Chrysoboullon but he made nothing worth calling an earthwork or a fortified encampment. The people of Tarsus received intelligence reports that he was heedlessly lying there, so they attacked him by night using the following stratagem. They had been reduced in numbers by their defeat at the hands of Andrew and were insufficient for a formal battle, so they gathered together a large number of horses, to the tails of which they attached dried pelts and set them on fire. At a given signal [145] they loosed these beasts at several points around the Roman encampment. Coming behind them, in charged the men of Tarsus with naked swords, making a great din with trumpets and drums. Fear and trembling now afflicted the Roman army. Horses and men were equally afraid and kept running into each other, so that the barbarians were able to get the upper hand and to inflict unlimited

---

[100] This refers to Exod. 19:5, Deut. 7:6, 14:2, 26:18, meaning Israel.
[101] A fortress commanding a pass which led into Cilicia: Hild and Restle, *Kappadokien*, 261–2. It was at the centre of the public domains or *episkepsis*: reign of John Tzimiskes, c. 22.
[102] This is the first mention of a member of that family which was to provide the state with so many officers, into the era of the Palaiologoi: O. Kresten, 'Zum Sturz des Theodoros Styppeiotes', *JÖB*, 27 (1978), 49–103.

slaughter on the Romans, most of whom perished ingloriously, trodden down or smothered by their own people.[103] When the men of Tarsus had carried off this unexpected victory and decimated the Roman forces, they broke out into barbarous howling of victory songs.

26. So much for eastern affairs; the narrative will now speak of the west. Here as elsewhere things had been badly neglected for a long time during the reign of Michael. Nearly the entire area of Italy which belonged to the Roman empire and the greater part of Sicily had been overcome by the Carthaginian forces and the people there were now paying taxes to the barbarians. Likewise those in Pannonia and Dalmatia and the adjacent Scyths, Croats, Serbs, Zachlouboi, Terbounitotes, Kanalites, Diocletians and Rhentanoi had renounced the Roman yoke to which they had long been subject and asserted their autonomy.[104] In due course the Hagarenes of Carthage attacked too with Soldan, Sabas and Kalphous[105] in command, men acknowledged [146] by their fellow countrymen to have given evidence of outstanding military experience. They dispatched a fleet of thirty-six warships against Dalmatia and were able to take several of its cities such as Boutoma, Rhosa and Kato Dekatora.[106] Since everything was going to plan for the Hagarenes, they appeared before the metropolis of the entire nation, Ragusa by name, and blockaded it for some time, those within putting up a determined resistance.[107] But in due course the Ragusans were worn down and reduced to a state of utter hopelessness. Compelled by necessity, they sent delegates to the emperor entreating him to come to the aid of those who were in danger of falling into the clutches of men who denied Christ. The emperor Michael died, however, before the delegates arrived; hence it was Basil whom they encountered. He gave them an attentive and entirely sympathetic hearing. He fitted out a fleet of one hundred vessels, put a man in command of it whom he knew to have distinguished himself above many others in experience and

---

[103] Stypeiotes fell on 14 September 883. The Arab commander was the famous Yazman, emir of Tarsus, who had just freed himself from the suzerainty of the Tulunids of Egypt: A. A. Vasiliev, *Byzance et les Arabes*, II: *Les relations politiques de Byzance et des Arabes à L'époque de la dynastie macédonienne*, ed. M. Canard (CBHB 2, 1, Brussels, 1968) 102–3. Yazman was so famous that according to the testimony of a Greek preserved by Mas'udi in his *Prairies of Gold*, the Greeks included his portrait among those of the most valiant Moslems which decorated some of their churches: Vasiliev and Canard, II, 123.

[104] An identical list of Dalmatian peoples appears in *DAI*, ch. 29. The listing of Slav princes in *De Cerimoniis* has been commented on by E. Malamut, 'Les adresses aux princes des pays slaves du sud dans le *Livre des cérémonies* 2.48: interprétation', *TM*, 13 (2000), 595–615.

[105] Sawdon (meaning the sultan), the emir of Bari,, Saba (or Sama) of Tarento and Kalfun, a Berber who had already attacked Bari in 841: J. Gay, *L'Italie méridionale et l'empire byzantin depuis l'avènement de Basil I jusqu'à la prise de Bari par les Normands (867–1071)* (Paris, 1904), 52.

[106] Butova, Rosa and Kotor.

[107] The Arabs launched two attacks on Ragusa (now Dubrovnik), one in 840 at which time they took Bari too, another in 866: Gay, *Italie*, 92.

Basil I the Macedonian

skill, the patrician Niketas Ooryphas, droungarios of the fleet,[108] and sent him against the enemy. The Hagarenes, while still persevering with the siege of Ragusa, learnt about the Ragusan delegation to the emperor from some deserters. Losing hope of taking [that city] in the immediate future, they now also began to be afraid that help might be arriving from the emperor. So they raised the siege and passed over into Italy, into what is now called Longobardia.[109] They plundered the fortified town of Bari[110] and set up camp there, raiding the environs on a daily basis. Continually advancing in this way, they gained control of the whole of Longobardia, almost as far as the once great and glorious city of Rome.

When the aforementioned races of Scyths, the Croats, Serbs and the rest of them saw what had happened in Dalmatia as a result of Roman intervention, [147] they sent delegates to the emperor requesting to be brought into subjection under Roman rule. This seemed to the emperor to be a reasonable request; he received them with kindliness, and they all became subjects of the Roman government and were given governors of their own race and kin.[111]

The emperor now gave thought to the problem of disposing of the Hagarenes who were using Ragusa as a base from which to coast around Italy, continually devastating it. Knowing that Ooryphas'[112] fleet was inadequate for such a campaign, he began negotiations with Doloichos [Louis II, 850–75], king of Francia, and with the pope of Rome, requesting reinforcements for his own troops, to take their place beside them in the struggle against the godless ones. He ordered the lands of the Slavs mentioned a little earlier and also the inhabitants of Ragusa to take their part in the campaign. When all these had gathered and a great army was assembled, since the Roman admiral was a man of considerable military experience, it was not long before Bari was taken.[113] The commander of

---

[108] Presumably a relative of the man of the same name who was droungarios of the watch under Theophilos.

[109] Longobardia usually means the area populated by Lombards, but the Byzantine theme of Longobardia was more or less Apulia. On that region when the Byzantine empire flourished: J.-M. Martin, *La Pouille du VIe au XIIe siècle* (Rome, 1993).

[110] Skylitzes has confused this one with the previous attack on Ragusa.

[111] These events probably led to the creation of the theme of Dalmatia, of which a strategos is first mentioned in 878 (whereas the *Taktikon Uspensky* only mentions archons): Oikonomides, *Listes*, 353.

[112] This must be Niketas, droungarios of the admiralty (mentioned above), who subsequently commanded the fleet in action against the Saracens in the Adriatic (see below), not the person of the same name who served under Theophilos and Michael II.

[113] The matter is more complicated than this. The '*archon* of Francia' must be the emperor Louis II who campaigned in southern Italy to counteract the growing influence of the Moslems there. He sought an alliance with Byzantium but their cooperation before Bari achieved little; Ooryphas

the Franks fell upon Soldan and his force of Hagarenes and led them off to [the Franks'] homeland in captivity. Such was the outcome of the emperor's first campaign in the west.

27. As we said, Soldan was taken prisoner by the king; he was brought to Capua, where he spent two whole years during which nobody ever [148] saw him laugh. The king promised to give gold to anyone who could make him be caught laughing. One day a fellow came to the king announcing that he had seen Soldan laughing and he produced witnesses to the event. The king summoned Soldan and asked what circumstances had come about that he had laughed. 'I saw a wagon,' he said, 'and noticed its wheels: how the lower part is raised up while the upper part is brought low. In this I saw a metaphor of the instability and uncertainty of human happiness. Then I laughed at the thought of how we are puffed up by such an uncertain thing; and I also recognised that it was impossible that I who have been brought low from so great a height should not be raised up again to greatness from ground level.' The king listened to this and reflected on his own situation. He reckoned the speaker an intelligent man who, in the course of his former command and long life, had experienced both good fortune and bad; whereupon he treated him as a free man, admitting him to his presence and conversation.[114]

28. Now Soldan was no fool, and very cunning; he devised an intrigue against the king[115] to drive him out of Capua and permit himself to return to his own land. The rascal was aware that those two Italian cities, Capua and Benevento, had not been in the king's possession for long and that they were not particularly loyal to him, but were always dreaming of being independent. Neither was he ignorant that it was a major concern of the king how to hold them firmly and securely in subjection. So he went to the king and said: 'I notice, O king, that it is a constant source of worry and concern to you how you are to maintain a firm hold on these Italian cities. I will give you some advice: you should be aware, most noble prince, that you will never have an unshakable hold [149] on these cities until you remove the leading inhabitants of them to the lands of the Franks. For those who are enslaved against their will naturally long for freedom and will break out in revolt to attain it if they are given the opportunity.'

arrived off the town with his fleet after the army of Louis II had already lifted the siege. Louis did return to besiege Bari and took it (February 871); it did not return into Byzantine hands until 875–6: V. von Falkenhausen, 'Bari bizantina', *Spazio, società, potere nell'Italia dei Comuni*, ed. G. Rosetti (Naples, 1986), 195–227.
[114] The same event is reported in *DAI*, ch. 29.
[115] Louis II was captured by the Lombards of Benevento and set free against his promise to take no revenge.

The king liked what he heard and, thinking it would be to his advantage, decided to do as follows. He had chains and fetters secretly forged, as if there were an urgent need of them. Having taken the king so cunningly in his snare, Soldan now turned to the leading citizens with whom he had also formed an acquaintance and maintained constant contact. To these he said: 'I wish to give you some top secret information which, if it were discovered, would, I fear, be my destruction and put you in great danger.' They swore silence and to keep what he said unspoken. 'The king wishes to send you all in chains to his own land of Francia, fearing that there is no other way for him to maintain a firm grasp on your cities,' he said. But they hesitated, thinking that what he said did not merit belief. When they asked for some credible confirmation of his allegations, he took one of the leading citizens and went off to the area of the blacksmiths and invited him to enquire what it was they were forging in such haste. When he learnt that it was chains and fetters, the citizen returned with the information that the man was speaking to them in good faith. His words were true and also advantageous to the Italian cities. When the leaders and counsellors of the said cities received this information they began searching for an opportunity of striking a counter-blow against the king. One day when he went out to hunt, they shut the city gates in his face and would no more permit him to enter. Since he could do nothing about the situation for the time being, he withdrew to his own land. Then Soldan came to the leaders demanding the reward for his revelation, which was to be set free and to be allowed to return to his own fatherland. He was released as one who was supposed to have benefited [the cities]; he returned to Carthage, resumed his command and mounted a campaign against Capua and Benevento.[116] He established a fortified camp and vigorously besieged the cities. Oppressed by the siege, [150] the citizens despatched an embassy to the king begging forgiveness for their offence and an ally in the fight, but he dismissed the embassy with scorn, saying that he rejoiced in their destruction. They were at a loss what to do when the ambassadors returned empty-handed. As there was nothing [else] they could do and they were being severely oppressed by the shortages occasioned by the siege, they sent a messenger to Basil the emperor of the Romans to ask for help. He received the envoy and quickly sent him back, urging them to hold fast because shortly reinforcements would arrive for them and deliver them out of their oppression. But as the envoy was returning he was taken prisoner by the enemy. Soldan had him brought before him and said: 'There are two paths open to you, of which

---

[116] Abd'Allah commanded the army despatched by the emir Mohamed ibn Ahmed.

you should take the one more beneficial to you. If you wish to save your own life, also to receive many gifts and favours, say – in my hearing – to those who sent you that the emperor of the Romans refuses to ally himself with you; thus, you will live. But if you insist on delivering your true message, sudden death awaits you.'[117] The messenger agreed to do what the Emir wanted; then, when he was a bowshot from the wall, he asked for the leading citizens to be present. When they were in place he began the following speech to them: 'O fathers, even though death is obviously at hand and the sword ready to strike, I will not conceal the truth. I only ask that you show your gratitude to my wife and children. I am in the hands of the enemy, my lords; but I have completed my embassy. You may expect help from the emperor of the Romans forthwith, so be of good cheer: your deliverer is coming, but not mine.' Even as he was saying these and similar things, he was immediately slashed into little pieces by the swords of Soldan's servants. Nevertheless Soldan was disquieted by the prospect of the arrival of relief from the emperor. He lifted [151] the siege and went back home.[118] But the cities of which we have been speaking thenceforth remained friends and allies of the Romans.

[Soldan] completely destroyed only the illustrious Italian city of Iontos and led its population captive back to Carthage with him. The emperor built another city to replace it. It was washed by the sea on all sides except at the point of entry, which is by a narrow strip of dry land that allows only a very narrow path for those going in that way. As this town stood in need of inhabitants, he brought people from the town of Herakleia in Pontos to live there and he called it Kallipolis. This explains why even today the inhabitants have the same customs, dress and political institutions as the Romans.[119]

29. It was at that time that Esman, the emir of Tarsus,[120] exulting in his recent victory, fitted out thirty large vessels of the kind the Saracens usually call *koumparia* and launched an attack on the city of Euripos.[121] The emperor had received prior intelligence of this so, by imperial command,

---

[117] The story of the heroic messenger is an oft-recurring commonplace.
[118] In fact the departure of the Saracens was due to the death of Abd'Allah (December 871 or January 872) and the victory of Louis II on the banks of the Vulturno that year. On these operations: Vasiliev and Canard, II, 50–1.
[119] The passage is only found in MSS ACEB. The town mentioned is Callipoli, on the Straits.
[120] Yazman, emir of Tarsus. Since the victory of Petronas over Amr of Melitenein in 863, it was the emir of Tarsus who took the initiative in leading the jihad and who was the principal adversary of the Romans.
[121] This was the principal fortress of Euboea: J. Koder and F. Hild, *Hellas und Thessalien*, Register von P. Soustal (TIB, 1, Vienna, 1976), 156–8. Violent currents swept the straits separating the town from the mainland: Koder and Hild, *Hellas und Thessalien*, 60.

the commander of the Helladikon theme, Oniates, had raised an army adequate for the defence of the city from all over that theme. He put the walls in the necessary state of repair and built machines for hurling stones and darts. In brief, he omitted no defence-work capable of resisting a siege. When the fleet from Tarsus arrived it drew near to the walls and attempted to dissipate the defending forces by constant discharges, but the men of Euripos abounded in energy and enthusiasm. They valiantly drove the enemy off with their machines for hurling stones, missiles and darts – to say nothing of stones thrown from the walls by hand. Each day they inflicted heavy losses on the barbarians. Having watched out for a favourable wind, they now brought their own ships up against the enemy and burnt many of them with 'Greek fire'. In the face of this action the barbarian was at a loss what to do; but, knowing that the desire for and love of money can bring many a man to despise death, he set up a great shield before [152] their line of defence and filled it with gold, saying that he would give this together with a hundred maidens chosen from the captives to the first man who scaled the wall and conferred victory on his fellow countrymen. As soon as they saw this, the men in the city realised what was going on. They encouraged each other with fortifying and inciting words to resist boldly, then, at a given signal, they opened the city gates and launched a dauntless attack on the barbarians. At the first encounter the emir received a mortal wound and fell;[122] many others there lost their lives with him while the rest took to their heels. They were pursued as far as the remaining ships, and there a great massacre of the barbarians took place. Those who remained alive manned a few of the ships and shamefully fled to their homeland; such was the end of the fleet from Tarsus.

30. Then another fleet was raised against [us], this one in Crete. When Saet,[123] the son of Apochaps, was ruling Crete, a warlike and energetic fellow named Photios was sent by him against the Roman empire with twenty-seven *koumparia* and many *myaparones* and *pentekontores* usually known as galleys.[124] Setting out from Crete, this Photios devastated the

---

[122] This is the emir Yazman. Skylitzes' report does not agree with the Arab historians who say the emir died in 891–2, killed by a stone propelled by a ballista at the siege of Salandu: Vasiliev and Canard, II, 56 and n. 1, also 122.
[123] Sa'íd ordered this raid in 872 or 873: Vasiliev and Canard, II, 53–4.
[124] *Koumparia* is a vessel designed both for war and for freight: H. Antoniadis-Bibicou, *Etudes d'histoire maritime de Byzance: a propos du 'thème des Caravisiens'* (Paris, 1966), 167–9. The *myoparon* or *satoura* was a heavy, rounded vessel, the *pentekontor* or *galea* a light vessel propelled by oarsmen: H. Ahrweiler, *Byzance et la mer: la marine de guerre, la politique et les institutions maritimes de Byzance aux VIIe–XVe siècles* (Paris, 1966), 410 and note 8, also 414.

islands and shores of the Aegean[125] and advanced as far as the Proconnesos of the Hellespont; he enslaved the people, looting and burning wherever he appeared. He was met at the mouth of the Aegean, near Kardia, by the patrician Niketas Ooryphas, droungarios of the admiralty now commanding the Roman fleet. A furious battle ensued in which he promptly disposed of twenty Cretan ships with 'Greek fire', dispatching the barbarians in them with the sword or by fire and water. They who managed to survive the perils of naval warfare and the sea saved their lives by running away.

31. [153] But although the Cretans had been so badly defeated, they were by no means ready for a quiet life. Once again they launched an attack on the maritime possessions [of the empire]. With the aforementioned Photios in command, they fitted out pirate ships as war vessels, terrorising the Peloponnese and the adjacent isles. The commander of the Roman fleet, the patrician Niketas Ooryphas, went out to meet them; profiting from a favourable and steady wind, he reached the Peloponnese in a few days and tied up in the harbour of Kenchreai.[126] He now learnt that the enemy ships were devastating the western parts of the Peloponnese: Methone,[127] Pylos, Patras and the approaches to Corinth, whereupon he adopted a wise and expedient plan. His head swam at the thought of circumnavigating the Peloponnese by way of Capes Maleas and Tainaron, uselessly measuring off thousands of miles only to arrive too late. So he did what he could: suddenly and by night, putting all hands to work, he transported his ships over dry land across the Isthmus of Corinth to the sea beyond. Then he embarked his men and went into action; thus he was able suddenly to fall on an enemy who had not the slightest idea of his whereabouts. His attack was so unexpected that it confounded their hopes with fear and threw their plans into confusion. They gave no thought to regrouping or fighting, but only to how they could immediately get away. He burnt some of their warships and sunk others; some of the barbarians he put to the sword, others he caused to drown in the deep. He executed the naval commander, and the remaining men were forced to disperse across the island. These he later netted alive and inflicted a variety of punishments on them. Some of them, [154] in particular those who had renounced their Christian baptism, he had flayed alive, saying that what was being taken away from them was

---

[125] At that time the inhabitants of Erissos on the western tip of Lesbos took refuge on the Athonite peninsula and there founded the future diocese of Hierissos.
[126] The port of Corinth.
[127] Modon, a port on the south-eastern coast of the Peloponnese which controls access to the Adriatic.

nothing of their own for they had shed it of their own free will. Other men had bands of skin most painfully torn off them, from the neck to the heel. Others still he raised up with ropes then let them down into vessels of boiling pitch – while on the rest he inflicted a diversity of torments. By doing this he inspired fear in them and made sure they would think twice before sending an expedition against the Roman empire again.[128]

32. There was another naval force, from the west, which crashed against the Roman empire like a hurricane or a squall.[129] The ruler of Africa[130] fitted out sixty exceedingly large ships and sent them out against the Roman government. They devastated as they went and took many people prisoner even as far as the islands of Kephalonia[131] and Zakynthos. There was immediately despatched a squadron of ships and other swift vessels under the successor of Niketas as commander of the naval forces, a man named Nasar.[132] Taking a direct route and profiting from a favourable wind, he soon reached Methone but he was prevented from attacking the enemy right away for the following reason. Many of the oarsmen had quietly deserted in small groups for fear of the danger which lay ahead, thus denying their commander the speedy action for which the situation called. He decided that he should not engage the enemy while his ships were so undermanned. He despatched a swift messenger to advise the emperor of what had happened, and *he* arrested the deserters in less time than it takes to tell and inflicted a punishment on them which was intended to strike terror in the hearts of the rest of the oarsmen. He ordered thirty [155] of the Saracens being held prisoner in the praetorium to be brought out by night and to be made unrecognisable by having their faces rubbed with soot. They were brought to the Hippodrome and flogged, then sent off in disgrace to the Peloponnese under the pretence that these were the instigators of the desertion and that they were being executed at the spot from which they had fled. And that is what happened: the thirty Saracens were impaled as though they were the deserters and a great fear was instilled in the entire Roman fleet. Every thought of comfort and well-being was cast aside; [the sailors] begged the commanding officer to take action against the enemy in all haste.

---

[128] Photios perished in this action: D. Tsougarakis, *Byzantine Crete: from the fifth century to the Venetian conquest* (Athens, 1988), 50; Vasiliev and Canard, II, 54–5.
[129] The date of this Moslem attack (880) is established by a letter from Pope John VIII to Charles the Fat: Vasiliev and Canard, II/1 99.
[130] Named Husayn b. Rabah: Vasiliev and Canard, II, 95.
[131] Kephalonia was already a theme at the beginning of the ninth century.
[132] According to the *Life of Elias the younger*, his name was Basil Nasar and he had forty-five vessels under his command: Vasiliev and Canard, II, 95–9.

33. Meanwhile [Nasar] brought his forces up to strength with some of the Peloponnesian fighting men and, being assured of the cooperation of the local commander, he was ready to attack. For their part, the Saracens had become very conceited and held the Roman fleet in deep contempt because of its earlier inertia. Becoming over-confident, they fearlessly disembarked from their ships and laid waste the surrounding area. Then, suddenly, the Roman admiral made his appearance close by and, at a given signal, launched a surprise attack on the enemy by night. The adversaries, not having the time either to regroup or to counter-attack, were ingloriously slaughtered and their ships given to the flames, together with those who were on board. Nasar, the commander, dedicated the undamaged ships to God as a kind of sacrifice by granting them to the church of Methone.[133] The emperor congratulated him on what he had accomplished and ordered him to advance yet further. As the morale of the army was high (thanks to the foregoing successes), he went over to Sicily and attacked all the cities which were subject to the Carthaginians. These he pillaged and destroyed, capturing many merchant vessels, some of which contained valuable cargoes, including a great quantity of oil so well priced that [156] a measure sold for one obol,[134] they say. This same fleet sailed on to Italy and was able to rendezvous with the Roman cavalry of the region, commanded by Prokopios,[135] the emperor's protovestiarios, and the patrician Leo Apostypes,[136] commander-in-chief of the Thracian and Macedonian themes. [The fleet] accomplished praiseworthy deeds, encountering and defeating a fleet setting out from Africa again off the island of Stylai,[137] and also freeing all but a few of the Hagarene-held fortresses of Calabria and Longobardia from the hands of the barbarians[138] and restoring them to Roman rule. Such then are the victories won with God's help by Nasar and the Roman fleet; he returned to the emperor loaded with booty and triumphal crowns.

---

[133] A seal suggests that this church might have been dedicated to St John the Evangelist: *DOSeals*, 11, 85.
[134] Meaning one *follis*.
[135] Prokopios had under his command the troops of the two themes consolidated, in other words the greater part of the troops of the west – soldiers normally engaged in Calabria and Sicily.
[136] *George the Monk, Continuatus*, ed. Bekker, 22, says that Leo Apostypes was commander of the Peloponnese.
[137] 'The island of Stylai' indicates a spot on the way to Rome via the straits of Messina where a column (*stylos*) stood. On the battle: E. Kislinger, 'Milazzo-Stelai (880 D. CR.): una battaglia navale cambia luogo', *Archivio storico messinese*, 69 (1995), 4–11.
[138] It was in this year (880) that the Arabs were expelled from Tarento and a Roman garrison installed.

34. The infantry of Longobardia was not entirely capable of escaping the enmity of destiny for, although they served with courage and distinction, in the midst of their striving for victory there arose enmity and jealousy which cost the highest-ranking commander his life. Leo had fallen out with Prokopios over some trifling matter and, before a reconciliation took place, there was an engagement with the enemy. Apostypes, fighting on the right wing with the Thracians and Macedonians, carried the day against the enemy and slew many Saracens. Prokopios, however, on the other wing, with the Sclavini and the western troops, was sorely pressed by the adversary. As no relief was sent to the distressed wing by the co-commander because of their preceding quarrel, the troops of Prokopios were put to flight and he himself was slain. He fell fighting valiantly in the midst of the fray.[139] Now Leo was desirous of performing some further illustrious deed to eclipse the shameful event which enmity had brought about. He took his own army, [157] joined to it the troops under Prokopios who had survived the rout and laid siege to the fortress of Taranto which was still in the hands of the Hagarenes. He took it and sold the entire population into slavery. From the spoils he was able to make generous provision for the soldiery and to bring booty to the emperor. But he was not able to propitiate the emperor in this way; when [Basil] learned the reason for the slaying of Prokopios, he dismissed [Leo] from his command and sent him into exile at Kotyaeon, where he had his estate.

35. Baianos, Leo's chief groom, and some others of those who waited on him[140] now laid a charge of treason against him. When his sons Bardas and David heard of this, first they slew Baianos then, fearing the wrath of the emperor at this audacious act, they fled into Syria, taking their father with them. When the emperor learned of this he despatched the commanding officer of the Hetaireia and some troops with orders to intercept and arrest them. [The envoys] hastened their journey and apprehended them in Cappadocia while they were only just on their way to Syria. Although [the troops] merely intended to prevent [David and Bardas] from going any further, they encountered resistance. An engagement took place in which [Leo's] two sons fell fighting, but he was taken alive and brought before the emperor. He was handed over to the courts and found guilty.

[139] According to *Vita Euthymii patriarchae CP. Text, translation, introduction and commentary*, P. Karlin-Hayter (Bibliothèque de *Byzantion*, 3, Brussels, 1970) (ch. 1) Prokopios was with Zaoutzes when Basil suffered his fatal hunting accident.
[140] According to *Theophanes Continuatus*, ed. Bekker, 307, the cubicularios Chamaretos was also one of the accusers.

He had one eye ripped out, one hand amputated and he spent the rest of his life an exile in Mesembria.[141]

36. While the emperor was accomplishing these things in the west by the agency of his commanders, the Arabs in the south began to revive and (under the impression that the emperor was inactive) to think of launching another attack against the domains which bordered on the sea. Ships were built in Egypt and in the coastal cities of Phoenicia and Syria with a view to launching a naval offensive against the Romans. [158] But first spies were sent out to find out what the emperor was up to. Nor was the emperor by any means blind to what was going on; he knew all about what was happening in Syria. He too fitted out a fleet ready for battle, which he kept at the capital, waiting to see what would happen. And to make sure that it did not become undisciplined for want of something to do ('Pointless inactivity brings forth no good thing,'[142] says the poet), he ordered [the sailors] to work at the construction of the church which was then arising in the imperial palace to the name of our Saviour Jesus Christ, of the Archangels and of Elijah the Tishbite. At the same time they were to remain in readiness, so that when the [enemy] fleet crossed the borders of Syria they would be completely prepared to be sent out to withstand them. That is how the emperor dealt with the situation. As for the Saracen spy,[143] he came to the capital, saw that everything was very well prepared, went back to those who had sent him and reported what he had seen. In their alarm, they chose rather to remain quietly [at peace].

37. Fearing, on account of their recent reverses, that a Roman fleet might be sent against their territories, the Carthaginians built a good number of ships. When spring began and no news arrived of any force being despatched by the emperor, thinking that he must be otherwise engaged, they launched a campaign against Sicily. When they came before Syracuse they laid siege to it, pillaging and laying waste all the surrounding countryside. When the commander of Sicily made this known to the emperor, he immediately sent out the fleet which was held in readiness to Sicily (even though [its men were] engaged in building the church) with the Patrician Adrian [159] in command. Sailing out of the capital, they had no easy voyage and indeed only just made it to the Peloponnese, where

---

[141] A port of some importance on the north shore of the Black Sea. The place of exile was well removed from the former residence of Apostypes.

[142] Sophocles, fragment 308 = Stobaeus, *Florilegium* 30.6.

[143] On espionage: N. Koutrakou, '"Spies of towns": some remarks on espionage in the context of Arabo-Byzantine relations, eighth–tenth centuries', *Proceedings of the Sixth International Congress of Graeco-Oriental and African Studies* (Nicosia, 30 April–5 May 1996), published in *Graeco-Arabica*, 7–8 (Nicosia, 2000), 243–66.

Basil I the Macedonian

they moored in the harbour called Hierax[144] at Monembasia to wait for a favourable wind. A long time [Adrian] delayed in this harbour, wishing neither to use the oars in periods of calm nor to struggle against an adverse sea. Meanwhile, the Hagarenes intensified their siege and took the city. Many of those within were slain; the rest were taken prisoner. The city was utterly destroyed, the holy churches it contained put to the flames. That city, so famous and illustrious until then, which had repelled so many attacks by barbarians, shorn of all its glory in the twinkling of an eye![145] Adrian got wind of what had happened in the following way. There is a place in the Peloponnese called Elos; it acquired its name from the adjacent thick forest.[146] That was where the Roman naval force was stationed. There were shepherds who, one night, heard the demons who inhabited that region telling each other that Syracuse had been captured and destroyed the day before.[147] Word passed from mouth to mouth, and then the tale came to Adrian's ears. He summoned the shepherds, interrogated them and found that what he had heard was confirmed by their words. Wanting to hear with his own ears, he went to the place with the shepherds and, putting a question to the demons by means of them, he heard that Syracuse was already taken. Overcome [at first] by anguish and distress, he pulled himself together again, judging that he ought not to believe the deceptive words of demons – yet he carefully noted the day. Ten days later some refugees arrived, reporting the disaster of which they had been eyewitnesses.[148] When Adrian heard their account, [160] he turned tail and quickly reached the capital with the fleet. There he fled to the Great Church for sanctuary, but this asylum did not protect him from prosecution. He was dragged out from there and sent into exile. Stephen Maxentios, the Cappadocian, was sent out as commander of Longobardia, with choice Thracian, Macedonian and Cappadocian troops. He arrived, but through lack of courage and too much love of comfort he achieved nothing worthy of report and was relieved of his command.

---

[144] Port to the north of Monembasia.
[145] There is an eyewitness account of the fall of Syracuse on 21 May 878 by one Theodosios the Monk. The siege had lasted nine months and a dreadful famine had ensued. The Moslems massacred part of the population when the final assault took place, including the garrison commander. The prisoners who survived the ordeal (of whom Theodosius was one) were liberated by an exchange of prisoners in 885: Vasiliev and Canard, II, 70–9.
[146] This place is close to Sparta. Skylitzes calls the place Elos; *Theophanes Continuatus* gives Helos which is preferable. The word means a swamp or marsh.
[147] On the persistence of paganism in Lakonia and a reference to this passage: A. Avraméa, *Le Péloponnèse du IVe au VIIIe siècle: changements et persistances* (Paris, 1997), 154.
[148] Among those of the garrison who survived were some Peloponnesian Mardaites who then went back home: *Theophanes Continuatus*, ed. Bekker, 311.

38. Nikephoros, surnamed Phokas, a man of nobility and action,[149] was sent to replace him, bringing with him forces equal to the task and a corps of Manichees under the command of that Diakonitzes who had served with Chrysocheir. Arriving at the appointed place, he joined forces with those under Stephen's command and then gained many glorious victories against the Saracens. First he threw back the enemy drawn up in battle order, then he captured the city of Amantia, Tropai and Saint-Severine.[150] He also got the better of the enemy in many other battles and engagements. Such were the military events in the time of Basil.

39. He also splendidly adorned [the church of] that greatest of martyrs, Diomedes, with extremely costly treasures and splendid offerings. He honoured it with grants of profitable estates and in many ways promoted and enriched it.[151]

40. The son of Danielis[152] (with whom he had entered into a bond of spiritual brotherhood) he promoted to the rank of protospatharios and [161] granted him complete freedom of access to his person. As for Danielis, now an old lady, he sent for her and, since she was no longer able to sit a horse, she made the journey reclining in a litter, which was carried in relays by three hundred strong young servants of her choosing. When she arrived at the capital there was the customary reception in the Magnaura,[153] at which she was brought before the emperor in great honour and there she offered costly gifts; it would be an offence against the canons of good taste to enumerate them.[154]

---

[149] Nikephoros Phokas 'the elder' – to distinguish him from his grandson of the same name, the future emperor. He may well have been the son of that Phokas whom Basil had singled out during his campaign in Asia Minor and made a *tourmarch*. Nikephoros had already served as commander of the Charisanon theme: J.-C. Cheynet, 'Les Phocas', *Le traité sur la guérilla de l'empereur Nicéphore Phocas*, ed. G. Dagron and H. Mihàescu (Le monde byzantin, Paris, 1986), 289–315, 292 = J.-C.Cheynet, *La société byzantine. L'apport des sceaux* (Bilans de recherche 3, Paris, 2008), 477.

[150] This town in the province of Catanzaro is still known by the same name. It was elevated to the rank of metropolis after being reconquered: V. Laurent, 'A propos de la métropole de Santa Severina en Calabre (quelques remarques)', *REB*, 22 (1964), 176–83.

[151] The *Patria* confirm this magnificent reconstruction. The monastery was still active in the time of Andronikos I (1183–5), who had his predecessor's (Manuel's) widow Mary of Antioch confined there: Janin, *Églises et monastères*, 1, 95–7; A. Berger, *Untersuchungen zu den Patria Konstantinopoleos* (Poikila Byzantina, 8, Bonn, 1988), 365–7.

[152] The *archontissa* of the Peloponnese who had assured Basil's future: above, c. 6.

[153] Normally receptions in the Magnaura were only offered to very distinguished guests such as the ambassadors of foreign princes.

[154] *Theophanes Continuatus*, ed. Bekker, 318, has no such reticence, saying that Danielis offered five hundred slaves, some of whom were eunuchs, one hundred women who could weave, hundreds of pieces of precious silk, many gold and silver objects. But, as E. Anagnostakis observes, 'The episode of Danielis', *Everyday life at Byzantium* (Athens, 1989), 375–90, this list is highly reminiscent of the gifts the Queen of Sheba brought to Solomon when he was building the temple (2 Chron. 9). It is a striking comparison: Basil, the new Solomon, is building his new temple (the Nea). On the silks offered by Danielis: D. Jacoby, 'Silk in western Byzantium before the Fourth Crusade,' *BZ*, 84/85 (1991–2), 458–60.

Basil I the Macedonian

She received hospitality befitting one so charitably disposed to Basil and stayed in the capital for as long as she pleased; she then returned to her homeland. She did pay another visit to the capital; after Basil died and Leo his son received the right to rule, the old lady came again with gifts of a similar kind. She embraced [Leo] and declared him in writing to be heir to all her worldly goods. Then she returned to her estates and died shortly afterwards. But that was later.

41. Many of the sacred churches had been damaged by previous disruptions and shaken by earthquakes, while some had been completely wrecked.[155] The emperor Basil took this matter in hand. Some he replaced with new buildings; of others he made good the damage, while in other cases he conferred additional beauty and ornamentation. First of all, the western apse[156] of the great [church of the] Wisdom of God, which is gigantic and towers into the sky, was badly cracked and in danger of falling down. By the skill of experienced builders he bound it around, thus restoring it to solidity and stability. Within [the Great Church] he depicted the image of the Mother of God with the baby cradled in her arms, together with the princes of the apostles, Peter and Paul, on either side of her. He also rectified the fissures and faults in the walls. He increased the income, which was rather diminished to the point that there was danger of the sacred lights being extinguished for want of oil. By the grant of a large estate known as Mantaia, he provided perpetual light in the lamps and he made provision for more generous salaries to be paid to the choristers of the sacred church [162] out of the income from the estate. The sacred church of the holy martyrs Sergios and Bacchos had sadly declined from its former glory, the holy icons therein having been effaced when John, formerly superior of the monks living there, became patriarch in the reign of the former emperor Theophilos. At the prompting of the blessed patriarch Ignatios, Basil decorated this church with sacred icons and made good the other deficiencies of the structure. They call this Hormisdas' church; it

---

[155] Among other things, the earthquake of 8 January 869 did severe damage. Skylitzes proceeds to reproduce the list of buildings constructed or repaired by Basil given in the *Vita Basilii, Theophanes Continuatus*, ed. Bekker, 323–5 and 338–41, obviously meant to redound to that emperor's glory. P. Magdalino observes (*Constantinople medievale: etudes sur l'evolution des structures urbaines, TM*, 9 (Paris, 1996), 27–8) that more than half the buildings that benefited from Basil's munificence were situated outside the Constantinian wall; also that the main churches of the city (apart from Saint Sophia and Holy Apostles) had been adequately preserved since the days of Justinian and Heraclius. For a somewhat different interpretation: R. Ousterhout, 'Reconstructing ninth-century Constantinople', *Byzantium in the ninth century: dead or alive, Papers from the Thirteenth Spring Symposium of Byzantine Studies*, ed. L. Brubaker (SPBS, 5, Aldershot, 1998), 115–30. On the role of Basil's constructions in the formation of the imperial ideology of the Macedonians: P. Alexander, 'The strength of empire and capital as seen through Byzantine eyes', *Speculum*, 37 (1962), 339–59.

[156] Literally, 'facing west'.

was first constructed by Justinian on the plan of the Great Church, as an inscription running round the inside of the church itself testifies:

> Other emperors have honoured the dead,
> Their labours were unrewarded. But
> He who now holds our sceptres, pious Justinian
> Honours with an illustrious house Sergios, servant
> Of Christ, King of the universe, whom neither the flickering flame,
> The sword, nor any other torture could hurt,
> But who was constant unto death for Christ our God
> And merits heaven by his blood. May he always
> Protect our ever-vigilant emperor
> And augment the sway of Theodora, crowned by God;
> She whose piety enlightens the soul; whose ceaseless
> Activity and unremitting good works bring
> Relief to those who are crushed by poverty.[157]

The sacred church of the Holy Apostles,[158] this too sadly declined from its former glory, he secured with buttresses and reinforcements to the dilapidated portions, rendering it 'glorious in the flower of youth',[159] as the poet puts it. He restored the church of the Mother of God at Pege,[160] which had lost its original beauty. He rebuilt the other church of the Theotokos, the one called the Sigma, from its foundations (for it had completely fallen down in an earthquake),[161] rendering it more substantial and beautiful [163] than before. He also raised up from its foundations [the church of St] Stephen the first martyr in the Aurelianai,[162] which had fallen down to the ground,

---

[157] The meaning is less than explicit towards the end. On this inscription and the medieval manuscript tradition, see the bibliography in D. Feissel, 'Les édifices de Justinien au témoignage de Procope et de l'épigraphie', *Antiquité tardive*, 8 (2000), 89.

[158] Janin, *Églises et monastères*, 1, 41–50. The core of Holy Apostles' was the heroon built by Constantine, the nearest he ever came to providing his new city with a shrine. Under Konstantios it became a church and subsequently one of the principal sanctuaries where a number of very important ceremonies were held. The emperors and the court went there on Easter Monday, Pentecost; also on the Sundays following Easter and Pentecost and on the feast of St Constantine. It also housed some significant relics. Most emperors were buried in the heroon until the eleventh century. Holy Apostles' was still standing in 1453, when it housed the patriarchs for a time.

[159] *Iliad*, 10.446.

[160] Janin, *Églises et monastères*, 1, 223–8; another very famous Marian shrine, outside the walls by the gate of the same name. The spring there produced miraculous healings: A.-M. Talbot, 'Two accounts of miracles at the Pege shrine in Constantinople', *Mélanges Gilbert Dagron*, ed. V. Déroche, D. Feissel, C. Morrisson, C. Zuckerman, *TM*, 14 (2002), 605–15.

[161] Janin, *Églises et monastères*, 1, 230; this church was near the Mese, across from the Peribleptos monastery. In 869 at the feast of St Polyeuktos, there was an earthquake. Leo the Philosopher [Mathematician?] tried in vain to get the people to evacuate the church, which was in danger of falling down: *Symeonis magistri*, 261–2.

[162] Janin, *Églises et monastères*, 1, 472–3. The existence of this church is attested in the fifth century; it too was near the Peribleptos monastery.

and the two shrines of the Baptist in Stobilaia[163] and in Makedoniai[164] respectively – the one he completely, the other he largely rebuilt. The [church] of Philip the Apostle[165] and the one to the west of it dedicated to Luke the evangelist,[166] both of which had suffered severe dilapidation, he rebuilt from their foundations. Add to these the great shrine of Mokios the martyr,[167] the sanctuary of which had fallen to the ground in such a way that the holy table was cracked. This too he took under his care and raised up what had fallen down. He restored to its former elegance the adjacent [church of St] Andrew the first-called[168] [apostle], which had also fallen down. He renovated the somewhat decrepit [churches of] St Romanos, St Anna in the Deuteron,[169] of the great martyr Demetrios[170] and of the martyr Aimilianos[171] in the Rhabdos. Besides these he restored [the church] of St Nazarios[172] which was falling down, and he magnificently reconditioned the very beautiful church of Christ's Resurrection and of St Anastasia the Martyr in the Arcades of Domninos,[173] replacing the wooden roof with one of stone. He restored the church of Plato,[174] that great martyr (which was falling down), and also turned his attention to the adjacent church of the victorious martyrs Hesperos and Zoe.[175] He snatched from the jaws of ruin the church of Akakios the martyr at Heptaskalon[176] (which was in danger of falling down) by reconstructing it. He similarly renewed in splendid fashion [the church] of the prophet Elijah at Petrion.[177] Within the imperial palaces he raised up a novel foundation in the names of the lord-and-master Christ, Michael the archangel,[178] Elijah the prophet and

[163] Janin, *Églises et monastères*, 1, 440, located on the Golden Horn.
[164] Janin, *Églises et monastères*, 1, 418, location unsure.
[165] Janin, *Églises et monastères*, 1, 493, located near to St Mokios at Ta Meltiadou.
[166] Janin, *Églises et monastères*, 1, 311, located near the cistern of Mokios.
[167] Janin, *Églises et monastères*, 1, 353, situated adjacent to the cistern of the same name; said to have been founded by Constantine on the site of a temple of Zeus, but probably earlier.
[168] Janin, *Églises et monastères*, 1, 28–31, probably the famous monastery of this name, St Andrew 'en Krisei', bought by St Philaret in 792; the burial place of Andrew of Crete.
[169] Janin, *Églises et monastères*, 1, 35. This church, built under Justinian I, was located near the Adrianople Gate and the cistern of Aspar.
[170] Janin, *Églises et monastères*, 1, 89, the oldest church of this dedication in the city.
[171] Janin, *Églises et monastères*, 1, 12. The only thing known about this church is that Basil restored it.
[172] Otherwise unknown.
[173] Janin, *Églises et monastères*, 1, 22–3, constructed in the fourth century in the quarter Ta Marianou: Berger, *Untersuchungen*, 444–7.
[174] Janin, *Églises et monastères*, 1, 404; similarly located in the Portico of Domninos.
[175] Janin, *Églises et monastères*, 1, 114.
[176] Janin, *Églises et monastères*, 1, 14: believed to be one of the oldest churches in the capital. The *Patria* says it was built by Constantine; its existence is attested in 359.
[177] Janin, *Églises et monastères*, 1, 137, Ta Antiochou.
[178] The *Nea* (new) church seems first to have been dedicated to Gabriel, subsequently changed to Michael.

also of the Mother of God and of Nicholas, the illustrious prelate. This is the exquisite church which is there now and which they call 'the New Church'.[179] In beauty, comeliness and magnificence it knows no rival and is beyond compare. Sufficient income was assured for the provision of light and [164] for the needs of those who sing praises to God [there]. But what point is there in going on at length? The work itself is there, offering its peculiar beauty and magnificence to the beholder. He founded a number of other sacred churches within the palace in the name of the prophet Elijah,[180] Clement the martyr,[181] Christ the Saviour, Peter the apostle[182] and the archangel Michael, to describe the beauty of which even the eloquence of poets would not suffice. He did a considerable amount of construction at the palace, creating (as it were) palaces within the palace; there is no need to list them all. The so-called 'house of Manganes'[183] is the work of this emperor, and 'the new palace'[184] (as they call it) is another; these were built for the following reason. Basil was unwilling to disburse public funds for his own needs, so he built these mansions and provided a generous income for them from his agricultural products so that there would always be an abundant and sufficient provision for his imperial banqueting and for the guests he entertained throughout the year. He built the palace at Pegai and renovated the one at Hiereia, where he cleaned out the cistern which the emperor Heraclius had filled with earth and transformed into a flower and vegetable garden. Heraclius did the same with other cisterns

---

[179] Janin, *Églises et monastères*, I, 361ff.; also P. Magdalino, 'Observations on the Nea Ekklesia of Basil I,' *JÖB*, 37 (1987), 51–64. A number of buildings constructed by Basil were known as 'new' (note in the same paragraph, above, the New House). As Magdalino observes (52–4), the epithet does not so much mean 'new' in our modern sense as rather superior, i.e. to what was there before. The Nea was inaugurated Sunday 1 May 880.

[180] Janin, *Églises et monastères*, I, 136. For some reason Elijah was particularly popular with the Macedonians; Leo VI inaugurated a foot-race on the prophet's feast day, 20 July, according to the *Kleterogion of Philotheos*: Oikonomides, *Listes*, 215.

[181] Janin, *Églises et monastères*, I, 281. This Clement, bishop of Ancyra, martyred under Diocletian, must not be confused with Pope Clement – whose relics had been recently discovered by Constantine and Methodios while they were living in Cherson (860–1), a very important event at the time, of which neither Skylitzes nor his source (*Theophanes Continuatus*) make the slightest mention.

[182] Janin, *Églises et monastères*, I, 398.

[183] Basil had merely renovated a personal residence in which Michael Rhangabe lived before he came to the throne and which subsequently became part of the imperial patrimony. It was the residence of the patriarch Ignatios, the son of Michael Rhangabe, who ceded it to Basil: E Malamut, 'Nouvelle hypothèse sur l'origine de la maison impériale des Manganes', *Mélanges Svoronos*, I (Rethymno, 1986), 127–34. There is mention of a curator of this property from the beginning of the eleventh century. He was the administrator of the emperor's private domain, together with the 'grand curator', replaced in the 11th century by the economos for pious institutions.

[184] This *neos oikos* may be the same as the palace of Marina: C. Mango, 'The palace of Marina, the poet Palladas and the bath of Leo VI,' *Mélanges Chatzidakis* (Athens, 1991), 321–30.

within the palace (the one before the Magnaura and the one between the refectory of Justinian and the Lausiakon) because he learnt from Stephen the philosopher (who had studied the astrological conditions at his birth) that he would die by water. So he had the cisterns filled in, as we said. [Basil] cleaned out the cistern in the palace at Hiereia and restored it to its original function, making it a reservoir (instead of a garden) providing an abundant supply of limpid water. He built a very elegant church of the Theotokos in the forum so that the merchants [165] could have a house of prayer when their business detained them. He reconditioned and ornamented the church of St Phokas in the Stenon and, establishing a residence for monks, he provided a sufficient income for the maintenance of those who were living the ascetic life there.[185] He restored the great but ruined church of the Archangel at Sosthenion[186] to the beautiful state in which it now appears.

42. By promising them rewards, making them grants and exchanging gifts with them, he was able to render many of the Jews worthy of sacred baptism.[187] He strengthened in the faith the Bulgar race (only recently turned to the worship of God) by a mission of exemplary monks and priests distinguished by virtue.[188] He concluded a pact with the Russians; he was responsible for them partaking of salvific baptism and he sent them a bishop.[189]

43. The wonder which came about at the hands of the bishop who was sent is worth reporting. While the ruler was still clinging to superstition – as

---

[185] Janin, *Églises et monastères*, I, 498–9; this is the former property of Arsavir, see Michael III, c. 4 (above).

[186] Janin, *Églises et monastères*, I, 346–9, one of the most celebrated sanctuaries dedicated to St Michael, already attested in 515.

[187] On compulsory baptism of Jews in the time of Basil I: G. Dagron, 'Le traité de Grégoire de Nicée sur le bapteme des juifs,' *TM*, 11 (1991), 357.

[188] Photios' correspondence bears witness to his connections with the infant Bulgar church. Towards the end of Basil's reign the disciples of Methodios were chased out of Moravia, notably Clement and Nahum. Basil bought back Nahum and a hundred priests sold into slavery on the Venetian market by Sviatopluk of Moravia and sent them into Bulgaria. They encountered Greek clergy who were by no means enthusiastic about their installation in that country: C. Hannick, 'Les nouvelles chrétientés du monde byzantin: Russes, Bulgares et Serbes', ed. G. Dagron, *Histoire du christianisme*, IV, *Evêques, moines et empereurs (610–1054)*, ed. G. Dagron, P. Riché and A. Vauchez (Paris, 1993), 927–31

[189] Following *Theophanes Continuatus*, ed. Bekker, 342–4, Skylitzes in paraphrasing gives the impression that there was a second mission, subsequent to that of Photios, instigated by the patriarch Ignatios who, on this occasion, sent them a dignitary of archiepiscopal rank. It is possible that this first establishment of christianity in 'Russia', i.e. not in the Kiev region, but in the lands to the north of 'Russia', near the Baltic Sea, did not survive after the disappearance of the first Russian state: C. Zuckerman, 'Deux étapes de la formation de l'ancien état russe', *Les centres proto-urbains russes entre Scandinavie, Byzance et Orient*, ed. M. Kazanski, A. Nersessian and C. Zuckermann (Réalités byzantines, 7, Paris, 2000), 95–121, at 104–6.

were his grandees and all the people – he, wishing to compare their former religion with the Christian faith, summoned the bishop who had just arrived among them and asked him what he was going to proclaim and teach them. The bishop produced the sacred book of the divine gospel and explained to them some of the wonders worked by God during his human incarnation: 'Unless we and the Russian people have the opportunity of witnessing something similar (especially what you told us happened to the three children in the furnace), we will not believe you in the least.' [166] The bishop believed in the unerring word of Him who said, 'Whatever you ask in my name, you will receive,' and 'He who believes in the works that I do will do even greater than these.' He said to them: 'Even though it is not permitted to put the Lord God to the test,[190] if you have decided with all your heart to come to God, ask whatever you like and God will certainly do it on account of your faith, even though we be the most unworthy of men.' Without hesitation they asked that the codex of the divine gospel be thrown into the bonfire they had lit; and, if it were recovered undamaged, they would embrace the God who had been proclaimed to them by him. This was agreed to; the priest raised his eyes and his hands to God, saying: 'Jesus Christ, our God, glorify your holy name' – and then in the sight of this pagan people, the book of the holy gospel was thrown into the inferno. The fire burnt on for many hours, and when it finally died down the sacred codex was found intact and undamaged, not harmed in any way by the fire. When the barbarians saw this, dumbfounded by the magnitude of the wonder they spontaneously and without hesitation presented themselves for baptism.

44. About that time Constantine, the eldest of the emperor's sons, died of a fever, plunging his father into inconsolable grief.[191] But the emperor suffered this with quiet dignity, even comforting his wife and children.

45. The officers of the treasury urged the emperor to send [tax-] inspectors[192] into the themes, so that the tax revenues would flow in more freely. He, pretending to approve this suggestion, ordered them to choose and instruct persons who would effectively discharge this duty and then to bring them before him. The *genikos* selected those whom he thought would perform such a task well and then presented a list of the names of the chosen ones. But he was held to be seriously at fault [167] if he supposed

---

[190] Matt. 21:22, John 14:12, Matt. 4:7.
[191] Constantine died of fever 3 September 879: F. Halkin, 'Trois dates historiques précisés grâce au *Synaxaire*,' *B*, 24 (1954), 14–17.
[192] The *epoptes*, officers of the treasury under the head of the *genikon*, had the task of determining the level of taxation for the tax payers. They could grant reliefs and also refuse them.

ministers like that would be adequate for such service. When, in self-defence, he said there were none better in the entire realm, the emperor went on: 'In my judgement, the effort required by the proposed undertaking is such that, if it were possible, I would go out myself to perform it. Since that is neither convenient nor possible, I have no choice but to put my confidence in the two [senior] magisters of the realm. Through time, experience and the many offices they have held and by which they have been put to the test in the course of a long life of political service, these have demonstrated their incorruptible integrity. It is by them, I feel sure, that this task will be discharged in a fitting manner. Do you yourself go then,' he continued, 'inform them of the nature of the undertaking – and of my will. If they are willing to go, I approve.' When the magisters heard, they were dismayed. As grounds for an appeal, they protested their great age as a reason for not going and the many services they had already performed for the administration, praying that this service be taken away from them. So the messenger came back empty-handed and reported to the emperor what they had said. He listened and then said: 'Since it seems impossible for me to go and the most distinguished magisters decline the mission, having no minister adequate for the undertaking, it is my will that the situation be left without inspectors. It is better to take the chance that a few defraud the treasury (which is not a good thing) than to run the risk of somebody being punished in a compromising and ruinous way because of false accusations. And because of this, through his entire reign, for the entire population under Roman rule in all the themes, there was no new tax evaluation; or rather, to express it correctly, they were free and untaxed.

46. After Constantine, the emperor's eldest son, departed this life (as we mentioned), [Basil] transferred his affection and his hopes to [168] Leo, his second son, for whom envy prepared a bitter blow; the following account will explain how. There was a monk among those whom the emperor held in great affection and trusted implicitly, a priest whose name was Santabarenos.[193] Even though the emperor cherished him, the others did not think much of him and for this reason he was often attacked by Leo, the emperor's son, as a deceiver and a charlatan who would distort the emperor's reasoning from the better into less desirable ways of thinking.

[193] This monk got his name from his native village, Santabaris in Phrygia. With the support of the caesar Bardas he entered Stoudios' monastery where he was for a time hegoumenos, after the deposition of his predecessor, one Nicholas. His fate was bound up with that of Photios who appointed him Metropolitan of Euchaita: *ODB*, III, 1839, and the introduction to *Vita Euthymii*, ed. Karlin-Hayter, 40–5. According to Pseudo-Symeon the Logothete, 693, a source hostile to Photios, Theodore Santabarenos was originally, and never really ceased to be, a Manichee.

Santabarenos was wounded in his soul by this and yearned for revenge against Leo for insulting him, so [the monk] pretended to be friendly towards [Leo] and said to him one day: 'O emperor, since you are a young man and well loved by your father, why do you not carry a sword or a dagger when you ride out into the countryside with your father, so you can hand it to him if he needs it to deal with a beast? Or if there is a secret plot against him – as there often is – you will not be unarmed, but will have to hand what you need to strike back at your father's enemies.' Never thinking there might be guile here or that a plot was being rigged, Leo accepted the advice and was persuaded to carry a dagger slipped into his boot. Once Santabarenos realised that his plan had worked, he went to the emperor and said: 'O emperor, you ought to know that your son is plotting against your life. If you don't believe me, the next time you are out hunting order his footwear to be brought to you. It will be found that he is bearing a knife and that my information is perfectly correct.' This was agreed upon. An imperial hunting expedition was announced and the entire company rode out in the usual way. Leo, the emperor's son, went too, and when they came to a certain spot the emperor pretended to need a dagger and made a great fuss about finding one. Completely ignorant of his father's suspicions, the son innocently drew out the dagger he was carrying and handed it over to the father. At this occurrence, the allegations of Santabarenos were instantly believed while Leo's explanations were treated as vain and empty words. The emperor went back to the palace very angry with his son and locked him up in one of the palace buildings [169] known as Margarites, removing his imperial insignia.[194] He was incited by Santabarenos to put out the light of his eyes too, but he was prevented from doing this by the patriarch and the Senate; but Basil still kept him in gaol. Much time went by,[195] during which the Senate often attempted to intercede on Leo's behalf but, for one reason or another, was always prevented from doing so. Then a good way was found to accomplish what was intended. There was a bird in a cage hanging in the palace – to delight the eyes and ears of those who saw or heard it; the animal was a parrot, a mimic and a chatterbox. Either because somebody had taught it or because it had picked it up spontaneously, this bird would often cry out: 'Poor Leo, poor Leo.' Once, when the emperor was holding a banquet and the leading senators

[194] For the chronology, see R. H. J. Jenkins, 'The chronological accuracy of the Logothete for the years AD 867–913', *DOP*, 19 (1965), 91–112, at 102, repr. *Studies*, no. 111. It would have been autumn 883 when Leo was arrested. It looks as though Leo really had been plotting against a father whom he hated for forcing him into a marriage he abhorred. He was no doubt buoyed up by the opposition to the politics of the ageing emperor: Tougher, *Leo VI*, 57–9.
[195] Three years.

were feasting with him, the parrot kept calling out the words mentioned above. The guests were saddened and the feasting came to a halt as the guests sat there, occupied with their thoughts. When the emperor noticed this he enquired why they were refraining from eating. With tears in their eyes they said: 'Sovereign Lord, how can we, who are so put to shame by the voice of this bird, touch food; we who are supposed to be rational creatures and devoted to our sovereigns? This animal, devoid of reason, calls upon its sovereign while we, besotted with delights, are completely unmindful of our sovereign who transgressed no law. If he had been found guilty of some crime and it was proven that he had raised his hand against his father, we would raise our own hands against him in an insatiable lust for his blood. But if they cannot prove him guilty of the crime of which they accuse him, how long is the tongue of the false accuser going to have its way with him?' The emperor was mollified by these words; he told the senators to bide their time for a while, promising to look into the matter himself. Soon after he reconsidered, released his son from prison and had him brought before him.[196] He changed his clothes of mourning, cut his hair which had grown too long during his [170] affliction and restored to him his former imperial dignity.

47. Before very long Basil fell prey to the disease of diarrhoea which slowly sapped his strength.[197] Having disposed of imperial business as seemed best to him and publicly designated his heir and successor, he departed this life. He had co-reigned with Michael, his predecessor, one year and then distinguished himself by governing the empire alone for another nineteen years. Leo, the first in age of his surviving sons, inherited complete control of the government.

---

[196] Leo was set free on 20 July 886, the feast of St Elijah: 'Clétorologe de Philothée', Oikonomides, *Listes*, 215. Skylitzes (following his source, *Theophanes Continuatus*) alludes to this conspiracy but places it incorrectly in the chronological sequence of the events of Basil's reign. It was a very serious conspiracy, organised by John Kourkouas, domestic of the Hikanatai, comprising more than sixty senators and persons in authority. Probably already quite ill, Basil had to occupy himself with the problem of succession: B. Vlyssidou, 'La conspiration de Kourkouas dans la *Vita Basilii*', *Symmeikta*, 6 (1985), 53–8 (in Greek). This Kourkouas is the first known member of this family of eastern origins which was to furnish the empire with so many officers, including the emperor John Tzimiskes.

[197] There are varying accounts of Basil's end. *Vita Euthymii*, Karlin-Hayter (ch. 1) is the most specific: it speaks of a hunting accident. Basil was unhorsed by a stag which wounded him severely in the belly. It is possible that this story is inspired by the death of Hippolytos: A. Markopoulos, 'Kaiser Basileios I und Hippolytos', *Lesarten. Festschrift für Athanasios Kambylis zum 70. Geburtstag* (Berlin and New York, 1998), 81–91. Some modern historians have tried to read into Basil's demise an attempt by Leo to seize power, but there are difficulties with this, not the least of which is the fact that Basil survived his wounds for some time. According to the curse which was hurled at the assassins of Michael III, Basil should have been the last to die a violent death.

{The emperor Basil reigned eighteen years, eleven months and four days. He acceded on 24 September and died on 29 August. He was buried in the church of the Holy Apostles in the heroon of Constantine the Great in a green sarcophagus, gold and green.[198]}

[198] {–} MS B only.

CHAPTER 7

Leo VI the Philosopher (the Wise) [886–912]

1. [171] Once Leo[1] became master of all he surveyed[2] he cared little or nothing for any of the affairs of state. He chafed with anger at the memory of the recent intrigue which Santabarenos had contrived against him and decided to take immediate vengeance. First he brought up some not unreasonable accusations to make it seem as though there were good grounds for proceeding to the attack and also to remove certain obstacles from his path. He was well aware that he could do no serious harm to Santabarenos as long as Photios was occupying the patriarchal throne, rightly suspecting that Photios would protect him and stand by him lest he be the object of any despotic action. So the word was now put around that Photios had been eyeing the imperial throne for one of his relations and had conspired with Santabarenos; but they could both see that there was no future to their project unless Leo was first put out of the way; that was why they brought the false charge against him mentioned above. Since he knew this, [Leo's] first action was to remove [Photios] from the patriarchal throne.[3] He promptly despatched the magister Andrew the stratelates together with the magister John Hagiopolites (who was logothete of the drome) to the Great Church. Their orders were to go up into the ambo of the church and to read out the charges against the patriarch Photios for all to hear. They were then to drag him from the throne and exile him to the monastery of Harmonianoi.[4] Not wasting a moment, the emperor appointed Stephen the synkellos[5] (his own brother) patriarch. [172] Because [the metropolitan of]

---

[1] A study of the reign of Leo VI has recently appeared, containing an up-to-date bibliography: S. Tougher, *The reign of Leo VI (886–912): politics and people* (The Medieval Mediterranean, 15, Leiden, 1997). Earlier works by R. J. H. Jenkins and P. Karlin-Hayter offer useful supplementary matter.
[2] 30 August 886.   [3] 29 or 30 September 886.
[4] R. Janin, *Les églises et les monastères des grands centres byzantins* (Paris, 1975), 84–5.
[5] Consecrated 25 December 886; Stephen presided over the church six years and five months, until May 893. He was nineteen years old when he became patriarch: R. H. J. Jenkins, 'The chronological accuracy of the Logothete for the years AD 867–913', *DOP*, 19 (1965), 91–112, at 99. This arbitrary choice worked out reasonably well as the new patriarch acquired a reputation for piety.

Herakleia had departed this life,[6] [Stephen] was consecrated by Theophanes the protothronos.[7] [The emperor] then sent [men] in all speed to Euchaita where the above-mentioned Theodore Santabarenos was presiding over the aforementioned church, with orders to bring that man to him.

2. While this was being done, he sent Andrew the stratelates and many other senators to the monastery of Philippikos[8] at Chrysopolis. Their orders were to take clergy with candles, incense and lights and exhume the assassinated emperor Michael. They were to lay [his body] in a coffin of cypress wood, dress it up in a manner worthy of an emperor and bring it into the city. There, accompanied by the emperor's brothers, Alexander and Stephen the patriarch, [the body] was to be brought in solemn procession with sacred hymns and songs to the church of the Holy Apostles where it was to be laid in a marble sarcophagus.[9] And that is what happened.

3. Stylianos Zaoutzes[10] he promoted magister and logothete of the drome. [The emperor] had already begun to frequent this man's daughter, even though the woman to whom he was legally married, the augousta Theophano, was still alive.[11] For her part, she saw and heard everything that was going on but did not in the least allow herself to give way to the passion of jealousy.[12]

4. In a short time the city of Hypsele in the theme of Charsianon[13] was captured by the Hagarenes and all its inhabitants taken prisoner

---

[6] Traditionally the metropolitan of Herakleia consecrated the patriarch because Byzantium had once been a dependency of his see.
[7] Metropolitan of Caesarea.
[8] A brother-in-law of the emperor Maurice named Philippikos built a monastery dedicated to the Virgin there in 594: Janin, *Grands centres*, II, 24–5. In reality the translation of the corpse of Michael III was the *first* decision of the new emperor: Jenkins, 'Symeon "the Logothete"', 106.
[9] This action of Leo has given weight to the arguments of those who believe he was the son of Michael. Tougher, *Leo VI*, 42–67, argues convincingly that Leo was trying to appease the Amorian elite and to secure the solidarity of the aristocracy.
[10] Zaoutzas or Zaoutzes derives from the Armenian word *zaoutch*, black; it is almost certain that the basileiopator was very dark. He was born in Thrace of an Armenian family, and was probably related to Tzantes, a variant of Zaoutzes [?], the stratego of Macedonia who brought the Byzantine prisoners (including the parents of Basil I) out of Bulgaria (reign of Basil I, c. 2, note 16). Stylianos had been promoted protospatharios then hetaireiarch at the end of Basil's reign: *Vita Euthymii patriarchae CP. Text, translation, introduction and commentary*, ed. P. Karlin-Hayter (Bibliothèque de *Byzantion*, 3, Brussels, 1970), 149–2; Tougher, *Leo VI*, 98–109. Tougher argues that Zaoutzes was not quite as influential upon Leo as we have sometimes thought. At the beginning of the reign Andrew the stratelates had the most influence.
[11] Leo married Theophano on his father's orders and against his own will. She was one of the Martinakioi (as was Eudokia, Basil's wife). This marriage reinforced the connection with the Amorian dynasty. They had one daughter, named Eudokia after her paternal grandmother.
[12] Theophano was chosen as Leo's bride after a beauty competition in 882.
[13] Doganhar today, 70 km north-east of Sivas. This fortress may have fallen in 888: A. A. Vasiliev, *Byzance et les Arabes*, II: *Les relations politiques de Byzance et des Arabes à l'époque de la dynastie macédonienne*, ed. M. Canard (CBHB 2, 1, Brussels, 1968), 121–2, F. Hild, *Das Byzantinische Strassensystem in Kappadokien* (TIB, 2, Vienna, 1977), 108.

5. and a fire occurred in the southern part of the city, namely in Sidera. It reduced the church of St Thomas the Apostle to cinders and ashes[14] [but] the emperor reconstructed it at great expense.

6. [173] Santabarenos was now brought into the city. Andrew the stratelates and the magister Stephen (whom Santabarenos had often denounced before the emperor Basil) proposed to the emperor that the libellous charges against the emperor himself be examined. They assured Leo that it would be possible to find proof that the patriarch Photios and Santabarenos had devised and staged the comedy themselves in order to elevate a relation of Photios to the rank of emperor. Imperial officers were dispatched to bring Photios and Santabarenos to the palace of Pege – with instructions to confine them apart from each other. The stratelates Andrew himself, the magister Stephen,[15] the magister [John] Hagiopolites[16] together with the patricians Krateros[17] and Gouber[18] were chosen to be the examining magistrates. They brought in Photios the patriarch and respectfully seated him on a throne; when they were seated themselves, the enquiry began. The stratelates said to the patriarch: 'Does your Grace know the monk Theodore?' 'I know many monks called Theodore,' he replied, 'but I cannot know to which of them you are referring.' When Andrew added the name Santabarenos, the patriarch testified: 'I know the man; he is the bishop of Euchaita.' When Santabarenos was brought in, Andrew said to him: 'The emperor would ask of you: Where are the monies and properties which are his due as emperor?' He responded: 'They are in the possession of those to whom the emperor of the day gave them. Since the emperor who has lately come to power is calling for them, he has the right to search them out and take them into his possession.' Andrew continued: 'Well now, just

---

[14] This happened in 887 according to Michael the Syrian: *Chronique de Michel le Syrien, patriarche jacobite d'Antioche (1166–1199)*, ed. J. B. Chabot (Paris, 1905–10), repr. 1963, III, 119. Janin, *Églises et monastères*, 1.252, distinguishes this St Thomas' from the St Thomas' *en tois Amantiou*, the famous sanctuary where the relics of John Chrysostom were temporarily laid to rest in 438. This church was well-situated close to the Iron Gate, as Skylitzes says. Leo VI delivered a homily there on the inauguration of the restored church: Antonopoulou, Th. Antonopoulou, *The homilies of the emperor Leo VI* (Leyden, 1997), 238–40.

[15] Stephen was the son of Kalomaria, a sister of the empress Theodora, who had married the patrician Arsavir. Stephen was thus the nephew of the patriarch John the Grammarian and a cousin of the emperor Michael III.

[16] The former logothete of the drome.

[17] The patrician Leo Krateros, strategos of the Anatolikon theme, was one of the god parents of Leo VI: *Constantine Porphyrogennetos, De administrando imperio*, ed. G. Moravcsik, tr. R. H. J. Jenkins (CFHB, 1, Washington, DC, 1967), 622.

[18] Gouber or Goumer (*PmbZ* 2527 = *PBE* Goumer 1) was logothete of the drome under Basil I. He had one sister called Theodosia (*PmbZ* 7792) who married the caesar Bardas and another, Eirene (*PmbZ* 1452), who was superior of the Chrysobalantou monastery. The name may be from the Bulgarian Kouber.

tell me: whom did you wish to make emperor when you proposed to the emperor's father to put out the eyes of his own son? A relation of yours, or one of the patriarch's?' [Santabarenos] swore that he knew nothing about the things of which he was being accused. The magister Stephen said to him: [174] 'O devious and crafty-minded one, then why did you lead the emperor to think one could condemn the patriarch on this score?' As soon as he heard this allegation, [Santabarenos fell down and] embraced the patriarch's feet saying: 'I beseech you, your Grace, in the name of God, first to depose me and to deprive me of the priesthood; then let them take me and punish me as an evil-doer. For my own part, I know nothing of this nor have I communicated anything of it to the emperor.' The patriarch raised him up and set him on his feet, saying to him: 'By my own salvation, monsignor Theodore, archbishop you are both now and in the world to come.' In anger Andrew the stratelates asked: 'Deceiver and charlatan! Did you not advise the emperor through me that you could condemn the patriarch on this score?' – but he again denied any knowledge of this matter and the leaders withdrew. The emperor was maddened with rage when the officials came back and told him what had been said, especially so because he could not find a charge against the patriarch that would stand up in court.[19] He sent [men] to flog Santabarenos mercilessly and exiled him to Athens. Then he sent others to blind him and deport him to the East. A long time afterwards he recalled him from exile and made an allocation for his maintenance from the resources of the New Church. He outlived Leo, dying in the reign of Zoe his wife and of Constantine his son.

7. In the second year of the reign of Leo when Agion, duke of Longobardia and son-in-law of the king of Francia,[20] heard of the death of the emperor Basil, he broke his treaty of friendship with the Romans and brought the entire region [of Longobardia] under his sway. When the emperor learned of this he dispatched the patrician Constantine, the superintendent of his own table, against him with the western thematic armies. [175] There was an engagement in which the forces of Constantine were soundly defeated and decimated; he himself only just escaped with his life.[21]

---

[19] The case against Photios collapsed, to the intense annoyance of the young emperor. It is not known what happened after the trial. Presumably Leo had some respect for the aged ex-patriarch for he describes him in favourable terms in the funeral oration on Basil I.

[20] Agion or rather Aigion, prince of Benevento, whose sister Agiltrude had married Guy II of Spoleto, who became western emperor in 891 after his coronation by pope Stephen V.

[21] June 887. The battle took place before the walls of Bari, the Romans having lost control of that town the year before: J. Gay, *L'Italie méridionale et l'empire byzantin depuis l'avènement de Basil I jusqu'à la prise de Bari par les Normands (867–1071)* (Paris, 1904), 134.

8. At that time there was an eclipse of the sun about the sixth hour of the day. The stars even appeared; violent winds blew; there were terrifying storms and dangerous lightning;[22] there were fire-bearing thunderbolts by which seven men were burned up on the steps of [the church of] St Constantine in the forum.[23]

9. Samos was besieged by the Saracens and the commander, the patrician Constantine Paspalas,[24] was taken prisoner.

10. Prompted by his passion for Zoe, the daughter of Zaoutzes, the emperor honoured her father with the newfangled title (which did not exist before) of basileopator[25] [father of the emperor]. Zoe was then in the full flower of her charm and beauty; she had previously been married to the patrician Theodore Gouniatzitzes but he was treacherously poisoned.[26] She, moreover, became the emperor's concubine while his wife was still living.

11. The following year, Stephen, the emperor's brother and patriarch, departed this life;[27] Anthony Kauleas was appointed in his stead.[28]

12. That is what was happening in the capital. Then Symeon, ruler of the Bulgars, found the following pretext for breaking off his treaty with the Romans, as he wished to do.[29] The basileopator had a slave, a

---

[22] 8 August, between 11 a.m. and 2 p.m., mentioned in *SynaxCP*, col. 878.
[23] A chapel was located at the base of Constantine's column: Janin, *Églises et monastères*, 1, 296.
[24] First mention of a strategos of this maritime theme, no doubt newly created to oppose the menace of the pirates from Crete. Paspalas was defeated between 891 and 893.
[25] Tougher, *Leo VI*, 99–100, reminds us that the post which Zaoutzes actually held was that of *basileiopator*, meaning (more or less) mayor of the palace (*basileia*). Skylitzes appears to attribute his obtaining this post to his daughter's standing in the emperor's eyes, probably because by the time the *Synopsis* was composed the term *basileiopator* had lost its original meaning. But Stylianos received his appointment prior to his daughter's marriage: there is nothing to suggest that his nomination had anything to do with her relations with Leo.
[26] According to the *VEuthymii*, ed. Karlin-Hayter, 45, the husband of Zoe, there named Gouzouniates, died shortly after the empress Theodora.
[27] May or June 899.
[28] Kauleas was the creature of Zaoutzes. The synkellos (the future patriarch Euthymios) was passed over on this occasion. It is to Anthony's credit that he put an end to the quarrel between the Photians and the Ignatians, the latter including most recently Metrophanes of Smyrna and Stylianos Mappas of Neocaesarea.
[29] On the personality of Symeon and what he hoped to achieve by war see J. Shepard, 'Symeon of Bulgaria – peacemaker', *Annuaire de l'Université Saint Clement d'Ochride*, 83.3 (Sofia, 1989), 9–48, for a fairly irenic view of the Bulgar. For a less favourable assessment, Tougher, *Leo VI*, 174, who recognises that Symeon, until recently the master of Bulgaria, had no wish to smooth over the crisis – which would have made him look like the creature of Constantinople. This opinion is shared by P. Stephenson, *Byzantium's Balkan frontier: a political study of the northern Balkans, 900–1204* (Cambridge, 2000), 20–1. At all events Leo had little appreciation of the consequences of his action and none of the mood the Bulgars were in. J. Howard-Johnston, 'Byzantium, Bulgaria and the peoples of the Ukraine in the 890s', *MAIET*, 7 (2000), 342–56. Having little confidence in the chronology of pseudo-Symeon the Logothete (which *Theophanes Continuatus*,

eunuch, named Mousikos who was friendly with some greedy merchants to whom he sought to bring some profit.[30] Trading upon his influence with Zaoutzes, [176] he had the goods coming into Constantinople[31] from Bulgaria rerouted through Thessalonike, where he appointed those greedy merchants as customs officers. These then exploited the Bulgars who were importing goods by demanding increasingly heavy customs duties. This the Bulgars reported to Symeon who brought it to the attention of the emperor, but he was so much under the influence of Zaoutzes that he wrote it off as nonsense which merited no response whatsoever. Now Symeon (who, as we said, was just looking for a credible pretext) exploded in rage and took up arms against the Romans. When the emperor heard of this, he too prepared for war. He furnished Prokopios Krinites (then serving as stratelates)[32] with a large army of officers and men, plus Kourtikios the Armenian[33] – and sent him out against Symeon. The armies met head on in Macedonia and the Romans got the worse of it. Krenites himself, the Armenian Kourtikios and many others who had been taken from the imperial Hetaireia were butchered. Symeon slit the noses of the prisoners who were the emperor's retinue[34] and sent them off to the city – to the disgrace of the Romans. Deeply ashamed by this disaster and by his humiliation at Symeon's hands, the emperor sent the patrician Niketas Skleros[35] across the Danube to persuade the Turks[36] and Hungarians (as

hence Skylitzes, follow), Howard-Johnston constructs a different schedule according to which the war with Symeon probably has to be placed earlier in the reign of Leo. It may have something to do with the troubles which followed the abdication of Boris-Michael and the abortive restoration of paganism by his son Vladimir.

[30] *Theophanes Continuatus*, ed. I. Bekker (CSHB, Bonn, 1838), 357, gives their names: Staurakios and Kosmas. They were probably both promoted kommerkiarioi for there is a seal of a kommerkiarios of Thessalonike for that time whose name is Staurakios (*DOSeals*, 1.18.44). It is not clear what exactly were the measures taken by Mousikos even though these obviously harmed the Bulgars: N. Oikonomides, 'Le kommerkion d'Abydos, Thessalonique et le commerce bulgare au 9e siècle, *Hommes et richesses dans l'empire Byzantine* (Paris, 1991), 241–8. Symeon began hostilities in 894.

[31] P. Magdalino, 'St Demetrios and Leo VI', *BS*, 51 (1990), 198–201, proposes an ingenious hypothesis to explain the benefit conferred on the friends of Zaoutzes and on the city of Thessalonike. Leo had a particular devotion to St Demetrios and, since this saint had appeared to him on the eve of his liberation, he would wish to show his gratitude to the city which housed the most significant shrine of that saint.

[32] It is hard to tell whether the term only means 'army chief' or has a more precise meaning, in which case it could mean 'the chief of the army' – in the absence of the domestic of the scholai. This army had been put together in a hurry because of the suddenness of the attack; the greater part of the army was campaigning elsewhere.

[33] The same Kourtikios who submitted to Basil.

[34] These were Khazars.

[35] The Skleroi were a military family of Armenian origin of which the first known member was strategos of the Peloponnese at the beginning of the ninth century: W. Seibt, *Die Skleroi. Eine prosopographisch-sigillographische Studie* (Byzantina Vindobonensia, 9, Vienna, 1976), no. 6.

[36] Hungarians, who do derive from the Turkic peoples of the Steppes.

they are called) to cross the river[37] and to devastate Bulgaria as best they could. [Niketas] made contact with the Turks, persuaded them to take up arms against the Bulgars, took hostages and returned to the emperor who, meanwhile, had decided to make war against the Bulgars by land and sea. He appointed the patrician and droungarios Eustathios to command at sea and, as commander of the land forces, the patrician Nikephoros Phokas, whom he appointed domestic of the scholai after the death of Andrew. [177] As these forces converged on Bulgaria, the emperor, still hoping for peace, sent the quaestor Konstantiniakos to Symeon – who promptly arrested him and threw him into prison, thinking that the man had not come to him in good faith. While Symeon was dealing with the army of Phokas, the Turks crossed the river and laid waste all of Bulgaria. When Symeon learnt of this, he abandoned Phokas and advanced against the Turks. They too were anxious to engage the Bulgars; they crossed the Danube, attacked them and severely defeated them. Symeon was only just able to save himself in Dorostolon (also known as Dristra). The victorious Turks offered the emperor the opportunity of ransoming the prisoners they were holding – which he seized and dispatched some citizens to redeem those people. But Symeon was so enfeebled that, by the agency of the droungarios Eustathios, he requested a peace treaty of the emperor – who acceded to his request. He sent Leo Choirosphaktes[38] to arrange the truce; Phokas, domestic of the scholai, and the droungarios were ordered home with their forces,[39] but when Leo Choirosphaktes arrived [in Bulgaria], Symeon flung him into prison without even hearing what he had to say and marched out against the Turks with a great army. On the occasion of this sudden and unexpected nature of this turn of events, the emperor could offer [the Turks] no help. [Symeon] put them to flight and overran all their land. Arrogant and haughty in his victory, he wrote to the emperor that he would not make peace until the Bulgar prisoners had

---

[37] The Hungarians had recently migrated in no great number from the plains of southern Russia and were in process of settling themselves in Pannonia, their future homeland: C. Zuckerman, 'Les Hongrois au pays Lébédia: une nouvelle puissance aux confins de Byzance et de la Khazarie ca. 836–889', *Byzantium at war: ninth–twelfth century* (Athens, 1997), 51–74. For a more general description of the early centuries of Hungary: *Les Hongrois et l'Europe: conquete et intégration*, ed. S. Csernus and K. Korompay (Paris and Szeged, 1999).

[38] Leo Choirosphaktes was related to the imperial family, hence the high rank of magister. He was an educated courtier some of whose writings have survived: G. Kolias, *Léon Choirosphraktès, magistre, proconsul et patrice* (Athens, 1939); and P. Magdalino, 'In search of the Byzantine courtier: Leo Choirosphaktes and Constantine Manasses', *Byzantine court culture from 829 to 1204*, ed. H. Maguire (Washington, DC, 1997), 141–65.

[39] It was a grave error on the part of Leo VI to recall the troops before the peace treaty was signed.

been returned, to which the emperor agreed.⁴⁰ Thus Theodore, one of the closest associates of Symeon, arrived together with Choirosphaktes and took charge of the prisoners.

13. When the basileopator Zaoutzes realised in what good stead Nikephoros Phokas, the domestic, stood with the emperor, he sought [178] to make him his son-in-law. Suspecting this would anger the emperor, Phokas would have nothing to do with it, which enraged Zaoutzes. So he trumped up a charge against Phokas and had him relieved of his command, replacing him with magister Katakalon Abidelas. But after a short period of inactivity, Nikephoros was appointed commander of the Thrakesian⁴¹ [theme]. He achieved many successes in all his commands and inflicted numerous defeats on the Hagarenes and other people before he died at a great age leaving two sons, Bardas and Leo.

14. As Symeon was unwilling to stand by the terms of the treaty, the emperor decided that he would have to fight and deliver the Bulgars an annihilating defeat. He now ordered all the thematic units and the professional troops of the east to cross [to the west]. He made the western [forces] ready for battle in addition to yet another by no means small army, and sent all these forces against Symeon. He appointed the domestic of the scholai, Katakalon⁴² [Abidelas], to be their leader and general, with the patrician Theodosios the protovestiarios as his colleague. They encountered the advancing Symeon at Bulgarophygon;⁴³ battle was joined and the Romans were put to flight with heavy losses. The protovestiarios himself

---

⁴⁰ Once the treaty was signed in 896 or 897, peace must have been fully established because in his *Kletorologion* composed in 899 Philotheos notes that two Bulgar 'friends' had their places at the emperor's table: N. Oikonomides, *Les listes de préséance byzantines des IXe et Xe siècles* (Le monde byzantin, Paris, 1972), 163 and 167.

⁴¹ This tale of the demotion of Phokas and his appointment to the Thrakesion theme invites caution. He was, after all, the favourite general of the emperor, as his own *Taktika* attests. *The Chronicle of the Logothete* (*Symeonis magistri et Logothetae chronicon*, rec. St. Wahlgren (CFHB series Berolinensis XLIV/I, Berlin–New York, 2006), 277) says that Symeon recommenced hostilities when he learnt of the death of Nikephoros Phokas: J.-C. Cheynet, 'Les Phocas', *Le traité sur la guérilla de l'empereur Nicéphore Phocas* (Le monde byzantin, Paris, 1986), 289–315, at 295–6 = J.-C. Cheynet, *La société byzantine. L'apport des sceaux* (Bilans de recherche 3, Paris, 2008), 479–80.

⁴² Probably to be identified with Leo Katakoilas, droungarios of the watch, related to Photios – which brought him into disgrace at one stage. It was Euthymios who persuaded the emperor to recall him. The monastery which the emperor built for Euthymios at Psamathia (south-west of the capital) was on an estate which had been confiscated from Katakoilas. Psamathia possessed a *metochion* – the Ta Agathou monastery – which had also been a property of the then droungarios (*Vita Euthymii*, ed. Karlin-Hayter 26–31, reign of Alexander, c. 1).

⁴³ For once the Roman army was at full strength, which makes the defeat all the more bitter. Symeon invaded Macedonia in spring 896, encountering the imperial forces at Bulgarophygon, a fortress of Thrace 160 km west of Constantinople: P. Soustal, *Thrakien (Thrake, Rodope und Haiminontos)* (TIB, 6, Vienna, 1991), 223–4.

Leo VI the Philosopher

lost his life, while the domestic shamefully saved his life and a few others' in Bulgarophygon.[44]

15. At one time the emperor went to what we call Damian's Fields[45] with Zoe, Zaoutzes' daughter, intending to stay there for a while. Zaoutzes' son Leo, Christopher Tzantzes[46] and some others mounted an uprising[47] against him, but he was wakened in time because Zoe heard the din. Alerted, the emperor promptly embarked from Pege and sailed to the [179] palace. He dismissed John, droungarios of the watch, for being careless concerning the emperor's security and Zaoutzes was out of favour for a time[48] – until the magister Leo surnamed Theodotakes, a friend of both, reconciled them.

16. After the augousta Theophano died,[49] the emperor Leo crowned Zoe, Zaoutzes' daughter, and [his marriage with her] was blessed by a clergyman of the palace[50] – who was promptly degraded. She lived one year and eight months after being proclaimed and then died. When the sarcophagus in which her body was to be laid was being prepared, they found an incised inscription which read: 'Daughter of Babylon, wasted with misery.'[51]

17. Basil, the emperor's *epeiktes*,[52] a nephew of Zaoutzes, was contemplating the unspeakable against the emperor.[53] He shared his secret with

---

[44] Skylitzes says nothing of the consequences of this defeat. Leo VI agreed to pay an annual tribute, which conferred a fairly pacific character on the rest of his reign, with the exception of one campaign by Symeon hoping to gain some advantage from the sack of Thessalonike by the Arabs.

[45] Damian, parakoimomenos under Michael III, had a monastery built on the European bank of the Bosporos, close to the present Ortaköy, and thus gave his name to the area: R. Janin, *Constantinople byzantine* (*AOC*, 4A, Paris, 1964), 470.

[46] Other chroniclers say this Tzantzes (often taken as an alternative form of Zaoutzes) was a son of the Basileopator: *Georgius Monachus Continuatus*, 830; *Theophanes Continuatus*, ed. Bekker, 360.

[47] Probably in 897, before Leo's marriage to Zoe. This uprising was no doubt the consequence of Byzantine reverses. *Theophanes Continuatus*, ed. Bekker, 360, and *George the Monk, Theophanes Continuatus*, ed. I Bekker (CSHB, Bonn, 1838), 855, say that the inhabitants of Cherson slew their commander and that the Arabs took Koron, the former capital of the theme of Cappadocia: F. Hild and M. Restle, *Kappadokien (Kappadokia, Charsianon, Sebasteia und Lykandos)* (TIB, 2, Vienna, 1981), 216.

[48] He replaced him with Pardos, son of the hetaireiarch Nicholas, a faithful supporter of the emperor: *Theophanes Continuatus*, ed. Bekker, 361; *George the Monk, Continuatus*, ed. Bekker, 856.

[49] Theophano probably died on 10 November 896: P. Karlin-Hayter, 'La mort de Théophano (10.11.896 ou 895)', *BZ*, 62 (1969), 13–19, but possibly as late as 897: V. Grumel, 'Chronologie des événements du règne de Léon VI', *EO*, 35 (1936), 22–3.

[50] His name was Sinapes: *Symeonis magistri*, 279. Leo VI did not marry Zoe before July 898: Tougher, *Leo VI*, 142.

[51] Ps. 136–7:8.

[52] This was an official serving under the count of the stables responsible for maintaining the supply of horses and pack animals: Oikonomides, *Listes*, 339. This conspiracy may be dated to the beginning of the year 900.

[53] With the death of Zoe, the Zaoutzes clan was attempting to retain its grasp on power.

the koubikoularios Samonas,[54] a Hagarene by birth, placing him under oath not to reveal it. Samonas gave his word – and then revealed the whole plan, for he leapt into the saddle and went straight to the emperor. Taking him aside, he said: 'O emperor, I want to tell you something which will bring about *my* death if it is spoken, *yours* if it is kept in silence,' and he revealed Basil's whole plot. At first the emperor would not believe it, so Samonas, hoping to convince him, proposed that two of the emperor's most trusted men be sent to his house. He asked that they remain in hiding when Basil arrived there and that, while he was there and they were speaking to each other, what was said by both of them be written down. To this the emperor willingly agreed. He sent Christopher the protovestiarios and Kalokyros, one of his chamberlains, who hid themselves when they got to Samonas' residence and waited to see what would happen. [180] Unaware of what was going on, Basil arrived at Samonas' house and fell into the trap. The conversation was uninhibited: the unspeakable was openly discussed and the emperor's envoys took down what was said in writing. Then, leaving the two conspirators at supper, they secretly left the house, went to the emperor and gave him their notes. As soon as he had read them, he sent Basil into Macedonia, allegedly to distribute alms on behalf of his late aunt Zoe;[55] he had Stypeiotes[56] arrest the droungarios of the watch[57] and banished Nicholas the hetaireiarch[58] from the city. He then had Basil brought back from Macedonia, subjected him to a trial, had him paraded through the city centre in disgrace and then banished him to Athens. He subsequently convened a plenary session of the senate and read out what Samonas had brought to light. The Senators praised him and pronounced him deserving of the highest honour, whereupon the emperor immediately conferred on him the rank of protospatharios and numbered him among his confidants.

---

[54] A eunuch born at Melitene c. 875, a member of the Zaoutzes household: R. Janin, 'Un Arabe ministre à Byzance: Samonas', *EO*, 34 (1935), 317–18; *V. Euthymii*, ed. Karlin-Hayter, 177.
[55] *Psychika* – donations which the deceased empress was offering for the salvation of her soul, to the tune of 24,000 pieces of silver: *Theophanes Continuatus*, 363.
[56] This could be Michael Stypeiotes, the future ambassador to Symeon of Bulgaria: reign of Romanos Lakapenos, c. 12.
[57] Relatives of Zaoutzes. Nicholas (who was his son-in-law) had at least two sons: Pardos, the recently promoted droungarios of the watch, and Basil the *epeiktes: Theophanes Continuatus*, ed. Bekker 363–4; *Symeonis magistri*, 281.
[58] Another relation of Zaoutzes – probably his son-in-law: Leo the Grammarian, ed. Bekker (CSHB, Bonn, 1842), 271.

18. On the death of the patriarch Anthony, Nicholas the Mystikos[59] was made [patriarch] on account of his outstanding intelligence and wisdom.[60]

19. As the emperor Leo was unable to perform the ceremonies as they are laid down in the formularies without an augousta, he crowned Anna, the daughter of Zoe, daughter of Zaoutzes. He married a beautiful and gracious maiden from the Opsikion [theme] named Eudokia[61] and crowned her too. She was expecting and about to give birth to a child when both she and the embryo died.[62]

20. In honour of his first wife, Theophano, the emperor erected a very beautiful church in her name, close by Holy Apostles'.[63] He built another church in the Topoi quarter dedicated [181] to St Lazaros. Here he brought and deposited the body of the saint [Lazaros] and also that of his sister, Mary Magdalene.[64]

21. While the navy was occupied with the construction of these buildings, the Hagarene fleet succeeded in capturing Taormina in Sicily[65] and many Romans were slain. The island of Lemnos[66] was also taken by the Hagarenes and a considerable number of people led into slavery. On the day of mid-Pentecost,[67] the customary procession to the church of St Mokios[68] was taking place, including the emperor and his entourage.

---

[59] On the position of *mystikos*, private secretary to the emperor: P. Magdalino, 'The not-so-secret functions of the mystikos', *REB*, 42 (1984), 229–40, repr. *Tradition and transformation in medieval Byzantium* (London, 1991).

[60] Anthony died 1 February 901; Nicholas was promoted 1 March 901. He was born in 852, in Italy. He came to Constantinople and became an associate of Photios. When Photios withdrew from public life, Nicholas retreated to St Typhon, which is where Leo VI went to find him, to make him his *mystikos*. A wealth of letters and other writings of Nicholas survives: *Nicholas I, Patriarch of Constantinople, Letters*, ed. and tr. R. J. H. Jenkins and L. G. Westerink (CFHB, 6, Washington, DC, 1973).

[61] Eudocia Baiane, *VEuthymii*, ed. Karlin-Hayter, 63, no doubt a relative of the Baianos who denounced the machinations of Leo Apostypes to Basil I. Eudocia gave birth to a boy (named Basil) but he died a few days after his mother.

[62] 12 April 901, Easter day.

[63] By imperial fiat Leo had Theophano listed as one of the saints, her rather meagre list of miracles notwithstanding: G. Dagron, 'Théophano, les Saints-Apôtres et l'église de Tous-Les-Saints', *Mélanges Zakythènos, Symmeikta*, 9 (1994), 211–18. Her shrine stood close to Holy Apostles, i.e. in the very centre of Constantinople: Janin, *Églises et monastères*, 1, 389.

[64] Some texts attribute this church to Basil I. It was located at Topoi, the lower part of the Serailpoint: Janin, *Églises et monastères*, 298–300.

[65] This, the last Byzantine stronghold of any significance in Sicily, fell on 1 August 902.

[66] On this large Aegean island: J. Koder, *Aigaion Pelagos (Die nordliche Agais)* (TIB, 10, Vienna, 1998), 205–9.

[67] Mid-Pentecost, 11 May 903. On the ceremonies for mesopentecoste: *De caerim.*, Vogt, 1.26, 92–100.

[68] This vast church, one of the extremely few pre-Constantinian foundations in the area, stood outside the Constantinian wall, close by the cistern of Mokios: Janin, *Églises et monastères*, 1, 355–8. Although the oikonomos was a monk at the time of the attack, the *monastery* of St Mokios did not

When it came time for the offertory, just as the emperor was approaching the holy doors, a man leapt from the ambo and dealt him a blow on the head with a massive, heavy club. He would have killed him immediately if the end of the club had not caught the hanging chandelier and lost something of its impetus. Blood was flowing freely from the emperor's head while the officials fled in disorder. Alexander, the emperor's brother, was not present at the offertory, allegedly taken ill – which led many to think that it was he who had hatched this plot.[69] The emperor's attacker was arrested and subjected to prolonged torture but he revealed nothing of any accomplice. They cut off his hands and feet then burned him in the sphendone [hairpin bend] of the Hippodrome. Henceforth, this procession was suspended, in spite of the repeated requests addressed to the emperor by Mark, the wisest of monks and oeconomus of this monastery (he who completed the Tetraodion for Holy Saturday by Kosmas the Great). When the emperor refused his request, the monk said: [182] 'O emperor, do not be angry or dismayed, for it is foretold in writing by the prophet David that you should suffer, when he speaks of "All evil the enemy accomplished in your sanctuary; and those who hate you have made their boast in the midst of your feast."[70] But you, Lord-and-Master, you are destined to rule the empire for ten more years from now,' and that is how it was. He died ten years later on the very day on which he was wounded.

22. The emperor Leo took a fourth wife, Zoe Karbonopsina,[71] who lived with him some considerable time uncrowned.

23. When the sons of Hagar learned that the Bulgarians were wearing down the Romans by their incursions, they armed a fleet and sent it against the Roman shores. They appointed a renegade Christian, Leo of Attaleia,[72] to command the fleet. He had taken up residence in Tripoli[73] and that was how he came by the name by which he was known [Tripolites]. The

---

exist prior to the reign of Basil II: P. Magdalino, *Constantinople médiévale: études sur l'évolution des structures urbaines* (Paris, 1996), 62.

[69] The detailed account of this assault in the *VEuthymii*, ed. Karlin-Hayter, 67, presents Alexander's attitude in a different light.

[70] Ps. 73:3b–4, *LXX*.

[71] Zoe 'of the coal-black-eyes' was of the same distinguished family as Theophanes Confessor, the chronicler. One of her great-grandfathers, Photeinos, had been strategos of the Anatolikon theme under Michael II: *Theophanes Continuatus*, ed. Bekker, 76; one of her sisters was married to Himerios: *VEuthymii*, ed. Karlin-Hayter, 109.

[72] Attaleia, the principal port of the Kibyrrhaiote (naval) theme, played a key role in the fight against the Arab pirates. Leo would have been captured as a youth and subsequently become a Moslem. There are inscriptions indicating that the walls of this town underwent reconstruction under Leo VI: H. Grégoire, *Recueil des inscriptions grecques-chrétiennes d'Asie Mineure* (repr. Amsterdam, 1968), 103–4.

[73] Tripoli in Lebanon.

news of Tripolites reached the emperor at Boaitios' Market[74] where he had gone for the dedication ceremony of the monastery of Christopher,[75] his protovestiarios. The messengers added that the object of the onslaught was the capital itself, no less. The emperor dispatched Eustathios, at that time droungarios of the fleet, with a fleet, but being unable to withstand Tripolites he returned empty-handed, pursued [by the Hagarene] into the straits of the Hellespont and as far as Parion.[76] When this was reported to the emperor, he succumbed to [183] despondency and uncertainty. He handed over the naval forces to Himerios, the protoasekretis, and sent him against Tripolites. Himerios sailed past Abydos into the Aegean Sea and anchored off Strobilos.[77] Then he set sail for Imbros, passed Samothrace and discovered the enemy in the harbour at Thasos.[78] But when he saw their superiority both in numbers and in strength, he dared not approach them.[79] Reversing his direction, Tripolites then came to Thessalonike, blockaded and captured it,[80] taking prisoner the commander, Leo Chatzilakios. There was much bloodshed and many went into slavery.

24. A koubikoularios named Rhodophyles had been sent to Sicily on business with a hundred pounds in gold. He fell sick and entered Thessalonike in the hope of being treated. When Tripolites laid hands on him, he tortured him at length because of the gold and killed him, because he insisted that he had none. He had in fact deposited [the gold] along the way and Symeon the asecretis recovered it on his way through. When Tripolites declared his intention of razing the city to the ground, Symeon persuaded him to accept the gold and spare the city, and so it was.[81] Tripolites took the gold and went back home. Such was the emperor's

---

[74] *Kata to emporion tou Boaitiou*, Flusin translates 'au comptoir du Boaition'; presumably the exact significance remains unknown.
[75] The name of the monastery is not known. It was in Asia, on the northern shore of the Propontis: Janin, *Grands centres*, II, 57.
[76] An archbishopric on the southern shore of the Marmora at the entrance to the Hellespont. Thus Leo was at this time aiming at Constantinople.
[77] Strobilos (Aspat today) was an important port of the Kibyrrhaiote theme, located in Caria. From there Himerios could intercept communications with Leo's fleet, which must have sailed out of the Propontis and returned to the Aegean: C. Foss, 'Strobilos and related sites', *History and archaeology of Byzantine Asia Minor* (Aldershot, 1990), no. XII.
[78] Himerios was now sailing into the northern Aegean. On Imbros: Koder, *Aigaion Pelagos*, 177–9; on Imbros, Koder, *Aigaion Pelagos*, 291–3.
[79] That neither Eustathios nor Himerios dared to confront the opposing fleet indicates that this was of unusual magnitude, combining as it did the forces of Leo, Damian and the Egyptians.
[80] 31 July 904. There is a narrative of the capture of Thessalonike by Kameniates, who says he witnessed the events – but Kazhdan did not believe he did: A. P. Kazhdan, 'Some questions addressed to the scholars who believe in the authenticity of Kameniates' Capture of Thessalonica', *BZ*, 71 (1978), 301–14.
[81] The same story is to be found in *VEuthymii*, ed. Karlin-Hayter, 101, where Symeon is praised for his action.

approval of what Symeon had done that he promoted him patrician and protoasekretis. When the admiral Himerios learnt that the Saracens were going back home, he took off in pursuit. Putting into Crete, they gave the Cretans a portion of their booty and then returned home unharmed, leaving Himerios sitting in Lemnos, nothing accomplished. The emperor now sent two most valiant commanders to the east: Eustathios, a scion of the house of the Argyroi and Andronikos of the Doukai, both of whom had gained many victories over the Hagarenes.[82]

25. [184] That same Samonas who had been granted such illustrious honours by the emperor for revealing the conspiracy now fled the country with treasure and horses, under pretence of visiting his monastery.[83] He cut the hamstrings of the government horses at each relay stage. The emperor sent the hetaireiarch, Basil Kamateros,[84] and George Krinites after him. It was the droungarios Nikephoros Kaminas[85] who caught up with him as he was about to cross the [river] Halys and arrested him, his many prayers and promises of gifts nothwithstanding. When [Samonas] could not prevail, he sought refuge at the cross of Syricha,[86] pretending that he was going there to pray. Then came Constantine, the son of Andronikos Doukas,[87] who took charge of him and returned to the city with him. When they entered Constantinople, the emperor ordered [the prisoner] to be detained in the palace of the caesar Bardas. As for Constantine Doukas, even though he knew full well that Samonas had been attempting to find refuge in Melitene, the emperor declared that he was not to say this before the senate, but rather to say that he was going to say his prayers at Syricha (for the emperor wanted Samonas to be pardoned). So, early in the morning he convened the Senate, brought Constantine into the midst of the house and questioned him under

[82] This is the second time that the names of Doukas and Argyros are associated in connection with fighting in Asia Minor. According to Arab sources (the Greeks being silent), Eustathios was *hypostrategos* (commander-in-chief) of the Anatolikon theme while Andronikos was probably domestikos of the scholai: D. I. Polemis, *The Doukai: a contribution to Byzantine prosopography* (University of London Historical Studies, 22, London, 1968), 16–21. This successful campaign was conducted in retaliation for the naval preparations being made by Leo of Tripoli.
[83] The monastery of Speira at Damatrys. The palace of Damatrys faced Constantinople from the other side of the Bosporos, a little way inland, on the slopes of Mount Auxentios: Janin, *Constantinople*, 147–8.
[84] Probably a relative of Petronas Kamateros, the builder of Sarkel.
[85] *Theophanes Continuatus*, ed. Bekker, 369, says the man's name was Nikephoros Kallonas; the family was related to Constantine VII.
[86] Fortress of Charsianon to the north of the Halys, probably today's Çukur, 50 km north-east of Caesarea. The monastery of the Holy Cross possessed a portion of the True Cross: Hild and Restle, *Kappadokien*, 281; also H. Ahrweiler, 'Sur la localisation du couvent de Timios Stauros de Syricha', *Geographica byzantina*, ed. H. Ahrweiler (Paris, 1981), 9–15.
[87] Constantine achieved so many successes against the Arabs that Michel Psellos, *Chronographie*, ed. É. Renauld (Paris, 1967), trs. E. R. A. Sewter (London, 1953), II, 140, cites him among the illustrious ancestors of his friend Constantine Doukas, the future emperor.

oath in these words: 'Before God and on my head, did Samonas flee to Syria or not?' Now Constantine (who had great respect for oaths) had been led to believe that it would be *without* oaths that he should conceal the truth. So he confessed before them all that Samonas had been heading for his own home town of Melitene. The emperor angrily dismissed him and ordered Samonas [still] to be detained in the caesar's [palace].[88] Some time later he was released from there and restored to his former rank.[89]

26. A boy child was born to the emperor by his fourth wife, Zoe. [185] At his birth a comet appeared, its tail towards the east, and it shone for forty days.[90] The patriarch Nicholas baptised the child in Hagia Sophia;[91] Alexander, the emperor's brother,[92] the patrician Samonas and the leading senators received him from the holy font. The marriage of Leo with Zoe was solemnised by Thomas the priest (who was also degraded for this) and [the emperor] proclaimed her augousta.[93] This is the reason[94] why the patriarch forbade the emperor to enter the church;[95] hence he traversed the right-hand section [of the church] to reach the mitatorion.[96]

---

[88] This house arrest lasted four months: Leo the Grammarian, ed. Bekker, 279. These events took place in the spring and summer of 904: R. H. Jenkins, 'The 'Flight' of Samonas', *Speculum*, 23 (1948), 217–35, repr. 'The 'Flight' of Samonas', *Studies*, no. x.

[89] The significance of this episode is unsure; but it does explain the avowed hatred of Samonas for the Doukai.

[90] Constantine VII was born 3 September 905: D. Pingree, 'The horoscope of Constantine VII Porphyrogenitus', *DOP*, 27 (1973), 217–31. Since the father was governing the empire when the birth took place, the child was *porphyrogennetos*, 'born in the purple', and it was by that title that Leo habitually referred to him. This is why he is so known to posterity, even though he was by no means the first child to be 'born in the purple': G. Dagron, 'Nés dans la pourpre', *TM*, 12 (1994), 105–42.

[91] 6 January 906.

[92] The reading 'the emperor's brother' is a correction of Thurn. All the MSS except M say simply 'the emperor Alexander'. Alexander had been co-emperor since 879. The choice of Alexander as a godfather is understandable. Leo, fully aware that his brother detested him, wanted to protect the child in the event that he (the father) should predecease Alexander (the uncle). This he did by placing one more ethical hurdle between Alexander and Constantine.

[93] It was in April 906 that Zoe Karbonopsina became empress in the full sense of the word, replacing the young Anna in official ceremonies.

[94] It was Leo's decision to marry Zoe which triggered the so-called Tetragamy affair. The church permitted second marriages but not third and Leo had himself confirmed that third marriages were not allowed in one of his novels. Hence his own fourth marriage was a scandal. Leo could not back down because only legitimate marriage could secure the succession of Constantine VII and thus secure the endurance of the dynasty. Although Alexander had been married twice, there was no issue. To complicate matters, Leo could rely on the support of the Roman church which was more tolerant concerning the marriage of widowers. Leo Choirosphaktes was sent to the court of Pope Sergius III. For a synopsis of this matter and full bibliography: G. Dagron, *Histoire du christianisme*, IV: *Evêques, moines et empereurs (610–1054)*, ed. G. Dagron, P. Riché and A. Vauchez (Paris, 1993), 188–94.

[95] On two occasions (Christmas 906 and Epiphany, 6 January 907) the emperor arrived in procession with the senate only to be denied entry. Nicholas tried to find a compromise, but Arethas of Caesarea led a very vigorous opposition party: Tougher, *Leo VI*, 160.

[96] This was a small chamber somewhere (it is not certain where) in the church where the emperor changed his robes and sometimes took light refreshment with the senior dignitaries. There may have been two such chambers: *ODB*, II, 1353.

27. The patrician Samonas, the emperor's most artful collaborator in all things wicked and illegal, was appointed parakoimomenos. It was he who put the emperor up to forcing the reluctant patriarch to receive him in the church. At the beginning of February [the emperor] summoned the patriarch and insistently requested to be received.[97] When he refused to grant this request, they put him on a warship at the Boukoleon and brought him over to Hiereia.[98] Then they conducted him on foot[99] to the Galakrenai monastery,[100] which he had founded. Before very long Euthymios the synkellos[101] was appointed patriarch, a man who possessed the highest degree of godliness and virtue. They say that at first he refused the patriarchate but was then persuaded to accept it by a divine revelation. It was the emperor's intention to proclaim a law permitting a man to have three or even four wives in succession and many illustrious persons were in favour of this move; but the patriarch [Nicholas had] opposed this with all his might.

28. [186] In the month of June the emperor Leo was invited by Constantine Lips[102] to come to the monastery he had renovated near to Holy Apostles' for the dedication service and a dinner. Suddenly a strong wind they call 'lips' blew up from the south-west which shook many buildings. It disturbed and frightened the people so much that they all fled from their houses into the open air.[103] Then a shower of rain put an end to this tempest.

---

[97] On 1 February, even though he was opposed to any compromise (*oikonomia*), the patriarch together with the metropolitan bishops participated in an imperial banquet – still refusing to give any ground: *Symeonis magistri*, 288–9. Nicholas' connections with the Doukai strengthened the emperor's determination to set the patriarch aside.
[98] A control post on the European bank of the Bosporos for the sea passage to the Black Sea: Janin, *Grands centres*, II, 35–6. This is where the iconoclast council of 754 was held. Nicholas resigned when faced with the alternative of being charged with high treason: *VEuthymii*, ed. Karlin-Hayter, 91.
[99] This detail is explained by the other chroniclers (e.g. *Theophanes Continuatus*) who report that it had been snowing heavily.
[100] The exact location of this monastery is unknown, but the route taken suggests it was on the Asiatic shore of the Bosporos.
[101] Euthymios was born *c.* 834 in a town named Seleukeia, possibly in Isauria but more likely the one in Pisidia. He had supported Leo when he was accused by his own father, Basil I, after whose death (886) he was appointed hegoumenos of the Constantinopolitan monastery of Psmathia. He became Leo's spiritual director and was made synkellos, i.e. patriarch designate (usually). In all probability he succeeded Nicholas in February 907. *VEuthymii*, ed. Karlin-Hayter is the main source of information about him.
[102] June 907. This is probably the same Constantine Lips mentioned in *DAI*. At the time of the inauguration of his monastery he was *anthypatos* and grand hetaireiarch: *ODB*, II, 1232–3. The monastery is still standing: now the Fenari Isa Camii in the Lykos valley: Janin, *Églises et monastères*, I, 307–10; W. Müller-Wiener, *Bildlexikon zur Topographie Istanbuls* (Tubingen, 1977), 126–31.
[103] According to *Theophanes Continuatus*, ed. Bekker, 371, whom Skylitzes is following here, many people thought that this violent disturbance presaged the end of the world. On the eschatological expectations of the Later Romans: (most recently) P. Magdalino, 'The year 1000', *Byzantium in the year 1000*, ed. P. Magdalino (The Medieval Mediterranean, 45, Lieden and Boston, 2003), 233–70.

29. When the Hagarene fleet put out to sea against the Romans, the emperor placed Himerios, logothete of the drome, in charge of the Roman fleet. Andronikos Doukas was ordered to accompany him to oppose the Hagarenes. But Samonas was the implacable enemy of the house of the Doukai because he had been apprehended by Constantine. He succeeded in persuading one of Andronikos' friends to write to him secretly not to go on board ship because Himerios had a directive from the emperor (at Samonas' instigation) to blind him. On receiving this letter, [Andronikos] became reluctant to accompany Himerios, so the latter was obliged to set out alone to engage the enemy – on 6 October.[104] Engage them he did; put them to flight and annihilated them. When Andronikos heard of this he lost all hope. Gathering up his things, his relations and his servants, he went and occupied a fortress named Kabala,[105] situated above Iconium, looking for an opportunity to rebel.[106] Seizing every opportunity that presented itself of aggravating and worrying the emperor, Samonas would say: 'I have known for a long time that this man was fomenting insurrection and that he should be nipped in the bud. But since the suitable and convenient chance of doing that has been lost by your procrastination, O emperor, and the enemy is now slipping out of our hands, we must use the second- [187] best method lest he secretly take further action rather than suffer punishment.' Spurred on by these words as though with a spear-point, the emperor sent Gregoras Iberitzes, domestikos of the scholai, a brother-in-law of Andronikos, with a considerable force against Andronikos.[107] On hearing this, and also that the patriarch Nicholas (on whom he was counting greatly) had been thrown out of the church, he abandoned Kabala and fled with his entire household to the Hagarenes. The amermoumnes gave him an honourable and magnificent reception, but when the emperor considered what a good strategist he had lost and what a dangerous enemy he would find in him, he became depressed and ill-humoured, casting about for some means of restoring him to the Romans. A letter imperial was drawn up granting him a complete amnesty for his misdeeds and the right to return to his home, where he would recover his former prosperity plus a myriad other gifts and benefits. The document was rolled in wax to give it the appearance of a candle; then they gave it to a Saracen whom they had brought out of the praetorium and

---

[104] The year is uncertain; Vasiliev and Canard, II, 185, note 1 gives 905 while Tougher, *Leo VI*, 209 opts for 906.

[105] Kabala is 11 km from Iconium: K. Belke and M. Restle, *Galatien und Lykaonien* (TIB, 4, Vienna, 1984), 182–3. Presumably Andronikos' behaviour is explained by the discovery of his compromising correspondence with the patriarch Nicholas which provided evidence of treason.

[106] September 905 or 906.

[107] Iberitzes was the father-in-law of Andronikos: Polemis, *Doukai*, 25.

won over with opulent [gifts], persuading him to go to Syria and hand the letter to Andronikos. As the Saracen was leaving, Samonas took him aside and asked him: 'Do you know what you have there?' – indicating the 'candle'. When the other confessed his ignorance, he said: 'The wax given to you is the destruction of Syria; if you have any concern for your race and co-religionists, deliver [the 'candle'] into the hands of Ouzer.' To ensure the man perform the requested service, he showered him with a diversity of valuable gifts. When he arrived in Syria the man handed the candle to Ouzer, who took it apart and found the letter, read what was in it and reported it to the *amermoumnes*. He immediately flung Andronikos and his company into prison where for a long time they were severely mistreated. Some of them, unable to tolerate the hardship of imprisonment, were compelled to deny their own faith. It was in these circumstances that Andronikos departed this life. Before that, and with his knowledge, Constantine his son [188] and some others who were with him were planning an escape (there were plenty of people still in gaol with him because they refused to abjure their own undeniable faith). These people 'broke their bonds asunder',[108] fled the prison, let themselves down with a rope, got some horses and made good their escape. Sometimes they eluded their pursuers by turning and fighting the soldiers sent to apprehend them, sometimes by scattering gold; thus were they able to reach the Roman boundaries. The emperor quickly summoned Constantine to his presence, showering him and his companions with diverse gifts.[109]

30. When the audience was over, just as Constantine was leaving the Chrysotriklinos (for that was where the emperor had received him), he called him back and, lifting his eyes to the icons of Christ and the Mother of God above the door,[110] said this to Constantine: 'Do not let your name betray you, Constantine, nor think to rule the Roman empire because of it, for the empire is being kept by God for my son, Constantine. This has been revealed to me by godly men empowered by their purity to foresee the future. Remain in the rank you have been assigned and do not aspire

---

[108] Ps. 2:3a.
[109] Constantine returned to the capital during the winter 907–8, Polemis, *Doukai*, 21–5: M. Canard, 'Deux épisodes des relations diplomatiques arabo-byzantines au xe siècle', *Bulletin d'études orientales*, Damascus 13 (1949–51), 51–69, repr. M. Canard, *Byzance et les musulmans du Proche-Orient* (London, 1973), no. XII; R. J. H. Jenkins, 'Leo Choerosphactes and the Saracen vizier', *ZRVI*, 8 (1963), 167–75, repr. Jenkins, *Studies*, no. XI.
[110] Michael III had restored the Chrysotriklinos; two of the epigrams in the *Anthologia palatina* describe its decoration: there was a representation of an enthroned Christ in the apse which housed the throne while the Virgin was portrayed above the western door, surrounded by the emperor, the patriarch and some saints: Janin, *Constantinople*, 115

insanely beyond your station. Otherwise, be assured that your head, the head of a pretender, will pass through this door separated from your body,' which is what eventually happened. After the death of Leo, Constantine did rebel; he was executed in the treasury and his head was taken to the emperor through the aforementioned door, dripping with blood and gore.[111]

On the grounds of some suspicion the emperor dismissed the magister Eustathios Argyros from his command (he was droungarios of the watch). He went to his home where he died of poisoning, much regretted by both the army and the navy, [189] where his heroic deeds were held in remembrance. He was buried in the Charsianon [theme], in the monastery of St Elizabeth which Leo, his grandfather, had renovated.[112] That Leo was the first to acquire the surname Argyros,[113] either from his purity of life, the comeliness of his body or from some aspect of his nobility. So outstanding was he among his contemporaries during the reign of the emperor Michael [III] that he alone, together with his household, dared oppose the Manichees of Tephrike and the Hagarenes of Melitene in battle – and easily defeated them. The mere mention of his name infused terror in every adversary.

31. There came from Tarsus and Melitene to the capital the notorious Abelbakes[114] and the father of Samonas, sent to arrange an exchange of prisoners.[115] The emperor received them in great style, especially decorating the Magnaura [palace] for the occasion. He also lavishly adorned the Great Church and took them there, where he showed them all the objects worthy of veneration and also the vessels, vestments and the like, which were used in divine worship. It was unworthy of a Christian state to expose to the eyes of persons of another race and of a different religion those things which are even hidden from Christian men whose lives are less than orderly.[116] When the father of Samonas saw the trust his son enjoyed with the emperor and beheld his glory and honour, he would have preferred to stay

---

[111] There is more on this failed revolt below: reign of Constantine VII as a minor, c. 2.
[112] This action has been mentioned already: reign of Michael III, c. 8. Leo was actually the father of Eustathios: J. F. Vannier, *Familles byzantines: les Argyroi (IXe–XIIe siècles)* (ByzSorb, 1, Paris, 1975), 22, reproduced in Cheynet, *Société*, 526–8.
[113] *Argyros* means 'that which is white', especially silver. The various explanations advanced by Skylitzes and his source *Theophanes Continuatus*, 374, suggest that the original meaning of the name had been lost. It may also refer to the immense riches of the Argyroi.
[114] Abd al-Baqi was a grandee of the emirate of Tarsus, sometime commander of the forces there: Vasiliev and Canard, II, 193, 230.
[115] The object of this embassy in spring 905 was to effect the exchange of prisoners which the desertion of Andronikos Doukas had interrupted.
[116] A rare expression of personal conviction by the author.

with his son and forsake his home town, Melitene, but Samonas would not agree to this, demanding that he go back home, retain his own religion and wait for his [son's] return at the first opportunity.

32. At the time of the feast celebrating the descent of the Holy Ghost in tongues of flame upon the Apostles, the emperor crowned his own son by the hand of Euthymios the patriarch.[117] Samonas, anxious to find favour for himself in the sight of the empress, presented to the augousta to wait upon her Constantine, [190] a eunuch originally from Paphlagonia, who was his own personal servant.[118] Constantine became so beloved both by her and by the emperor Leo that Samonas became jealous and spoke evil of him to the emperor, hinting that he was too familiar with the augousta. Believing this to be the case, the emperor sent and had him tonsured as a monk at St Tarasios' monastery;[119] it was Samonas who executed the order. A little later, however, the emperor changed his mind and wished to have him back, so – again with the same Samonas as his agent – he transferred him to the Speirai monastery.[120] Now, one day the emperor went out to Damatrys and was dining at Samonas' monastery where he saw Constantine. He ordered him immediately to take off the monastic habit and put on lay clothing; also that, when he held a feast, it was by Constantine that the cup should be handed to him at dinner, and he returned to the palace taking [the eunuch] with him. But when Samonas noted the emperor's growing affection for Constantine he devised a plot against him; this was the nature of it. He conspired together with Megistos[121] the *koitônitês* and Michael Tzirithon[122] to put together a very poisonous note against the emperor (it was Constantine of Rhodes,[123] secretary to Samonas, who composed it). When it was written and sealed, they threw it into the mitatorion. As the emperor was going to the Great Church in a public procession, he came to the mitatorion and,

---

[117] 15 May 908, feast of Pentecost.
[118] Constantine had been previously in the service of Basil the magister and prefect of the inkstand (*epi tou kanikleiou*). In the tenth and eleventh centuries Paphlagonia produced a number of eunuchs who had flourishing careers: P. Magdalino, 'Paphlagonians in Byzantine high society', *Byzantine Asia Minor (sixth–twelfth centuries)* (Athens, 1998), 141–50.
[119] Monastery founded by the patriarch Tarasios (784–806) on the European shore of the Bosporos (hence outside Constantinople).
[120] Monastery located at Damatrys: Janin, *Grands centres*, II, 50–1.
[121] A family of this name supplied a few minor personages, among them a physician known from a letter of Tzetzes in the eleventh to twelfth century: Ioannès Tzetzès, *Epistulae*, ed. P. Leone, Leipzig 1972, Letter 74, 108–9. The meaning of *koitônitês* (hapax in Skylitzes) is unsure.
[122] This is the first mention of a family which would provide several civil servants, mostly in the eleventh century.
[123] Constantine was born on the island of Rhodes between 870 and 880. He became a civil servant but is best known for his literary creations which include a description of the seven wonders of the world, a description of Holy Apostles' church and various satirical poems: P. Lemerle, *Le premier humanisme byzantin* (Paris, 1971), 174.

seeing the letter introduced into that place where he usually prayed, took it up and read it. Great was the helplessness of those present, each man in doubt and none knowing who had deposited it there. The emperor too was profoundly disturbed and wanted to discover the perpetrator. At that very time a major eclipse of the moon took place,[124] so the emperor summoned the Metropolitan Synades Pantaleon,[125] an adept in the science of astronomy, [191] seeking to learn what the effects of this eclipse might be. As the adept was coming to the emperor, Samonas took him aside and asked him privately who was going to suffer misfortune. 'You are,' he replied, 'but if you can come through the thirteenth day of June unscathed, you will suffer no further evil.' Questioned on the same matter by the emperor, he said that the evil would befall 'the second person', which led the emperor to think 'the second person' was his own brother, Alexander. As the narrative proceeds, we will discover how this prophecy was fulfilled. Michael Tzirithon came to the emperor of his own accord and advised him that it was Samonas who had composed the note, whereupon that man was immediately placed under house arrest and given the monastic tonsure. He was then brought to the monastery of the patriarch Euthymios whence, derided and insulted, he was transferred to Martinakios' monastery; this happened before the time stipulated by the metropolitan elapsed.[126] Leo appointed Constantine parakoimomenos in [Samonas'] stead and he also built for him a monastery at Nosiai[127] dedicated to the Saviour, of which he celebrated the consecration ceremonies together with Euthymios the patriarch.

33. The Hagarenes sailed out with three hundred ships under the command of Damian, emir of Tyre and Leo Tripolites. In the month of October Himerios the logothete, admiral of the Roman navy, encountered them off Samos[128] (where the Commander was Romanos

---

[124] 20 March 908.
[125] C. Mango, 'The legend of Leo the Wise', *ZRVI*, 6 (1960), 68, repr. *Byzantium and its image* (London, 1984), XVI.
[126] Samonas was turned away *c.* 13 June 908.
[127] Location unknown, probably in the area around Chalcedon. The monastery was still in existence in the time of John II Komnenos for he attached it to his new foundation of the Pantokrator. Eighteen monks were then living at Nosiai: Janin, *Grands centres*, II, 59.
[128] Himerios prepared an expedition probably intending to eliminate the Arab naval forces in the Mediterranean rather than to liberate Crete, where he does not appear to have attempted to disembark: J. F. Haldon, 'Theory and practice in tenth-century military administration, Ch. II, 44 and 45 of the *Book of Ceremonies*', *TM*, 13 (2000), 202–352, at 239–43. We know from Constantines Porphyrogenitus, *De cerimoniis aulae byzantinae libri duo*, ed. J. J. Reiske (CHSB, Bonn, 1829–30), 651–64, that Himerios had assembled 177 ships with 34,200 hands, capable of transporting an army of 20,000 men. Himerios set sail for Crete in the summer of 911 and

Lekapenos).[129] Battle was joined but he and those with him got the worse of it. His ships were scattered and he only just managed to get to Mytilene in safety.

34. The emperor caught a disease of the bowels and remained in its grip for some considerable time until he was completely exhausted. He was scarcely able to deliver the traditional public discourse at the beginning of Lent.[130] And when the Senate was in session, he began [192] to say something like this: 'Worn out by disease, O friends, my carcass has melted away and my strength has deserted me. I will not much longer be among you in the land of the living; indeed I will not live to celebrate the Lord Christ's resurrection. I now ask this one, final favour of you: that you bear in mind the gentle disposition which I have had towards you and, in return, remain faithful to my wife and son.' Such was the emperor's speech; with weeping and lamentation the Senate asserted that it would experience inconsolable grief at the loss of such a master and emperor; that it would remain loyal to his Lady, 'And to our Lord-and-master and emperor, his son, for whose sake we would, if necessary, die a thousand deaths.' Thus spoke the Senate; a last embrace was offered to the emperor and the session adjourned. But the emperor did not die immediately; diseased and wasting away, he hung on until 11 May,[131] when he was released from life, bequeathing the imperial sceptre to Alexander, his own brother. Seeing this man approach him for their last meeting, he is said to have remarked: 'Behold, evil times after thirteen months!'[132]

This emperor was much given to learning and especially the effects of astronomical occurrences. He set verses to music for singing in church, verses of great sweetness. Letters and other works of his are still extant, very learned and written in the old style. He was a devoted reader of Archimedes, more so than anybody else at that time.[133]

---

attacked but without success. It was on his way back in April (?) 912 that he fell foul of the Muslim fleet and was soundly defeated.

[129] The future emperor Romanos I.

[130] On the occasion when the emperor delivered this oration: *De Cer.* 2:10, *CSHB*, 545–8. Three 'homilies' of Leo VI the Wise for the beginning of Lent have survived: T. Antonopoulou, 38.

[131] 912.

[132] For a different account of the death of Leo VI, quite hostile to him (possibly a fragment of V*Euthymii*): B. Flusin, 'Un fragment inédit de la vie d'Euthyme le patriarche 1, Texte et traduction', *TM*, 9 (1985), 119–31; 11, 'Vie d'Euthyme ou Vie de Nicétas?' *TM*, 10 (1987), 233–60 (commentary). On the meaning of the proverbial expression 'a year of thirteen months': Mango, 'Legend', 69.

[133] Interpolation of MS ACEB. The chroniclers pay scant attention to the 'wisdom' of Leo VI, even though some of his contemporaries mention it; see Tougher, *Leo VI*, ch. v, 'The reality of Leo the Wise', 110–32.

Having disposed of the imperial government in the way indicated, [the emperor Leo] most insistently requested that his son, Constantine, be given a decent education and be raised in the way befitting to his rank; also that [Alexander] would designate him as his eventual successor. And so [the emperor] died.

CHAPTER 8

Alexander [912–913]

1. [193] Alexander[1] the brother of Leo was still a young man just going into his twentieth year.[2] When Leo died, he took over the direction of the empire with Constantine the son of Leo as co-emperor. As soon as he became ruler he sent and brought back the patriarch Nicholas [the mystikos] from Galakrenei, deposed Euthymios and installed Nicholas[3] for the second time. Seating him beside himself for a *silention*[4] in the Magnaura, he confirmed the deposing of Euthymios. Those clergy who were supporters of Nicholas set upon Euthymios like wild beasts once he was deposed. They struck him with their fists, slapped his face, plucked out his reverend beard, beat him on the neck and inflicted other unbearable tortures, calling him interloper, adulterer and defiler of other men's wives.[5] That reverend man endured all this humbly and quietly.[6] He was exiled to Ta Agathou[7] and died shortly after. He was brought into the city and buried

---

[1] On Alexander: P. Karlin-Hayter, 'The emperor Alexander's bad name', *Speculum*, 44 (1969), 585–96, also in *Studies*, no. IV. In spite of the statement of his nephew (Constantine VII) to the contrary, Alexander was indeed the youngest son of Basil I and the only one whose paternity is beyond doubt: R. H. J. Jenkins, 'The chronological accuracy of the Logothete for the years AD 867–913', *DOP*, 19 (1965), 91–112, at 99.

[2] This is a very odd statement since Alexander (born on 23 November, almost certainly in 870) must have been forty-one when he became the ruling emperor.

[3] Alexander systematically rid himself of those who had been close to Leo VI, starting with the patriarch Euthymios; then the empress Zoe, followed by the logothete Himerios. There is another version according to which Leo himself, on his deathbed, recalled Nicholas. This is somewhat unlikely, even though Nicholas seems to give credence to it in his correspondence.

[4] A *silention* was a solemn conclave presided over by the emperor, at which he, having caused the silentiaries to impose *silence* on the assembly, let his decisions be known: *ODB*, 1896.

[5] This report is confirmed in *Vita Euthymii patriarchae CP. Text, translation, introduction and commentary*, P. Karlin-Hayter (Bibliothèque de *Byzantion*, 3, Brussels, 1970), 121. A man named John Manolimitis struck the old man and would have knocked him senseless if Petronas Triphyllios and some others had not intervened and led Euthymios away.

[6] Like his source (*Theophanes Continuatus*, 378), our author is following a source kindly disposed towards Euthymios, possibly *V Euthymii*, ed. Karlin-Hayter 129.

[7] A district on the Asiatic shore of the Bosporos to the north of Chrysopolis. The Patriarch Nikephoros founded a monastery there which at one time belonged to Leo Katakoilas. Leo VI gave it to Euthymios: *V Euthymii*, ed. Karlin-Hayter, 29.

in his own monastery.[8] The cleric who had plucked out his grey beard, on returning to his own house at the same hour, found it burned down and his daughter sitting paralysed and dumb beside it. She survived for several years, obtaining the necessities of life for herself by begging.

2. The emperor Alexander's former way of life was luxurious and unbridled, his passions being hunting and other [194] licentious, habitual practices, for he knew nothing of behaviour worthy of an emperor, preferring to devote himself to debauchery and immorality.[9] From the time he came into possession of the empire and of plenary powers he neither conceived nor accomplished anything worthy of note. When he became sole ruler he appointed as rector a vagabond named John Lazares, a wretched fellow not worth mentioning, who shortly after died a shameful death: he, a cleric, playing ball in the Hebdomon! Then, there were his accomplices before he acceded to the throne, Gabrielopoulos and Basilitzes, partakers and ministers of his wicked deeds. These he showered with money and raised to the dignity of patrician. They say it was his intention (if God had not intervened) to promote Basilitzes to the imperial throne and make a eunuch of Constantine, his own nephew. This he would have done too if God first, and then those who remained faithful to Leo, the child's father, had not stood in his way. For these would say sometimes 'he is a child', sometimes, that he was an infant and sickly and, in this way, they were able to save the child by deflecting Alexander for a little – until death overtook *him*.[10]

3. While he reigned a comet appeared in the west which those who are skilled in such matters called the swordfish. They said it presaged the shedding of blood in the capital.[11]

4. The emperor put his trust in deceivers and wizards and asked them about his reign, whether it would be of long duration. [195] They promised him a long life if the bronze wild boar standing in the Hippodrome were to receive from him the genitals and tusks it lacked, for they pointed out that he was in competition with Leo [=lion] his brother.[12] This made sense

---

[8] Euthymios died on 4 or 5 August 917; he was interred at Psamathia.

[9] This assessment of the character of Alexander reappears in the *Historia Syntomos* of Psellos, 78–80, where it constitutes the sum total of what is said of this emperor.

[10] Alexander did not have the young Constantine featured on the coins of his day. Alexander was the first emperor to have himself shown standing and being crowned, not by the Theotokos, but by a protector saint, John the Baptist: N. Thierry, 'Le Baptiste sur le solidus d'Alexandre (912–13)', *Revue numismatique*, VIe série 34 (1992), 237–41.

[11] Halley's comet, visible from 9 July to 3 August 912: R. H. J. Jenkins, 'The chronological accuracy of the Logothete for the years AD 867–913', *DOP*, 19 (1965), 91–112, at 111; repr. R. H. J. Jenkins, *Studies on Byzantine history of the ninth and tenth centuries* (London, 1970), no. 111.

[12] On the magical significance attached to some monuments in the capital: G. Dagron, *Constantinople imaginaire: études sur le recueil des 'patria'* (Paris 1984), 127–90.

to that truly piggish man and he provided the pig with the missing parts. While he was prey to such mad thoughts, he ordered that the holy tapestries, the sacred lamp stands and candelabra be brought from the churches during the chariot races. With these he adorned the chariot races, thus profaning what had been dedicated to God, or rather dedicating it to idols in his vileness.

5. He arrested Himerios the logothete when that man returned to the capital from his defeat at the hands of the Hagarenes and sent him into exile at the monastery of Kalypa,[13] threatening to treat him as an enemy for having often plotted against him in the days of his brother. Himerios survived a short time in exile and then died, consumed by sorrow.

6. The Bulgar ruler, Symeon, sent a delegation to enquire whether he would maintain the peace and continue to pay the subsidy which his brother, the former emperor, had paid.[14] But Alexander shamefully sent the delegates away, uttering pompous, boasting and insolent phrases, making threats against Symeon under the impression that this would intimidate him. When the delegates returned to Symeon he did not take Alexander's haughty insolence and threats lightly; he declared the peace treaty void and decided to take up arms against the Romans.

7. On 6 June Alexander bathed, dined, drank plenty of wine and when he had slept came down to play ball. A pain [196] arose in his entrails which had been overloaded with an excess of food and excessive drinking. He went back up into the palace haemorrhaging from his nose and his genitals; after one day he was dead, leaving as regents the patriarch Nicholas, the magister Stephen, the magister John Eladas,[15] John the rector, Basilitzes and Gabrielopoulos.[16] He bequeathed the throne to Constantine his own nephew. When he was dead he was laid with Basil his father.[17]

He governed the empire one year and one month, just as his brother Leo prophesied.[18]

---

[13] A monastery within the palace.
[14] In other words, the ambassadors came to demand the annual tribute. Nicholas Mystikos, *Letters*, ed. tr. Jenkins and Westerlink: *Nicholas I, Patriarch of Constantinople, Letters*, ed. tr. R. J. H. Jenkins and L. G. Westerink (CFHB, 6, Washington, DC, 1973): nos. 6, 40, promised just after the death of Alexander to respect the agreements and to have the tribute delivered to Debeltos.
[15] John Eladas had served in the treasury under Leo VI: *DAI*, ed. Moravcsik and Jenkins, 256.
[16] Thus the empress Zoe was excluded from the regency council; the last three members named were all creatures of Alexander.
[17] Alexander died on 6 June 913.
[18] Addition of MS E.

CHAPTER 9

Constantine VII, Porphyrogennetos [913–959]

1. [197] Alexander died in the way we described and the imperial authority passed to Constantine, the son of Leo, now in the seventh year of his life, but it was exercised by the regents specified above. Nicholas the patriarch came to power as one of the regents and was directing the affairs of state together with the others.

2. Such being the state of affairs and the realm being governed by regents, as we said, Constantine Doukas, son of Andronikos, domestic of the scholai and a man invested with very great powers,[1] was provoked by letters from friends and relations in the capital[2] which alleged that the empire was without a head; that it was being badly administered and that it was in grave peril of falling into the gravest danger. The letters called upon him as a prudent and courageous fellow, the only one capable of adequately governing the illustrious Roman state, to return. They added that both the Senate and the people of the city were in favour of him and that he should make haste to come as soon as possible; Nicholas the patriarch was aware of, and approved of, these letters (they said); this was because the will of Alexander had not yet been published and he was as yet unaware that he was named as regent for the child in it. Artabasdos was serving in that capacity and for this he later became dean of the clergy of the Great Church. He was the father of Andreas the famous portrait painter. Now Constantine had already been dreaming of becoming emperor and was always aiming in that direction, to the exclusion of every other aspiration. When he received the letters he was readily convinced and quickly arrived at the [198] capital accompanied by a choice body of

---

[1] He was assembling an army to counter Symeon of Bulgaria.
[2] There had long been a faction of the Doukai at Constantinople, of which the patriarch Nicholas was an adherent. According to the *Vita Euthymii patriarchae CP. Text, translation, introduction and commentary*, P. Karlin-Hayter (Bibliothèque de *Byzantion*, 3, Brussels, 1970), 131–3, it was Nicholas who summoned Constantine Doukas, prior to the unexpected death of Alexander. Once Alexander gave Nicholas authority over the regency council, the patriarch did everything in his power to restrain Constantine.

troops. He entered the city in the depth of night by way of the wicket-gate of Michael the protovestiarios which is near the Acropolis.[3] Then he went to the house of the magister Gregoras Iberitzes,[4] his father-in-law, and passed the night there, he and those with who were with him. As soon as Niketas the asekretis was made aware of Constantine's arrival, he immediately advised the patrician Constantine Eladikos[5] (who happened to be a monk) and, taking him along, went to be with Doukas that very night. A discussion took place and then, before dawn broke, they went to the gates of the Hippodrome with torches, many soldiers and a crowd of people, proclaiming Constantine emperor. But the people inside the Hippodrome vigorously withstood them and would not open the gates. Constantine's commander of horse who had great confidence in his own courage and strength undertook to open up the gates by a powerful (but, in truth, disorderly) [assault] but was speared by someone within through the gap between the two gates. He died on the spot but Constantine, even though he had been driven back, was besotted like a drunken man with the desire to be emperor and was no longer thinking clearly. He got up and advanced towards the Hippodrome.[6] The slaying of his commander of horse may have been a bad omen for him but it did not deflect him in the least from his pronounced intent. From the Hippodrome, cheered on his way, he reached what we call the Chalke [Gate],[7] went through it and came to the [barracks of the] Exkoubitors.[8] The magister John Eladas (who was one of the regents) made the best choice he could in the circumstances from the Hetaireia and the Elates,[9] armed them with whatever each man had could lay hands on and sent them against Doukas. They approached the Doukas detachment and engaged it in a battle in which a great slaughter ensued on both sides. Gregory, the son of Doukas, fell[10]

---

[3] Where Topkapi is today.
[4] Gregoras had been domestic of the scholai under Leo VI, probably the successor to his relative by marriage, Andronikos Doukas.
[5] Another Eladikos, Niketas, protovestiarios under Leo VI, was beaten when his master was accused by Santabarenos before Basil I. He became *papias* under Romanos Lekapenos: Prodolzenie chroniki Georgija Amartola po Vatikanskomu spisku no. 153, dans V. Istrin, *Knigy vremennyja i obrazniya Georgija Mnicha. Chronika georgija Amartola v drevnem slavjanorusskom perevode. tekst, izsledovanie i slovar*, II (Petrograd, 1922), 1–65, at 23.
[6] The precise meaning of this and the following sentences is less than clear.
[7] Having failed to force the gates of the Hippodrome, Constantine continued along the Mese and arrived at the main gate of the palace which, apparently, was not closed.
[8] Once he had gained entrance into the palace, Constantine had succeeded in passing through the barracks of the scholai and had arrived at the Exkoubitors. On the quarter of the Exkoubitors: R. Guilland, *Études de topographie de Constantinople byzantine* (Amsterdam, 1969), I, 14–24.
[9] The oarsmen of the imperial fleet.
[10] Slain by John Garidas: *VEuthymii*, ed. Karlin-Hayter, 131.

as did Michael, his nephew, and Kourtikios the Armenian,[11] which considerably disturbed Constantine. [199] As he sped forward to encourage and fortify his own side, his horse (which he spurred on to bring him into the front line) slipped on the paving stones which are there, throwing its rider to the ground. While he lay there all alone (for all the others had dispersed) somebody cut his head off with a sword and brought it to the emperor Constantine at the run. It was already known to the regents that such a fate would befall him – this for a completely different reason. There was a certain Nicholas functioning as tax collector in Chaldia who had spent some of the income and did not have the wherewithal to pay back what was owing. He fled to Syria where he renounced our holy religion and took up astrology instead. He wrote a message on a black sheet and sent it to Thomas the Logothete;[12] when the sheet was washed with water the letters appeared. This is what they said: 'Do not be afraid of that flashy bird[13] Doukas; he will rashly raise the standard of revolt but will immediately be eliminated.' When his revolt ended in this way, the magister Gregory, the father-in-law of Constantine, fled immediately to the church of the Divine Wisdom together with the patrician Leo Choirosphaktes. The regents dragged them out from there and tonsured them monks at Stoudios' monastery. The patrician Constantine Eladikos was mercilessly flogged with ox tendons, paraded through the city centre and imprisoned at the monastery of Dalmatos. The patricians Leo Katakalitzes[14] and Abessalon,[15] son of Arotras, were blinded and sent into exile. Philotheos the eparch[16] had Constantine, son of Eulampios, beheaded in the hairpin of the Hippodrome and others with him. Niketas the Asekretis and Constantine Lips were searched for diligently but could

---

[11] Probably a descendant of the Kourtikios who fell before Symeon of Bulgaria. This confrontation cost 800 deaths: *VEuthymii*, ed. Karlin-Hayter, 131.

[12] This Thomas was the son of Constantine, droungarios of the watch under Michael III and the father of Genesios the historian, of whom no text (other than, somewhat belatedly, Skylitzes') supplies the first name: A. Markopoulos, 'Quelques remarques sur la famille des Genesioi aux IXe–Xe siècles', *ZRVI*, 24–5 (1986), 103–8, repr. in A. Markopoulos, *History*, no. XI (taking up the various references to these persons in the versions of the logothete). On the relations between the Genesioi and the Armeniakon theme: E. Kountoura-Galake, 'The origins of the Genesios family and its connection with the Armeniakon theme', *BZ*, 93 (2000), 464–73.

[13] *Tou pyrrou peteinou*, 'cet oiseau fauve' *pace* Flusin; meaning obscure.

[14] Possibly a variant (diminutive?) of Katakalon, in which case this person would be related to the magister and domestic of the scholai, Leo Katakalon.

[15] There exists a seal of an Abessalom, protospatharios and strategos of Macedonia: G. Zacos, *Byzantine lead seals*, compiled by J. W. Nesbitt (Berne, 1985), II, no. 78. He could be related to the Krinitai, for a Krinites Arotras is known: *DAI*, ed. Moravcsik and Jenkins, 234.

[16] Philotheos was the son of Lampoudios: *Theophanes Continuatus*, 384. He was a friend of Zaoutzes and he had agreed to the slandering of Euthymios: *VEuthymii*, ed. Karlin-Hayter, 43 and 45.

not be found. The patrician Aigides, famous for his courage, and other by no means undistinguished commanders were impaled along the way from the [statue of the] heifer in Chrysopolis all the way to what we call [200] the Leukation.[17] Many another senator would have been destroyed without mercy and without cause by the regents mentioned already if some of the judges had not spoken out boldly and restrained them from their unjust procedures, saying: 'Since our emperor is a child and has no knowledge of what has taken place, how dare you take such action without his command?' The regents tonsured Doukas' wife and packed her off to her estates in Paphlagonia and they castrated Stephen, her son.[18]

3. While these things were happening in the city, Symeon, ruler of the Bulgars, invaded Roman territory with heavy forces and, reaching the capital, entrenched himself on a line between Blachernae and the Golden Gate.[19] His hopes soared that he would now easily take [the city]. But when he realised how strong the walls were, the number of men defending them and the abundant supply of stone-throwing and dart-discharging devices they had to hand, he abandoned his hopes and withdrew to Hebdomon, requesting a peace treaty. The regents received his request favourably, whereupon Symeon despatched his own magister Theodore to hold peace talks. There were lengthy discussions when he came, then the patriarch and the regents, taking the emperor with them, came to the palace of Blachernae.[20] When suitable hostages had been given, Symeon[21] was brought into the palace where he dined with the emperor. He then bowed his head before the patriarch who said a prayer over him and placed his own monastic cowl (they say)[22] on the barbaric brow instead of a crown.

---

[17] Leukation is probably to be identified with Leukate, a cape adjacent to the route to Nicomedia between Pendik (Penteichion) and Darica (Ritzion): R. Janin, *Constantinople byzantine* (*AOC*, 4A, Paris, 1964), 500–1. This fierce repression must have severely depleted the officer-class, which would partly explain the dismal showing of the Roman army when it was confronted with Symeon.

[18] The object of the exercise appears to have been to eliminate all the male issue of this family, but in fact at least one son survived (see below).

[19] Symeon appears to have advanced on Constantinople unopposed in August 913. The army under the command of Constantine Doukas was not yet ready for action and was no doubt in some confusion as a result of its commander's revolt.

[20] This ceremony actually took place at Hebdomon where Symeon and his army had retreated. The place was well chosen because that is where Roman emperors had been proclaimed or crowned in former times.

[21] *Theophanes Continuatus*, 385, and the *Chronicle of the Logothete* (*Symeonis magistri*, 301) say that the patriarch had the son of Symeon come to the palace and that they dined with the emperor, but that the patriarch *went out* to place his *epirriptarion* on the head of the Bulgar sovereign. This suggests that Symeon remained outside the walls.

[22] *Epirriptarion*. The author is trying to disguise the fact that Nicholas agreed to crown Symeon emperor of the Bulgars. In fact Symeon would have been under no illusions concerning Byzantine practices,

After the meal, although no peace treaty had been concluded,[23] Symeon and his children returned to their own land, gratified with gifts. That is what happened in this matter.

4. [201] The emperor Constantine was constantly complaining and calling for his mother (she had been expelled from the palace by Alexander) so they brought her back in, against their better judgement. Once she was in, she seized the reins of government and made a pact with Constantine the parakoimomenos together with the two Gongylios brothers,[24] Anastasios and Constantine, as her associates. On the advice of John Eladas, those who had been close to Alexander were sent packing: John the Rector, Gabrielopoulos, Basilitzes and the rest of them.[25] Zoe the augousta appointed Dominikos – who seemed to be a man of action and was certainly under her thumb – commander of the Hetaireiai. It was on his advice that the patriarch was ejected from the palace.[26] The magister John Eladas stepped down of his own accord, for he had a sickness from which he died. Now Constantine the parakoimomenos wanted to gather all the reins of government into his own hands with nobody opposing him, so he maligned the commander of the Hetaireiai to the augousta, saying that he was trying to appropriate the position of emperor for his own brother. She, convinced by him, conferred the title of patrician on Dominikos then, when he came down to receive the customary blessing,[27] she ordered him to remain in his home. John Garidas[28] was appointed commander of the

---

for he had lived at the capital. The presence of the young Constantine is explained by the proposal to unite him in marriage with Symeon's daughter. There has been much discussion concerning exactly what it was that the Patriarch placed on Symeon's head. *Epirriptarion* means a scarf-like cloth with which the patriarch covered his head; Symeon was surely too familiar with Byzantine procedures to have been taken in by that! J. Shepard, 'Symeon of Bulgaria – peacemaker', *Annuaire de l'Université Saint Clement d'Ochrid*, 83, 3 (Sofia, 1989), 9–48, at 21–2 (including complete bibliography).

[23] *Nicholas Mystikos, Letters*, no. 7, 42–4, however, states that some things were agreed upon. See Shepard, 'Symeon of Bulgaria', 20–5, who takes into account the information contained in the *Oratio* pronounced on the occasion of the marriage of Peter of Bulgaria and Maria Lekapenos. In seeking to ensure the payment of tribute Symeon does not seem to have had any other object than to promote his own prosperity and that of his boyars; also to ensure the development of his capital, Preslav. A marriage with a member of the imperial family was a way of ensuring that the tribute would continue to be paid: P. Stephenson, *Byzantium's Balkan frontier: a political study of the northern Balkans, 900–1204* (Cambridge, 2000), 18–23.

[24] Like many other eunuchs, these brothers were from Paphlagonia: Leo the Deacon, ed. Hase, 7, tr. Talbot and Dennis, 59. Constantine led the ill-fated expedition against Crete in 949: reign of Constantine VII and an adult, c. 15

[25] Evidently something of a *coup d'état* took place, bringing those close to Leo VI back into power. The patriarch's attempts at conciliation were not acceptable to the army.

[26] When Euthymios refused to return to resume the office of patriarch (he was now very old), Zoe reconciled herself with Nicholas who, for his part, recognised her as augousta.

[27] On the making of patricians: *De Cer.*, ed. Vogt (Paris, 1939), 2:51–60.

[28] P. Karlin-Hayter, 'L'hétéreiarque. L'évolution de son role du *De cerimoniis* au *Traité des Offices*', *JÖB*, 23 (1974), 107–8, repr. *Studies in Byzantine political history* (London, 1981), no. XVIII.

Hetaireiai in his place and the eunuch Damian (a recent arrival) droungarios of the watch.[29]

5. The augousta consulted those in authority on the problem of how to put a stop to the inroads of Symeon who was devastating and plundering in the regions of Thrace. John Bogas[30] said that if he were granted the title of patrician, he would bring the Patzinaks[31] against [the invader]. He got what he asked for and went off to the Patzinaks with gifts in hand. He made a treaty, received hostages and returned to the city; the Patzinaks had agreed to cross the Danube [202] and make war on the Bulgars. It was then that the famous Asotios [Ashot], son of the 'ruler of rulers',[32] switched allegiance. It was said of him that if he took an iron bar in his hands by each end he could bend and twist it by the strength of his hands, the force of the iron being overcome by that of his hands. The Sovereign Lady gave him a hospitable reception but eventually arranged for him to go back home.

6. After a long-drawn-out siege of Adrianople which accomplished nothing, Pankratoukas,[33] an Armenian by race, appointed to defend the city, was corrupted with gold and delivered it into Symeon's hands. But shortly afterwards the patrician Basil, the prefect of the inkpot, and Niketas Helladikos were despatched by the augousta and were able to buy it back again with gold and many gifts.

7. In that year Damian, the emir of Tyre, launched an attack against Roman possessions with many warships and considerable forces; he

---

[29] A seal of this man has survived: J. Nesbitt, 'Overstruck seals in the Dumbarton Oaks Collection', *SBS*, 2:84. The presence of eunuchs among these highly placed personages is remarkable.

[30] In 917 John Bogas, then strategos of Cherson, was spying on the negotiations between Symeon and the Patzinaks: Nicholas Mystikos, *Letters*, no. 9, 58.

[31] Petchenegs: these people had replaced the Hungarians in southern Russia and were consequently in contact with the Bulgars – whom they were capable of attacking from the rear. The mission to the Patzinaks would have been in 917, the year in which hostilities were resumed: J. Howard-Johnston, 'The *De Administrando Imperio*: a re-examination of the text and a re-evaluation of its evidence about the Rus', *Les centres proto-urbains russes entre Scandinavie, Byzance et Orient*, ed. M. Kazanski, A. Nersessian and C. Zuckerman (Réalités Byzantines, 7, Paris, 2000), 301–36, esp. 324.

[32] Ashot II was the son of Sembat, the chief Armenian prince, whence the title 'ruler of rulers'. Sembat had recently been captured by the emir Yousouf and put to death (913). Ashot negotiated with the patriarch Nicolas via the Katholikos John V; Ashot came to Constantinople at the end of 914. For the most recent references to the history of Armenia in the tenth century: B. Martin-Hisard, 'Constantinople et les archontes du monde caucasien dans le *Livre des cérémonies* II 48', *TM*, 13 (2000), 359–530, 370–5.

[33] *DAI*, ed. Moravcsik and Jenkins, 238, says that Pankratoukas and his brothers were received by Leo VI, who appointed him chief of the Hikanatoi, then commander of the Boukellarioi. He must subsequently have been promoted to the command of Thrace since it was he who surrendered Adrianople in 914.

Constantine VII Porphyrogennetos (as a child) 197

reached Strobelos and laid vigorous siege to it. He would have taken it too if he had not fallen sick and died, whereupon the Saracens returned home empty handed.

8. The empress Zoe could not tolerate Symeon's continual onslaughts. Wishing to put an end to them, she came to the decision together with the Senate that it would be advantageous to conclude a treaty with the Saracens and bring all the forces in the east over into the west, then wage war with the combined eastern and western armies against the Bulgars and utterly eliminate them. This plan was approved; the patrician Rhadenos[34] and Michael Toxaras were sent to Syria where they came to an agreement with the Saracens.[35] Relieved in her mind on that score, the empress ordered the customary [203] distribution of pay to the troops to take place. She committed the forces to the magister Leo Phokas,[36] domestic of the scholai at that time, and ordered him to strike the Bulgars. All the thematic and tagmatic troops were assembled at Diabasis (the plain of Diabasis is large and well-suited for accommodating an army). The dean of the palace clergy was sent with the relic of the True Cross and all men were obliged to venerate it, swearing that they would die for each other. When the swearing was done, the entire army set off against the Bulgars. John Grapson, a warlike man who had often distinguished himself by bravery in battle, was in command of the Tagma of the Exkoubitors; Olbian Marsoules, a well-tried soldier, commanded the Hikanatoi; Romanos and Leo, the sons of Argyros[37] and Bardas Phokas,[38] commanded other units. Accompanying them was the magister Melias with the Armenians and many other commanders of themes. The patrician Constantine Lips went along too, perhaps as an adviser to Leo, the domestic of the scholai. On the sixth of August in the fifth year of the indiction[39] the Romans and the Bulgars joined battle near the fortress on the Achelous;[40] the Bulgars were thoroughly routed and many of them slaughtered. The domestic [of the scholai] was perspiring

---

[34] This is the first mention of one of the Rhadenoi, a family whose members occupied high office for some centuries.

[35] In 915 and 916 the Romans, under Melias, kleisourarch of the Lykandos, gained some success in the east as a result of which Zoe was able to gain a truce and the exchange of prisoners with the Arabs of Tarsus and Melitene. In 917 Toxas and Redenos led the sumptuous embassy that was received with munificence by the caliph of Baghdad, according to the reports of the contemporary Arab historians: Vasiliev and Canard, 11/1, 238–43.

[36] This is the son of the Nikephoros Phokas who was domestic of the scholai under Leo VI.

[37] The sons of Eustathios Argyros.

[38] Brother of Leo Phokas and father of the future emperor Nikephoros Phokas: Cheynet, 'Les Phocas', 296–9, reproduced in Cheynet, Société, 480–3.

[39] August 917.

[40] The fortress shared the name of the neighbouring small river which flows south of Mesembria.

freely and feeling faint so he dismounted at a spring to wash away the perspiration and to refresh himself, but his horse broke free of the reins and went careering through the battle lines without a rider. This horse was well known so, when the soldiers saw it, they assumed that the domestic had fallen. They panicked; their enthusiasm evaporated and they halted the pursuit, while some of them actually turned back. Symeon witnessed all this from some high ground (for his retreat had not been disorderly), whereupon he launched the Bulgars against the Romans whose morale, as we said, was broken. At first they were stupefied to see the Bulgars suddenly coming at them; the entire army turned tail and there occurred a most horrendous running away, some being [204] trodden underfoot by their own comrades, others slain by the foe. Leo the domestic was saved by fleeing to Mesembria. They were not only ordinary soldiers who fell but also a considerable number of commanders and officers in charge of units. Constantine Lips was slain and also the magister John Grapson, commander of the Exkoubitors.

9. They sent out the patrician Romanos Lekapenos, droungarios of the fleet[41] at the time, with orders to cruise the coastline, to give support to Leo and to ferry across the Patzinaks Bogas had brought as allies for the Romans. But a difference of opinion arose between Romanos and Bogas; the Patzinaks, seeing them at odds with each other, went back to their own country; hence the help they were supposed to give evaporated and was of no avail.[42] Others say that the overthrow of the Romans came about, not like that, but in another way. When Phokas had put Symeon to flight and was following in pursuit, a report suddenly came to his ears announcing that the droungarios of the fleet had taken off with the entire fleet, intending to seize the throne. He was thunderstruck by this report for he too was looking for a chance to usurp the imperial power. He abandoned the pursuit and returned to camp, perhaps intending to learn what was really going on. When word got around among the army that the domestic had fled, the rest of the pursuers were so discouraged that they did likewise. When Symeon saw them running away (for he was standing in a place well-suited to observing the outcome of the struggle) he poured his entire forces into the fray and reversed the direction of the retreat. That is the second version of the story. Whichever of the two is the true one, the Romans were

---

[41] The former commander of the naval theme of Samos had been promoted to command the entire fleet.
[42] There is no doubt that the proposed joint operation with the Patzinaks miscarried but it is impossible to say to what extent the droungarios of the fleet was responsible.

defeated and the result was as stated above.[43] After the defeat and the return of those who had survived the war, there was an enquiry into the affair of Romanos and Bogas. Things looked so bad for the droungarios [205] that a sentence of 'guilty' was handed down to him by the judges condemning him to have his eyes put out because, either by negligence or with malicious intent, he had failed to ferry the Patzinaks over immediately and because he had not picked up men returning from the defeat. He would have suffered that punishment too had not the magister Stephen, one of the regents, and the patrician Constantine Gongyles (who had a great deal of influence with the Sovereign Lady) intervened on his behalf.

Puffed up and arrogant with his victory, Symeon took his entire army and led it against the capital. Leo Phokas the domestic, John the commander of the Hetaireiai and Nicholas, the son of Constantine Doukas,[44] had to go out again with what troops they could find to oppose him. They ran into a detachment of Bulgars sent out to forage at a place called Katasyrtai,[45] clashed with and easily routed them. Another detachment almost immediately fell upon them, but this they withstood as well, easily and bravely. There followed a violent and long-drawn-out battle in which the Bulgars were defeated;[46] but Nicholas, the son of Doukas, was slain fighting manfully, and the Romans owe their victory to him. That was how the war turned out.

10. Things were not going well in the city; many of those in powerful positions were out of their minds, burning with a desire to appropriate the position of ruler,[47] and the chief offender was Phokas. He was the brother-in-law of Constantine [the parakoimomenos], whose sister he had married, and Constantine was one of the most powerful of the eunuchs who then held sway in the palace. [Leo Phokas] thought that by putting a great deal of confidence in him it would be easy to usurp the imperial throne. So [Phokas] was talked about far and wide; nor did he go about the matter

[43] Here Skylitzes is following two different accounts of the battle, one of them hostile to Romanos Lekapenos, the other to Phokas. It is clear that they belonged to different camps. Only rarely does Skylitzes use two conflicting sources for the same episode without opting for one of them.
[44] Thus one of the Doukai had escaped the massacre of his family.
[45] A location near to Constantinople; it was here that Basil I was wounded by the stag: *VEuthymii*, ed. Karlin-Hayter, 5.
[46] *Theophanes Continuatus*, ed. Bekker 390, and the *Chronicle of the Logothete* (*Symeonis magistri*, 306) say quite the opposite: that the Bulgars surprised the domestic by night and got the better of him again. Skylitzes wishes to present the accomplishments of a Doukas in the best possible light because in his day the Doukai were sharing the reins of government with the Komnenoi. This is not the only time that Skylitzes adjusts his text to adopt it to contemporary circumstance: C. Holmes, *Basil II and the governance of empire (976–1025)* (Oxford Studies in Byzantium, Oxford, 2005), 223–4
[47] Zoe had staked her chances on an offensive policy towards Symeon and lost. Now she was obliged to look for a co-emperor capable of stopping Symeon in his tracks.

secretly, but quite openly, as though [the throne] were a family inheritance and a legacy [206] coming down to him from his ancestors. He tended more and more to imagine that he would soon accede to the position as a legitimate successor. But Theodore (who was tutor to the emperor Constantine) was frightened that the man's ambition was beyond control; fearing the emperor might suffer some harm, he suggested to him that he secretly attach himself to the patrician Romanos, droungarios of the fleet, a servant of his father, whose interests he had always served. Romanos would be with the emperor to protect him and, if necessity arose, to fight on his side and proffer assistance. When overtures to this end were first made, Romanos refused; Theodore's assistants tried again and again but still he refused. Then the emperor himself wrote a letter[48] (which he signed in purple characters) and sent it to him. Romanos yielded when he had the letter in his hands and undertook to put a stop – insofar as he was able – to the designs of Constantine the parakoimomenos and his relatives. The negotiations and agreement had come about in such a way that there was whispering on this score in marketplaces, in highways and byways. The parakoimomenos was clearly no stranger to what was being planned against him, but he set no store by it, never for a moment thinking that anybody would dare to undertake a move against him. So he came out [of the palace] to make the customary distribution of pay to the sailors. While encouraging Romanos to put to sea without delay, he fell into a trap. Romanos came to meet him in a subservient manner and, by letting it be known that he was quite ready to perform what was required of him, gently and gradually led [the parakoimomenos] into the snare. Unable to perceive what was being planned and conversing without guile or suspicion, the parakoimomenos drew even closer to Romanos, asking whether there were good men and true to hand, to row the imperial yacht. Romanos said there were and that they were indeed close at hand. Then, with a nod of the head, he ordered some of the finest-looking men to approach. Constantine inspected them, [207] apparently approved of them and made as though he would leave; but as they came abreast of the flagship, Romanos (who was walking next to him) laid hands on Constantine and said no more than this: 'Take him.' Romanos stood still while men trained for the task took him aboard the flagship where they put him under lock and key. None of his retinue dared come to his aid; they all dispersed right away.

The whole city was disturbed when the news of what had happened went abroad, thinking (not unreasonably) that a *coup d'état* had taken place.

---

[48] The young emperor was then only thirteen years old.

When the news reached the empress Zoe, both she and the senior officials were at a loss what to do; so she summoned the patriarch Nicholas and the leading senators and, after coming to a consensus with them, she sent a delegation to Romanos wishing to learn the reason for what had taken place. When the emissaries arrived there where the ships were moored and were about to make an enquiry into the arrest of the parakoimomenos, the undisciplined men of the fleet rose up and drove them off with stones. Early next morning the empress came down to the Boukoleon, sent for her son and questioned his retinue how this insurrection had come about. When nobody said anything, the emperor's tutor, said: 'This uprising took place because Leo Phokas has destroyed the army, while Constantine the parakoimomenos has destroyed the palace, Sovereign Lady.'

11. Intending to take over the reins of government from his mother, the emperor brought Nicholas the patriarch and the magister Stephen back into the palace. Next day they sent John Toubakes to remove the augousta from there, but she clung to her son with shrieks and tears and moved him to feel the compassion and pity one ought to have for his mother. He said to those who were taking her away, 'Let my mother be with me'; and they let her be as soon as he said that. [208]

The emperor appointed the magister John Garidas domestic of the scholai to replace Leo Phokas whom he feared might break out in revolt. At John [Garides'] request Symeon, his son, and Theodore Zouphinezer,[49] his wife's brother, were appointed to command the Hetaireiai. Deceived by oaths taken by the emperor, [Leo] went down to his residence; then his relations were immediately expelled from the palace. He was overcome with grief and fear when he learnt of this; he rode off at once to the naval station and reported the outrage and humiliation he had suffered to Romanos the droungarios. Now they made common cause together, sealing the bond with oaths to each other and completing a marriage contract between their children; but they kept quiet about what they had in mind. Romanos sent[50] an explanation of what had happened to the palace, swearing that neither insurrection nor mutiny had been committed. He said that he had forestalled an attack by Phokas and was apprehensive for the emperor's safety and anxious that he come to no harm. For these reasons he would like to come up to the palace and provide a guard for the

---

[49] A Zephinezer, relative by marriage of St Athanasios, the founder of the Great Lavra, the oldest of the monasteries on Mount Athos, was strategos of the Aegean Sea: *Vitae duae anti`quae sancti Athanasii Athonitae*, ed. J. Noret (CCSG, 9, Tornhout, 1982), *Vita* A, 5; *Vita* B, 130.

[50] Theodore Matzoukes and a priest named John conveyed the explanation: *Theophanes Continuatus*, ed. Bekker, 393.

emperor. But Nicholas the patriarch neither trusted him nor believed what he said, so Theodore the Tutor told Romanos to make haste and bring all the fleet into the palace harbour at Boukoleon.[51] While Romanos delayed and tried to keep out of it, they who were encouraging him to execute the secret plan prevailed upon him to do as he was commanded [by the Tutor] even against his better judgement. And indeed, setting sail on the very day of the Feast of the Annunciation, the fleet arrived off the Boukoleon in battle order. The magister Stephen immediately quit the palace while the patrician Niketas,[52] who was related to Romanos by marriage, went in and expelled the patriarch. Those close to the emperor sent the holy and life-giving relic of the True Cross to Romanos, and when they had been assured with the most solemn oaths and deadly curses that he intended the emperor no harm they permitted him to enter the palace with a few men. Up he came and made an act of obeisance before the emperor, who received him and conducted him to the church of the Lighthouse.[53] [209] There assurances were given and received, whereupon [Romanos] was appointed commander in chief of the Hetairiai. A letter was immediately despatched to Leo Phokas telling him not to alarm himself or to lose courage, but not to enter into any shady conspiracy either, and to possess his soul in patience for a little while on his own estates, as provision was going to be made for him before too long. Constantine the parakoimomenos was coerced into writing a similar letter to him. When Phokas received these letters, he remained quietly at home, in Cappadocia.

12. In the fifth week of Lent the emperor Constantine was engaged to be married to Helen, daughter of Romanos, and on the Tuesday known as 'Galilee'[54] the emperor was married to her by the patriarch Nicholas. Romanos was proclaimed *basileopator*[55] and his son, Christopher, replaced him as commander of the Hetairiai.[56]

[51] This little port communicated directly with the palace.
[52] Niketas, better known as the magister Niketas (a title which he later acquired), had given his daughter Sophia in marriage to Romanos' elder son, Christopher. His origins were Slav; he *may* be the same person as Niketas Eladikos, also known as Rentakios: L. G. Westerink, *Nicétas Magistros, Lettres d'un exilé (928–946)* (Paris, 1973), introduction, 23–38.
[53] This was the church in which Michael I took refuge after his abdication. It was renovated by Michael III who provided it with numerous New Testament relics: Photios, homily 10, tr. C. Mango, *The homilies of Photius, patriarch of Constantinople* (DOS, 3, Cambridge, MA, 1958), 177–90.
[54] They were married on the feast commemorating the wedding at Cana in Galilee (John 2:1–11) Tuesday 4 May 919: R. H. J. Jenkins, 'The chronological accuracy of the logothete for the years AD 867–913', *DOP*, 19 (1965), 91–112, 109.
[55] 'Father of the emperor', but originally 'guardian of the palace' – a title formerly (and first) held by Stylianos Zaoutzes.
[56] The frequent changes of *hetairiarch* in the year 919 emphasise the importance of this position, crucial for the security of the emperor. It was thanks to the men under his command (the *hetaireiai*) that the revolt of Constantine Doukas had failed.

13. Shortly afterward, Leo Phokas was enticed by his relatives and his troops to foment an uprising. He summoned to his side Constantine the parakoimomenos, the Gongylios brothers, Constantine and Anastasios, together with Constantine of Malelia.[57] He proclaimed to them that he was taking up arms on behalf of the emperor Constantine, but Romanos put out chrysobulls containing a denial of Phokas' stated intent – confirmed by the emperor's signature and seal. These letters he sent into Leo's camp by the hand of a woman of questionable virtue who was later known as 'the imperial'[58] for having performed this service. Other letters were sent with a churchman named Michael containing promises of honours and gifts to the unit commanders and men of the army, the intention being to incite [210] them to mutiny, but he was apprehended by Phokas, cruelly flogged and cropped of his ears. But the woman eluded arrest and spread throughout the army the [statement] she was bringing. Constantine the son of Michael Barys,[59] commander of the unit of the Hikanatoi, was the first to abandon Leo and go over to Romanos; he was followed by Balantes[60] and Atzmoros, both of whom were governors of fortresses. Meanwhile Leo Phokas arrived at Chrysopolis[61] and terrified the people in the city by drawing up his army across [the Bosporos] from the stone heifer standing on a column. Romanos then despatched Symeon, the prefect of the inkpot, in a galley to the army of the rebel, entrusting to him a chrysobull addressed to Leo and sealed by the emperor which he was instructed to communicate to the army at large by any means within his power. The sense of the letter was this: 'Our Imperial Majesty having found no protector to hand so distinguished and faithful as Romanos, it is to him (after God himself) that we have entrusted the task of guarding our person in place of a father. And as he has shown us fatherly compassion, we have accepted him as standing *in loco parentis* to us. As for Leo Phokas, he has always fought against our rule; has always lain in wait for it and now openly displays his hidden animosity. It is now our will that he be no longer domestic; nor is he judged to be one of our subjects, but an apostate and usurper who has generated this uprising against our declared will, in order to arrogate the imperial government to his own person. And you, our army: do you willingly perform your duty, now that you know

---

[57] These were all faithful friends of Zoe; Constantine was protoasekretis.
[58] *Basilike.*
[59] Scion of an important aristocratic family in the tenth to eleventh centuries.
[60] First mention of another important family, a military family in this case, very likely from Cappadocia, often mentioned in the tenth century in connection with the Phokai.
[61] Phokas camped in full view of the capital. This proximity explains why it was so easy for Lekapenos' emissaries to slip into the enemy camp.

these things. Recognise us, your hereditary ruler, and do you segregate yourselves from this bitter attempt at usurpation.' Symeon arrived at the [enemy] camp and published the chrysobull to the troops. As they read it and understood its intent, they all went over to the side of 'the father of the emperor', Romanos. Phokas tried at first to prevent the circulation of the chrysobull but when he failed in that, seeing his forces gradually flowing away, [211] he fell into deep despair and saved himself by taking to his heels. He came to the fortress of Ateo with a few of his most trusty comrades and, when he was denied entrance there, they moved on to a village called Oe-Leo ['woe is Leo']. There he was captured by Michael Barys leading a number of others who had rallied to his support. John Toubakes and Leo Pastilas were sent to bring [Leo] to the capital and, while he was in their charge, they blinded him. Some say this was on secret instructions from Romanos but sources close to Romanos deny this, claiming that the captors acted on their own authority. And indeed Romanos seemed to be dismayed, as though this had been done against his will. Such was the ending of the uprising of Leo.

14. There was another conspiracy against Romanos, this one led by a certain Constantine Ktematinos,[62] David Koumoulianos[63] and Michael, kourator of the Mangana. They armed some young men and instructed them to lay murderous hands on Romanos when he went out hunting. But when word of this leaked out, the instigators of the plot were arrested, deprived of their eyes and paraded through the city centre. Leo Phokas also participated in this disgraceful procession, mounted on a mule. The empress Zoe was accused of plotting against the life of Romanos too. She was expelled from the palace and tonsured at St Euphemia's monastery.[64] The patrician Theophylakt,[65] Theodore, [212] the emperor's tutor, and Symeon his brother were expelled from the city and ordered to reside in the Opsikion theme on suspicion of contemplating action against Romanos. It was John Kourkouas,[66] droungarios of the watch, who carried

---

[62] This name indicates that the man was charged with caring for the imperial properties (*ktemata*), much the same as a caretaker and *pronoetes*: J.-C. Cheynet, '*Episkeptitai* et autres gestionnaires des biens publics (d'après les sceaux de l'IFEB), *SBS*, 7 (2002), 87–117 = Cheynet, *Société*, 237–72.
[63] Last known mention of a member of a family dating back to the time of Constantine V. Nicholas Mystikos (*Letters*, nos. 69 and 70) addressed two letters to him.
[64] She took the monastic name of Anna: *V Euthymii*, 137; this was in August 920. A basilica dedicated to St Euphemia was built over her tomb at Chalcedon. This saint had several sanctuaries dedicated to her in the capital. Zoe was confined in the women's monastery of St Euphemia at Petrion, a property of Basil I in which he confined his daughters: Janin, *Églises et les monastères*, I, 127–9.
[65] Theophylact was count of the stable: *Theophanes Continuatus*, 397.
[66] One of Romanos Lekapenos' partisans whom he later made domestic of the scholai.

out the sentence of ostracism against these men by suddenly arresting them and transporting them over to the other shore in ships. On 24 September Romanos was promoted to the rank of caesar and in the month of December he was crowned with the imperial diadem at the behest of the emperor Constantine, the patriarch Nicholas placing it on his brow.[67]

[67] 24 December 920.

CHAPTER 10

Romanos I Lekapenos [919–944]

1. [213] After Romanos[1] had received the imperial diadem, he crowned Theodora his wife[2] on the same day, Epiphany; and at Pentecost in the month of May he had his son Christopher crowned by Constantine [VII], who managed to give the appearance of doing it willingly although he was being coerced; but he was distraught when not in the public eye and deeply lamented this misfortune in private. Only the two emperors [Constantine and Romanos] took part in the procession that day.[3]

2. In the month of July, the eighth year of the indiction, the church was united. The metropolitans and clergy who had been at odds and differed with each other in support of the patriarch Nicholas or of Euthymios were reconciled.[4] The emperor Romanos exiled the magister Stephen[5] to the island of Antigone for aspiring to be emperor and tonsured him a

---

[1] S. Runciman, *The emperor Romanus Lecapenus and his reign: a study of tenth-century Byzantium* (Cambridge, 1929), repr. 1990, can still be read to advantage.

[2] 6 January 921. The origin of this, Romanos' second wife, remains unknown. She bore him Theophylact who eventually became patriarch.

[3] Christopher was older than Constantine when he became emperor, 20 May 921. The question of the order of precedence of the emperors arose nevertheless. Numismatic evidence reveals when Constantine VII was relegated to second position and when he slipped to third, indeed, disappeared from the effigies. It is also significant that he is sometimes shown with a beard, sometimes without one, for a beardless emperor is not considered 'of age' no matter how many years he has lived: Grierson, *DOC*, III, 2:526–40 for a detailed study.

[4] July 920 or 921. The object of this tome of union was to re-establish the unity of the church now that the protagonists of the former conflict were disappearing one by one. It may be that the famous mosaic in St Sophia showing the emperor prostrate before Christ was made at this time, symbolising the triumph of the church. The tome established a compromise between church and state concerning the number of legitimate unions one might contract. The church accepted second marriages (except for clergy) and even third marriages in outstanding circumstances. On the evolution of aristocratic marriage: A. E. Laiou, 'Imperial marriages and their critics in the eleventh century: the case of Skylitzes', *DOP*, 46 (1992), 165–76.

[5] This person enjoyed the confidence of Leo VI who had supported him in the Santabarenos affair: reign of Leo VI, c. 6 and note 15. He was subsequently made one the regents for the young Constantine VII.

monk. Theophanes Teicheotes[6] and Paul the Orphanotrophos, his closest associates,[7] went with him too. While a solemn procession was making its way to the tribunal,[8] the emperors suddenly returned to the palace: they had received information that a conspiracy was afoot. The leading conspirators, the patrician Arsenios[9] and Paul Manglabites,[10] were arrested, blinded, deprived of their property and sent into exile. That was the year in which the emperor Romanos made Leo Argyros his son-in-law by marriage to his daughter, Agatha. Leo was a man of great nobility and distinguished appearance, endowed with wisdom and intelligence.[11]

3. Also in the same year the affair of Rentakios took place. A native of the Helladikon theme,[12] he attempted to slay his own father. Terrified by the disorderly conduct of his son, the parent boarded a vessel and sailed to [214] Byzantium in the hope of persuading the emperor to put a stop to the son's recklessness, but on the way there he was taken captive by the Saracens of Crete. Rentakios, now left in possession of his father's wealth, came up to the capital with it, hastened to the sacred church of the Divine Wisdom where he installed himself and proceeded to dissipate his father's fortune. This did not escape the notice of Romanos who decided, once he knew of it, to get him out of the church and discipline him. When Rentakios got wind of this he forged an imperial letter supposedly from the emperor to Symeon with the intention of deserting to the Bulgars. Condemned for this, he lost both his wealth and his eyes.

4. At the death of Adralestos, he was succeeded as domestic of the scholai by Pothos Argyros.[13] The Bulgars now advanced as far as Katasyrtai, so out marched Pothos with the troops and made his camp at the place called Thermopolis.[14] From there he sent out the unit commander Michael,[15] son

---

[6] This name is really an office; the 'count of the walls' was responsible for the maintenance of the walls of the palace: Oikonomides, *Listes*, 336–7
[7] *Theophanes Continuatus*, 398, says these two officials were creatures of the magister Stephen.
[8] A building on the forum of Constantine.
[9] *Theophanes Continuatus*, says it was a creature of Arsenios who apprised Romanos. There is no other mention of this Arsenios (which was usually a monastic name at that time).
[10] Literally, 'the [emperor's] strap-bearer'; probably an imperial footman.
[11] In fact Agatha married Romanos, the son of Leo Argyros: J. F. Vannier, *Familles byzantines: les Argyroi (IXe–XIIe siècles)* (ByzSorb, 1, Paris, 1975), 33, with all the references. Romanos was the grandfather of the future emperor Romanos II.
[12] The Rentakioi were an old Helladic family of which the first one known was the patrician Sisinnios who plotted with the Bulgars against Leo III and lost his life: *Theophanis Chronographia*, 1, ed. C. de Boor (Leipzig, 1883–5), 400.
[13] Being the brother of Leo, Pothos was the uncle of the husband Romanos chose for his daughter Agatha.
[14] Near to Katasyrta, hence in Thrace and not too distant from the capital.
[15] Michael was deputy commander (*topoteretes, locum tenens*) of the scholae: *Theophanes Continuatus*, 400.

of the patrician Leo the Fool, to reconnoitre the Bulgars but, from lack of forethought, he fell into an ambush of the barbarians. As no escape was possible, he opted to fight. Many Bulgars were killed or put to flight but he too received a mortal wound and was carried back to the capital where he died shortly afterwards.

5. Then a plot against the emperor Romanos was betrayed to him.[16] Its leader was Anastasios the sakellarios,[17] allegedly working for the emperor Constantine. The principal conspirators[18] were arrested and each was punished as the emperor Romanos thought fit, Anastasios being tonsured as a monk.[19] This was the pretext for the demotion of Constantine to the rank of second emperor, Romanos being first – for he claimed that this was the only possible way of putting an end to conspiracies. Thus, for ephemeral gains and for a fleeting, corrupt reign, he distanced [215] himself from God by perjury. That is what was happening in the city.

6. Symeon, for his part, again sent a powerful force against the Romans, commanded by Chagan,[20] one of his leading subjects, and Minikos, commander-in-chief of the cavalry, with orders to attack the city itself as soon as possible. When the emperor Romanos learnt of this advance, realising that when they came they might burn down the most beautiful of the palaces and dwellings close to the city, he sent John the rector[21] with Leo and Pothos Argyros, leading a fairly large troop drawn from the imperial Hetaireiai and from the regular soldiers. With them was the patrician Alexios Mosele, droungarios of the fleet,[22] and his ships. In the

---

[16] The informer was a eunuch named Theokletos, a lawyer attached to the furnishers of the imperial table (*hypourgia*) who appears to have had access to the emperor: *Theophanes Continuatus*, 400.

[17] The sakellarios controlled the financial services of the state. Anastasios was also the officer in charge of the *chrysocheion* (bullion store), in which capacity he left a seal to posterity: V. Laurent, *Le Corpus des sceaux de l'empire byzantin*, v, *L'Église*, 1–3 (Paris, 1963–72), II, no. 663.

[18] The conspirators were: Theodoret the koitonites, Demetrios, imperial notary of the eidikon, Nicholas Koubatzes and Theodotos the protokarabos (commandant of the imperial yacht), all of them enthusiastic supporters of Constantine VII: *Theophanes Continuatus*, 400.

[19] He was sent to the monastery of Elegmoi in Bithynia: *Theophanes Continuatus*, 400, a monastery (also known as Elaiobomoi) which was of sufficient importance in 787 for its then superior to sign the acts of the council held in that year: Janin, *Églises et monastères*, 142–8.

[20] Chagan is a title (not a name) borne by the chiefs of tribes of Turco-Mongolian origin (Avars, Khazars, Rhos, etc.). The same was true of the Bulgars until the Christianisation of the kingdom.

[21] This man is not to be confused with the John the rector who was one of the regents for Constantine VII; he perished after the death of Alexander: R. Guilland, *Recherches sur les institutions Byzantines*, 4 vols. (Berlin and Amsterdam, 1968), II, 214.

[22] Alexios was probably Romanos' successor at the admiralty and was undoubtedly the husband of one of his daughters. He was a descendant of that Alexios Mosele who was for a time the heir presumptive and son-in-law to Theophilos: Theophilos, c. 13, above.

fifth week of Lent they drew up their men on the plains of Pegai[23] and waited. The Bulgars came upon them there with a horrendous shouting and launched a furious attack on them. John the rector ran away, while the patrician Photeinos, son of Platypous, and not a few others died fighting for him. But the rector got away by the skin of his teeth and boarded a galley. Alexios the droungarios tried to do likewise but was unable to get up; he fell into the sea under the gangway leading to the galley and was drowned, together with his first lieutenant. Leo and Pothos Argyros fled to Kastellion[24] and were saved. As for the rest of the men, some were drowned as they fled from the enemy, some fell prey to their swords, while others fell into the hands of the barbarians. As there was virtually nobody to stop them, the Bulgars burnt down the palaces of Pegai and set fire to the entire straits.[25]

7. On 20 February, tenth year of the indiction,[26] Theodora, the spouse of Romanos, died and was buried at the Myrelaion.[27] [216] Sophia, wife of the emperor Christopher, was promoted augousta. Then the kouropalates Iber came from Iberia. He proceeded through the richly decorated forum and was received with great honour and glory. The emperor sent him to the [church of the] Holy Wisdom of God to behold its beauty and magnitude. He was overcome by its loveliness when he came there and astounded at the diversity of its adornment. He declared that this sacred spot was indeed the dwelling place of God[28] – and returned to his own land.

8. The Bulgars now made a further attack on Roman territory, and approaching the palace of the empress Theodora[29] set fire to it as there was no one to withstand them. The emperor Romanos gave a splendid banquet to which he invited the commanders of the army units. Among them

---

[23] The plains of Pegai lay on the other bank of the Golden Horn, which permitted the fleet to cover the army's rear. By this manoeuvre the Romans hoped to prevent the Bulgars from reaching the suburban palaces (such as St Mamas) on the Bosporos.

[24] The fortress of Galata.

[25] *Hapan to Stenon*, i.e. the Bosporos. In the eleventh century Stenon was a theme, probably to be identified with the 'Euxine' in the Taktikon of the Escorial: Oikonomides, *Listes,* 358.

[26] 20 February 922.

[27] The family monastery of the Lekapenoi. On the circumstances of this choice: A. Müller, 'Wiederverwendete Sarkophage?', *JÖB*, 48 (1998), 49–56.

[28] Gen. 28:16–17. The person ruling the section of Georia known as Iberia traditionally received the elevated title of kouropalates from Constantinople: B. Martin-Hisard, 'Constantinople et les archontes du monde caucasien dans le *Livre des cérémonies* II.48', *TM*, 13 (2000), 359–530, at 437–50. The kouroplates referred to here was most likely Ashot, who had replaced his father, Ardanas, who died in 922–3. The chronology is not very secure; it rather looks as though Skylitzes (following *Theophanes Continuatus,* 444–9) is presenting a series of brief notices which did not necessarily succeed each other within the framework of a single year.

[29] This was a palace situated near to the church of St Theodora mentioned already by John Malalas; it was at the far end of the Golden Horn: Janin, *Constantinople,* 467.

there was a man whose surname was Saktikios, an officer commanding the corps of the Exkoubitors. When the banquet was in full swing, conversation turned towards the matter of the Bulgars and the emperor gave a fiery speech, which elicited an enthusiastic response, urging them valiantly to go forth against the foe and to fight for their own fatherland. They all declared themselves ready to march out and fight for the Christian cause. Early next morning Saktikios took up his arms, went behind the Bulgar lines, entered their camp (for most of the Bulgars had dispersed through the countryside in search of booty) and slew everybody he found within the camp. When the majority of the Bulgars learnt of this from escapees, they returned to the camp and an engagement ensued: fresh Bulgars fighting against tired [Romans]; they were in good condition, while our forces were already worn down by the preceding battle before they received the first onslaught of the enemy. Together with only a few men Saktikios put up a heroic fight and killed many of the foe, but when he was overwhelmed [217] he gave his horse rein and fled. Then, when he came to a river and was crossing it, his horse became bogged down in the mud; he was overtaken by the Bulgars and received a mortal wound in the seat and thigh. The horse now got free of the mud, thanks to the care and cooperation of his attendants. Sometimes fleeing, sometimes turning back again, he and his attendants and cavalrymen slashing at the Bulgars, he came safely to Blachernae. There he was laid in the church of the Holy Casket[30] and died the following night, to the great sorrow not only of the emperor, but of the army and of all the Roman people.

9. There was yet another uprising against the emperor, this one in Chaldia, at the instigation of the local governor, the patrician Bardas Boilas.[31] The leaders of the revolt were a man named Adrian Chaldos[32] and the Armenian Tatzates,[33] both very rich men. They captured a fortress called Paiperte[34] and there they armed themselves against the emperor, but John Kourkouas,[35] commander of the scholai, made a sudden appearance

---

[30] A section of the church at Blachernae so called because it housed the casket (*soros*) which contained the shawl or veil (*maphorion*) of the Theotokos.
[31] The name suggests Slavic origins.
[32] Skylitzes mentions other Chaldoi a little later, with whom this Adrian was most likely connected.
[33] This surname means (in Armenian) one who has converted to Chalcedonianism (diophysitism). A strategos of the Boukellarion theme bearing this name deserted to the Arabs in 782: Theophanes, I, 456.
[34] Bayburt on the river Akampsis, protecting the approach to Trebizond from Erzeroum.
[35] John succeeded Pothos Argyros in June 922 and remained in office for twenty-two years, until autumn 944. He was one of Romanos' best military officers (the emperor, having no experience of land warfare, did not lead his armies in person): Runciman, *Lecapenus*, 135–50. John's brother Theophilos was another commander who acquired a great reputation.

(he happened to be staying at Caesarea) and dispersed the gathering. He blinded the most important of the men he arrested and confiscated their property, but the poor and insignificant he let go scot-free, ordering them to go wherever they pleased. Tatzates alone remained in possession of a fortress built on a high hill. Having asked for and received the word of the domestic [of the scholai] that he would suffer no ill, he came into the capital where he was honoured with the rank of Manglabitos and interned in the Mangana palace. But he was detected trying to escape and deprived of his eyes. As for Bardas Boilas (to whom the emperor [218] was amicably disposed), he was tonsured a monk and suffered no worse affliction.

10. Symeon, the Bulgar chief, now advanced on Adrianople and, surrounding it with palisades and ditches, laid vigorous siege to it. The commander of the city was that patrician Leo whom they called Leo the Fool[36] on account of his rash impetuosity in battle. He valiantly withstood the siege, sometimes bravely driving the invading Bulgars from the very walls themselves, sometimes opening the gates and launching an irresistible onslaught against the foe whom he easily repelled. But when shortage of grain began to afflict those within the city and famine tormented them, as there was no hope of supplies from any side, victims of necessity, they surrendered the city, themselves and the governor to the Bulgars. Once Symeon got him in his hands he remembered all the anguish Leo had caused the Bulgars. He punished him with innumerable tortures and finally put him to a bitter death. Then he stationed a Bulgar garrison there and withdrew, but when the garrison heard of the approach of a Roman army they abandoned the city and fled; Adrianople passed back under Roman rule.

11. It was then that Leo of Tripoli sailed out with a considerable naval force against the Romans. While he was moored off the island of Lemnos,[37] the patrician John Rhadenos,[38] droungarios of the fleet, suddenly appeared and easily put him to flight, killing nearly all the Hagarenes. [Leo] of Tripoli alone saved his life by fleeing.[39]

12. In the month of September, second year of the indiction,[40] [Symeon] the Bulgar chieftain campaigned against Constantinople with his entire army. He devastated Macedonia, set fire to the regions of Thrace and ravaged [219] everything that came to hand. He pitched his camp close to

[36] His son, Michael, had recently fallen fighting the Bulgars.
[37] This island played a key role in the fight against the Arab naval forces.
[38] This is he who was ambassador to Baghdad in 917: reign of Constantine VII, c. 8.
[39] This was the last campaign of Leo Tripolites: reign of Leo VI, c. 23.
[40] September 924; actually the thirteenth of the indiction.

Blachernae and set about getting Nicholas the patriarch[41] and some senior officials to undertake peace negotiations. Each side took hostages from the other to ensure that no hostile act should ensue. As the patriarch had confidence in the [Bulgars'] oaths, there followed a discussion as to which of the senators should accompany him; the patrician Michael Stypeiotes[42] and John the private secretary with executive authority[43] were chosen (for John the rector had been maligned before the emperor and was expelled from the palace, to have his layman's hair shorn in his own monastery). When the delegates came to Symeon and were about to open the peace negotiations, he sent them back because, having learnt that the emperor Romanos was a man of intelligence and integrity, he wanted to see him in person. Romanos welcomed this proposal. He sent to the Kosmidion shore and had a secure jetty built out into the sea, at which the imperial vessel could tie up in absolute safety when it had sailed there. He hemmed it around with fortifications and ordered a raised platform to be set up in the midst of it where they could speak with each other. But Symeon sent and burnt the church of the All-holy Mother of God at Pege[44] (the one the emperor Justinian built) and burnt everything around it. From this it was clear that he was in no mood for peace. The emperor came to the church of Blachernae together with the patriarch; they entered the [church of the] Holy Casket where intercessory hymns were offered to God, then he left the church taking with him the shawl of the Mother of God, escorted by protective weaponry. The squadron which accompanied [the shawl] was decked out in glorious array as it arrived at the appointed location; this was on the ninth of November. Symeon too appeared with numerous hosts in several formations of varying appearance. Some had golden shields and spears, some had silver shields and some copper, while the rest were distinguished by whatever colours they chose. [220] They had Symeon in the midst of them and were acclaiming him emperor in the Roman language. All the officials and the population of the city saw from the walls what was happening. First Romanos arrived at the jetty mentioned just now – and waited for Symeon. They exchanged hostages and the Bulgars carefully inspected the jetty to ensure that it concealed

---

[41] The patriarch maintained a regular correspondence with Symeon 920–4: *Nicholas I, Patriarch of Constantinople, Letters*, ed. and tr. R. J. H. Jenkins and L. G. Westerink (CFHB, 6, Washington, DC, 1973), 14–30.
[42] Might this be the same Stypeiotes who took part in the suppression of the revolt of Basil Epeiktes against Leo VI?: see reign of Leo VI, c. 17.
[43] *Ho mystikos kai paradynasteuon. Mystikos* we know, but *paradynasteuon* is not an official title found in the Taktika. Clearly the *paradynasteuon* coordinated the entire function of the civil service, but the emperors did not appoint such an officer on any regular basis. See cc. 13 and 14 following.
[44] This church must be distinguished from Pegai; it was one of those restored by Basil I.

no trap or snare. Then they invited Symeon to dismount and come and join the emperor on the fortified platform. These embraced each other and began the peace negotiations. They say that Romanos addressed Symeon in these words: 'I have heard that you are a Christian and a God-fearing man, but I see deeds which are totally incompatible with this report. If you are truly a Christian, stop these unjust slayings and this unholy bloodshed at once. Deal with us Christians as one who bears the name of and truly is a Christian; decline to soil the hands of Christians with the blood of their fellow Christians. For you too are a man: death lies ahead of you, resurrection, judgement and the reward of what you have done in life. You are here today, tomorrow you will dissolve into dust and ashes. If it is for love of wealth that you commit these deeds, I will give you your fill of riches.[45] Only do you embrace peace and cherish concord so that you can live a peaceful life without bloodshed and Christians can finally desist from raising weapons against each other.' Thus spoke the emperor; Symeon was put to shame by his humility and promised to make peace. They embraced each other and separated, the emperor showering Symeon with magnificent gifts. A portent occurred that day which is worth reporting. They say that two eagles flew in the sky above where the emperors were conversing; they shrieked, paired up and then separated, one flying towards the city, the other into Thrace. Those who prognosticate from the flight of birds were afraid that this augured no good; [Romanos and Symeon] had parted without concluding a peace treaty, they said. When he returned, Symeon enthusiastically told his officials about [221] the modesty of the emperor, likewise of his generosity and freedom with money.

13. At Christmas, second year of the indiction,[46] the emperor Romanos crowned his sons, Stephen and Constantine, in the Great Church. The patriarch tonsured his remaining son, Theophylact, making him a cleric. He ordained him sub-deacon and appointed him synkellos[47] once he had taken his place in the sanctuary with the company of sub-deacons. He promoted John the private secretary with executive authority patrician and proconsul.

14. On 15 May, third year of the indiction,[48] the patriarch Nicholas died,[49] his second patriarchate having lasted thirteen years, and Stephen,

---

[45] Romanos appears to be promising to restore the tribute.
[46] 25 December 924.
[47] Clear indication that he was destined for the patriarchate. The appointment was totally uncanonical as Theophylact (born in 917) was only seven years old.
[48] 15 May 925. *Theophanes Continuatus*, 410, says, correctly, that it was the thirteenth year of the indiction.
[49] Nicholas was buried in the Galagrenai monastery, *Theophanes Continuatus*, 410.

metropolitan of Amaseia, was enthroned as patriarch in the month of August.[50] But the private secretary was accused of trying to appropriate the imperial throne at the instigation of the patrician Kosmas, logothete of the drome, who wanted to make him his son-in-law by marrying him to his own daughter. He was expelled from the palace but still allowed to come and do obeisance to the emperor – who held him in high esteem and was unwilling to be totally deprived of his company. His accusers, however, would not be silenced and indeed produced evidence to support their charges. The emperor had the matter investigated and found that what they said of John was true. He was about to have him arrested and tortured when [the secretary] got wind of it and fled to the monastery called Monokastanos,[51] where he received monastic tonsure. Then the emperor tortured the patrician Kosmas the logothete[52] at the Horologion[53] and deprived him of his command. John the protovestiarios was appointed to replace John as private secretary with executive authority.

15. It was at that time that an earthquake occurred in the Thrakesion theme; alarming fissures yawned in the ground which swallowed up many villages and churches together with the people.

16. [222] In the month of May, the fifteenth year of the indiction,[54] Symeon the Bulgar chieftain launched an attack against the Croats. When he encountered them he was worsted by them in the fastnesses of the mountains and lost his entire army.[55]

17. An astronomer named John came to the emperor and said that if he would send someone to cut off the head of the statue standing above the apse of the Xerolophos[56] and facing west, Symeon would immediately

---

[50] Theophylact could not succeed Nicholas on account of his youth. It is uncanonical for a bishop to leave one church for another but Romanos had no doubt obtained assurances that the newly elected bishop would not in any way frustrate his plans.

[51] Monastery in Bithynia, but it is not known exactly where: Janin, *Grands centres*, II, 58–9 and 168–9.

[52] This Kosmas must be distinguished from the great jurist, the nephew of Photios, who may have published the Novel of 934: *ODB*, 1152.

[53] From the context this would appear to be a *horologion* (timepiece) in the Grand Palace, not to be confused with the better-known *horologion* at St Sophia.

[54] 927 AD.

[55] Symeon had fought against the Serbs whom Romanos had incited to intervene against him. Two brothers, Zachariah and Paul, were contending for power and both were perfectly ready to change sides when it was to their advantage so to do. At first Zachariah favoured the Romans, then he was able to seize the reins of Serbia with the support of Symeon – whom he promptly betrayed, whereupon the Bulgar obliged him to take refuge with the Croats. It was at this point that a Bulgar army ventured into Croatia only to be destroyed: *DAI*, ed. Moravcsik and Jenkins, c. 32.

[56] The seventh hill of Constantinople, to the west of the city, where the forum of Arkadios lay. Here stood a column with a statue of Arkadios on the top of it.

die – for his fate was magically linked to that of the statue. Convinced by this speech, [Romanos] had the head of the statue cut off and in that very same hour (as the emperor precisely discovered) Symeon died in Bulgaria, carried off by a heart attack.[57]

18. On the death of Symeon, Peter took command of the Bulgars. He was the child of his second wife, the sister of George Soursouboules whom Symeon had appointed guardian of his children. While he was still alive, Symeon obliged Michael, born by his first wife, to receive monastic tonsure. When the neighbouring peoples, Turks, Serbs, Croats and the rest of them, learnt of Symeon's death they immediately made plans to campaign against the Bulgars. The Bulgar nation was suffering a severe famine and a plague of locusts which was ravaging and depleting both the population and the crops,[58] so the Bulgars were very fearful of an incursion by these other peoples, but they were especially apprehensive of a Roman onslaught. So Peter took counsel with his entourage and decided they had better launch a deterrent attack on the Romans. They penetrated into Macedonia [223], but when they learnt that the emperor was moving against them Peter the Bulgar chieftain and George, the guardian of Symeon's children, secretly despatched a monk[59] carrying a letter saying that they were ready to treat with the Romans if they chose to do so and to enter into a marriage agreement with them. The emperor warmly welcomed this proposition when it arrived and immediately sent off a monk named Theodosios[60] and Constantine of Rhodes,[61] a palace chaplain, in a galley to undertake peace negotiations with the Bulgars at Mesembria.[62] They arrived, carried on the necessary conversations one might expect and returned overland together with a very distinguished Bulgar named Stephen. Later the guardian George Soursouboules arrived and other illustrious Bulgars. While they were in the presence of the emperor, they saw Maria, the daughter of the emperor Christopher, and were highly pleased with her; she was indeed of outstanding beauty. They wrote asking Peter to come with all haste (this after they had reached a peace agreement). The magister Niketas,[63]

---

[57] Symeon died on 27 May 927, leaving a somewhat weakened Bulgaria at the end of his life. Leo the Grammarian says nothing about the business of the statue.
[58] This is a reference to the terrible winter of 927–8, mentioned again below, from which the people of the empire also cruelly suffered.
[59] His name was Kalokyros and he was of Armenian descent: *Theophanes Continuatus*, 413; *Symeonis magistri*, 327.
[60] Known as Aboukes: *Theophanes Continuatus*, 413; *Symeonis magistri*, 327.
[61] The former secretary of Samonas: reign of Leo VI, c. 32.
[62] Peter had the problem of getting himself accepted as the new sovereign, especially by his restless brothers (see c. 23 below). This was not really a show of hostility.
[63] The accession of Romanos must have brought Niketas promotion; he was a simple *asekretis* at the time of the conspiracy of Constantine Doukas in 914.

the emperor Romanos' co-father-in-law, was sent to meet Peter and bring him to the capital. When [Peter] reached Blachernae the emperor came by water, embraced him and warmly welcomed him. They said what needed to be said to each other to confirm the terms of both the peace agreement and the marriage alliance, Theophanes the protovestiarios serving as mediator. Then on 8 October out came the patriarch Stephen together with Theophanes the protovestiarios and the entire senate and blessed [the marriage of] Peter and Maria in the church of the most holy Mother of God at Pege with the protovestiarios and Soursouboules as witnesses.[64] When the wedding had been magnificently and extravagantly solemnised, the protovestiarios returned to the city with the emperor's daughter. The third day of the marriage celebrations the emperor gave a banquet [224] at the jetty of Pege, dining with Peter while the imperial galley was moored there. The emperors Constantine and Christopher were at the banquet; in fact the Bulgars caused quite a commotion by insisting that Christopher be acclaimed first, and *then* Constantine. The emperor Romanos gave in to them and ordered that it should be so.[65] When everything that is customarily done in these circumstances had been accomplished, Maria and her husband departed and turned their faces towards Bulgaria. They were brought on their way as far as Hebdomon[66] by her parents and the protovestiarios. This is the way that things happened in the city.

19. The magister John Kourkouas, domestic of the scholai, was ravaging Syria[67] and sweeping aside all resistance. He took possession of many fortresses, strongholds and cities of the barbarians[68] and then came to the renowned Melitene which he besieged, reducing the inhabitants to such straits that they were contemplating coming to terms with him. So Apochaps, the descendant of Amr, emir of Melitene, came to him together

---

[64] The ceremonies were held outside the walls to prevent any unexpected action.

[65] This adjustment of the imperial order of precedence is attested by the coins. The Bulgarian marriage in 927 was obviously a pretext for fading Constantine VII (now an adult) into the background. Christopher died in 931: *Theophanes Continuatus*, 420.

[66] Constantine VII severely criticised this marriage: *DAI*, ed. Moravcsik and Jenkins, 72–4. On the marriage of Maria Lekapena: J. Shepard, 'A marriage too far? Maria Lekapena and Peter of Bulgaria', *The empress Theophano: Byzantium and the west at the turn of the first millennium*, ed. A. T. Davids (Cambridge, 1995), 121–49. Shepard emphasises that the places where the marriage celebrations were held (Blachernae, the Marian church at Pege) recall the visits of Symeon who had been received in the palace and who burnt the church.

[67] The term is used to designate the whole area under Arab domination, i.e. the entire eastern frontier as far as Armenia, to the north of the Syria of today.

[68] The chronology of events has been compressed here. A first campaign took place in June–July 926, when the Bulgar peril had abated, allowing reinforcements to be sent to the east; but it only succeeded in ravaging the territory around Melitene, not in taking the town. It was not until the autumn of 931 that John Kourkouas succeeded in imposing peace on the main parts of the Melitene district.

with Aposalath, the commander of its garrison. The domestic cheerfully welcomed them and sent them off as honoured guests to the emperor. They met him and concluded a peace treaty, then returned to their own land, having joined the ranks of the Romans' friends and allies, ready to fight against people of their own race on Rome's behalf. But when Apochaps and Aposalath died, this peace treaty was abolished,[69] so the above-mentioned domestic went to war with them, taking with him the magister Melias and his Armenians.[70] First they made an armed assault to drive back within the walls those who had been so bold as to establish themselves in open country. Then they surrounded the city, vigorously besieged it, captured it and placed it under martial law. They overran all the surrounding territory and brought it into subjection under Roman rule. The emperor constituted Melitene [225] and all the adjacent populated area a 'curacy' by which means he brought a great deal of tribute into the public purse.[71]

20. The magister Niketas, father-in-law of the emperor Christopher, was accused of having incited Christopher against his own father, to depose him as emperor. He was ejected from the city and obliged to receive monastic tonsure.[72]

21. On 15 July, sixth year of the indiction, Stephen of Amaseia died having been patriarch for two years and eleven months. In the month of December[73] they brought in Tryphon the monk and ordained him patriarch *pro tempore* – until Theophylact, the emperor's son, attained the canonical age.

---

[69] The reality of the matter is that the Arab emir of Mossoul, Saïd ben Hamdam, the first of the famous Hamdanid dynasty, came to the help of the people of Samosata then sent a detachment to retake control of Melitene: Vasiliev and Canard, *Byzance et les Arabes*, II.1:266–8.

[70] This Melias (Mleh in Armenian) is very famous for the exploits which he and his band accomplished fighting against the Arabs. He was the creator of the frontier theme of Lykandos: G. Dédéyan, 'Mleh le Grand, stratège de Lykandos', *REArm NS*, 15 (1981), 73–102.

[71] The final capitulation of Melitene took place on 19 May 934: Vasilev and Canard, II, 1:269. The 'curacy' of Melitene was the first to be established as a result of the Byzantine reconquest. It is extraordinary that the land was not redistributed but remained the property of the state. This, however, was totally in accord with the policy of combating the growth of great landed aristocrats. The income accruing amounted to thousands of pieces of gold and silver: *Theophanes Continuatus*, 416–17; Leo the Grammarian, 318. For a novel interpretation of the role of the kourator of Melitene as an administrator emerging from the former Moslem elite: J. Shepard, 'Constantine VII, Caucasian openings and the road to Aleppo', *Eastern approaches to Byzantium*, ed. A. Eastmond (SPBS, 9, Aldershot, 2001), 19–40; and C. Holmes, 'How the east was won in the reign of Basil II', *Eastern approaches*, 41–56.

[72] A part of the correspondence of Niketas has survived in which he repeatedly urges his former friends (from his estate in Bithynia) to intervene in his favour with Romanos I then with Constantine VII: L. G. Westerink, *Nicétas magistros: Lettres d'un exilé, 928–946* (Paris 1973), especially Letter no. 7.

[73] This information is incorrect. Stephen mounted the patriarchal throne on 29 June 925 and died on 18 July 927, the fifteenth year of the indiction in fact.

22. The same month an intolerable winter suddenly set in; the earth was frozen for one hundred and twenty days.[74] A cruel famine followed the winter, worse than any previous famine, and so many people died from the famine that the living were insufficient to bury the dead. This happened in spite of the fact that the emperor did his very best to relieve the situation, assuaging the ravages of the winter and the famine with good works and other aid of every kind.[75]

23. Peter, the chieftain of the Bulgars, was opposed by his brother John with other powerful men of Bulgaria. [John] was apprehended, beaten and imprisoned, while those acting with him suffered horrible deaths. Peter let the emperor Romanos know what had happened and he, when he learnt of it, despatched the former rector, John the monk, ostensibly for exchange of prisoners, but in fact to find John and, somehow or other, get him to Constantinople; which is what happened. The [ex-] rector was able to abduct John, get him aboard a ship [226] at Mesembria and come to the capital with him. Shortly after that he put aside the monastic habit, got permission to marry a wife and acquired both a house and great deal of property. Now Michael, Peter's other brother, aspired to become ruler of the Bulgars. He occupied a powerful fortress and greatly agitated the Bulgar lands. Many flocked to his banner but, when he died shortly after, these people, for fear of Peter's wrath, entered Roman territory. They reached Nicopolis[76] by way of Macedonia, Strymon and the Helladikon theme, laying waste everything that came to hand, and there, finally, took a Sabbath rest. In due course and after a number of reverses, they became Roman subjects.

24. About that time that piece of masonry which they call the keystone fell from the apse of the forum killing sixty men.[77] There was also a terrible fire near the church of the most holy Mother of God in the forum.[78] The arcade was burnt down as far as the place called Psicha.[79]

---

[74] A further reference to the winter of 927–8, a winter which accelerated the concentration of land in the hands of the powerful. Some years later (in 934) Romanos promulgated a celebrated novel intended to eliminate the damage done to the social structure by that terrible winter: M. Kaplan, *Les hommes et la terre, à Byzance, propriété et exploitation du sol du VIe au XIe siècle* (ByzSorb, 10, Paris, 1992), 421–4 (presentation and translation of the Novel); E. McGeer, *The land legislation of the Macedonian emperors* (Toronto, 2000), 49–60. On the development of huge estates: J. Lefort, 'The rural economy, seventh to the twelfth centuries', *EHB*, 283–93.

[75] Romanos urged the controllers of the public purse and the monasteries to make distributions of goods and money to the poor: *Theophanes Continuatus*, 418; *Symeonis magistri*, 330–1.

[76] Nicopolis in the Epirus.

[77] Other sources say six men: *Theophanes Continuatus*, 420; *Symeonis magistri*, 332.

[78] A church built by Basil I in the forum of Constantine. It either escaped the flames or was immediately rebuilt, for Nikephoros Phokas made a halt there in the course of his triumphal entry in 963: Janin, *Églises et les monastères*, 1, 236–7.

[79] The fire was nourished by the material in the candle-makers' and furiers' shops which were located there: *Theophanes Continuatus*, 420; *Symeonis magistri*, 332.

25. The emperor Christopher died in the month of August, fourth year of the indiction, and was buried in his father's monastery.[80]

26. When the time to which the patriarch Tryphon had agreed came to an end, he was unwilling to vacate the throne as he had promised he would. He asked for reasons to be given and charges to be laid against him justifying his expulsion from the church. The emperor's hands were tied in this matter and he was at his wits' end when [the metropolitan] of Caesarea, Theophanes 'Hog skin' as they called him, a real chatterbox, saw the emperor's dilemma and his chagrin at being trapped and deceived. He promised to bring about what the emperor longed for in the end and the emperor believed in his promise. Now Theophanes set about getting around the patriarch. He went to him and said: 'Lord-and-master, the emperor's attacks [227] on you are multiplying; he is seeking reasons for expelling you from the throne. But much as he tries, none does he find. How indeed could he find fault with one who is without fault? There is, however, one point that they allege, those who would see you deposed: they claim that you do not know how to write. If we could refute this point, it would silence your accusers. [To quote the proverb] they would prove to be "wolves with open jaws". If you will take my advice, you will inscribe your name and priestly rank on a fresh leaf – this in the presence of the entire Synod – and send it to the emperor. This way he will be convinced and, being disappointed in this hope, he will abandon his assault on your position.' This seemed like good advice; the Synod was summoned immediately, and when it was assembled the patriarch addressed it in these words: 'O sacred fellow ministers, those who wish to eject me from the throne unfairly have contrived in many ways to find a good reason for ostracising me and have found none. Finally they have brought this charge against me: they say I cannot write. So now, before the eyes of you all, I am going to inscribe these letters for my accusers to see and know, hence to abandon their unjust harassment of me.' When he had spoken, he took a fresh leaf and, in the presence of them all, wrote as follows: Tryphon by the mercy of God archbishop of Constantinople, New Rome, and ecumenical patriarch. When he had written it, he sent it to the emperor by the hand of the protothronos. This man took it in his hand, and attached another clean sheet above it on which he wrote a [letter of] resignation as of one unworthy and abandoning the throne to whomsoever might desire

---

[80] The Myrelaion. *Theophanes Continuatus*, 420, says that Romanos wept bitterly for his oldest son, whom he probably hoped would succeed him. Christopher's daughter, Maria, the wife of Peter of Bulgaria, came to Constantinople with her three children after the death of her father: *Theophanes Continuatus*, 422.

it. This 'resignation' was presented to the Synod and Tryphon was put out of the church, bitterly decrying the deceit which had been practised on him and reproaching the protothronos. A year and five months later (which was how long it needed for Theophylact fully to attain the required age for archiepiscopal ordination) in February, second year of the indiction, Theophylact, the emperor's son, was ordained patriarch.[81]

27. [228] A Macedonian whose name was Basil gave it out that he was Constantine Doukas; many were deceived and rallied to him. He went around troubling and disturbing the cities, inciting them to revolt. Then he was arrested by a subordinate officer[82] surnamed Elephantinos; he was brought before the emperor and deprived of one of his hands. Later, when he was released, he equipped himself with a hand of bronze and had a huge sword made. He stalked around the Opsikion theme deluding the simpler folk into believing that he was Constantine Doukas, and when he had gathered a large following he broke out into revolt.[83] He gathered a large fighting force, rebelled and seized the stronghold known as Plateia Petra,[84] and laid up all kinds of provisions there. From that base he ravaged and pillaged the surrounding countryside. The emperor sent an army against him which took both him and his followers prisoner. The emperor also made a detailed enquiry to discover whether any persons of significance were behind his insurrection, but when nothing definitive came to light, they had him put to the flames at the place called Amastrianon.[85]

28. The emperor Romanos married Anna,[86] daughter of Gabala, to his son Stephen and invested her with the imperial diadem at the same time as she received the marriage crown.

29. In the month of April, seventh year of the indiction,[87] the Turks invaded Roman territory and overran all the west right up to the city. The patrician Theophanes the protovestiarios was sent out and concluded an

---

[81] This story is found neither in *Theophanes Continuatus* nor in Leo the Grammarian nor in *Symeonis magistri et logothetae chronicon* but it is given by pseudo-Symeon the Logothete, *Symeon Magister*, ed. I. Bekker (Bonn, 1838), 603–760, at 742–3. Tryphon resigned in August 931; Theophylact was elevated on 2 February 933, sixth year of the indiction.

[82] A *tourmarch* had been established in the Opsikion theme, which rather suggests that this was the region in which Basil caused trouble. It was the eparch Peter who carried out the punishment inflicted on Basil: *Theophanes Continuatus*, 421; *Symeonis magistri*, 333.

[83] This uprising shows how popular the Doukai were in Asia Minor, at least in the themes some distance from the frontier.

[84] Symbatios took refuge in this fortress when he was in revolt against Basil I.

[85] A square on the Mese beyond the forum of Theodosios where executions sometimes took place: Janin, *Constantinople*, 68–9.

[86] Anna was also the granddaughter of a Katakylas, no doubt Leo: Theodore of Melitene, 231.

[87] April 934. The Magyars, now well-established in Pannonia, began serious raiding and pillaging mostly in the Latin west, which was less well defended.

agreement with them; the emperor did not stint in pouring out money with which to ransom the prisoners.

30. Constantine, the remaining son of the emperor, was married to a maiden named Helen, member of a family in the Armeniakon theme, [229] the daughter of the patrician Adrian, but she died a little later, whereupon Romanos married him to another, a maiden named Theophano, a member of the Mamas family.

31. In the month of June, fourteenth year of the indiction, there was an assault on the city by a Russian fleet of ten thousand ships.[88] The patrician Theophanes, the protovestiarios, sailed out against them with the fleet and tied up at the Hieron, while the enemy was moored off the Lighthouse[89] and the adjacent shore. Waiting for the right moment [Theophanes] attacked in full force and threw them into disorder. Many of their vessels were reduced to cinders with Greek fire while the rest were utterly routed.[90] The surviving Russians passed over to the eastern shore and turned towards the spot called Sgora. The patrician Bardas, the son of Phokas, was patrolling the shore with cavalry and picked men when he encountered a considerable body [of Russians] sent out to forage,[91] which he overcame and slew. And when Kourkouas, the domestic of the scholai, arrived immediately after with the army, he found the Russians dispersed, wandering hither and thither; he dealt them a bitter blow. The atrocities they had committed before they were defeated exceed the horror of a tragedy. They crucified some of their prisoners and staked others out on the ground. Others they set up as targets and fired arrows at them. They drove sharp nails into the heads of any of the prisoners who were priests and burnt down not a few sacred churches.[92] But that was before; after they had been defeated at sea (as we explained, above) and no less severely mauled on land, they sat quietly in their own ships; and, as they were already running short of supplies, they decided to return to their homeland. But they were intimidated by the [Roman] fleet standing nearby, preventing them from sailing away.[93] Seizing a chance, however, they cast off at a given signal and sailed off, but this did not escape the notice of the

---

[88] This attack which took place in 941 was led by Oleg and Igor.
[89] Meaning the lighthouse at the northern entry into the Bosporos.
[90] After this first setback Igor returned directly to Kiev, abandoning the great part of his forces.
[91] Bardas, the brother of Leo, the former rival of Romanos Lekapenos, was no longer on active service at this time: *Theophanes Continuatus*; but he was called out to deal with this emergency before Kourkouas could return.
[92] They ravaged the straits (Stenon).
[93] The Russians were held in check all along the coast, by the army of Kourkouas on land and by Theophanes' fleet on the high sea.

patrician Theophanes, the protovestiarios. Realising what was happening, he immediately confronted them and a second naval encounter took place. Again the Russians were defeated. Some of their boats went down into the deep, some were destroyed by fire and sword and others, along with their crews, fell into Roman hands. Only a few escaped the perils of war and reached their homeland.[94]

32. The emperor gave the protovestiarios a warm welcome and rewarded him by promoting him to be parakoimomenos. Animosity arose among the other emperors against John Kourkouas, domestic of the scholai, because the emperor Romanos wanted to marry the domestic's daughter, Euphrosyne, to his own grandson, Romanos, the son of his youngest son, Constantine. [The emperor] was obliged to relieve the domestic of his command after he had exercised it for twenty-two continuous years and seven months, conquered practically the whole of Syria and subdued it. Anybody who wishes to learn of his excellent record should consult the work composed by one Manuel, protospatharios and judge. He wrote in eight books all about the brave exploits of this man. From these one will know what kind of a man he was in military matters.[95] And his brother Theophilos too, the grandfather of that John who later became emperor, dealt similarly with the Saracen towns in Mesopotamia when he became commander there, subduing and subjugating the sons of Hagar.[96] And the patrician Romanos, son of John the domestic when he became commander, seized many strongholds and was responsible for a great deal of booty accruing to the Romans. After John was relieved of his command, a relative of the emperor Romanos called Pantherios[97] was appointed domestic of the scholai.

33. [231] To propitiate the deity for the oaths he had broken and in repentance of his misdeeds in breaking pacts, the emperor Romanos

---

[94] Led by Oleg, these refugees did not dare enter their own country; they travelled along the coast of the Black Sea (*Vita Basilii iunioris*) before attempting a raid (together with the Khazars) on Bardha'a on the edge of the Caspian Sea. On the chronology of this campaign: C. Zuckerman, 'On the date of the Khazars' conversion to Judaism and the chronology of the kings of the Rus Oleg and Igor', *REB*, 53 (1995), 264–8.

[95] This work (with which Skylitzes was certainly not personally acquainted) is lost. From *Theophanes Continuatus*, 426, we know that the Kourkouas family was originally from a village near Dokeia (Tokat) in the Armeniakon theme, that John was the grandson of a domestic of the Hikanatoi also named John, and that he had been educated by one of his relatives, Christopher, metropolitan of Gangra. The same chronicler compares him with Trajan and Belisarios, affirming that his conquests reaped great taxes for the state.

[96] On the achievements of Theophilos: *Theophanes Continuatus*, 428; *DAI*, ed. Moravcsik and Jenkins, 208.

[97] A member of the Skleros family no doubt, one who had faithfully served Lekapenos: J.-C. Cheynet, 'Notes arabo-byzantines', *Mélanges Svoronos* (Réthymno, 1986), 145–7.

undertook a number of good works which it would be a severe task to list. In his fear he paid the debts owed to the city by both rich and poor, contributing (they say) nineteen *kentenaria*, and he burnt the promissory notes at the porphyry *omphalos* of the Chalke [gate].[98] He paid the rents of the citizens from the greatest to the least and, as for the annual income which for the salvation of his soul he had settled on the monastery of the Myrelaion[99] recently founded by him, it is common knowledge that it is paid to this day.

34. In the first year of the indiction the Turks made another attack on Roman territory. Theophanes the parakoimomenos went out, concluded a treaty with them, received hostages and returned.[100]

35. In the second year of the indiction the emperor sent Paschal, protospatharios and commander of Longobardia, to Hugh, King of Francia, hoping to engage his daughter[101] to Romanos, the son of [Constantine] Porphyrogennetos. She was brought with great wealth and married Romanos; she lived with him for five years and then died.

36. There was a terrific storm in the month of December; what are called the *Demes* collapsed and broke the steps below as well as the balustrades.

37. The city of Edessa was besieged by Roman forces, and when the people of Edessa were oppressed by the privations of the siege they sent

---

[98] C. Mango, *The brazen house: a study of the vestibule of the imperial palace of Constantinople* (Copenhagen, 1959), 231; see *Theophanes Continuatus*, 429.

[99] This foundation of Romanos Lekapenos was constituted an imperial peculiar and endowed with a fortune. The arrangement obviously worked since the donations stipulated by Romanos were still being made in Skylitzes' time. The foundation of the Myrelaion was responsible for nuns, aged persons and the sick. Its officers were responsible for distributing 30,000 loaves of bread each day to the poor: *Theophanes Continuatus*, 430. P. Magdalino, *Constantinople médiévale: études sur l'évolution des structures urbaines* (Paris, 1996), 24–5, suggests that Romanos may have attached the bakeries restored by the empress Eirene to the Myrelaion foundation. *Theophanes Continuatus*, ed. Bekker, 403–4, reports (but Skylitzes does not) that Romanos had what passed for the tombs of the emperor Maurice and his family transferred from St Mamas to the Myrelaion. On the Myrelaion: C. L. Striker, *The Myrelaion (Bodrum Camii) in Istanbul* (Princeton, NJ, 1981). On the Bodrum Camii: W. Müller-Wiener, *Bildlexikon zur Topographie Istanbuls* (Tübingen, 1977), 103–7.

[100] In 943.

[101] In September 944 the five-year-old Bertha of Provence, illegitimate daughter of Hugh of Provence, king of Italy (927–47), came to the Byzantine court and took the name of Eudokia, which had been her grandmother's name and also that of the sister of Constantine VII: *DAI*, ch. 26, ed. Moravcsik and Jenkins, 112. According to *Theophanes Continuatus*, Skylitzes' source here, Eudokia died young in 949. The claim that this is the couple portrayed in the famous ivory depicting the marriage of an emperor named Romanos with an Eudokia is still opposed by some scholars who think (e.g. I. Kalavrezou) the couple are Romanos IV Diogenes and Eudokia Makrembolitissa: A. Cutler and J.-M. Spieser, *Byzance médiévale 700–1204* (Paris, 1996), 181; I. Kalavrezou-Maxeiner, 'Eudokia Makrembolitissa and the Romanos ivory', *DOP*, 31 (1977), 307–25. See (most recently) Maria Parani, 'The Romanos Ivory and the New Tokali kilese: imperial costume as a tool for dating Byzantine art', *Cahiers archéologiques* 49 (2001) 15–28.

a delegation to the emperor asking for the siege to be lifted [232] and promising to hand over the sacred *mandylion* of Christ as a ransom. The siege was lifted, and the likeness of our God was brought to the capital where the emperor had it ceremonially received by the parakoimomenos Theophanes with impressive and fitting pomp.[102]

38. In those days a monstrous thing came to the imperial city from Armenia: a pair of Siamese twins, males sharing a single belly, but they were driven out of the city as an evil portent. Then they came back in the [sole] reign of Constantine [VII]. When one of the twins died, some experienced doctors tried to excise the dead portion – and they were successful, but the living twin survived only a short while and then died.

39. The emperor Romanos held all monks in high honour, but this was especially true of the monk Sergios, nephew[103] of the patriarch Photios, a man rich in virtue and adorned with every excellence. He was always warning the emperor to watch out for his children and not to let them grow up undisciplined, lest he himself suffer the fate of Eli.[104] In the same year of the indiction they expelled the emperor Romanos from the palace, brought him to the island of Prote and tonsured him a monk.[105] Exactly who put him out of office and how they did it will be related in the following pages.

---

[102] The solemn entry of the *mandylion* from Edessa (15 August 944) was one of Romanos' major triumphs. There is a contemporary account of its reception: A.-M. Dubarle, 'L'homélie de Grégoire le référendaire pour la réception de l'image d'Edesse', *REB*, 55 (1997), 5–51. Another account written somewhat later is attributed to Constantine VII himself and may well have been produced in his entourage; it contains the prophecy retailed here by MSS ACE: 'A voice was heard in the air saying: 'Constantinople, receive glory and joy and do you, Constantine Porphyrogennetos, receive your empire': E. von Dobschütz, *Christusbilder: Untersuchungen zur chrislichen Legende*, Leipzig 1899, 78xx (text A) and 79xx (text B). Text A is the Synaxarist's; text B was written in the entourage of Constantine VII, but not by him. The *mandylion* was deposited in the palace church of the Virgin at the Lighthouse (Pharos) where it still lay on the eve of the Fourth Crusade, 1204: B. Flusin, 'Didascalie de Constantin Stilbès sur le Mandylion et la Sainte Tuile (*BHG* 796m)', *REB*, 55 (1997), 62–3.

[103] Grand-nephew in fact. Sergios was the brother of the magister Kosmas, first of the judges: *Theophanes Continuatus*, ed. Bekker, 433.

[104] The father of undisciplined sons, Hophni and Phineas: 1 Sam. 2:12–36; LXX 1 Kings 2 and 4.

[105] 16 December 944.

CHAPTER 11

Constantine VII [944–959]

1. [233] As the emperor Constantine had been left an orphan in very early childhood, affairs of state were conducted by Zoe his mother and the regents whom we listed above. Constantine the parakoimomenos exercised considerable influence over the empress while the magister Leo Phokas, domestic of the scholai for the east, was his brother-in-law, having married his sister. Thus Constantine effectively held all the reins of state and could direct it wherever he wished. Night and day he searched for a way of getting rid of [the emperor] Constantine and of transferring the imperial office to his own brother-in-law. When Theodore, the tutor of the porphyrogennetos, realised this, he endeavoured (as we said above) to appropriate the elder Romanos who was then droungarios of the fleet and bring him into the palace in the hope that he would be the protector and defender of the emperor. Romanos was brought in and, little by little, gained possession of all the levers of power. Not content with the powers assigned to him though, he broke his oaths (and he had bound himself with the most awesome oaths that he would never aspire to be emperor) and proclaimed himself emperor. It was the porphyrogennetos who placed the diadem on his brow, willingly to all appearances, 'but with a most unwilling heart' to cite Homer.[1] And it was not only himself but also Christopher, his son, whom Romanos proclaimed emperor, a short time after. He let some more time go by and then proclaimed his sons Stephen and Constantine. Now, although he was proclaimed emperor, he did not like the ranking: it displeased him to be in second place. So he expelled the tutor and any others who seemed to be opposed to him, then he proclaimed himself first emperor and took over the administration of all [234] the affairs of state. His sons ranked after him and Constantine [VII] came last of all. By now Constantine had only the appearance and name of emperor, for he was deprived of all the privileges; therefore his constant endeavour and most

---

[1] *Iliad*, 4.43.

fervent wish was to get rid of the usurpers and assume his father's supreme command. He thought that this could not be brought about other than by setting the sons against the father. Now it so happened that Christopher departed this life, but there were still Stephen and Constantine. He decided to sound them out to see whether it would be possible to carry out his plan. He did not dare put Constantine [Lakapenos] to the test for he was of a very intractable character, so he decided to direct his entire intrigue and approach to Stephen, who was of a more frivolous turn of mind and more easily turned in the direction one desired. As his collaborator and co-worker [the porphyrogennetos] won over a very gifted man who was wondrously skilled in contriving deceptions and intrigues: Basil, surnamed Peteinos, enrolled in the corps of the Hetaireiai, a familiar friend of Constantine [porphyrogennetos] from his youth up. With him he shared his plan and through him he deceived Stephen into thinking he was his friend, misleading him with insidious phrases which confused his thinking by duplicity and artifice. Peteinos left no stone unturned to make Stephen like him and, when he had succeeded, he hung around him, filling his ears with speeches and advice which massaged his vanity and shortly almost drove him out of his mind. 'O emperor,' he would say, 'why do you who are in the vigour of youth, distinguished by the fervour of your soul and the power of your intellect, why do you only observe and not react to the fact that affairs of state are hanging by a thin, antiquated thread near breaking point?' – by which he meant Stephen's father. 'Why do you not rise up against him, get rid of him as an obstacle to your own noble aspirations and take the administration into your own hands, you who are capable of governing not only the Roman empire, but [235] many others too? Come now, accept my beneficial advice; rise up and take control of affairs of state; contrive to put Roman fortunes back on an upward course and to abase those of the enemies. Demonstrate by actual deeds that it was not in vain or for nothing that your youth and the other spiritual advantages were given to you by God. You will have your brother-in-law, the porphyrogennetos, to fight with you and aid you in this undertaking, he who ardently prays and beseeches God to be rid of the heavy burden of your father and to see the Empire governed by you.' Stephen was taken in by these words and won over by a longing to rule. He fell prey to a burning desire to depose his father from the throne.[2] Just as he was

---

[2] The sons of Romanos had good reason to be apprehensive about their father's intentions. After the death of Christopher, Constantine VII alone (still without a beard) appears at the side of their father on the gold coins. Romanos showed remorse towards the end of his life, or at least he became concerned about the salvation of his soul. Moreover, in 944 he provided a wife, Bertha-

about to execute his design, he breathed some cryptic remarks about what he intended to his brother, but that one was inflexible from the very first word and warned him not to have any confidence in their brother-in-law, urging him to remain faithful and loyal to their own family. So Stephen abandoned Constantine [Lekapenos] as likely to be an obstacle rather than an advantage and decided to go ahead insofar as it was possible to do so with his project. Besides the aforementioned Basil [Peteinos] he took as his associates the monk Marianos, son of Leo Argyros,[3] greatly honoured and trusted by the emperor Romanos, and some others.[4] When the time was ripe, he overthrew his own father on the sixteenth of December, third year of the indiction, AM 6453, in the twenty-sixth year of his reign,[5] and exiled him to the island of Prote where he was tonsured an unwilling monk.

2. Immediately after the overthrow of Romanos, Stephen energetically took matters of state in hand,[6] with his brother-in-law and his brother as colleagues. But as they were not always of like mind and sometimes actively disagreed, from this beginning the shoots of discord sprang forth; they regarded each other askance and with suspicion, Stephen the porphyrogennetos [236] and vice versa, and there arose among them reckless and boundless quarrels. Stephen made extraordinary efforts to rid himself of his brother and brother-in-law in order to be left in sole charge of the administration but, as the poet says, 'there are things hotter than fire';[7] he failed to notice that he was the prey rather than the huntsman. Once Constantine [porphyrogennetos] realised that *he* was under attack, he did not hesitate to set his plan in motion and his wife, Helen, strongly encouraged him to depose the brothers. He revealed the secret [plan] to Basil

---

Eudokia, for his grandson, the future Romanos II, who was still very young. Hence his sons were suspecting that he intended to restore the reins of government to his son-in-law, Constantine VII, the only one who had a legitimate title to rule as emperor.

[3] Marianos, still a monk, was the son of Leo Argyros, the domestic of the scholai defeated by the Bulgars; hence he was the brother of Romanos, the husband of Agatha Lekapena: (most recently) Cheynet, *Société*, 530–1, for the articles of J.-F. Vannier mentioned above.

[4] In reporting the plot of Stephen, *Theophanes Continuatus*, 435, names Manuel Kourtikios as one of the conspirators. Elsewhere, 438, he makes the point that many of the conspirators who were in favour of Constantine VII met a miserable end. It is revealed that a strategos named Diogenes, a Kladon and a Philip took part in the plot against Romanos. A similar misfortune befell the friends of the founder of the Macedonian dynasty, Basil I, in their case for being guilty of the assassination of Michael III.

[5] 16 December 944.

[6] *Theophanes Continuatus*, 436, tells a different tale, saying that Constantine VII took the helm and surrounded himself with men he could trust: Bardas Phokas (made magister and domestic of the scholai); Constantine Gongyles (commander of the fleet); Basil Peteinos (patrician and grand hetaireiarch); Marianos Argyros (count of the stable); and Manuel Kourtikios (patrician and droungarios of the watch). Skylitzes notes these appointments elsewhere.

[7] Aristophanes, *Equites*, 382.

Peteinos and, by his agency, rallied to the cause Marianos, Nikephoros and Leo the sons of Bardas Phokas, Nicholas and Leo Tornikios[8] and not a few others.[9] Stephen and Constantine [Lekapenoi] suspected nothing and were in fact arrested while they were at table, dining with [Constantine porphyrogennetos] and removed from the palace; this on 27 January, the same third year of the indiction.[10] They were put aboard ship and exiled, one of them to the island of Panormos,[11] Constantine to Terebinthos.[12] They were both tonsured clerics by Basil of Caesarea[13] and Anastasios of Herakleia, then, a little later, the emperor moved Stephen to the Prokonnesos and then to Rhodes and finally to Mytilene, Constantine to Samothrace.[14] Stephen bore the misfortunes which befell him with good courage and survived nineteen years on Lesbos. But Constantine was of a less placid disposition and resisted with greater fervour than was called for. He often attempted to escape and the second year after his fall from power he slew his gaoler,[15] then was himself killed by the other gaolers. [237] And in July, the sixth year of the indiction, Romanos their father paid the universal debt[16] and was buried at the Myrelaion.

3. Once he had purged his circle of suspicious elements, now girded with exclusive imperial authority, at Easter of the same year of the indiction[17] Constantine placed the diadem on the brow of his son, Romanos, while the patriarch Theophylact offered prayers. It had been expected that he would be a capable and energetic ruler, one who would devote himself

---

[8] They were the sons of the Armenian prince of Taron, Tornik, son of Apoganem. After a dispute with his cousin, Bagarat, Tornik bequeathed his country to the empire. Romanos Lekapenos brought his family to Constantinople, including the sons (or grandsons?) Leo and Nicholas: *DAI*, ed. Moravcsik and Jenkins, 194–6. On the Tornikioi: N. Adontz, 'Les Taronites en Arménie et à Byzance', *B*, 11 (1936), 21–42.

[9] Liutprand of Cremona claims that the Amalfitan colony at Constantinople gave its support to Constantine VII: *Opera Liutprandi Cremonensis*, ed. P. Chiesa (Turnholt, 1998); *Antapodosis*, 5.21.

[10] 27 January 945.   [11] One of the Prinkipo islands, better known as Antigone.

[12] Another of the Prinkipo islands, the one on which the patriarch Ignatios built a monastery.

[13] This bishop was quite close to Constantine VII, to whom he dedicated his Commentary on the *Orations* of Gregory of Nazianzos.

[14] Islands were frequently used as places of confinement because the Roman navy controlled all shipping movements.

[15] The *protospatharios* Niketas: *Theophanes Continuatus*, 438.

[16] 15 June 948: P. Grierson, 'The tombs and obits of the Byzantine emperors (337–1042) with an additional note by C. Mango and I. Ševčenko', *DOP*, 16 (1962), 29. According to *Theophanes Continuatus*, 439–40, Romanos had a dream in which he saw his son Constantine having his throat cut and Anastasios, metropolitan of Herakleia, conducted by two bodyguards; Anastasios was thrown into the fire – this on the very day they both died. Romanos also sent money to many monks asking them to pray for the forgiveness of his defects. He particularly singled out Dermokaites, a monk of Bithynian Olympos.

[17] The dating is defective since Skylitzes omits to say *which* year of the indiction he means. It could be the third (April 945) or the fourth (946). C. Zuckerman has recently argued for Easter 946: 'Le voyage d'Olga et la première ambassade espagnole à Constantinople en 946', *TM*, 13 (2000),

to state affairs with diligence once he became sole ruler. In the event he proved to be weaker than anticipated and achieved nothing that measured up to the expectations one had of him. He was addicted to wine and always preferred to take the easier way. He was implacable towards defaults and merciless in inflicting punishment. He was indifferent to the promotion of officials, unwilling to appoint or promote according to birth or merit[18] (which is the function of a truly admirable government). He entrusted a command – military or civil – indiscriminately to whomsoever happened to be on hand. Thus it invariably happened that some base and suspicious character would be appointed to the highest of civil offices.[19] Helena his wife was much engaged in this with him and so was Basil the parakoimomenos;[20] they were responsible for the buying and selling of offices.

Yet Constantine was not totally devoid of good works, and the praiseworthy and wondrous qualities about to be related are enough to eclipse and obfuscate many of his shortcomings. On his own initiative he brought about a restoration of the sciences of arithmetic, music, astronomy, geometry in two and three dimensions and, superior to them all, philosophy, all sciences which had for a long time been neglected on account of a lack of care and learning in those [238] who held the reins of government. He sought out the most excellent and proven scholars in each discipline and, when he found them, appointed them teachers, approving of and applauding those who studied diligently. Hence he put ignorance and vulgarity to flight in short order and aligned the state on a more intellectual course.[21] He also concerned himself with practical arts and handicrafts and brought

---

647–72, at 669. It is, however, surprising that Constantine did not choose to crown his son at the first celebration of Easter after he became sole emperor.

[18] An implied criticism of the choices of Bardas Phokas as domestic of the scholai (echoed even by Bardas' own son, Nikephoros) and of Constantine Gongylios as commander of the naval forces, the man who, in that office, would be responsible for the failure of the expedition to Crete in 949.

[19] A source hostile to Constantine VII is being followed here. In fact, this emperor had some quite remarkable civil servants: the quaestor Theophilos who had been eparch under Romanos Lekapenos, drafted certain novels, including the novel of 947 against the encroachments of magnates on the lands of the poor, translated in E. McGeer, *The land legislation of the Macedonian emperors* (Toronto, 2000), 63–7. There was also the judge and magister Kosmas and, last but not least, Constantine the mystikos and professor of philosophy who became eparch, the most learned man in the Senate according to *Theophanes Continuatus*, 444.

[20] The illegitimate son of Romanos Lekapenos, born *c*. 925 by a 'Scyth' slave. He was castrated in infancy, which qualified him for the position of parakoimomenos. He supported Constantine VII in 945 and from then until 985 played a principal role in Byzantine political life, in addition to acquiring phenomenal wealth: W. G. Brokkaar, 'Basil Lecapenus', *Studia bizantina et neoellenica Neerlandica*, 3 (1972), 199–234.

[21] For a commentary on this passage: Lemerle, *Premier humanisme*, 264–6.

about great progress in them. In addition to this he was pious and reverent in his approach to God, never appearing empty-handed before Him in the processions which tradition required to be made to the various churches, but offering splendid sacrificial gifts, such as befit an emperor who is the friend of Christ. He rewarded those who had worked with him to overturn his stepbrothers with the following benefits: Bardas Phokas was made magister and domestic of the scholai for the east; of his two sons, Nikephoros and Leo, the first was made commander of the Anatolikon theme, the other of Cappadocia, while Constantine the other son received the command of Seleucia.[22] Basil Peteinos was made commander of the Great Hetaireiai, Marianos Argyros became count of the stable, Manuel Kourtikios droungarios of the watch. Romanos the son of Stephen (who later became sebastophoros) the emperor castrated; likewise Basil who was born to Romanos the Elder by a slave woman.[23] He tonsured as a cleric Michael, the son of the emperor Christopher.[24]

4. [The emperor] now thought he had secured the empire with links of iron and had shaken off all resentment. Yet, while he believed he was securely installed, he came within a hair's breadth of falling prey to two major offensives which nearly cost him his life. Theophanes the parakoimomenos[25] sought to bring Romanos the Elder back into the palace from the island of Prote and there were not a few others [239] who shared his purpose. Then there were others (Leo Kladon, Gregory of Macedonia, Theodosios, Stephen's head groom and John the Rector) who aimed at bringing Stephen from Mytilene and installing him as emperor, but some of the conspirators let it be known what they were up to.[26] Theophanes and his collaborators were exiled; Stephen's protagonists

[22] Thus the emperor gave control of the army to the Phokas family. Bardas Phokas (who had discharged the office of commander with a measure of success according to the *De Velitatione*: *Traité*, ed. Dagron and Mihàescu, 35, received a check to his career with the advent of Lekapenos – who came to power by distancing Bardas' brother, Leo, from it. Bardas was married to a member of the Maleinos family whose brother Michael was revered as one of the Byzantine saints. They had three sons of whom one, Nikephoros, named after his paternal grandfather (in accordance with an aristocratic tradition), became emperor in 963.
[23] This information is incompatible with what was said earlier: that Basil was a eunuch from infancy. This would also have been a very odd way of rewarding such a strong supporter.
[24] Constantine had him deprived of the purple buskins which he wore as the elder son of Christopher, the heir apparent who died in 931. He was compensated by being promoted magister and rector: *Theophanes Continuatus*, 438.
[25] One would have thought that Romanos' chief minister would have lost (or have been about to lose) his influence on the course of events.
[26] This second conspiracy was denounced by a man named Michael Diabolinos: Leo the Grammarian, 309.

received a beating, lost their property to the state, had their noses slit and were sent into exile.

5. The Turks did not discontinue their raiding and ravaging of Roman land until their chieftain, Boulosoudes, came to the city of Constantine under pretence of embracing the Christian faith. He was baptised and received [from the font] by the emperor Constantine who honoured him with the title of patrician and put him in possession of great riches; then he went back to his homeland.[27] Not long afterwards, Gylas[28] who was also a chieftain of the Turks came to the capital where he too was baptised and where he too was accorded the same honours and benefits. He took back with him a monk with a reputation for piety named Hierotheos who had been ordained bishop of Turkey by Theophylact. When he got there, he converted many from the barbaric fallacy to Christianity.[29] And Gylas remained faithful to Christianity; he made no inroad against the Romans nor did he leave Christian prisoners untended. He ransomed them, took care of their needs and set them free. Boulosoudes, on the other hand, violated his contract with God and often invaded Roman land with all his people. He attempted to do likewise against the Franks but he was seized and impaled by Otto their emperor.[30]

6. [240] The wife of the Russian chieftain who had once sailed against Roman territory, Olga by name, came to Constantinople after her husband died. She was baptised and she demonstrated fervent devotion. She was honoured in a way commensurate with her devotion, then she went back home.[31]

---

[27] On the Turks/Magyars, see *DAI*, ed. Moravcsik and Jenkins, c. 40, where it is confirmed that Boultzous (Bulscu), who stood third in rank with these people with the title of Karhas, did go to Constantinople.

[28] The Romans knew that Gylas was a title and not a name (*DAI*, 178). A peace treaty was concluded in 948 and the baptism of the chieftains took place shortly afterwards: P. Stephenson, *Balkan frontier: a political study of the northern Balkans, 900–1204* (Cambridge, 2000), 40.

[29] Hierotheos left in 953 but the bishopric of Turkey remained in existence, for a seal confirms its existence in the eleventh century: *DOSeals* 1, 36.1. In the twelfth century its centre was moved to Bacs.

[30] In 955 Otto dealt the Magyars a decisive blow at the battle of Lechfeld, which had two consequences: Otto restored the empire in the west and the Magyars settled in the territory which would become Hungary. Thanks to Latin missionaries this eventually became a Christian kingdom, but the Greek church must have maintained its institutions for three bishoprics are mentioned in a source dated 1020.

[31] There has been a great deal of discussion of the visit of Olga, wife of Igor and mother of Sviatoslav, concerning both the date (946 or 957) and the object of the visit. A Christian community was already in existence at Kiev. Olga received baptism having made a personal decision to do so, then she returned home accompanied by some Greek priests, but her conversion provoked no sympathetic movement towards Christianity among the Russian aristocracy: (most recently) O. Kresten, *'Staatsempfänger' im Kaiserpalast von Konstantinopel um die Mitte des 10. Jahrhunderts. Beobachtungen zu Kapitel II 15 des sogennante 'Zeremonienbuches'* (Vienna, 2000), opining that

7. When the fiancée of Romanos, the daughter of Hugh [king of the Franks], died still a virgin (as we said), his father the emperor engaged him to another woman, not the scion of a distinguished family, but one born of humble folk whose trade was innkeeping. Her name was Anastaso but [the emperor] changed it to Theophano.[32]

8. While the emir of Tarsus was campaigning against the Romans he sent a foraging party to the village of Herakleos. A priest named Themel was offering the unbloody sacrifice[33] when he learnt that the Saracens were approaching. He interrupted his liturgy and went out in the vestments he was wearing, seized the church's semantron[34] in his hands and repelled the attackers with it. He wounded many, killed a few and put the rest to flight. But he was inhibited from his ministry by the bishop who could not be persuaded to forgive him. So he went over to the Hagarenes and renounced Christianity. He joined forces with them, and not only ravaged Cappadocia and the adjacent themes but penetrated as far as what is called Asia Minor. It would be unpardonable to set down in writing the atrocities he committed.

9. After Bardas Phokas was appointed domestic of the scholai (as we said) [241] he did nothing worthy of record. Whenever he served under another, he showed himself to be a fine commander; but once authority over the entire land forces depended on his own judgement, he brought little or no benefit to the Roman realm. He was consumed by greed as if it were an illness which dulled his mind. It even happened that he once unexpectedly encountered the forces of Chambdan;[35] everybody deserted him (they say), and he would have been taken prisoner if his servants had not rallied round him and delivered him from captivity. He received a

---

there were two visits of Olga to Constantinople but that Olga was baptised in 946. Zuckerman, 'Olga', 660–9, argues on the basis of a study of the structure of Constantines Porphyrogenitus, *De caerim*, ed. Reiske, II, 15, that Olga only came once to Constantinople, 946–7, the object of the visit being to discuss the commercial relations of Byzantium with the Russians laid out in the treaty of 944. She remained several months in the Christian metropolis and it was in the course of this, her one and only visit there, that she received baptism. See also M. Featherstone, 'Olga's visit to Constantinople in the *De Cerimoniis*', *REB*, 61 (2003), 241–51, arguing (as others have done) that the baptism took place in 957.

[32] There are two contradictory traditions concerning the origin of Theophano. According to one tradition (*Theophanes Continuatus*, 458) she was the daughter of Krateros while the other, followed by Skylitzes and by Leo the Deacon, asserts that she was of lowly origins and no better than she ought to be. But such a marriage would have been quite contrary to normal procedure; for only the daughters of 'good' families could participate in the 'beauty contests' by which so many brides were selected for princes in former centuries. The name of Krateros moreover inspires confidence; it denotes a family which had links with the Macedonian house. See Leo VI, c. 6, above.

[33] He was celebrating the sacred liturgy of the holy eucharist.

[34] A large piece of wood or iron struck repeatedly to announce the commencement of services.

[35] Sayf ad-Daula was the son of Hamdan.

serious and deep wound on the forehead and bore the scar of it to his dying day.[36] His sons, Nikephoros and Leo, were well above taking any ill-gotten gain.[37] They treated those under their command as favoured sons and greatly benefited the Roman realm. We will speak of the distinguished accomplishments of Nikephoros in the section devoted to him, in order not to interrupt the continuous flow of the history. As for Leo, he routed Apolasaeir, a distinguished man related to Chambdan, who was campaigning against the Romans with an innumerable host, arrested him and sent him to Constantinople. One part of his army he had already eliminated in battle; the other part he now took into captivity.[38] When [Apolasaeir] arrived at the capital the emperor Constantine exhibited him in a triumph, placing his foot on the man's neck, but then demonstrated his benevolence by bestowing honours and gifts on him. Chambdan took prisoner Constantine, the remaining son of Phokas, and carried him off to Aleppo where he made every effort to convert him to their miserable religion but, failing in his efforts, murdered him by poisoning.[39] Bardas was deeply pained on hearing of this and put all the prisoners he held who were relations of Chambdan to the sword. This is why the magister Paul Monomachos (who had been sent to conclude a treaty) returned empty-handed.[40] Prey to unassuageable grief at the loss of his relatives, Chambdan set off on campaign [242] against the Romans. With him he took the patrician Niketas Chalkoutzes[41] (whom the emperor had despatched as ambassador for peace negotiations) and took prisoner many a good man from among the bravest and most noble of the Romans. But Niketas secretly let Phokas know all Chambdan's plans and by which route he intended to effect his retreat, so Phokas was able to set up an ambush at a place to which there was only a narrow and steep entry between cliffs. Once Chambdan was there and had advanced well into the narrow passage, he was surrounded by the forces lying in ambush. Men posted for

---

[36] This is a reference to a battle near Marash in 953 where, in spite of superior strength of numbers, Bardas was defeated and wounded by Sayd-ad-Doula, Constantine his son being taken prisoner: Vasiliev and Canard, *Byzance et les Arabes*, 11.1, 350–1.

[37] The supposed virtue of Leo is given the lie by Skylitzes himself (below) in describing his speculation in grain when his brother was on the throne.

[38] Leo fought Abul Asair, cousin of Sayf-as-Doula, near Duluk in 956: Vasiliev and Canard 11.1, 358–9.

[39] In fact Constantine was well cared for; he died of an illness and was buried by the Christians of Aleppo: Vasiliev and Canard, 11.1, 351.

[40] The setback of the embassy of Monomachos in 954 probably had nothing to do with the death of Constantine Phokas.

[41] This is the first appearance of the name of a very important family which supplied the state with many civil servants and military officers: A. Savvidès, 'La famille byzantine Chalkoutzès' (in Greek), *Archeion Euboïkon Meleton*, 28 (1988–9), 63–73.

this purpose rose up from their concealed positions, rolling great stones down on them and shooting all kinds of missiles at them. Chalkoutzes was prepared for the event; he had corrupted some of the Saracens with gifts to facilitate his flight and got away unnoticed with his entire entourage. An innumerable multitude of the Hagarenes fell. As for Chambdan, after slaying all the prisoners he was holding, he and a few others managed to make an inglorious and disorderly escape from danger.[42]

10. In the twelfth year of the reign of Constantine, AM 6464, 27 February, fourteenth year of the indiction, the patriarch Theophylact departed this life[43] after an episcopate of twenty-three years and twenty-five days. He was sixteen years old when he took control – uncanonically – of the church. [243] He fulfilled his episcopal rule under tutors for a while, thank goodness, and would to God it had always been so. For in those days he gave the impression that he was capable of behaving with dignity and the necessary restraint; but as he approached the age of maturity and was allowed to lead his own life, there was nothing disgraceful or even frankly forbidden to which he was stranger. He put ecclesiastical advancement and elevation to the episcopate up for sale and did other things which a true bishop would certainly have eschewed. He had a mania for horses and went out hunting much of his time. He also indulged in other unseemly activities which it would be both tedious and improper to set out in detail. But there is one which it would be right to mention as an indication of how crude he was. He had this absolute passion for acquiring horses (he is said to have procured more than two thousand of them) and their care was his constant concern. He was not satisfied with feeding them hay and oats but would serve them pine-seeds, almonds and pistachios or even dates and figs and choicest raisins, mixed with the most fragrant wine. To this he would add saffron, cinnamon, balsam and other spices and serve it to each of his horses as food. It is said of him that once when he was celebrating the great supper of God on the Thursday of Holy Week and was already reading the prayer of consecration, the deacon charged with the task of caring for the horses appeared and gave him the glad tidings that his favourite mare – he mentioned its name – had just foaled. [Theophylact] was so delighted that he got through the rest of the liturgy as quickly as possible and came running to Kosmidion where he saw the newly born foal, took his fill of the

---

[42] Skylitzes ignores the chronological sequence of the successes of the sons of Bardas. It was in October 950 that Leo inflicted this crushing defeat on the emir in one of the passes of the Taurus. Sayf-ad-Doula slaughtered four hundred Christian prisoners. Niketas Chalkoutzes succeeded in escaping with his attendants by bribing those who were guarding them.
[43] 27 February 956.

sight of the animal and then returned to the Great Church, there to complete the singing of the hymn on the sacred sufferings of the saviour. It was he who instigated the present custom of insulting God and the memory of the saints on greater festivals by performing the early morning service with indecent howling, bursts of laughter and wild cries, whereas it should be offered to God with compunction and a contrite heart, for our own salvation. He gathered a band of disreputable men, set over them a fellow named Euthymios Kasnes (whom he promoted domestic of the church) and taught them satanic dances, [244] scandalous cries and songs gathered at crossroads and in brothels. Such was the life he led, and he lost his life by reckless riding; thrown from his horse at a section of the sea wall, he began to haemorrhage from the mouth. He sickened for two years and then died, a victim of dropsy.

11. On 3 April, the same year of the indiction, the monk Polyeuktos was ordained patriarch in his stead, a man born and raised in Constantinople,[44] castrated by his parents, a monk of many years' exemplary experience. The emperor made him patriarch on account of his exceptional wisdom, the austerity of his way of life and his indifference to worldly possessions. His ordination, however, was not performed by [the metropolitan] of Herakleia as was the custom, but by Basil of Caesarea for Nikephoros, bishop of Herakleia, had offended the emperor in some way and was not permitted to perform the ordination. From this, unusually severe blame was laid not only on him who had authorised and on him who had performed the ordination, but also on the one who was ordained for receiving an irregular ordination. He was nevertheless ordained and began speaking the truth boldly, condemning the greed of the relatives of Romanos the Elder,[45] and when the emperor came to the Great Church on Holy Saturday[46] he urged the emperor to rectify his misdeeds, to which he reluctantly agreed. Basil who later became parakoimomenos, born of a slave-woman to Romanos the Elder, now came to the support of his [step-] sister Helena, the Sovereign Lady. He so worked upon Constantine that he not only came to regret the patriarch's appointment, but also encouraged Basil to search out a pretext for expelling him from the throne; in this he had the strong encouragement of Theodore of Kyzikos.

---

[44] *ODB*, III, 1696.
[45] In 956 the patriarch could only have been referring to Helena, the wife of Constantine VII, and her half-brother Basil who – as Skylitzes alleges above – were encouraging the porphyrogennetos to confer the highest positions in the state on those who offered most for them: Brokkaar, 'Basil Lacapenus', 214.
[46] Easter eve.

12. [245] Time seemed to make a special effort to produce similar patriarchs simultaneously: it fell to John, son of Alberich, to direct the church of the western Romans, a man who inclined to every kind of wanton violence and evil. Otto, the emperor of the Franks, drove him out and installed another pastor for the church in his stead.[47]

13. In the first year of his episcopate Polyeuktos inserted the name of the patriarch Euthymios in the sacred diptychs, the one who received the emperor Leo into communion after he had married his fourth wife. For this reason some of the bishops refused to communicate with Polyeuktos for a while, but shortly afterwards they fell into line with the ruler's wishes and this provided discerning people with an occasion for laughter.

14. At the same time the venerated hand of John the Baptist was brought to the capital from Antioch where it had been stolen by a monk named Job. The emperor sent out the imperial yacht when it reached Chalcedon and out went the cream of the Senate, the patriarch Polyeuktos and all the clergy with candles, incense and lights to bring the relic into the palace.[48]

15. Bardas, the domestic of the scholai, campaigned against the Hagarenes of the east and overturned things wherever his foot trod. He captured quite a number of strongholds and laid siege to the renowned city of Adata.[49] It was the emperor's wish to intimidate the Saracens in Crete who were incessantly raiding the shores of Roman territory, pillaging and ravaging them. He wanted to put a stop to their unchecked onslaught. He put a large army together and prepared a fleet of no mean

---

[47] The papacy went through some severe troubles in the tenth century because Rome was in the hands of Theophylact, of Marozia his daughter and of Alberic her son. Octavian, the son of Alberic, was elected pope with the name of John XII when he was sixteen years old, in 955; it was he who crowned Otto at Rome on 2 February 962. The new emperor decided to rid himself of a pope who was a disgrace to his office; John XII was deposed forthwith: P. Dagron, *Histoire du christianisme* IV: *Evêques, moines et empereurs (610–1054)*, ed. G. Dagron, P. Riché and A. Vauchez (Paris, 1993), 781–5; and especially P. Toubert, *Les structures du Latium médiéval: le Latium méridional et la Sabine du ixe à la fin du xiie siècle* (Rome and Paris, 1973).

[48] On this relic which came to Constantinople in 956: I. Kalavrezou, 'Helping hands for the empire: imperial ceremonies and the cult of relics at the Byzantine court', *Byzantine court culture*, ed. H. Maguire, (Washington DC, 1997), 67–72. Theodore Daphnopates composed an oration on the arrival of the arm of the Prodromos: Kalavrezou, 'Helping hands for the empire', 77–8 and note 97. The transfer of this relic of one of the most popular of Byzantine saints, to whom several dozens of churches were dedicated within Constantinople alone: Janin, *Églises et les monastères*, I, 410–42, occurs in the context of a whole series of entrances of relics to the capital (e.g. of the sacred *mandylion* from Edessa under Romanos Lekapenos), usually at the initiative of an emperor. See the account of the entry of the relics of Gregory the Theologian on whom Constantine Porphyrogennetos composed a panegyric: B. Flusin, 'Le panégyrique de Constantin VII Porphyrogénète pour la translation des reliques de Grégoire le Théologien *(BHG 728)*', *REB*, 57 (1999), 5–97.

[49] It is difficult to tell to which campaign of Bardas Phokas this refers, for all the expeditions that went by Adata (which controlled one of the eastern passes of the Taurus) ended up in reverses.

dimensions, and sent the entire force to the island[50] under the command of the patrician Constantine Gongylios, an effeminate, sedentary fellow with no experience of war, [246] one of the eunuchs of the bedchamber at the palace.[51] He got to the island but did nothing there worthy of a general. He failed both to make a secure encampment and also to post a guard and watch as a protection against attacks by the barbarians; hence, he fell into very severe danger. The islanders noted the inexperience and carelessness of the general and, when the time was ripe, launched a sudden attack on the army. In this they were easily successful; many of the Romans were taken prisoner or put to the sword. The encampment itself was occupied while the Romans shamefully ran away. Gongylios would have been taken too had his attendants not rallied around him, rescued him from being captured, then got him on board a ship and safely away.

16. Romanos the son of Constantine had now reached the age of maturity;[52] he could not bear seeing the way in which the affairs of state were handled by his father, so he decided to get rid of him by poison and this with the full knowledge of his wife, the innkeeper [-'s daughter]. When Constantine was about to take a purgative drink, they secretly mixed a noxious substance with it and prevailed upon Niketas the butler to serve it to the emperor. It was standing before the sacred icons when Niketas was about to take it up and – perhaps accidentally, perhaps on purpose – he knocked it over and spilled most of it. The remainder (which Constantine drank) proved itself inert and ineffectual, deprived of its power because there was so little of it. Nevertheless, Constantine was only just able to survive, for the poison lodged in his lung and tormented him considerably.

17. In the fifteenth year of his reign, in the month of September, third year of the indiction, AM 6468, [247] the emperor Constantine set out for Mount Olympos, ostensibly to arm himself with the prayers of the fathers there and, so armed, to campaign against the Saracens in Syria. But in truth it was to meet with Theodore, bishop of Kyzicos,[53] who was

---

[50] In 949. The documents intended for the preparation of this expedition are extant: Constantine Porphyrogenitus, *De cerimoniis aulae byzantinae libri duo*, ed. J. J. Reiske (CHSB, Bonn, 1829–30) 664–78; J. F. Haldon, 'Theory and practice in tenth-century military administration. Chs 11, 44 and 45 of the *Book of Ceremonies*', TM, 13 (2000), 202–352, at 219–35. Constantine mobilised nearly 9,000 men and almost 20,000 marines at a cost in excess of 120,000 nomismata, approximately 546 kg of gold.

[51] Constantine and his brother Anastasios have already been mentioned as members of the council assisting Zoe the mother of Constantine VII during her regency: reign of Constantine VII (minor), c. 4. They were probably sent away from the palace during the reign of Romanos I; Constantine could no longer have been young.

[52] He was twenty-one: *Theophanes Continuatus*, 469.

[53] Some of the correspondence between Constantine and Theodore of Kyzikos has survived: J. Darrouzès, *Epistoliers byzantins du Xe siècle* (Le monde byzantin, Paris, 1960), 317–41.

staying there at that time, and to take counsel with him concerning the deposition of Polyeuktos. While he was there, on account either of some physical defect or of being poisoned by his son again, he fell ill and had to return to the capital which he reached towards the end of October riding in a litter. On 9 November he died leaving his intention [to depose Polyeuktos] unaccomplished. He had lived a life of fifty-four years and two months;[54] he had co-reigned with his father, his uncle Alexander and his mother thirteen years then with Romanos the intruder twenty-six [years]. Subsequently, after [Romanos] fell from power, he had ruled alone for fifteen years.[55] When he died he was buried with his own father. To his last breath he was maliciously disposed toward Polyeuktos and making plans to depose him.

18. Some days before his death and for some considerable time, as evening drew on, stones thrown from above would fall in the place where he was staying with great violence and a very loud crash. He thought they were coming from the upper stories of the Magnaura and ordered guards to be posted there for many nights in the hope of catching whoever dared to do such a thing. But he failed to realise that this was a wasted effort; the happening was not the work of men but of a higher power.

---

[54] This is correct; *Theophanes Continuatus*, 468, gives fifty-five years and two months.
[55] MSS C and E (the latter in the margin) add: 'Not fifteen years but fourteen, ten months, twenty-four days. For he came to power on 16 December, the third year of the indiction, AM 6453 and he died on 9 November, the thirteenth year of the indiction, AM 6468.' There are other sources which say he died on 19 November: Grierson, 'Tombs', 58.

CHAPTER 12

Romanos II the Younger [959–963]

1. [248] After Constantine [VII] had departed this life and passed on to the hereafter, Romanos his son came to power. He appointed officials who were fervently loyal to him and, once he had assured his hold on the empire as securely as possible, he crowned his son Basil at the feast of Easter, still in the third year of the indiction,[1] by the hands of the patriarch Polyeuktos, at the Great Church.

2. The following year another son was born [to Romanos], this one in the palace at Pege, whom he called Constantine after his father.

3. [Romanos] was young and devoted to pleasure; he abandoned the supervision of every matter to Joseph Bringas,[2] the praepositos and parakoimomenos, for he himself would have nothing to do with anything but the pursuit of ribald behaviour in the company of silly young men who frequented prostitutes, wantons, actors and comedians. There was a cleric, a eunuch who, warned by the emperor Constantine about his disorderly behaviour, had adopted the monastic habit and kept himself out of sight

---

[1] 22 April 960. It is not certain when Basil was born. Psellos (*Chronographia*, 1:24) says that Basil died in his seventy-second year, which would mean he was born in 954. This is unlikely for several reasons. Romanos II (born in 939) would have been a very young father; also this would imply that Basil was considerably older than his brother, whereas the sources all agree that he was only three years older than Constantine. *Theophanes Continuatus*, 469, and *Pseudo-Symeon the Logothete*, 775 and 757, say that Basil was one year old when his grandfather died, which would mean he was born in 958, and this is probably correct. According to Yahya of Antioch, 1, 480, Basil was sixty-eight when he died on 12 December 1025, meaning that he was born in 957. For the most recent word on this matter: M. Featherstone, 'Olga's visit to Constantinople in *De Cerimoniis*', *REB*, 61 (2003), 250–1.

[2] A. Markopoulos, 'Joseph Bringas: problèmes prosopographiques et question idéologiques' (in Greek), *Symmeikta*, 4 (1981), 87–115, trs. *History and literature of Byzantium in the ninth-tenth centuries* (Aldershot, 2004), no. IV. Constantine VII had made this eunuch his confidant and awarded him the title of patrician. He was successively praepositos, sakellarios, droungarios of the fleet and finally parakoimomenos. As he lay dying the emperor made him swear to assist Romanos in governing: *Theophanes Continuatus*, 466. Joseph made a series of appointments at the accession of Romanos II: John Choirinas became great hetaireiarch, Sisinnios eparch of the City, subsequently logothete of the genikon when Theodore Daphnopates replaced him as eparch.

until the emperor's death. But as soon as Romanos came to power, he made him throw off the monastic habit and put on the garb of a secular cleric, associating himself with the attendants of the imperial bedchamber.[3] Now Polyeuktos, full of zeal, importuned and besought the emperor at great length to discharge this man [249] from his service for having renounced the monastic profession. The emperor refused, claiming that [John] had never really taken the monastic habit or had the office [of clothing] said over him by any one of the priests; he had feigned the monastic way of life for fear of the emperor and, taken in by this, Polyeuktos let the matter drop – Joseph also having worked hard to attain that result. [As for John], he lived a secular, disorderly life until the death of Romanos, after which he again assumed the monastic habit. But he did not change his state of mind.

4. In this year [Romanos] sent the magister Nikephoros Phokas (who had already been promoted domestic of the scholai for the East by the emperor Constantine and had achieved many victories against the Saracens of the East, completely subduing Karamnes, emir of Tarsus, Chambdan, emir of Aleppo and Izeth, emir of Tripoli) against the Saracens of Crete, providing him with an army of picked soldiers and a well-equipped fleet.[4] [Nikephoros Phokas] made the passage to the island and immediately on disembarkation became embroiled with the Hagarenes who were there and offering him resistance. These he put to flight and safely disembarked both himself and his army. Then he set up a strong palisade surrounded by a deep ditch fortified with stakes and staves. He moored the fleet in a calm harbour and, when all was in order, set about laying vigorous siege to the cities of the island. For seven months in all he employed every kind of siege-engine; he threw down the walls of the cities and occupied the strongholds. On 7 March, fourth year of the indiction, he ravaged the strongest city of all (known locally as Chandax) and took prisoner the emir of the island, Kouroupes[5] by name, [250] together with Anemas,[6] the

---

[3] The man is otherwise unknown; he may well have been appointed *epi tou koitonos* (koitonites).
[4] Nikephoros Phokas, now domestic of the scholai for the West, sailed from the port of Phygela to the south of Ephesos in the spring of 960 and arrived in Crete on 13 July. This expedition, which numbered 250 vessels, was bigger than the previous ones. It was being prepared during the last years of Constantine VII, probably at the instigation of Basil Lekapenos, the parakoimomenos: D. Tsougarakis, *Byzantine Crete: from the fifth century to the Venetian conquest* (Athens, 1988), 58–63.
[5] The name of the emir was 'Abd al-'Aziz ibn Shu'ayb et-Qurtubi. Kouroupes may come from the *nisba* of the emir.
[6] This man entered the service of the empire and provided it with a long line of generals reaching into the twelfth century: e.g. B. Skoulatos, *Les Personnages byzantins de l'Alexiade* (Louvain, 1980), 200–2.

most important person on the island after him. After he had subjugated the entire island he was going to remain there for some time in order to set its affairs in order,[7] but word went round that the Roman who conquered the island would perforce reign over the empire. So as soon as it was known that Nikephoros had the upper hand in Crete, Romanos (at Joseph's insistence) recalled him from there. And when Nikephoros protracted his stay in Crete to ensure against it being overrun by the Arabs of the East (especially by Chambdan, the emir of Aleppo, who was a fiercer warrior than the others), Romanos honoured Leo Phokas, Nikephoros' brother, with the title of magister and sent him out to discharge the office of domestic.[8] He crossed the sea and encountered Chambdan at a place called Adrassos where he not only repulsed him with great vigour, but virtually annihilated him.[9] It would be impossible to state in numbers how many fell in the encounter, and as for the prisoners which were taken and sent into the city, they were so many that both urban and rural properties were filled with slaves. Only Chambdan their chieftain and a very few others with him escaped the danger and got away home. When Leo returned he was most warmly received by the emperor who accorded him the celebration of a triumph and honoured him with fitting endowments. He also awarded promotions and distinctions to all those who had been his associate in valour.

5. In the second year of the reign of Romanos many senior officials were arrested for plotting against him. The leaders and instigators of this conspiracy were the magister Basil Peteinos[10] and some other distinguished personages, the patricians Paschalios[11] and Bardas Lips;[12] also Nicholas Chalkoutzes.[13] Their plan was to seize the emperor as he was going [to the

---

[7] The Roman forces entered Chandax on 7 March 961, massacred part of the population and took immense booty. Having completed the conquest of the island, Nikephoros left behind a garrison mainly of Greeks and Armenians: Leo the Deacon, 7–16 (tr. 60–9) and 24–9 (tr. 76–81) is the best source on the taking of Crete and is very favourable to Nikephoros. See Tsougarakis, *Crete*, 63–74, for a good modern overview.

[8] It was under Romanos II that the office of domestic of the scholai was first divided into two, one for the East and one for the West. Leo was domestic for the East, his brother for the West: Oikonomides, *Listes*, 239.

[9] This new victory of Leo (leading substandard troops on that occasion) took place on 8 November 960.

[10] One of those who had supported Constantine VII against the Lakapenoi: reign of Constantine VII as an adult, c. 1.

[11] Possibly the strategos of Longobardia mentioned above.

[12] Otherwise unknown, but very likely a relative of Constantine Lips, the contemporary of Leo VI.

[13] Almost certainly *Niketas* Chalkoutzes, the patrician, who saved some of the prisoners taken by Sayd-ad-Doula shortly before this and who served under Nikephoros Phokas at the conquest of Crete. On Niketas: reign of Constantine VII as an adult, c. 9.

Hippodrome] the day when there was horse racing, to put Basil on the imperial throne [251] and proclaim him emperor. But the plot was betrayed to the emperor by one of the conspirators named Ioannikios, a Saracen by birth. Before the appointed day arrived, they were arrested by Joseph, condemned and ruthlessly tortured (with the sole exception of Basil). On the day of the horse races they were paraded for public derision, sent into exile and tonsured as monks. When they had suffered this humiliation for a short time, they were recalled by Romanos, now charitably disposed towards them. The exception was Basil Peteinos who had gone out of his mind and died in the Proconnesos: justice had overtaken him for the deceit he had practised on the emperor Stephen when he betrayed him to Constantine.

6. Romanos Saronites[14] was the brother-in-law of Romanos the Elder[15] by marriage to his sister. When he saw what had befallen Basil Peteinos and the others, he was frightened that the same fate might befall him, for his elevated status attracted envy and suspicion. So he divided his fortune among his children as he pleased, distributed the rest to the poor, assumed the monastic habit and entered the Elegmoi[16] monastery. He remained there for many years and was held in high honour by subsequent emperors.

7. In those days a man appeared whose name was Philoraios, a bodyguard to the magister Romanos Moseles and a grandson of Romanos the Elder.[17] He could ride around the track of the Hippodrome standing upright on the saddle of a racehorse running at full speed, bearing in his hands a sword which he would turn like a windmill without in the least declining from his upright position.

8. In those days the cattle disease was raging which had plagued the Roman empire for some time, a disease known as *krabra* that wastes and destroys bovines. [252] They say that it originated in the days of Romanos the Elder. It is said that when he was constructing a palace in which to

---

[14] The Saronitai (not to be confused with the Taronitai) belonged to the highest aristocracy. A lawsuit challenging the legitimacy of the marriage between Theophylact, son of the patrician Romanos Saronites, and Theophano, daughter of the protospatharios John Parsakoudenos, reveals something of the marriage alliances contracted by this illustrious family: with the Taronitai, twice with the Lekapenoi, and with the Radenoi: A. Schminck, 'Vier eherechtliche Enscheidungen aus dem 11. Jahrhundert', *Fontes Minores*, 3 (1979), 240–51.

[15] Hence Romanos was the uncle of Romanos II; his wife's name is not known.

[16] The Bithynian monastery of Elegmoi (or Elaiobomoi) was sufficiently illustrious in 787 for its hegoumenos to sign the acts of the council held in that year: Janin, *Grands centres*, 11, 142–8.

[17] Thus Moseles was first cousin to Romanos II and nephew to Romanos Saronites. This relationship explains why both enjoyed the elevated title of magister.

gain relief from the summer heat close to the cistern of Bonos,[18] the head of a marble ox was found while the foundations were being dug. Those who found it smashed it up and threw it into the lime kiln; and from that time until this there was no interruption in the destruction of the bovine race in any land that was under Roman rule.

9. Romanos was urged by his own wife to try to expel his mother, Helena, and his sisters from the palace and to banish them to the palace of Antiochos.[19] When Helena learnt of this she managed to change his mind by using tears and threats, for he was afraid of her curses. He let *her* remain where she was, but he had his sisters[20] taken out and tonsured as nuns by John, hegoumenos of Stoudios' monastery. Once [their brother] was no more, they put aside both the monastic habit and vegetarianism. [Meanwhile] Helena was deeply pained by her daughters' fate; she lived a short while and then departed this life, 20 September, fifth year of the indiction.[21] She received an imperial funeral and was interred in the sarcophagus of her father.[22]

10. As we mentioned earlier, Nikephoros Phokas was commanded to return from Crete but was refused permission to enter the capital;[23] he was ordered to the East with his entire army. Chambdan had been recovering from his recent defeat and was now ready for action again. He had assembled an army ready for battle and it was anticipated that he would launch an attack on Roman territory. However, when Phokas arrived in Syria [253] he put [the Hagarenes] to flight in a pitched battle and severely crushed them, repelling them into the remoter parts of Syria. He pillaged the city of Berroia, all except the citadel; he acquired great riches, much booty and many prisoners. He released the Christians who were being held prisoner there and sent them home.[24]

---

[18] The exact location of this covered cistern constructed by the patrician Bonos at the beginning of the seventh century has not yet been established. It is, however, clear that both the cistern and the palace which had the same name were in the general vicinity of Holy Apostles: Janin, *Constantinople*, 128–9, 206–7.

[19] Located to the north-west of the Hippodrome: Janin, *Constantinople*, 310.

[20] Zoe, Theodora and Theophano.

[21] September 961.

[22] i.e. at the Myrelaion where Romanos I had decided to establish the family mausoleum.

[23] This is not correct for the sources nearer to the event than Skylitzes report that Nikephoros celebrated a triumph: Leo the Deacon, 23–4 (tr. 76) and see below: reign of Basil II.

[24] In 962 Nikephoros, once again domestic of the scholai for the East, led several campaigns against Sayf-ad-Doula. He defeated the forces of Tarsus in the spring and took Anazarba. In December, with the support of John Tzimiskes, strategos of the Armeniakon theme, he surprised the Hamdanid and took his capital, Aleppo (Berroia in Greek), but did not succeed in storming the great fortress which was its acropolis. He withdrew in the last days of December.

11. The emperor Romanos died on 15 March, sixth year of the indiction, AM 6471. He had reigned for thirteen years, four months and five days;[25] some say he had precociously worn out his constitution with debauchery and excess, but according to another report he was carried off by poison.

[25] These numbers do not make sense. Counting from the day of his coronation as co-emperor (945 or 946) he reigned seventeen or eighteen years. Thirteen is probably an error for *three* years of independent rule, counting from the death of his father – if one accepts Skylitzes' opinion that Constantne VII died on 9 November 959.

CHAPTER 13

Basil II Bulgaroktonos and Constantine VIII
[976–1025]

1. [254] Romanos was succeeded as emperor by his sons, Basil and Constantine, together with Theophano, their mother, who bore a daughter whom they named Anna,[1] two days before [Romanos'] death.

2. Romanos was tall, but less tall than his father. He was courteous and gentle in his ways and not without brains. Even as a young man his mind was sharp and quick; he would have been perfectly capable of governing the state if he had been allowed to do so by the attendants but his closest companions encouraged him to give free rein to his youthful excesses. In order to keep themselves in office running the state and free to acquire wealth for their own use, they portrayed him as a useless, idle fellow.

3. In April of the same (sixth) year of the indiction[2] Nikephoros Phokas came to Constantinople at the Sovereign Lady's request, in spite of Joseph [Bringas'] repeated protests. He celebrated a triumph in the Hippodrome with the spoils of Crete and of Berroia.[3] He also brought a portion of the raiment of John the Baptist which he had found conserved at Berroia.[4] Bringas regarded him with fear and suspicion but [Nikephoros] was able to lead *him* astray by deceiving him in the following way. Taking one of his bodyguards with him, he went to Joseph's house around supper time. [255] He knocked at the door and told the doorkeeper to announce who had come. He was announced and invited in, whereupon he took Joseph apart and showed him the hair shirt he was wearing under his clothes. He told Joseph (and swore that it was true) that he would have embraced the monastic way of life, donned the habit and delivered himself from worldly cares long ago, had he not been detained by his attachment to

---

[1] Anna was born on 13 March 963.   [2] April 963.
[3] Berroia is the Greek name of Aleppo. The triumph is described by Leo the Deacon, 32 (tr. 84). The booty went to augment the imperial treasury. On the two triumphs of Nikephoros see M. McCormick, *Eternal victory: triumphal rulership in late antiquity, Byzantium, and early medieval west* (Cambridge, MA, 1986), 164–70.
[4] The arm of John the Baptist had been imported from Antioch some years earlier: reign of Constantine VII as an adult, c. 14.

the emperors Constantine and Romanos;[5] now he was going to do what he had so long intended to do as soon as possible. He implored the other not to be suspicious of him without grounds. Joseph fell at his feet when this was revealed, begged his pardon and assured him that he would never again lend any credence to anyone who spoke ill of him.[6]

4. But Bringas was suspicious of the emperor Stephen, still in the land of the living, exiled to Methymne,[7] and endeavoured to have him imprisoned more securely. He, however, after receiving the holy mysteries on the feast of Holy Saturday, suddenly and unexpectedly died, for no apparent reason. Yet even though she was living far away, it was Theophano who procured his death.

5. When the wife of Peter, the emperor [sic] of the Bulgars, died, he made a treaty with the emperors ostensibly to renew the peace, surrendering his own sons, Boris and Romanos,[8] as hostages. He himself died shortly afterwards,[9] whereupon the sons were sent to Bulgaria to secure the ancestral throne and to restrain the 'children of the counts'[10] from further encroachments. David, Moses, Aaron and [256] Samuel, children of one of the powerful counts in Bulgaria, were contemplating an uprising and were unsettling the Bulgars' land.

6. After Bringas was beguiled by Nikephoros in the way which we have explained he let him go home. Afterwards he thought better of it and was very angry with himself for having had the prey in the net and then been so foolish as to let it go; so he set about thinking by what subterfuge

---

[5] At the time of the conquest of Crete Nikephoros had already spoken to Athanasios, the future founder of the Great Lavra on Mount Athos, of his desire to embrace the monastic life: *Life of Athanasios*, Vita A, chs. 30–1, 15; Vita B, ch. 11, 137.

[6] The account of Leo the Deacon, ed. Hase, 32–4, is quite different: Nikephoros was contemplating revolt but he no longer had the regiments of the east at his disposal, they having been sent back to their homes. So he decided to come to Constantinople in order to celebrate his triumph. Thwarted by Bringas (who would have imprisoned him), Nikephoros denounced the intentions of his enemy to the patriarch Polyeuktos who, in great anger, came before the Senate and had the command of the forces of the east conferred on Nikephoros [again] – even in the presence of Bringas – with orders to make no move whatsoever prejudicial to the young emperors.

[7] On the island of Mytilene (Lesbos): J. Koder, *Aigaion Pelagos (Die nordliche Agais)* (TIB, 10, Vienna, 1998), 228–30; reign of Constantine VII as an adult, c. 2.

[8] Maria Lecapena must have died in 963.

[9] Peter of Bulgaria died 20 January 969. Skylitzes is simplifying matters here for Peter crossed swords with Nikephoros in 966 when the latter was unwilling to continue paying the tribute established in the time of Symeon, which led to hostilities (see below, on the reign of Nikephoros Phokas, c. 20).

[10] Or 'sons of the count', *kometopoloi*: J. Ferluga, 'Le soulèvement des Comitopoules', *ZRVI*, 9 (1966), 75–84; W. Seibt suggests that the *kometopoloi* were of Armenian origin: 'Untersuchungen zur Vor-und Früh-geschichte der "bulgarischen" Kometopoulen', *Handes Amsorya*, 89 (1975), 65–100. Skylitzes is anticipating an uprising which came about after the death of John Tzimiskes in 976. On the shaky chronology of the Bulgar wars: C. Holmes, *Basil II and the governance of empire (976–1025)* (Oxford Studies in Byzantium, Oxford, 2005), 102–3.

he might be relieved of his concern over the matter. The most effective measure he could think of was to write to the magister John Tzimiskes, a high-spirited man of action and the most distinguished of the Roman commanders after Phokas himself, at that time serving as commander of the Anatolikon theme;[11] and also to the magister Romanos Kourkouas, another distinguished general serving in the east. He would send them letters inciting them with promises of friendship, honours and gifts to overthrow Phokas. The letters were written and this is their substance: if [the addressees] would rise up and depose Phokas,[12] tonsuring him a monk or [removing him] by any other way, John would receive the supreme appointment of domestic of the scholai for the East while Romanos would become domestic for the West. As soon as the letters had been delivered to the men in question, they immediately read them to Phokas (to whom they were very loyal) and besought him to react in no uncertain way or to devise some noble and audacious stratagem. They threatened to kill him with their own hands when he delayed and procrastinated. Since he feared that his life was in danger, he permitted them to proclaim him [emperor] on 2 July, the same year of the indiction, and he was indeed acclaimed emperor of the Romans by the entire army of the east assembled by Tzimiskes.[13]

7. [257] That is what one version of the story says. There is another version which is more likely to be true, according to which Phokas had long been labouring under the impression that he ought to be emperor, and that he burned not only with this passion, but also with desire for the empress Theophano whom he had encountered while he was staying in the capital. He frequently sent his most trusted servant, Michael, to her; which fact Bringas noted and, consequently, became suspicious of him. When news of his acclamation[14] reached Constantinople and everything was in

[11] John, surnamed Tzimiskes, a word of Armenian origin referring to his small stature, was of the Kourkouas family which had Armenian blood in it. His grandfather, Theophilos, had been strategos of Chaldia and had gained some brilliant victories over the Arabs. John's mother (who bore him *c.* 925) was the sister of Nikephoros Phokas; his first wife was the sister of Bardas Skleros. He was a highly successful warrior, as the Arab as well as the western sources attest. In 958 he defeated Naga al-Kasaki, one of the emirs of Sayf ad-Dowla, then routed ad-Dowla himself before Ra'ban: A. A. Vasiliev, *Byzance et les Arabes* 11, 362–3. He had been serving as strategos of the Anatolikon theme since Leo Phokas abandoned that position to become domestic of the scholai for the East in 959.

[12] Romanos was a first cousin of John Tzimiskes, the strategos of an important theme – probably the Armeniakon theme, for he seems to be the next strategos in order of precedence after John.

[13] The army of the east had been concentrated under the pretext of opposing Sayf ad-Dowla and Nikephoros had established it at Caesarea in Cappadocia; that is where he was proclaimed emperor. The account of Leo the Deacon, 38–40 (tr. 89–90), gives more detail; Leo is one of the sources named by Skylitzes in his *Proimion*.

[14] Nikephoros had sent a letter addressed to the patriarch Polyeuktos, to Joseph the parakoimomenos and to the Senate, asking to be received as emperor. Joseph was so angry that he flung the person

a state of disarray, Joseph (who was effectively in charge of everything) was very worried and at a loss what action to take, for he himself was by no means beloved of the citizens on account of being so unapproachable. When Nikephoros Phokas came with his entire army right down to Chrysopolis, acclaimed all the way, Bringas decided to set up some other emperor, under the impression that in this way he would somewhat abate the fervour of the army's advance.[15] When the acclamation of Phokas took place in the way we described, his father, Bardas, who was living at the capital, took refuge in the Great Church while Leo [Nikephoros'] brother managed to escape, even though he was held under tight security, and joined his brother. These events caused Bringas to lose heart and reduced him to inactivity, for he was totally incapable of flattering and swaying public opinion in adverse circumstances. It would have been necessary to massage the crowd's attitude with soft and flattering speeches, while he tended rather to prickle and aggravate them. Everybody came running to the Great Church and, to put fear into the multitude, he spoke arrogant and savage words, saying: 'I will put an end to your impudent and disgraceful behaviour; I will make you pay one piece of gold for as much grain as you can carry in your bosom.' Less than one full day [258] after he had said that (it was a Sunday, 9 August), in the evening of the same day, Basil the parakoimomenos of the emperor Constantine (who was antipathetic and hostile to Joseph) mingled his own servants[16] with his friends and relations, then sent them into many parts of the city, to the houses of those who were opposed to him. From the first hour of Monday unto the sixth they ravaged and destroyed many citizens' houses, of which Joseph's was the most significant; and not only the houses of distinguished men and officials who seemed to be of the opposition, but of many other lesser folk too. There was no numbering the many houses that were overthrown. Whoever had a difference with another person would take a band of desperadoes with him and slaughter that person with nobody intervening on his behalf. Many men were murdered in this lawless time, and while this was going on in the squares of the city, in the main thoroughfares, the marketplaces and the back streets they were acclaiming Nikephoros

---

bringing the letter (Philotheos, metropolitan of Euchaita) into prison: Leo the Deacon, 44–5 (tr. 95).

[15] Leo the Deacon, 45 (tr. 95), says that Joseph attempted to mobilise the western army by placing it under the command of Marianos Argyros, at that time *katepan* of the west: *Theophanes Continuatus*, 480. He also appointed Paschalios and the Tornikioi brothers to command it. But there was a disturbance at the capital in the course of which Marianos was mortally wounded by a tile thrown by a woman. This completely disorganised the defence: Leo the Deacon, 46 (tr. 96).

[16] There were 3,000 of them: Leo the Deacon, 47.

the conqueror. This drew Bardas, the father of Phokas, out of the Great Church where he had pitiably sought refuge, for he perceived that he was no longer in danger. But Joseph the parakoimomenos, formerly so high and mighty, now took his place as a humble suppliant, fearing for his life. The partisans of Basil the parakoimomenos prepared some ships, took the imperial galley and passed over to Chrysopolis with the entire fleet. There they brought Nikephoros on board and conveyed him to Hebdomon, from where they and all the city population bore him in procession through the Golden Gate, [259] into the capital, with cheering and applause, with trumpets and cymbals. When they arrived at the Great Church, they contrived to have the patriarch Polyeuktos place the imperial diadem on his brow. Polyeuktos did indeed crown him, in the ambo of the Great Church of God, on Sunday, 16 August, sixth year of the indiction.[17]

---

[17] The date is confirmed: P. Schreiner, *Die byzantinishen Kleinchroniken* 1, Historicher Kommentar (CFHB, 12, Vienna, 1975–7), 153, no. 3.

CHAPTER 14

Nikephoros II Phokas [963–969]

1. [260] [Nikephoros][1] despatched the synkellos, a Stoudite monk named Anthony,[2] to expel Theophano from the palace and sent her to the Petrion[3] palace. Shortly after that he sent Joseph the parakoimomenos into exile in Paphlagonia then, before long, transferred him to a monastery known as Asekretis in Pythia[4] [Thessaly] where he lived for two whole years and then died. [Nikephoros] also promoted his own father, Bardas,[5] to the rank of caesar.

2. On 20 September he put aside all pretence and play-acting by taking Theophano to be his lawful wife. It was then that he started eating meat again; he had been abstaining from it ever since the death of Bardas, the son born to him by his first wife. This son had been horse-riding on the plain, sporting with his own nephew Pleuses, when he was accidentally but mortally wounded with a spear.[6] Only Nikephoros and God know whether this was really an abstinence or merely an affectation to deceive

---

[1] There is no recent monograph on this emperor. It is still possible to profit enormously from G. Schlumberger, *Un empereur byzantin au Xe siècle: Nicéphore Phokas* (Paris, 1890). Important modern works include: R. Morris, 'The two faces of Nikephoros Phokas', *BMGS*, 12 (1988), 83–115; Dagron and Mihàescu, *Traité*; E. McGeer, *Sowing the dragon's teeth: Byzantine warfare in the tenth century* (DOS, 33, Washington, DC, 1995). Morris (using earlier work by A. Kazhdan) remarks that there are two traditions, one favourable to Nikephoros, e.g. Leo the Deacon, and one hostile – which Skylitzes used. The chroniclers probably gained their information from a Phokas family chronicle.

[2] As synkellos Anthony was 'heir apparent' to the patriarchal throne. He did not, however, succeed Polyeuktos directly, but he did succeed Basil Skamandrenos in 973: J. Darrouzès, 'Sur la chronologie du patriarche Antoine III Stoudite', *REB*, 46 (1988), 55–60. Anthony was patriarch until 978.

[3] A district of Constantinople adjacent to the Golden Horn which gave its name to both a port and a palace: Janin, *Constantinople*, 407–8.

[4] This is the only known reference to this monastery: Janin, *Grands centres*, 11, 86. Pythia, close to Pylai (now Yalova) was famous for its baths.

[5] Bardas Phokas had attained many ranks in the imperial hierarchy and was now magister. The title of caesar had not been given since the demise of Bardas, the uncle of Michael III. Leo Phokas was appointed curopalates at this time.

[6] The Peus[t]ai probably came originally from Pontos.

those in power. The marriage was celebrated at the New Church in the palace. When it came to the point of entering the sanctuary, Polyeuktos, leading the emperor by the hand, approached the sacred enclosure and entered the sanctuary himself but forced the emperor to remain outside, saying that he would not allow him to enter the sanctuary [261] until he had performed the penance required of one who marries a second time.[7] This offended Nikephoros and he never ceased being indignant with Polyeuktos until the day of his death. Now a rumour went out in all directions, a rumour that disturbed the church in no small way, that Nikephoros had stood godfather for one of Theophano's children at his holy baptism. Taking this rumour as an opportune pretext, Polyeuktos demanded that Nikephoros either separate from his wife (as the canon required)[8] or that he stay away from church – which in fact he did, cleaving to Theophano. Polyeuktos summoned the bishops residing in the city together with the leading senators and invited their opinion on this matter. They all said that [the canon in question] was a law of [Constantine V] Kopronymos and that, in their estimation, it need not be observed.[9] They put their signatures to a statement to that effect and delivered it to him. When Polyeuktos *still* delayed in admitting the emperor to communion, the caesar [Bardas Phokas] asserted that [his son] had not stood godfather; and Stylianos, the dean of the clergy[10] of the Great Palace (who was reputed first to have put the rumour in circulation), came before the Synod and the Senate and swore that neither had he seen Bardas or Nikephoros stand godfather nor had he told anybody that he had. Whereupon Polyeuktos, fully aware that Stylianes was perjuring himself, withdrew the charge of marrying the mother of his godchild. He who had been demanding the penance for a second marriage now turned a blind eye to that grave offence.

3. In the first year of his reign Nikephoros despatched the patrician Manuel against the Saracens in Sicily with an army and navy of

---

[7] For both Theophano and for Nikephoros this was a second marriage, which the church did not forbid, but for which it did require a penance to be done: two years for a second marriage, five for a third. Thus the fourth canon of Basil, commented on by Theodore Balsamon at the end of the twelfth century: G. Rallès and M. Potlès, *Syntagma ton theion kai hieron kanonon*, IV (Athens, 1868), 103.

[8] 'God'-relationships were counted in the same way as other relationships in determining whom one could or could not marry. On such relationships: E. Patlagean, 'Christianisation et parentés spirituelles: le domaine de Byzance', *Annales ESC* (1978), 625–36, repr. E. Patlagean, *Structure sociale, famille, chrétienté à Byzance IVe–XIe siècle* (London, 1981), no. XII.

[9] To invalidate a precedent completely it only had to be attributed to an iconoclast emperor, preferably to Constantine V Kopronymos.

[10] *Protopapas*.

considerable size. Manuel was the illegitimate son of his father's brother, Leo, the former domestic of the scholai who was blinded by Romanos the elder.[11] [262] [Nikephoros] felt that he would be assailed by disgrace if the Roman empire were to pay tribute to the Saracens during his reign.

4. We must quickly explain what this tribute was that was paid to the Saracens and how it started. When the city of Syracuse was taken by the Saracens of Africa in the time of Basil [I] the Macedonian,[12] the whole of the island also fell under their control. Its cities were devastated; Palermo alone was spared as the Hagarenes maintained it as a base for operations against the land at the other side [of the water]. From there they sailed out to ravage the islands as far as the Peloponnese; the chances of them attacking were greater than ever before. The emperor Basil was at a loss what to do. He searched for a servant capable of undertaking this mission and his choice fell on the domestic of the scholai, Nikephoros, surnamed Phokas after a distinguished ancestor.[13] He was the grandfather of the emperor Nikephoros, a noble and wise man, devout in his relations with God, just towards his fellow men. He sailed to Italy with an army of sorts and promptly put the Saracens to flight, forcing them to bide their peace in Sicily. The Italians are said to have built a church to perpetuate the memory of his excellence, not only for having secured their freedom, but in gratitude for another deed which is worth recording. When the Romans were about to return home with their commander, they were holding many Italians whom they intended to take overseas as slaves. Nikephoros became aware of this but said not a word. He gave no hint of what he intended to do until they arrived in Brindisi, from where [263] they were to cross to Illyria. When they got there, he personally supervised the embarkation of each one of the soldiers in preparation for the crossing. By this intervention he permitted the local inhabitants freely to occupy their own land. Thereupon Italy remained at peace until the time of Constantine Porphyrogennetos and his mother, when the Saracens stirred themselves again and, since there was nothing to stop them, overran Italy. Those in power realised that they were incapable of withstanding the Saracens both in the east and in the west (for the Bulgars had just broken the peace treaty) so they decided to negotiate with the Saracens in Sicily. An agreement was

---

[11] On Leo Phokas the elder: reign of Constantine VII as a minor, c. 13. On Manuel: Cheynet, 'Phocas', 306, reproduced in Cheynet, *Société*, 488.
[12] See above, the reign of Basil I, c. 37.
[13] Basil I, c. 38 (above). Nikephoros the elder did not yet have the title of domestic of the scholai at the time of the Italian campaign.

reached by the commander of Calabria,[14] Eustathios, one of the imperial chamberlains, that an annual tribute would be paid to the Saracens of twenty-two thousand gold pieces.[15]

5. When the treaty had been made, the patrician John Mouzalon was promoted commander of Calabria, but he governed the people of the land with such a heavy hand that they slew him and went over to Dandulf, the king of Longobardia.[16] This was just after Romanos the Elder came to rule over the Romans. He judged it expedient for soldiers and ships to be sent there to recover the portion which had been separated from the whole. The patrician Kosmas of Thessalonike was sent, a man known to Dandulf. When he had crossed to Italy and made contact with Dandulf,[17] he advised him to withdraw from the land of the Romans and to become a friend of the emperor, thus gaining a friend and an ally in place of an enemy. At first Dandulf would not accept his advice; then Kosmas, a wise and intelligent man, said to him: 'I have to give salutary advice to a friend, [264] but if you are unwilling to heed me when I offer advantageous counsels, you will quickly learn how great a mistake you have made when, after plunging yourself and all your people into the most severe danger, you come to grief. For you cannot withstand so great and strong a power.' Dandulf realised the patrician was showing him the path he should take; he accepted his exhortation and concluded a treaty. He instructed the rulers of the apostate themes to return to their former allegiance and acknowledge their own emperor. When they had returned to obedience profound peace reigned over the affairs of Italy and of Longobardia.

6. Symeon, the chieftain of the Bulgars, became over-confident on account of the many victories he had won against the Romans and began to dream of becoming their emperor. He sent to Phatloum, hereditary ruler of the Africans,[18] urging him to despatch a fleet against the imperial city, promising that he would come through Thrace leading a powerful army.

---

[14] We do not know the exact date at which the theme of Calabria was created; it was, however, prior to 950: Oikonomides, *Listes*, 356. If the title attributed by Skylitzes to Eustathios and John Mouzalon (or Byzalon) is official, these are the first known strategoi of that theme.

[15] This agreement (only mentioned by Skylitzes) would have been made in 920: Vasiliev and Canard, *Byzance et les Arabes*, II.1:228.

[16] John would have been levying very heavy taxes to pay the tribute owing to the Moslems of Africa. He was contemplating a revolt against the emperor when he was killed by those under his supervision in 921–2: V. von Falkenhausen, *La dominazione bizantina nell' Italia meridionale dal IX all' XI secolo* (Bari, 1978), 102–3.

[17] In 935 the patrician Kosmas was sent to Landulph, prince of Capua and Benevento, who had rebelled a second time. According to Haldon, 'Military administration', 202–352, at 235–7, Kosmas went with an army of 1,453 cavalrymen: Falkenhausen, *Dominazione*, 131–2.

[18] At this time the Maghreb was dominated by the Fatimid al-Mahdi: *Islamic Egypt, 640–1517*, ed. C. F. Petry (*The Cambridge History of Egypt*, 1, Cambridge, 1998), 129–30.

Then, when the two forces came together, they would besiege the capital by land and water and share her riches equally, whereupon he would return home leaving Phatloum at Constantinople. The Bulgars sailed to Africa unnoticed, where Symeon's proposals met with approval. They took some eminent Saracens to ratify the agreement with them but, on the way home, they ran into some Calabrians who sent them to Byzantium together with the Saracens. When the emperor (Romanos the Elder) saw them and learnt all about their common strategy, he realised what a sea of troubles he would have experienced had it been realised. He considered it necessary to restrain the Saracens from this present endeavour by means of magnanimity and benefits. He flung the Bulgars into prison but honoured the Saracens with extravagant gifts. He even sent sumptuous presents to their ruler and returned the men unharmed. He told them to declare to their master that this was the way the Roman emperors knew how to reward their enemies. He apologised for the annual tribute, [265] saying that the delay was not due to a postponement or deferment of payment, but to the disturbance which at that time had the region in its grip. The Saracens went running back to their own ruler, reporting on how they had fared when they were with the emperor and singing the praises of his benevolence to them. They handed over the presents they had brought to Phatloum and he was so pleased with everything he heard that he remitted half the tribute that the Romans owed him, cutting eleven thousand from the twenty-two thousand [pieces of gold]. That is how much the Romans gave to the Saracens from that time until the proclamation of Nikephoros.[19] And as long as the land had wise and just rulers, their subjects led an untroubled life and the tribute owing to the Saracens was easily paid. But once the task of ruling was entrusted to unjust and greedy men, their subjects experienced hard times and the treaty with the Saracens no longer held fast. Then came Krinites Chaldos, appointed commander of Calabria by [Constantine VII] Porphyrogennnetos.[20] The Saracens of Africa and Sicily were then at the point of being completely exhausted both by famine and also by their war against the Saracens of Cyrene. Motivated by pure greed [Krinites] aided them to recover while he severely maltreated those under his authority. What he did was to buy up all the necessities of life at a ridiculous price from the people of the land then sell them dearly

---

[19] The truth of the matter is that the Fatimids needed peace in order to accomplish their grand design of conquering Egypt, which they succeeded in doing by 969: *Islamic Egypt*, ed. Petry, 133–41.
[20] Once Constantine was rid of the Lekapenoi he brought in some new men, including Krinites, who was sent to Calabria in 945: Falkenhausen, *Dominazione*, 103.

to the Saracens – who paid his price without arguing. They disbursed gold generously, pressed as they were between the two millstones of famine and war. But Krinites was relieved of his command by Constantine; having suffered the confiscation of his fortune he grew old and died in disgrace. Now, during the war, the Romans had accepted deserters fleeing from Carthage, and these the Carthaginians made no effort to reclaim. In fact, they had even waived the annual tribute, perhaps for fear that the Romans would take offence and prevent the purchase of the necessities of life, thus putting [the Saracens] in danger of being destroyed by famine. But afterwards, when the war was over, they demanded both the deserters [266] and the tribute and, when nobody paid any attention to them, they broke the peace treaty; each day they sailed over and ravaged Calabria.

7. Constantine, who was now emperor, had not the slightest wish to treat the Saracens as gently as his father-in-law had done nor to renew the peace treaty. His preference was to have the matter decided by war, so he assembled a battle-worthy force, put the patrician Malakenos in charge of it and sent it off to Calabria with orders to join forces with the commander of the region, Paschalios, who was mentioned a little earlier.[21] Together with him they were to wait in readiness for the war which the Carthaginians and Sicilians were threatening. Makroioannes was put in command of the fleet that was sent along. When [the soldiers] arrived in the land, they inflicted a myriad evils on the people there; they went looting and committing other atrocities which even the enemy would hesitate to perpetrate. When the emir of the Saracens, Aboulchare,[22] heard this (for Phatloum was already dead), he encouraged his men and urged them to have no fear of an army which could treat its own people with such brutality. He provoked a great battle and gained a splendid, glorious victory in which even the senior officers only just escaped being taken alive.

8. After this, the emperor Constantine sent John Pilatos, the asecretis, to hold peace talks with the Saracens. As it was not their custom to take advantage of their victories, but to conclude a peace while they held the upper hand,[23] they were willing listeners and a short-term peace agreement was concluded. However, once this expired they sailed across and were ravaging Calabria again, so Constantine sent another expedition

---

[21] It was in 951 that Malakenos was sent to reinforce Paschalios, the strategos of Calabria. Both were defeated near Gerace by the governor of Sicily, Hasan, on 7 May 952: Falkenhausen, *Dominazione*, 82–3; A. A. Vasiliev, *Byzance et les Arabes*, 11: *Les relations politques de Byzance et des Arabes à l'époque de la dynastie macédonienne*, ed. M. Canard (CBHB 2, 1, Brussels, 1968), 366–8.

[22] Hasan, the governor of Sicily, had received reinforcements from al-Manlur, the successor of al-Mahdi.

[23] Unusual praise from the hand of a Roman!

against them, by land and by sea. The navy was under the command of Krambeas[24] (that was his surname) and of Moroleon ('Leo the Mad') [267] while the patrician Marianos Argyros[25] was in charge of the land forces. They arrived at Hidrous,[26] drew their boats up onto the shore and prepared for the voyage to Sicily. Now the Saracens were disturbed by the rumour [of this] – rumour which makes mountains out of molehills and reports things as yet more terrifying than they really are. They were frightened that the sudden appearance of the enemy nearby might betoken some disaster for themselves, for they were as yet unprepared. Panic-stricken, they abandoned their camp, fled out of Reggio[27] and passed over to Sicily. As they were approaching Palermo, they encountered a severe storm; their boats were capsized by the waves (or rather by Christ who is God, blasphemed by them) and they all perished. Then they made a treaty with the Romans and peace was maintained until the accession of Phokas.[28]

9. As soon as he was proclaimed emperor, considering it indecent to pay tribute to the Saracens,[29] he sent Manuel against them with a contingent of troops, as we said. Manuel was quite young and better suited to be in the ranks than to be in a position of command. He was also addicted to several bad habits and paid no attention whatsoever to those who gave him good advice. By getting himself and the entire army enclosed in some rugged and inaccessible part of Sicily, he brought about its entire destruction. The droungarios of the fleet, the patrician Niketas, a eunuch, was taken alive and sent off to Africa, a prisoner. Such was the catastrophe which befell Manuel, and that was how he was responsible for the annihilation of the whole army.[30]

10. In that year the emperor sent the magister John Tzimiskes, already appointed domestic of the scholai for the east, against Cilicia. When he

---

[24] This is the only mention of this person, otherwise unknown. There was a property of this name in Thessalonike: P. Gautier, 'Le typikon du Christ Sauveur Pantocrator', *REB*, 32 (1974), 121.
[25] Marianos had participated in the overthrow of Romanos Lekapenos (above, reign of Constantine VII, cc. 1 and 3).
[26] Otranto.
[27] Reggio in Calabria.
[28] In fact Marianos embarked in 955 with soldiers from Thrace and Macedonia. He won a victory over the Neapolitans, then over the Arabs, before suffering a severe defeat at the hands of the latter in 957–8: Falkenhausen, *Dominazione*, 83–4.
[29] There was the added consideration that the emperor could count on the support of the Christians living on the eastern side of the island; they had continued their resistance well after the fall of Taormina.
[30] Leo the Deacon, 66–8 (tr. 115–17), gives a detailed report of this unfortunate campaign. Manuel was somewhat successful at first but he became overconfident, letting himself be surprised, routed and killed at Rametta in October 964.

came to the town of Adana[31] [268] he encountered a considerable number of hand-picked Hagarenes gathered from all over Cilicia. He joined battle with them and thoroughly routed them. Some of them were hewn in pieces according to the rules of war but a portion of the army, about five thousand in number, dismounted and took refuge on foot on a very rugged and precipitous mountain. Taking full advantage of their location, they stoutly repelled their assailants. John surrounded them and, since there was no approaching them on horseback, he ordered his men to dismount and then he advanced together with them, on foot. He prevailed against the foe and slew every one, for not a man got away and blood ran down the mountainside onto the plain like a river; it is on account of this incident that the mountain is called 'the mountain of blood'. This accomplishment enhanced the reputation of John yet more; it was the beginning of the complete defeat of the Saracens.[32]

11. In July of the second year of his reign, seventh year of the indiction, Nikephoros advanced against Cilicia with a massive army of Romans together with Iberian and Armenian allies.[33] Theophano and her children were with him too. He left her in a fortress known as Drizion[34] before entering Cilicia and then advanced into that region where he destroyed the cities of Anazarbos, Rhossos[35] and Adana in addition to no small number of other fortresses. He hesitated to approach Tarsus or Mopsuestia[36] as winter was already drawing on. He left an adequate detachment there and withdrew to pass the winter in Cappadocia.

12. At the beginning of spring he advanced into Cilicia again where he divided the army into two parts: he left his brother Leo [269] to besiege Tarsus with one part, while he took the other one and advanced on Mopsuestia. There he conducted a vigorous siege and, with famine working in his favour, was able to take part of the city. This city is divided

---

[31] One of the main fortified towns of Cilicia: F. Hild and M. Restle, *Kappadokien (Kappadokia, Charsianon, Sebasteia und Lykandos)* (TIB, 2, Vienna, 1981), 154–8.

[32] By annihilating the best soldiers of the emir Sayf ad-Doula this victory prepared the way for the emperor's wars of annexation: M. Canard, *Histoire de la dynastie des Hamdanides de Jazira et de Syrie* (Paris, 1953), 818–19.

[33] July 964, but according to Yahya of Antioch, 1, 793, the emperor must have set out earlier since he utterly defeated the army of the emir of Tarsus between 16 May and 14 June. Yahya's date is to be preferred because the commanders avoided fighting in Cilicia in the hottest times of the year. Nikephoros Phokas relied on the heavy cavalry known as *kataphraktoi*: McGeer, *Byzantine warfare*, 301–17.

[34] The ruins of this fortress lie close to Nigde: Hild and Restle, *Kappadokien*, 172–3.

[35] A port to the south of Alexandria: Hild and Restle, *Kappadokien*, 392–3.

[36] One of the oldest towns of Asia Minor, located on the banks of the Pyramos. It was often fought over by the Arabs and Romans in the seventh and eighth century: Hild and Restle, *Kappadokien*, 351–9.

in two by the river Saros, giving it the appearance of two cities.[37] The one part he took, as we said but, when it fell, the Saracens fled to the other one, burning everything in the captured half. The emperor intensified the siege and the other half fell to him; nobody escaped from there. But now Leo, the emperor's brother who was besieging Tarsus, suffered a setback. He sent out a detachment of his army under the command of Monasteriotes[38] to gather forage and other necessities of life. They had posted no guards and were well spread out when the men of Tarsus sallied forth by night without them being in the least aware of it; these fell on the dispersed soldiers and brought down no small number of them, including Monasteriotes himself. But when the people of Tarsus became aware of the fall of Mopsuestia, exhausted by siege and famine, they sent a delegation to Leo. They begged the emperor to let them go unharmed if they would surrender their city. Having permitted each man to carry away a specified amount of booty, he[39] took possession of all the remaining wealth of the city himself.[40]

13. Three days after the city was taken a very large fleet arrived from Egypt to relieve Tarsus, filled with grain and other necessities of life. It was prevented from approaching land and discharging its cargo by the soldiers who had been posted by the emperor to guard the coast. Since they were unable [270] in these circumstances to be of any use, the ships returned. Many of them were wrecked either by stormy winds or by the attacks of the imperial warships.

14. After pillaging and burning down the remaining cities of Cilicia the emperor returned to Constantinople in October, ninth year of the indiction, bringing the gates of Tarsus and of Mopsuestia with him. These he had covered with gold on the surface and made an offering of them to the

---

[37] Setting out again in November 964, Nikephoros captured Adana, Anabarza and more than twenty other strongholds before appearing before the walls of Mopsuestia. A difficult siege ensued, but the emperor succeeded by placing mines under the two towers, which collapsed: Leo the Deacon, 52–3 (tr. 101–3). The city fell 13 July 965, the Romans taking a multitude of prisoners; Yahya of Antioch, I, 795–6. Under the command of a strategos, a garrison was installed in what was to be the capital of a new theme, the existence of which is attested by the *Taktikon Scorialensis*: Hild and Hellenkemper, *Kilikien,* 354; Oikonomides, *Listes,* 359.

[38] Yahya of Antioch does not mention this (no doubt minor) occurrence.

[39] Leo or the emperor? The text is unclear; probably the latter, competent to make such decisions.

[40] Nikephoros became master of Tarsus in August 965; here too he installed the strategos of a theme: Hild and Hellenkemper, *Kilikien*, 431. The city was particularly well fortified for it was encircled by two very high walls and protected by a moat fed by the river Kydnos: Leo the Deacon, 51–61 (tr. 101–9), gives a different account in which he distinguishes between an expedition of autumn 954 during which Mosuestia fell, and one in the summer of 965 which saw the taking of Tarsus. The only Moslem leader who sent any aid to his correligionists in Cilicia was Kafur, the Ikhchidite master of Egypt: Canard, *Hamdanides*, 823.

city; one pair was set up on the acropolis, the other on the walls by the Golden Gate.[41] He also offered to God as a gift and as a tithe of his expedition the precious crosses captured when Stypeiotes, then domestic of the scholai, was besieging Tarsus and brought his entire force to utter destruction by lack of foresight.[42] These were deposited in the all-sacred Church of the Wisdom of the Divine Word.[43]

15. In that same second year of his reign Nikephoros restored the entire island of Cyprus to Roman rule and expelled the Hagarenes from it by the hand of the patrician Niketas Chalkoutzes, the commander.[44] In the third year of his reign the emperor made another expedition against Syria at the beginning of spring. When he arrived before Antioch he did not attack it, in the hope that the mere mention of his name would terrify the Antiochenes in their trepidation at what had befallen the cities of Cilicia. So he passed it by and penetrated into the inner parts of Syria where he devastated many cities and much land down the coast towards Lebanon, returning in the month of December. [271] Now the Antiochenes were confidently ready to do battle because a considerable number of men from the surrounding countryside had come into and reinforced the city. The Roman army was suffering from a shortage of supplies[45] [and had to contend with] extensive marshes (from which there was no egress) caused by incessant rain falling from the sky, so the emperor retreated empty-handed and came back to the capital. Along with him came the tile which bore an imprint not-made-with-hands of the features of Christ our God found in Hierapolis[46] when it was taken;[47] also a lock of the hair of John the Baptist, matted with blood.

[41] M. McCormick, *Eternal victory: triumphal rulership in late antiquity, Byzantium, and the early medieval west* (Cambridge, MA, 1986), 169–71.
[42] Above, Basil I, c. 25.
[43] On the crosses of Tarsus : N. Thierry, 'Le culte de la croix dans l'empire byzantin du VIIe au Xe siècle dans ses rapports avec la guerre contre l'infidèle. Nouveaux témoignanges archéologiques', *Rivista di Studi Bizantini e Slavi*, 1 (1981), 224–5. This incident achieved great fame; the cross is portrayed on f.152r of Codex Matrit. Bibl.nat. Vitr.26–2, the 'Madrid Skylitzes'.
[44] On Chalkoutzes: reign of Constantine VII as an adult, c. 9; reign of Romanos II, c. 5. As Cyprus was neutral the Moslems and the Romans shared the island's revenues: C. P. Kyrris, 'The nature of the Arab-Byzantine relations in Cyprus', *Graeco-arabica*, 3 (1984), 149–75. In 965 Nikephoros took advantage of the empire's ascendancy to annex the island again, which he did without great difficulty.
[45] Thurn's text is less than coherent here.
[46] Membidj-Hierapolis was situated to the north-east of Aleppo, halfway towards Edessa; it was besieged in October 966: Canard, *Hamdanides*, 825. The city was occupied briefly by the Romans in 1069 under Romanos IV Diogenes.
[47] Leo the Deacon, 70–1 (tr. 121), says that it was from Edessa that Nikephoros removed the miraculous tile (*keramidion*) which he ordered to be set in a casket decorated with gold and to be deposited in the palace church of the Theotokos at the Lighthouse. Leo the Deacon, 165–6 (tr. 207–8), is again at odds with Skylitzes concerning the hair of the prodromos (John the Baptist). He says that John Tzimiskes removed this relic in the course of his campaign in Syria in 975.

260   *John Skylitzes: a synopsis of Byzantine history*

16. That is the kind of man Nikephoros was; such was the strategy he employed and that is the extent to which he increased the Roman domains, for he captured more than a hundred cities and fortresses in Cilicia, Syria and Phoenicia in Lebanon, of which the largest and most significant were Anazarbos, Adana, Mopsuestia, Tarsus, Pagras,[48] Synnephion,[49] Laodikeia[50] and Aleppo, while he obliged Phoenician Tripoli and Damascus to pay tribute. Nevertheless, he was hated by all men and everybody longed to see his fall; this narrative will list the reasons why in due course.

17. When Nikephoros was returning to the capital from Antioch,[51] as he was crossing the Taurus [mountain range] at a place in the heart of the mountains known locally as the Black Mountain, he built a fortress on a practically impregnable hilltop. [272] He gave Michael Bourtzes[52] the title of patrician[53] and left him in the fortress, naming him commander of the Black Mountain.[54] His orders were to keep constant watch and to use every means to prevent the Antiochenes from coming out to obtain the necessities of life. He also left a dynamic slave named Peter, one of his eunuchs, whom he appointed camp commander in Cilicia,[55] with orders to disperse the army for the winter and await his return in the following spring. It was said that the emperor could have taken Antioch by assault but that he did not want to; that he purposely delayed and postponed taking it out

---

[48] This fortress commanded the approach to Antioch from the north. It was on the road which crosses the Amanos coming from Adana by way of Alexandretta.
[49] An unidentified fortress near to Antioch: Honigmann, *Ostgrenze*, 96, n. 7, and Hild and Hellenkemper, *Kilikien*, 423.
[50] Laodikeia in Syria, now Lattakeia.
[51] After leading his army in northern Syria, Nikephoros left Antioch 22 October 968, having remained no more than two days before that city: Yahya of Antioch, 1, 815.
[52] First mention of this family which was to distinguish itself in the following century; a family whose origins remain obscure, maybe from Arab stock: J.-C. Cheynet and J.-F. Vannier, *Etudes prosopographiques* (ByzSorb 5, Paris, 1986), 7–122, at 15–16 = Cheynet, *Société*, 341–7.
[53] This is a very high dignity for the strategos of a small theme; maybe this man was related to the Phokai. Or it may be that Nikephoros wanted to bring to his side a member of the Arab-Christian aristocracy in order to gain the support of a section of the population of Antioch. This would explain why Michael Bourtzes was repeatedly appointed duke of that city when it was restored to Roman rule. But see Holmes, *Basil II*, 330–47, who does not think Michael Bourtzes was at Antioch as duke under Tzimiskes.
[54] The Black Mountain or Amanos lies between the plain of Antioch and the Mediterranean coast. Several monks chose this wooded area as their place of retreat: Hild and Hellenkemper, *Kilikien*, 174–5. There were Georgians among those living there: W. Z. Djobaze, *Materials for the study of Georgian monasteries in the western environs of Antioch on the Orontes* (Louvain, 1976).
[55] *Stratopedarches*. That Nikephoros should have appointed one of the eunuchs of his household head of the army rather suggests that he did not have complete confidence in the officers he left behind. He appears to have set aside John Tzimiskes, his domestic of the scholai. Peter, being a eunuch, could not be appointed domestic. He is sometimes erroneously named Peter Phokas in the literature: Cheynet, *Société*, 488.

of fear engendered by a rumour that was going the rounds. In fact, everybody was saying that the emperor would die at the same time as Antioch was taken. It was indeed because of this that he did not approach Antioch himself and that he ordered Peter and Bourtzes to take no action against it whatsoever.[56] After making these arrangements, he returned to the capital, as we said. But Bourtzes was lying close to Antioch and he yearned to obtain an immortal reputation for himself. Paying scant attention to the emperor's stipulations, day and night he was racking his brains to find a way of capturing the city. He went a number of times and held treaty negotiations with the Antiochenes but they were quite conceited and they rejected his proposals. So he secretly befriended one of the Saracens (it was Aulax) whom he corrupted with gifts and promises until he was able to discover the dimensions of one of the western towers of Antioch known as Kalla.[57] Then, with him, he had ladders constructed capable of reaching the top of the tower and, on a moonless, rainy night, he surreptitiously leaned the ladders against the wall. Up he went with three hundred of his men and slew those guarding that tower and the one next to it. When the three hundred had a secure hold on the two towers he promptly sent a messenger to the camp commander urging him to make haste and come with the entire army for the city was already taken. When Peter received the message he hesitated and delayed, fearing the emperor's wrath and the punishment he might suffer for disobeying his orders. But Bourtzes [273] insisted, sending one messenger after another, demanding his speedy arrival and letting it be known that he could not hold out much longer against the forces surrounding him. For when the Antiochenes learnt that the towers had been seized they came running from all sides and tried to retake them. They hurled missiles of every kind, used various engines,[58] lit fires underneath and took other action such as men have to take when they are in danger of being destroyed, together with their wives and children, and also of losing a city superior to all other cities of the East. The

---

[56] Here Skylitzes' narrative (which echoes rumours hostile to Nikephoros) is less than coherent for it has already been explained that the rain and the number of defenders caused the emperor not to attempt an assault. Yahya of Antioch, 1, 822, says the Antiochenes were no longer on their guard and that there were divisions in the garrison.

[57] Antioch was protected by such extensive defence-works that it was almost impossible to take it by assault. The number of its towers was between 136 (Mas'udi) and 450 (*Gesta Francorum*): all refs. in K.-P. Todt, 'Region und griechisch-orthodoxes Patriarchat von Antiocheia in mittelbyzantinischer Zeit und im Zeitalter der Kreuzzüge (969–1204)', unpublished thesis (Wiesbaden, 1998), 483–4. Thus in 1097, at the time of the First Crusade, Bohemond too could only gain possession of the capital of Syria by coming to an agreement with one of the defenders who was responsible for a section of the walls.

[58] An addition found only in MS B has to be inserted here to make sense.

camp commander, fearing that the Roman state might suffer the loss of so many such brave men and of such a city through his disobedience, reluctantly and against his will made haste and arrived with the entire army. He found the troops with Bourtzes[59] in very sore straits for they had been surrounded for three days and nights. But when the Antiochenes heard of his approach they lost heart and relaxed their efforts. Seizing his chance, Bourtzes went down to the gate, cut the bar of the retaining device with his sword and opened the gates. Peter entered with his entire force and that was how Antioch the great, the illustrious, was taken.[60] Nikephoros ought to have rejoiced at the capture of such a city when he heard of it and left his own fate in the hands of God. On the contrary: it made him sick at heart. He brought charges against the camp commander and, as for Bourtzes, not only did he refuse to acknowledge his initiative and courage and grant him rewards befitting his excellence; he roundly insulted him, relieved him of his command and obliged him to remain at home.

18. For this and other reasons which we are about to mention, Nikephoros came to be hated and abominated by everybody. Even at the very beginning when there was a movement in his favour, his soldiers were committing thousands of confiscations [274] and he did nothing to stop them. 'It is hardly surprising if a few misbehave in such a large body of men,' he remarked. Then, when he entered the city, many citizens, both high and low, were plundered without him doing a thing to bring the culprits to justice. He simply overlooked their misdeeds and took pleasure in the atrocities the undisciplined troops permitted themselves, mistreating the very citizens who had made no small contribution to his rise to power. Then when he went off on one of his many expeditions, he maltreated his subjects atrociously, not only by imposing additional taxes[61] and requisitioning all kinds of supplies, but also by unimaginable plundering. In addition to what has been said, he also suppressed a portion of the customary perquisites of the Senate, allegedly because he was short of money for the wars, and he completely suppressed the income which some of the God-

---

[59] It is known that he had an Armenian officer at his side whose name was Isaac Brachamios: Cheynet and Vannier, *Etudes prosopographiques*, 19 = Cheynet, *Société*, 377–9.
[60] 28 October 969: Yahya of Antioch, 1, 823. The camp commander Peter continued his march towards Aleppo and got from the emir Gargawaih a treaty signed in December 969/January 970 which made his emirate a dependency of the empire. This permitted the Romans to levy commercial taxes even on Aleppo: Canard, *Hamdanides*, 832–6; W. Farag, 'The Aleppo question: a Byzantine–Fatimid conflict of interests in northern Syria in the later tenth century', *BMGS*, 14 (1990), 44–60.
[61] On the fiscal policy of Nikephoros, see P. Magdalino, 'The Byzantine army and the land: from *stratiotikon ktema* to military *pronoia*', *To empolemo Buzantio (Byzantium at war, ninth to the twelfth centuries)*, ed. N. Oikonomides (Athens, 1997), 15–36.

fearing emperors had instituted as grants to religious houses and churches. He even promulgated a law that churches were not to increase their real estate holdings,[62] for (he wickedly alleged) the bishops were disposing of income which should be going to the poor and the soldiers were in need.[63] But, worst of all, he made a law (to which some feeble-minded and flattering bishops subscribed) that no bishop was to be elected or consecrated without his knowledge and permission. And when a bishop died he would send out an imperial agent with orders to control the expenses [of the diocese] and he would confiscate [the income] in excess of expenses. He made some other regulations which could by no means whatsoever be justified by need, of which it would be beyond the wit and tongue of a powerful narrator to give a detailed report.

He endeavoured to establish a law that soldiers who died in war were to be accorded martyrs' honours, thus making the salvation of the soul uniquely and exclusively dependent on being in action on military service. He was pressing the patriarch and the bishops to agree to this doctrine but some of them vigorously withstood him and frustrated his intent. They produced as evidence the canon of Basil [275] the Great which requires a man who has slain his enemy in battle to remain three years excommunicate.[64] He reduced the gold coin and devised the so-called *tetarteron*.[65] From then on there were two sizes of gold coin; for the collecting of

---

[62] This refers to the novel of 964 which forbade further donations of real estate to churches and monasteries. Nikephoros was motivated by the poor management of several monasteries which possessed quantities of arable land but were unable to exploit them for want of capital. On this passage: M. Kaplan, *Les hommes et la terre*, 434–5; McGeer, *Land legislation*, 86–96, gives an English translation of the novel together with all other documents dealing with real estate under the Macedonian emperors.

[63] The protection of soldiers was a major concern for the officers who were associated with the Phokai: Dagron and Mihàescu, *Traité*, 259–74.

[64] According to Canon XIII of Basil the Great, the penance is two years' exclusion from communion: N. Oikonomides, 'The concept of "Holy War" and two tenth-century Byzantine ivories', ed. Miller and Nesbitt, *Peace and war*, 62–86, at 65. Leo VI complained that the empire was at a disadvantage in not having anything equivalent to the Moslem jihad. He could have been echoing the complaints of the officers of the Eastern army, which included the Phokai. When Nikephoros made his suggestion, he ran into the objections of the upper echelons of both state and church: G. Dagron, 'Byzance et le modèle islamique au Xe siècle. A propos des *Constitutions Tactiques* de l'empereur Léon VI', *Comptes rendus des séances de l'Académie des Inscriptions et Belles-Lettres* (1983), 219–42, at 231–2. See also A. Kolia-Dermitzaki, *The Byzantine 'Holy War': the idea and propagation of religious war in Byzantium* (Athens, 1991) (in Greek but with a summary in English) and more recently J-Cl. Cheynet, 'La guerre sainte à Byzance au Moyen Âge: un malentendu' in *Regards croisés sur la guerre sainte. Guerre, religion et idéologie dans l'espace méditerranéen latin (XIe-XIIIe siècle)*, ed D. Baloup and Ph. Josserand, Toulouse 2006, 13–32.

[65] On the *tetarteron*: H. Ahrweiler, 'Nouvelle hypothèse sur le tétartèron et la politique monétaire de Nicéphore Phokas', *ZRVI*, 8 (1963), 19, repr. *Etudes sur les structures administratives et sociales de Byzance* (London, 1971), no. III; also M. Hendy, 'Light-weight solidi, tetartera, and the Book of the Eparch', *BZ*, 65 (1972), 57–80.

taxes he demanded the heavier one but used the small one for his expenditure. And though law and custom required that every [coin bearing] the emperor's effigy, even if it were of short weight, should be of equal value, he stipulated that his own should be preferred, thus lowering the value of others. For this reason his subjects suffered greatly from the exchange rates and the worst of it was that although the government oppressed them like this, the supply of commodities on the market was by no means assured. But it was the building of the palace wall which distressed the people more than any of the other things, exceedingly onerous though those were. There were many structures of size and beauty around the palace which he tore down in order to raise up an acropolis; a tyrant's dwelling over against the wretched citizens. He built warehouses and granaries with kitchens and bakehouses which he filled with provisions. It was foretold to him that he would die within the palace; apparently he was unaware that 'Except the Lord keep the city, the watchman waketh but in vain'.[66] When the wall was finished it happened that he died the very day on which the overseer of the building project brought the keys and handed them over.

19. In addition to the above there was something else which even further intensified the hatred in which he was held. At the very feast of the Holy Easter itself a skirmish occurred between members of the navy and some Armenians, in which many lives were lost and the magister Sisinnios, the eparch, was almost killed. From this event the rumour went the rounds that Nikephoros [276] was exasperated with the citizens whom he suspected of being responsible for the skirmish and that he was going to punish them by setting a trap for them on a day when the Hippodrome was functioning. And in fact, shortly afterwards, when the horse races were taking place, Nikephoros ordered some men to take naked swords and make pretence of fighting each other as though they were enemies, to entertain the audience. He wanted to show the citizens what a military skirmish was really like; perhaps to frighten them too. But when the 'skirmish' took place, the audience – knowing nothing of why it was being mounted – assumed that the current rumour was proving to be true. They charged up the exit ramps, which were all steep and treacherous, fell one on top of another and [many] died. They would all have died, trodden under foot by one another, if they had not noticed that the emperor was sitting on the throne, fearless and serene. When the mob saw him sitting

---

[66] Ps. 126:1b. MSS FH add: 'It happened that while they were building the palace wall, one night, somebody out there at sea on a boat called out: "Ah emperor, you are building ramparts; but even if you build up to the sky, the evil is within and your city is easily taken." They searched for a long time to find the man who uttered this cry, but found nothing.'

there, unmoved, and realised that what had taken place was not what he intended, they put an end to the stampede.

20. On the feast of the Ascension[67] of Christ, Nikephoros went in solemn procession to Pege, and on the return journey he received relatives of those who had lost their lives in the Hippodrome at the breadmakers' square.[68] They began rebuking him in an insulting manner. They called him unpunished murderer; defiled assassin, stained with the blood of his own people. They were pelting him with dirt and stones all the way to the forum of Constantine the Great. He would have been transfixed by fear if some more honourable citizens had not intervened, driven off the miscreants and accompanied him to the palace, singing his praises along the way. It was for this reason, that is, when he learnt that the citizens were hostile to him, that he built the [palace-] fortress. But there was no escaping his destiny; it was just when he thought he had set everything to rights for himself that his life was snatched away (we shall tell how at the appropriate moment).

In June of the fourth year of his reign, tenth year of the indiction, [the emperor] set out to visit the towns in Thrace[69] [277] and when he came to the Great Dyke[70] (as it is called) he wrote to Peter, the ruler of Bulgaria, to prevent the Turks from crossing the Danube to raid Roman land. [Peter] paid no attention to this but rather took every opportunity of doing the opposite; so Nikephoros raised Kalokyros (son of the prince[71] of Cherson) to the rank of patrician and sent him to Sphendoslav,[72] the ruler of Russia, to persuade him with promises of gifts and honours to campaign against the Bulgars.[73] The Russians agreed and set out against Bulgaria in the month of August, eleventh

---

[67] For the ceremonies of Ascension Day: *De caerim*, ed. Vogt, I, 101–5. The emperor processed to Pege. The route by which he returned is not known but a reception at the breadmakers is indicated for the second Monday after Easter (*ibid.*, 1.5, ed. Vogt, I, 44). The breadmakers' quarter was on the central avenue (Mese) between the forum of Theodosios and the forum of Constantine: Janin, *Constantinople*, 315.

[68] *He ton artoprateion agora.*

[69] This was in June 967. Skylitzes is not presenting things in chronological order. The same is true a little further on, when he reports the deaths of the patriarchs of Jerusalem and Antioch.

[70] This was a wall and ditch stretching 130 km to protect the Roman frontier, from Maritsa to lake Mandra: P. Soustal, *Thrakien (Thrake, Rodope und Haiminontos)* (TIB, 6, Vienna, 1991), 261–2.

[71] *Proteuon.* The theme of Cherson was more or less coterminous with the town of the same name at that time. As the most illustrious personage of the town in the Crimea, Kalokyros was obviously the appropriate person to negotiate with the Russians of Kiev.

[72] Prince of Kiev, the son of Olga but, unlike his mother, a pagan. While Nikephoros was negotiating with him, Spendosthlav had destroyed the Khazar state and destroyed Sarkel: *ODB*, III, 1979.

[73] Leo the Deacon, 63 (tr. 111–12), says Nikephoros promised 1,500 pounds of gold.

year of the indiction, the fifth year of Nikephoros' reign. They laid waste many of the Bulgars' cities and lands, collected a large amount of booty and then returned to their own lands.[74] They campaigned against Bulgaria again in the sixth year of his reign and did similar or even worse things than the first time.

At the twelfth hour of the night on 2 September, eleventh year of the indiction,[75] there was an exceptionally severe earthquake which badly damaged the Honoriad and Paphlagonia. There were fierce, burning winds in the month of May, the same year of the indiction, which destroyed the crops, even the vines and trees, with the result that in the twelfth year of the indiction there was an intense famine. The emperor (who ought to have been concerned for his subjects' well-being) now shabbily sold the imperial grain, profiting from the misfortune of those in need, and he congratulated himself as though it were some great deed that, when [grain] was selling for one gold piece a bushel, he ordered it to be sold for two. He certainly was not following in the footsteps of the emperor Basil the Macedonian. When *he* came to the church of the Great Apostles on the Sunday of Renewal[76] he saw some pious and decent citizens who were clearly depressed and downcast. He had them brought to him [278] and asked them why they were not wearing festal robes at this celebration but rather wore the gloomy look of men whose city was in great adversity. One of the citizens answered him: 'It is right and proper that you, majesty, and those around you should wear festal robes and rejoice, but not for those for whom the expectation of death is here. But maybe you are unaware that two bushels of grain are selling for one piece of gold on account of the ferocity of the winds?' At these words the emperor heaved a great sigh and shed sympathetic tears. He comforted them with generous aid, then went back up to the palace where he convened a meeting of the administrators of civic and imperial affairs. These he upbraided with many bitter reproaches and curses for not telling him about the shortage of grain and he immediately put

---

[74] This first campaign took place in the summer of 968. The Bulgars sent a delegation which was well received; Nikephoros required that Peter abdicate to enter a monastery and that he be succeeded by his son, Boris. The Russians were the more willing to depart as Kiev was under attack from the Patzinaks: Stephenson, *Balkan frontier*, 48–9.

[75] 2 September 967.

[76] The emperor used to go to St Sophia on the first Sunday after Easter: *De caerim*, 1.25, ed. Vogt, I, 90–1, and n. 91 which adds this observation: 'It should be known that on this Sunday after Easter the emperor proceeds in state, on horseback, to the Holy Apostles. This was decided recently.' Skylitzes has portrayed a procession in the time of Basil which had not yet taken place.

the imperial and public grain [reserves] on the market, stipulating that twelve [bushels] were to be sold for one piece of gold.[77] God approved of this good work and provided great abundance for men. But this was said to the credit of that emperor; Nikephoros rejoiced not in coming to the assistance of his subjects, but rather in seeing them afflicted; and not only he but Leo his brother too who, by trading in commodities,[78] filled the world with a host of varied woes. The citizens very willingly derided them for their sordid swindling. Once when the emperor came onto the plains to exercise the army a grey-headed fellow came by and tried to get himself enlisted in the army. [Nikephoros] said to him: 'Why are you, old fellow, in such a hurry to get yourself enlisted as one of my soldiers?' He boldly replied: 'Because I am much stronger now than when I was young.' 'How can that be?' asked the emperor. 'Because it used to require two asses to carry as much grain as you could purchase for one piece of gold; but under your government I can easily carry two gold pieces' worth of grain on my shoulders.'[79] Aware of the joke, the emperor went his way not in the least troubled by it.

21. After the cities of Syria and Cilicia were taken, the Saracens burnt John, archbishop of Jerusalem, alive because it was [279] at his instigation that Nikephoros might have been going to arrive there;[80] they also burnt the exquisite church of the Holy Sepulchre. The Antiochenes did likewise, slaughtering their archbishop, Christopher.[81] The brothers Gregory and Pankratios now took refuge with the emperor, having fled from their own

---

[77] Basil put an end to speculation on commodity prices by opening up the public granaries. In this way he re-established what seems to have been the normal price between the ninth and eleventh centuries in Constantinople: J.-C. Cheynet, E. Malamut and C. Morrisson, 'Prix et salaires dans les sources byzantines (Xe–XVe siècle)', *Hommes et richesses* (Paris, 1991), II, 339–74, at 357 and 361; Cheynet and Morrisson, *EHB* 823.

[78] Leo had been appointed logothete of the drome by his brother; the charge against him of profiteering had an adverse effect on the popularity of the emperor at the capital. This partly explains the somewhat feeble public reaction to the murder of Nikephoros.

[79] By this riposte the soldier states that in his youth the grain which two mules could carry (fifteen modii) was worth one piece of gold, which was a good price; whereas now he is old, two pieces of gold will only buy as much grain as can be carried on one shoulder, maybe two or three modii. This may be an exaggeration but there is little doubt that the price of grain had risen very sharply, perhaps by 600 per cent: *EHB*, 823.

[80] Yahya of Antioch, I, 799–802, gives more information about this murder, brought about by the personal intervention of the Arab governor of Jerusalem. Fearing for his life, the patriarch took refuge in the church of the Resurrection. The mob set fire to the church and the fire brought down the dome. The church was subsequently restored.

[81] The patriarch was killed by some of the leading Moslems on the pretext that he had incited the Greeks to take the city. The patriarchal residence and the church of Kassian were pillaged. The assassins were punished after Bourtzes took Antioch: Yahya of Antioch, I, 807–10; Habib Zayat, 'La Vie du patriarche melkite d'Antioche Christophore (*ob* 967) par le protospathaire Ibrahím b. Yuhanna. Document inédit du Xe siècle', *Proche Orient Chrétien*, 2 (1952), 11–38.

country of Taron.[82] He raised them to the rank of patrician and granted them estates which produced good revenues.[83] There was an eclipse of the sun on 22 December[84] about the third hour: the stars could be seen.

22. Having terminated her relations with Nikephoros, the empress Theophano sent one of Tzimiskes' men to summon him. Tzimiskes was kicking his heels on his own estate, the emperor having previously relieved him of his command as domestic on suspicion of something or other and commanded him to remain confined to his own estates. The messenger brought him from there, for the adulteress had arranged for him to receive letters permitting him to make the journey. He arrived at Chalcedon; the emperor, when asked whether he should enter the capital, replied that he should wait a while. But on the night of 11 December, thirteenth year of the indiction, AM 6478,[85] the empress sent and brought him into the port that had been hollowed out below the palace, from which she had him and all those who were with him brought up in a basket. There was the patrician Michael Bourtzes, the *taxiarches* Leo Abalantes, and of Tzimiskes' most trusted [comrades] Atzypotheodoros and two others. Up they went and entered the emperor's bedchamber, sword in hand. When they did not find him in the bed where they expected him to be, they thought they had been [280] betrayed and would have leapt to their death if they had not come across a manikin from the women's quarters and been led by him.[86] They chanced upon the emperor lying on the floor, on a mattress of scarlet-dyed felt and bearskin which he had received from his uncle, Michael Maleinos,[87] the monk. He had only just gone to sleep and was not in the least aware of the arrival of those who were about to slay him. Tzimiskes roused him with a kick. When he was awake he placed his right elbow on the ground and raised his head just as Leo Abalantes struck him a terrible wound with his naked sword on his unprotected head (for his

---

[82] Taron is a region of Armenia to the south-west of lake Van, the capital of which is Mus. It became a theme (mentioned in the Taktikon of the Escorial) after annexation: Oikonomides, *Listes*, 355–6.

[83] Such is the origin of the powerful family of the Taronitai which allied itself with the Komnenoi in the second half of the eleventh century: *ODB*, III, 2012–13. Gregory became duke of Thessalonike under Basil II; see also below, Michael IV, c. 26.

[84] 22 December 967.

[85] 11 December 969.

[86] R. Guilland has carefully reconstructed the atmosphere in the capital at the time of this murder and traced the steps of the conspirators: they looked for the emperor in his bedroom at the Great Palace before discovering his place of retreat: Guilland, *Topographie*, 1, 334–67.

[87] This is the only time Skylitzes mentions the maternal uncle of Nikephoros, a saint who died 12 July 961. There is a *Life* of him written shortly after his death by one of his disciples: (most recently) A. Laiou, 'The general and the saint: Michael Maleinos and Nikephoros Phokas', *EUYUCIA, Mélanges offerts à Hélène Ahrweiler*, ed. M. Balard *et al.* (Paris, 1998), 399–412.

head-covering had fallen off as he was getting up) and his skull was split. Then they got him up out of the bed and brought him to Tzimiskes who was sitting on the imperial bed. They abused him, they reproached him, they cursed him, but the only thing he said was 'Lord have mercy' and 'Mother of God, help!' Finally, when the palace footmen got wind of what was going on and a group began to form of would-be attackers, they slew him. They cut off his head and showed it through a window to those who were rushing to his assistance. These were so taken aback by this that it allowed Tzimiskes' party to do all they wanted to do, without fear or danger of reprisals.

23. It is said that, ten days before his death, the emperor found a document lying in his chamber, warning him to protect himself as he was the object of a conspiracy led by Tzimiskes. Also that, [281] in the evening before his murder, some clergyman gave him a letter the purport of which was: 'Protect yourself, O emperor, for no small danger is being prepared for you this very night.' There are others who say that the emperor thought the letter was a petition and read it not; others that he read it but was indifferent concerning his safety, because his own destiny stood in his way, and after he was dead [the letter] was found bearing that writing. Yet others claim that he read it and ordered the protovestiarios to look into the matter and check the security. He also wrote to his brother, Leo, who was at home, to collect an armed band and come to the palace as quickly as possible. When Leo received the missive he did not open it as he was playing at dice with some people and enjoying a run of good luck; he put it under a cushion in his couch. He came across the letter when the game was over, and when he had got the sense of what the writing meant he put together a company such as the occasion called for and set off for the palace. But when he got to the western end of the Hippodrome he heard some people saying to each other that the emperor Nikephoros would be dead [by now] and there were voices in the highways and in the byways acclaiming John. He was immobilised by this unexpected turn of events and could think of no bold stroke, so he came as quickly as possible to the Great Church together with Nikephoros, his son. That is what they say; true or false I cannot tell, but Nikephoros certainly died, murdered in the palace.

He was fifty-seven years old at the time. In the evening of the same day he was buried at John's command, in the very late evening. They put him in a wooden coffin that came to hand and brought him to the sacred church of the Apostles in the middle of the night and buried him in one of the imperial sarcophagi there in the heroon, where the body of the divine and ever-memorable Constantine lies. This is what he looked like: his features inclined to dark rather than pale. He had thick, dark hair, black eyes that were thoughtful and concerned, beneath thick eyebrows. The nose was of average size and thickness, slightly turned up at the end. The moustache (no larger than it ought to be) merged into the beard on his cheeks, which was of loose texture and grey. [282] The body was stooped but robust, the chest and shoulders unusually wide. His strength and vigour equalled the famous Hercules and he outstripped every man of his generation for wisdom and intelligence.

John, bishop of Melitene,[88] inscribed these words on his sarcophagus:

> Who once sliced men more sharply than the sword
> Is victim of a woman and a glaive.
> Who once retained the whole world in his power
> Now small, is housed in but a yard of earth.
> Whom once it seems by wild beasts was revered
> His wife has slain as though he were a sheep.
> Who chose to sleep but little in the night
> Now sleeps the lasting slumber of the tomb.
> A bitter sight; good ruler, rouse yourself!
> Take footmen, horsemen, archers to the fight,
> The regiments and units of your host –
> For Russians, fully armed, assail our ports,
> The Scyths are anxious to be slaughtering
> While every people does your city harm
> Who once was frightened by your graven face
> Before the gates of your Byzantium.
> Do not ignore these things; cast off the stone
> Which now detains you here and stone the beasts,
> Repel the gentiles; give us, built in stone,
> A firm foundation, solid and secure.
> Or if you would not leave your tomb a while,
> At least cry out from earth against the foe –
> For that alone might scatter them in flight. [283]
> If not, make room for us there in your tomb
> For death, as you well know, is safety and
> Salvation for th'entire Christian folk,
> Nikephoros, who vanquished all but Eve.

That is how it goes. [89]

---

[88] John of Melitene, a former soldier and a great admirer of Nikephoros, must be distinguished from John the Geometres, a faithful friend of Basil the parakoiomenos: M. Lauxtermnan, 'John Geomètre, poet and soldier', *B*, 68 (1998), 356–80.

[89] MSS ACE only.

CHAPTER 15

John I Tzimiskes [969–976]

1. [284] After Nikephoros died, John Tzimiskes assumed responsibility for the Roman government with Basil and Constantine, the sons of Romanos [II], as co-emperors; Basil was in the seventh year of his life, Constantine in his fifth.[1] [John] immediately summoned Basil the parakoimomenos[2] by night and made him his associate in power. It was in no small measure owing to this man that the emperor Nikephoros gained the imperial throne, for which he was appointed president [of the Senate] – a position which did not exist before; Nikephoros was the first to name anybody to it.[3] [John made this man his associate] because he had been involved in affairs of state for many years, under Romanos [I] the Elder, his own father, then under his half-brother, Constantine [VII] Porphyrogennetos. Many times he had campaigned against the Hagarenes[4] and he was especially skilled in smoothly adapting himself to difficult situations. He quickly took matters in hand and expelled all those who remained in favour of Nikephoros. He exiled Leo the kouropalates[5] to Lesbos and his son, Nikephoros the vestes, to Imbros.[6] He wrote to Bardas the

[1] There is something wrong with the arithmetic here, because in December 969 Basil was more than ten years old, his brother seven. Nor do these figures agree with the regnal years; Basil had been emperor in name since 22 April 960, Constantine since March 962. John Tzimiskes was forty-five at this time: Leo the Deacon, 96, trad. 146.
[2] Basil appears to have taken no active part in Tzimiskes' plot; nor did he try to prevent it: Leo the Deacon, ed. Hase, 94; hence he was able to retain his position as parakoimomenos.
[3] The exact time at which this new senatorial office (*proedros*) was created is not known; certainly it was after the accession of Nikephoros. Basil used the title on his seal: 'Basil, very glorious proedros of the Senate and parakoimomenos to the emperor beloved of Christ': Zacos II, no. 794. It is also found on a chalice now in St Mark's, Venice, and on a reliquary, the famous Staurotheke of Limbourg.
[4] In particular he had been joint commander with John Tzimiskes in 958 of an army which had prevailed over Saif ad-Doula and taken Samosata on the Euphrates: M. Canard, *Histoire de la dynastie des Hamdanides de Jazira et de Syrie* (Paris, 1953), 795.
[5] Leo the Deacon, 95, trad. 144, reproves Leo for failing to avenge his brother (even though an army loyal to the Phokades was stationed at Constantinople) and for not dipping into his immense riches to stop Tzimiskes in his tracks.
[6] An island in the north-east of the Aegean Sea which, together with Tenedos, controls the entry to the Dardanelles: J. Koder, *Aigaion Pelagos (Die nordliche Agais)* (TIB, 10, Vienna, 1998), 177–9. Both these islands are now part of Turkey.

younger,[7] then duke of Chaldia and Coloneia, relieving him of his command and transferring him to Amaseia.[8] And he dismissed those others who held civil or military commands from their positions, appointing his own men, supporters of the new emperor.[9] [285] He permitted those whom Nikephoros had exiled to return, especially those bishops he had exiled for refusing to sign the bill by which that emperor sought to restrict and humiliate the church, as this narrative has already reported.

2. After taking these measures, in that same night the emperor, accompanied by only a few men, went to the Great Church without the slightest apprehension; his intention was to receive the diadem at the hand of the patriarch. But when he was about to enter the church, Polyeuktos would not allow it. He said that a man whose hands were dripping with the steaming blood of a newly slain kinsman was unworthy to enter a church of God; that he had better start showing deeds of repentance and thus gain permission to tread the floor of the house of the Lord. John quietly accepted a penance and obediently declared that he would perform it all. He did, however, advance the justification that it was not by him that Nikephoros had been killed, but by Balantes and Atzypotheodoros; and they at the instigation of the Sovereign Lady. On hearing this the patriarch ordered her to be ejected from the palace and sent to some island, Nikephoros' murderers to be banished, and the bill by which Nikephoros sought to throw church affairs into disarray to be torn up. John immediately expelled [the two men] from the city and banished Theophano to the Prokonnesos. She subsequently escaped from there and secretly fled to the Great Church, from which she was expelled by Basil the parakoimomenos and exiled to the Damideia monastery, newly founded by the emperor, in the Armeniakon theme,[10] but not before she had roundly upbraided the emperor and Basil (whom she called Scyth[11] and barbarian), leaving the

---

[7] He is called 'the younger' to distinguish him from his grandfather. Bardas the younger began his career under his uncle; he had already obtained an important command in the east: Trebizond and its hinterland: J.-C. Cheynet, 'Les Phocas', *Le traité sur la guérilla de l'empereur Nicéphore Phocas*, ed. G. Dagron and H. Mihàescu (Le monde byzantin, Paris, 1986), 307–9, reproduced in J.-C. *La société byzantine. L'apport des sceaux* (Bilans de recherche 3, Paris, 1986), 489–91

[8] One of the principal towns of the Armeniakon theme (Amasya today) where Tzimiskes and his friends were particularly influential (which meant that Bardas Phokas would be under strict surveillance there). Tzimiskes exempted those who lived in that theme from taxation – to increase his popularity: Leo the Deacon, 100, tr. 149.

[9] We have no detailed knowledge of the measures taken but at Antioch Eustathios Maleinos (who was related to Nikephoros Phokas on his mother's side) was replaced by Michael Bourtzes who had been bitterly disappointed when Phokas did not give him the command of a city whose conquest owed so much to his efforts.

[10] The Kourkouas-Tzimiskes commanded solid support in the Armeniakon theme, n. 95, p. 222.

[11] Basil's mother was a concubine of unknown nationality; probably a Bulgar or a Magyar – both could be described as Scyth, meaning nomad of the northern Steppes.

marks of her knuckles on his temple. Her mother was exiled at the same time, [286] she to Mantineion.[12] The bill was brought in and ripped up; the church then enjoyed her former liberties.

3. Once these measures had been taken, John promised that, in propitiation for his sin, he would distribute among the poor whatever he had possessed as a private citizen, whereupon Polyeuktos allowed him into the church. On the feast of the Nativity of Christ our God he entered [the Great Church] and received the imperial diadem.[13]

The empire was now considerably disturbed, both in the east and in the west. The cities which had been taken from the Hagarenes in Cilicia, Phoenicia and Cœlo-Syria were contemplating revolt, for [after their capture] Nikephoros did not have time to set them in order and assure their security. The ill-advised project of inciting the Russians against the Bulgars had now turned into a gravely dangerous threat to the empire, while a five-year famine afflicting Roman lands was now sorely oppressing the towns.[14] The emperor gave careful thought and attention to how these ailments might be remedied and the resulting apprehension for the future be eliminated. Meanwhile a most virtuous monk named Thomas was appointed archbishop for Antioch on the Orontes (which was without a bishop).[15] This was the monk who foretold the emperor's proclamation and warned him not to be in a hurry, as God was going to raise him up to imperial heights; but he had to beware lest by foolishly rushing to possess the throne he destroy his own soul. He also requested that the Manichees who were ravaging all the east and corrupting it by spreading their miserable religion should be transported to the west and settled in some remote wilderness. This was done later on; they were transported and settled

---

[12] A monastery in the Boukellarion theme, see below: reign of Romanos Argyros below, c. 18. The name of Theophano's mother (Maria) is recorded on a seal: Zacos and Veglery, *Byzantine lead seals*, I, no. 2675.

[13] The emperor proceeded to the Great Church at Christmas: *De Cer.*, 1.32, ed. Vogt, I, 119–26, at 122–3 for the entry. On this occasion, by virtue of the twelfth canon of the council of Ankyra, the patriarch declared by an act of Synod that the (symbolic) anointing of an emperor eliminated the foregoing murder just as baptism eliminates all previous sin: Grumel, *Les regestes du patriarcat*, II, no. 794.

[14] This explains the rising grain prices in the time of Nikephoros Phokas. Leo the Deacon 102–3, trans. 152, mentions not only a third year of famine, but also the speedy arrival of relief which brought this catastrophe to an end.

[15] On the patriarchs of Antioch after its return to Roman rule: V. Grumel, 'Le patriarcat et les patriarches d'Antioche sous la seconde domination byzantine (969–1084)', *EO*, 33 (1934), 129–47, and K.-P. Todt, 'The Greek patriarchate of Antioch in the period of the renewed Byzantine rule and in the time of the first Crusades (969–1204)', *History of the Antiochian Greek Orthodox Church: what specificity?* (Balamond, Lebanon, 1999), 33–53. Theodore II (970–6) was hegoumenos of the monastery of St Anthony in the Armeniakon theme. It was no doubt as a neighbour of the Tzimiskes that he was able to make such predictions.

at Philippoupolis.[16] Thirty-five days after the proclamation [of John], Polyeuktos departed this life[17] [287] and the monk Basil Skamandrenos[18] was appointed in his stead, a man who had demonstrated virtue to perfection; such were matters in the city.

4. The capture of Antioch and the other cities which we listed above was an affront to the Saracens all over the world and to the other nations who shared their religion: Egyptians, Persians, Arabs, Elamites, together with the inhabitants of Arabia Felix and Saba.[19] They came to an agreement and made an alliance, whereupon they assembled a great army from all parts and put the Carthaginians[20] in charge of it. Their commander was Zochar, a man of vigour and military skill with an accurate understanding of land and sea operations. Once all the forces had been brought together, they marched out against the Romans, numbering one hundred thousand fighting men. They approached Antioch by Daphne[21] and laid vigorous siege to it, but those within resisted courageously and with excellent morale, so the siege dragged on for a long time. When this concentration of peoples was made known to the emperor, he quickly despatched letters to the commander of Mesopotamia ordering him to gather up the forces he had there and go to the relief of the besieged. He also sent as commander-in-chief (who came with other forces) the patrician Nicholas who was one of the emperor's personal eunuchs. [Nicholas] met up with the other force and engaged the myriads of barbarians whom he decisively put to flight and dispersed in a single battle, thus restoring the security of the cities under Roman rule.[22]

---

[16] These are the Paulicians – who eventually formed a unit in the Roman army which still existed in the time of Alexios I Komnenos. Philippoupolis is the present Plovdiv: Anna Comnène, *Alexiade*, ed. B. Leib, Paris 1967 2:43–5; *Annae Comnenae Alexias*, ed. Reinsch and Kambylis, *CFHB* 40/1, Berlin-New York 2001, 170–1.

[17] 5 February 970.

[18] The surname is derived from the fact that he had founded a monastery on the Bithynian river of that name: R. Janin, *Les églises et les monastères des grands centres byzantins* (Paris, 1975), II, 212.

[19] The Yemen and Ethiopia.

[20] Meaning the Fatimids, who set out from north Africa (hence 'Carthaginians'), made themselves masters of Egypt and were now – thanks to the actions of their general Jawhar (Zochar) threatening to overrun Palestine and Syria: *Islamic Egypt, 640–1517*, ed. C. F. Petry (*The Cambridge History of Egypt*, I, Cambridge, 1998), 138.

[21] Affluent Antiochenes frequently maintained a residence at Daphne, which was pleasantly watered.

[22] The report of Yahya of Antioch, 11, 350–1, is somewhat different: the Fatimid army lifted the siege because it was itself under attack in Palestine by the rebelling Qarmathe. Yahya names the real commander of the Fatimid army sent against Antioch as Foutou. He remained before Antioch for five months in 971: P. E. Walker, 'A Byzantine victory over the Fatimids at Alexandretta (971)', *B*, 42 (1972), 431–40.

5. We have already described the way in which the Russian people occupied Bulgaria and were holding the two sons of Peter, [288] Boris and Romanos, as prisoners of war. The Russians now had no wish whatsoever to return to their homeland. They were charmed by the fertility of the place and, without paying any attention whatsoever to the agreement concluded with the emperor Nikephoros, they thought it would be to their advantage to remain in that country and take control of the land.[23] They were further encouraged in this by Kalokyros when he said that if they would accept him as emperor of the Romans he would withdraw from Bulgaria and make an eternal peace with them. He would pay them the subsidies to which they had agreed many times over and hold them to be his allies and friends for life. Gratified by these words, the Russians treated Bulgaria as conquered territory, and when the emperor sent an embassy promising to fulfil all the obligations that Nikephoros had undertaken, they would not receive it. They returned answers brimming with barbaric arrogance; this obliged him to seek a military resolution of the situation. By letter he promptly ordered the eastern forces to cross over to the west and he appointed as commander of those forces the magister Bardas Skleros[24] (whose sister the emperor had legally married while he was still a private citizen) with the rank of general;[25] he was going to set out himself at the beginning of spring. When the Russians and Sviatoslav, their chieftain, learnt that the Romans had crossed over, they made common cause with the Bulgars whom they had already made their subjects,

---

[23] The truth of the matter is that Sviatoslav (Sphendosthlav *pace* Skylitzes, son of Igor and Olga) was obliged to return to Kiev because it was being menaced by Patzinaks, with his mother manning the defence. Sviatoslav resumed his offensive against the Bulgars at the end of 969. Meanwhile Nikephoros Phokas had concluded an agreement with the Bulgars to repel the Russians, a change of allegiance which is explained by the fact that Nikephoros had secured the submission of the Bulgars: Leo the Deacon, 79–80. It was not the intention of Sviatoslav to conquer Constantinople but to take up residence at Little Preslav (which must be distinguished from Preslav, the Bulgar capital) because this would offer more facilities for trading with the empire: S. Franklin and J. Shepard, *The emergence of Rus, 750–1200* (London, 1996), 147.

[24] This is the first mention of the brother-in-law of John Tzimiskes. Bardas was probably the son of Pantherios Skleros, last domestic of the scholai under Romanos Lekapenos, which would explain why he received no important command under Nikephoros Phokas. He was now a soldier with wide experience but also quite old, for he must have been born around 920: W. Seibt, *Die Skleroi: Eine prosopographisch-sigillographische Studie* (Byzantina Vindobonensia, 9, Vienna, 1976), 29–58.

[25] *Stratelates*, the former *magister militum*, came to designate no more than a dignity in the course of the seventh century before disappearing in the eighth, even though it is still cited in the *Kletorologion* of Philotheos. It re-appears in the *Taktikon Scorialensis* to mean somebody who really commanded troops. There is no doubt that this was the title Bardas held but it is not always easy to see what exactly it meant: the officer in charge of the unit known as the *stratelates*, or merely 'officer in charge': N. Oikonomides, *Listes*, 332.

taking as their allies the Patzinaks[26] and the Turks[27] settled to the west, in Pannonia. When all the army was assembled its fighting force numbered three hundred and eight thousand.[28] They crossed the Haemos [mountain-range], burning and laying waste the whole of Thrace, then set up camp before the walls of Arkadiopolis[29] where they waited for battle to be joined. But when the Magister Bardas Skleros realised how short he was of men (his entire army numbered about twelve thousand) he decided to get the better of the enemy by military cunning; [289] to gain the upper hand over so great a number by skill and dexterity, which indeed he did. He enclosed himself and his army inside the walls, and no matter how much the enemy invited him to come out and fight once and for all, he paid no attention. He stayed where he was, giving the impression that he was afraid — and watching the enemy doing whatever they liked. This behaviour earned the great contempt of the barbarians, for they thought that it really was because he was afraid that he had enclosed the Roman units within the walls, and that he *dare* not come out. They began to disperse without caution; they became negligent about camp security and careless as to the posting of proper guards. They passed their nights in drinking and drunkenness with flutes and cymbals, in barbaric dancing with not a care for the precautions which ought to have been taken. Bardas seized the opportune moment. When he had carefully studied the matter of how the enemy might best be attacked and had stipulated the day and hour, he set up ambushes and traps by night in some suitable places. Then he despatched the patrician John Alakasseus[30] with a small detachment whose orders were to advance and reconnoitre the enemy; he was to remain in frequent contact and to keep [the commander] informed of wherever he might be. When he encountered the enemy he was to give battle, but as soon as blows were struck he was to turn his back and give the impression of running away. He was not to flee at full tilt, giving the horses their

---

[26] The relations between the Russians and the Patzinaks, who occupied the Steppes to the south of Russia, were very complex and mainly hostile. Yet Sviatoslav appears to have won them over to fight with him; no doubt they were lured by the prospect of booty.

[27] Since the victory over them won by Otto I in 955, the Hungarians/Magyars were no longer free to wander in the Latin west so they turned towards Pannonia, which would have reminded them of the Steppes from which they came.

[28] Clearly a gross exaggeration. Nikephoros had granted Kalokyros the sum of 1,500 pounds of gold (*ca.* 490 kg), sufficient to maintain an army of around 10,000 men. Sviatoslav could have eventually added a significant number of auxiliaries.

[29] The present Luleburgaz, situated on the road leading from Adrianople to the capital, which explains why the Roman army had to give battle.

[30] First mention of a family of soldiers which was active into the time of the Komnenoi, especially in the Balkans. The title 'patrician' means that John was the commander of a unit or of a theme.

bridle, but gently and without breaking ranks. Then, wherever it was possible, [his men] were to turn about and set upon the enemy again. Their orders were to keep on repeating the operation until [the enemy] was well within the ambushes and traps; at that point they were to retreat in disorderly and headlong flight. Now the forces of the barbarians were threefold: the first third consisted of Bulgarians and Russians, the second was Turks only, the third Patzinaks, likewise alone. When John came on, he chanced to encounter the Patzinaks. He pretended to run away as he was ordered to do, but made quite a leisurely retreat. The Patzinaks for their part came in pursuit, breaking their ranks in the hope of utterly annihilating them. The Romans, however, now making an orderly retreat, now turning to defend themselves, drew closer to the [290] ambuscades and, when they were in the midst of them, gave the horses their heads and fled for all they were worth, with the Patzinaks strung out in disorderly pursuit. Then the magister suddenly appeared with the whole army and, taken by surprise, the Patzinaks halted the pursuit. This, however, was not with the intention of running away, for they stood their ground, waiting for whatever might befall them. Those who were accompanying the magister violently attacked them; then so did the rest of the army which was following in good order and rank by rank, with the result that even the bravest of the Scyths[31] fell. The Roman forces were now completely parted and the Patzinaks fell right into the trap; the two wings came together again, which meant the enemy were perfectly surrounded. They resisted for a short time and then surrendered; almost all of them were slain.

6. Thus Bardas put them to flight; he then learnt from the prisoners that the rest of the Patzinaks were biding their time, unwearied and drawn up in battle line. He directed himself to them forthwith. At first when they learnt of the [other] Patzinaks' misfortune, their morale had collapsed at the unexpected nature of the disaster, but they rallied each other and reintegrated those who had been dispersed as they took to their heels. They then launched an attack on the Romans, the cavalry leading the charge, the infantry following behind. At the first onslaught the impetus of the cavalry was interrupted by the Romans, who seemed to be irresistible; the horsemen turned back and were forced up against the infantry. When they got back to where they were before, they regrouped and waited the coming of the Romans. For some time the battle hung in the balance until a Scyth who outstripped the others in the size of his body and the courage of his soul leapt on the magister himself as

---

[31] 'Scyths' usually means all people from the north; here, Russians and Bulgars.

he was riding by encouraging the ranks, and with his sword dealt him a blow on the helmet. But the sword slipped off and the blow achieved nothing. Then the magister dealt *him* a sword blow on the helmet; so strong was his arm and such the temper of the steel that the blow was powerful enough to slice the Scyth in two all the way down. The patrician Constantine,[32] the magister's brother, came to his brother's aid [291] and tried to wound in the head another Scyth who was coming forward even more recklessly to the aid of the former one, but he leaned his body to one side and Constantine missed his mark, hitting the horse's neck and severing the head from the throat. As the Scyth fell, Constantine dismounted, seized the fellow's beard in his hand and cut his neck. This deed heartened the Romans and put new courage in them, while it filled the Scyths with fear and dread. They quickly lost their courage; they turned their backs and shamefully fled in grave disorder. The Romans pursued them and covered the plain with dead, but more were taken alive than fell and all but a very few of the survivors were wounded. Nobody would have escaped the danger if night had not fallen, whereupon the Romans halted their pursuit. Of those tens of thousands of barbarians, very few survived while twenty-five Romans fell in the battle but almost everybody was wounded.[33]

7. Skleros had not yet completed the war against the Scyths nor had the Romans yet cleansed themselves of the gore of battle, when letters arrived from the emperor summoning him to the imperial presence. When he arrived there, he was ordered to pass over into Asia with an army adequate for the conflict which awaited him. For Bardas Phokas had absconded from Amaseia where he had been condemned to reside, accompanied by some relations, friends and acquaintances to whom he had secretly sworn that he would come to Caesarea in Cappadocia.[34] There they were to assemble no small force under the command of Theodore and Nikephoros, the sons of the patrician Theodoulos Parsakoutinos;[35] also of another patrician, [292]

---

[32] Constantine Skleros had married Maria, daughter of the curopalates, Leo Phokas, brother of the emperor Nikephoros Phokas: Seibt, *Skleroi*, 58.

[33] On this classical tactic used in combat see the commentaries of E. McGeer, *Sowing the dragon's teeth: Byzantine warfare in the tenth century* (DOS, 33, Washington, DC, 1995), 294–300. This battle took place in spring, 970 (not in autumn, as McGeer claims). The report of Skleros' successful operations (very similar to the one given by Leo the Deacon, 108–11, trans. 158–61) probably comes from communiqués sent to Constantinople to announce the victory.

[34] It was in this city, the capital of the Charsianon theme, that his uncle Nikephoros had been proclaimed emperor. Caesarea was central to the lands under the influence of the Phokades and their friends.

[35] Leo the Deacon, 112, trans. 162, mentions a third brother, Bardas, adding that the brothers were cousins of the rebel. Parsakoutenos (*pace* MSS ACV and ND) is the more usual form of the name.

Symeon Ampelas.[36] Then [Bardas Phokas] would assume the diadem and the rest of the imperial insignia and raise the standard of revolt against the emperor. His father, Leo the kouropalates, had already gained some supporters, some with gifts, others with promises of honours and lands, the bishop of Abydos serving as his agent in this matter. [Leo] himself intended secretly to travel from Lesbos to the district of Thrace, together with his son, Nikephoros. When the emperor learnt of this (for the bishop was arrested and, being unable to refute the mass of evidence produced against him, brought everything out into the open) the kouropalates was handed over to the justices and it was their unanimous opinion that he and his son should die. The emperor, being of a gentler nature, condemned them both to perpetual banishment and the loss of their eyes, but it is said that the emperor secretly instructed the executioners not to harm their eyes in any way; merely to go through the motions of blinding them and in fact to leave them the light of their eyes. But they were to conceal the fact that they had these instructions from the emperor and attribute the deed to themselves, as though they had given them the gift of sight out of compassion;[37] and that is how the matter of the kouropalates came to an end.

Skleros crossed Asia and came to Dorylaion;[38] first he tried to see whether with promises of benefits he could persuade Phokas and his associates to refrain from what they were planning. In fact he had orders from the emperor to do everything in his power to keep his hands clean of the blood of his fellow countrymen. But when he realised that this was wasted effort (for the rebels treated his overtures with ever-increasing arrogance and impertinence) he judged it to be time for action. He mobilised the army and advanced on Caesarea. When Phokas' associates realised this, they abandoned their hopes of an uncertain future in favour of an advantage in hand: when night fell they accepted the gifts proffered to them by the emperor and deserted to Skleros. Diogenes Adralestos[39] came first, then Ampelas and the sons of Theodoulos (who had fomented the whole uprising) [293] followed by all the rest, until Phokas was left alone with his own servants. Abandoned and devoid of all support, he was plunged into

---

[36] Symeon derived his name (which he bequeathed to his posterity) from his original trade: vine-dresser. Either he or one of his relatives endowed the monastery of Xerochoraphion near Miletos, which suggests that he might have been from that area: *Life of Nikephoros of Miletos*, ed. H. Delehaye, *AnalBoll*, 44 (1895), 151.

[37] Tzimiskes (who was not yet firmly established on the throne) had to be careful not to offend any section of the army. A further consideration is that the Phokades were his close relations.

[38] Dorylaion marked the second stage (after Malagina) on the military road to Cappadocia.

[39] He was a nephew of the rebel leader: Leo the Deacon, 120, trans. 168.

bitterness and sorrow against those who had incited him to revolt and then betrayed him. Sleep overcame him (night had now fallen) and, as he slept, it was as though he raged and fretted against them who had wronged him and that he lectured God saying: 'Plead thou my cause, O Lord, with them that strive against me,'[40] but as he was about to recite the rest of the psalm, he heard a voice telling him not to go any further because Skleros had anticipated him and appropriated the rest of the poem. He stood up, trembling, in the realisation that there was no hope left for him. He mounted and fled to the fortress of Tyropoion[41] together with those who were with him. When this was made known to the magister Bardas Skleros he sent swift horsemen to overtake and capture him before he could enter the fortress. They gave vigorous pursuit and overtook him on the plain, just as he was approaching the foothills of the fortress. One of the pursuers, more daring and brave than the other, Constantine surnamed Charon,[42] outstripped his fellows and, riding full out, overtook Phokas who was protecting his men in the rear, ready boldly to receive whatever might befall. Charon recognised him at a distance and began hurling unseemly and indecent insults at him, calling him ignoble and unmanly, demanding that he stand and take the reward of his rebellion. When he heard the insults, by no means unaware of who was speaking, Phokas drew rein and turned to him saying: 'O man, you ought to take into account the unstable nature of human fortune and not insult or revile a man borne down by its caprices. Rather should you have pity and compassion for me in my misfortune, for my father was kouropalates, my grandfather caesar, my uncle emperor, and I, who was myself once duke and numbered among the highest in the land – I am now fallen to the ultimate degree of calamity and disgrace.' [294] 'O wicked man,' said the other, 'it is permissible to say things like that to children who can be led astray, but you do not deceive me with such fables'; and he spurred on his horse and increased his speed. Phokas seized the mace hanging on his saddle, met him head-on and dealt him a blow on the helmet which killed him instantly, for the helmet was not able to withstand the force of the blow. Then Phokas reined about and continued on his way. The rest of the party riding in pursuit came up to where Charon lay dead, and they were so amazed at the irresistible force

[40] Ps. 34/35:1; the verse continues 'Fight against them that fight against me', and the following verses are in the same vein, as the righteous man calls for divine aid against the enemy who is oppressing him.
[41] Location unsure; it must have been in the district of Trypia: Hild and Restle, *Kappadokien*, 298. Bardas Phokas probably fled to the east in order to take refuge with the Moslems.
[42] This man is otherwise unknown but an Alexios Charon was the father of Anna Dalassene, thus the grandfather of Alexios I Komnenos: Nikephoros Bryennios, *Hylē historias, Nicephori Bryennii historiarum libri quattuor*, ed. P. Gautier (CFHB, 9, Brussels, 1975), 77.

of the blow that they all desisted from the chase, nobody daring to go any further. No longer in fear of his life, Phokas entered the fortress. Skleros came along afterwards; he sent him frequent messages and wrote to him swearing that he cared for him as a kinsman (his brother Constantine was in fact married to Sophia, Phokas' sister). He counselled Phokas to approach the emperor and to gain his benevolence by giving himself up. When he had received sworn assurances that no evil would befall him, Phokas delivered himself and those with him into Skleros' hands. The worst the emperor did to him was to force him to receive holy orders and to banish him to the island of Chios. But he commanded Skleros and the light [-ly armed] units to cross over to the west again in all haste.[43]

8. John took to himself as wife Theodora, the sister of Romanos [II] and daughter of Constantine Porphyrogennetos, which pleased the citizens greatly for it kept the imperial power within the family [of Basil I].[44]

9. In the second year of his reign, as he was about to campaign against the Russians, [John] conciliated the soldiers with bounties and appointed commanders [295] known for their skill and experience in military matters. He gave careful attention to other preparations to ensure that the army not go short of anything. He also concerned himself with the fleet by the agency of Leo, then droungarios of the fleet but afterwards protovestiarios. Old vessels were refitted, new ones built to put a fleet worthy of the name on the water. When everything was to his satisfaction, at the beginning of spring he made departure offerings to God, took his leave of the citizens and left the capital. When he came to Raidestos,[45] he was met by two Scythian ambassadors who gave the appearance of fulfilling an embassy but in fact had come to spy on the state of Roman affairs. In response to their grumbling and complaints about mistreatment the emperor ordered them to pass through the entire camp and to inspect the ranks, for he was under no delusions as to why they were there. When they had been all around and seen everything, he enjoined them to take themselves off and tell their commander with what a well-

---

[43] The revolt of Phokas obliged Bardas Skleros to abandon the main front on which he had been fighting for a few months; the regiments were ordered into winter quarters on their return, probably in the autumn of 970. After the Russians were defeated, they satisfied themselves with occupying the lands to the north of the Hæmos.

[44] Leo the Deacon, 127, trans. 174, says that when the widowed John Tzimiskes married Theodora in November 970 she was not particularly attractive, but that she was very intelligent. Yahya of Antioch, I, 830, tells us it was stipulated that if the marriage produced a son (Theodora was in her thirties) the child would be an emperor, the two porphyrogennetoi [Basil and Constantine] taking precedence over him.

[45] A town on the European banks of the sea of Marmara, the present Tekirdag. This was an important stage on the Via Egnatia and a depot for the grain raised on the adjacent plains.

organised and disciplined host the Roman emperor had come fortified in order to make war on him. When he had thus dismissed the ambassadors he himself next took some swift soldiers (five thousand infantry and four thousand cavalry) and, ordering all the rest of the army to follow at a more leisurely pace under Basil the parakoimomenos,[46] he crossed the Haemos mountains, made an unforeseen advance into enemy territory and pitched his camp close by the city of Great Preslav where the palace of the Bulgar kings lay.[47] This happened so unexpectedly that the Scyths were dumbfounded and reduced to inactivity. Kalokyros chanced to be staying there, he who was the cause and prime mover of these present disasters and who could not even bear to hear the sound of the trumpet! When he became aware that the emperor was present to supervise the war in person, he secretly left the city and fled to the encampment of the Russians. When they saw him and learnt of the emperor's arrival they were disturbed in no small way but they pulled themselves together when Sviatoslav made a rallying speech and uttered the bombastic [296] phrases the situation called for. Then they came and pitched camp over against the Romans' camp. Meanwhile the force that was with the emperor came onto the plain before the city and suddenly fell on the enemy, taking them completely unawares. They surprised eight thousand five hundred fully armed men engaged in training outside the city; these resisted for a time but then, overcome, turned and fled. Some were ingloriously slain, some reached safety inside the city. While this was happening the Scyths inside the city saw the unexpected arrival of the Romans and the subsequent engagement with their own troops. They each did what they could, seizing whatever weapon came to hand and rushed out to help. The Romans met them as they advanced, disorganised and well spread out, and they massacred them. The foe was unable to resist even for a short time, but turned in flight. However, a detachment of Roman cavalry ran ahead of them and closed off the path leading to the city. They were overtaken as they dispersed over the plain in flight; they were annihilated until every piece of level ground was covered with bodies and even more of them were taken prisoner. Sphangelos, commander-in-chief of the army in Preslav (he was second in rank to Sviatoslav among the Scyths) was now apprehensive for the city itself and not without reason; he had

---

[46] On the strengths of the imperial army when campaigning, see the contemporary military treatise: G. T. Dennis, *De re militari: three Byzantine military treatises, text translation and notes* (DOT, 9, Washington, DC, 1985), 246 and 274.
[47] In the course of their second campaign against the Bulgars the Russians took their capital, capturing Tsar Boris and his children.

the gates closed and secured with bars. Then he went up onto the walls and repelled the attacking Romans with every kind of missile including stones. The siege was relaxed when night fell but with the morning there came the President [of the Senate] Basil [the parakoimomenos] with the host that was bringing up the rear – and this made the emperor very happy. He went up onto a hillock to make himself visible to the Scyths while the host, now assembled in the same place, surrounded the city. He urged the Scyths at some length to abandon their obstinate resistance and not rush to their destruction, but they would not be persuaded to come down from the walls. Full of righteous indignation, the Romans intensified the siege, forcing back the defenders who were above with arrows and leaning ladders against the walls. A valiant soldier, [297] his sword held high in his right hand, his shield held over his head, was the first to climb up one of the ladders. Then, repelling missiles with his shield and driving off with his sword attackers and those who got in his way, he penetrated beyond the parapet, scattered the people there and thus opened the way for those who were coming up after him.[48] One did likewise, then another, followed by many others. As [the Romans] got into formation, the Scyths were overcome and began throwing themselves down from the battlements. Many other Romans went up ladders in different places and onto the walls with all the zeal of the first ones. The Scyths were in such disorder that some Romans effortlessly evaded them and came to the gates; these they flung open wide and admitted the army, and in this way the city was captured. The Scyths who fled down the alleyways were apprehended and slaughtered; the women and children were taken prisoner. Boris the king of the Bulgars was taken still wearing the royal insignia, together with his wife and children. They were brought to the emperor who received them graciously, calling [Boris] emperor[49] of the Bulgars. He released all the Bulgars they had captured – leaving them free to go wherever they would, saying that he was not come to enslave the Bulgars but rather to free them.[50] It was only the Russians whom he regarded as enemies and intended to treat as adversaries.

10. The more dauntless of the Scyths occupied a fortress within the palace which was in the city, eight thousand of them in all, and for some time they were able to seize and kill many of those who went reconnoitring and looking for spoils – without anyone being aware of it. When

---

[48] This man is named by Leo the Deacon, 135–6, trans. 181–2: Theodosios Mesanyktes.
[49] *Basileus*!
[50] Tzimiskes was not intending to conquer Bulgaria at that time but to restore a Bulgar state which would be an ally of the Romans. That is why he greeted Boris with the title of *basileus*.

the emperor learnt of this he sent a sizeable detachment against them,[51] but the men he sent were reluctant to, indeed dared not, attempt an assault; not because they were afraid of the Russians [298] but because the location was very well fortified and impregnable. The emperor soon solved that problem; he seized his weapons and set off on foot, ahead of everybody. When the soldiers saw that, they all took up their weapons and every man tried to catch up with the emperor; then, shouting and bellowing, they attacked the fortress. The Russians resisted the attack courageously, but the Romans started fires at a number of points and thus overcame the defenders. Unable to withstand the heat of the fire and the strength of the Romans, they flung themselves down the precipice and escaped. Many lost their lives in the fire, others from falling down the precipice; the rest either fell victim to the sword or were taken prisoner. That is how the city was taken; its resistance did not even last two full days. Once he had captured it, the emperor rebuilt it. He stationed an adequate garrison there with appropriate supplies of the necessities of life. When he celebrated the day of the holy resurrection,[52] he renamed the city Ioannoupolis[53] after himself; then, the next day, he set out for Dorostolon, also known as Dristra.

11.[54] Sviatoslav was deeply troubled when he heard that Preslav had fallen (which is hardly surprising) but that did not in the least diminish his arrogance. He rallied his comrades, demanding of them that they now show themselves to be men of even better mettle. He set things in order to the best of his ability, slaying those Bulgars of whom he was at all suspicious (around three hundred of them),[55] and then set out against the Romans. The emperor captured the cities that lay on his route and posted governors in them. He plundered many fortresses and buildings, handed them over for the soldiers to take the spoils and then went his way. When the scouts let it be known that some Scyths were approaching, he

---

[51] This detachment was commanded by Bardas Skleros: Leo the Deacon, 137, trans. 183.
[52] Easter 971.
[53] The renaming of Preslav is an aspect of John's attempt to legitimise the rule of a usurper and a murderer by victory.
[54] Skylitzes' description of the operations around Dorostolon/Dristra is one of his best. His account can be compared with the one written by Leo the Deacon which is even more detailed. The two writers appear to have used a common source, possibly official reports of the victory. On the action and the way in which it was reported: S. McGrath, 'The battles of Dorostolon (971)', Miller and Nesbitt, *Peace and War in Byzantium*, 152–64.
[55] Sviatoslav was afraid that the liberation of Preslav would unleash a general insurrection of the Bulgars (still under the Russian yoke) for many towns surrendered to Tzimiskes without resistance: Leo the Deacon, 139, trans. 184. The massacre of the Bulgar elite made it easier for the Romans to establish their hegemony later on.

despatched a company of picked men and put Theodore of Mistheia[56] in command of their number with orders to advance ahead of the army, look out for the main body of the enemy and to keep the emperor informed. [299] If they drew near, they were to test the strength of the enemy by skirmishing with them. He himself came after them with the whole army in order of battle. When the men with Theodore came into contact with the enemy, they launched a violent assault on them but the Russians would advance no further for fear of an ambush. Many of them were wounded and some fell, then they broke ranks and dispersed into the neighbouring mountains and the thick, dark forest which covered them; by way of the mountains they reached safety in Dristra. They were seven thousand in number, while the number of the Romans who attacked them and put them to flight was three hundred.

When the Scyths were reunited around Sviatoslav they set out with him and set up camp twelve miles before Dorostolon together with their whole army: there were three hundred and thirty thousand of them, eagerly and confidently awaiting the arrival of the emperor. Exulting in their recent victories, the Romans were looking forward to a decisive battle, knowing that they had God on their side, He who has no wish to come to the aid of princes with unclean hands, but always helps the victims of injustice. Thus the Romans were eager and bold (not only the outstandingly courageous, but also the faint-hearted and timorous) – all champing at the bit to be in action. When the armies came within sight of each other, the emperor and Sviatoslav each encouraged his own men with heartening words, addressing them in appropriate language. Then, when the trumpets gave the signal for battle, the hosts charged each other with equal ardour. At the first encounter such was the impetus of the Romans' charge that they killed many barbarians and broke their ranks, but there was no retreat on the part of the enemy nor any definite rout by the Romans. What happened was that the Scyths regrouped and came at the Romans again, hurling cries. For some time the battle was equally matched [300] but when it drew on towards evening on that day the Romans rallied each other and somehow stiffened their determination with exhortations. Then they charged the Scyths' left wing and put down many of them by the irresistible nature of this manoeuvre. The Russians now concentrated their forces there where the danger lay, at which the emperor despatched reinforcements from those who accompanied him

---

[56] A town in the Anatolikon theme, the present Beyhehir: K. Belke and M. Restle, *Galatien und Lykaonien* (TIB, 4, Vienna, 1984) 205–6.

and he himself came after them, the imperial insignia openly displayed. His lance at the ready, he spurred on his horse and rallied his troops with frequent shouts. A bitterly contested battle ensued in which there were many reverses of fortune; it is said that twelve times the balance tipped this way and that. Then, not by any means without having put up a stiff resistance, the Russians broke into disorderly flight before the dangers which confronted them and scattered over the plain. The Romans gave pursuit and slew those whom they overtook; many fell and more were taken prisoner. Those who succeeded in getting out of danger found refuge in Dorostolon.

12. The emperor made offerings for the victory to George, the gloriously triumphant martyr (for it was on his feast day[57] that he had charged the enemy), and then himself set out for Dorostolon [Dristra] on the following day. When he arrived there, he established a well-fortified camp. He did not yet lay siege to the city, for fear that the Russians might have been able to escape in their ships since the river was unguarded. So he remained in camp, awaiting the Roman fleet. Meanwhile Sviatoslav put the Bulgars he had captured alive (they numbered about twenty thousand) in iron fetters and other kinds of restraints for fear they might mutiny; and he made preparations in anticipation of a siege. Once the fleet arrived, the emperor attempted an assault on the walls. Frequent sallies of the Scyths were repulsed but one day, when the Romans were dismissed for supper and evening was drawing on, the barbarians split into two sections, cavalry and infantry, and poured out of two of the city gates: the one to the east which Peter the camp commander[58] had been stationed to guard with Thracian and Macedonian troops, and the one to the west, the security of which was entrusted to Bardas Skleros [301] with the troops of the East. Out came the Scyths in battle order, and this was the first time they had been seen on horseback; in the previous battles they had fought on foot. The Romans withstood their charge and opposed them vigorously. For some time it was an equal contest but eventually the Romans with their superior qualities thrust the barbarians back and shut them up inside the walls. The barbarians suffered many casualties in the battle, especially of horsemen, but not a single Roman was wounded, except for the three horses that fell. Trounced like this and shut up within the walls, the barbarians remained awake as night fell, mourning all night long for those who had fallen with wild and frightful wailing. To those who heard them it sounded like the roaring and bellowing of wild beasts rather than the

[57] 23 April.   [58] *Stratopedarches*, appointed by Nikephoros Phokas: above, c. 1.

grief and lamentation of humankind. At daybreak all those who had been detached to guard various fortresses were summoned back to Dorostolon and they came in haste as soon as they were called. Now the emperor concentrated all his forces and advanced onto the plain before the city where he tried to goad the barbarians [to fight]. But as they did not come out, he returned to camp and bided his time. A delegation now came to him from Constantia and the other fortresses established beyond the Danube. They sought an amnesty for their misdeeds [in return for] handing over themselves and the strongholds. He received them kindly, despatching officers to take charge of the fortresses and with sufficient troops to secure them.

When it was already evening, all the city gates were flung open and the Russians (in far greater numbers than before) fell on the Romans – to their great surprise, for it was now night. At first the Russians seemed to have the upper hand but, shortly after, it was the Romans who were prevailing. And then it happened that Sphangelos went down, fighting heroically, but the Russians faltered when they were deprived of him and their impetus was slackened. They gave no ground, however; they held fast all night long and the following day until high noon. At that point the emperor sent a detachment to cut off the barbarians' retreat into the city, and once the Russians realised this they turned and fled. When they found the ways into the city blocked [302] they fled over the plain, where they were apprehended and slain. When night fell Sviatoslav threw a deep trench all around the city wall to prevent the Romans from easily approaching the wall when they attacked. But he knew that, having secured the city like that, he had to expect a very severe siege. The better part of the army lay wounded and famine was afflicting them, for they had already consumed their supplies. Since the arrival of any relief from outside was prevented by the Romans, one dark and moonless night when heavy rain was falling from the sky, atrocious hail pelting down, thunder and appalling lightning all around, he embarked in drakkars [*monoxyloi*] with two thousand men and went off to forage. Each one gathered whatever he could of the necessities of life: grain, millet and so forth. Then they returned upstream towards Dorostolon in their drakkars. While they were sailing upstream they saw a considerable number of soldiers' orderlies on the river bank. Some of them were watering horses, some reaping hay, while others were collecting wood. They disembarked from their vessels, quietly made their way through the woods and then fell on the unsuspecting orderlies who had not even seen them. Many of them were killed; the rest were obliged to disperse through the nearby bush. The barbarians got back into their ships and, profiting from a favourable wind, returned to Dorostolon.[59] This greatly disturbed the emperor when he heard of it; he was particularly incensed with the commanders of the fleet for not having noticed the embarkation of the barbarians from Dorostolon. He threatened them with death if any such fault should ever occur even once again and, for their part, they kept a very careful watch on both banks of the river. When the emperor had spent in all sixty-five days on the siege, fighting every day without respite, he thought he should reduce the city by blockade and famine. To this end he cut all the roads with ditches at which he stationed guards [303] to prevent anybody going out in search of supplies; he then sat down to wait. That is how things were at Dorostolon.

13. Although Leo the kouropalates and Nikephoros his son appeared to have been mutilated, their eyes were still unharmed, as we said above; they now made a further attempt to seize the throne. They had corrupted many of those set to guard the city and the palace guards; when all was ready for what they had in mind, they hired a ship, went on board and sailed away from the island on which they had been condemned to reside.[60] They arrived on the shore opposite the city, at an estate called Pelamys,[61] and from there they came into Byzantium at first cockcrow. But one of the conspirators revealed the affair to Leo, droungarios of the fleet, who was charged with the security of the palace together with Basil the Rector,[62] who dispatched an adequate detachment to arrest the kouropalates and his son. When they learnt of this they took refuge in the Great Church, but they were dragged out of there and sent to the island of Prote where their eyes were gouged out.[63]

At that time something else came to light which is well worth reporting. A plaque of Prokonnesian marble was found lying around in the garden of one of the senators. On the good side of it two human figures were portrayed, one of a man, the other of a woman. On the upper margin of the plaque was inscribed an epigram which went something like this: 'Long live the friends of Christ, John and Theodora.' Some people were astonished to see the actual state of affairs so accurately portrayed, but others thought the matter was not innocent of deception and chicanery; maybe the proprietor of the estate was seeking to get into the good graces of the

---

[59] This episode is not mentioned by Leo the Deacon.
[60] Leo and his son were at Methymna on the island of Lesbos: Leo the Deacon, 145, trans. 189.
[61] There was a monastery on this estate which was near to Chalcedon: Janin, *Grands centres*, 11, 35.
[62] Basil was also logothete of the *genikon*: *Actes de Lavra*, 1, *Des origines à 1204*, ed. P. Lemerle, N. Svoronos, A. Guillou, D. Papachryssanthou (Archives de l'Athos, 5, Paris, 1970), 125.
[63] Yahya of Antioch, 1, 831, says the empress Theodora ordered the arrest and blinding of Leo.

emperor by this artifice. Whether it was those or these people who spoke the truth I cannot say.

14. [304] The Scyths were severely oppressed by famine within the city and afflicted by the siege-engines outside, especially in the quarter which the magister John, the son of Romanos Kourkouas,[64] was stationed to guard, for the rock-hurling machine which was there inflicted no small damage on those within. So the Scyths selected some of their most heroic heavily armed men mingled with some light infantry and sent them against that machine, to see whether they could incapacitate it. When Kourkouas got wind of this he took the strongest men who were with him and hastened off to help. When he was in the midst of the Scyths his horse fell, wounded by a missile, bringing him down too, and he was killed, cut to pieces. The Romans charged on, engaged the Russians and prevented the machine from being damaged; they drove the Scyths back and shut them up in the city.[65] Then in the month of July, the twentieth day, the Russians sallied forth in great numbers, engaged the Romans and did battle with them. They had someone encouraging them and urging them on in the battle, a man who was a great celebrity among the Scyths. His name was Ikmor and he was the most honoured man after Sphangelos, who had been killed. It was not because he was born of a noble line that he was held in such high honour, nor merely because he was well-liked. He was revered by all for nothing other than his excellence. Anemas, son of Kouroupes, emir of the Cretans, was one of the emperor's bodyguard.[66] When he saw Ikmor engaging so valiantly in the fray, encouraging the others to do likewise, urging them on and throwing the Roman battle lines into confusion, he was neither dismayed by the stature of the man nor afraid of his strength. His heart burned within him and, turning his horse this way and that, he drew the sword which was hanging at his thigh and charged the Scyth with irresistible force. He struck him on the left shoulder about the clavicle with his weapon, and cut his neck in such a way that he severed the head together with the right arm and he fell to the ground. The Scyth lay prostrate [305] while Anemas, for his part, returned to camp unhurt. Great shouting greeted this deed, the Romans cheering the victory, the Scyths uttering unseemly groans, their resistance weakening. When the

---

[64] Domestic of the scholai under Romanos Lekapenos. John was a cousin of the emperor.
[65] Leo the Deacon, 148, trans. 192, describes the death of Kourkouas (a first cousin of John Tzimiskes) differently. He says drunkenness was the reason for the ineffective defence and that Kourkouas was mistaken for the emperor because he was wearing gilded armour. Leo also suggests that his sad end was his punishment for pillaging Bulgar churches to fill his own pockets.
[66] This was the son of an emir; he had been captured by Nikephoros at the reconquest of Crete (reign of Romanos II, c. 4). The emperor's bodyguard consisted of men from the leading families.

Romans fell on them again, the Scyths were put to flight and ingloriously sought refuge in the city. Many of them fell that day, trodden underfoot by others in the narrow defile and slain by the Romans when they were trapped there. Sviatoslav himself would have been taken too, if night had not fallen and delivered him. When those who escaped danger were within the defence-work, they raised a mighty lamentation over the death of Ikmor. When the Romans were robbing the corpses of the barbarians of their spoils, they found women lying among the fallen, equipped like men; women who had fought against the Romans together with the men.

15. The war was going badly for the barbarians and they had no hope of any ally, for their fellow countrymen were far away and the barbarian nations close by refused to help for fear of the Romans. They were running short of supplies too and there was nowhere that they could obtain provisions, as the Roman fleet was keeping a strict watch on the banks of the river. But all kinds of goods accrued to the Romans day by day, as though from a bottomless well, while their cavalry and infantry forces were ever being augmented. Nor were [the barbarians] able to run away by embarking in their vessels because, as we said, the waterways were heavily guarded. A council was held: some were of the opinion that they should take advantage of the night to steal away; others that, since there was no other possible way of retreating, they ought to seek pledges and guarantees from the Romans [306] and then take off for their homeland. Others also gave their opinion, each one saying what he thought the situation demanded, but while they all wanted to see an end, once and for all, to the war, Sviatoslav was rather in favour of meeting the Romans in one more encounter. Then they would either win, having fought well and triumphed over the enemy, or lose, having preferred a noble and happy death to a life of shame and disgrace. Life would be unliveable for them if they sought safety in flight, for they would then be despised by the adjacent peoples who formerly lived in acute fear of them. The opinion of Sviatoslav won the day; everybody agreed to risk the extreme danger of [losing] their lives and all their troops. Accordingly they sallied forth from the city next day in full force, closed its gates so that nobody could turn back and find refuge in the city – and charged at the Romans. A violent battle ensued in which the barbarians fought courageously. As the sun was very hot and they were suffering from thirst (for they were heavily armed and it was towards high noon), the Romans began to give ground. When the emperor became aware of this, he and his retinue rushed to their aid, he himself wading into the thick of the battle, ordering skins filled with wine and water to be supplied to the soldiery suffering from the sun and from thirst. This they

could use to overcome their thirst and the heat of the sun. Then, pulling themselves together, they charged the Scyths with violent impetus, but the foe boldly withstood the shock and the battle stood undecided until the emperor noted how narrow the place was, and that it was due to this factor that the enemy's resistance was possible: the Romans had so little elbow room they were unable to display the kind of performance which was appropriate to their valour. So he ordered the commanders to retreat towards the plain, withdrawing from the city, thus giving the impression of running away. They were not, however, to be in a hurry, [307] but to take their time and retreat only little by little. Then, when they had drawn their pursuers some distance from the city, they were suddenly to turn about, give their horses their heads and attack those men. The Romans did as they were commanded; the Russians, thinking the withdrawal of the Romans was a retreat, urged each other on and came in pursuit with loud shouts. When the Romans approached the appointed spot, they turned about and boldly charged the foe. Now there ensued a bitter conflict, in the course of which there fell the commander Theodore of Mistheia, his horse injured by a lance. An intense action was fought around him as the Russians tried to kill him and the Romans strived to stop them from doing so. In fact, as Theodore fell from his horse, he grabbed one of the Scyths by the belt, swinging him this way and that by the strength of his arm, like a light shield, fending off the weapons aimed at him. Little by little and walking backwards, he made his way to where the Romans were. Finally the Romans fell on the Scyths, forced them back and delivered the man from danger. Then the forces disengaged from each other, the battle remaining completely undecided.

16. The emperor realised that the Scyths were fighting with more tenacity than before. He was concerned about how much time the action was taking; he was also moved with compassion for the wretched Romans who were faring so badly in the war, so he came up with the idea of having the matter decided by single combat. And indeed he sent a delegation to Sviatoslav challenging him to fight alone: for (he said) it was better for the decision to be made by the death of one man than to massacre and gradually wear the people down; the winner would take all. But [the Scyth] would not accept the challenge. He answered derisively that he could look after his own affairs better [308] than his enemy; and that, if [John] was weary of life, there were ten thousand other ways of dying; let him embrace whichever one he chose. And with this effrontery he fell to preparing for action even more vigorously. So, abandoning the project of single combat by challenge, the emperor took every measure to close off access to the city

for the barbarians, sending the magister Bardas Skleros with the regular troops under his command to attend to this. Then he ordered an attack on the enemy by the patrician Romanos, son of the emperor Constantine [Lekapenos], the son of Romanos the Elder, and Peter the camp commander, with the forces under their orders. These men charged and fought violently but the Scyths offered stiff resistance so that the battle saw many turns of fortune; indeed, it hung in the balance for some time. That was when Anemas, the son of the emir of Crete, turning his horse this way and that, spurred it forward and came with impetuous determination right up to where Sviatoslav was. Cutting his way through the enemy ranks, he unhorsed [the Scyth] with a blow to the middle of the head with his sword; not a mortal blow on account of the armour the man was wearing. [Anemas] was now assailed on every side and killed, the victim of many blows. His was a heroic death; he was greatly admired even by the enemy.

17. The Romans are said to have benefited from enhanced supernatural aid at that time, for a storm arose in the south and blew into the Scyths' faces, preventing them from performing in battle the way they would have preferred. And a man appeared to the entire Roman army mounted on a white horse, thrusting forward, routing the enemy ranks and throwing them into confusion, a man previously and subsequently unknown to anyone; they say he was one of the [two] gloriously victorious martyrs named Theodore, for the emperor always used [the icons of] these martyrs as allies and protectors against the foe.[67] And it also happened that the engagement in question took place on the very day on which we are accustomed to celebrate the memorial of [St Theodore] the commander.[68] At Byzantium, [309] a trustworthy woman confirmed that the apparition was due to supernatural forces, for she had a dream the day before the engagement in which it appeared that she was in the presence of the Mother of God and heard her saying to a soldier: 'Theodore, sir; John, my [friend] and yours, is in distress; go quickly to his assistance.' She reported this to her neighbours at sunrise; so much for visions. Anyway, the Scyths were driven back again and, finding that the city gates had been closed by Skleros, they dispersed over the plain. Some of

---

[67] On the use of icons on the battlefield: (most recently) B. Pentchevna, *Icons and power: the Mother of God in Byzantium*, Pennsylvania State University Press, 2006, 61–103.

[68] 8 June. Once again the intervention of the supernatural underlines the divine support for imperial action. The choice of St Theodore *stratelates* was dictated partly by the day (which happened to be his feast day), partly by the popularity of this saint with the eastern armies. On the two saints Theodore: N. Oikonomides, 'Le dédoublement de saint Théodore et les villes d'Euchaïta et d'Euchania', *An.Boll.*, 104 (1986), 327–35, and Ch. Walter, *The Warrior Saints of Byzantine art and tradition*, Aldershot, 2003, 44–66.

them died as they trod each other under foot, while even more of them were slaughtered by the Romans and almost all of them were wounded. To honour the martyr and repay him for his timely aid, the emperor tore down to the ground the church in which his sacred body lies and built a large and most beautiful new one which he endowed with splendid estates. The name [of the place] was changed from Euchaneia to Theodoropolis.[69]

18. Sviatoslav had now tried every possible device and had been worsted every time. Realising there was no hope left for him, he contemplated coming to terms. He sent a delegation to the emperor asking for assurance that he could be counted among the allies and friends of the Romans; that he would be allowed to return in safety to his homeland with his men and that any Scyth who wished to do so could freely visit [the empire] for trade purposes. The emperor received the delegation and, repeating the famous saying that it was the custom of the Romans to conquer their enemies with alms rather than with arms, agreed to all the requests.[70] When the treaty had been ratified, Sviatoslav asked also to speak with the emperor and this was agreed to. When he arrived for the interview they met each other, spoke of whatever they pleased and then parted.[71] The emperor also conceded this at Sviatoslav's request: that a delegation be sent to the Patzinaks inviting them too to become friends and allies; allies who would not cross the Danube to prey on the [310] Bulgars but who would allow the Russians to pass through their lands unharmed on their way home. It was Theophilos, bishop of Euchaita,[72] who discharged this mission. When the Patzinaks received the delegation, they agreed to all the other terms but they would not allow free passage to the Russians. Once the Russians had sailed away, the emperor turned his attention to the fortresses and cities along the banks

---

[69] Skylitzes must be mistaken here, for there is no mention in the episcopal lists of the name Theodoropolis for Euchania (which certainly housed a shrine of St Theodore). On the other hand Leo the Deacon, ed. Hase, 158, while he says nothing of the building of a church, does affirm that Dristra was renamed Theodoroupolis – and this is verified by a seal of a *katepan* of Theodoroupolis found at Preslav: I. Jordanov, *Pecatite ot strategijata v Preslav* (Sofia, 1995), nos. 228–31.

[70] Leo the Deacon also attributes the terms of the agreement between Sviatoslav and Tzimiskes to imperial generosity. In fact, it looks as though the emperor was not on the point of taking Dristra and that the better course was negotiation with a view to restoring the situation that obtained prior to the initiative of Nikephoros Phokas, especially as this would leave the emperor in control of Bulgaria.

[71] That the two men met in person may explain why Leo the Deacon, ed. Hase, 156–7, depending on official documentation, has left us an unflattering portrait of the Russian chieftain's physical appearance.

[72] Euchaita was in the Armeniakon theme – which is where the Kourkouai came from. This explains why it was Theophilos (no doubt a good friend of Tzimiskes) who was chosen as amabassador.

of the river and then he returned to Roman territory.[73] The archbishop of the city, the Synod and all the distinguished citizens met him, bearing crowns amid paeans of praise and victory songs. They had prepared a most splendid carriage drawn by four white horses abreast, into which they invited the emperor to step in order to celebrate his triumph. He, however, not wishing to be arrogant but rather to appear modest, while he accepted the proffered crown, rode the triumphal path on a white horse. He placed the royal insignia of the Bulgars in the carriage together with (but above them) the icon of the Mother of God, protectress of the city, and ordered it to precede him.[74] When he arrived at the Forum, surfeited with cheering, he offered thanksgiving for his victories to the Mother of God and to her Son then, in full sight of the citizens, he stripped Boris of the Bulgar regalia:[75] a crown of gold, a tiara of woven linen[76] and scarlet buskins. From there he proceeded to the Great Church where he presented the Bulgar crown as an offering to God. He next promoted Boris to the rank of magister[77] and then went to the palace. When Sviatoslav was making his way back home, as he passed through the land of the Patzinaks, he fell into ambushes already prepared to take him.[78] He and the entire host that accompanied him were completely annihilated, so angry were the Patzinaks with him for having made a treaty with the Romans.

19.[79] [311] In gratitude to Christ the Saviour for his victories, starting afresh, the emperor rebuilt the church above the vault of the Chalke, sparing nothing that might enhance its splendour and beauty.[80] He also excused all taxpayers from the tax called *kapnikon*.[81] He also ordered that

---

[73] Seals found at Preslav make it possible to understand the military organisation set out by Skylitzes: N. Oikonomides, 'A propos de la première occupation byzantine de Bulgarie (971–*ca* 986)', *EUYUCIA, Mélanges offerts à Hélène Ahrweiler*, ed. M. Balard *et al.* (Paris, 1998), 581–9.

[74] The ostentatious humility of the emperor again attests to the divine support which gives legitimacy to his rule. On the new elements introduced into the triumphal ceremonies: M. McCormick, *Eternal victory: triumphal rulership in late antiquity, Byzantium, and the early medieval west*, (Cambridge, MA, 1986), 171–4.

[75] Tzimiskes reorganised Bulgaria into a number of commands each strengthened by a great fortress: Preslav, Dristra and the renovated fortresses at the mouth of the Danube: P. Stephenson, *Byzantium's Balkan frontier: a political study of the northern Balkans, 900–1204* (Cambridge, 2000), 55–8.

[76] *Byssos*, see Luke 16:19, the rich man (Dives) 'clothed in purple *and fine linen*'.

[77] In this way Boris was integrated into the Byzantine honours system at a high level.

[78] His skull was made into a drinking cup, a tradition among nomad peoples.

[79] Many things are passed over in silence here, e.g. the marriage of Tzimiskes' niece to Otto II, son and heir of the emperor Otto I, in spring 972. This marriage signalled complete acceptance of John's *coup d'état*, while assuring the security of the empire's possessions in Italy.

[80] This church was built by Romanos Lekapenos, who endowed it with twelve clergy. Tzimiskes enlarged it, increased the staff to fifty and deposited the relics he had brought back from his campaigns there: Janin, *Églises et monastères*, I, 529–30.

[81] This tax on fireplaces probably amounted to two pieces of silver per hearth: Oikonomides, *Fiscalité*, 30. Tzimiskes had already offered tax relief to those living in the Armeniakon theme.

the image of the Saviour be inscribed on the gold and copper coins, something which had not happened before, and on one of the sides there was written Roman letters saying, 'Jesus Christ, king of kings' – a practice which subsequent emperors retained.[82] Charges were laid against the patriarch Basil and he was deposed by the Synod;[83] Anthony the Stoudite was promoted in his stead.[84]

20. In the month of August, third year of the indiction,[85] a comet appeared called 'bearded' and it remained visible until the month of October, fourth year of the indiction. It presaged the death of the emperor and the irreparable damage which was to befall the Roman lands through civil war.

21. The cities which (as we said above) had been appropriated by the emperor Nikephoros and made subject to the Romans had now kicked up their heels and thrown off Roman domination; so the emperor set out against them and advanced as far as Damascus.[86]

22. Some of them he won back by persuasion and negotiation, others with arms and violence; then, when he had restored everything to a state of decency, he turned back towards the capital. When he came to Anazarbos, as he was proceeding along the Podandos and through the other areas, inspecting what he came across, he noted that the properties were affluent, the estates prolific in every respect. He asked the people he

---

[82] On the coins of Tzimiskes: Grierson, *DOC*, 3, 2:588–9.

[83] According to Leo the Deacon, 163, trans. 205, the patriarch Basil was accused of plotting against the emperor, perhaps in favour of Bardas Skleros whom we know was almost blinded in this reign; he was exiled to his monastery of Skamander.

[84] The patriarchate of Anthony extended from December 973 to June 978: J. Darrouzès, 'Sur la chronologie du patriarche Antoine III Stoudite', *REB*, 46 (1988), 55–60.   [85] AD 975.

[86] The accounts of both Skylitzes and Leo the Deacon are very unbalanced for they have little to say about the east – which was the principal field of operations under Tzimiskes. Skylitzes gives only four lines to the largest expedition, omitting the campaigns of 972 and 974. Yahya of Antioch and Matthew of Edessa, 28–33, provide more detailed accounts, they being more sensitive to what went on in the east. These campaigns carried the emperor beyond the Euphrates; he took Nisibis in autumn 972, but then Melias, the domestic of the scholai whom he left behind in the east, allowed himself to be beaten and captured before Amida in June 973: Yahya of Antioch, II, 353–4. On the eastern campaigns of Tzimiskes: M. Canard, 'La date des expéditions mésopotamiennes de Jean Tzikmiskès', *Mélanges Henri Grégoire*, 11, *AIPHOS*, x (1960), 99–108, repr. Canard, *Byzance*, no. XIII. Tzimiskes was also obliged to oppose the Fatimids in view of their rising military power. The campaign of 975 saw the emperor in Syria where he was able to compel the emir of Damascus to pay tribute in order to avert an attack on his city. Matthew of Edessa provides the text of a letter sent allegedly to the Bagratid king Ashot III by Tzimiskes in which he boasts of the victory of the Christians over the Moslems, mentioning the relics of Christ and of John the Baptist which he had seized at Djabal in Syria: Matthew of Edessa, 28–33. Yahya of Antioch, 11, 368–9, says the emperor took Baalbek, made the emir of Damascus a tributory of the empire, took Beirut, but failed before Tripoli before conquering the fortresses of Balanias and Saone, thus establishing the borders of the duchy of Antioch which held for a century. On the extension of Tzimiskes' campaign southward: P. E. Walker, 'The 'crusade' of John Tzimiskes in the light of new Arabic evidence', *B*, 47 (1977), 301–27.

encountered whose land this might be and learnt from his interlocutors that it all belonged to Basil the parakoimomenos: 'This estate and that one were recently added to the Roman lands by the emperor Nikephoros, [312] the one over there by the domestic of the scholai, the next one by such-and-such, the one after it by you – and all these estates have been given to Basil.' Yet of these acquisitions he saw nothing worthy of note which had been left to the public treasury.[87] He was deeply troubled and heaved a great sigh, saying: 'Oh, gentlemen, what a terrible thing it is if, when public funds are expended, the Roman armies are reduced to penury, the emperors endure hardships beyond the borders and the fruits of all this effort become the property of one – eunuch!' Thus spake the emperor, and one of those present reported what the emperor had said to Basil, which provoked him to wrath; so that, henceforth, he was looking for an opportunity to rid himself of the emperor. In due course he won over the emperor's usual wine pourer with flattery and bribed him with gifts. He prepared some poison, not the most deadly or one which speedily brings on ill effects, but one of those that gradually sap the strength of those who drink them. This toxin was served to the emperor in wine; he drank it and gradually fell ill, losing his energy. Finally, boils broke out on his shoulders and there was a copious haemorrhaging from the eyes.[88] He returned to the capital and departed this life after reigning a little more than six years and as many months;[89] he left to succeed him in life Basil and Constantine, the sons of Romanos.

{This is what he looked like: he had a white face and high colouring. His hair was fair but thin; he let it hang down over his forehead. His eyes were lively and clear, his nose narrow and well-proportioned. His moustache was red and stretched out a long way at the sides while his beard was of normal length and thick. He was not tall but the chest and back were broad. He was enormously strong; the dexterity and vigour of his arm was irresistible. He was possessed of a heroic soul, fearless and intrepid, displaying supernatural courage in so small a body. He would not hesitate to charge a whole rank single-handed, after which he would speedily [313] return to his own ranks having slain many victims. He surpassed all the men of those days in jumping, handball, javelin-throwing and archery. He

---

[87] The normal procedure was for conquered lands, whether they had been taken from a private owner or belonged to a conquered emir, to be managed by public trustees or *episkeptitai*. On this transfer: J. Howard-Johnston, 'Crown lands and the defence of imperial authority in the tenth and eleventh centuries', *Byz. Forsch.* 21 (1995), 75–100.

[88] It is by no means certain that he was poisoned.

[89] This calculation is not correct: John reigned from 11 December 969 to 10 January 976, the day he died: Leo the Deacon, 178, trans. 220.

would line up four saddle-horses, take a run at one side, fly through the air like a bird and end up astride the fourth horse. He could shoot arrows through a ring and hit his mark. He would put a leather ball at the bottom of a glass vessel, spur on his horse to great speed and hit the ball with a stick to make it jump up and fly while the vessel remained in its place intact. He loved giving, and giving on a grand scale; nobody who asked for anything ever went away empty-handed – unless Basil the parakoimomenos restrained him. He did have this fault that sometimes he allowed himself to drink more than was proper, and he was violently excited by the pleasures of the flesh. He was forty-five years old when he began to reign and he had lived in all fifty-one years when he died. The bishop of Sebasteia says that Basil [II] began to reign on 11 January, and he is to be believed.[90]}

---

[90] {...} Interpolation of MSS AE.

CHAPTER 16

Basil II and Constantine VIII bis *[976–1025]*

1. [314] John met his end in the way described; the right to rule now passed to Basil[1] and Constantine, the sons of Romanos [II],[2] in the month of December, AM 6468, fourth year of the indiction,[3] Basil being then in his twentieth year, Constantine three years younger. But they only became emperors in appearance and name, for the administration of the affairs of state was undertaken by Basil [Lekapenos] the president on account of the youth of the emperors, their immaturity and their as yet undeveloped aptitude.[4] As soon as the right to rule had passed to the sons of Romanos [II], [the president] sent messengers speeding to bring their mother back

---

[1] Skylitzes is the only chronicler to provide a record – albeit somewhat patchy – of the reign of Basil II; both Zonaras and Kedrenos depend on him for their information. In order to control what he reports we have to turn to Asolik of Taron (who is only mainly concerned with affairs in the Caucasus region) and Yahya of Antioch, who provides an excellent report but is mainly interested in eastern affairs. The portrait of Basil II given by Psellos in his *Chronographia* (1:2–4) offers no new factual information but offers a picture of the emperor (that being the aim of the historian) that has largely contributed to the modern idea of a severe and austere Basil II. No modern work covers the reign as a whole. C. Holmes, *Basil II and the governance of empire (976–1025)* (Oxford Studies in Byzantium, Oxford, 2005), presents a study of the methods of government in the time of the great emperor. On his subsequent reputation: P. Stephenson, *The Legend of Basil the Bulgar-slayer* (Cambridge, 2003). We still use the monumental work that remains remarkable for its period: G. Schlumberger, *L'épopée byzantine à la fin du dixième siècle: Basile II le tueur de Bulgares* (Paris, 1900). Individual aspects of the reign have been dealt with in more recent works: politics in Cheynet, *Pouvoir* and in *Byzantium in the year 1000*, ed. P. Magdalino (The Medieval Mediterranean, 45, Leiden, 2003), there are articles on Basil's matrimonial policy (J. Shepard), the role of the elites (C. Holmes), foreign policy (J.-C. Cheynet, P. Stephenson, V. von Falkenhausen), the influence of millenarism (P. Magdalino) and other aspects, including Basil's relations with intellectuals of the period. On millenarism see also I. Ševčenko, 'Unpublished Byzantine texts on the end of the world about the year 1000 AD', *Mélanges Gilbert Dagron*, ed. V. Déroche, D. Feissel, C. Morrisson, C. Zuckerman, *TM*, 14 (2002), 561–78.
[2] The succession was somewhat simplified by the fact that John Tzimiskes had no children.
[3] 976.
[4] The second reason seems better than the first since Basil was already eighteen years old, his brother sixteen. Constantine may have already been married (see the reign of Constantine VIII, c. 3 where there is mention of his wife, the daughter of Alypios) seeing that his second daughter, Zoe, was born around 978.

from exile and into the palace. He feared an uprising against the government, and more than any other he feared the magister Bardas Skleros who was always lying in wait for a chance to rule and forever labouring to bring forth an uprising. He had been arrested for conspiring against the emperor John and condemned to have his eyes put out but the punishment was stayed by the same emperor. He was especially to be feared as the entire Roman army was now in his hands; he could easily take it wherever he wished and take risks with it for he had been promoted commander of the entire east.[5] [Basil the president] thought it would benefit the security of the empire to cut down this great force, rendering Skleros less powerful for undertaking the uprising which he was suspected [of fomenting]. So he relieved Skleros of his command and appointed him duke of the regular troops in Mesopotamia;[6] his orders were to watch over and guard against the inroads of the Saracens. He devised the same fate for Michael Bourtzes, [315] who also was suspected, quickly detaching him from Skleros' company (for he was with Skleros, in command of a unit). This [Michael] he raised to the rank of magister and appointed him duke of Antioch on the Orontes.[7] As superintendent and overseer of all the forces of the east he appointed the patrician Peter, the creature of Phokas, with the title of camp commander;[8] he was a eunuch but very dynamic and highly experienced in military matters. This all grieved Skleros severely, so much so that he was not man enough to keep his grief to himself but flung out accusations and reproaches. Was demotion[9] the kind of reward he was to receive for all the courageous deeds and victories which he had brought about? And that with the parakoimomenos caring little or nothing about it, but rather telling him to be content with the command he had received and not to try to gain more than he had been given, unless he preferred confinement on his own estates rather than exercising a command.

---

[5] Skylitzes' narrative is less than coherent. Skleros had narrowly escaped having his eyes put out under Tzimiskes on suspicion of conspiracy and yet now we find him in total command of the armies of the east. Basil the parakoimomenos would scarcely have approved of such an appointment as he was concerned to limit the influence of Skleros.

[6] It seems as though Skleros was not appointed strategos of the theme of Mesopotamia but commander (duke) of the regular army units stationed in that theme.

[7] Bourtzes was one of the conquerors of Antioch in 969.

[8] *stratopedarches*; Peter had already held this appointment under Tzimiskes.

[9] Holmes (*Basil II*, 324–7) considers that, since Skleros remained at the head of an army powerful enough to challenge the Hamdanides of Mosul, this was not really a demotion. That may be so from a military point of view but, in terms of prestige, it was indeed a demotion. The post of duke of Mesopotamia is two ranks lower down than that of stratelates in the *Taktikon scorialensis*. It is, however, slightly higher than a strategos of Mesopotamia, which is the point of reference in this case: Oikonomides, *Listes*, 263.

2. When things had been arranged in this way by the parakoimomenos, Bardas quickly left the city and took up the command which had been entrusted to him. In his former commands he had often given the impression of vigour and dynamism, so that he was loved by the whole army one might say. So now he could reveal the secret of what he was about to attempt to many people in whom he had confidence, especially among the units of the camp commander. Then, when he thought the time was ripe to proclaim his intentions openly, he consulted with his immediate colleagues and gave birth to the uprising with which he had been in labour for so long: he took arms against the emperors[10] and against his fellow countrymen. He immediately despatched a man named Anthes Alyates[11] to the capital. This was the most dynamic of his subordinates; he was to attempt to seize Bardas' son, Romanos,[12] who was then residing at the capital, and bring him to his father. When he arrived at the capital, Anthes spread unflattering reports about Skleros as he left no stone unturned to throw people off the scent. In this way he was able to dispel suspicion, deceive everybody, get possession of Romanos [316] and to bring him to Skleros. Now Bardas had openly declared what his intentions were; he donned the diadem and the rest of the imperial insignia and was proclaimed emperor by the entire Roman army there present, the Armenians leading the way in the acclamation. He was well aware that in a game of chance such as this there had to be plenty of money and that, without money, nothing of what ought to be would be accomplished (as the orator says)[13] so he immediately set about acquiring money. He arrested the state tax collectors and appropriated public funds.[14] He apprehended and extracted money from people suspected of being affluent, while others brought him their wealth of their own free will in the hope of receiving even greater wealth eventually. By these means he collected a large amount of money in a short time. He seized a strongly fortified bastion in Mesopotamia named Charpete[15] which he rendered fully secure in every way and adequately garrisoned. Here he concentrated and deposited the money; this

---

[10] There is a considerable bibliography on the rebellion of Skleros: Seibt, *Skleroi*, 35–48; Cheynet, *Pouvoir*, 33–4; Holmes, *Basil II*, 241–98. Skylitzes' chronology is often confused. As usual he has sythesised different sources and may have added some literary elements such as the single combat of the two Bardas, Skleros and Phokas.
[11] This is the first mention of a family which supplied many strategoi in the course of the century. Anthes is a rare Christian name: it was held by a person close to Constantine V: *PBE*, Anthes, 3.
[12] On Romanos: Seibt, *Skleroi*, 60–5.   [13] Demosthenes, *Olynth.*, 1.20.
[14] Skleros had the *basilikos* of Melitene arrested and laid his hands on six hundred pounds of gold. With this treasure in hand he had himself proclaimed emperor: Yahya of Antioch, 11, 372.
[15] The Hisn Ziyâd of the Arabic texts, now Harput in eastern Turkey.

he kept in reserve as a base for operations should things not go well and as a harbour of safe refuge. He exchanged assurances with the neighbouring Saracens, Apotoulph[16] the emir of Amida (which they called Emet) and Apotagle[17] emir of Martyropolis (which they call Miepherkeim).[18] He secured friendship with them by marrying and giving in marriage;[19] he also received much money in addition to three hundred Arab horsemen as auxiliaries. As word of all this went out in every direction, there flocked to him the sort of people who rejoice in reckless undertakings. When summer arrived he advanced on the capital with his entire army, full of hope and under the impression that all he had to do was to occupy the palace. He had been emboldened and further encouraged in the undertaking by the vision which a virtuous monk claimed to have had one night. It was as though he saw some [317] fiery men who took Bardas and brought him to a lofty point where he encountered a woman of superhuman appearance; she presented him with the imperial scourge. Bardas took the scourge to be symbolic of ruling the empire, but it was the wrath of God against the Romans.

3. When news [of the uprising] reached the capital the emperors were greatly distressed and despair overcame those of the citizens who had intelligence and integrity. The only ones who were pleased were those who delight in political disruptions and taking spoils. A letter was sent in all haste to Peter the camp commander and the loyal portion of the army was hastily assembled at Caesarea. While this was happening Stephen the synkellos, bishop of Nicomedia, a man of learning, well known for his wisdom and virtue,[20] possessing the ability of calming rough and wild minds by persuasion – this Stephen was sent as an envoy to Skleros to see whether he could persuade him to lay down his arms. But Skleros had his mind set on one thing: his desire to be emperor. The synkellos made many a cogent and persuasive argument but Skleros did not waste words. He stretched out his right foot to show the scarlet buskin, saying: 'It is impossible, sir, for a man who has once publicly worn that boot voluntarily to take it off again. Tell those who sent you that either they accept me willingly as

---

[16] Abu Dulaf, governor of Amida/Diyarbakir until 979–80 on behalf of Abu Taglib.
[17] Abu Taglib, Hamdanid emir of Mosul, who died in Palestine 979–80: T. Ripper, *Die Marwâniden von Diyâr Bakr: eine kurdische Dynastie im islamischen Mittelalter* (Würzburg, 2000), 498.
[18] Martyropolis, Mayyafariqin in Arabic, is now Silvan to the north-east of Amida: *ODB*, II, 1308–9.
[19] It is possible that Bardas married his son Romanos to the sister or the daughter of Abu Taglib: Seibt, *Skleroi*, 65.
[20] Together with Symeon the logothete he had given an optimistic interpretation of the passage of the comet in the reign of John Tzimiskes: Leo the Deacon, 169, trans. 211–12.

emperor or I will attempt to seize the throne against their will.' Those were his words; he granted a delay of forty days and sent him on his way. When the synkellos returned and reported Skleros' reply to the emperors and to Basil who was ruling the empire, the camp commander was instructed by letter not to instigate a civil war, [318] but he was to maintain a close watch on the roads and to repel anybody who came a-warring. Then Skleros advanced on Caesarea, sending out scouts and observers to reconnoitre and to inform him of the enemy's dispositions; also to prepare the way for him. He appointed Anthes Alyates to command this detachment which, finding itself in a narrow pass (they call that place Cuckoo Rock), encountered a section of the imperial army under the command of the magister Eustathios Maleinos.[21] An engagement was attempted and there was some exchange of blows. In fact the armies kept thrusting at each other for some time without either side giving way, until Alyates could contain himself no longer. Swept away by an excess of zeal he put spur to his horse and charged the enemy at an insane speed. He achieved nothing worthy of note for he fell, mortally wounded, and all his company melted away into the adjacent woods and bushes. At that time Bardas' hetaireiarch[22] was denounced as a would-be deserter to the emperor's army. Skleros had him brought into his presence and scolded him, then let him go without openly doing anything else to him in public; but he secretly instructed the Saracen mercenaries to slay him. Milling around him as he passed through their midst, they cut him down with their swords, in broad daylight.

4. The commanders of the imperial forces were now more apprehensive than ever of an onslaught by Skleros, so they judged it prudent to occupy the strategic points on the road. Taking the entire army, they set up camp over against him and took possession of the roads he was going to follow. Skleros became inactive when he learnt of this and hesitated to advance. He wasted time with this delay, waiting to see what the outcome would be. He was spurred to action and rendered more eager by a deserter, a high-ranking officer Sachakios Brachamios[23] by name. [This person] arrived urging Skleros [319] to waste no more time for (he said) delay earns contempt and, since his words seemed judicious, he was appointed commander and guide for the journey. He led, Skleros followed, and in three

---

[21] Without consulting Bardas, now head of the Phokas family, the parakoimomenos nevertheless makes use of that man's close friends, Peter the stratopedarches and Maleinos.
[22] Skleros has distributed military appointments as though he were already emperor. The hetaireiarch was the commander of foreign contingents.
[23] This general of Armenian extraction had participated at the taking of Antioch: Yahya of Antioch, 1, 822.

days they reached Lapara, a district of Cappadocia now called Likandos[24] (it used to be called Lapara on account of its fertility and abundance). When the camp commander learnt of this he marched by night for fear of not overtaking Skleros; then he pitched camp in face of the enemy. The opponents delayed and postponed an open engagement for some time, seeking to gain victory by subterfuge. Bardas outmanoeuvred his enemy by preparing a great amount of food as though he were going to give a banquet for his army. Thus he deceived his adversary into thinking that he would not instigate a battle that day, whereupon they too gave themselves to feasting. When Skleros became aware of this (he had his troops already prepared for battle), the trumpet suddenly sounded the 'attack' and he fell on the enemy soldiers as they feasted. They, however, withstood the onslaught, each one seizing whatever weapon came to hand; nor were they unduly disturbed by the suddenness of it. For some time they stood firm but then Bardas effected an outflanking movement which made the enemy afraid of being surrounded. Then he sent the mercenaries round behind and put the foe to flight; a great slaughter ensued. Bourtzes, the duke of Antioch, was the first to break ranks, either out of cowardice or malice; both are alleged. [Bardas] captured the encampment with all the baggage; he also acquired an enormous amount of wealth. From there he came to the place called Tzamandos,[25] a city situated on a beetling precipice, rich in people and in wealth; wealth which the people of the region willingly handed over to him, hence he collected a considerable fortune there. This victory disturbed many of those remaining faithful to the emperor and prompted them to desert to Skleros. Bourtzes was the first to desert,[26] then the patrician Andronikos Lydos and his sons. The people of Attalia put the emperor's droungarios in chains and, with all the fleet, rallied to [320] Michael Kourtikios who had been sent by Skleros to command the Kibyrrhaiote theme.[27]

5. When these things were reported to the emperor and to the parakoimomenos a council was held and it was proposed that somebody close

---

[24] A Greek word for abundance/fertility is *liparon*; it was a region where there was an abundance of forage for the cavalry.

[25] Continuing his march westward, Bardas came to this town situated about 60 km east of Caesarea in Cappadocia: F. Hild and M. Restle, *Kappadokien (Kappadokia, Charsianon, Sebasteia und Lykandos)* (TIB, 2, Vienna, 1981), 300–1. His victory here allowed him to continue his march on the capital. It also opened up central Asia Minor to him, probably causing many landowners in the area to join his cause rather than have him as their enemy.

[26] This defection meant the loss of Antioch and its vast resources to Basil. Bardas Skleros appointed an Arab convert to Christianity named Oubeidallah duke of Antioch with the title of magister: Yahya of Antioch, 11, 373. On this person: Holmes, *Basil II*, 379–81.

[27] The principal naval theme of the empire, base of a large provincial fleet.

to the emperor should be sent against the usurper, a plenipotentiary not answerable for his decisions, with powers to award honours and also to enrich with gifts those who rallied to his support. This proposal was approved; Leo,[28] the emperor's protovestiarios, was sent with a patrician named John as his colleague, a distinguished person renowned for his oratorical skills. Leo was granted authority by the emperor to do whatever the emperor might do. He departed and came to Kotyaion in Phrygia[29] where he joined up with Peter the camp commander and there he pitched his camp; Bardas was now encamped at Dipotamon, an imperial estate which the local people call Mesanakta.[30] [Leo] quietly tried to draw away the insurgents with promises of gifts and honours and to gain their support for the emperor but he was not successful; rather did he strengthen the enemy cause, for his overtures were interpreted as a sign of weakness. So he abandoned that plan of action and, leaving Kotyaeon, marched past the camp of Skleros by night and headed further east. This manoeuvre sowed fear in the hearts of Skleros' men; they were afraid not only for their money and property, but also for those whom they held most dear.[31] So, many of them renounced the uprising and flocked to the protovestiarios, putting the uprising in danger of disintegrating like dust. Fearing that this might happen, Skleros sent the magister Michael Bourtzes (who, as we said, had joined his ranks) and the patrician Romanos Taronites with a light unit; their orders were to oppose the protovestiarios by obstructing him by attacking him as soon as contact was made. They were also to prevent him from sending out raiding parties as much as they could, but to avoid a full-scale battle if possible. However, [321] when Bourtzes and his men drew near to the imperial army they were obliged to fight willy-nilly, contrary to Skleros' instructions, for the following reason. It became known that Saracens from Berroia-in-the-east[32] were travelling to the capital to pay their annual tribute and that on a certain day they were

---

[28] Possibly the droungarios of the fleet under John Tzimiskes who succeeded in arresting Leo the kouropalates: R. Guilland, *Recherches sur les institutions Byzantines, I–II* (Berlin and Amsterdam), I, 220.

[29] The imperial forces attempted to stop Skleros in Phrygia as he advanced along the military road leading to Malagina then on to Nicomedia.

[30] The exact location of this Phrygian fortress is not known, but it was near the lake of the Forty Martyrs: Belke and Mersich, *Phrygien und Pisidien*, 338. Bardas Skleros would know the region well for he advanced as far as this when he was fighting against the rebel Bardas Phokas in 970. The vast imperial estate in Phrygia may have been used for raising horses: a most important resource from a military point of view. On the *metata* of Phrygia: Haldon, *Welfare State*, 141–2.

[31] The stratopedarch uses exactly the same intimidation tactics as his adversary, the object being to put an end to the conflict without a formal battle being fought.

[32] Aleppo. The Hamdanid emir of Aleppo had been forced to become a client of the empire by the victorious campaigns of Nikephoros Phokas; a treaty was signed in 970.

to pass between the two armies. When the appointed day arrived and the Saracens were about to pass the fortress called Oxylithos,[33] Bourtzes' colleagues armed their men and the officers of the protovestiarios did likewise; then they charged into battle. For both sides the gold the Saracens were bringing lay before them as a prize to be won; as they drew near they fell on each other and fought. Bourtzes was put to flight and many of those with him were slain, especially among the Armenians. In fact the Romans slew every Armenian they captured without quarter, for they had been the first to join the uprising.[34]

6. When this reverse was reported to Bardas he wasted no time in hastening to confront his adversaries. He came to a place called Rhageas and pitched camp there, in wait of an opportune time to give battle. But as the imperial forces were in no hurry, the time for battle was delayed and many of the rebels, discouraged by the former defeat, went over to the protovestiarios. The inexperienced men in the imperial army, puffed up by and exulting in the recent victory, were eager for action, but the battle-seasoned veterans were for holding back and postponing the conflict.[35] But, as the proverb says, 'He who urges in haste follows the path to woe';[36] the protovestiarios was convinced by the younger men. He sounded the 'attack' and led [322] his troops into battle. Bardas divided his army into three parts; he led the middle one himself, his brother Constantine led the right wing while he set Constantine Gabras[37] to command the left wing. When battle was joined the commanders of the wings sent the cavalry against the foe and, unable to withstand the charge, the protovestiarios' troops were put to flight with severe loss of life. That was when the patrician John fell, Peter the camp commander and many of the

---

[33] A fortress to the south-west of Mesanakta in Phrygia: Belke and Mersich, *Phrygien und Pisidien*, 353.

[34] Skleros' ancestry was partially Armenian. He was also very influential in the *Armeniaka themata*, those frontier themes with an Armenian population. According to Asolik de Taron, *Histoire universelle*, tr. F. Macler (Paris, 1917), 56–7, Armenian troops, particularly those lead by Taronitai, were especially distinguished by their gallantry in civil war, 'putting many enemies to the sword'. Hatred clearly escalated in the course of a civil war.

[35] The experienced officers argue that time is on their side as people were deserting Skleros. That is why Skleros was anxious to bring things to a head.

[36] Sophocles, *Fragment* 860 Pearson = 785 Nauck, quoted by Plutarch, *Artaxerxes*, 28.

[37] The first mention of this family (originally from Trebizond) which distinguished itself in the army during the eleventh and twelfth centuries, especially during the reign of Alexis Comnenos: A. A. M. Bryer, 'A Byzantine family: the Grabades *c.* 979–*c.* 1653', *University of Birmingham Historical Journal*, 12 (1970), 174–87; also A. A. M. Bryer, S. Fassoulakis and D. M. Nicol, 'A Byzantine family, the Grabades: an additional note', *BS*, 36 (1975), 38–45. See also A. A. M. Bryer, A. Dunn and J. Nesbitt, 'Theodore Gabras, duke of Chaldia (†1098) and the Gabrades: portraits, sites and seals', *Byzantium, state and society: in memory of Nikos Oikonomides*, ed. A. A. Avramea, A. Laiou and E. Chrysos (Athens, 2003), 51–70.

nobility. The protovestiarios was taken prisoner with other senior officers. [Bardas] ordered the protovestiarios to be imprisoned and in the sight of the whole army he put out the eyes of the brothers Theodore and Niketas Hagiozacharites[38] for having broken the oaths they took to him and gone over to the protovestiarios.

7. As a result of this victory Bardas' prestige rose higher and higher, with everybody (one might say), great and small, flocking to his standard, while the emperor's cause was close to collapse, except that it was firmly secured by one anchor, and that a sacred one: the help of God. Yet while the parakoimomenos was concerned about what was happening on land, he was far more concerned about what was going on at sea. He was deeply disturbed by the commander of the enemy fleet, Michael Kourtikios, who after ravaging every island now seemed to be about to blockade Abydos[39] on the Hellespont. Fitting out the best fleet he could, the parakoimomenos sent it out against Kourtikios under the command of the patrician Theodore Karantenos.[40] Out he sailed, passed through the straits of the Hellespont and engaged Kourtikios off Phokaia. A bitter naval conflict ensued, then Kourtikios' [ships] were put to flight and dispersed; Karantenos got the upper hand and thus gained mastery of the seas.[41] Once things [323] were well dealt with at sea, the parakoimomenos turned his attention to matters on land. He despatched the patrician Manuel Erotikos, a man distinguished by birth, virtue and courage,[42] to defend Nicaea.[43] Shortly afterwards Skleros approached; he set fire to all the villages around Nicaea and finally came to the city itself. He attempted to take it by storm, using siege-engines and other devices, but Manuel bravely withstood the assault, repelling the ladders from the walls and burning the siege-engines with Greek fire, so that Skleros gave up the idea of taking it by storm. But he hoped to reduce it by depriving it of the necessities of life. The siege went

---

[38] Bardas inflicts the punishment reserved for those guilty of treason against the legitimate emperor; meaning, in this case, against himself.
[39] Skleros did not have a hope of taking Constantinople unless he could attack it by sea. In order to do that he had to control the Dardanelles/Hellespont, to which Abydos is the key.
[40] This victory gained him the title of magister, as we learn from an inscription at Hadrianople in Phrygia: W. M. Calder, *Eastern Phrygia, Monumenta Asiae Minoris Antiqua*, VII (Manchester, 1928), no. 190. Henceforth the Karentenoi figure among the military elite of the empire.
[41] Skylitzes has no doubt conflated two engagements into one: Holmes, *Basil II*, 456 and note 27.
[42] Manuel (also known as Komnenos: Bryennios, ed. Gautier, 75) was of an illustrious line, but not the first. A certain Nikephoros Erotikos was sent by Nikephoros Phokas to negotiate with the Bulgars in 969: Leo the Deacon, 79. Probably Skylitzes is attempting to enhance the ancestry of the Komnenoi.
[43] Skleros is still following the great military road towards Constantinople but he cannot afford to leave a well-protected enemy garrison in his rear – behind the impressive walls of Nicaea.

on for some time and those within ran short of grain. Manuel did not know what to do nor from where to get sufficient supplies for Abydos to keep body and soul together, because Skleros was keeping a tight watch on the approaches. Then he decided to outwit Skleros with a trick. He had the granaries of Nicaea filled with sand in secret and then a little grain was spread over the sand, enough to deceive the eyes of the beholder. Then he summoned some of the enemy they had taken prisoner, showed them the granaries and sent them back with orders to say: 'I have no fear of the siege causing famine, for I have enough supplies of food for two years and the city is impregnable by assault. But I am really on your side; I am prepared to surrender the city to you if you will engage yourself by oaths to let me and those with me go free wherever we choose.' Bardas willingly accepted this proposition and gave the undertakings. Manuel went out with the citizens of Nicaea, his own army and everything they possessed and proceeded to the capital. Skleros occupied Nicaea and discovered the trick that had been pulled on him concerning the grain; he was furious to have been deceived like that. Nevertheless he left an adequate garrison in Nicaea with a man named Pegasios[44] in command while he went on to subsequent adventures.

8. [324] The parakoimomenos was greatly perplexed by all this (for Skleros was already on his way to the capital) and could produce only one adequate solution: to bring back Bardas Phokas from exile, thinking him to be the only effective antidote to Skleros. Quicker than it takes to tell he recalled him, secured his loyalty with oaths, showered him with wealth, raised him to the rank of magister and appointed him domestic of the scholai, then sent him out to do battle with Skleros. Accepting this challenge on which everything depended, Phokas first tried to cross to Abydos from Thrace but Romanos, the son of Skleros, was guarding the area of the Hellespont; he was driven back and returned to the capital. There he took shipping and, slipping unnoticed past the enemy and successfully disembarking on the opposite shore, he made his way by night marches to Caesarea[45] where he joined up with the magister Eustathios Maleinos and Michael Bourtzes (who had undergone a change of heart

---

[44] This Pegasios (with the elevated title of patrician) had a command in the region of Antioch in 1004/1005: Yahya of Antioch, II, 466. Another official of the same name is known during the reign of Alexis Comnenos: *Alexiade*, II, 227; *Alexias*, 314.

[45] Bardas Phokas was no doubt bringing along some troops from the west, but it was in Cappadocia that he was counting on amassing those faithful to the emperors. His aim was to cause the disintegration of Skleros' army by threats to the families of the soldiers and officers of which it consisted. At the beginning of 978 Antioch and its duke, Oubeidallah, switched their loyalties back to the emperors: Yahya of Antioch, II, 376–8.

and joined up with the imperial forces again). Together they prepared for battle; he assembled whatever army the situation would allow and gathered up those who had been dispersed in the rout, then they marched on Amorion. When Skleros heard Phokas had set out, he thought that now for the first time the fight would be against a true soldier, one who well knew how to conduct military operations with courage and skill; not, as formerly, against pitiful fellows, eunuchs, fostered in chambers and raised in the shade. He took off from Nicaea and went to Amorion[46] where he encountered Phokas and joined battle with him. Phokas' troops were unable to withstand the charge, mainly because the edge of their morale and courage had been blunted by the previous reverses; thus Skleros got the upper hand. Nevertheless, Phokas' army did not by any means disperse in a disorderly retreat. It gave ground, [325] but withdrew in an unhurried way, giving the impression that this retreat was not from fear of being pursued, but in obedience to a commander's instructions, well organised and without breaking ranks. And even as the soldiers turned their backs and started to retreat, there was Phokas commanding the rearguard, repelling attackers and preventing them from striking in full force and vigour. It was now (they say) while he and his men were pursuing the retreating enemy that the excessively ambitious Constantine Gabras got it into his head that he could acquire great distinction if he could make Phokas his prisoner. He spurred on the horse he was riding and came up at great speed to where Phokas was. Phokas looked at him, realised who he was, quietly brought his horse about, came within arms length of Gabras and struck him on the helmet with his mace. The man was stunned by the irresistible force of the blow and immediately fell from his horse. A little more at his ease, Phokas continued on his way, proceeding at a gentle pace and certainly not giving the horse its head. When Gabras' men saw that their own commander had fallen they held back from the pursuit in order to attend to him. Meanwhile, Phokas and his forces arrived at the place called Charsianon[47] where they lodged, waiting to see what would happen. Here he received many people coming over to his side with gifts from the emperor while the zeal of those already with him was intensified with favours. Skleros came after him and pitched camp at a place called

---

[46] Phokas has achieved what he was aiming at: Skleros has turned about and headed for Caesarea in Cappadocia by the most direct route, which goes through the capital of the Anatolikon theme. The battle took place on the plain of Pankaleia: Leo the Deacon, 170, on 19 June 978: Yahya of Antioch, II, 375.
[47] Phokas has now returned to the theme from which he set out and taken refuge in the fortress of the same name.

Imperial Hotsprings,[48] calling upon his namesake to come out and fight. The other did not hesitate to accept this challenge; battle was immediately joined. Phokas' troops prevailed for some time while he rode in all directions, breaking down the ranks of the enemy with his iron mace and slaying thousands. But yet again his men turned their backs and were put to flight.

9. [326] Then Phokas went to Iberia with all the speed he could muster. He came to David,[49] the ruler of the Iberians, asking for an army to support him. This was readily granted[50] for David was well disposed towards Phokas since the time when he served as duke of Chaldia.[51] He received a considerable body of troops and also reassembled his men who had been dispersed in the rout. He came down to Pankaleia[52] where Skleros was already encamped.[53] At Pankaleia there is an open plain lying by the river Halys, well suited to cavalry manoeuvres. Another violent battle took place in the course of which Phokas saw his men giving way little by little and contemplating the possibility of retreat. Judging a glorious death to be preferable to an ignoble and shameful life, cutting his way through the enemy ranks he came rushing up to Skleros himself. Skleros firmly withstood the other's charge and, when none of the soldiers came to his aid (for they preferred the matter to be decided by a contest between the commanders and, indeed, thought that it would be a magnificent and astounding sight for the beholders, two men of courageous and valiant heart locked in single combat with each other), the two brought each other up short and engaged in hand-to-hand fighting. Skleros struck Phokas' horse with his

---

[48] *Basilika therma*, Sarikaya today, then a bishopric located about 100 km to the north of Caesarea: Hild and Restle, *Kappadokien*, 156–7.

[49] David belonged to the Georgian branch of the Bagratids and reigned until 961 over Tao-Klartjetie, a province of south-west Georgia bordering on Chaldia. On this family: C. Toumanoff, 'The Bagratids of Iberia from the eighth to the eleventh century', *Museon*, 74 (1961), 37–40.

[50] A different version of the story circulated among the Georgians: a eunuch who had been sent to Constantinople met Tornikios, a former general of David now become a monk on Athos. Tornikios went to David's help and then supported Phokas with an army of 12,000 cavalrymen: B. Martin-Hisard, 'La vie de Jean et Euthyme et le statut du monastère des Ibères sur l'Athos', *REB*, 49 (1991), 89–91.

[51] Yet again Bardas Phokas puts his personal relations to good use. His friendship with David illustrates the degree of freedom which the commanders of great themes and frontier *katepans* enjoyed.

[52] There is confusion here. The battle took place at Aquae Seravenae, halfway between Ankyra and Caesarea, 24 March 979: Seibt, *Skleroi*, 47. On the number of battles in which Phokas and Skleros faced each other (two or three?) and the confused chronology: (most recently) Holmes, *Basil II*, 453.

[53] Meanwhile Skleros had not been idle. He had attempted to retake Antioch which had changed sides again, this time at the instigation of its new patriarch, Agapios. But Isaac [Sachakios] Brachamios, sent out by the rebel, failed in his mission in spite of the support of the local Armenian population: Yahya of Antioch, II, 375–8.

sword, cutting off the right ear together with the bridle, but Phokas struck him on the head with his mace, forcing him down onto the neck of the horse with the strength of the blow. Phokas spurred his horse on and, cutting through the ranks of the enemy, got away. He went up onto a hillock and rallied his men from the rout. Skleros' men could see that their commander was far from well as a result of his wound; indeed he was so seriously injured that his life was ebbing away. They brought him to a spring to wash away the gore, under the impression that Phokas had been given to final destruction.[54] Then his horse reared and managed to get away from the man who was holding it. This horse, which was called Egyptian, now got the bit between its teeth and went rushing riderless through the soldiers, all covered with blood. They realised whose horse it was and, thinking their leader [327] had fallen, turned in disorderly flight. They flung themselves into ravines and into the river Halys, perishing ingloriously, and there was nobody in pursuit of them. Phokas saw this from his hillock and surmised, not without reason, that it was an act of God. He and those with him came down to pursue the fugitives who were treading each other underfoot without a thought for courage. Some he slaughtered, some he took prisoner.[55] As for Skleros, he and a few others got safely away to Martyropolis[56] from where he sent his own brother, Constantine, to Chosroes, the ruler of Babylon,[57] requesting a relief force and an alliance. But the Persian was in no hurry; he neither granted nor refused the request and Constantine was so long away that Skleros himself was obliged to go to Chosroes together with all those who were with him.

10. When the rout of Skleros and his flight to Babylon were reported to the emperor by Phokas in a letter, this man was received by the emperor and honoured accordingly. He sent the vestes Nikephoros Ouranos[58] as an

---

[54] Or: 'that Phokas had been gifted with the final destruction [of Skleros]' but the intrusion of the name of Phokas here is highly suspect.

[55] The account in Martin-Hisard, *Vie de Jean et Euthyme*, 91–3, credits the Georgians with this victory, adding that Tornikios returned with a huge amount of booty which he distributed among his soldiers, keeping for himself some objets d'art and 1,200 pounds of gold, with which he was able to found the Athonite monastery of Iviron.

[56] i.e. to his ally, the emir Marwanide: Ripper, *Marwâniden*, 112–13.

[57] This is not a reference to the Abbasid caliph but to the Buyid 'emir of emirs' Adud ad-Daula, 975–83, who was the effective power in the land: Ripper, *Marwâniden*, 50–60, and especially A. Beihammer, 'Der harte Sturz des Bardas Skleros. Eine Fallstudie zu zwischenstattlicher Kommunikation und Konflikführung in der byzantinische-arabischen Diplomatie des 10 Jahrhunderts', in R. Boesel and H. Fillitz, *Roemische Historische Mitteilungen* 45 (Vienna 2003), 21–57.

[58] This is the first mention here of Basil's faithful servant who was prefect of the inkstand and one of his best generals, on whom: E. McGeer, *Sowing the dragon's teeth: Byzantine warfare in the tenth century* (DOS, 33, Washington, DC, 1995). The Ouranos family served Constantine VII; the patrician Michael Ouranos helped to organise the Cretan expedition of 949: Haldon, 'Military

ambassador to Chosroes, *amermoumnes* of Babylon,⁵⁹ beseeching him not to allow the rebel to return nor to be willing to furnish (he who was himself an emperor) a thoroughly bad example to his progeny: the example, that is, of one who failed to come to the aid of an emperor who was being wronged, by supporting a wicked usurper and traitor. The ambassador carried a letter bearing the imperial seal which granted Skleros and those with him a complete pardon if they would remember where their duty lay, recognise their sovereign and go back home. When Ouranos reached Chosroes this imperial letter came to light; Chosroes became suspicious, so he imprisoned the ambassador, Skleros and all the Romans with him.⁶⁰ While they were in gaol some of the rebels who had not gone off with Skleros – [328] Leo Aichmalôtos,⁶¹ the sons of duke Andronikos Lydos⁶² (who had since died), Christopher Epeiktes⁶³ and Bardas Moungos – these captured Armakourion, Plateia Petra⁶⁴ and other fortresses lying in the Thrakesion theme and held onto them until the eighth year of the indiction,⁶⁵ making raids from these bases which devastated land belonging to the empire. Nor did they desist from these raids and become loyal subjects of the emperor again until they had received an amnesty for their wrongdoings by the intervention of the patrician Nikephoros Parsakoutinos.

11. It was then that the patriarch Anthony died, having resigned his ministry during the rebellion of Skleros. Nicholas Chrysoberges⁶⁶ was appointed patriarch after the church had been without a pastor for four and a half

---

administration', 202–352, at 223. Here Basil first appears to be gathering the reins of government into his own hands. Hence this marks the beginning of the gradual deterioration of his relations with his great-uncle, Basil the parakoimomenos.

⁵⁹ This embassy was doubtless sent not to the 'emir of emirs' but to the Calif, who was indeed the emir of believers, even though one negotiated with Adud ad-Doula.

⁶⁰ The Buyid emir called in vain on the emperor to honour the promise made by Skleros to restore those lands taken from the Arabs. He also held Ouranos prisoner, suspecting that he intended to poison Skleros: Yahya of Antioch, II, 401.

⁶¹ Literally, 'the captive', but it is a family name; an Orestes of the same name is mentioned below, c. 38. Other members of the family are attested into the time of the Comneni and there is Basil, secretary to the bureau of the *oikeiaka*, in 1087: *Byzantina eggrapha tês monês Patmou A – Autokratorika*, ed. É. Vranoussi, Athens 1980, Act no. 46.

⁶² No doubt one of the Doukai.

⁶³ This surname is probably derived from the position of epeiktes which Christopher would have filled, a position associated with several activities. The one most closely associated with military matters concerned the stables: the epeiktes ensured that the animals were properly equipped: Oikonomides, *Listes*, 339.

⁶⁴ This is where the rebel Symbatios had taken refuge: reign of Basil I, c. 13, above.

⁶⁵ September 979–August 980.

⁶⁶ Nicholas was from a family which supplied several prelates in the following centuries, notably patriarchs of Constantinople and of Antioch.

years.⁶⁷ There was an eclipse of the sun about midday such as to render the stars visible. After the death of the emperor John the Bulgars rebelled, appointing four brothers to rule them: David, Moses, Aaron and Samuel, sons of a count who was one of the powerful men among the Bulgars, Nicholas by name;⁶⁸ their mother was Ripseme; that is why they were known as Kometopoloi.⁶⁹ Death had removed the other relatives of Peter while his sons, Boris and Romanos, had been brought to the capital (as we explained above) and stayed there. Boris was honoured with the title of magister by the emperor John while Romanos was deprived of his genitals by Joseph [Bringas], the former parakoimomenos. Then when the death of the emperor John occurred, [329] {when Skleros rebelled against the emperor and their relative Basil invaded the regions of Thrace}⁷⁰ Boris and Romanos escaped [from the capital] and managed to arrive in Bulgaria. Boris was wounded by an arrow as he was passing through some bushes, shot and killed by a Bulgar who thought he was a Roman (he was in fact wearing Roman clothing). Romanos made his way safely {to Bidine}⁷¹ and eventually returned to the capital – as will be reported in the appropriate place. Of these four brothers David died right away {killed between Kastoria and Prespa, at a place called Kalasdrys [beautiful oaks], by some vagabond Vlachs}.⁷²

Moses died at the siege of Serres, struck by a stone thrown from the walls.

{Others write that it was not by a stone thrown that Moses [died] but that his horse fell, bringing him down, and he was slain by one of duke Melissenos' men.⁷³}

Samuel slew his brother Aaron and all his family too, because he was said to be pro-Roman, on 14 June at a place called Rametanitza.⁷⁴

The only survivor was his son, Sviatoslav (also known as John), saved by Rodomir (also known as Romanos), the son of Samuel. [330] In this way Samuel became the sole ruler of all Bulgaria;⁷⁵ he was much given

---

⁶⁷ The interval was really just under two years. Anthony resigned around June 979 and Nicholas was promoted in April or May 980: J. Darrouzès, 'Sur la chronologie du patriarche Antoine III Stoudite', *REB*, 46 (1988), 60.
⁶⁸ MS U only.
⁶⁹ 'The children of the counts': W. Seibt, 'Untersuchungen zur Vor-und Frühgeschichte der 'bulgarischen' Kometopulen', *Handes Amsorya*, 89 (1975), 65–100. The account of the Bulgar wars is confused. C. Holmes gives an account of this question and discusses the chronology in several chapters of her *Basil II*, especially in ch. 7.1.
⁷⁰ MS U only.   ⁷¹ MS U only.   ⁷² MSS ACRU only.   ⁷³ MSS AE only.
⁷⁴ MSS ACU only.
⁷⁵ On Samuel see (most recently) Sr. Pirivatrić, *Samuilo's state: its extent and character* (Belgrade, 1997), 199–210 (in Serbian with English summary). The Bulgar princes often had double names: one Slavic, one Greek, e.g. Radomir/Romanos, Vladislav/John.

to waging war and not at all to possessing his soul in peace. When the Roman forces were occupied with the war against Skleros he seized his chance and overran all the west, not only Thrace, Macedonia and the region adjacent to Thessalonike, but also Thessaly, Hellas and the Peloponnese. He also captured several fortresses of which Larissa[76] was the outstanding example. He transferred the inhabitants of Larissa, entire families of them, into further Bulgaria where he enrolled them among his own forces and used them as allies to fight against the Romans. He also translated the relics of St Achillios, who had served as bishop of Larissa under Constantine the Great and who was present at the First Ecumenical Council with Reginos of Skopelos and Diodoros of Trikka,[77] and deposited them at Prespa[78] where his palace was located, constructing a most beautiful and large church in his name.[79]

12. Once the emperor was relieved of his concern about Skleros, eager to restrain [Samuel] from his activities he assembled the Roman forces with the intention of leading an invasion of Bulgaria in person.[80] He did not, however, consider this worth mentioning to Bardas Phokas, domestic of the scholai, nor to the other eastern commanders. He entered Bulgaria by way of the Rhodope mountains and the river Hebro, leaving the magister Leo Melissenos behind with orders to guard the danger points. The emperor himself advanced through the passes and wooded valleys which lie beyond Triaditza, formerly known as Sardica, where the synod of the three hundred western bishops was held at the command of Constans in the west and Konstantios in the east, the sons of Constantine the Great.[81]

When he arrived at a place named Stoponion, [331] he threw up a fortification and applied himself to the question of how he might take Sardica by storm. He heard that Samuel was in possession of the heights of the surrounding mountains and that, reluctant to engage in hand-to-hand fighting, he had set up ambushes in all directions in an attempt to do the adversary some harm. Meanwhile, such being the emperor's plan, Stephen, the domestic of the scholai for the west, came to the emperor by night. On

---

[76] There is information on the fall of Larissa provided by a descendant of the Byzantine defender: Kekaumenos, an eleventh-century aristocrat who has left us some advice allegedly intended for children, advice which is based (among other things) on his own experience and on a number of matters that touched members of his family: Kekaumenos, *Strategikon*, 250–2.
[77] MSS ACEU only.
[78] On lake Mikre Prespa, in western Macedonia around Preslav. The Bulgar state did not rise again in its original location but much further to the west, in a region where the Byzantine military presence was much weaker.
[79] MSS ACEU only.
[80] In common with the other Greek sources, Skylitzes reports no event between 979 and 986.
[81] MSS ACEU only.

account of his small stature he was known as Stephen the short[82] and he was the sworn enemy of Leo Melissenos. He now called upon the emperor to strike camp and return to the capital giving this operation priority over everything else, because Melissenos was envious of the throne and was marching on the capital at great speed.[83] The emperor was frightened by what Stephen said and signalled immediately for camp to be struck. Now Samuel suspected that their disorderly withdrawal was a retreat (as well he might), so he attacked in full force with yelling and shouting, thoroughly scared the Romans and forced them to run for their lives. He captured the camp and took possession of all their baggage, even the emperor's tent and the imperial insignia. The emperor was only just able to get through the passes and find safety in Philippoupolis.[84] When he arrived there, he found that Melissenos had not moved an inch but was carefully maintaining the guard which had been entrusted to him. So he reviled Stephen the Short as a liar and the instigator of so great a misfortune. Stephen did not humbly endure this reproach but protested firmly that he had given good advice. The emperor was provoked by his effrontery to leap down from the throne and, seizing him by the hair and the beard, to throw him to the ground.

13. In the fifteenth year of the indiction, AM 6494, the month of October, there was a great earthquake; [332] many mansions and churches fell down, as did a portion of the dome of the Great Church of God.[85] This the emperor zealously restored, providing ten *kentenaria* for the machines alone by which the workmen standing [above] receive the materials being brought up, with which to rebuild the fallen portion.

14. Certain powerful Romans, Bardas Phokas and some of his associates, were angry with the emperor for ignoring them when he went on campaign in Bulgaria, not even according them the respect due to a mercenary. They

---

[82] Kontostephanos, 'Stephen the short'. This is the first mention of a distinguished military family related to the Komnenoi in the twelfth century: A. G. K. Savvidès, 'A prosopographical note on the first member of the Byzantine family of Contostephanus', *In honour of Prof. V. Tàpkova-Zaimova* (Sofia, 1997), 159–64.

[83] In the preceding year Leo Melissenos, duke of Antioch, had raised the siege of Balanea on the false report of a revolt by Basil the parakoimomenos. The emperor Basil had given him the choice of taking Balanea or of paying the cost of the campaign out of his own pocket: Yahya of Antioch, II, 417.

[84] August 986. It is claimed that it was the Armenian infantry which surrounded the emperor and saved his life: Asolik of Taron, tr. Macler, 127.

[85] In the night of 25–26 October 986 the western apse and the dome of Hagia Sophia were damaged. The restoration work took six months under the direction of the Armenian architect Tiridathe: Asolik of Taron, tr. Macler, 133. Yahya of Antioch (II, 428–9) dates this earthquake in 989. His chronology is less reliable than Skylitzes'.

all complained of different insults and injuries, the magister Eustathios Maleinos[86] especially of having been ungraciously excluded from the campaign in question. They assembled in the Charsianon [theme], in the house of the same Maleinos on 25 August, fifteenth year of the indiction, and proclaimed Bardas Phokas emperor; they invested him with a diadem and the rest of the imperial insignia. He had just been acclaimed when it was announced that Skleros was returning from Syria. Arrested (as we said) by Chosroes together with his men, he had remained in Babylon where he was held in prison and denied all comforts. He was worn out by the misery of confinement and the brutality of the warders. Then he suddenly saw his fortunes take a turn for the better when, against all expectation, he and his associates were let out of prison. How he came to be released from his bonds and subsequently returned to Roman lands this narrative is about to report.

15. The Persian race having had the office of ruler stolen away from it by the Saracens never ceased to be indignant and bear a grudge against them on this account. [The Persians] were ever on the lookout for the opportunity and means of striking down those who held power over them, in order to restore their ancestral rule. There was a man among them of noble birth, Inargos[87] by name, a skilful orator and a fearsome warrior too. Noting that Chosroes was an easygoing and paltry ruler, [333] he thought the time had come for which the Persians were looking. He stirred up the entire race of the Achaimenides and created a rebellion against the Saracens. He obtained a troop of about twenty thousand mercenaries from the eastern Turks and went pillaging and overrunning the Saracens' land, completely eliminating those he took without even sparing the children. Chosroes frequently took action against them, by the agency of his generals and sometimes personally, but he got the worse of all the battles. He began to lose heart as he realised that he was no match for the Persians in arms. So often were his armies cut to pieces that they could no longer bear to hear the name of Persians. Then the thought came to his mind that he was holding some Roman prisoners and he calculated very intelligently that if the [chief] prisoner had not been one of the famous and even distinguished [Romans], courageous in body and soul, he would not have risen up against his own sovereign and run the

---

[86] At Caesarea in Cappadocia, 15 August 987.
[87] The Buyid emir Samsam al-Daula succeeded his father, Ahud ad-Daula, but ran into opposition from his brother, Sharaf ad-Daula, who may be the person referred to here as Inargos (Inaros further on), one who relied on the Fars (Persians). See *EI* sv Samsam ad-Dawla.

risk of falling into such a wretched situation. Moreover, having managed to escape he had been proclaimed emperor by so many people of such quality! [Chosroes] consulted with his council of elders then released the Romans from gaol, made all services available to them and finally put his request to them concerning the war. Skleros was reluctant at first; how could men who had been so long imprisoned and had been sated with the affliction of captivity manage their arms, he asked sardonically. But Chosroes kept insisting and asked him to accept an enormous amount of money and a numerous host, splendidly equipped to fight the war. He begged him to take command of the war and not to bear a grudge about his incarceration, for he could erase the ill treatment and discomfort of prison by the good things and the delights which were to come. In the end Skleros agreed and undertook to accomplish what was required of him. But he absolutely refused to lead an army made up of Arabs or Saracens or of other races under Chosroes; he asked for a search to be made in the prisons of the cities of Syria and the Romans being held there to be released [334] and armed; otherwise (he said) it was not possible for him to confront the Persians in war. When Chosroes agreed to this, the prisons were quickly opened and the Romans in them set free; three thousand men were assembled from those prisons. After he had sent them to the baths and purged them of the filth of confinement, Skleros clothed them with new garments and raiment, arming each man in an appropriate and adequate manner. Then he engaged guides to show them the way and out they went against the Persians. When a formal battle took place and Skleros' men repeatedly and violently charged the Persians, these were perplexed by the strange nature of their armament, the unusual sound of their speech, their previously unknown battle order and, most of all, by the violence and speed with which they charged. Thus the Persians were roundly put to flight and every one of them fell. There was not even a messenger left (so the saying goes) to report the disaster. Inaros[88] himself fell in the fray. The Romans collected a great amount of booty and many horses, then decided not to go back to Chosroes again but to take the road leading to Roman lands. They pressed the pace and succeeded in evading detection until they arrived safely in their homeland. According to another account, Chosroes accorded them a generous reception as they returned from the victory against the Persians and, some time later, when the end of his life was approaching, he urged his son and namesake (who reigned after him) to make a treaty with the Romans and send them

---

[88] Inargos above.

home.[89] By one of these means Skleros regained Roman territory and, finding that Bardas Phokas had been proclaimed emperor, he too was likewise proclaimed by his companions.

16. When Skleros realised how things lay he was in two minds what to do. He realised that he was too weak to instigate, conduct and pursue the uprising all by himself, but he was convinced that it would be both ignoble and unmanly to go over to the side [335] either of Phokas or of the emperor. After debating at length with his associates he finally came to the conclusion that to be proclaimed emperor would be a hazardous and reckless undertaking, given his lack of support; yet he still hesitated to throw his weight behind one of those vying for power and to abandon the other, this on account of the unpredictable nature of the outcome. He decided to conciliate both of them insofar as he could so that, if one came to grief, he would have the other to aid and protect him. So he sent a personal letter to Phokas proposing to make common cause with him and to share the rule if he prevailed against the emperor. But he secretly sent his son Romanos (as though he were deserting) to the emperor, having very intelligently calculated and come to the verdict that if Phokas won the day he would ensure the safety of the son, whereas if the emperor's side prevailed the son would plead for the father, in this way releasing him from the embarrassing position he would be in.[90] So, making a pretence of fleeing, Romanos went to the emperor – who received him with great benevolence and much joy. He immediately honoured him with the rank of magister and henceforth regularly employed him as a counsellor in his campaigns.[91] In fact, after Skleros withdrew into Syria the emperor, relieved of anxiety, now applied himself more strenuously to affairs of state. He was aware that the parakoimomenos was by no means pleased with what he was doing. He was complaining and aspiring to do terrible things if the occasion presented itself. For this reason the emperor dismissed him from his

---

[89] This second version is nearer to the truth. Skylitzes' account of Skleros is well developed and sympathetic towards his actions. Holmes thinks our author had access to a source well disposed towards Skleros: *Basil II*, ch. 5.2.4. Skleros negotiated his return with the Buyid emir and concluded a treaty with him the text of which is extant: M. Canard, 'Deux documents arabes sur Bardas Sclèros', *Studi bizantin e Neoellenici*, 5 (1939), 55–69, repr. *Byzance et les Musulmans du Proche-Orient* (London, 1973), xi. Bardas made an agreement with the local Moslem powers who provided him with troops in return for land and the return of Moslem prisoners: Ripper, *Marwâniden*, 121–3.

[90] Yahya of Antioch, II, 422, says that Romanos was indeed at odds with his father concerning the strategy they were to adopt, and not at all in favour of the arrangement with Phokas.

[91] This 'defection' of Romanos explains why the Skleroi did not come to grief after the failure of their uprising but remained among the first families of the empire until the accession of the Komnenoi.

powerful position and ordered him to stay at home.[92] Then, seeing that he would not remain quietly there but was forever conjuring up some unwelcome thing and endeavouring to regain his former power, he exiled him to the Bosporos and confiscated most of his property so that he would not have access to the means of committing any criminal offence.[93] Now the emperor was deprived of the parakoimomenos' counsel; he was also devoid of friends and colleagues to assist in the difficulties which confronted him. It was then that he willingly accepted Romanos, a man whom he knew to be skilful, energetic and highly competent in warfare.

17. When Bardas learned that the return of Skleros [336] was public knowledge he sent him a letter indicating his agreement and guaranteeing the undertakings he was making with oaths. 'If we attain what we hope for,' he said, 'you shall rule Antioch, Phoenicia, Cœlo-Syria, Palestine and Mesopotamia while I shall be the ruler of the capital itself and the rest of the peoples.'[94] Skleros gladly embraced these propositions and, confidently trusting the oaths, went to meet Phokas in Cappadocia, intending to ratify their cooperation. But once Phokas had him in his net, he stripped him of the imperial insignia and sent him to the fortress of Tyropoion[95] where he set a by no means ignoble guard over him. He then entrusted a portion of the army to the patrician Kalokyros Delphinas[96] and sent him

---

[92] It is not clear at what point in the sequence of events the parakoimomenos was put down from his seat: B. Crostini, 'The Emperor Basil II's cultural life,' *Byzantion* 64 (1996), 59–64. He may have been confined to his residence before 986 and exiled before the Bulgarian campaign; or, as Skylitzes suggests, when Skleros returned to the empire, which would have cleared the way for the return of Nikephoros Ouranos, the faithful servant of Basil II.

[93] Basil became so antipathetic to his great-uncle that he not only had the monastery of St Basil founded by him destroyed but also annulled all the chrysobulls issued during the years when the parakoimomenos was in power which had not been personally confirmed by the emperor. This effectively destroyed the party supporting the parakoimomenos by withdrawing the favours he had granted to his friends. He died of heart congestion shortly after his exile: Michel Psellos, *Chronographie*, trans. E. R. A. Sewter (London, 1953), 1, 12–13.

[94] Psellos, *Chronographia*, trans. Sewter, 1, 9, gives a different version of the negotiations between Skleros and Phokas, stating that Skleros came to Phokas as an inferior. This is understandable since Phokas had the greater part of the army of the east at his back. It is inconceivable that Phokas would have accorded the other the title of emperor. He probably created an important eastern command for him, putting the Armenians under his rival's command and leaving him free to enter into negotiations with the neighbouring emirs. It is interesting to note that, at the time when Skylitzes was composing his work, the area in question was a semi-autonomous region under Philaretos Brachamios, the man who was going to be recommended to Bohemond the Frank by Alexios Komnenos with the title of domestic of the scholai: Cheynet, *Société*, 390–410.

[95] This fortress must have been Phokas' base for operations for it was here that he took refuge when his abortive uprising under John Tzimisces came to grief.

[96] This man had been appointed *katepan* of Italy in 983–5, i.e. when the Phokai had influence at court: V. von Falkenhausen, *La dominazione bizantina nell' Italia meridionale dal IX all' XI secolo* (Bari, 1978), 183–5.

to Chrysopolis, opposite to the capital.⁹⁷ Then he took all the remaining army with him and went to Abydos in the hope that, once he controlled the straits, he could reduce the citizens by famine.⁹⁸ The emperor repeatedly asked Delphinas to withdraw from Chrysopolis and not to set up camp over against the capital. When he refused to obey, the emperor fitted out some ships by night and embarked some Russians in them, for he had been able to enlist allies among the Russians and he had made their leader, Vladimir,⁹⁹ his kinsman by marrying him to his sister, Anna.¹⁰⁰ He crossed with the Russians, attacked the enemy without a second thought and easily subdued them. He hung Delphinas on a gallows at the very spot where he had pitched his tent and he sent Phokas' brother, Nikephoros the Blind, to prison. {He also impaled Atzypotheodoros at Abydos}¹⁰¹ and inflicted whatsoever punishments he thought fit on the rest of the prisoners. Then he returned to the capital.

18. After Phokas arrived at Abydos he tightly besieged it [337] but those within withstood the siege vigorously, for the emperor had sent Kyriakos, droungarios of the fleet, to relieve and encourage them.¹⁰² In a little while Constantine, the emperor's brother, crossed over and afterwards the emperor himself came. When these had passed over, Phokas ordered a portion of the army to prosecute the siege of Abydos while he and the rest of the army took up positions against the emperors. Just as battle was about to commence, Phokas (who was of the opinion that it was better to die gloriously than to live ignobly) saw the emperor riding to and fro, mustering his ranks and encouraging them. Phokas thought to himself that if he could get to the emperor, the rest of them would easily be overcome, so he spurred on his horse and furiously charged towards him, cutting through the enemy ranks and appearing to be unstoppable. Then, just

---

⁹⁷ In contrast to the progress of Skleros in his first revolt (which was a series of battles), Phokas' forces advance unopposed.
⁹⁸ As Phokas had no fleet at his command, no blockade of Constantinople was possible.
⁹⁹ The son of Sviatoslav; he became the master of Russia c. 978 by eliminating his brothers.
¹⁰⁰ The marriage of the princess Anna Porphyrogenita to the prince of Kiev took place on condition that the bridegroom would accept baptism. For his part, Vladimir sent his new brother-in-law a contingent of fighting men, four or six thousand depending on the sources. Much has been written on this event on account of its connection with the conversion of Russia: (most recently, with bibliography) Franklin and Shepard, *Rus*, 160–3; also V. Vodoff, *Naissance de la chrétienté russe* (Paris, 1988), 63–107.
¹⁰¹ {...} MS U only.
¹⁰² According to Yahya of Antioch, ii, 424–5, the two opponents launched massive offensives. Basil II (who had mastery of the sea) tried to draw Phokas off by dispatching a contingent of Armenian warriors into the area around Trebizond so they could strike him in the rear. To counter this move Phokas sent his son and appealed to his Georgian allies who, in fact, carried the day but withdrew when news of the imperial victory at Chrysopolis arrived.

as he was approaching the emperor, he suddenly came about, rode up a hillock, dismounted from his horse, lay down on the ground – and died. He might have sustained a mortal wound at the hand of a soldier in his reckless charge or he may have been overcome by some physical disorder,[103] although there was no wound whatsoever found on his body, hence the rumour went round that he had been killed by poison. It was said that Symeon, his most trusted servant, had been bribed by the emperor with gifts to poison him. For Phokas was in the habit of drinking cold water before a battle when he was at war and this he did at that battle, unwittingly ingesting poison together with the water. He lay on the hillock for some time, everybody thinking he was allowing himself a little respite because of some physical weakness. But as he continued to lie there, somebody coming up to him found him dead and speechless. His death became general knowledge[104] whereupon the insurgents immediately turned and ran. [338] This put new heart into the emperor's troops who gave pursuit without looking back, capturing alive Leo and Theognostos Melissenos, Theodosios Mesanyktes and many others. These the emperor took to the capital with him and paraded them in triumph through the forum, mounted on asses. The only one he spared was Leo Melissenos, for it was said that he urged with many tears and begged his own brother to desist from his impudent words and stop shamefully insulting his rightful sovereigns, for the brother was standing out in front of the troops, hurling foul language and offensive abuse at the time. When Theognostos would not heed his words Leo gave him many blows with his barbed lance. Witness to this, the emperor said to those who were present: 'Look you men: a cross and a winnowing fan from the same tree!' It is for this reason that Leo is said to have been spared the parade.[105]

19. As soon as Phokas was dead, in April, second year of the indiction, AM 6497, and his uprising had disintegrated, Skleros picked himself up again and reactivated his former insurrection.[106] When the emperor learnt

---

[103] The battle of Abydos took place on 13 April 989.
[104] Phokas probably died of a heart attack. Many versions of the story of his death circulated, as Psellos reports: *Chronographia*, ed. Renauld, 1, 11, trans. Sewter, 1.17. Basil's brother, the co-emperor Constantine, boasted that he had killed Phokas.
[105] Leo Melissenos had supported Phokas and had blockaded Abydos with his fleet on the usurper's account (Leo the Deacon, 173, trans. 215), yet he was pardoned and obtained a command in the east in 993: Yahya of Antioch, II, 440–1. Thanks to this act of clemency the Melissenoi were able to maintain their high rank into the eleventh century and to insinuate themselves into the imperial family of the Komnenoi.
[106] Psellos, *Chronographia*, ed. Renauld, 1, 15–16, trans. Sewter, 1.24, reveals that Skleros reconstituted his forces and rallied his faithful supporters, thus causing all the emperor's projects to miscarry.

Basil II and Constantine VIII

of this he sent him a letter counselling him to consider whether he had not now had a surfeit of shedding Christians' blood; that he too was a man with death and judgement ahead of him;[107] that he should learn even at this late hour where his advantage lay and acknowledge the ruler God had provided; {that he should not be led astray by the prophecy derived from his name. For there was a popular saying going round, started by some of those star-gazers: 'B will chase out B and B will rule.' By this both Skleros and Phokas had been deluded into raising their rebellions.}[108] Skleros was mollified by this letter and, receiving assurances that he would come to no harm, [339] he laid down his arms and made his peace with the emperor, who appointed him kouropalates.[109] But it was not granted to him to see the emperor with his own eyes for he was stricken with blindness while still on the road and lost his sight. He was brought to the emperor a blind man and the emperor, seeing him being led by the hand, said to those present: 'He of whom I stood in fear and dread is approaching led by the hand.'[110]

20. Relieved of civil wars and their attendant worries, the emperor now turned his attention to the problem of how to deal with Samuel and the other local chieftains who had taken advantage of his involvement with the uprisings to inflict considerable damage on Roman territory with impunity. Marching out into the regions of Thrace and Macedonia he came to Thessalonike, intending to make thank-offerings to Demetrios the martyr.[111] There he left Gregory Taronites as commander with a capable army to exclude and intercept the incursions of Samuel. The emperor came in person to the capital and then proceeded to Iberia. David the kouropalates had died recently, having declared in writing that the emperor was to inherit all his possession.[112] The emperor arrived there and took possession of his inheritance. He prevailed upon George, the brother of David

---

[107] Skleros would have been approaching seventy.
[108] {...} MSS UE only.
[109] By this title Skleros ranked second to the emperor. It will be recalled that the emperor Nikephoros Phokas granted his brother Leo this title. This concession appears to indicate that Basil did not consider himself capable of vanquishing Skleros. Yahya of Antioch, II, 427, says Skleros also obtained a large, lucrative emolument in the east and promotions for his supporters. Yahya also says that Leo Phocas, son of the rebel, who was holding Antioch, held out for a long time, finally surrendering on 3 November 989.
[110] It was at Didymotika in Thrace that Basil met Bardas Skleros and his brother Constantine for the last time, in the fortress which had been assigned to the two brothers as their residence, well removed from their eastern bases. Bardas died shortly after this visit, 31 March 991, his brother Constantine five days later: Yahya of Antioch, II, 430–1.
[111] The campaign of 991 was the emperor's response to Samuel's attack on Thessalonike and his inroads into Greece.
[112] Skylitzes does not present events in their chronological order here. This expedition of Basil II took place in 1001; two different campaigns have been confused. It was in 990 that Basil (angry

the kouropalates and ruler of the Iberian interior,[113] to be satisfied with his own [territories] and not to covet another's. The emperor made a treaty with him and, taking his son as hostage, made his way into Phoenicia. He had with him the hereditary chieftains from his own part of Iberia; the most outstanding ones were the brothers Pakourianos, Theudatos and Pherses, whom he raised to the dignity of patrician.[114] [340] While he was in Phoenicia[115] he did everything in his power to ensure that the emirs of Tripoli, Damascus, Tyre and Beirut remain in subjection to the Romans, for these emirs had recently conspired together and taken up arms against Antioch while the emperor was occupied with the war against Phokas. They killed the governor of Antioch, the patrician Damian, when he went to war with them and put the city in considerable danger. The emperor took hostages from the emirs so that he could be assured of their remaining in subjection to the Romans and then made his way back to Byzantium.[116]

21. As he was travelling through Cappadocia the magister Eustathios Maleinos received him and the entire army as his guests, giving him and his men whatever they needed without counting the cost. As though he approved of this and was praising him, the emperor took him to the capital with him but would not allow him to return afterwards. He made

---

with David for supporting the revolt of Phokas) obliged that Bagratid ruler to recognise the emperor as his heir. Matthew of Edessa, ed. Dostourian, 39, says that David was dead, assassinated by his inner circle which included Hilarion, archbishop of Georgia. *Aristakes de Lastivert, Récit des malheurs de la nation arménienne*, French translation and commentary by M. Canard and H. Berberian following the edition and Russian translation of K. Yuzbashian (Bibliothèque de *Byzantion*, 5, Brussels, 1973), 4–5, says the soldiers of his bodyguard poisoned him.

[113] The king of Georgia, another Bagratid, was not in fact the brother of David: C. Toumanoff, *Les dynasties de la caucasie chrétienne de L'Antiquité jusqu'au XIX siècle: tables généalogiques et chronologiques* (Rome, 1900), 130.

[114] On the interpretation of this passage and the question of the relationship between these three persons: *Actes d'Iviron*, I, 19. Pakourianos (Bakouran) was named patrician and strategos of Samos, Phebdatos (Theudatos) patrician and count of the Opsikion theme: B. Montfaucon, *Palaeographia graeca sive de ortu et progressa literarum Graecarum* (Paris, 1708), 46.

[115] The Fatimids were trying to get their hands on Damascus and Aleppo to secure their hold on Syria. Since the victories of Nikephoros Phokas the Romans regarded Aleppo as their protectorate. It looks as though Basil II did not give the retention of Aleppo high priority but, on the other hand, the loss of Antioch could not be countenanced. Basil did intervene after Michael Bourtzes, duke of Antioch (having come to the aid of the people of Aleppo, tributaries of the empire), was defeated by the Fatimids at the so-called battle of Gue (on the Orontes). Basil arrived before Antioch in April 995 and sent the Fatimid troops packing: Yahya of Antioch, II, 440–2. He returned after the new duke, Damian Dalassenos, was defeated and killed on 19 July 998. He captured the Syrian fortress of Shaizar and burnt the church of St Constantine at Homs, but once again he failed to take Tripoli. Learning of the death of David, he proceeded into Iberia, leaving Nikephoros Ouranos as the new governor of Antioch. He also concluded a ten-year truce with the Calif al-Hakim: Yahya of Antioch, II, 454–60, 457–61. On these events: Th. Bianquis, *Damas et la Syrie sous la domination fatimide (359–468/969–1076)*, Damascus 1986 and Holmes, *Basil II*, 345–9, perhaps a little too sceptical about the existence of a duchy of Antioch at that time.

[116] It was now that Basil learnt of the death of David and took the road to Iberia.

generous provision for his needs but held onto him as though he were raising a wild beast in a cage until he reached the end of his life. And when he died, all his property was appropriated by the state.[117] The emperor promulgated a law which restrained the powerful from augmenting their lands by the agglomeration of villages.[118] His predecessor and grandfather Constantine Porphyrogennetos had done likewise and so had *his* father-in-law, Romanos.

22. Nicholas Chrysoberges departed this life[119] after administering the church for ten years and eight months; the magister Sisinnios was appointed [to succeed him], a man of great renown and most highly skilled in the art of medicine, AM 6503, [341] eighth year of the indiction.[120] It was he who reconciled the parties divided by the fourth marriage {of the emperor Leo, because Euthymios received him into communion}.[121] He departed this life after shepherding the church for only three years[122] and then Sergios[123] was appointed, he who was hegoumenos of the monastery of Manuel[124] and a relative of the patriarch Photios.

23. Samuel was campaigning against Thessalonike. He divided the majority of his forces to man ambushes and snares but he sent a small expedition to advance right up to Thessalonike itself. When duke Gregory [Taronites] learnt of this incursion he despatched Asotios, his own son, to spy on and reconnoitre the [enemy] host and to provide him with intelligence and then he himself came along afterwards. Asotios set out and came into conflict with the [enemy] vanguard which he put to flight, only to be taken unwittingly in an ambush. On hearing of this Gregory rushed to the help of his son, striving to deliver him from captivity, but he too was surrounded by Bulgars; he fell fighting nobly and heroically.[125] When the

---

[117] After the confiscation of most of the Phokas properties this Maleinos may have been the richest man in the empire.

[118] The Novel of 996 was the most severe of all the laws intended to defend the small land owners: (most recently) M. Kaplan, *Les hommes et la terre á Byzance, propriété et exploitation du sol du VIe au XIe siècle* (ByzSorb, 10, Paris, 1992), 437–9. For English translation of the two versions of the Novel: E. McGeer, *The land legislation of the Macedonian emperors* (Toronto, 2000), 111–32. For an a-political rather than a social interpretation of this Novel: C. Holmes, *Basil II*, 468–72, who considers that its purpose was to obliterate the last traces of the influence of Basil the parakoimomenos.

[119] 16 December 992.   [120] 12 April 996 in fact.   [121] {...} MS U only.

[122] 24 August 998.   [123] June or July 1001.

[124] This monastery was founded in Constantinople by the magister Manuel in the reign of Theophilos. Damaged in an earthquake, it was restored by the patriarch Photios whose remains were transferred there in the tenth century. The monastery had in all probability become a property of the Photios family, which would explain why a member of that family was hegoumenos there in AD 1001: Janin, *Les églises et monastères*, I, 320.

[125] Samuel's object was to gain control of the Via Egnatia; he had already taken Dyrrachion and married the daughter of John Chryselios, a leading citizen of that town. It was about this time (996–7) that Samuel proclaimed himself *basileus* in the belief that he had restored the Bulgar borders to where they were in Symeon's time: Pirivatric, *Samuilo's state*, 207.

death of the duke was reported to the emperor he despatched the magister Nikephoros Ouranos[126] as commander-in-chief of the west; he had purchased his release from Babylon and arrived at the capital. When he came to Thessalonike he learnt that Samuel was so elated by the killing of the duke Gregory Taronites and the capture of his son that he had passed through the vale of Tempe, crossed the river Peneios and advanced through Thessaly, Bœotia and Attica then into the Peloponnese by way of the isthmus of Corinth, ravaging and devastating all these lands. [Nikephoros Ouranos] set out with the forces under his command, crossed the heights of Olympos and came to Larissa, where he left the baggage. Then with his army relieved of its burdens he crossed Thessaly, the plain of Pharsala and the River Apidanos by forced marches and pitched his camp on the banks of the Spercheios, on the bank [342] opposite to where Samuel was bivouacked. There was torrential rain falling from the sky; the river was in flood and overflowing its banks so there was no question of an engagement taking place. But the magister, casting up and down the river, found a place where he thought it might be possible to cross. He roused his army by night, crossed the river and fell upon the sleeping troops of Samuel, taking them completely by surprise. The better part of them were slain, nobody daring even to think of resistance. Samuel and Romanos his son both received severe wounds and they only got away by hiding among the dead, lying down as though they were slain, then secretly slipping away into the Ætolian Mountains by night. From there they went through the peaks of those mountains and, crossing the Pindos, reached safety in Bulgaria. The magister released the Romans who were prisoners and despoiled the fallen Bulgars. He also occupied the enemy camp, capturing a huge amount of wealth. Then he returned to Thessalonike with his army.[127]

24. When Samuel returned safely to his homeland he took Asotios, son of Taronites, out of prison and made him his son-in-law by marrying him to his daughter. For she, Miroslava,[128] had fallen in love with him and was threatening to kill herself unless she could be legally married to him. Once the marriage was a fait accompli, he sent him off with her to Dyrrachion to ensure the security of the district. When he got there, however, he

---

[126] Thessalonike now became one of the principal bases for operations against Samuel. Ouranos (who must have come out of prison in Baghdad, reign of Basil II, c. 10) did not succeed Gregory Taronites directly. The latter was killed in 995, the year John Chaldos became duke: *Iviron*, 1, 153–4. John was captured in the following year and remained in prison for twenty-two years: below, reign of Basil II, c. 41, reign of Romanos Argyros, c. 5.
[127] The victory of Spercheios was won in 997; it was significant enough to permit Basil to return to the east: McGeer, *Byzantine warfare*, 344–5.
[128] MS U only.

persuaded his wife to join him in fleeing to the Roman ships which were coasting by that place as a safeguard. In those vessels he came in safety to the emperor who honoured him with the title of magister, and his wife with the decoration of the girdle.[129] Asotios came bearing a letter from one of the powerful men of Dyrrachion named Chryselios in which he undertook to deliver the city of Dyrrachion [343] to the emperor in return for him and his two sons being raised to the dignity of patrician. The emperor issued a letter endorsing the undertaking and Dyrrachion was duly handed over to the patrician Eustathios Daphnomeles. The two sons were designated patricians, the father having died in the meantime.[130]

25. It was at that time that two men were accused of being sympathetic to the Bulgars:[131] the magister Paul Bobos, one of the leading citizens of Thessalonike, and Malakenos,[132] distinguished by his intelligence and eloquence. Paul was transferred to the plain of the Thrakesion [theme], Malakenos to Byzantium.[133] Certain distinguished citizens of Adrianople who had also gained renown in military commands fled to Samuel because they too were under suspicion: Vatatzes with his entire family,[134] Basil Glabas alone, whose son the emperor imprisoned and held for three years, then let him go. At that time the emperor gave the daughter of Argyros (sister of the Romanos [III Argyros] who later reigned as emperor) in lawful marriage to the Doge[135] of Venice to conciliate the Venetians.

---

[129] *Zoste patrikia*, 'belted patrician', was the one title reserved for women only. It was the highest rank to which a woman could attain: *OBD*, III, 2231 and J.-Cl. Cheynet, 'La patricienne à la ceinture; une femme de qualité', in *Au cloître et dans le monde: Femmes, hommes et société (IXe-XVe siècle)*; Mélanges en l'honneur de Paulette L'Hermite-Leclerq, ed. P. Henriet and A.-M. Legras, Paris 2000, 179–87, rpr. in Cheynet, *Société*, 163–73.

[130] This shows how much power over the cities depended on relations between the central government (Basil's or Samuel's) and the local aristocracies who would bid against each other to command support.

[131] This is probably to be explained by the pressure which Samuel's forces kept up on the towns, which is where the aristocracy resided.

[132] There was a person of this name commanding an army against the Arabs in Sicily in 952: Falkenhausen, *Dominazione*, 103–4.

[133] This is a Peloponnesian family known from different sources, especially from several seals, the most remarkable being that of a Malakenos who was commander of Longobardia in the middle of the tenth century: *DOSeals*, 1.3.1.

[134] First mention of a family later interrelated with the Komnenoi and which provided emperors: J. S. Langdon, 'Background to the rise of the Vatatzai to prominence in the Byzantine *oikoumene* 997–1222', *To Hellenikon: studies in honor of Speros Vryonis, Jr*, I, *Hellenic Antiquity and Byzantium* (New Rochelle, NY, 1993), 179–210.

[135] *Archon*. Maria Argyropoulina married Giovanni Orseolo, the elder son of the Doge Peter II, in 1005–6. The bridegroom (who had accompanied the emperor on an expedition against Bulgaria) was honoured with the title of patrician. The marriage took place in Constantinople; the couple took back to Venice the precious relic of Barbara, one of the martyrs of Nicomedia. They had one son but the entire family was carried off by an epidemic in 1007: J. F. Vannier, *Familles byzantines: Argyroi, IXe–XII siècles* (ByzSorb, I, Paris, 1975), 43–4.

The emperor also invaded Bulgaria by way of Philippoupolis[136] and stationed the patrician Theodorokanos[137] to guard that city. He overthrew many fortresses in Triaditza and then returned to Mosynoupolis.[138]

26. In AM 6508, thirteenth year of the indiction, the emperor sent a large and powerful force against the Bulgar strongholds beyond the Haemos range, under the command of the patrician Theodorokanos and the protospatharios, Nikephoros Xiphias. [344] Greater and Lesser Preslav were taken; Pliskova too;[139] then the Roman army returned, triumphant and intact.[140]

27. In the following year the emperor set out against Bulgaria again, this time through Thessalonike. Dobromir, governor of Berrœa {who was married to a niece of Samuel}[141] joined the emperor's ranks and surrendered his town[142] to him, for which he was honoured with the title of anthypatos/ proconsul. The officer-commanding at Kolydros,[143] {Demetrios Teichonas, refused to surrender his town, but asked to be allowed to withdraw from it, to which request the emperor acceded, allowing Demetrios and his men to rejoin Samuel}.[144] Then there was the officer-commanding at the fortress called Serbia, Nicholas, nicknamed Nikoulitzas[145] on account of his small stature; he withstood and vigorously resisted the siege which was laid against him. The emperor intensified the blockade and took both the fortress and Nikoulitzas himself. He transported the Bulgars out of there and put Romans in to guard it. That accomplished, he returned to the capital taking with him Nikoulitzas, whom he then honoured with the title of patrician. But he was an unreliable fellow; he ran away and came safely to Samuel, with whom he now came to besiege the fortress of Serbia.[146] But the emperor reappeared in

---

[136] This was Basil's second choice as a base for operations to check the advances of Samuel.
[137] A Georgian: one of Basil's most faithful generals.
[138] Basil's strategy was to divide Samuel's territory in two by holding on to Sofia.
[139] Samuel was beginning to lose his somewhat tenuous control over eastern Bulgaria. This was the part which it was in Basil's great interest to control for thus he could protect Thrace and also gain access to the functioning ports of the lower Danube.
[140] On the disputed location of Little Preslav: N. Oikonomides, 'Presthlavitza, the Little Preslav', *Südost-Forschungen*, 42 (1983), 1–19.
[141] {...} MS U only.
[142] A town of Macedonia, to the south-west of Thessalonike. A seal indicates that a person named Dobromir, *anthypatos* and patrician, was duke of Thrace and of (western) Mesopotamia: Jordanov, *Preslav*, nos. 237 and 238. It is most unlikely that two persons with the name of Dobromir would have obtained the same dignity at that elevated level.
[143] A fortress located to the south of lake Dojran, now Kalindria.
[144] {...} MS U only.
[145] Not necessarily the same as the person of the same name who defended Larissa, the grandfather of Kekaumenos: *Strategikon*, 250–2, ed. Spadaro, 202–4.
[146] A town of Macedonia to the south of Berroia. Basil was in the process of liberating the whole of Macedonia from the Bulgars in order to re-establish the security of the region around Thessalonike and to deny Samuel access to the themes of Hellas and the Peloponnese.

haste and put an end to the siege, Nikoulitzas and Samuel fleeing for their lives. Yet that faithless fellow could not entirely escape; he was captured in a Roman ambush, brought to the emperor as a prisoner, sent to Constantinople and thrown into gaol.[147] Then the emperor marched into Thessaly and rebuilt the fortresses which Samuel had overturned; the ones they still held he besieged and transported the Bulgars to a place called Boleron.[148] [345] He left a battle-worthy garrison in each of them and marched off to the place called Vodena.[149] This is a fortress located on a precipitous crag around which the waters of lake Ostrovos flow. They travel some way underground then surface again here. Since the people within the fortress were not willing to surrender it, he was obliged to take the place by siege, transporting its defenders to Boleron as well. He secured the place with a guard worthy of the name and then returned to Thessalonike.

28. Draxanos, the governor of the fortress, a true warrior, asked permission to reside at Thessalonike. The emperor agreed, and he took for his wife the daughter of the first priest of the church of the victorious martyr Demetrios, who bore him two sons. Then he ran away and was captured, but was set free at the intercession of his father-in-law. A second time he ran away, was apprehended and then set free yet again; he engendered two more children while at liberty, then he ran away a third time. This time, however, he was not only arrested but impaled.

29. Because the Noumerite and Ataphite Arabs[150] were making devastating raids into Cœlo-Syria and even Antioch itself, the emperor sent the magister Nicephoros Ouranos[151] to be governor of Antioch, appointing the patrician David Areianites to succeed him at Thessalonike. He stationed the protospatharios Nikephoros Xiphias[152] at Philippoupolis (Thedorakanos had retired because of old age). When the magister Nikephoros Ouranos arrived in Antioch he fought two or three battles against Kitrinites, the

---

[147] The emperor's strategy was to win over the Bulgar chiefs by assuring them not only of high titles but also of the income that went with them, for the treasury was in very good shape.

[148] Boleron was to the east of the river Nestos, south of the Rhodope mountains, not too far from Mosynopoulis, one of Basil's military bases. In 1047 a new fiscal region of this name is noted; this may well have been a theme: *Iviron*, II, no. 29.

[149] Present-day Edessa, a south-Macedonian bishopric to the west of Thessalonike, on the Via Egnatia. Vodena was a major prize in the confrontation of Basil II and Samuel.

[150] These two Arab tribes had been living in Syria since the seventh century. At the time Skylitzes writes of the Numerites were under the sway of Wattab b. Sabiq, emir of Harran. The identity of the Ataphites is a matter of dispute: W. Felix, *Byzanz und die islamische Welt im früheren II. Jahrhundert* (Byzantina Vindobonensia, 15, Vienna, 1981), 53, notes 29 and 30.

[151] He was duke of Antioch (Skylitzes writes *archon*) from December 999 to *c*. 1006.

[152] A new name among the office holders. A relative (a brother?) of this man named Alexios was appointed *katepan* of Italy by Basil II, *c*. 1007: Falkenhausen, *Dominazione*, 189–90.

Arab leader,[153] put him to flight and obliged him to keep the peace. Thus a state of great calm prevailed.

30. [346] The following year, fifteenth year of the indiction,[154] the emperor campaigned against Vidin[155] and took it by storm after the siege had dragged on for eight months.

Here the ingenuity of the Bulgar chieftains was displayed. By the use of a very large earthenware vessel they were able to extinguish Greek fire.[156]

While the emperor was engaged in this siege, Samuel mounted a lightning attack on Adrianople with a light and rapid force on the very day of the *Koimesis*[157] of the most holy Mother of God. He suddenly fell on the fair which is customarily held at public expense [on that day], took a great deal of booty and went back to his own land. The emperor further improved the defences of Vidin, then set off back to the capital with his forces intact, ravaging and destroying every Bulgar stronghold he came across on the way home. As he approached Skopje[158] he discovered Samuel encamped without foresight at the other side of the river Axios,[159] which is now called Bardarios because Bardas Skleros diverted it from its former bed into the course which it now follows.[160]

Samuel was putting his trust in the high waters of the river – which he thought it was impossible to cross for the time being; so he encamped giving no thought to security. But one of the soldiers discovered a ford and brought the emperor across by it. Taken completely by surprise, Samuel fled without a backward glance. His tent was captured and all his encampment. The city of Skopje was handed over to the emperor by Romanos whom Samuel had appointed as its governor. This Romanos was the son of King Peter of the Bulgars and the brother of Boris; he had changed his name to that of his grandfather, Symeon. The emperor rewarded his

---

[153] Some Noumarite Bedouins had come together under the leadership of a chief (al-Aflar) who claimed to be a new Mahdi. He was detained at Aleppo in April–May 1007 with the consent of Ouranos: Yahya of Antioch, II, 466–7; Felix, *Byzanz und Islam*, 52–4. On the general situation in Syria: T. Bianquis, 'Les frontières de la Syrie au XIe siècle', *Castrum*, 4 (1992), 135–48.

[154] The war against the Bulgars started up again in 1002 and went on for three or four years, but it is not clear exactly how the campaigns succeeded each other.

[155] A bishopric on the Danube to the north of Bulgaria near the Iron Gates. By penetrating so far Basil could have been preparing to strike Samuel in the rear.

[156] *To medikon pyr* MS U only.

[157] The Dormition (falling-asleep) of the Virgin Mary, 15 August.

[158] Skopje controls the Vardar valley which leads to Thessalonike. The defeat of Samuel was in 1003 or 1004: Stephenson, *Balkan frontier*, 56.

[159] 'Axios': 'Naxios' – MS U.

[160] MS U only. The name of the river (Vardar) resembles the name of Bardas, pronounced Vardas.

submission with the titles of patrician and prefect,[161] awarding him a command of Abydos.

31. [347] From there the emperor crossed over and came to Pernikos[162] where Krakras was on guard, a most excellent man in warfare. He spent considerable time laying siege to that place and lost quite a number of men. Realising that the defence-works were too good to be taken by siege and that Krakas could not be deflected by flattery, promises or other suggestions, he went on to Philippoupolis and from there struck camp and proceeded to Constantinople.[163]

32. In the same year of the indiction[164] he made an ordinance that magnates were to pay the taxes of deceased common folk; this arrangement was called *allelengyon*.[165] The patriarch Sergios, many bishops and a good number of monks begged for this unreasonable burden to be withdrawn but the emperor was not persuaded. Samuel laid ambushes in suitable locations and captured alive the patrician John Chaldos, duke of Thessalonike.[166]

33. In the eighth year of the indiction, AM 6518, Azizios, the ruler of Egypt, broke his truce with the Romans on a small pretext and for minor infringements scarcely worthy of notice. He destroyed the magnificent church which had been erected over the tomb of Christ the Saviour in Jerusalem;[167] he devastated the illustrious monasteries [there] and dispersed the monks who lived in them to the four corners of the earth.

---

[161] Romanos was a eunuch, hence he qualified for the position of prefect (prepositos), a palatine office reserved for eunuchs.
[162] Pernikos commanded the road from Naissos (Nish) to Sofia; it was to the south-west of Sofia.
[163] Now Skylitzes interrupts his account of the Bulgar wars for a while without mentioning whether Basil and Samuel made a treaty after the success of the emperor: Stephenson, *Balkan frontier*, 69.
[164] This appears to be still in 1004.
[165] The object of the exercise was to bring the rich and powerful back into the system of corporate taxation, from which they had escaped by managing to get their holdings taxed separately. The point is that the rich paid what the displaced peasantry would have paid but, contrary to the old principle of village solidarity, they did not work the land on which they were taxed: Kaplan, *Les hommes et la terre*, 439–40.
[166] MSS UE only, E in the margin. The remark about Chaldos is out of place for the duke was captured before the battle of the Spercheios.
[167] The destruction of the church of the Holy Sepulchre commenced on 28 September 1009: Yahya of Antioch, II, 492, which agrees with the date given by Skylitzes, AM 6518, being the eighth year of the indiction (which began on 1 September 1009): M. Canard, 'La destruction de l'Eglise de la Résurrection par le calife al-Hakim et l'histoire de la descente du feu sacré', *B*, 25 (1955), 16–43, repr. M. Canard, *Byzance*, no. xx. Basil II did not react to this act of aggression on the part of the Fatimid Calif al-Hakim (996–1020/1021) to whom Skylitzes gives the name of his father, al-Azíz.

330   *John Skylitzes: a synopsis of Byzantine history*

34. The following year[168] there was a most severe winter; every river and lake was frozen, even the sea itself. And in January of the same year of the indiction a most awesome earthquake occurred; it continued to shake the earth until the ninth of March. On that day, about the tenth hour of the day, [348] there was a frightful shaking and trembling at the capital and in the themes, so much so that the domes of the churches of the Forty Saints[169] and of All Saints[170] fell down (which the emperor immediately rebuilt). These things presaged the uprising which followed in Italy. A magnate of the Bari area named Meles[171] incited the people in Longobardia and he took up arms against the Romans.[172] The emperor sent Basil Argyros,[173] commander of Samos, together with the man they called Leo the Short,[174] commander of Kephalonia, to restore Roman fortunes. Meles opposed them in a formal battle and inflicted a crushing defeat. Many fell, many were taken prisoner, while the rest opted for a life of shame by taking to their heels.[175]

35. The emperor continued to invade Bulgaria every year without interruption, laying waste everything that came to hand.[176] Samuel could do nothing in open country nor could he oppose the emperor in formal battle. He was shattered on all fronts and his own forces were declining, so he decided to close the way into Bulgaria with ditches and fences. He knew that the emperor was always in the habit of coming by way of what is

---

[168] Winter, 1010–11.
[169] There were several churches in the capital dedicated to the Forty Martyrs, of which the most famous was adjacent to the Mese: Janin, *Églises et monastères*, 1, 482–6.
[170] This church was built by Leo VI for his first wife, Theophano. It was adjacent to Holy Apostles, in the centre of the city: Janin, *Églises et monastères*, 1, 389.
[171] The only thing known about this person is that he was one of the most influential nobles of the region. His uprising prospered because he was able to enlist some Norman mercenaries: J. France, 'The occasion of the coming of the Normans to Italy', *Journal of Medieval History*, 17 (1991), 185–205.
[172] It is not clear when this revolt started; the Italian chronicles vacillate between 1009 and 1011.
[173] This is the brother of Maria Argyropoulina and a relative of the emperor: Vannier, *Argyroi*, 9–41, rpr. in Chenier, *Société*, 540–1.
[174] Tornikios Kontoleon succeeded Basil Argyros as *katepan* of Italy in 1017: Falkenhausen, *Dominazione*, 89–90.
[175] This is erroneous for, according to the Italian sources, Basil Argyros retook Bari (capital of the theme of Longobardia) after it had fallen into the hands of the rebels. This *katepan* (surnamed Mesardonites) has left an inscription commemorating the construction of a fortress inside Bari: (most recently) A. Guillou, *Recueil des inscriptions grecques médiévales d'Italie* (Rome, 1996), 143, 154–9. It is correct that the *katepan* Basil Boioannes decisively defeated Meles at Cannae, with the help of some Russians.
[176] Nowadays there is much discussion of this statement for there is no indication that Basil took any action against the Bulgars between 1004 and 1014, the date of the Battle of Kleidion: Stephenson, *Balkan frontier*, 69–71. It has to be borne in mind that Skylitzes abandons the narrative of important events now and again: witness his omission of some of Tzimiskes' eastern campaigns.

called Kiava Longos and Kleidion,[177] so he determined to block this pass and thus prevent the emperor from entering. He constructed a very wide fortification, stationed an adequate guard there and waited for the emperor who duly arrived and attempted to force a way in. But the guards stoutly resisted, killing the assailants and wounding them by hurling [weapons] from up above. The emperor had already abandoned the attempt to pass when Nikephoros Xiphias, then commander of Philippoupolis, made an agreement with the emperor that he would stay there and make repeated attacks on the enemy's line while Xiphias would (according to his own words) go and see if he could do anything profitable and likely to solve their problem. He led his men back the [349] way they had come. Then, trekking around the very high mountain which lies to the south of Kleidion and which is called Valasitza, passing by goat-paths and through trackless wastes, on 29 July, twelfth year of the indiction,[178] he suddenly appeared above the Bulgars and came down on their backs with great cries and thundering tread. Completely taken aback by the unexpected nature of this attack, the Bulgars turned and fled. The emperor dismantled the abandoned defence-work and gave chase; many fell and even more were taken prisoner. Samuel was only just able to escape from danger, by the cooperation of his own son who stoutly resisted those who attacked, got his father onto a horse and led him to the fortress called Prilapon.[179] They say that the emperor blinded the prisoners, about fifteen thousand in number, with orders that one man for each hundred be left one eye so he could be their guide,[180] then sent them back to Samuel. He, when he saw them arriving in such numbers and the state they were in, lacked the moral fortitude to endure the shock; fainting and darkness came upon him and he fell to the ground. By applying water and perfumes to get him breathing again, his attendants succeeded in bringing him back to himself somewhat. As he revived, he called for cold water to drink. He got it, drank it and then suffered a heart attack; two days later he died on 6 October.[181]

---

[177] A pass between the valleys of the Strymon and the Vardar.
[178] 29 July 1014.
[179] This town of northern Macedonia is still known by the same name. It lies on the route to Ochrid, which means that Basil was now threatening Samuel's capital.
[180] The number of prisoners said to have been blinded is quite unreasonable, for the loss of so many men would have brought the Bulgar army to its knees – whereas it showed itself to be ready for combat the following year: Stephenson, *Balkan frontier*, 72, for references. In the second half of the century, however, Kekaumenos (*Strategikon* 152) put the number of prisoners at 14,000. Blinding was the legal punishment for a rebel subject. Thus the emperor considered the Bulgars to be rebels in recovering their independence after the conquest of Bulgaria by John Tzimiskes.
[181] MS U only.

The governing of Bulgaria now fell to Gabriel, his son (also known as Romanos),[182] who now reigned over the Bulgars after him. He surpassed his father in vigour and strength but was sadly inferior to him in wisdom and understanding. He was born to Samuel by a woman captured at Larissa[183] {by Agatha, daughter of John Chyselios, proteuon of Dyrrachion}.[184]

His reign began on 15 September, thirteenth year of the indiction,[185] but before a full year was out, he was slain [350] when he was out hunting, by John also known as Vladisthlav, the son of Aaron, whom he had himself redeemed when he was about to die.

{Rodomir had to wife the daughter of the Kral of Hungary.[186] For reasons unknown to me he took to hating her and sent her away when she was already pregnant to him. Then he took the fair Irene who had been taken prisoner at Larissa.}[187]

36. Before this happened, when Theophylact Botaneiates had been sent to command Thessalonike after Areianites, David Nestoritzes, one of the great Bulgar magnates, was sent against that city with a powerful force by Samuel. Theophylact and Michael, his son, offered resistance to them and, when battle was joined, repelled them in no small way, taking much booty and many prisoners, which he sent to the emperor who was then engaged before the defence-work in the pass of Kleidion. The emperor overcame that obstacle (as we said) and advanced to Stroumbitza[188] where he took the fortress called Matzoukis (close to Stroumbitza). He then despatched Theophylact Botaneiates, duke of Thessalonike, commanding a detachment with orders to cross the Stroumbitza mountains and to burn all the defence-works he encountered on the way, clearing the road to Thessalonike for him. As Theophylact departed he was permitted to pass unimpeded by the Bulgars who were set to guard the place, but when he was about to return to the emperor after discharging his commission he fell into an ambush prepared for this purpose, set up in a long defile. Once he was in there, he was assailed from all sides by stones and weapons thrown from above. Nobody could do anything to defend himself on

---

[182] Romanos/Rodomir in MS U and this is confirmed by the *Chronicle of the Priest of Diokleia, Letopis Popa Dukljanina*, ed. F. Sisic (Belgrade and Zagreb, 1928), 336. This chronicle has, however, little historical value; it was in fact put together long after the events it records, as has recently been shown: S. Bujan, 'La Chronique du prêtre de Dioclée: un faux document historique', *REB* 66 (2008), 5–38.
[183] Thus John/Vladisthlav would be first cousin to Gabriel.   [184] MS U only.
[185] 15 September 1014.
[186] We do not know the name of this first daughter of Stephen I of Hungary.
[187] MS U only.
[188] Located in the south of the present republic of Macedonia, Stroumbitza controls the access roads to Skopje.

account of the press of men and there being no way out of the pass; [351] the [duke] himself fell without being able to use his own hands {Rodomir spilled out [the duke's] entrails with the spear he bore}[189] and a large portion of the army was destroyed with him. When this was reported to the emperor he was greatly distressed and he decided to advance no further on this account. He turned back and came to Zagoria where there stands the very secure fortress of Melnikos.[190] It is built on a rock ringed around on all sides by beetling crags and deep ravines. All the Bulgars of the area took refuge there and were not too much concerned about the Romans. But the emperor sent to them Sergios, a eunuch and one of his most intimate chamberlains, an able man and a fine speaker, to test their state of mind. When he got there he managed (by the use of many persuasive arguments) to convince the men of what they had to do: to lay down their arms and surrender to the emperor both themselves and the fortress. These the emperor received and rewarded them accordingly.[191] He appointed a sufficient detail to guard the fortress then went on to Mosynoupolis. It was while he was there that the death of Samuel was reported to him, the twenty-fourth of October. The emperor immediately left Mosynoupolis and came to Thessalonike, from where he proceeded to Pelagonia,[192] destroying nothing on the way except that he burnt the palace of Gabriel at Voutele. He sent out troops which took the fortresses of Prilapon and Stypeion, then he came to the river called Tzernas which he crossed on rafts and inflated bladders,[193] then he returned to Vodena and from there to Thessalonike where he arrived on the ninth of January.

37. [352] At the beginning of spring [the emperor] returned to Bulgaria again and headed for the fortress of Vodena, for the people there had broken faith with him and taken up arms against the Romans. By a long-drawn-out siege he forced those within (when they had received assurances) to surrender themselves. He deported them again to Boleron[194] and

---

[189] MS U only.

[190] The first mention of this fortress situated in the upper Strymon valley.

[191] After the death of Samuel some of the Bulgar nobles came to the conclusion that they had more to gain by serving the emperor – who, having the advantage of being able to dispose of immense riches, richly rewarded them for joining his side.

[192] Today Bitola, very close to Ochrid; Basil was making a show of force.

[193] Certain of the tenth-century treatises on tactics recommend this method of crossing rivers: *Three Byzantine military treatises,* text, translation and notes by G. T. Dennis, *CFHB* series Washingtoniensis ix, Washington 1985, index under the word *potamos.*

[194] 'At the beginning of spring, setting out on the very day of Holy Saturday, he came and took Vodina and deported the inhabitants to Boleron, installing in the city to replace them some Romans who are called *kontaratoi,* wild and murderous fellows, merciless bandits. And he erected two fortresses, etc.', MS U only. *Kontaratoi* means light infantry armed with lances (*kontos*):

he erected two new fortresses well within that difficult pass, calling the first one Kardia and the other St Elijah. Then he went back to Thessalonike. There Romanos-Gabriel undertook (by the agency of a certain Roman who had lost an arm) to be the emperor's subject and servant. But the emperor was suspicious of the letter; he sent the patrician Nikephoros Xiphias and Constantine Diogenes[195] (who had succeeded Botaneiates as commander of Thessalonike) into the region of Moglena[196] with an army. The emperor arrived when they had ravaged the whole area and were besieging the city. He diverted the river that flows by the city and excavated the foundations of the walls. Wood and other combustible materials were put into the excavations and set on fire; as the fuel burnt, the wall came down. When those within saw this, they fell to prayers and groans, surrendering themselves together with the fortress. Domitianos Kaukanos,[197] a powerful man and an adviser of Gabriel, was captured; also Elitzes, the governor of Moglena, many important people and a considerable number of fighting men. The emperor sent those capable of bearing arms to Asprakania;[198] he ordered the remaining mass of the people to be cut to pieces and the fortress to be put to the flames. He took another fortress, this one called Enotia, not far from Moglena.

38. [353] On the fifth day the one-armed Roman came bringing a servant of John-Vladislav, the son of Aaron, bearing a letter claiming that Gabriel had been slain by him at Peteriskon[199] and that plenary power had been passed to him.[200] He promised to show the proper degree of respect and servitude to the emperor. When the emperor had read this he acknowledged its contents with chrysobulls which he sent to John. A few days later the one-armed Roman was back with letters from John and from the governors of Bulgaria affirming themselves to be subjects and servants of the emperor. Kaukanos {Theodore Kpachanes,[201] the brother of Domitianos and of Meliton,[202]} who was taken at the fall of Moglena,

---

T. Kolias, *Byzantinische Waffen. Ein Beitrag zur byzantinischen Waffenkunde von den Anfängen bis zur lateinischen Eroberung* (Vienna, 1988), 191–213.

[195] Formerly the Diogenai were connected with the Phokai but Adralestos Diogenes had betrayed Bardas at the time of his revolt. Constantine was the father of the future emperor Romanos IV.

[196] In south-east Macedonia.

[197] On Kaukanos and the other members of Samuel's entourage: G. Nikolov, 'The Bulgarian aristocracy in the war against the Byzantine empire (971–1019)', *Byzantina et Slavica Cracoviensia*, III, *Byzantium and East central Europe* (Cracow, 2001), 41–158. Kaukanos is an ancient Bulgarian title designating the second in command to the Chagan.

[198] A province of the east, near to lake Van, also known as Vaspourakan.   [199] MSS EU only.

[200] The internecine strife within the bosom of the ruling family accelerated the disintegration of the Bulgar state.

[201] MS U only.   [202] MS U only.

also submitted to the emperor. Thereupon he was received with honour and respect, and he promised the emperor that he would slay Vladisthlav. He returned to Bulgaria together with the servant of John who, having been heavily bribed, was to slay John with his own hand; but it was he who was slain by [John] at the Stoupion hostel. The place where the murder of Theodore took place was originally called Diabolis.[203]

Once the emperor realised it was to beguile and deceive him that John had set down what he had written – that he intended the exact opposite of what he had written – he turned back to Bulgaria again, devastating the regions of lake Ostrovos, Soskos and the plain of Pelagonia. He blinded all the Bulgarians taken prisoner. He advanced as far as the city of Ochrid where stood the palace of the kings of Bulgaria.[204] He took the city, rendered the situation secure and was about to advance further by taking the road to Dyrrachion where the situation demanded his presence. As long as Vladimir,[205] the husband of Samuel's daughter, was ruling Tribalia[206] and the nearer parts of Serbia, things were calm at Dyrrachion, for he was a man of integrity, peace [354] and virtue. But when Gabriel was slain by John, Vladimir also was betrayed. He had put his trust in the oaths which John had sworn by the agency of David, archbishop of Bulgaria, and surrendered to him, only to be slain by him a little later. The situation around Dyrrachion then became very disturbed and distressed because John repeatedly attempted to take the city, often by sending his commanders, sometimes coming in person. This is why the emperor wished to go there and render aid, but for a reason worth noting he was prevented from doing so. When he was leaving for Ochrid, he left behind the commander George Gonitziates and the protospatharios Orestes 'the prisoner' with numerous troops and orders to overrun the Pelagonian plain. But they were taken in an ambush by the Bulgars under the illustrious and experienced command of Ibatzes and all killed. Broken with grief at their loss, the emperor returned to Pelagonia and went off in hot pursuit of Ibatzes; then he returned to Thessalonike. From there he went over to Mosynoupolis, having despatched a detachment against Stroumbitza under the command of David Areianates, who made a surprise attack and took the fortress known as Thermitza. The emperor sent another detachment against the

---

[203] MS U only. [204] Only since the time of Samuel.
[205] Vladimir was the prince of Zeta or Diokleia, a region at the inlet of Kotor, to the north of the theme of Dyrrachion. According to the *Chronicle of the Priest of Diokleia*, ed. Sisic, ch. 36, he married a daughter of Samuel named Kosara. This chronicle also gives a very similar account of the assassination of Vladislav, 22 May 1016, but this is not an original source: n. 182, above.
[206] A name for the coastal region of Serbia.

stronghold of Triaditza under the command of Xiphias; he razed all the open country and then took the stronghold known as Boio[207] by storm.

39. The emperor returned to Constantinople in January, AM 6524, and sent a fleet against Chazaria[208] under the command of Mongos,[209] the son of Andronikos, duke of Lydos. With the cooperation of Sphengos, the brother of Vladimir and brother-in-law of the emperor, he subdued the region and actually captured its governor, George Tzoulas,[210] in the first engagement. It was then that Senacherim, governor of Upper Media [355] (the region they now call Asprakania), came to the emperor with all his family as a refugee and handed over to him the entire land which was his to command.[211] He was made patrician and commander of Cappadocia and received in exchange the cities of Sebasteia, Larissa,[212] Abara and many other domains. It was because he had been under great pressure from the Hagarenes and was unable to withstand them that he took refuge with the emperor and handed over his own land.[213] This the patrician Basil Argyros was sent to rule but he failed in everything and was relieved of his command. The protospatharios Nikephoros Komnenos[214] was sent to succeed him; when he arrived there, he brought the land into subjection to the emperor by the alternate use of persuasion and force.

40. AM 6524, fourteenth year of the indiction,[215] the emperor left the capital and went to Triaditza where he encamped before the fortress of Pernikos and besieged it, but those within resisted with endurance and determination; many Romans fell. When the siege had dragged on for eighty-eight days, he realised there was no possibility of succeeding so he withdrew, empty-handed, and fell back on Mosynoupolis. There

---

[207] The present Bojana, near to Sofia.　　[208] Here this means the region of Cherson.
[209] Yet again a former rebel (in this case, a supporter of Skleros) obtains an important command.
[210] Member of an important family known mainly by seals.
[211] Senacherim surrendered his country during the winter 1021–2: *Matthew of Edessa*, ed. Dostourian, 44–5. The first attacks of the Turks may have unnerved him, but there was probably a certain amount of pressure from Basil who was campaigning against the Georgians at that time and wintered over in Trebizond. According to Matthew, Senacherim handed over to the emperor seventy-two fortresses and 4,400 villages and monasteries.
[212] Larissa on the eastern frontier (not to be confused with the town of the same name in Greece, mentioned above) was the headquarters of a *tourma* dependent on the theme of Sebasteia until it became itself the residence of a stratego in the eleventh century.
[213] See E. Honigmann, *Die Ostgrenze des byzantinischen Reiches von 363–1071 nach griechischen, arabischen, syrischen un armenischen Quellen* (CBHB, 3, Brussels, 1935), 168–71; also W Seibt, 'Die Eingliederung von Vaspurakan in as byzantinische Reich (etwa Anfang 1019 bsw. Anfang 1022)', *Handes Amsorya*, 92 (1978), 49–66.
[214] We do not know the relationship between Nikephoros and Manuel Komnenos Erotikos (the hero of the struggle against Skleros); he could have been a slightly younger brother or a cousin.
[215] 1 September 1016 to 31 August 1017.

he rested his army then, at the beginning of spring, he marched out of Mosynoupolis and entered Bulgaria. He encamped at the fortress called Longos and took it by siege. He sent David Areianates and Constantine Diogenes to the plains of Pelagonia and took possession of many beasts and numerous prisoners. The emperor burnt the fortress when it was taken and divided the spoils of war into three parts. One part he assigned to the Russian allies; a second part to the Romans; the third he kept for himself. Then he advanced further and came to Kastoria, but having made an attempt on the city he concluded that it was inexpugnable and turned back. He was in receipt of a letter from [356] the commander of Dorostolon, Tzotzikios, son of the patrician Theudatos the Iberian,[216] to the effect that Krakras had assembled a large army and had joined forces with John. Once he had gained the cooperation of the Patzinaks[217] he was going to make an assault on Roman lands. Disturbed by this letter, the emperor returned in haste, capturing and burning the fortress of Vosograd along the way, and also taking Berroia. Having devastated and burned the countryside surrounding Ostrovos and Moliskos he refrained from going any further, for it was reported to him that the attack on Roman territory planned by Krakras and John was frustrated by the Patzinaks not providing them with allies.[218] So he turned around and laid siege to another fortress, Setena, which contained a palace of Samuel and where much grain was stored. This he ordered the army to pillage; all that remained he consigned to the flames. Then he sent the scholai of the west[219] out against John (who was lying not too far away) and the unit of Thessalonike with Constantine Diogenes in command, but John set an ambush for them as they marched along. When the emperor learnt of this he leapt into the saddle and galloped off with no other words but: 'Let every true warrior follow me!' When John's spies got wind of this they came to John's encampment in great fear and filled it with anxiety and distress, shouting nothing else but: *bezeite ho tzesar*.[220] They all beat a disorderly retreat together with John, Diogenes taking fresh courage and following in pursuit. They killed many and took prisoner two hundred soldiers with all their arms and with their

---

[216] So this man was a Georgian and the son of one of the three closest associates of David the Kouropalates, who had come over to Basil's side.

[217] The alliance of Krakras with the Patzinaks living at the mouths of the Danube explains why the commander of Dristra–Silistria, capital of the Paristrion, was worried.

[218] There may have been an intervention of Byzantine diplomacy.

[219] The units of the scholai had been divided into two distinct regiments since the reign of Romanos II.

[220] Here the Greek texts gives the Bulgar words for 'Look out! the emperor (Caesar)!'

horses, plus all the equipment of John and his nephew too {who was promptly deprived of his eyes}[221]

That accomplished, the emperor returned to Vodena, set everything in order there and took the road back to Byzantium, 9 January, fifteenth year of the indiction, AM 6526.[222]

41. [357] Now John seized his opportunity and went off to besiege Dyrrachion with barbaric insolence and arrogance. When the siege was laid, an engagement took place in which he fell; with no man known to have been the cause of his death {a mounted engagement took place with the commander and patrician Niketas Pegonites and he fell, mortally wounded in the entrails by two foot soldiers running through the melee[223]}.

He had ruled Bulgaria for two years and five months. When the death of John was reported to the emperor by the commander of Dyrrachion, the patrician Niketas Pegonites,[224] he immediately set out on campaign. At Adrianople he was met by the brother and the son of the famous Krakras, announcing that they were ceding to him the celebrated fortress of Pernikos and thirty-five others. He honoured them accordingly, raising Krakras to the dignity of patrician; then he came to Mosynoupolis. To that place came ambassadors from Pelagonia, Morovisdos and Lipenios, surrendering those towns to him.[225] From there he came to Serres where Krakras arrived accompanied by the governors of the thirty-five fortresses which had made their submission to him; he was well received. Dragomouzos also made his submission, surrendering the fort of Stroumbitza with all it contained, and was promoted patrician. With him he brought the patrician John Chaldos, recently delivered from his interminable imprisonment; for after being captured by Samuel he had spent twenty-two years in gaol. No sooner had the emperor approached Stroumbitza than David,[226] archbishop of Bulgaria, came to him bearing a letter from Maria, the wife [widow] of John, in which she undertook to depart from Bulgaria if she got what she was asking for. He came into contact with Bogdan, governor of the interior fortresses; [358] he too was honoured with the dignity of

---

[221] MS U only.   [222] 9 January 1018.   [223] MS U only.
[224] This man's daughter married John Doukas, brother of the future emperor Constantine X Doukas. So Nicetas was the great-grandfather of Irene Doukaina, the wife of Alexis Komnenos.
[225] After the death of John-Vladislav the boyars tried to make the best of their surrender. When Krakras was made patrician he outranked many strategoi of themes at that time.
[226] John, also known as David, was maintained by the emperor as archbishop of Bulgaria, a post which he retained until his death in the reign of Michael IV: Theophylact of Bulgaria, *Opera*, 30.

patrician because he had long favoured the emperor's cause and had slain his own father-in-law, Matthaitzes.[227] From there he went to Skopie where he was met by Nikoulitzas the younger, he who had led the first and most warlike engagement under Samuel; he was honoured with the titles of protospatharios and commander.[228] In that city the emperor left the patrician David Areianites as commander plenipotentiary naming him *katepan* of Bulgaria.[229]

He returned by way of the fortresses of Stypeion and Prosakon where he was honoured and acclaimed with processions and hymns. Then once again he turned to the right[230] and courageously took the road to Ochrid where he set up camp. All the people came out to meet him with paeans of praise, clapping of hands and acclamations.[231] Ochrid is a city located on a high hill close by a large lake {called Lychnidon. That is where the city gets its name of Lychnidos from, the same name as the lake; it was originally called Dassarites. An innumerable quantity of fine fish is taken from this lake.}[232] Out of this lake the river Drinos flows to the north. {It comes from the Diabolis region to the south and crosses the said lake (just as they say the Alpheios crosses the sea then flows towards Arethousa) then proceeds in a northerly direction. At the end of the lake are found what is locally called the Strougai with which it comes together to form a very large river.[233]} Further on it turns towards the west and flows into the Orinos near the fortress of Eilissos. It is at Ochrid, the metropolis of all Bulgaria, [359] that the palace of the kings of Bulgaria lies and where their treasure was stored. When the emperor opened it he found a great deal of money, crowns with pearls, vestments embroidered in gold and one hundred *kentenaria* of gold coin[234] which he had distributed to his army as a bonus.[235] He appointed the patrician Eustathios Daphnomeles governor of the city, providing him with an adequate guard, then went out to his encampment where he received

---

[227] MS U only.   [228] MS U only.
[229] MSS CVOU only.   [230] Thus MSS BMNUH.   [231] March 1018.
[232] MSS CEBOU.   [233] MSS ACEOU.
[234] Not a large sum; equivalent to ten times what was spent on the repair of the Great Church after the earthquake. Certainly not much in comparison to the 200,000 talents which Basil II would leave when he died, according to Psellos, *Chronographia*, ed. Renauld, 1, 19, trans. Sewter, 1.32; or, according to an officer of the Fatimid court, 6,000 *qintar* of Baghdad in pieces of gold and 54 million dinars and jewels: O. Grabar, 'The shared culture of objects', *Byzantine court culture*, ed. Maguire, 124. The tsar's shortage of negotiable resources at an especially difficult time for him indicates that a money economy was not yet well developed in that part of Bulgaria.
[235] He was particularly generous to the Russian soldiers; they appear to have played an important part in the final victory over Bulgaria.

the wife of John-Vladisthslav who had been brought to him, together with three sons, six daughters, the bastard son of Samuel, two daughters of Rodomir, son of Samuel, and five sons of whom the first had lost his sight having been mutilated by John when he slew Rodomir, son of Samuel together with his wife and Vladimir his brother-in-law. Maria had borne John three other sons but these had fled to Mount Tmoros, a peak of the Ceraunian range. He accorded her a gentle and benevolent reception and ordered her to be detained with the others. Then some others of the great ones of Bulgaria came to him: Nestoritzes, Lazaritzes and Dobromeros the younger, each with his own detachment of troops. They were kindly received and given imperial honours. Then Prousianos and his two brothers {Alousianos and Aaron[236]}, children of Vladisthlav who had fled to Tmoros (as we said above). Having endured a protracted siege (for soldiers had been posted on the emperor's orders to oversee the paths leading to the mountain), they communicated with the emperor and asked for assurances, announcing that they would surrender their persons. The emperor returned a humane answer to them also. Then he departed from Ochrid and came to the lake they call Prespa. As he crossed the mountain between [the two lakes?] he constructed a fortress up the mountainside and called it Basilis and another one in the lake mentioned above {(a smaller one) which he called Konstantios[237]}. [360]

After leaving Prespa he went to the place called Diabolis[238] where he constructed a high tribune on which to receive Prousianos and his brothers when they arrived. Soothing them with indulgent and merciful words, he named Prousianos magister,[239] the others patricians. Ibatzes was also brought to him, his eyes destroyed; the way in which he came to be blinded is worth reporting, for it is a pleasant and wondrous story.

42. After the death of John Vladisthlav and the submission of his wife, Maria, also of her children {Preasianos, Alousianos, Aaron, Trajan and Rodomir <and Clement>[240]}, and the compliance of every other important person throughout Bulgaria, Ibatzes fled to an inaccessible mountain, Brochotos by name, in which there is a very lovely palace

---

[236] MS U only. [237] MS U only.
[238] It was in this very town that Alexios Komnenos made a peace treaty with Bohemond the Norman in September 1108. Alexios' choice of venue was probably dictated by a desire to emulate his great predecessor, Basil II.
[239] The same dignity which John Tzimiskes had accorded the king of the Bulgars after capturing him: reign of Tzimiskes, c. 18.
[240] MSS EU only, <…> E only.

called Pronista which has gardens and pleasure grounds of no mean beauty. He had no wish to obey the will of God, but rather gradually assembled a force by inciting the surrounding countryside, fomenting an uprising with dreams of seizing the Bulgarian throne. This greatly perturbed the emperor and for this reason he abandoned the direct route and turned south, coming to the aforementioned Diabolis. His aim was to oblige the upstart to lay down his arms by whatever means he could, or to coerce him by force of arms. While the emperor was enjoying a stay at the place just mentioned he urged Ibatzes by letter not to be the only one to raise his hand against him now Bulgaria was subdued; nor should he dream of the unobtainable, since he knew perfectly well that what he had undertaken would end up bringing him no advantage. Ibatzes received the letter and replied in kind pleading every kind of extenuation, delay and procrastination, with the result that the emperor, beguiled by his promises, was obliged to remain there for fifty-five days. The meat of this matter, to wit that the emperor would like to have done with Ibatzes, [361] was made known to Eustathios Daphnomeles, the governor of Ochrid; so, when the right opportunity presented itself, he took two of his most trusted servants into his confidence, revealed what he had in mind and addressed himself to the task. Ibatzes was holding a public celebration of the feast of the *koimesis* of the all-holy Mother of God. On that day it was his custom to invite to a banquet not only his close neighbours and those of adjacent lands, but also many who came from a great distance. Off went Eustathios to the feast as a self-invited guest and gave orders to the guards he encountered on the way to announce who he was and that he was come to make merry together with the governor. Ibatzes was dumbfounded when they told him this; astounded that an enemy would come of his own volition and deliver himself into the hands of the foe. Yet he said the man should come and, when he arrived, gave him a warm welcome and joyfully embraced him. When the morning liturgy was concluded and all the guests had dispersed to their several lodgings, Eustathios approached Ibatzes and asked the others to stand back for a moment, as though he had something important and advantageous that he would like to discuss privately with him. Not suspecting any guile or deceit but rather supposing that Eustathios wanted himself to become one of those who was supporting him in the uprising, Ibatzes told his servants to stand aside a little. He took [his guest] by the hand and led him into a garden of thick bushes in which there was a recess from which no sound could be heard, so dense were the trees. When Eustathios was alone with Ibatzes in there, he suddenly threw him to the ground, planted his knee on the man's chest (for he was a strong man) and throttled him, calling his two servants to come quickly and help. They were standing close by according to the pre-arranged plan, waiting to see what would happen. They came running as soon as they heard their master's voice, seized Ibatzes and stuffed his tunic into his mouth to prevent him from calling out, thus summoning the crowd and frustrating the undertaking. Then they blinded him and led him, blind, out of the garden into the courtyard while they ran [362] to the upper storey of a high building, drew their swords and stood in wait for those who might attempt to follow them. A large crowd gathered when the matter became known, some with swords in their hands, some with spears, some with bows, some with stones, some with clubs, some with lighted torches, others with firewood. They all came yelling and shouting: 'Let them be slaughtered, let them be burnt, let them be torn limb from limb, let them be buried with stones, these assassins and murderers; let there be no quarter for these wretches.' Eustathios despaired of his life when he saw this onslaught, yet he called upon those who accompanied him to play the man and not weaken; not to surrender and fall into the hands of those who sought their destruction, expecting to be delivered by them, only to receive a miserable and painful death. Leaning out of a window he silenced the crowd with his hand and addressed these remarks to them: 'As you are fully aware, you men who are assembled here, there was no personal enmity between me and your chief because he is a Bulgar and I a Roman; not a Roman living in Thrace or Macedonia, but a Roman of Asia Minor; some of you know how far distant that is. And the more intelligent will perceive that I did not undertake this present task lightly or wantonly, but because something obliged me to do so. I would not have insanely thrown myself into the midst of such evident danger and set such a low value on my life if there had been no other reason compelling me to embrace this undertaking. I would have you know that what I have done, I did it at the command of the emperor; in obedience to him, I served as his instrument. If you now wish to kill me, here I am, surrounded by you on all sides. But it will be no easy or straightforward [363] task putting me to death; I will not lay down my arms and surrender myself to you so you can treat me as you wish. Rather will I fight to the death for my own life and, together with my companions, repel my attackers. And if we die (the fate which of necessity awaits those who are assailed by many attackers), we will reckon our death a happy and blessed end, since we have one who will avenge and demand payment for our blood. Just ask yourselves how long you will be able to withstand *him.*' When the assembled men heard these words, they were stricken by their fear of the emperor. The crowd melted away, going off in different directions; the older and wiser acclaimed the emperor and became his subjects. Eustathios took his time in transporting Ibatzes and bringing him to the emperor, who approved his initiative and immediately rewarded him by appointing him commander of Dyrrachion, endowing him with all the moveable property of Ibatzes – whom he consigned to prison.

43. Nikoulitzas, who had often been captured and had many times escaped, went into hiding in the mountains. When a force was sent against him, some of his supporters went over to them with his consent while others were taken prisoner. Now, of his own free will, he came to the [imperial] camp and knocked on the gate with his hand, announcing who he was and that of his own free will he was surrendering his person to the emperor. The emperor, however, declined to see him but rather sent him to Thessalonike with orders that he was to be imprisoned. He then made whatever seemed to him to be the most propitious arrangements for Dyrrachion, Koloneia[241] and Dryïnoupolis;[242] he appointed guards and commanders for the themes and ordered those Roman prisoners who wished to stay where they were to do so while the rest were to follow him, for there were many Roman and Armenian soldiers who had been taken prisoner by Samuel and settled by him in Pelagonia, Prespa and Ochrid, of whom the most distinguished were the sons of Basil Apochaps, Gregory and ...[243]

He came to Kastoria and here two of the daughters of Samuel were brought to him. When they saw [364] Maria the wife of John standing beside the emperor, these women set about her as though they would kill her.[244]

The emperor was able to appease their wrath by promising to ennoble and enrich them. As for Maria, he honoured her with the dignity of belted patrician and sent her to the capital with her sons and all her relatives including the youngest, Samuel's bastard.[245]

---

[241] A town in Epiros, not to be confused with the town of the same name in Asia Minor, of which Bardas Phokas was duke.
[242] A town in Epiros to the south of Dyrrachion, a bishopric dependent on Naupaktos.
[243] MS U (+ *lacuna*).   [244] MS U only.
[245] MS U only.

By the agency of Xiphias he tore down all the strongholds at Serbia and at Soskos, levelling them to the ground, then he went to the fortress of Stagoi. Elemagos,[246] the governor of Belgrade,[247] came there too, clothed as a slave, together with his fellow governors.

The fortress of Belgrade is difficult to approach, indeed it is inaccessible to enemies, being ringed with precipices to the south with a river flowing by, Ason by name. There is only one entrance to the fortress. The prince of Rhakova[248] also came to the emperor.[249]

He left there and came to Athens and, as he was crossing the Zetounion, he saw the bones of the Bulgars who had fallen there when the magister Nikephoros Ouranos defeated Samuel; he saw them and was amazed. He was more amazed at the sight of the wall at Thermopylae, recently known as Skelos, which Roupenios[250] built to repel the Bulgars. When he came to Athens, he offered up thanks for his victory to the Mother of God and adorned her church with magnificent and splendid offerings, then returned to Constantinople.[251]

{The conspiracy of the two governors and patricians Elinagos and Gabras[252] by which they sought to restore the Bulgar ascendancy was revealed at Thessalonike. Gabras had already fled to his homeland; he was arrested and blinded; but when Elinagos was put to the question he consistently denied everything, so he was restored to his former rank. When the emperor returned to Constantinople[253]}, entering through the great doors of the Golden Gate and crowned with a crested golden diadem, [365] he celebrated a triumph preceded by Maria, wife of Vladisthlav, and the daughters of Samuel {plus the rest of the Bulgars and the Bulgar archbishop[254]}. This was in the second year of the indiction, AM 6527. Thus he came, joyful and triumphant, and entered the Great Church where he sang hymns of thanksgiving to God then went his way to the palace. As he came in after the triumph, Sergios the Patriarch strongly

---

[246] Elenagos Phrantzes MS U.
[247] This is Berat in Albania, not the Belgrade of today.
[248] This name now denotes a rivulet in western Macedonia, Rakovaa.
[249] The fortress of Belgrade MS B only.
[250] This is the first known member of the Armenian family of the Roupenids who ruled Little Armenia (Cilicia) in the twelfth century.
[251] The famous portrait of Basil II in the Marcian Psalter which shows him standing with four persons prostrating themselves before him has often been thought (incorrectly, it would appear) to have some connection with his victory over the Bulgars: A. Cutler, 'The Psalter of Basil II', *Arte Veneta*, 30 (1976), 9–19 and 31; (1977) 9–15, repr. *Imagery and ideology in Byzantine art* (Aldershot, 1992), no. III.
[252] This is the second mention of a member of this family (cf. reign of Basil II, c. 6). The absence of a forename precludes a precise identification of this person.
[253] MS U only.   [254] MS U only.

urged him to suppress the allelengyon,[255] which he had been promising to do if he overcame the Bulgars; but he was not persuaded to do it. After serving as pastor of the church of God for twenty whole years, Sergios migrated to the Lord in the month of July,[256] second indication, AM 6527, and Eustathios, the dean of the palace clergy, was promoted to be patriarch.

{The emperor again confirmed that the <arch>-bishop[-ric] of Bulgaria was autocephalous as it had been formerly under Romanos the Elder. This was because he drew the conclusion from the constitutions of the emperor Justinian that it was Justiniana Prima which that emperor claimed to be his fatherland and which then had Kastellion as its bishop.[257]}

44. Once Bulgaria was subject to him, the neighbouring people of the Chorbatoi came over to the emperor's side. Their rulers were two brothers; these were given high rank when they joined the emperor and their people became his subjects. The ruler of Sirmium[258] alone, the brother of Nestongos of Sirmium, refused his obedience, so the governor of those parts, Constantine Diogenes,[259] feigned friendship and despatched an embassy to him to say that, upon his oath, he really wished to meet with him and discuss some pressing matters. And if there were any fears in his mind, he would bring three only of his subordinates and meet with him in the middle of the river which flowed by [366] while the other, for his part, was to come there likewise with three attendants. The man was convinced; he came to the river and met Diogenes – who was carrying a knife in his bosom. Just as the conference was beginning he suddenly drew the weapon, stabbed the other in the side and killed him. His troops turned and fled while Diogenes concentrated his forces and marched on Sirmium with a considerable army. This terrified and confused the wife of the dead man but he mollified her by making huge promises. [Thus he] persuaded her to submit to him and to surrender Sirmium to the emperor. She was sent to Byzantium where she was married to one of the important citizens of the capital. As for Diogenes, he was appointed governor of the newly conquered land.

---

[255] A tax; see reign of Basil, c. 32, above.   [256] AD 1019.
[257] MSS EU. On the series of *sigillia* of Basil II concerning the church of Bulgaria: Stephenson, *Balkan frontier*, 75; also M. Mullett, *Theophylact of Ohrid: reading the letters of a Byzantine archbishop* (Birmingham, 1997), 64–6.
[258] Sirmium, today Sremska Mitrovica near to Belgrade, was lost once and for all in 582 when it was taken by the Chagan of the Avars.
[259] The evidence of seals shows that Diogenes held a very important military command which included Serbia: *DOSeals*, 1.34.1.

45. The emperor renovated the aqueduct of the emperor Valentinian[260] to provide the citizens of Constantinople with a plentiful supply of water. When George, the ruler of Abasgia, broke his treaty with the Romans by invading the frontier regions, the emperor campaigned against him in full force,[261] leaving behind the patricians Nikephoros Xiphias[262] and Nikephoros,[263] the son of Bardas Phokas. These complained bitterly about being left out of the campaign; they raised what army they could in Cappadocia at Rhodantos and in the surrounding regions, then they broke into open revolt. When this was reported to the emperor, disquiet and anguish overtook the camp, for fear that being caught between the Abasgians and the rebels (for the rumour was going round that the supporters of Xiphias had announced their intention of effecting such a manoeuvre to the ruler of Abasgia) they might suffer the worst of fates. The emperor wrote and sent letters to both Xiphias and Phokas, with orders to the messenger to take every care to ensure that he deliver each letter to each recipient without the other being aware of it. He did as he was commanded; when he had discretely delivered the letters, Phokas immediately read his to Xiphias; but Xiphias hid his letter and denied having ever received a word. Then one day he invited the other [367] to confer with him and, when he came, had him put to death by men who were lying in wait for that very purpose;[264] the coalition of the rebels immediately collapsed.[265] When the emperor learnt of Phokas' death, Theophylakt, the son of Damian Dalassenos, was sent; he arrested Xiphias[266] and sent him in chains to John the protonotarios[267] at the capital. John had him tonsured on the island of Antigonos. Once the emperor was relieved of the fear of rebels, he attacked the Abasgians. Many Romans fell, yet the two armies disengaged and it was left undecided which was the victor. Then on the

---

[260] This, usually called 'the aqueduct of Valens', was in fact built by Hadrian: C. Mango, *Le développement urbain de Constantinople, ive–viie siècles* (Paris, 1990), 20.
[261] For some time Basil had wished to regain his legacy from David the kouropalates, which George had seized. The death of the Fatimid Calif al-Hakim on 13 February 1021: Yahya of Antioch, III, 444, meant he now had nothing to fear from the direction of Syria.
[262] The hero of the Balkan wars was now strategos of the Anatolikon theme: Yahya of Antioch, III, 462.
[263] On this person: N. Adontz, 'Nicéphore au col roide', *B*, 8 (1933), 203–312.
[264] It has been claimed that it was David, the son of Senacherim, who killed Phokas. The head of the chief conspirator, Nikephoros Phokas, was brought to Basil's camp and displayed to the whole army to revive their faltering loyalty: *Aristakes de Lastivert*, ed. Canard and Berberian, 19–20.
[265] Phokas was assassinated on 15 August 1022: Yahya of Antioch, III, 464.
[266] He also succeeded him as strategos of the Anatolikon theme: Yahya of Antioch, III, 464.
[267] This is none other than John the Orphanotrophos, brother of the future emperor Michael IV. He remained a confidant of Basil II until the end of the reign.

eleventh of September, sixth year of the indiction, AM 6531, a second engagement took place; Liparites fell (he was George's commander-in-chief) together with all the leading men of Abasgia.[268] George fled to the interior mountains of Iberia but he shortly sent a peace delegation to the emperor, relinquishing whatever lands he pleased to him and offering his own son, Pankratios, as hostage. The emperor promoted him magister and then returned. As for the others who had participated in the uprising of Xiphias and Phokas, he confiscated their goods and imprisoned them. An exception was the patrician Pherses whom he put to death because he had been the very first to join the rebels.[269] He had killed the curators of four neighbouring governors and had beheaded one of the imperial eunuchs with his own hands. And an imperial chamberlain condemned of having tried to poison the emperor on Xiphias' behalf was fed to the lions.[270]

46. Anna, the emperor's sister, died in Russia, predeceased by Vladimir, her husband. Then a man named Chrysocheir, a relative of his, embarked a company of eight hundred men and came to Constantinople, ostensibly to serve as mercenaries.[271] [368] The emperor ordered him to lay down his arms and then he would receive him but [the Russian] was unwilling to do this and sailed on through the Propontis. When he came to Abydos he gave battle to the commander there whose duty was to protect the shores and easily defeated him. He passed on to Lemnos where, beguiled by offers of peace, they were all slaughtered by the navy of the Kibyrrhaiote [theme], the commander of Samos, David of Ochrid, and the *duke* of Thessalonike, Nikephoros Kabasilas.

---

[268] Liparites, a member of one of the most influential families in Georgia, actually died during Basil's first campaign: *Aristakes de Lastivert*, ed. Canard and Berberian, 13 and n. 2. Skylitzes' chronology of the Iberian wars is unsatisfactory. Basil led a first onslaught in 1021, gained a difficult victory and ravaged the land of the Abasges; he then wintered over at Trebizond. While he was there he invited Peter, the Armenian Katholicos, to visit him and received him most graciously. Then he set out for Georgia but suspended the campaign until the revolt of Phokas was dealt with. His final victory came in autumn 1022: Yahya of Antioch, III, 462–8, *Aristakes de Lastivert*, ed. Canard and Berberian, 11–23, and 'The Book of K'art'li', in *Rewriting Caucasian history: the medieval adaptation of the Georgian chronicles*, the original Georgian texts with the Armenian adaptation translation with introduction and commentary by Robert W. Thomson, Oxford 1996, 282–5.
[269] One of the Georgians in the entourage of David the Curopalates, see c. 20, above.
[270] The presence of lions in the palace is not inconceivable. Constantine IX Monomachos received the gift of a giraffe from the Fatimid Caliph, which suggests there was a menagerie there: Attaleiates, 37, and N. P. Sevcenko, 'Wild animals in the Byzantine park' in *Byzantine gardens culture*, ed. A. Littlewood, H. Maguire and J. Wolschke-Bulmahn, Washington, DC, 2002, 77.
[271] This episode reveals how the Varangian Guard was replenished.

47. It was the emperor's wish to campaign against Sicily and he sent ahead Orestes, one of the most trusted eunuchs, with a considerable force, but he was prevented from setting out because fate intervened. In the month of December, ninth year of the indiction, AM 6534, he suddenly fell ill and died;[272] and a few days before his death, the patriarch Eustathios also died. {It is said of Eustathios that while he was exercising his priesthood at one of the greater feasts, partly through old age (for he was old), partly through infirmity (for he was ill), since the entrance of the Holy Gifts was happening at a more leisurely pace than usual, he could not remain standing after completing the prayer. At his request the throne on which he habitually reposed himself was brought and he sat on it in wait of the arrival of the Holy [Gifts]. While he sat there, he fell asleep and saw a terrible vision (a real vision, not a dream). He saw wild beasts dressed as priests coming in; they had human bodies but their heads were in the form of beasts. Meanwhile the deacon alerted him of the presence of the Holy [Gifts] and was rewarded for his pains by a severe reproof for having deprived [the patriarch] of an awesome vision. He claimed to have seen eleven bishops in that terrifying form with others coming after them, but their entry had been cut short by the deacon coming to alert him. He said the beasts were donkeys, lions, panthers, domestic felines of the kind we call cats, wolves, bears and other similar beasts. So much for that.[273]}

The emperor appointed the monk Alexios, hegoumenos of Stoudios' monastery, to succeed [Eustathios] [369] as patriarch, he having visited the emperor with the venerable head of St John the Baptist. He sent him to be enthroned by the protonotarios John, whom he employed as aide in the administration of public business. In the evening he died, having lived seventy years;[274] he had reigned over all and ruled for fifty years. He asked his brother (whom he designated successor to the throne) to bury him in the church of [St John] the Evangelist and Theologian adjacent to the Hebdomon,[275] and so it was done.

---

[272] 15 December 1025: some sources give 12 December though, e.g. Yahya of Antioch, III, 480; P. Schreiner, *Die byzantinischen Kleinchroniken*, I, Enleitung und Text, ii, Historicher Kommentar (CFHB, 12, Vienna, 1975–7) c. 7, I, 158. Yahya of Antioch says expressly that Basil II had prepared a splendid sarcophagus at Holy Apostles' to be buried in, close to other emperors, then he changed his mind shortly before his death.

[273] MSS ACE.   [274] See the note at the beginning of this reign on this information.

[275] Basil broke with the tradition of the Macedonian dynasty in having his body buried somewhere other than in Holy Apostles'. The unfortunate fate which awaited his imperial remains is recorded by G. Pachymeres, *Relations historiques*, ed. A. Failler, tr. V. Laurent (Paris, 1984), 175–7. He gives the circumstances of the discovery of the remains in 1260 by persons close to Michael VIII in the ruined monastery of Hebdomon. They recognised the body by an inscription on the empty tomb. The emperor had it laid in the monastery of the Saviour at Selymbria.

CHAPTER 17

Constantine VIII [1025–1028]

1. [370] Although Constantine[1] now assumed total authority and the power to do whatever he wished, his delight was in perverse behaviour and he was the cause of many ills for the community. He neither accomplished nor planned to accomplish any of the things he ought to have done but rather entertained himself with horse races, actors and comedy shows, passing his nights playing silly games. He did not appoint those who had demonstrated their worth by deed or word to civil and military positions, but wine-sodden, servile eunuchs, bloated with every kind of disgusting abomination. These he promoted to the most conspicuous and high offices, cursorily passing over those distinguished by birth, virtue and experience. He promoted Nicholas, his first chamberlain, to be domestic of the scholai[2] and parakoimomenos; Nikephoros, the second one, to be protovestiarios, Symeon, the third, he made droungarios of the watch, and he gave them all the title of proedros. Eustratios, the most junior of the chamberlains, was made grand hetaireiarch. A eunuch named Spondyles[3] became duke of Antioch, Niketas of Pisidia duke of Iberia, both of them notoriously evil

---

[1] On this emperor (most recently): K.-P. Todt, 'Herrscher in Schatten: Konstantin VIII (960/1–1028)', *Thetis*, 7 (2000), 93–105. Little is known of the role played by Constantine VIII at his brother's side; doubtless it has been underestimated on account of the silence of the Greek sources, but at the conclusion of her study of Basil II, C. Holmes avers that Constantine never had any real influence on his brother: *Basil II and the governance of empire (976–1025)* (Oxford Studies in Byzantium, Oxford, 2005, 523–4. An Arab source informs us of his presence in the army which opposed the Fatimids in 995: Todt, 'Herrscher in Schatten', 97 and n. 43.

[2] This is not the first time a eunuch commanded the Roman armies. Nikephoros Phokas (whom nobody could accuse of softness in the way he governed the empire) set a certain Peter in charge of them, admittedly with the title only of stratopedarch, while others with beards were appointed domestic of the scholai. Skylitzes' account indicates that Constantine retained a number of the commanders appointed by his brother, e.g. Constantine Diogenes at Sirmium, Nikephoros Komnenos in Vaspourakan. Skylitzes' negative attitude to eunuchs reflects the spirit of his age (the time of Alexios I Komnenos).

[3] This is the only eunuch whose family name is given, which rather suggests he was a person of some significance. Persons with this name are known to have held civil appointments in the eleventh century.

men. They so disturbed and confused everything[4] that they very nearly overturned the state, [371] the very state which had been so well ruled since the reign of Romanos [II], the father of the two emperors, by Nikephoros [II], John [I] and Basil [II] as they succeeded each other on the throne and rendered [the empire] a terror to the neighbouring peoples. And it was not only that he was undiscriminating in his appointment of officers, promoting whoever came to hand; he also persisted in oppressing the worthier and more experienced [candidates] and schemed against the distinguished [citizens]. He blinded the patrician Constantine[5] too, the son of the magister Michael Bourtzes, for having harmed him before he became emperor by advising the emperor Basil of his unruly behaviour; and he eliminated not a few other good men as the narrative will explain in due course. Such was the prologue to his reign; as for what came after, who could ever present an adequate history of it? For, as we said, he was exclusively besotted with comedy shows and actors and (more than anybody else) gaping at horse races. These he held to constitute his only obligation, and everything else to be of no account; he even reckoned that the rest of his disorderly practices took second place to horse races.[6] Nikephoros Komnenos[7] was an intelligent man, famed for virtue and courage. As commander of Media, also known as Vaspurakan, he had brought the neighbouring peoples into subjection. For no reason whatsoever, out of envy for his virtue, the emperor trumped up a charge of treason against him and blinded him. Nikephoros had frequently engaged the Saracens adjacent to Media in action and noted that his own soldiers were somewhat languid, prone to turning their backs and making a disorderly retreat. He rebuked them for this but also besought them not to flee in shame but, rather, boldly to withstand the enemy – and he won them over. When [Nikephoros] asked them to confirm with oaths their undertaking that they would die with him fighting against the enemy, they gave him a written [372] letter corroborating with violent curses and appalling oaths that they would vigorously

---

[4] Skylitzes presents the same critical portrayal of Constantine VIII which Michael Psellos gives, but there is no justification for this so far as external affairs are concerned. Nothing is said of the two invasions (one by the Patzinaks, the other by the Arabs) which were repelled, nor of the successful campaign of Nicholas the parakoimomenos against the Abasges, known to us from eastern sources: Yahya of Antioch, III, 486; Aristakes de Lastivert, 27 – who incorrectly names the parakoimomenos Symeon. A certain number of his appointees, moreover, served under his successors.
[5] Nothing is known of the career of this man but he appears to have been a respected adviser to Basil II.
[6] Psellos tells the same tale: Psellos, *Chronographie*, ed. Renauld 29–30, trs. Sewter, 57.
[7] The second member of that family to distinguish himself after Manuel. Writing in the reign of Alexios Komnenos, Skylitzes may have blackened the name of Constantine VIII for having harmed one of the Komnenoi unjustly.

maintain the line of battle and die together with the commander. When this came to the ears of Constantine, he immediately relieved Nikephoros of his command and brought him to the capital. He set up a judgement seat and tribunal, condemned him of plotting against the emperor and deprived him of his sight. And when he became angry with the patrician Bardas (the grandson of the magister Bardas Phokas) and some others, by the agency of one of the informers he maintained, he trumped up a charge of attempted usurpation against him and immediately blinded him together with those defamed alongside him.[8] There was an uprising in Naupaktos[9] against George, the commander there, the one they called 'mad George' on account of the instability of his mind. They killed the commander and seized all his goods because he had mistreated the inhabitants there and afflicted them with frequent taxes of his own devising. The emperor not only mercilessly punished those responsible for the killing, but he even blinded the bishop of Naupaktos. The patrician Basil, the son of Romanos Skleros, came into conflict with the magister Prousianos the Bulgar, commander of the Boukellarion [theme], and became so incensed that they fell to fighting each other. Constantine judged this quarrel to be an outrage against the imperial dignity and exiled them both, one to the island of Oxeia, the other to Platea;[10] a little later he condemned Basil on the charge of planning to escape and blinded him. Prousianos came very close to suffering the same fate too but he was set free. He also blinded Romanos Kourkouas who was married to the sister of Prousianos;[11] also Bogdan,[12] Glabas and Goudelios; and he cut out the tongue of the monk Zacharias, a relative of the Vestes Theudatos, falsely accusing these men of plotting against him.[13]

2. [373] In this year the Patzinaks invaded Bulgaria, killing and taking prisoner many soldiers together with their commanders and officers. The emperor Constantine therefore appointed Diogenes, governor of Sirmium,

---

[8] Constantine completed a task of his brother in suppressing the last of the Phokai with any influence. Yahya of Antioch, III, 482, has a different story: the accomplices of Phokas and Xiphias had been released from prison (reign of Basil II, c. 45); then a conspiracy was formed around one of the sons of Phokas – and that was when the emperor struck.

[9] This town must have been the capital of the theme of Hellas at that time since the strategos was in residence there.

[10] Two of the Princes' Islands, adjacent to Constantinople.

[11] This is another example of a marriage between a descendant of one of the great families of the east (the one from which John Tzimiskes came) and a member of the Bulgar royal family.

[12] Bogdan was one of the last Bulgar chieftains to hold out against Basil II, who raised him to patrician status. Not all these Bulgar chieftains would be resigned to the loss of their independence.

[13] The names of some of those who opposed Basil (Glabas, c. 25; Bogdanos, a former Bulgar adversary now reconciled, c. 41) are included in the list.

to be duke of Bulgaria too. He frequently engaged the Patzinaks as they spread out and repelled them, forcing them to go back over the Danube and to remain at peace.

Throughout the years of Constantine's reign there was a severe drought; even unfailing springs and rivers dried up.

The emperor Basil used to spare the poor by not insisting that taxes be paid on time, granting a delay or postponement to those who asked. When he died, two years' taxes were owing; these payments Constantine demanded immediately and he also stipulated that taxes be paid on time for the three next years (for that is how long his reign lasted). By demanding five years' payments in three he ruined not only the poor and indigent but also those who were well off.[14]

A Hagarene fleet invaded the Cyclades islands. George Theodorokanos,[15] commander of Samos, together with Beriboes, commander of Chios, engaged and repulsed it, capturing twelve fully equipped and manned ships while scattering the others.[16]

3. On 9 November, twelfth year of the indiction, AM 6537,[17] Constantine suddenly fell ill and when the doctors despaired of his life he set his mind to designating someone to succeed him on the throne. He decided to summon Constantine Dalassenos[18] (who had retired to his own estates in the Armeniakon theme) to marry him to one of his daughters and proclaim him emperor. One of the most trusted eunuchs, [374] Ergodotes by name,[19] was sent to fetch him. But Symeon, a close friend of the patrician Romanos

---

[14] Yet again Yahya of Antioch, III, 482, gives a different report: he says that Constantine VIII forgave the taxes that were in arrears and offered a reduction of the tax which was levied on uncultivated land. Yahya may be nearer the truth for Psellos says that Basil II left 2,000 *kentenaria* in the treasury (*Chronographie*, 1.19, trans. Sewter, 1.31) – which would certainly permit his successor to be generous.

[15] This may be the son of the faithful general of Basil II who was relieved of his command in Bulgaria on account of his advanced age.

[16] Skylitzes' account omits some aspects of this emperor's foreign policy, such as his good relations with the west (especially with the emperor Conrad II) and the embassy despatched to Cairo asking for the restoration of the Holy Sepulchre (destroyed by al-Hakim in 1009), and also that those Christians who had been forcibly converted be allowed to resume their former religion: Todt, 'Herrscher in Schatten', 93–105, and 102–3.

[17] AD 1029.

[18] This is the son of the Damian, duke of Antioch, who was killed in 998. A prisoner of the Fatimids for ten years, Constantine was then appointed to his father's old command. This was before 1024, for in that year he led a campaign against Aleppo without the emperor's sanction. Replaced by Michael Spondyles, he retired to a quiet life on his estates in the Armeniakon theme – where he continued to be well thought of: Cheynet and Vannier, *Etudes*, 80–1, rpr. in Cheynet, *Société*, 417–419.

[19] The palace eunuchs are playing a new role in the succession procedure, a role which will become increasingly important.

Argyros,[20] intervened and this directive was set aside. A messenger was sent as though from the emperor telling Dalassenos to stay wherever he might be when the message reached him; meanwhile Romanos was brought into the palace. When he arrived, he was confronted with two alternatives: either to divorce his legitimate wife, marry the emperor's daughter and be proclaimed emperor, or to lose his eyes. He was speechless and undecided before this choice but his wife, fearing lest her man suffer pain, willingly accepted monastic tonsure, thus obtaining for her husband both his sight and the empire.[21] Constantine had three daughters by the daughter of the patrician Alypios,[22] whom he married while Basil was still living. Eudokia, the first in age, had received the monastic tonsure; the third, Theodora, refused to marry Romanos, either because he was a relative or because his wife was still living. But Zoe, the second in age, gladly accepted when the proposal of marriage was put to her. The question of consanguinity arose[23] but the church with the patriarch dispensed with the impediment; Romanos was married to Zoe and proclaimed ruler and emperor. Constantine died three days later, having lived in all seventy years and ruled one month short of three years.[24]

[20] Romanos was at that time eparch of Constantinople.
[21] The same story is told both by Psellos and by Yahya of Antioch, III, 486.
[22] Alypios is otherwise unknown. Should the name be Alopos, the name of a family well attested in the eleventh century which provided many high officers of state?
[23] Romanos and Zoe were only related in the eighth degree. Since Romanos' first wife had retired to a convent 'of her own free will', the marriage was legal: V. Grumel, *Les regestes du patriarcat de Constantinople*, I: *Les actes des patriarches;* II *and* III: *Les regestes de 715–1206*, 2nd edn revised and corrected by J. Darrouzès (Paris, 1989), no. 836; Laiou, 'Marriages', 165–76, at 168–9.
[24] He died on 12 November 1028, probably aged sixty-eight: Schreiner, *Kleinchroniken*, no. 15, c. 7, 158. This was the last emperor to be buried in Holy Apostles'.

CHAPTER 18

Romanos III Argyros [1028–1034]

1. [375] Thus, contrary to all hope and expectation, Romanos escaped the danger of losing his eyes, [surviving] to be girded with imperial authority and proclaimed ruling emperor together with Zoe, daughter of Constantine. No sooner was he seated on the throne than he honoured his subjects with preliminary bounties and inaugural gifts. His earliest benefactions were in the religious domain. He knew that the income of the Great Church was insufficient because he had previously served as the oikonomos[1] of this and of the other churches which were customarily served by the clergy of the Great Church. He now stipulated that an additional advance of eighty pounds of gold was to be made to it from the imperial treasury each year.[2] He suppressed and completely eliminated the allelengyon, which Constantine had intended to do but never did. He emptied the prisons of those who were detained there for debt, excusing unpaid taxes and paying private debts in full.[3] He ransomed the prisoners held in Patzinakia. He honoured three metropolitan [bishops][4] with the title of synkellos: Kyriakos of Ephesus, the patriarch's brother; Demetrios of Kyzikos, with whom he had been close friends before becoming emperor; and Michael of Euchaita, who was related by blood to Demetrios

---

[1] The position of oikonomos of the Great Church was now occupied by a high-ranking layman whose task was to manage the considerable revenues of the foundation. Romanos had been appointed to this position by Constantine VIII: Yahya of Antioch, III, 486.

[2] It may well have been this donation which was celebrated by a mosaic in the south gallery of Hagia Sophia showing the empress Zoe and her husband offering a purse to the church. The mosaic was reworked when Zoe married Constantine Monomachos to change the face and the name of the emperor. Thus it cannot be said with certainty that Romanos III was originally in the picture: it could have been Zoe's second husband, Michael IV. The figure of Christ was also modified to bring it more in line with the 'type' of the Christ Antiphonetes to whom Zoe entertained a particular devotion: A. Cutler and J.-M. Spieser, *Byzance médiévale 700–1204* (Paris, 1996), 326–7.

[3] There was a precedent for this in the reign of Romanos I Lekapenos.

[4] These appointments indicate the progressive devaluation of this ecclesiastical title: there was only ever one synkellos at a time until the reign of John Tzimiskes.

as they were both born into the family of the Rhadenoi.[5] He sent for John who had served as protonotarios under the emperor Basil,[6] already tonsured as a monk, honoured him with the title of synkellos and appointed him guardian of his own wife's sister, Theodora. He restored many of those servants of God who had come to the ultimate degree of penury because of the allelengyon [376] and granted relief to others whom distress and oppression had brought into tight straits. He provided a very large amount of money for the salvation of the soul of his father-in-law and he did likewise for those who had suffered under that man, appointing some of them to offices, comforting some with properties, others with money. He raised to the distinction of magister his brother-in-law on his sister's side, Romanos Skleros,[7] whom, as we said, [Constantine] had blinded and he recalled from his long, long exile Nikephoros Xiphias who, of his own free will, received the monastic habit at Stoudios' monastery.

2. In those days God caused an adequate amount of rain to fall and the crops were abundant, especially the olives. On the day of Pentecost there was a fracas concerning the order of seating at the liturgy [in the Great Church], for the metropolitan [bishops] would not suffer the synkelloi to take precedence over them in the clergy seats.[8]

3. At that time the magister Prousianos the Bulgar was accused of conspiring with Theodora, the empress' sister, to seize the throne. He was incarcerated at the monastery of Manuel[9] and when the charge stood up under investigation they blinded him and expelled his mother, a belted patrician, from the city. Constantine Diogenes, who was related to the emperor by his marriage to the daughter of his brother Basil [Argyros][10] and who had been transferred from Sirmium to become duke of Thessalonike, was now

---

[5] Skylitzes has already mentioned John Rhadenos, the admiral of the fleet who defeated the Arabs in the time of Romanos I Lekapenos. From the beginning of the eleventh century the Rhadenoi, in common with members of many other military families, increasingly occupied important positions in both the civil and the ecclesiastical orders; e.g. two Rhadenoi served as eparchs of Constantinople in the course of that century.

[6] This is the brother of the future emperor Michael IV, already raised up by Basil II.

[7] Skylitzes has confused Romanos with Basil who was indeed the husband of Pulcheria, the sister of Romanos, and was certainly blinded and sent into exile by Constantine VIII.

[8] *synthronon* designates the semicircle of rising benches set in the apse of a church, which was where the clergy sat – in order of precedence. This quarrel was a consequence of naming three bishops synkellos. The single synkellos certainly took precedence over the metropolitan bishops. The new appointees, however, unwilling to concede precedence to their colleagues, required that they all remain in their former stations so far as the order of seating (i.e. of precedence) was concerned.

[9] The future patriarch Sergios had been hegoumenos of this monastery.

[10] The name of this woman is not known. This marriage brought together two military families which had faithfully served Basil II. Diogenes now became a nephew-by-marriage to Romanos III.

accused of preparing a revolt by Orestes, the servant of the emperor Basil. He was sent out as commander of the Thrakesion theme but when the truth of the charge became evident he was brought into the capital as a prisoner and thrown into a tower. His fellow conspirators were severely flogged, paraded down the principal artery and sent into exile: the protonotarios and synkellos John, the patrician and commander Eustathios Daphnomeles, [377] the two grandsons of the magister Michael Bourtzes,[11] Michael Theognostos and Samuel and George Barasbatzes, founder of the monastery of Iberon on Mount Athos,[12] the nephews of the patrician Theudatos.[13] Theodora also was taken out of the palace and confined at the place called Petrion.[14]

In October, the thirty-first of that month, the fall of a star occurred, following a path from west to east, and on that day the Roman army suffered a severe defeat in Syria, Michael Spondyles being commander of Antioch the Great.[15] And rain fell in torrents continuously until the month of March. The rivers overflowed and hollows turned into lakes, with the result that nearly all the livestock was drowned and the crops were levelled. This was the cause of a severe famine in the following year.

In his desire to remedy the recent disaster in Syria, the emperor set out on campaign against Berroia.[16] He despatched the patrician Constantine Karantenos,[17] his sister's husband, with a light force, to keep a watch on the approaches and do all he could to damage the enemy, but he was to avoid any general engagement until the emperor arrived. While he was assembling his army, George, the ruler of Abasgia,[18] fell ill and died. His widow sent a delegation to the emperor bearing gifts, requesting a peace treaty and also a wife for Pankratios [Bagrat], her son.[19] The emperor received

---

[11] More of Basil's faithful soldiers.
[12] The Iberians are the companions of David the kouropalates. George Barasbadzes, actually the third hegoumenos of Iberon, was related to his two predecessors.
[13] The nephews of Theudatos *might* be the sons of Pherses, executed on the orders of Basil II in 1022, but this is no more than a possibility: *Actes d'Iviron*, II: *Du milieu du XIe siècle à 1204*, ed. J. Lefort, N. Oikonomidès, D. Papachryssanthou (Archives de l'Athos, 16, Paris, 1990), 17–19.
[14] The empress Theophano was buried at this monastery in Constantinople.
[15] 31 October 1029. The Arab sources assert that Spondyles was defeated by the Mirdassides on 15 July 1029: W. Felix, *Byzanz und die islamische Welt im früheren 11. Jahrhundert* (Byzantina Vindobonensia, 15, Vienna, 1981), 82.
[16] = Aleppo. On Aleppo in the eleventh century: S. Zakkar, *The emirate of Aleppo, 1004–1094* (Beirut, 1971).
[17] The Karantenoi supported Basil II against Skleros.
[18] George I of Iberia died 16 August 1027: C. Toumanoff, *Les dynasties de la Caucasie chrétienne de l'Antiquité jusqu'au XIXe siècle: tables généalogiques et chronologiques* (Rome, 1990), 135.
[19] Ruling under the supervision of his mother, Mary, daughter of Senacherim of Vaspourakan, the young Bagrat [Pankratios] attempted to regain those fortresses which his father had surrendered

her delegation;[20] he ratified the peace treaty and sent off his niece, Helen, daughter of his brother Basil,[21] to Abasgia as a bride. He raised Pankratios the bridegroom to the dignity of kouropalates.[22]

4. About that time an amazing wonder occurred in the Thrakesion theme, on the heights of Mount Kouzenas[23] where [378] a spring of excellent, pellucid water is located. A voice was heard, moaning and weeping in lamentation, similar to the voice of a grieving woman. And this was not just once or twice but every day and night, from March well into June. When some people came to the place where the voice was heard to investigate, the moaning happened somewhere else. It seemed as though this [voice] presaged the Roman disaster in Cœlo-Syria which is about to be reported.

The emperor Nikephoros [II] brought most of the cities of Syria and Phœnicia into subjection; John [I] his successor tightened his hold on what was already taken and extended his domains to Damascus. But Basil [II] who followed them was distracted by civil wars at first, then by his efforts against Samuel [of Bulgaria]; hence he did not have the opportunity of securing the eastern part of the empire properly and in a fitting manner. All he could do was make an appearance in the east and deal with the most pressing situations before returning to his constant concern and worry: the subjection of the Bulgar race. This provided an opportunity for the more powerful [eastern] cities to throw off the [Roman] yoke and seek their freedom. As long as Basil was alive they meditated insurrection, but in secret and not openly. But once he had paid the common debt and his brother Constantine was ruling in an indolent and uncaring manner, his only concern being for those things which I itemised in this narrative, treating all else with contempt and as of no account, then the Saracens seized their chance, diminishing the garrisons in the cities and killing the guards. This was especially true of the prince of Berroia which they also call Aleppo. He made frequent excursions to the detriment of Antioch as

---

to Basil II, but the parakoimomenos laid waste Georgia in 1028 and forced Bagrat to sue for peace: Yahya of Antioch, III, 484.

[20] Maria, Melchisedech (the katholikos of Iberia) and other notables came to Constantinople: Yahya of Antioch, III, 488.

[21] Basil Argyros was known in the east because he had served as *katepan* of Vaspurakan: Basil II, c. 39, above. The marriage took place in 1032.

[22] To a certain extent Bagrat of Georgia assumed the role David of Iberia had played under Basil II. Since the ninth century Byzantium had been in the habit of conferring this high distinction on the Iberian princes: B. Martin-Hisard, 'Constantinople et les archontes du monde caucasien dans le *Livre des cérémonies* II', 48, *TM*, 13 (2000), 359–530, at 437–50.

[23] St Lazaros founded a monastery at Kouzenas near to Galesion, hence between Ephesos and Magnesia: R. Janin, *Les églises et les monastères des grands centres byzantins* (Paris, 1975), II, 241.

well as the adjacent and neighbouring peoples who were Roman subjects. Spondyles, the officer commanding at Antioch as we said, marched out against him while Constantine was still in the area, hoping no doubt to perform some audacious act of bravery. [379] He joined battle with the prince of Berroia and was soundly defeated with heavy loss of troops, but he saved his own life by shamefully taking refuge in Antioch.[24] And an Arab named Mousaraph[25] got the better of him by the following subterfuge. This Mousaraph was held as a prisoner of war at Antioch having been captured by Pothos Argyros. When the reins of leadership fell to Spondyles, knowing him to be impressionable, the Arab promised to be very useful to the Romans if he were released from captivity and given every support in his undertakings. He announced that he would do his fellow countrymen great harm and that, if a fortress were erected at a place which he indicated and himself put in charge of it, he would be of no small advantage to the Romans. Spondyles failed to perceive the stratagem; he had his irons struck off, constructed the fortress as requested[26] and put him in charge of it with a thousand Roman guardsmen stationed there. When the awaited opportunity arrived, Mousaraph entered into secret negotiations with the emir of Tripoli and with Tousber,[27] the commander-in-chief of the Egyptians. He then received the army which they sent, wiped out the thousand guardsmen and handed over the fortress.[28] From then on the Saracens made no end of sallying forth from their advantageous position to ravage and destroy lands subject to the Romans in Syria.

5. Romanos relieved Spondyles of his command and sent Constantine Karantenos, his sister's husband, to replace him while the emperor himself prepared to set out after him against the Saracens. He had already reached Philomilion[29] when a delegation arrived from Berroia bearing a

[24] 12 May 1029. Halih ibn Mirdas, prince of Aleppo, having been killed fighting against an army despatched by the Fatimids, Michael Spondyles concluded that the time was ripe for an attack on Aleppo; but he was surprised and beaten by the sons of Halih – who nevertheless demanded peace of Romanos: Yahya of Antioch, III, 492.

[25] Nalr ben Musaraf was a local magnate who controlled several villages in the mountains of Rawadifi to the south of Antioch and on the frontier with the emirate of Tripoli, between Laodikeia and Emesa.

[26] Musaraf obtained written permission from the *katepan* Spondyles to construct the fortress of Maniqa: Yahya of Antioch, III, 502. A seal with the figure of St George on the face and an Arabic inscription on the reverse attests that he also received the title of patrician from the emperor: J.-C. Cheynet, C. Morrisson and W. Seibt, *Les sceaux byzantins dans la collection Henri Seyrig* (Paris, 1991), no. 395.

[27] Duzbari, a former slave of Turkish origin, had been appointed governor of Syria and given the task of taking Aleppo.

[28] In fact Musaraf also took one other Roman fortress, Bikisa'il: Yahya of Antioch, III, 504.

[29] A staging post on the military road to Antioch.

large quantity of gifts and asking for clemency; they would assume their former state of servitude and gratefully pay the annual tribute which was due. Many of the excellent commanders who were with him on campaign (one of them was the patrician John Chaldos)[30] urged him to accept these proposals and not to wage war in Syria [380] in summer time as water was in short supply there; hence it would not be possible to oppose the Arabs as they were accustomed from birth to the local temperatures and the scorching heat whereas the Romans, in full armour, could not tolerate that season. The emperor was not in the least deflected by any of this, for he had the recent example of his immediate predecessors before his eyes and longed to distinguish himself by some courageous deed.[31] Off he went to Syria, established his camp at a fortress two days' march from Berroia (its name was Azazion)[32] and waited to see what would happen. While he was encamped there he sent out the officer commanding the Excoubitores, the patrician Leo Choirosphaktes and his corps of soldiers,[33] on reconnaissance, to see whether any Arabs were likely to attack and to where it might be advantageous to move the camp. But the Arabs who were lying in wait, guarding the intervening plain, seized their chance. They suddenly attacked and captured Leo, scattering the troops with him. They became so bold and intrepid that they openly prevented the Romans from gathering forage and other necessities of life. They did even worse harm to the Romans by depriving them of water for they, their horses and pack animals were so oppressed by thirst that they openly exposed themselves to danger, and were captured and slaughtered. Then the patrician Constantine Dalassenos[34] was sent out to beat back the attacking forces and to accomplish something bold and daring. He joined battle with them but then fled in disorder, breathing confusion and dismay into the Romans and into the emperor himself. When he returned in person in great disarray he threw the entire camp into chaos and consternation; there was no longer any question of fighting as each man looked to his own safety as best he could. A council was held at which it was decided that [381] they should break camp at dawn and return to Antioch; on the second of August, thirteenth year

---

[30] This is the former duke of Thessalonike who had been the prisoner of Samuel for twenty-two years: Basil II, c. 41, above.
[31] There was nothing seriously threatening the Syrian border. It is Psellos' opinion that Romanos was motivated by a desire to emulate former emperors.
[32] This fortress – still known as Aazaz – lies to the north of Aleppo.
[33] The Exkoubitores.
[34] The former duke of Antioch was particularly well qualified to fight the Bedouins; his reverse caused him to fall under suspicion of conspiracy.

of the indiction, AM 6538,[35] the gates were opened on all sides according to plan and they took the road to Antioch. Many of them were sick with dysentery; many were worn out by the pangs of thirst. As they came out of the camp, the Arabs attacked in force. Since the Romans were not in the least capable of withstanding the impetus, a most terrible rout took place; some were trodden under foot by their comrades and killed, others were captured alive.[36] Yet something amusing happened. Neither among the commanders (who had a reputation for bravery) nor among the soldiers was there anybody bold enough to withstand the danger; they all ran away ingloriously. There was, however, a eunuch there, one of the attendants of the imperial bedchamber who, seeing his baggage and his servants being carried off, could not contain himself. Turning his horse this way and that he charged the Saracens at full tilt. Bending his bow, he shot one of them and put the others to flight; he seized what was his and gleefully rode back. {It was not from military experience but from love of money that this wretched gelding risked his own life, the love of money pushing away the thought that his life was in danger.}[37] The emperor came very near to being captured and then found refuge in Antioch. The imperial Hetaireiai fought valiantly, thus saving both themselves and the emperor.

6. George Maniakes[38] was at that time commander of the Telouch theme.[39] Eight hundred Arabs returning from the rout came to him all puffed up with pride and ordered him to surrender as soon as possible and abandon the city as the emperor was taken and the entire Roman army completely destroyed; he need not deliver himself into such obvious danger. As soon as day broke, he and those with him would be encircled and mercilessly destroyed. [382] George made pretence of accepting their warning and doing as he was told. He sent a plentiful supply of food and drink out to them, telling them to rest awhile for at daybreak he and those with him would surrender themselves and make the Arabs masters of Telouch together with all the money of the Romans. Deceived by his

---

[35] 10 August 1030: Yahya of Antioch, III, 498.
[36] Yahya of Antioch, III, 498, is more precise: the victims were few in number. Only one officer was killed, two taken prisoner. The evidence for this is that Ximal the Mirdassid, the master of Aleppo, sent an embassy to Romanos III asking for reinstatement in his status as an ally of the Roman people, which he had enjoyed in the time of Basil II and Constantine VIII.
[37] MS U only.
[38] This is the first mention of one of the greatest military heroes of this *Synopsis*. The origins of his family are unknown.
[39] Telouch is a town between Aleppo and Marash. It was taken from the Hamdanids in 962 by Nikephoros Phokas but only later became the administrative centre of a theme.

words and deeds and expecting to receive everything on the morrow, they gave themselves up to drinking and drunkenness, passing the night without the least concern or provision for their safety. But in the middle of the night, when they had drunk well and were sleeping without a care in the world, George attacked them and slew them all. He captured two hundred and eighty camels fully laden with all kinds of Roman goods. He cut off the noses and ears of the fallen and sent them to the emperor in Cappadocia (for after his flight he had arrived at the estate of Phokas and was residing there). In approval of what he had done the emperor designated him *katepan* of Lower Media.[40]

7. On leaving Syria [the emperor] designated Symeon who had served Constantine, his father-in-law, domestic of the scholai and Niketas of Mistheia governor of Antioch. He charged them to do everything in their power to put the defences of the fortress named Menikos built by Mousaraph to the test, in order to see if they could relieve Syria of his incursions. They, however, conducted the assault in such an unprofessional and inexperienced way that Mousaraph sallied forth from the fortress by night, burnt their siege-engines and chased them away in disgrace.[41] The emperor could not bear the outrage when he heard of it; he despatched to Syria one of his most trusted servants, the protospatharios Theoktistos, the grand hetaireiarch of that day, with a considerable army of Romans and of non-Romans, appointing him sovereign commander. His orders were to make contact with Pinzarach,[42] [383] emir of Tripoli, and to join him in damaging and destroying Arab possessions. It appears that this Pinzarach had recently renounced his allegiance to the *amermoumnes* of Egypt because of some offence and had taken up arms against him. The Egyptian had sent Tousper the Turk, his chief of the armed forces, with a sufficient army to suppress Pinzarach. When Pinzarach perceived that he was unequal to the task of confronting the might of the Egyptians alone, he had recourse to the emperor of the Romans whom he sought as an ally. Romanos did not refuse his request; he sent Theoktistos with a considerable host, ordering him to provide Pinzarach with allies and also to attack the fortress of Menikos on his way. [Theoktistos] set out, made contact with Pinzarach and set about the task. The Egyptian commander-in-chief, Tousber, was so

---

[40] Media seems to have formed two themes for a time. It is known that upper Media was connected with lake Van and that the term indicated the whole or part of the *katepanate* of Vaspurakan. It could be that lower Media was interchangeable with the theme of the towns beyond the Euphrates (such as Samosata) for Maniakes occupied this post some years later.
[41] Niketas and Symeon actually captured Aazaz in December 1030, which obliged the Mirdassid to enter into peace negotiations: Yahya of Antioch, III, 506.
[42] Al-Hassan ben al-Mufarrig al Garrah, emir of Tripoli, 1013/14–1041/2.

nonplussed by the suddenness of the offensive and the size of the host that he went back home; and neither could Mousaraph face the onslaught of the foe. He abandoned Menikos and fled, but he was taken and killed in the area around Tripoli.[43] Theoktistos' men occupied the fortress of Menikos (it was delivered to them by a nephew of Mousaraph)[44] and another fortress, this one called Argyrokastron,[45] located on a precipitous rock. When he had thus disposed of matters, Theoktistos returned to the capital bringing Alach, the son of Pinzarach, with him, whom the sovereign honoured with the title of patrician. Afterwards Pinzarach came, preceded and escorted by Niketas of Mistheia who was then serving as governor of Antioch. The emperor received him most graciously, rewarded him with a quantity of gifts and favours and sent him home rejoicing. He also ransomed Choirosphaktes out of captivity and delivered him to his kinsmen.[46]

8. As the narrative has already reported, the protospatharios Orestes was sent to Sicily by the emperor Basil [II]. He was inexperienced in war and had no administrative ability. [384] Seizing their opportunity, the Saracens of Sicily launched a surprise attack on the Romans (who were already feeble with dysentery from extravagant living) and slaughtered many of them.[47] To efface this disgrace the emperor assembled a battleworthy force from Hellas and Macedonia, then sent it to Italy, but it was unable to accomplish anything of distinction because the commander was a good-for-nothing simpleton. In that year, AM 6539,[48] fourteenth year of the indiction, Prousianos was tonsured a monk of his own free will and his mother was transferred from the Mantineion monastery in the Boukellarion theme to the Thrakesion theme. Also the patrician Constantine Diogenes was released from the tower and tonsured a monk in Stoudios' monastery. The emperor Romanos purchased the estate of Triakontaphyllos and transformed it into a monastery dedicated in the name of Our Sovereign Lady the Mother of God.[49] No expense was spared

---

[43] Yahya of Antioch, III, 521–7, gives a detailed account of the campaign waged by the *katepan* Niketas against Musaraf, completed in 1032 with the taking of hundreds of prisoners.
[44] 1 December 1031. Niketas took 810 prisoners, including several members of the family of Musaraf: Yahya of Antioch, III, 512.
[45] Meaning 'silver castle', now 'Ullaiqa, to the south of Maniqa and the west of Balanea.
[46] The situation had been completely restored in northern Syria with no regrettable consequences for the emperor's expedition, so far as one can tell.
[47] This information is confirmed by the *Chronica Siculo-Saracena*. Although he had the cooperation of the *katepan* of Italy, Christopher Bulgaris, the successor of Boioannes, Orestes was defeated at Reggio late in 1028 or early in 1029: Felix, *Byzanz und Islam*, 201.
[48] 1 September 1030 to 31 August 1031.
[49] Romanos founded the Peribleptos on land by the sea of Marmora purchased from a great Constantinopolitan family, not far from Stoudios' monastery. The substructure is there to this

but the subjects were sorely oppressed as they were obliged to convey the stones and other building materials. He adorned the capitals of the Great Church and of the church of the all-holy Mother of God at Blachernae with silver and gold. In the course of restoring the sanctuary at Blachernae he found an ancient icon hanging there and ordered it to be restored. When he noted that the silver on the plaster of the wall had peeled off he ordered it to be stripped off and replaced. When the old plaster was removed an icon was found painted on wood, a panel of the Mother of God holding our Lord and God against her bosom. It had remained intact since the days of the [emperor Constantine V] Kopronymos until that day, three hundred years.[50]

9. AM 6540,[51] fifteenth year of the indiction, in the month of September, Amr, the son of the emir of Aleppo, came to the emperor Romanos [385] bearing many gifts, asking that the peace treaty be renewed and that the tribute be paid as before. The protospatharios Theophylact of Athens was sent; he ratified the treaty and entered into various agreements with the people of Aleppo. After the Exultation of the Holy Cross [September 14] the empress Zoe suddenly came to Petrion and tonsured her sister, Theodora, for (she said) there was no other way to put an end to her plots and her scandalous behaviour. The emperor Romanos gave his own niece in marriage to the supreme ruler of Greater Armenia with a large dowry.[52] Making as though he would attack Syria for a second time, the emperor marched out to Mesanakta. While he was there it was made known to the empress Zoe through Theophanes [bishop] of Thessalonike that Constantine Diogenes was plotting with her sister Theodora with the intention of fleeing to Illyricum, and this with the full knowledge of the metropolitan of Dyrrachion and the bishop of Peritheorion.[53] The

---

day, known as Sulu Manastir: R. Janin, *La géographie ecclésiastique de l'empire byzantin*, I: *Le siège de Constantinople et le patriarcat Ocuménique*, III: *Les églises et les monastères* (Paris, 1969), 218–22; C. Mango, 'The monastery of St Mary Peribleptos (Sulu Manastir) at Constantinople revisited', *REArm*, n.s. 23 (1992), 473–93. The foundation included a hospital and a guest house: Yahya of Antioch, III, 536.

[50] The form of the Virgin known as Blachernitissa immediately became very popular, as its appearance on many contemporary seals testifies: W. Seibt, 'Die Darstellung der Theotokos auf byzantinischen Bleisiegel, besonders im 11. Jahrhundert', *SBS*, 1 (1987), 35–56, esp. 43–4; B. Pentcheva, 'Rhetorical images of the Virgin: the icon of the "usual miracle" at the Blachernai', *RES: Journal for Anthropology and Aesthetics*, 38 (2000), 34–5.

[51] September 1031.

[52] John-Smbat ruled Armenia 1020–41. Romanos III had become his uncle by marriage between the families of the two principal Christian sovereigns of the Causasus region.

[53] A bishopric in Thrace subordinate to Traianoupolis in the Rhodope mountains: P. Soustal, *Thrakien (Thrake, Rodope und Haiminontos)* (TIB, 6, Vienna, 1991), 394–5. It is obvious that Constantine Diogenes had support among the western regiments which he had commanded; also

bishops and Diogenes were immediately seized; while Constantine was being examined in the palace of Blachernae by John the praepositos (who afterwards became orphanotrophos, the brother of Michael who became emperor) he hanged himself from the walls, broke his neck, died and was buried among those who had killed themselves. The bishops were sent to the emperor at Mesanakata and there set free.

10. On Friday, 28 July,[54] at the second hour of the night, a star fell from south to north, lighting up the whole earth, and shortly afterwards there were reports of disasters afflicting the Roman empire: of Arabs ravaging Mesopotamia right up to Melitene,[55] of Patzinaks crossing the Danube and doing damage to Mysia, of Saracens coasting off Illyricum as far as Corfu and setting it on fire.[56] For the most part [386] these enemies returned home unharmed, but the Saracens fared badly at the hands of the citizens of Ragusa and of the patrician Nikephoros Karantenos, commander of Nauplion,[57] who opposed them in force and captured many of their boats. The survivors put the Roman prisoners they were holding to death but were then shipwrecked on the high seas off Sicily as they were returning home and killed.

11. This year[58] famine and pestilence afflicted Cappadocia, Paphlagonia, the Armeniakon theme and the Honoriad, so grave that the very inhabitants of the themes abandoned their ancestral homes in search of somewhere to live. The emperor met them on his return to the capital from Mesanakata and, unaware of the reason for this migration, obliged them to return home, providing them with money and the other necessities of life. And Michael, who was then governing the church of Ankyra, performed virtuous works, sparing nothing which might procure the survival of the victims of famine and pestilence.

12. On Sunday, 13 August, at the first hour of the night, AM 6540,[59] there was a severe earthquake. The emperor came into the capital and Helena, his former wife, having died, he distributed much alms on her behalf. In that year on 20 February a star traversed from north to south with noise

---

that rumours of sedition were rife in the camps of Dyrrachion, Thessalonike and Mosynoupolis, not far from Peritheorion.

[54] AD 1032.
[55] The Arabs were probably reacting to the loss of Edessa, reported by Skylitzes a little later.
[56] Pirates from Sicily and the Magreb, owing allegiance to the Zirid emirs.
[57] This mention of a strategos of Nauplion (a *hapax*) is surprising. Perhaps it should be of Naupaktos – which was nearer to the Adriatic sea (where the Arabs were attacking) and to the allied city of Ragusa.
[58] Still 1032, because Romanos III meets the refugees on the road from Mesanakata to Constantinople.
[59] 13 August 1032.

and commotion. It was visible until 15 March,[60] and there was a bow above it. On 6 March, third hour, there was an earthquake.

13. At that time there was an invasion of Africa by the Saracens with a thousand boats carrying ten thousand fighting men on board; they did much damage to the islands and coasts. [387] Nikephoros Karantenos joined battle with a portion of them and put them to flight, sending five hundred Saracens to the emperor in chains. And in that year the protospatharios George Maniakes, the son of Goudelios Maniakes, the commander of the cities on the Euphrates who resided at Samosata, attempted to take the city of Edessa in Osroene. This city was controlled by Salaman[61] the Turk, having been entrusted to him by the emir of Miepherkeim/Martyropolis but, bribed with gifts, promises and honours, he surrendered it to Maniakes in the middle of the night. Maniakes secured three heavily fortified towers and vigorously repulsed the would-be besiegers, summoning aid from without. When Apomerbanes, the emir of Miepherkeim,[62] heard of their fall, he promptly appeared with a considerable army and laid siege to the towers, but George stoutly withstood him. The emir was thrown back and was at a loss what to do. He razed the finest buildings and pillaged what was of beauty in that city, even in the Great Church itself. He loaded the finest objects onto camels and, putting the rest of the city to the flames, returned to Martyropolis.[63] Now that Maniakes was free to do so, he captured the fortress situated in the centre of the city atop a lofty rock, summoned forces from outside and secured his hold on the city.[64] And finding the autograph letter of the Lord and Master Jesus Christ which was sent to Abgar, he despatched it to the emperor at Byzantium.

14. Azizios[65] [Hakem] the Egyptian was mad and the cause of many woes for the Christians. He tore down the church of our Lord and Saviour

---

[60] AD 1033.
[61] After he had surrendered the citadel of Edessa (October 1031) Sulayman ibn al Kurgi later came to Constantinople carrying a letter (thus Skylitzes) or two letters: the letter of Abgar and the reply of Christ to it. These relics were received by the emperor, the patriarch and the high officers of state; they were conserved in the imperial palace: Yahya of Antioch, III, 514–16, giving the text of the two letters.
[62] Naīr ad-Doula ibn Marwan was Emir until 1061.
[63] For a detailed account of the taking of Edessa and confirmation that it was put to the flames: Matthew of Edessa, 51–5.
[64] Yahya of Antioch, III, 518, describes the operations; commentary in T. Ripper, *Die Marwâniden von Diyâr Bakr: eine kurdische Dynastie im islamischen Mittelalter* (Würzburg, 2000), 299–303, based on several eastern sources.
[65] The form of the name which most of the MSS give and which the editor of the Greek text retains (Azios) is incorrect. MSS B and U give the correct form: Azizios.

Jesus Christ at Jerusalem but, after he had died the most horrible of deaths, his son (born to him by a captive Roman woman) [388] permitted those who wished to do so to rebuild the church.[66] The emperor generously hastened to send [resources] for the reconstruction, but he was interrupted by death and it was Michael,[67] his successor, who completed the task.

15. The magister Basil Skleros, the husband of the emperor's sister, the man who was blinded by Constantine, was of an unstable and fickle mind. Even though he had been promoted magister by Romanos, from whom he also received many benefits, he began plotting against him. But this was brought to light and he was expelled from the city together with his wife.

16. Maniakes sent an annual tribute of fifty pounds [of gold] to the emperor from Edessa. Pinzarach, the emir of Tripoli, overcome by the Egyptians, fled and came to the capital;[68] the emperor sent him back to Syria with a numerous army accompanied by the hetaireiarch Theoktistos. He also sent a fleet to Egypt with the protospatharios Tekneas of Abydos[69] [in command]; his orders were to do as much damage as possible to the mouth of the Nile and even to Alexandria itself. He sailed there directly and pressed on to Alexandria. He captured a large quantity of shipping, seized a great deal of booty and returned unharmed. Alim the Saracen handed over the fortress he was holding called Perkrin[70] (it lies very near to Babylon) to the emperor of the Romans in the hope of receiving the title of patrician and many other rewards;[71] he had made contact with the emperor through his son. The fortress was received by the patrician Nicholas[72] the Bulgar who went by the name of Chryselios; the Saracen's son came into Byzantium but on

---

[66] In the course of the negotiations between Romanos III and the Fatimid caliph al-Hahir the emperor insisted on three conditions before a truce could be signed: permission for himself to rebuild the church of the Holy Sepulchre at his own expense and undertakings by the caliph that he would neither take any action against Aleppo nor render any support to the Arabs in Sicily. These conditions were unacceptable; it was only in the reign of Michael IV that the truce was concluded: Yahya of Antioch, III, 532.

[67] In fact it was Constantine Monomachos.

[68] Kekaumenos (who calls him Apelzarach and says he was chief – *phylarchos* – of the Arabs) reports that the emir's last visit to Constantinople was not uneventful. He returned to the capital expecting to receive yet more honours but was in fact imprisoned and only succeeded in escaping on the death of the emperor: Kekaumenos, 302.

[69] This is not a Greek name; it may be of Turkic or Caucasian origin. We are not obliged to assume that Tekneas was commander of Abydos. This expedition can be dated to spring 1033; the object of the exercise appears to have been to hasten the conclusion of the truce.

[70] Berki, Mouradie today, to the east of lake Van, quite some distance from Babylon (Baghdad).

[71] This emir was in conflict with his uncle, the emir of Azerbaidjan.

[72] The family which had handed over Dyrrachion to Basil II.

account of the emperor's illness he received no attention whatsoever. He returned in anger and persuaded his parent to take back his own fortress. [Alim] made a secret accord with the local Persians then took the fortress in a surprise night attack, killing six thousand Roman fighting men who were in it, due to the carelessness and negligence of Chryselios. But before long the patrician Niketas Pegonites[73] was sent out to govern there; [389] he maintained a protracted siege with Russians and other Roman forces and eventually took the fortress by storm, killing Alim and his son. It was then that Alde, the wife of George of Abasgia, an Alan by race,[74] came over to the emperor and surrendered to him the extremely well fortified stronghold of Anakouphia;[75] the emperor honoured Demetrios, her son, with the dignity of magister. Karantenos gained another victory against some Saracens out looking for booty; he sent six hundred of them in chains to the emperor.[76]

17. AM 6547,[77] on the seventeenth of February, there was an earthquake and the cities of Syria suffered severely. Orestes was relieved of his command and Leo Opos[78] was sent to take charge of the infantry in Italy while John, one of the bedchamber attendants of the emperor Basil, was put in command of the fleet. For some time the eastern themes had been consumed by locusts, compelling the inhabitants to sell their children and move into Thrace. The emperor gave to every one of them three pieces of gold and arranged for them to return home. The locusts were finally carried away by a powerful wind, fell into the high sea off the Hellespont and perished. They were washed up onto the shore where they covered the sand of the beach. The emperor renovated the ducts which bring water into the city and also the cisterns which receive that water. He restored the leper house[79] and every other hospice which

---

[73] An experienced officer who had successfully conducted the defence of Dyrrachion against the last Bulgar offensive.

[74] This princess was the daughter of the king of Alania and the second wife of George I: Toumanoff, *Dynasties*, 134.

[75] Anakouphia (Anakopia in the Georgian texts, also known as Trachis) lies on the Black Sea to the north of Sebastoupolis. This fortress was of strategic importance as it controlled access to Alania, whence there came valued mercenaries to the empire in the eleventh century.

[76] This victory of Karantenos could be a doublet of his former success, for Skylitzes' chapter on Romanos III is not very well organised.

[77] Better to follow those MSS which give AM 6542; the earthquake happened on 17 February 1034.

[78] According to the Italian sources, this man's Christian name was Constantine and he came to Bari on 1 May 1033: V. von Falkenhausen, *La dominazione bizantina nell' Italia meridionale dal IX all' XI secolo* (Bari, 1978), 92–3.

[79] MSS MNUDH give 'orphanage'.

had been damaged by the earthquake. In a word, every good work was his concern. But he was afflicted by a chronic disease; his beard and his hair fell out. It was said he had been poisoned by John, who later became orphanotrophos. This John [390] had served Romanos before he became emperor and, when he acceded to the throne, became very powerful. He had brothers, Michael, Niketas, Constantine and George, of whom John, Constantine and George were congenital eunuchs and rascals by profession. Niketas still had his genitals intact and was showing the first down of a beard but Michael had already achieved maturity and was a fine figure of a man to look at. They were both money changers by trade; they used to adulterate the coin. Through John they were all familiar to the emperor and, fate having designated them to wield power in the future, constantly increased their influence. The others were assigned various offices while Michael was appointed governor of the Pantheon[80] by the emperor. The empress fell madly and demonically in love with this man; she used to have secret meetings with him and shady intercourse.[81] They say this is why the emperor wasted away with a painful disease under the influence of slow poison, the empress taking the opportunity of getting rid of him without attracting suspicion, so that she could raise up Michael to the imperial throne. That is why (as we said) the emperor dragged out his wretched and excruciating life contaminated not with poisons that obtain an early demise, but with those that bring on a slow and lingering death. He was bedridden and praying with all his might for extinction. He lasted until 11 April, second year of the indiction, AM 6542.[82] Then, on the Thursday of Holy Week, after making the distribution of the senators' emoluments, he expressed a desire to bathe in the baths of the Great Palace. He went in and was pitilessly suffocated by Michael's henchmen in the swimming pool of the baths[83] after a reign of five years and six months. And that very night, while they were singing of the Saviour's sufferings, the patriarch Alexios was summoned, allegedly by the emperor Romanos, [391] to come up to the palace. When he got there, he found the emperor Romanos dead. The Chrysotriklinos was all decked out; sitting on a throne, Zoe brought in Michael and would have the patriarch marry

---

[80] One of the state rooms in the imperial palace.
[81] Psellos has a great deal to say about these goings-on in the palace.
[82] 11 April 1034.
[83] Psellos gives the same report of the emperor's death, but according to Yahya of Antioch, III, 536, he died of consumption.

him to her. Alexios was astounded at her demand and stood there speechless, at a loss whether or not to comply.[84] But John, together with Zoe, gave fifty pounds of gold to the patriarch and fifty to the clergy – which convinced them to perform the priestly office.

[84] This would only be the second marriage of Zoe, but the conventions of widowhood demanded some delay. Worse still, palace gossip accused her of adultery, alleging that she wanted to be united to her lover who was also the murderer of her first husband. It has been suggested that the presentation of the marriage in such an unfavourable light may originate from a priestly source, probably Demetrios of Kyzikos, to whom Skylitzes alludes in his Prologue: A. E. Laiou, 'Imperial marriages and their critics in the eleventh century: the case of Skylitzes', *DOP*, 46 (1992), 165–76, at 170–2.

CHAPTER 19

Michael IV the Paphlagonian [1034–1041]

1. [392] After the emperor Romanos had been exterminated in the way we just described he was interred on that same Good Friday in the Peribleptos monastery which had recently been constructed by him.[1]

2. Zoe thought that, once she had established Michael on the imperial throne, she would have a slave and servant rather than a husband and an emperor. She had already moved her father's eunuchs into the palace and was taking a closer interest in state affairs but, in the event, everything turned out for her in a strikingly different way. John [the Orphanotrophos], the emperor's brother, was an energetic man of action.[2] He was concerned for his brother's safety from when he first set foot in the palace, for he had the example of Romanos [III] before his eyes. He expelled the empress' eunuchs from the palace and packed off the most faithful of her servants, appointing women who were related to him to be her warders and guardians. There was nothing that she could do, great or small, without his permission. She could neither go for a walk nor visit the baths unless he gave assent; he deprived her of all recreation.

When he had dealt with all aspects of the palace situation, he sent letters throughout the inhabited world making it known to all that the emperor Romanos had paid the debt of his mortality; also that Michael, having been proclaimed while Romanos was still alive and with his approval, was now married to the empress. Everybody else willingly accepted this and acclaimed the new emperor with the voice of praise; [393] only the patrician Constantine Dalassenos (who was residing on his estate) did not take kindly to the news. He could scarcely endure what they were saying and wondered aloud why, when there were so many excellent men of distinguished families and noble birth, a vulgar threepence-a-day man should

---

[1] 12 April 1034; Psellos was present at the interment: Michael Psellos, *Chronographia*; tr. E. R. A. Sewter (London, 1953), 4.5, 89.
[2] According to Psellos it was this man who persuaded Zoe to crown Michael: *Chronographia*, tr. Sewter, 4.2, 88.

be preferred above all others and be proclaimed emperor. When John learned of this he was (not surprisingly) deeply troubled and concerned; he gave his care and attention to the question of how he might ensnare this man in his net. One of the eunuchs was sent to him, Ergodotes[3] by name, particularly suited for this kind of mission; he was to exchange oaths with the man and bring him to the emperor. Off he went to Dalassenos while John manipulated the Senate and the people. He gained general approval by advancing the senators to higher ranks while he mollified the commoners with gifts and favours,[4] conciliating the subjects once and for all. But it was clearly shown from the outset that what had transpired was not pleasing to God. At the eleventh hour of Easter Day there was an unendurable hailstorm, so violent that not only the trees (fruit-bearing and otherwise) were broken down, but also houses and churches collapsed. Crops and vines were laid flat to the ground; hence there ensued a great shortage of all kinds of produce at that time. There was a falling star about the third hour of the night on the Sunday after Easter; the brilliance of its shining put all the stars into the shade and, for many, it looked like the rising sun. And the emperor became possessed of a demon; those close to him, using fine phrases, called it a madness-causing disease[5] but it endured to the end of his life. He received no relief either by divine might or from doctors but was grievously tormented and tortured.

3. When Ergodotes came to Dalassenos, [394] he found him unwilling to trust the oaths or to accompany [the eunuch] to Byzantium [i.e. Constantinople]. Sending one of his most trusted servants, he demanded yet more firm undertakings that he would suffer no evil, promising that then he would come. Constantine Phagitzes, a eunuch from Paphlagonia, closely associated with the emperor,[6] was now sent bearing the Wood of the True Cross, the holy Impression,[7] the autograph letter of our Lord and Saviour Jesus Christ to Abgar and an icon of the more-than-holy Mother of God. He arrived, exchanged oaths with Constantine and set off with

---

[3] This faithful servant of Constantine VIII had already been ordered to bring Dalassenos back to Constantinople in 1028, then the order was rescinded; reign of Constantine VIII, c. 3.

[4] From this time emperors mounting the throne demonstrated great generosity towards the senators and to the tradesmen of Constantinople. This was because they were unsure of their position and, lacking any dynastic legitimacy, they were forced to depend on the citizenry of the capital.

[5] Michael was subject to epileptic fits.

[6] The family of Michael IV was of obscure origins. His ancestors came from Paphlagonia, a province which provided the palace with many eunuchs, one of the more famous ones being Michael's brother, John the Orphanotrophos: P. Magdalino, 'Paphlagonians in Byzantine high society', *Byzantine Asia minor (sixth–twelfth centuries)* (Athens, 1998), 141–50.

[7] i.e. of the Saviour's face: a reference to the *mandylion* of Edessa brought to Constantimople in 944: reign of Romanos, I, c. 37; *ODB*, II, 1082–3.

him for Byzantium. The emperor gave him a warm reception, raised him to the proconsular dignity,[8] showered him with substantial gifts and directed that he enjoy free and unimpeded occupation of his residence located in the Kyros suburb[9] without let or hindrance.

4. In that year something else worthy of note took place. There were some Varangians dispersed in the Thrakesion theme for the winter.[10] One of them coming across a woman of the region in the wilderness put the quality of her virtue to the test. When persuasion failed he resorted to violence, but she seized his Persian-type short sword, struck him in the heart and promptly killed him. When the deed became known in the surrounding area, the Varangians held an assembly and crowned the woman, presenting her with all the possessions of her violator, whom they threw aside, unburied, according to the law concerning assassins.

The swarms of locusts which had expired (as we reported) on the sands of the shore of the Hellespont now spontaneously regenerated and overran the coastal regions of the Hellespont again, devastating the Thrakesion theme for three whole years. Then they appeared in Pergamon but perished there, as one of the bishop's servants saw beforehand in a vision [395] (not a dream, for he was awake). It was as though he saw a eunuch dressed in white, of radiant appearance. [This apparition] was ordered to open and empty the first of three sacks lying before him, then the second and, after that, the third. He did as he was commanded; the first sack poured out snakes, vipers and scorpions; the second, toads, asps, basiliscs, horned serpents and other venomous creatures; the third, beetles, gnats,[11] hornets and other creatures with a sting in the tail. The man stood there speechless; the bright apparition stood close to him and said: 'These came and will come upon you because of your transgression of God's commandments and the desecration of the emperor Romanos which has taken place and the violation of his marriage bed.' That is what happened so far.

5. As the emperor Michael was afflicted by the demonic disease and was also too sluggish and indolent to undertake affairs of state, he had the

---

[8] *Anthypatos*, a rather modest rank, one step down from patrician.
[9] Thus he was assigned a residence in Constantinople where it would be much easier to keep track of his activities than on his estates in Paphlagonia, where he would have been able to hold clandestine meetings with other military chieftains. The suburb known as *Ta Kyrou* lay to the west of the city, between the cistern of Mokios and the Gate of St Romanos: Janin, *Constantinople*, 378–9.
[10] Ever since Basil II recruited the company of Varangians they had manned the palace guard or accompanied the emperor on his campaigns. From that time some of them were also stationed in the provinces, usually in the Thrakesion theme, but normally in eastern Asia Minor.
[11] *sknipas*, the word used in LXX for the third Plague of Egypt, Exod. 8:16ff.: lice, sand flies or fleas.

trappings and name of emperor but the entire responsibility for matters both civil and military lay in the hands of John.[12] He promptly appointed his own brother Niketas duke of Antioch, but when he got there, the citizens of Antioch would not allow him to enter the city. This was because a little earlier a tax collector by the name of Salibas[13] had been given the task of ensuring that they paid; but he was killed by the populace of Antioch because his demands on people were excessive. Then the Antiochenes were afraid they might suffer some implacable punishment for this murder and that is why they shut Niketas out. He swore oaths that there would be an amnesty of crimes for them and that nothing disagreeable would happen to them on account of Salibas' murder; then they let him in. Once he was in possession of the city and master of its affairs, he paid little or no attention to his oaths. He put a hundred men to death by decapitating or impaling them; he arrested eleven prominent and exceedingly rich men of noble birth (the patrician Elpidios was the most distinguished) and sent them in chains to Byzantium. He wrote [396] in a letter to his brother John that it was not because of the murder of Salibas that he was prevented from entering Antioch but because that city was well disposed towards Dalassenos.[14] This was a spark to ignite John's smouldering resentment of Dalassenos, which now burst into open flames. He brought him to the capital right away and exiled him to the island of Platea on the third of August, second year of the indiction.[15] His son-in-law, Constantine Doukas, was also thrown into a tower because he protested the injustice of it and condemned the breaking of the oaths, calling God as his witness.[16] Three other high-born and affluent gentlemen of Asia Minor also suffered on his behalf: Goudelios, Baianos[17] and Probatas.[18] Their goods were confiscated and allocated to the emperor's brother Constantine. The protovestiarios Symeon, one of the servants of the emperor Constantine, was expelled from the city because he did not like what had happened, protesting the injustice done to Dalassenos and the setting aside of the

---

[12] Psellos attributes rather more qualities to Michael, allowing that he *did* occupy himself with matters of state: *Chronographia*, 4.8–11, trans. Sewter, 90–2.
[13] This person is unknown elsewhere; the name could be Syriac or Arabic.
[14] Dalassenos had been duke of Antioch towards the end of the reign of Basil II: Yahya of Antioch, III, 477.
[15] 3 August 1034.
[16] The first wife of Constantine Doukas was a daughter of Dalassenos; presumably she died young and childless.
[17] The Baianos family was related to the Macedonian dynasty. There was a Baianos serving in Italy under Basil I; the third wife of Leo VI was Eudokia Baïane: reign of Leo VI, c. 19.
[18] The inclusion of this name is suspicious for a George Probatas served on delicate missions on behalf of Michael IV and John the Orphanotrophos; see below.

emperor's oaths. He came to Olympos and put off his layman's hair, being tonsured in the monastery recently erected by him.

6. In the same year there was an earthquake from which Jerusalem suffered severely. Many lives were lost for dwellings and churches collapsed as the earth shook for forty days. In the month of September, AM 6543,[19] a pillar of fire appeared in the east, the apex inclined towards the south. In those days the Saracens captured Myra[20] and the people of Berroia, also known as Aleppo, chased out the moderator[21] sent to them by the emperor Romanos and, ostensibly to avenge the emperor Romanos, his wife's uncle, the sebastos Pankratios[22] renounced his peace treaty with the Romans, repossessing all the fortresses and strongholds he had previously handed over. [397] The Patzinaks crossed the Danube and devastated Mysia right up to Thessalonike and the Africans' ships did no small damage in the Cyclades. None of these matters was of any concern to John whose sole and abiding concern was how to keep a firm hold on Dalassenos and ensure that he not slip unnoticed through the net prepared for him. So he had him brought from Platê and imprisoned in a secure tower where he set guards who were by no means low-ranking men over him. The patrician George Maniakes he transferred from Edessa and sent to govern Upper Media, also known as Vaspurakan, while he despatched Leo Lependrenos to Edessa. The Orphanotrophos was now afflicted with an ulcer in the mouth which defied all medical treatment. Nicholas, the great miracle-worker, appeared to him in a dream commanding him to come to Myra as quickly as possible, for that was where he would be healed. Quicker than it takes to tell he went there and conferred upon the sacred church of the great saint incense of various kinds and other costly offerings. He also encircled the city of Myra with a very strong wall.[23] Having received his cure he then returned in good health.

7. Niketas, the commander of Antioch in Syria, having departed this life, another of [John's] brothers, Constantine, was appointed his successor while the remaining brother, George, became protovestiarios, Symeon

---

[19] September 1034.
[20] This city in the Kibyrrhaiote theme was the site of the most famous of all the shrines of St Nicholas.
[21] The term 'moderator' (*harmostes*) does not denote an official position. This is probably a representative of the emperor sent to supervise the application of the peace treaty signed after the unfortunate campaign of Romanos III.
[22] Michael IV would appear to have promoted Bagrat [Pankratios] of Georgia, for Romanos III only made him kouropalates. This would be the first mention of the title *sebastos*.
[23] The wall was to protect this city in Lycia (Demre today) against the attacks of Arab pirates such as the one which had just taken place. In gratitude for his healing, John had St Nicholas portrayed on his seals: G. Zacos and A. Veglery, *Byzantine lead seals*, I, (Basle, 1972), no. 2677.

having assumed the monastic habit, as we reported. The emperor released those Antiochenes from their lengthy imprisonment and elevated his sister Maria's son Michael to the sublime rank of caesar. To the very end he lamented the offence he had committed against the emperor Romanos, propitiating the Divinity by doing good works, distributing alms to the poor, erecting new monasteries and installing monks in them and by accomplishing other blameless deeds. And these might have attained their end if he had renounced the purple for which he had committed such misdeeds, repudiated the adulteress and wept [398] for his sin, alone. But he did none of these things; he continued to live with her, wholeheartedly enjoying his imperial role. And he financed what were supposed to be his good works out of the common and public purse, expecting to receive absolution as though from a mindless and unjust God from whom repentance could be purchased with the money of others.

8. AM 6543, third year of the indiction, in the month of May,[24] [Saracens from] Africa and Sicily who had been overrunning the Cyclades and the shores of the Thrakesion theme were finally vanquished by the troops posted to guard those areas. Five hundred of the enemy were brought to the emperor alive; all the rest were impaled along the coastline from Adramytion to Strobilos.[25] John sent George Probatas as an ambassador to Sicily for peace negotiations with the emir of that place.[26] He went there and negotiated so skilfully that he returned to the capital bringing the emir's son with him. There was an earthquake that year which created fissures in the Boukellarion theme and five whole villages were engulfed. The proedros Nikephoros, the eunuch of the emperor Constantine, who was staying there, came within a hair's breadth of his life, and when he escaped the danger against all hope he was tonsured a monk at Stoudios' monastery.

9. Apolaphar Mouchoumet, the ruler of Sicily, made an alliance with the emperor and was honoured with the title of magister. His brother Apochaps rose up against him and, when he was defeated, had recourse to the emperor for help.[27] The patrician George Maniakes was sent with

[24] May 1035.
[25] i.e. these Arabs were executed all along the shore of the Thrakesion theme. This expedition has probably been confused with the one led by Constantine Chage, strategos of the Kibyrrhiaote theme (mentioned a few lines further on).
[26] The mission of Probatas was to the emir Ahmad al-Akhal who theoretically owed allegiance to the Zirids of Africa. A treaty was arranged and the emir's son was sent to the court at Constantinople: Felix, *Byzanz und Islam*, 205.
[27] The army of Sicily consisted of Arabs from Africa and of Sicilians. The emir of Africa despatched an army to secure his hold on the island, thus provoking the revolt of Abu Hafs (Apochaps), the brother of Ahmed al-Akhal (Apolaphar for Skylitzes), who sought refuge with Constantine Opos in 1036/7: Felix, *Byzanz und Islam*, 204–5.

forces to Longobardia[28] as commander plenipotentiary.[29] The patrician Stephen, the emperor's brother-in-law on his sister's side, went with him, commanding the fleet. When African and Sicilian [Saracens] invaded the islands and coast with many ships, the commodore of the Kibyrrhaiote theme, Constantine Chage, [399] engaged them with the local fleet and severely routed them. He sent five hundred prisoners to the emperor and drowned the rest. There was unbearably cold weather; the Danube froze and Patzinaks crossed, doing considerable damage in Mysia and Thrace, as far as Macedonia. The Thrakesion theme suffered another plague of locusts and the crops were damaged.

10. AM 6544, fourth year of the indiction, in the spring,[30] the Patzinaks made three assaults on the Romans wreaking utter destruction wherever they went.[31] They slaughtered all those who were old enough to bear arms and subjected the prisoners to unspeakable tortures. They captured five commanders alive: John Dermokaites, Bardas Pitzes, Leo Chalkoutzes, Constantine Pterotos and Michael Strabotrichares.[32] The Russian rulers Nesisthlav and Hierosthlav also perished and a relative of the deceased was chosen to rule the Russians: Zinisthlav.[33] Serbia, having revolted against the Romans after the death of the emperor Romanos, now made a treaty again. On the death of Amr,[34] the *amermoumnes* of Egypt, his wife (who was a Christian) sent a delegation to the emperor together with her son[35] for peace negotiations. The emperor responded to her initiative

---

[28] Maniakes arrived in Sicily with an army composed of Varangians (among whom was the famous Harald of Norway), Russians, Norman mercenaries, Lombards and some contingents from the eastern themes: Felix, *Byzanz und Islam*, 208.

[29] According to the *Vita Philareti* of Nil he received imperial orders to assemble troops from all over the empire: Felix, *Byzanz und Islam*, 207. Skylitzes errs in stating that Maniakes set out for Sicily at that time. On Skylitzes' treatment of matters Sicilian: J. Shepard, 'Byzantium's last Sicilian expedition: Skylitzes' testimony', *Rivista di Studi Bizantini e Neoellenici*, n.s., 14–16 (1977–9), 145–59.

[30] 1036.

[31] From now on Patzinak raids were an annual event.

[32] The Dermokaitai and the Chalkoutzai are families with a military tradition. The form Chalkotoubes found in several manuscripts should be preferared to Chalkoutzes for it is attested by a seal of Theophylact, archegetes of the west: G. Schlumberger, *Sigillographie de l'empire byzantin* (Paris, 1884), 326, now in Vienna. This reading is confirmed by A.-K. Waisiliou and W. Seibt, *Die byzantinischen Bleisiegel in Österreich, II: Zentral- und Provincialverwaltung* (Vienna, 2004), no. 240.

[33] According the Russian chronicles, Mstislav of Chernigov (Nesisthlav *pace* Skylitzes), the most powerful of the sons of Vladimir, died in 1036. His brother and rival, Iaroslav, then seized his domains and ruled the Russian lands until he died in 1054. The security of the capital (Kiev) was only assured after the defeat of the Patzinaks who were besieging it: S. Franklin and J. Shepard, *The emergence of Rus, 750–1200* (London, 1996), 206–8. Skylitzes' Zinisthlav can probably be identified as Iziaslav, son of Iaroslav, who reigned at Kiev. It is possible that the growing power of the young Russian state diverted the Patzinaks towards the Danube and against the affluent Byzantine provinces.

[34] Amr died on 13 June 1036.

[35] Al-Mustansir, 1036–94.

and arranged a thirty-year peace with her.[36] In the month of December, fifth year of the indiction, AM 6546, the eighteenth day of the month,[37] the fourth hour of the night, there were three earthquakes: two small and one large. As we said, the patrician George Maniakes had been transferred from Edessa and Lependrenos appointed to govern there. The Arabs living in Mesopotamia[38] made a pact with each other, [400] advanced on Edessa and besieged it. It would have fallen too[39] if Constantine, the emperor's brother, had not sent the necessary help from Antioch and delivered it from a hopeless situation.[40] To reward him for this deed the emperor promoted him domestic of the scholai for the east. The eunuch Anthony Paches was appointed bishop of Nikomedeia. He was a relative of the emperor and had no quality befitting a bishop but he knew well when to keep his mouth shut.[41]

{As John, archbishop of Bulgaria, was now dead the emperor named another: a Paphlagonian by birth who had distinguished himself in the service of the Great Church, having served there as chartophylax for many years. But for love of silence and in full awareness that religious affairs were not well managed, he had declined to be involved in the midst of the hurly-burly. To avoid crossing swords with the Patriarch, he lived a private, retired life. His name was Leo and he was well versed in all learning, both secular and ours. As primate of Bulgaria he left behind many a souvenir of his virtue.}[42]

Because there was a drought and for six whole months no rain had fallen, the emperor's brothers held a procession, John carrying the holy *mandylion*, the Great Domestic the Letter of Christ to Abgar, the protovestiarios George the holy Swaddling Bands. They travelled on foot from the Great Palace to the church of the exceedingly holy Mother of God at Blachernae.[43] The patriarch and the clergy made another procession, and not only did it not rain but a massive hail-storm was unleashed which

---

[36] According to the Arab sources a ten-year peace was concluded in 1035/6, before the death of Az-Zahir: Felix, *Byzanz und Islam*, 107.
[37] 18 December 1036.
[38] Nasr ad-Daula the Marwanid and Sabib ibn Wahhab the Numairite, emir of Harran, 1019/20 – 1039/40.
[39] This was in 1036. Roman soldiers took refuge in the citadel: Felix, *Byzanz und Islam*, 148–9.
[40] *Armenia and the crusades tenth to twelfth centuries: the chronicle of Matthew of Edessa*, tr. A. E. Dostourian (New York and London, 1993), 55–6, accuses the emperor's brother of having allowed the enemy to escape in the direction of Melitene unopposed.
[41] There is a reference to the proverb 'he carried the ox of silence on the tongue' here.
[42] MSS U and E only. On Leo of Bulgaria: *Théophylacte d'Achrida*, *Opera*, 30–1 and D. Stiernon, *DS*, 9 (1976), 623–5.
[43] Thus the procession went the length of the city, passing along the Golden Horn.

broke down trees and shattered the roof tiles of the city. The city was in the grip of famine so John purchased one hundred thousand bushels of grain in the Peloponnese and in Hellas; with this the citizens were relieved.

11. In Sicily, as we said, two brothers were contending with each other, and when Apolaphar got the better of it the other brother summoned Oumer,[44] ruler of Africa, to his aid. Oumer promised to fight with him if he might receive some possession on the island. The Sicilian readily agreed to this; he arrived and engaged Apolaphar whom he thoroughly routed, [401] because the force which had been sent with the patrician George Maniakes to fight with Apolaphar was delayed.[45] Apolaphar fled to the governor of Longobardia, Leo Opos, asking for aid. Leo gathered up what forces were at his disposition and crossed into Sicily where, as a result of several successful encounters with the African commander, he was able to interrupt the foe's ruthless advance. But then, when he heard that the brothers had made peace with each other and were about to make a united attack on the Romans, he crossed back into Italy taking with him in his ships about fifteen thousand Roman prisoners who landed safely in Italy and then dispersed to their homes. The Carthaginian was now free to stay in Sicily and to pillage it at his convenience; that is how things were in Sicily.

12. John had an excessive desire to secure the [patriarchal] throne of Constantinople. Demetrios of Kyzikos, Anthony of Nikomedia, the bishops of Side and of Ankyra who were brothers and other metropolitans made common cause with him, debating how to expel Alexios and put John on the throne in his stead. The patriarch Alexios, with the support of the remaining portion of the church, sent a memorandum to them to this effect: 'If, as you claim, it was not by a vote of the bishops but uncanonically, at the command of the emperor Basil, that I acceded to the throne, then let all the metropolitans I ordained during the eleven and a half years that I have directed the church be deposed; and let the three emperors I have crowned be declared anathema and then I will vacate the throne for anybody who desires it.' When Demetrios' circle received this pronouncement they were filled with shame and fear – for most of them had been ordained by him. They said not another word and, in the end, John had to keep his yearning to attain the throne to himself.

---

[44] 'Abdallah b. al'Mu'izz was the name of this son of the Zirid emir, 'the Carthaginian'.
[45] Presumably it had taken longer than anticipated for Maniakes to assemble his army, hence he had not yet arrived in Italy.

13. [402] In AM 6546, sixth year of the indiction, there was an earthquake on 2 November[46] about the tenth hour of the day, and the earth continued to tremble into and throughout the month of January. There was a famine in Thrace, Macedonia, Strymon and Thessalonike, right into Thessaly. When the clergy of Thessalonike accused Theophanes the Metropolitan of withholding their customary allowance, the emperor (who was staying there) tried admonishing him, urging him not to deprive the personnel of the church of the allowance stipulated in the law. When the bishop showed himself recalcitrant and inflexible, the emperor realised he would have to circumvent him with a subterfuge to punish his avarice. He therefore sent one of his servants to him requesting the loan of one *kentenarion* until gold was delivered from Byzantium. The bishop denied with oaths that he had any more than thirty pounds on hand but the emperor did not let this stand in his way. He sent and scrutinised the man's treasury and found thirty-three *kentenaria* of gold. Out of this he paid the clergy what was owing to them since the first year of Theophanes' episcopate until the present hour: the rest he distributed to the poor. He expelled the metropolitan from the church and restricted him to an estate. He appointed Prometheus to the see, stipulating that Theophanes should receive an allowance from him and was to live alone.

14. Because Pankratios, the strong man of Abasgia, was oppressing Iassites,[47] the katepan of Iberia, John despatched his brother, Constantine, the domestic of the scholai, with the entire army and promised to send Dalassenos with him as an adviser and comrade in the wars. But this he did not do and, in the end, the domestic returned empty-handed.

15. [403] The empress Zoe knew that John was about to take a purgative. She bribed the doctor to mingle poison with the medicine. This she did by the intermediary of one of her personal eunuchs (his name was Sgouritzes), offering many gifts and the promise of an elevated position in life plus much wealth. However, a young slave who served the doctor betrayed the plot to the emperor. When it became known the doctor was condemned for conspiracy and exiled to Antioch, his home town.[48]

---

[46] 2 November 1037.
[47] Michael Iasites occupied some high positions (including the duchy of Antioch) under Michael IV and Constantine IX. One of his descendents married Eudokia, daughter of the emperor Alexios I Komnenos: J.-C. Cheynet, 'Les ducs d'Antioche sous Michel IV et Constantin IX', *Novum millennium: studies on Byzantine history and culture dedicated to Paul Speck* (Aldershot, 2001), 56–7, repr. in Cheynet, *Société*, 200–2.
[48] It was possible for physicians to enter the court, then to be appointed to elevated positions: A. P. Kazhdan, 'The image of the medical doctor in Byzantine literature of the tenth to twelfth centuries', *DOP*, 38 (1984), 43–51.

The man who had prepared the poison, the protospatharios Constantine Moukoupeles, was expelled from the city, while the empress herself came under increasing suspicion.

16. No sooner had the patrician George Maniakes reached Sicily than the two brothers who ruled there made peace with each other and turned their attention to chasing him off the island.[49] They summoned five thousand allies from Africa and, when they arrived there was a fierce battle at Rhemata[50] in which Maniakes most certainly put the Carthaginians to flight. There was so much killing that the river which flowed by overflowed with blood. He proceeded to take thirteen Sicilian towns and then, little by little, to conquer the whole island.[51]

17. AM 6546, sixth year of the indiction,[52] there was an attack on Edessa and it was all but taken, but God preserved it. The commander there was the protospatharios Barasbatzes the Iberian; there came twelve Arab chieftains with five hundred horses and five hundred camels carrying a thousand chests containing a thousand [404] heavy-armed troops. They came to Edessa saying they were on their way to the emperor, bearing gifts; their aim was to bring the chests into the city, let the soldiers out by night and take the city. The commander received the chieftains graciously and feasted them, but he ordered the horsemen and baggage to remain outside [the city]. Now a poor Armenian went a-begging where the Saracens were quartered and he heard one of the men in a chest asking where they were. The beggar, who understood the Saracen language, ran off and reported this to the commander. He left the chieftains at their meal, went out with armed men, broke open the chests and, finding the soldiers within, utterly annihilated them all, together with the horsemen and camel-drivers. He then returned to the city and killed eleven of the chieftains, while one was sent home with his hands, ears and nose cut off – judged to be the best person to report what had taken place.[53]

18. In AM 6547, seventh year of the indiction, intensifying his animosity towards Dalassenos, John banished his brother, the patrician Theophylact, and the other brother too, the patrician Romanos, together with their

---

[49] The emir of Africa had already caused Ahmed al-Akhal, a refugee in the citadel of Palermo, to be assassinated; it is not known what became of Abu Hafs.
[50] A stronghold in the eastern part of the island, controlling the road from Messina to Syracuse. It was here that the Romans were defeated under Manuel Phokas in 964 by the Arabs of Sicily.
[51] In the course of 1039 Maniakes conquered a large portion of the island, including Syracuse, which had the largest concentration of Greek-speaking people.
[52] 1038.
[53] We do not know which Arab chieftains were engaged in this action. Certainly not the emirs who had attacked Edessa previously.

nephew Adrian and all the other close relations, the object being to obliterate the family. He was so resourceful in whatever evil undertaking you might mention and capable of discovering every path of wickedness. He added this over and above the public taxes: that every village should pay an *aerikon* tax, each one according to its ability: one village four pieces of gold, another six and so on up to twenty,[54] plus other shameful tolls to generate income which it would be a disgrace to mention.

{They say that he was responsible for the empress becoming besotted with his brother. Knowing that she passionately desired to produce a child, he arranged for some women to come to the Sovereign Lady calling upon her to compel this man by ordinance to support the children they had borne him. She surmised that [405] if she lay in sin with him, she would bear a child and the empire would have an heir. So she became intimate with him as was formerly stated and had carnal knowledge of him in a hole in a corner, not so much because she was overwhelmed by his beauty, but because she desired the endowment of offspring from him.}[55]

The emperor was still afflicted by the demon and, finding no relief, he sent two pieces of gold for each priest in all the themes and the islands, one for each monk. He also stood godfather at the baptism of newborn children, giving each one a single piece and four miliarisia, but none of this did him any good. In fact, the condition worsened and in addition he was afflicted by dropsy. That year there were continuous earthquakes and frequent heavy rainfalls while, in some of the themes there was such an epidemic of quinzy that the living were unable to carry away the dead.

19. On 2 February, eighth year of the indiction, AM 6548, there was an appalling earthquake; other places and cities suffered too. Smyrna[56] was a pathetic sight for its most beautiful buildings fell down and many of the inhabitants lost their lives.

20. As for Sicily, the Carthaginian[57] had picked himself up again, assembled a force much larger than the former one and come to Sicily intending to chase Maniakes out of there. He encamped on an inclined plain called Draginai[58] and there he waited for battle to commence. When Maniakes

---

[54] The *aerikon* tax is very old, for it is mentioned by Prokopios, but its exact nature is unknown. It appears to have been a supplementary tax which was imposed (at least in the eleventh century) on cattle. John did not create this tax; he simply increased it: Oikonomides, *Fiscalité*, 80–2 and, for a different hypothesis: J. Haldon, 'Aerikon/Aerika: a reinterpretation', *JÖB*, 44 (1994), 136–42.
[55] MS U only.
[56] Izmir today. Smyrna was already replacing Ephesos (which was becoming silted up) as the principal port of the Thrakesion theme.
[57] i.e. the emir of Africa, Abdallah ben al-Mu'izz.
[58] Now Troina, to the west of Etna.

learnt of this, he mobilised the forces under his command and went out to meet him, first directing the emperor's brother-in-law Stephen who, as we said, was in charge of the fleet, to secure the coast, thus ensuring that, when battle was joined, the defeated Carthaginian could not run off unnoticed and return home. The fray commenced and the foe was severely routed; a multitude of Africans [406] (about five thousand in number)[59] fell while, their chieftain fled out of danger, came to the shore, boarded a rapid yacht (unknown to Stephen's guardsmen) and got away to his homeland. Maniakes was furious when he learnt of this. When Stephen came to meet with him, he assailed him with excessive abuse and, raising his whip, dealt him several blows on the head. He called him a lazy, cowardly fellow who had betrayed the emperor's interests. Stephen did not take lightly to being dragged in the mud and insulted; without delay he sent a letter to the Orphanotrophos advising him that Maniakes was hatching an uprising against the emperor. Maniakes was immediately brought to the capital under arrest and imprisoned, together with the patrician Basil Theodorakanos.[60] The entire command was transferred to Stephen and a eunuch was sent out to join him, the praepositos Basil Pediciates. In due course these two ruined the whole situation and lost Sicily by greed, cowardice and carelessness. As Maniakes took the towns of the island, he constructed citadels in them, stationing an adequate garrison in each one; this was to prevent the local people from retaking the cities by assault. But now that he was a prisoner, carried off to Byzantium (as we said), the local people took advantage of the timidity and laziness of the commanding officers. They allied themselves with some Carthaginians and attacked the cities. Razing the citadels once they had defeated the defending forces, they repossessed all the cities with the exception of Messina. Here it was the protospatharios Katakalon Kekaumenos,[61] officer commanding the unit of the Armeniakon theme, who was in charge of security. He had three hundred cavalry and five hundred infantrymen with him. In their haste to leave no ember of Roman power smouldering on the island, [407] the local people had pressed everyone capable of bearing arms into service. With these and a significant allied force of Carthaginians they marched on Messina and invested the city. Katakalon closed the gates and let nobody

---

[59] The number is obviously excessive.
[60] A relative of the famous general who served under Basil II; also of George Theodorakanos, commander of Samos under Constantine VIII, possibly a son or a brother.
[61] Skylitzes seems to be remarkably well informed concerning the deeds of this officer, who now makes his first appearance. It has been suggested that the historian either consulted a dossier on him or was in direct communication with him: J. Shepard, 'A suspected source of Scylitzes' *Synopsis Historion*: the great Catacalon Cecaumenus', *BMGS*, 16 (1992), 171–81.

set foot beyond the moat for three days, thus giving the appearance of timidity. The Saracens were filled with disdain; they dispersed, fearing nothing, and disported themselves with drinking, with flutes and cymbals, by night and by day, as though they were going to capture the city next morning. Katakalon noted the nonchalance and inattention of the Saracens and that they were acting incautiously, not paying the slightest attention to those inside the walls. On the fourth day (it was the Wednesday on which we are accustomed to celebrate mid-Pentecost)[62] he rallied his own troops, ordered the priests to celebrate the unbloody sacrifice, partook of the divine mysteries with them all and, at the hour of the main meal, flung open the city gates. He charged out against a drunken and hung-over enemy, himself in the lead with his men, riding full tilt for the tent of Apolaphar, the island chieftain, whom he slew on the spot, staggering with drunkenness, and his tent was ripped apart. The rest of the Saracens were falling as they tripped over the heap of the fallen in their drunkenness; they were utterly incapable of offering any resistance on account of the unexpected nature of the assault and the entire army was put to flight. The Saracens died treading each other underfoot and killing their own; the whole plain, the nearer ravines and the rivers were filled with corpses, so that out of so many tens of thousands only a very few reached safety in Palermo. The entire encampment was captured; it was full of gold, silver, pearls and precious stones, which (it is said) the soldiers measured out in bushels. So it was that the whole of Sicily, recently vanquished by Maniakes, was shortly repossessed by the Saracens, thanks to the nonchalance and ineptitude of the commanders. Only Messina was retained (in the manner we described): Stephen and Pediates fled into Longobardia. That is how things were in Sicily.

21. [408] Most of the time the emperor Michael resided at Thessalonike where he frequented the tomb of the wondrously victorious martyr Demetrios in the sincere hope of finding relief from his illness. He had nothing whatsoever to do with affairs of state other than those which were absolutely necessary; the administration and the handling of public business rested entirely on John's shoulders and there was no imaginable form of impurity or criminality that he did not search out for the affliction and mistreatment of the subjects. It would be a Herculean task to list them all. Everybody living under this grievous tyranny persisted in interceding with the Deity, appealing for some relief. God frequently shook the

---

[62] The year is uncertain: probably 1041, since he was at Constantinople in April 1042: reign of Michael V, c. 1.

earth; the inhabited world was assailed by awesome and fearful [portents]: comets appearing in the sky, storms of wind and rain in the air, eruptions and tremblings on earth. In my opinion, these things presaged the forthcoming unparalleled catastrophe for the tyrants. In the month of May, AM 6548, eighth year of the indiction,[63] Maria, the emperor's sister, the mother of the Caesar, went to Ephesos to worship [at the tomb of] the beloved [disciple, John]. On her way she learned a great deal about the unreasonable things that had been done. On her return to Byzantium she reported them all to her brother, John, asking that there be some restraint in his wrongdoing. He sent her away with a laugh saying that this was woman's thinking and that she had no idea what was appropriate for the Roman state. John sent ten *kentenaria* of gold to the emperor who was residing (as we said) at Thessalonica but the ship encountered stormy winds and was wrecked on the Illyrian coast.[64] The gold was acquired by the chieftain of Serbia, Stephen-Boisthlav,[65] who had recently fled from the capital and acquired the land of the Serbs by chasing out Theophilos Erotikos.[66] John put the officials' appointment up for sale and gave everybody [409] his head in wrongdoing, filling the world with ten thousand woes. Judges were levying taxes on the people with impunity and nobody cared a farthing for what was going on.

22. When the emperor heard in Thessalonike about the loss of the gold he wrote to Stephen to send him his own [gold] and not to engage in a war on his own account. When he made no reply, the emperor sent an army against him with the eunuch George Probates in charge. He reached the place but inadvertently encountered some very exacting, broken and inaccessible terrain in which he lost his whole army, extracting himself only with great difficulty.

23. That year[67] there was an uprising in Bulgaria {the twenty-first year of its enslavement and subjection};[68] it happened like this. A Bulgar named Peter Deleanos, the slave of a citizen of Byzantium, escaped from the city and was wandering in Bulgaria. He came to Moravos and Belgrade, fortresses of Pannonia lying across the Danube, neighbours to the Kral of

---

[63] May 1040.
[64] It appears that John ordered the officials in Dalmatia to deliver the taxes of their region, not to Constantinople, but directly to Thessalonike, where the emperor was residing, for a ship sailing from Constantinople to Thessalonike could scarcely have found itself off the Illyrian coast.
[65] This person is mentioned by Kekaumenos too (*Strategikon*, 170–2), calling him Voisthlav of Dioclea, toparch of the fortresses of Zeta and Ston in Dalmatia. The prince of Diokleia overcame the commander of Ragusa, Katakalon Klyzomenites, by trickery.
[66] A relative of the Komnenoi who rebelled under Constantine IX, c. 4
[67] Still AD 1040.   [68] MS U only.

Michael IV the Paphlagonian

Turkey, and let it be known that he was the son of Romanos, son of Samuel, {born to him by the daughter of the Kral of Hungary[69] whom Samuel hated when he was still alive, drove her out and married the very beautiful Eirene of Larissa,}[70] and he stirred up the Bulgars who had recently bowed the neck in subjection and were yearning for freedom. They believed what he said and proclaimed him emperor of Bulgaria. They then left that place and passed through Naissos and Skoupoi,[71] the metropolis of Bulgaria, proclaiming and acclaiming him, mercilessly and inhumanely putting to death every Roman they encountered. [410]

When Basil Synadenos who was then commander of Dyrrachion learnt of this, he took the local troops and hastened to confront Deleanos before the disaster got out of hand and become a raging inferno. When he was at the place called Debris[72] he had an argument about something or other with one of his subordinates, Michael Dermokaites, who then denounced him to the emperor for fostering an attempt at usurpation. He was immediately relieved of his command, brought to Thessalonike and thrown into gaol while Dermokaites was appointed commander in his stead. But Michael was so inexperienced and incompetent in exercising his command that he brought disorder everywhere. The men under his command were so defrauded and badly treated, deprived of their own horses, their arms and anything else they possessed of value, that they rose up against their commander. He, however, realising there was a plot against him, secretly fled by night. The dissidents were so afraid of the emperor that they now contemplated open revolt. They proclaimed one of their company emperor of Bulgaria, a soldier named Teichomeros, well known for his courage and intelligence. So now there were two Bulgar uprisings: one proclaiming Deleanos, the other Teichomeros.[73] Writing a conciliatory letter to Teichomeros inviting him to cooperate, Deleanos persuaded him to come. When the two Bulgar factions were together, Deleanos assembled everybody and asked whether, knowing him to be a descendant of Samuel, they chose to be ruled by him and to rid themselves of Teichomeros; or if

---

[69] By claiming to be the descendant of a Hungarian princess in a region close to Hungary (or Turkey) Deleanos hoped to rally the local people more easily to his cause. On the role of Hungary in the world of the steppe: J. Shepard, 'Byzantium and the Steppe-Nomads: the Hungarian dimension', *Byzanz und Ostmitteleuropa 950–1453*, ed. G. Prinzig and M. Salamon (Wiesbaden, 1999), 55–83.

[70] MS U only.

[71] This should be Skopje (ut MS U). Deleanos was travelling south, along the Morava valley, towards Thessalonike.

[72] Probably Debar, a fortress lying halfway between Dyrrachion and Skopje.

[73] This officer was most likely a member of one of the leading Bulgarian families. Note that he had served at Dyrrachion.

(this being unacceptable) they would prefer to disencumber themselves of him and be ruled by Teichomeros. 'One bush cannot sustain two robins,'[74] he said; 'neither can a country fare well which is governed by two rulers.' A great clamour arose when he had said this; they declared that they wanted him alone to be their sovereign leader. The decision was no sooner made [411] than they picked up rocks and stoned the wretched Teichomeros; thus he who had dreams of becoming ruler lost both the throne and his life. All authority was now transferred to Deleanos who promptly sent men to tear down the fortress of Basilis.[75] On assuming full authority he marched on Thessalonike, against the emperor who, for his part, when he learnt of this, fell back on Byzantium in disorder leaving behind all the regalia, the tent, and whatever there was of gold, silver and vestments. Manuel Ibatzes,[76] a close associate of the emperor, was ordered to collect all this up and follow on but he seized it and went over to Deleanos together with a certain chamberlain, one of the eunuchs of the bedchamber.

24. There was a drought that year, so severe that copious springs and ever-flowing rivers almost dried up. There was a fire at the Arsenal on 6 August and all the ships that were moored there were burnt together with their fittings.

25. Once Deleanos had disposed of Teichomeros (as we said) and had achieved complete mastery, he addressed himself energetically to the tasks in hand. First he dispatched an army with a man named Kaukanos[77] in command and took Dyrrachion. He sent another army into Hellas, commanded by Anthimos; this was encountered and engaged by Alakasseus[78] at Thebes, but he was routed and a large number of Thebans lost their lives. It was then that the theme of Nicopolis went over to the Bulgars (except for Naupaktos) for the reason about to be given. A man of Byzantium, one John Koutzomytes, had been sent there as public tax collector and he oppressed the people of the region so heavily that he brought about his own destruction by provoking a rebellion of the Nicopolitans. Unable to tolerate his exactions, [412] they rose up and tore him limb from limb then, hurling insults against the emperor of the Romans, they went over to the Bulgars. It was not so much out

---

[74] *Erithakos*, Lat. *erithacus rubecula*, 'a solitary bird' (Souda 2983.1). The proverb is well known, e.g. Souda, 1023.1.
[75] MS U only.
[76] Ibatzes was of Bulgarian extraction, possibly a son of the famous general who destroyed an army of Basil II: reign of Basil II, c. 42.
[77] Another former luminary of Samuel's empire in the service of Deleanos. Two brothers, Demetrios and Dometianos, have already been mentioned by Skylitzes. The disbanding of the army set to guard it facilitated the taking of Dyrrachion.
[78] Probably the commander of the theme of Hellas.

of affection for Deleanos that they rebelled and threw off the Roman yoke as on account of the Orphanotrophos' greed and insatiate desire for riches. When the emperor Basil brought the Bulgars into subjection he had no desire whatsoever to bring in new measures or to disturb the existing state of affairs. He wanted matters to remain on the same footing and to be administered in the way Samuel had ordained: that each Bulgar possessing a yoke of oxen should give to the public purse a measure of grain, the same amount of millet and a jar of wine.[79] But the Orphanotrophos had stipulated payment in gold coin, not in kind. The people of the land did not take kindly to this so, seizing on the appearance of Deleanos as a propitious occasion, they threw off Roman rule[80] and returned to the former custom.

26. At that time there was an attempted insurrection against the emperor led by Michael Keroularios,[81] John Makrembolites and several other citizens, who were likewise deprived of their goods and exiled.[82] There was another mutiny, this one against the grand domestic, Constantine, at Mesanacta.[83] When this was reported to [the domestic], Michael Gabras,[84] Theodosios Mesanyktes and many other officers in charge of units lost their eyes. And as for the patrician Gregory Taronites, Constantine completely enclosed him in a fresh ox skin with only a sufficient opening to see and breathe through (this because he was said to have been instigator of the mutiny) and sent him to the Orphanotrophos.

27. In the month of September, ninth year of the indiction, AM 6549,[85] [413] the patrician Alousianos, commander of Theodosioupolis,[86]

---

[79] If this information is accurate, the Bulgars were very lightly taxed: the equivalent of one or two *miliaresia* for a peasant of substance. P. Stephenson (*Balkan Frontiers*, 135–6) does not think that taxation was the cause of these uprisings. The reforms of John the Orphanotrophos were justified by the increasing needs of the Byzantine administration but the people resented them as an added burden

[80] This passage is not altogether coherent; it is attempting to explain a revolt in the theme of Nicopolis, which is by no stretch of the imagination a Bulgar theme.

[81] The Keroularioi (candle-makers) were a craft guild at Constantinople. In this case Keroularios might be Michael's family name, not his nickname; other cases of this as a family name are known from seals.

[82] Makrembolites was the brother-in-law of Michael Keroularios. When the plot failed he was compelled to become a monk while his brother (also implicated in the affair) took his own life: J.-C. Cheynet, *Pouvoir et contestations à Byzance (963–1210)* (Paris, 1990), 52–3.

[83] There was an assembly-point for troops at Mesanacta, located on the road from Dorylaeon to Antioch. It was here that Romanos III was stopped in his campaign against the emir of Aleppo, both going to and returning from the campaign: reign of Romanos III, cc. 9 and 11.

[84] Probably a relative of Constantine Gabras who had fought in the army of Bardas Skleros against Bardas Phokas.

[85] September 1040.

[86] A town in Armenia, known locally as Karin, conquered by the Arabs in 949. The fortress of Theodosioupolis was separate from the great commercial centre of Arz from which the present Erzeroum developed. Basil II had established several members of the Bulgar nobility in the east.

the second son of Aaron,[87] suddenly fled from the city and went over to Deleanos; this for the following reason. While he was still commander in Theodosioupolis he was accused of unjust dealing. Even before he had been given a statement of the charges against him, John demanded fifty pounds of gold from him while a magnificent estate of his wife's which he had in the Charsianon theme was confiscated. He repeatedly petitioned the emperor about this but, receiving no satisfaction, he lost all hope. Disguising himself as an Armenian and under pretence of being a servant of Basil Theodorakanos on his way to the emperor at Thessalonike he slipped away, unknown to all, and found refuge in Ostrovos where Deleanos and his entire forces happened to be encamped. Deleanos accorded him a warm welcome because he was somewhat afraid that the Bulgars might rather declare themselves in favour of [Alousianos] who was reportedly of royal blood. Hence to all appearances he accepted the man as partaker of his 'royalty'; he gave him an army of forty thousand with orders to storm Thessalonike. At that time the city of Thessalonike was governed by the patrician Constantine, the emperor's nephew; he went out and by digging an excavation around [that city] resolutely withstood the siege. For six days Alousianos assaulted the city with siege-engines and other devices but he was repelled at all points, so he withheld the attack and decided to attain the desired end by blockading it. Now one day the people of the region went to the tomb of the great martyr Demetrios and held an all-night intercession, anointing themselves with the myrrh which flows from the sacred tomb. Then with one accord they flung open the gates and went out against the Bulgars; the unit of the Megathymoi[88] was with the men of Thessalonike. Out they went, throwing the Bulgars into disorder by the unexpected nature of the attack and beating them back. [The Bulgars] were not in the least willing to offer a sustained or courageous resistance for the martyr was leading the Roman army and smoothing a path for it [cf. Isaiah 40:3]. This was attested to with oaths by some Bulgars who were taken prisoner. They said they had seen a young horseman leading the Roman ranks, exuding [414] a fire which burnt up the enemies. At least fifteen thousand fell and no fewer were

---

[87] Skylitzes correctly stated above that he was the son of John-Vladislav; hence he was the brother of Prousianos and Catherine, wife of the future emperor Isaac Komnenos. His daughter married the future emperor Romanos IV Diogenes. Aaron, one of the *comitopololoi*, was his grandfather.
[88] The great-hearted? This is the one and only time a unit of that name is mentioned. It might have been formed under Michael IV and not have survived the Paphlagonian dynasty.

taken prisoner.[89] The rest of them, including Alousianos, shamefully ran for safety to Deleanos.

28. In this year, ninth year of the indiction, on 10 June,[90] about the twelfth hour of the day, there was an earthquake.

29. When Deleanos and Alousianos came together after being vanquished they became suspicious of each other: one of them disgusted with the defeat, the other suspecting that he had been betrayed. So they plotted against each other, watching for the appropriate moment. Alousianos conspired with some of his close associates; he prepared a banquet and invited Deleanos, then blinded him when he was hung-over and intoxicated but without giving the Bulgars the slightest hint of what had taken place. Then he fled to Mosynoupolis[91] in search of the emperor,[92] who sent him to the Orphanotrophos at Byzantium after raising him to the rank of magister. The emperor meanwhile left Mosynoupolis and made his way to Thessalonike. From there he went into Bulgaria,[93] captured Deleanos and sent him to Thessalonike while he himself penetrated deeper into Bulgaria. Manuel Ibatzes had previously built a wooden barricade at Prilapon under the impression that this would impede the advance of the imperial army and prevent it seizing the interior. But once the emperor arrived there, he dismantled the wooden barricade in less time than it takes to tell, dissipated the Bulgar host and captured Ibatzes. After he had put everything in order in Bulgaria and appointed commanders in the themes, he entered the capital bringing with him Deleanos and Ibatzes. But as he was wasting away [415] from the disease which had him in prey and was totally despairing of his life, he accepted monastic tonsure at the hands of the monk Kosmas Tzintziloukios,[94] who was always at his side advising him

---

[89] Kekaumenos gives a completely different account of the battle. He says the reason for the Bulgar reverse was the inexperience of Alousianos, who neither rested his men nor established a camp: *Strategikon*, 160–2.

[90] June 1041.

[91] This town served as a base for operations against the Bulgars in the time of Basil II.

[92] The negotiations between Michael IV and Alousianos are confirmed by Psellos, *Chronographia*, 4. 45–9, trans. Sewter,113–15.

[93] According to Michael Attaleiates, 10, Michael IV passed through Sardica (Sofia) and from there got to Illyricum where he put his adversaries to flight.

[94] This is the first mention of the Tzintziloukioi, a family which provided many important officials, civil and military, from now until 1204. Kosmas the Monk (of whom a seal has survived, Laurent, *Corpus*, v/2, no. 1271, founded a monastery which bore his family name in the diocese of Mosynopoulis; this is attested by a document and by a seal (Laurent, *Corpus*, v, no. 1270). In the reign of Constantine Monomachos Kosmas was given the task of inspecting the monasteries of Mount Athos prior to that emperor establishing a new typikon for the Holy Mountain: Protaton, 8 (1045), ed. D. Papachryssanthou, *Actes du Protaton* (Archives de l'Athos, 7, Paris, 1975), actes nos. 8 and 9.

what he ought to do. He died on 10 December AM 6550, tenth year of the indiction,[95] penitent and confessed, deeply regretting the wrong he had done the emperor Romanos. He had reigned seven years and eight months, a decent and honest man who in everything else other than his offence against the emperor Romanos[96] seemed to have lived a kindly and devout life; and many laid that fault at the door of the Orphanotrophos.

---

[95] 10 December 1041.
[96] Michael IV was buried in the monastery of the Saints Anargyroi (Kosmas and Damian), which he had founded outside the city: P. Grierson, 'The tombs and obits of the Byzantine emperors (337–1042) with an additional note by C. Mango and I. Ševčenko', *DOP*, 16 (1962), 59.

CHAPTER 20

Michael V Kalaphates [1041–1042]

1. [416] After Michael met his end in that way the supreme power passed to the empress Zoe, she being the heir. She addressed herself with youthful vigour to state business in cooperation with her father's eunuchs whom the narrative has frequently touched on above. But she did not remain in the same state of mind. Faced with the enormous responsibility of the empire, she realised she could not adequately administer the public business all alone. She thought it was detrimental for such a dominion to be without ruler and director and judged it necessary to procure an emperor capable of dealing with matters in the various circumstances which might arise. For three whole days she considered this matter, then she received as her adoptive son[1] and proclaimed emperor of the Romans the [late] emperor's nephew and namesake, the son of that Stephen who had ruined the situation in Sicily. [This Michael was already] caesar[2] and seemed to be both a man of action and a capable administrator. She had previously bound him with awesome oaths to hold her as his mistress, his Sovereign Lady and mother for as long as she lived and to do whatever she commanded.[3] She took him as her adopted son and proclaimed him emperor of the Romans, placing the imperial diadem on his brow,[4] but first she got rid of the Orphanotrophos by banishing him to the Monobata monastery.[5]

---

[1] The ceremony took place in the church of the Theotokos at Blachernae: *Ioannis Zonarae epitomae historiarum*, ed. M. Pinder (CSHB, Bonn, 1897), III, 597.

[2] This promotion placed Michael second only to the empress herself, thus paving the way for his accession to the throne.

[3] The oath was taken on the most precious relics including the hand of John the Baptist: Atteleiates, *Historia*, 9.

[4] Psellos confirms that Michael V swore perfect obedience to his adoptive mother: Psellos, *Chronographia*, 5.4, trans. Sewter, 122. Michael was proclaimed 11 December 1041: Schreiner, *Kleinchroniken*, 159, 166, i.e. the morning after the death of his uncle: which indicates that the succession was prearranged and was not dependent on the will of the empress.

[5] According to Psellos and Zonaras, John was absent from Constantinople, together with a number of senators, under the impression that Michael would recall him: Psellos, *Chronographia*, 5.12–13, trans. Sewter, 128–9; *Zonaras*, III, ed. Pinder, 607–8. But Michael banished him. The precise location of the monastery of Monobata is unknown; it was somewhere on the borders – possibly

She also relieved Constantine,[6] the domestic of the scholai, of his command, exiling him to his estate of Apsis in the Opsikion theme[7] [417] and likewise sent off the protovestiarios George to his estate in Paphlagonia.[8] In the very same hour at which he received the diadem Michael was afflicted with vertigo and swimming in the head. He almost fell over; they were only just able to revive him with sweet oils, perfumes and other aromatic substances. The earth was a-tremble throughout the four months of his reign. Meanwhile, after he had been crowned by the patriarch and was established as emperor, he conciliated the Senate with honours and promotions, the people with distributions of bounties. The Sovereign Lady acceded to his request to recall the domestic Constantine from exile; [Michael] honoured him with the title of nobelissimos[9] and retained him at his side. Then, just when he thought he was firmly established, he suddenly fell. It was letters from the Orphanotrophos and the domestic's advice which were his undoing; for they frequently told him not to trust the Sovereign Lady but to be on his guard against her, lest he suffer the same fate as his uncle, the emperor Michael, and of Romanos *his* predecessor, who had been done away with by wizardry[10] (they said). Their advice to him was to get rid of her if possible and to strive to prevent her from getting the better of him. By harping on the same theme they succeeded in persuading him to hatch a plot against her. He decided to sound out the people of the city first, to find out what their opinion of him might be. If there was evidence that they esteemed him and held him in affection, then he would put his plan into action; if not, he would keep quiet. So he proclaimed a public procession to the church of the Holy Apostles for the Sunday after Easter, judging that in this way he could test the climate of public opinion. Together with the Senate he set out in procession wearing the diadem, and the whole city came out to see the spectacle. Those whose homes were on the main artery [*Mese*] hung out gold and silver objects, apparel and other fabrics worked with gold, and they cheered

---

the eastern borders – of the empire. Alexander of Nicaea was sent there: Darrouzès, *Epistoliers*, 69, 744, 88; and so was George Barasvatzé, hegoumenos of Iviron: *Iviron*, I, Introduction, 42.

[6] Psellos says it was Constantine who instigated the measures taken against his brother John, of whom he was very jealous.

[7] Remember that Constantine had received the confiscated wealth of several conspirators in this theme: reign of Michael IV, c. 5.

[8] The accession of Michael V signalled a break with the policy of his uncles Michael IV and John the Orphanotrophos, since he recalled George Maniakes and Constantine Dalassenos from exile: reign of Michael V, c. 5. He also restored the church of the Theotokos to the monks of Iviron (which had been confiscated): *Iviron*, I, Introduction, 47–8.

[9] This dignity ranked immediately below that of caesar: it was rarely granted at that time.

[10] MS U says 'assassination' – which makes more sense.

vigorously enough to pour out their souls had it been possible. The wretched fellow was deceived into thinking that this was because they were well disposed to him. He returned to the Great Palace [418] and instructed the patriarch to go to his monastery in the Stenon and wait for him to come the following day. He even gave him four pounds of gold for the reception he was supposed to be going to accord the emperor. Then, by night, he expelled the empress from the throne and banished her to Prinkipo [island]; her conductors were ordered to tonsure her, bringing her hair back to Michael, and these orders they obeyed. At dawn[11] he wrote a proclamation and gave it to the eparch of the city with instructions to read it out to the citizens in the forum of Constantine the Great. The proclamation stated: 'Because Zoe has shown herself ill-disposed to my rule,[12] she has been banished by me and Alexios her like-minded accomplice has been expelled from the church. As for you, my people, if you maintain your favourable disposition towards me, you will acquire great honours and benefits, living an untroubled and quiet life.' When the eparch had read the proclamation in the hearing of the people, a voice was heard (and it was never discovered who called out): 'We don't want a cross-trampling caulker for emperor, but the original and hereditary [ruler]: our mother Zoe';[13] and the entire people immediately broke out into shouts of: 'Let the bones of the caulker be broken' and, each one picking up stones, pedestals and leftover pieces of wood, they all but killed the eparch. This was the patrician Anastasios who had served Zoe's father; he only just saved his life by taking to his heels. The crowd then went running to the Great Church where the patriarch happened to be (having bribed his way back to the city), denigrating the emperor and demanding the restoration of the empress.[14] All her father's eunuchs now came running together with the patrician Constantine Kabasilas[15] and all the rest of the Senate. By common consent they despatched persons to bring Theodora from Petrion[16] to

---

[11] 20 April 1042.
[12] *Zonaras*, III, ed. Pinder, 609, says that Michael accused the empress of trying to poison him.
[13] Thus the population of the city remained attached to the former legitimate dynasty. On the fall of Michael V: T. Lounghis, 'Chronicle of the fall of Michael V', *Byzantiaka*, 18 (1998), 75–117 (in Greek).
[14] Ibn al-Athír reports that the patriarch Alexios was removed from the city by Michael V who had ordered the Varangians to arrest and execute him. But Alexios was able to bribe those sent to do him violence, get to the Great Church and have the semantron struck to alert the multitude against the emperor: Cheynet, *Pouvoir*, 55. There is one chronicle which says that the rebels forced the patriarch's hand: Schreiner, *Kleinchroniken*, 166.
[15] Probably a relative of the Nikephoros Kabasilas whom Basil II appointed duke of Thessalonike.
[16] It would be easier to bring Theodora out of her prison at Petrion (within Constantinople) than to cross the straits in search of Zoe.

the Great Church where they dressed her in imperial purple and proclaimed her empress [*anassa*] together with Zoe her sister. Then they charged to the palace, in eager haste to drag [419] Michael down from the imperial residence. He, terrified by the rage and uprising of the people, immediately sent and brought Zoe into the palace, stripped off the monastic habit[17] and clothed her with imperial robes. Looking out from the imperial box at the Hippodrome,[18] he attempted to address the people [saying] that he had brought back the empress and that everything was the way they wanted it to be; but they would have none of it. Insults were hurled at him from all sides; stones and arrows shot up from below. In the end he gave up hope and decided to go to be tonsured at Stoudios' monastery, but the domestic would not permit him to do so, saying that he should not so readily abandon the throne and retire. He should put up a brave resistance and either triumph completely or die a great-hearted and imperial death, as befitted an emperor. As this opinion prevailed, he armed everybody in the palace as best he could; the nobelissimos summoned all his own men-at-arms from his private residence (the commander Katakalon Kekaumenos had just arrived from Sicily bringing the news from Messina) and courageously took matters in hand.[19] The rabble was divided into three parts: one advancing by way of the Hippodrome, the other through the barracks of the Exkoubitores, the rest by way of the Tzykanisterion.[20] The emperor's men divided their forces into three and defended themselves vigorously. There was heavy loss of life among the citizens, for they were naked and unarmed except for sticks and stones and whatever material came to hand; yet they were fighting against men-at-arms. They say that on that day, the second Tuesday after Easter, about three thousand men were killed. In the end though it was the citizens who prevailed, overwhelming the emperor's men by sheer weight of numbers.[21]

[17] *Zonaras*, III, ed. Pinder, 611, says that, on the contrary, the sight of Zoe in monastic habit revived the anger of the Byzantines, for she reminded them of the mistreatment of her by Michael V.
[18] The imperial box at the Hippodrome, from which there was direct access to the Great Palace.
[19] The presence of troops from Messina is confirmed by Kekaumenos, 288–90. The author of *Consilia et narrations* had recently returned from Sicily and was in Constantinople while these events were taking place. He expresses his amazement at having been present at the fall of an emperor in the space of one day.
[20] The palace was attacked from three sides: from the Hippodrome to the north, from the Gate of the Exkoubitores to the east and from the Tzikanisterion (polo park) to the south. The struggle was between the partisans of Theodora and those of Michael V, Zoe remaining apparently undecided as yet. At least a portion of the palace was pillaged, for a large quantity of gold and of silk fabric was removed from the *eidikon* and from the mint: Schreiner, *Kleinchroniken*, 166.
[21] As was usually the case in disturbances of this nature, the rioters attacked and pillaged the mansions of the emperor's relatives, making off with the riches which had been accumulated at their expense, or so they said: Attaleiates, *Historia*, ed. Perez Martin, 12.

They forced the palace gates and entered, seizing the gold laid up in the offices and the rest of the things they found. They tore up the tax rolls and then pressed on to apprehend the emperor, [420] but he realised he was beaten and went aboard the imperial yacht together with the nobelissimos and some close associates, leaving Zoe in the palace. He fled to Stoudios' monastery early on the Wednesday and, together with his uncle, was immediately clothed with the monastic habit.

2. The fighting which broke out at the second hour of the second Monday after Easter came to an end during the following (Tuesday) night. When Zoe was once again in control of the empire she was of a mind to eject her sister Theodora[22] but she was thwarted by the crowd demanding that she co-reign with her. So Theodora left the Great Church and came to the palace. When the Senate had been convened Zoe made a speech to that assembly, then she spoke to the crowd from a high and clearly visible position. Naturally she thanked them in appreciation of their support for her, inviting their opinion concerning the emperor and what should become of him. They all cried out with one voice: 'Death to the murderer! Get rid of the criminal! Impale him! Crucify him! Blind him!' She, however, shrank from punishing him, for she was beginning to feel sorry for the miserable wretch. But Theodora, filled with wrath and determination, ordered the newly appointed eparch (it was Kampanares)[23] to go and make sure that he plucked out the emperor's eyes and his uncle's too. Off he went with the entire crowd following and came to Stoudios'. When Michael and his uncle became aware of the presence of the crowd, they fled into the sanctuary of the [monastery] church of [John] the Baptist, but the crowd, burning with anger on account of those who had lost their lives, forced its way into the sacred church, snatched them out of there and dragged them across the forum by the feet. They took them up above the illustrious [Stoudios'] monastery to the place called Sigma[24] and blinded them both.[25] Michael fervently entreated that his uncle [421] be blinded before him because he was the cause and instigator of all the evils that had taken place and that

---

[22] It was Zoe who had relegated her sister to the Petrion: reign of Romanos III, c. 9.
[23] The evidence of two minor chronicles gives his first name, Nikephoros: Schreiner, *Kleinchroniken*, 142 and 159. This man had received the prediction of St Lazaros of Galesion that troubles would break out at Constantinople: *Life of Lazaros the Galesiote, BHG* 979, *AASS* Nov. III, 539.
[24] So called on account of its shape: C. Mango, *Le développement urbain de Constantinople, IVe–VIIe siècles* (Paris, 1990), 50.
[25] 21 April 1042, a Tuesday. The decision to blind both men arose from a suspicion that Zoe might change her mind and re-establish Michael V on the throne: Psellos, *Chronographia* 5.48–50, trans. Sewter, 150–1.

is what happened. Blinded, they were banished, Michael to the Elegmoi monastery[26] on 21 April, tenth year of the indiction, AM 6550; he had reigned four months and five days; his relatives scattered in different directions.

[26] In Bithynia.

CHAPTER 21

Constantine IX Monomachos [1042–1055]

1. [422] The wheel of fortune having decreed that Zoe should once again rule the empire, she reluctantly allowed her own sister, Theodora, to reign with her,[1] as we said. The Senate was rewarded with promotions to honours, the people with the distribution of gifts. The administration found itself conducted with befitting foresight; letters and directives were sent out in all directions promising that offices would not be for sale and could no longer be purchased the way they used to be; also stipulating that any wrongdoing was to be cast out from among them. When these regulations had come into effect to the rulers' satisfaction, the nobelissimos Constantine was recalled from exile and questioned concerning public monies. Terrified by what he was threatened with, he showed the fifty-three *kentenaria* of gold[2] hidden in a cistern at his house near Holy Apostles' church. The sum was delivered to the empress while he returned into exile. She appointed her father's eunuch, Nicholas the proedros, domestic of the scholai for the east; the patrician Constantine Kabasilas[3] duke of the west. She sent off George Maniakes, already released from prison by Michael, to be commander plenipotentiary of the army units in Italy with the rank of magister. This is how it went; then a conference was held concerning the [office of] emperor and the unanimous opinion was that an emperor ought to be appointed and married to Zoe. Her inclination was to marry the *katepan* Constantine Artoklines, so called from the position in which he had served.[4] He was a man of pleasing appearance, said

---

[1] The two empresses reigned together, without husbands, from 21 April to 11 June 1042: Schreiner, *Kleinchroniken*, no. 15, ch. 11, 159 and no. 16, ch. 13, 160. There is numismatic evidence of this brief cohabitation on which the empresses, decked in imperial regalia, are portrayed as equals: Grierson, *DOC*, III, 731–2.

[2] 381,600 pieces of gold (nomismata), almost 1.75 tonnes of gold, which would certainly have sufficed for most of the largesse accorded to the Constantinopolitans.

[3] This was his reward for playing an active part in the overthrow of Michael V.

[4] The task of the *artoklines* was to draw up the order of precedence at court and to ensure that it was followed. According to Michael Psellos, *Chronographia*, 6.15, trans. Sewter, 162, this man was

to have been Zoe's secret lover, [423] but his wife expelled him from this life with poison,[5] not because she did not love him any more, but because she was about to be deprived of him even while he was alive. Anyway, the empress, frustrated in her plan, recalled Constantine Monomachos[6] from exile. He had been condemned to live on the island of Mytilene by the Orphanotrophos because everybody said he was going to rule the empire.[7] When she was intending to elevate the other Constantine to the imperial throne, she appointed this one judge of the theme of Hellas,[8] and when the former Constantine [Artoklines] succumbed to poison (as we related) the said Monomachos, namesake of the departed, seemed to be a likely candidate to the empress.[9] He was brought to the church of the Commanding Archangel at Damokraneia, the one which lies nearest to Athyra,[10] and Stephen of Pergamon, one of the empress' eunuchs of the bedchamber, was sent to divest him of his private citizen's garb and clothe him in imperial purple. Then he took Monomachos aboard a vessel and brought him to the palace. The empress was united to him in the bonds of marriage when he arrived;[11] the office was celebrated by the first priest of the New Church[12] who was called Stypes and it was 11 June, AM 6550.[13] Next day Constantine was crowned by the patriarch.

2. Once he had grasped the sceptre, he advanced all the senators in rank according to each man's worth and conciliated the people with the distributions of gold. He sent out proclamations to all the themes reporting that he had been acclaimed, promising a generous affluence of every good thing

a former secretary to Romanos III. It is unlikely that he had ever had a military career; he was probably *katepan* ('officer in charge') of ranks and dignities.

[5] Psellos, *Chronographia*, 6.14, trans Sewter, 161, says he was carried off by a sudden illness.

[6] Constantine is said to have been a scion of the ancient house of the Monomachoi (Psellos) and a member of the aristocracy (Attaleiates). The first known Monomachos was Niketas who served under Eirene as commander of Sicily: D. Papachryssanthou, 'Un confesseur du second iconoclasme: la Vie du patrice Nicetas (*ob.* 836)', *TM*, 3 (1968), 310–51. Subsequently the family history can be traced as it provided the state with servants on a more or less regular basis; see Paul Monomachos, who was sent as ambassador to Baghdad under Constantine VII (c. 9).

[7] Constantine's father, Theodosios, 'judge supreme' of the empire (*Aristakes de Lastivert*, 42), was compromised in a conspiracy against Basil II: Psellos, *Chronographia*, 6.14, trans. Sewter, 161.

[8] The status of Constantine prior to his promotion is only known from two seals which indicate that he had made his career in the civil service.

[9] Because he had taken as his second wife the daughter of Pulcheria Argyropoulina and Basil Skleros, Constantine became the nephew by marriage of the emperor Romanos III, thus permitting his family to re-enter the highest levels of society: Psellos, *Chronographia*, 6.15, trans. Sewter, 162.

[10] Athyra, Buyuk-cekmece today, is on the European coast of the Propontis, halfway between Selymbria and the capital.

[11] This was the third marriage for both bride and groom but apparently no grave objections were raised to this infraction of the Law of Leo VI: Laiou, 'Marriages', 165–76, 173.

[12] A palace church founded by Basil I: reign of Basil I, c. 41.

[13] 11 June 1042.

and the suppression of all evil.[14] He transferred John the Orphanotrophos with everything he possessed from the Monobata monastery to the island of Lesbos, Michael the previous emperor to Chios, and Constantine the nobelissimos to Samos. Those were the first deeds of Monomachos [424] in the tenth year of the indiction. On the eleventh of October, eleventh year of the indiction, AM 6551,[15] a comet appeared travelling from east to west and it was seen shining during the whole month; it presaged the forthcoming universal disasters. Indeed, Stephen-Boisthlav[16] (as stated above) had fled from Byzantium and established himself in the Illyrian mountains. He was now overrunning and despoiling the Triballes (the Serbs)[17] and the neighbouring peoples who were Roman subjects. Refusing to tolerate these raids, Monomachos issued a letter instructing the then commander of Dyrrachion, the patrician Michael, the son of Anastasios the logothete,[18] to assemble the army of Dyrrachion under his command, likewise the armies of the adjacent themes which were subordinate to him, and to proceed together with the subaltern commanders into the country of the Triballes there to confront Stephen. But Michael, like a man raised in the shade and nourished with affection, was a long way from having any notion of military science. He undertook the operation devoid of aptitude or ability and became the cause of great misfortune to the Roman state. He assembled the forces according to orders (they say there were about sixty thousand men) and entered the Triballes' country travelling by paths that were steep, rough, precipitous and so narrow that two horsemen could not advance abreast. The Serbs (they say) quite deliberately permitted them free passage, yet the commander never gave a thought to the return journey or posted an adequate guard at the passes. While he entered the interior, pillaging and setting fire to the plains, the Serbs seized and manned the narrow and precipitous passes of the track and waited for his return. When Michael thought he had done enough pillaging (for now he was encumbered with a great deal of booty and many prisoners) it seemed to be time to go back. But while [his men were] winding their way

---

[14] *Aristakes de Lastivert*, 42, gives a short extract from this proclamation; it confirms the words that Skylitzes puts in the mouth of the new emperor. *Aristakes de Lastivert, Récit des malheurs de la nation arménienne*, French translation and commentary by M. Canard and H. Berbian following the edition and Russian translation of K. Yuzbashian (Bibliotèque de *Byzantion*, 5 Brussels, 1973).

[15] 6 October 1042.

[16] As ruler of Diokleia he was the next-door neighbour of the theme of Dyrrachion.

[17] Triballes appears to be an older term for Serbs.

[18] It is not known whether this is the same Anastasios as the eparch of the same name who confronted the people of Constantinople when the exile of Zoe was announced; he appears to have had a great reputation. A seal testifies that he was magister and logothete of the drome: Laurent, *Corpus* II, no. 342. His son Michael came from the administrative chambers of the capital, hence his inexperience.

through the narrow defiles the enemy decimated them by bombarding them from above with stones and arrows [425] and all kinds of missile-hurling machines, also by rolling down huge rocks. Michael's men could use neither their hands nor their weapons, nor could they perform any acts of bravery. Some fell where they were struck; others leapt from the crags and perished miserably so that the subjacent gorges and ravines were filled up with corpses and served as pathways for the pursuers. About fourteen thousand men fell and seven commanders were killed. The remainder hid themselves in the bush, the forests and the hollows of the mountain and escaped detection by the enemy then, scaling the heights, found refuge by night. On foot and unarmed, they presented a pitiful, forlorn and truly lamentable sight to the beholder. Michael also got away to safety with them, sharing the same experiences.[19]

3. As it was stated in the foregoing narrative, the magister George Maniakes was sent to Italy by the empress Zoe to stabilise the situation there;[20] for everything was in a sickly state and the land had suffered badly from the inexperience and incompetence of its commanders. George was now contemplating insurrection and it is well worth rehearsing the reasons why, in order to supply those who encounter this book with accurate information. When he was first sent into Italy by the emperor Michael it was to sustain the ruler of Sicily, Apolaphar Mouchoumet, against whom his own brother and the Africans [Zirids] were fighting. George was joined by five hundred Franks summoned from transalpine Gaul and led by a man named Ardouin, a ruler who acknowledged no suzerain. It was together with these that he gained his victories over the Saracens. Then George was falsely accused, relieved of his command, brought to the city and flung into prison while the [426] protospatharios Michael Dokeianos[21] was sent to govern Italy in his stead, an inept man, not at all gifted for administering public affairs. He wasted no time in reducing everything to confusion

---

[19] According to the report of this campaign by Kekaumenos, *Strategikon*, 168, the ruler of Serbia was named Tribounos. (Kekaumenos, *Sovety i rasskazy kekavmena (Cecaumeni consilia et narrationes)* ed. G. G. Litavrin (Moscow, 1972), Michael had mobilised the zoupans (who were allies of the empire) to form his army; Boisthlav blasted the hopes of Michael and his officers by carrying the day in spite of his much smaller number of men. After his victory Boislav annexed the territory bordering on Zachlumia, but he died some time after 1043, leaving his sons to fight over his inheritance: Stephenson, *Balkan frontier*, 134–5.
[20] Maniakes landed at Otranto in April 1042 and remained shut up in the town while the Normans ravaged the region of Oria: *Annales Barenses, Monumenta Germaniae Historica. Scriptores*, v, 52–6, 54.
[21] The family name suggests that this man came from Dokeia (Tokat today) in Paphlagonia. The ineptitude of the protospatharios and *katepan* Michael Dokeianos was not apparently held against him, for he went on to have an illustrious career under Constantine Monomachos, see below, c. 22.

and disaster. He failed to provide the Franks with their monthly allowance on time and there was worse to come, according to what they say. When their leader arrived to ask him to use the soldiers kindly and not to deprive them of the reward for their labours, he reviled him and administered a humiliating flogging, which provoked the [Franks] to mutiny.[22] When they were up in arms, Michael was reluctant to assemble the entire Roman forces and do battle with Franks. He took one unit (the Opsikion) and part of the Thracesian and joined battle with them at Cannae near the river Amphidos, the very place where in ancient times Hannibal cut down many myriads of Romans. Michael was defeated and lost the better part of his army, he shamefully taking refuge in Cannae.[23] Crippled like this he was none the wiser for his wound, unlike the fisherman in the proverb,[24] nor did he first strengthen his hand with the whole army and then attack the enemy but, governed it seems by reckless imprudence, took back into battle his defeated forces together with the Pisidians and Lycaonians who make up the unit of the foederati and fell on the enemy at a place called Horai. Again he was severely defeated by the Franks who had now allied with themselves a considerable host of Italians living around the river Po and in the foothills of the Alps.[25] The emperor Michael [IV] relieved the man of his command when he heard of this and sent out Boioannes who seemed to be a dynamic man, well tried in action, a descendant of that Boioannes who was sent to Italy by the emperor Basil, the one who brought the whole of Italy as far as Rome into subjection to the emperor.[26] He went there but did not receive fresh and flourishing troops; he was obliged to counter the enemy with men who had already been defeated, an enemy firmly entrenched in [427] Monopolis and holding the land as firmly as if it were his own. Boioannes was defeated and captured,[27] likewise the army

---

[22] According to the Italian sources, Ardouin revolted against Maniakes over a dispute concerning booty taken from the Moslems. He nevertheless remained in imperial service, for he was subsequently appointed *topoteretes* (garrison commander) at Melfi, probably by Michael Dokeianos after his arrival in Italy, November 1040. Ardouin then rebelled at Melfi in November 1040 and let in the Normans, thus initiating a period of great perturbation for the imperial possessions in Italy: G. A. Loud, *The age of Robert Guiscard: southern Italy and the Norman conquest* (London, 2000), 78–80.

[23] The Italian sources confirm this, saying that many Russians and some soldiers from the Opsikion theme were killed: *Annales Barenses*, v, 54. This first confrontation took place near Melfi on 17 March 1041, just after the rebellion of Ardouin: Loud, *Guiscard*, 92–3.

[24] 'Once stung, the fisherman will be wiser' – *piscator ictus sapiet*: Erasmus, *Adagia*, 1.1.29.

[25] At this second battle which took place at Cannae on 4 May 1041, 2,000 Normans and Lombards carried the day against 18,000 'Greeks' (obviously exaggerated): *Annales Barenses*, v, 54–5.

[26] This is Basil Boïammès, *katepan* of Italy from 1017 to 1025: Falkenhausen, *Dominazione* 105 and 185–7.

[27] The battle of Montepoloso (September 1041) opened up the road to the coast for the rebels.

with him. Those who escaped being put in irons scattered in all directions, [some] finding refuge in fortresses still loyal to the Romans. So the Franks took possession of Italy by right of conquest and the people of the land transferred their allegiance to them, some willingly, some by coercion and force, except for Brindisi, Hidrous, Tarento and Bari. Those four cities kept faith with the Romans. After the emperor Michael died and his successor was ejected from the throne, Maniakes was sent to Italy by Zoe (as it says above) and even though he did not have adequate forces, even with what he had he was able by the use of devices and strategems to chase away the Franks of Italy from around Capua, Benevento and Naples and introduce a measure of order and calm to the state of things.[28] Now this man Maniakes possessed estates in the Anatolikon theme. There he was the neighbour of Romanos Skleros,[29] of whom he fell foul. Skleros tried on many occasions to kill him but he got himself to safety by running away. But when the Roman sceptre passed to Constantine Monomachos, the fortunes of Skleros rose steeply because his sister was the emperor's mistress.[30] He was honoured with the titles of magister and protostrator, and when he recalled George's attempts on his life, asserting his authority and profiting from the absence of Maniakes, he pillaged and destroyed the villages which belonged to him and desecrated his marriage bed. When, in Italy, Maniakes learnt of this he was very angry, burning with rage; then when, at Romanos' instigation, he was relieved of his command, he despaired of everything. He knew very well that his arrival in Byzantium would serve no useful purpose so he stirred up the troops in Italy, alienating their affections (the soldiers were thirsting to see their homeland again), [428] and took up arms against the emperor. He slew the man sent out to succeed him, the protospatharios Pardos,[31] a citizen of Byzantium, despatched to govern such a country for no other good reason than that he was well known to the emperor. Maniakes placed the diadem on his own brow,

---

[28] Our author is using a source favourable to Maniakes who, since he could not count on a network of associates similar to that on which his highly aristocratic colleagues could draw, also won the sympathy of Psellos. He speaks warmly of the military skills of the general whereas the Italian sources emphasise his cruelty and the violence of his character.

[29] Not the son of the famous rebel Bardas Skleros, mentioned above in the reign of Basil II and Constantine VIII, but one of his great grandsons: Seibt, *Skleroi*, 76–7.

[30] Maria Skleraina was also a first cousin of the second wife of Monomachos: Seibt, *Skleroi*, 71–6.

[31] Pardos, whom Psellos says 'came off the street' (Psellos, *Chronographia*, 6.80, trans. Sewter, 194), was killed in October 1042. It is a name frequently encountered in the theme of Hellas and in the Peloponnese, e.g. *Les Récits édifiants de Paul, évêque de Monembasie*, ed. J. Wortley (Paris, 1987), 36. A Peter Pardos, protospatharios and exkoubitor of Longobardia, is known from a seal: V. Laurent, 'Contributions à la prosopographie du thème de Longobardie', *Byzantino-Sicula*, 2 (Palermo, 1975), 317. The Chronicles of Bari mention the death of Pardos in 990; he may have been chosen on account of his knowledge of the Italian situation.

assumed the imperial insignia and was proclaimed emperor. He embarked his troops and passed over into Bulgaria.[32] When the emperor learnt of this he was far more troubled than one might imagine. He sent Maniakes a letter telling him and those with him not to be afraid, exhorting him to lay down his arms and promising him a totally benign reception, but Maniakes was not to be diverted from his goal. The emperor therefore assembled what forces were available, appointed as commander plenipotentiary[33] the sebastophoros Stephen (the man who had brought the news of his elevation to emperor to Monomachos at Damokraneia) and sent him against the apostate. The expeditions encountered each other at the place called Ostrovos[34] in the Marmarion; there was an engagement in which Stephen's troops were defeated with Maniakes himself leading the charge, cutting through their ranks, and they too acclaimed him emperor. But even as this was happening, he fell from his horse and died – with no visible sign of any wound; he was [later] found to have a mortal wound in the chest. When this became known to the opposing army, they cut off George's head and all those who had been party to his uprising were taken prisoner, for they threw down their arms and gave themselves up when their chieftain fell. A messenger was sent to the emperor with the news of the victory and some days later Stephen arrived bringing the head of Maniakes and the prisoners of war. He processed in triumph down the main artery [*Mese*], the head going first on top of a lance, then the rebels mounted on asses while he followed after riding a white horse. Such was the end of the Maniakes affair.[35]

4. [429] At that time there was another uprising in Cyprus of which the instigator was Theophilos Erotikos,[36] commander of the island, one with a constant passion for revolutions. When he heard that [Michael IV] Kalaphates had been overturned and the state thrown into confusion, he thought the time was ripe for what he had in mind. He whipped up all the

---

[32] Maniakes was followed by the best Roman units, some Albanian soldiers: (*Miguel Ataliates, Historia*, ed. I. Perez Martin (Madrid, 2002), 15) and above all, some Latin troops: Psellos, 'Eloge de Monomaque', Βιβλιοθήκη ἢ Συλλογὴ Ἀνεκδότων Μνημείων τῆς Ἑλληνικῆς Ἱστορίας, ed. K. N. Sathas (Venice, 1876), *MB* V, 138–9. He disembarked at Dyrrachion in February 1043, thrusting aside the first army he encountered, under the command of the duke of the west: Psellos, 'Eloge de Monomaque', ed. Sathas.

[33] This office (usually held by a eunuch) was created between 963 and 975 and carried with it the right to display the imperial banner: Oikonomides, *Listes*, 308. By the eleventh century it appears to have become simply a dignity.

[34] Ostrovo (Armissa today) was on the Via Egnatia, between Ochrid and Thessalonike.

[35] The Latin contingent was incorporated into the imperial army and so remained at least into the reign of Alexios Komnenos: *Alexiad*, 2:117.

[36] A relative of the Komnenoi: reign of Michael IV, c. 21.

people of Cyprus, inciting them to kill the magistrate and tax collector, the protospatharios Theophylact, whom he accused of making very heavy demands. But Monomachos did not have to fear him for long because the patrician Constantine Chage, admiral of the fleet,[37] was sent out. He arrested him, pacified all the Cypriots and brought him to the emperor. When he arrived the emperor dressed him in woman's clothing, paraded him in the Hippodrome on a race day, confiscated his goods and then released him.

5. On the twentieth of February, eleventh year of the indiction, the patriarch Alexios departed this life and Michael Keroularios was installed on his throne on the Feast of the Annunciation;[38] he had been a monk ever since the Orphanotrophos exiled him for conspiracy. It was reported to the emperor that there was gold stored up in Alexios' monastery;[39] he sent and seized it, to the sum of twenty-five *kentenaria*. On the second of May, the same year of the indiction, the Orphanotrophos was blinded in the village called Marykatoi,[40] some say on Theodora's orders and against the emperor's wishes. Most people, however, believe the report that it was on the orders of the emperor who carried a grudge against him for the periods of exile he had endured. The man died on the thirteenth of the same month, the same year of the indiction. In [430] the sebastophoros Stephen was denounced for plotting against the emperor with the intention of raising to the throne the patrician Leo, commander of Mytilene, the son of Lampros. Stephen was stripped of his property, tonsured a monk and sent into exile. Lampros was cruelly tortured, blinded and paraded through the forum; he died shortly after.

6. In the month of July, the same year of the indiction, the Russians attacked the capital.[41] Until then they had been allies of the Romans and at peace with them. [The two peoples] had mingled with each other without fear and sent merchants to each other.[42] But at this time a dispute arose with some Scyth merchants at Byzantium; the matter escalated

[37] This man was commander of the maritime Kibyrrhaiote theme under Michael IV, now promoted to command the entire fleet.
[38] 25 March 1043. On Keroularios: F. Tinnefeld, 'Michael I. Keroularios, patriarch von Konstantinopel (1043–58)', *JÖB*, 39 (1989), 96–124.
[39] This monastery formed part of the patriarchal palace: Janin, *Églises et monastères*, 18–19.
[40] If this is the same village as *ta tou Marykatou* mentioned in the *Life of St Paul the Younger*: *AnalBoll*, 11 (1892), 21 it was situated in Phrygia.
[41] Some historians think that the Russian attack was coordinated with the offensive of Maniakes but there is no source which gives credence to this theory: A. Poppe, 'La dernière expédition russe contre Constantinople', *BS*, 32 (1971), 1–29; and J. Shepard, 'Why did the Russians attack Byzantium in 1043?', *Byzantinische-neugriechische Jahrbücher*, 22 (1979), 147–212.
[42] This as a result of the treaty of 972 between John Tzimiskes and Sviatoslav.

out of hand and an illustrious Scyth was killed. Vladimir, an impulsive man who often gave free rein to his wrath, was at that time ruler of [the Russian] race.[43] When he heard what had happened, he exploded in anger. Without the slightest delay he raised up all the fighting force under his command and took as allies a considerable number of the people inhabiting the islands to the north of the ocean.[44] They say he assembled a host of around one hundred thousand men,[45] put them aboard the ships the local people call drakhars[46] and set out against the city. When the emperor learnt of this he sent an embassy asking [Vladimir] to lay down his arms and promising reparations for anything untoward which had taken place; also requesting him not for a little matter to break the peace which had been so long established nor to inflame the peoples against each other. When he received the letter he chased the ambassadors away ignominiously, returning an answer at once haughty and disdainful, whereupon the emperor gave up any hope for peace and himself made the best preparations he could. The Scythian merchants dwelling at the capital and those who were present under treaty arrangements he dispersed into the themes, and he put a guard over them to prevent them [431] striking a blow from within as the occasion might allow and the nature of the situation facilitate. He made ready the imperial war ships and plenty of other well-equipped and light vessels, manning them with the soldiers who chanced to be in Byzantium at the time. The emperor himself went aboard the imperial yacht,[47] sailed out and confronted the Scyths who were moored in the mouth of the Black Sea at the place called Pharos. He had a considerable detachment of cavalry following by land. Although the two naval forces stood face to face, neither went into action. The Scyths remained inactive in the harbour where they were moored, the emperor waiting for them to make a move. As the day was slipping by and it was towards the evening hour, the emperor again sent a peace delegation and again the barbarian sent them back ignominiously. The emperor was told that if he wanted them to lay down their arms he would have to give three pounds of gold to each soldier in the army that was following Vladimir. As this reply

---

[43] It was Vladimir's son, Iaroslav, who was then reigning at Kiev, 1036–54: Franklin and Shepard, *Rus*, 186–93.
[44] According to Psellos the Russians no longer regarded the empire as a serious power but as a fine prize, ripe for the picking: Psellos, *Chronographia*, 6.91–5, trans. Sewter, 199–203.
[45] Obviously an exaggeration; the boats – of which Attaleiates, *Historia*, ed. Perez Martin, 16, says there were four hundred – were of small capacity.
[46] *Monoxyloi*, Viking longboats.
[47] Psellos, an eye witness of the engagement, says he observed it from a hill some distance away: Psellos, *Chronographia*, 6.33, trans Sewter, 172.

appeared to be outrageous, the emperor realised he would have to act. As the enemy was still not moving he summoned Basil Theodorakanos, ordering him to take three swift vessels and test the mettle of the Scyths, to see whether they could be provoked to battle by skirmishing. He took the ships and approached the Scyths; he did not, however, taunt them with skirmishing but himself sailed right into the midst of them, burned seven vessels with Greek fire and sunk three more of them, together with their crews. He captured one ship by boarding it himself, slaying some of the people within and routing others who were dumbfounded at his daring.[48] The Scyths now sighted the emperor approaching with the entire fleet. They asked themselves (not surprisingly): if they had suffered such losses resisting only three hostile ships, what would they suffer if they were obliged to join battle with the entire fleet? They decided to beat a retreat but, in retreating, [432] they sailed into waters where there were reefs and submerged rocks, on which most of their vessels foundered. Whereupon [their people were] attacked and destroyed by the soldiers following on dry land; subsequently, about fifteen thousand corpses were found lying on the beach. The emperor remained two whole days after the defeat of the Scyths then returned to the capital on the third day, leaving behind two units as well as the [troops] called Hetaireiai, under the command of Nicholas the parakoimomenos and of the magister Basil Theodorokanos. Their orders were to keep a watch on the shores, to patrol and guard them, thus averting any invasion by barbarians; he commanded the entire fleet to remain at Pharos.

Having made these arrangements, the emperor returned to Byzantium [Constantinople]. As the men with the parakoimomemos and Theodorokanos patrolled the shore where, after the disaster, the corpses of barbarians had been washed up, they laid their hands on a great deal of booty and much equipment, stripped from the vanquished. A detachment of twenty-four ships followed the fleeing barbarians but, in their pursuit, sailed right past them, for they were moored in an inlet. The Scyths now knew how few their pursuers were; certain that there were no more of them than those which had appeared, they made an outflanking movement by sailing out from the two headlands [of the inlet] and, by determined rowing, they succeeded in surrounding their enemy. The Romans were both weary from the rowing they had already done in pursuit and frightened by the multitude of barbarian vessels, so they backed water, intending to

---

[48] Basil had fought with Maniakes in Sicily under Michael IV. Attaleiates, *Historia*, 17, also gives high praise to his military capabilities.

flee. But since the barbarian ships had made a circle and closed it, there was no egress from the inlet to the high sea. The patrician Constantine Kaballourios,[49] commander of the Kibyrrhaiote theme,[50] nobly volunteered to do battle using his own ship and ten others. He was cut down fighting courageously; four ships (including the flagship) were captured with their crews and everybody in them slain. The remaining Roman vessels ran into shallows, headlands and reefs which they fouled; some [433] went down to the bottom of the sea, others were captured by the barbarians and [their crews] put to the sword or enslaved. The survivors found refuge, on foot and unarmed, in their own encampment.[51]

Disappointed in their hopes, the Scyths turned their thoughts to the homeward journey. They returned by land as well as by sea, because there were not enough ships for everybody, some having been sunk or captured in the foregoing sea battles, others lost in storm and tempest: that is why most of the [Scyths] were going home on foot. But the vestes, Katakalon Kekaumenos, governor of the Danubian cities and lands, intercepted them near the island called Varna;[52] he attacked and defeated them,[53] killing many and capturing eight hundred alive, whom he sent to the emperor in chains. When the Scyths first came out of their own lands and made for the capital it was in the territory which this man governed that they disembarked and went foraging. He assembled the troops under his command and attacked them. He fought nobly and thoroughly defeated them, compelling them to flee to their ships. Then he kept a careful watch on the regions under his command which were adjacent to the river in anticipation of the end of the affair. He was there to receive them with firm resistance when they returned, and then accomplished what was reported above.

7. In the month of September, twelfth year of the indiction, AM 6552 a wind blew so violently that almost the entire fruit of the vine was destroyed.

---

[49] Another Constantine Kaballourios (the grandson of the commander?) founded a monastery at Strobelos and Constantine possessed lands in the area, on the islands of Kos and Leros. Thus the Kaballourioi were important landowners in the Kibyrrhaiote theme: *Patmos*, 1, no. 4, lines 39, 51.

[50] Monomachos appears to have been warned of the Russian attack soon enough to be able to summon the main provincial fleet to Constantinople.

[51] Skylitzes is our only informant for this event.

[52] Ever since the tenth century this had been a traditional stage on the route the Russians took towards Constantinople, but the town actually belonged to the Bulgars: *DAI*, ed. Moravcsik and Jenkins, 62, line 100.

[53] This means that Kekaumenos (of whose heroic actions this is the second mention here) was duke and *katepan* of Paristrion.

{The patriarch Michael struck the pope of Rome from the diptychs[54] as soon as he was appointed for raising the question of the unleavened bread.[55] Peter, Patriarch of Antioch,[56] and Leo, archbishop of Bulgaria,[57] [434] and all the better-educated churchmen supported him. He had an altercation with Michael Mermentoulos[58] who was then hegoumenos of Stoudios' monastery and he excised St Theodore the Stoudite from the synodikon which is read in church. Mermentoulos could not suffer this; he went to the emperor and told him about it and, at the emperor's command, the synodikon was read on the Sunday of the Samaritan woman.[59] Everything else was read as usual but the patriarch stood up and himself spoke the name of the great Theodore in a loud and clear voice. In this way the uprising of Mermentoulos and the monks on this score was put to rest.}[60]

This year when they were celebrating the feast of the holy Forty Martyrs on 9 March, just as the emperor was about to go in public procession to venerate the [forty] Saints there was a disturbance among the people. The emperor left the palace on foot, well guarded and accompanied by cheering; he had arrived at the church of the Saviour at the Chalke from where he was going to proceed on horseback to the Martyrs' shrine when a voice broke out in the crowd: 'We don't want Skleraina for empress and we don't want our mothers, the porphyrogennetoi Zoe and Theodora, put to death on her account.'[61] Suddenly everything was confusion; the crowd was in

[54] This alleged removal of the name of the pope from the diptychs is questionable. If it is true, the pope in question would be Benedict IX (1032–44). In fact it was probably many years since the pope was last commemorated: ever since Basil II failed in his attempt to have the patriarch recognised as *oecumenical*, which created tension between the two Christian capitals.
[55] i.e. the bread at the eucharist, of which the Latins and the Armenians used the unleavened variety, the Greeks leavened.
[56] Peter, who hailed from Antioch, was first the judge of a theme then Sacristan (*skeuophylax*) at Hagia Sophia. Michael Kerularios consecrated him patriarch of Antioch in spring, 1052: V. Grumel, *DTC*, 12 (1807–12); K.-P. Todt, 'Region und griechisch-orthodoxes Patriarchat von Antiocheia in mittelbyzantinischer Zeit und im Zeitalter der Kreuzzüge (969–1204)', thesis (Wiesbaden, 1998), 668–93.
[57] A former archivist (*chartophylax*) of Hagia Sophia, Leo became archbishop of Bulgaria in 1025. Together with Peter of Antioch he was very active in discussions with the Latins, especially on the question of the primacy of Rome: *ODB*, II, 1215. Skylitzes' note on Kerularios and the Latins is not in its correct chronological place for reference is made to events which occurred after the revolt of Tornikios.
[58] This personage is otherwise unknown, but there are seals of officials with the same surname, e.g. Nicholas who was droungarios of the watch under Alexios Komnenos: Laurent, *Corpus*, II, nos. 894 and 1042.
[59] The fourth Sunday after Easter.
[60] Interpolation of MSS ACE
[61] This disturbance of 9 March 1044 is a repetition of the one which brought down Michael V, except that in this case Constantine was saved by the empresses, Zoe apparently not resenting the presence of Skleraina. The citizens were uneasy about the fact that, with the title of *sebaste*,

tumult, trying to get its hands on the emperor, and if the empresses had not promptly shown themselves from a place high up and calmed the crowd many would have perished, possibly including the emperor himself. When the disturbance had quieted down he returned to the palace, abandoning the visit to the [Forty] Martyrs.

{There was plenty of complaining by the people, the Senate and by the sisters, the Sovereign Ladies, about the daughter of Skleros being the emperor's mistress. A particularly eminent monk of that time whose name was Stethatos[62] reproved him but achieved nothing for the emperor was completely under the spell of her beauty. This Stethatos was engaged in attaining the highest degree of virtue, moulding his body with fasting, austerity and every other discipline so that sometimes he went for forty days without food, tasting nothing whatsoever during that period.}[63]

8. [435] In the thirteenth year of the indiction war broke out in the principality of Ani;[64] but first we should tell why and how it came about that the emperor Constantine declared war on the ruler[65] of Ani, who was living in peace and had done nothing untoward. When George, the chieftain of the Iberians, raised arms against the Romans, Iovanesikes, ruler of the country of Ani, fought alongside him. Then when (as we said above) the emperor Basil went into Iberia and fought against George in battle order, defeating and overthrowing him, Iovanesikes was afraid that the emperor, enraged by his alliance with George, would do him some severe damage. So he took the keys of the city, deserted to the emperor, surrendered himself voluntarily into his hands and gave him the keys. The emperor accepted him for his sagacity, honoured him with the title of magister and appointed him ruler for life of Ani and of the so-called Great Armenia. In return he demanded (and got) a written guarantee that, after his death, all this dominion would pass under the emperor's sway and become a part of the Roman empire.[66] These things happened; the emperor died and,

---

Skleraina was addressed in public as *despoina*, a form of address reserved for empresses: Zonaras III, 620.

[62] Niketas Stethatos, disciple and biographer of Symeon the New Theologian, was a monk and eventually the hegoumenos of Stoudios. He appears to have exercised a degree of moral authority; he was party to the discussion with the delegates of the papacy in 1054. Several members of the same family are known in the eleventh and twelfth centuries, notably Nicholas, drungarios of the watch then eparch in the time of Alexis Komnenos: Wassiliou-Seibt, *Bleisiegel*, II, no. 12.

[63] Interpolation of MSS ACEU.

[64] Ani was the capital of the Armenian Bagratids.

[65] The affairs of Armenia were of not great concern at Constantinople since neither Attaleiates nor Psellos mentions them.

[66] According to *Aristakes de Lastivert*, 45–6, Constantine VIII, on his deathbed, delivered this document to an Armenian who wished to betray his country. He retained it only to sell it dearly to Michael IV.

in due course, Iovanesikes died too.[67] After his death, his son Kakikios [Gagic] succeeded to the principality,[68] living in peaceful alliance with the Romans; except that he retained his father's lands and would not surrender them to the Romans, as his father's letter required.

When Monomachos found the letter in the palace, he demanded (as Basil's heir) the submission of Ani and the whole of Great Armenia. As Kakikios was willing to confess himself a Roman subject but *not* to renounce his father's lands, the emperor thought war should be declared on him.[69] He raised an army and entrusted it to the vestes Michael Iassites [436] who had already been proclaimed governor of Iberia; he was now looking for the chance to do battle with Kakikios.[70] He set out and did his very best to accomplish what he had been commissioned to do. When Kakikios became aware of this and realised that he was no longer regarded as a friend and ally, but as a foe, he also assembled his forces and resisted the invaders to the best of his ability. When things took a turn for the worse for Iassites, they sent out the proedros Nicholas, domestic of the scholai and parakoimomenos to the emperor Constantine [VIII], with a powerful army, to oppose Kakikios with superior numbers and strength. A letter from the emperor was sent to Aplesphares, ruler of Tivion[71] and that part of Persarmenia[72] on the river Araxes, asking him to do everything in his power to ravage Great Armenia and the land ruled by Kakikios.[73] Nicholas came and addressed the task in hand. He sent the letter to Aplesphares, adding a personal letter inciting him with gifts and promises

---

[67] John/Sembat and his brother, Asot who governed Armenia, both died in 1041. At least there is an inscription which attests that Gagic was reigning before 10 March 1042: Shepard, 'Scylitzes on Armenia', 269–311, at 286.

[68] Gagic II was in fact the son of Asot; he was nineteen years old at his accession.

[69] The Armenian nobility was divided into two opposing factions: there were those opposed to annexation, led by the great family of the Pahlawuni (who had put Gagic on the throne), and there was a pro-Byzantine party led by the vestes Sergios (Sarkis) Haykazn who was (according to an inscription of 1033) *anthypatos*, patrician, vestes and duke of the east: *Aristakes de Lastivert*, 46–7; Felix, *Byzanz und die Islam*, 154–5.

[70] Gagic reigned for two years without the emperor reacting in any way, for he had to deal with both Maniakes and with the Russians in 1043. This permitted Gagic to strengthen his hold, most notably by arresting Sergius/Sarkis.

[71] Abu'l-Aswar, of the Kurdish dynasty of the Saddadides. Tivion = Dvin on the Araxes, to the south of the present Erivan.

[72] The old name for Azerbaidjan. The Araxes rises in the mountains of Armenia and discharges into the Caspian Sea.

[73] It is odd that Matthew of Edessa is not aware of this Machiavellian plan of the Romans. He makes no connection between the attack of the emir of Dvin and that of the Romans. He thinks he knows that David, Prince of the Albanians, successfully opposed the invader and that Gregory Pahlawumi gained a victory on behalf of Kakikios of Ani: *Armenia and the crusades tenth to twelfth centuries: the chronicle of Matthew of Edessa*, trans. Dostourian, 63–5, 67–8.

to put the emperor's plan into action. When Aplesphares received the letters he responded that he would accomplish all that was required of him on condition that an imperial letter were sent stating that he was guaranteed sovereign rights over those fortresses and villages now in Kakikios' hands which he might be able to capture, by right of conquest.[74] The emperor agreed to this and affirmed by chrysobull whatever Aplesphares had demanded. When the latter received the letter, he went into action; he stormed and captured many of Kakikios' fortresses and villages. As for Kakikios, assaulted by Roman forces and ravaged by the ruler of Tivion, he abandoned all hope. He made contact with the parakoimomenos and gave his allegiance to the emperor through him, [437] to whom he surrendered the city.[75] When he came before the emperor he was honoured with the title of magister, receiving lucrative estates in Cappadocia, Charsianon and Likandos; from then on he led a peaceful and quiet life.[76]

But now Monomachos demanded the fortresses and villages which the ruler of Tivion had captured as parts of Ani. When Aplesphares refused to part with them, adhering to the letter of the chrysobull, the emperor declared war on him. Again he ordered the parakoimomenos to attack Aplesphares using the Roman troops, the Iberian army and the forces in Great Armenia which the prince of Ani commanded.[77] All these forces were assembled; the vestarches Michael Iassites was appointed to direct them together with his servant, the magister Constantine the Alan; then he sent them against Tivion. But Aplesphares was a truly gifted

---

[74] The negotiations took place during 1044.
[75] The Armenian chroniclers tell a different tale. According to *Aristakes de Lastivert*, ed. Canard and Berberian, 50–5, followed by *Matthew of Edessa*, ed. Dostourian, 71–3, who emphasise the perfidy of the Romans, Monomachos succeeded in getting the Armenian prince to Constantinople where he was obliged to exchange Ani for some considerable estates within the empire. This stratagem succeeded because Peter, catholicos of the Armenain church since 1019, was of the pro-Byzantine party, and the Pahlawuni family (which controlled the army) preferred to negotiate with the Romans. Gregory, the principal scion of that family, attained the dignity of magister with a significant command and considerable estates in the east. Ani was surrendered in 1045.
[76] *Matthew of Edessa*, ed. Dostourian, 121–2, has a different version of this story, according to which Gagik proves to be a determined adversary of the Romans. But this is wrong if the seal of Gagik of Ani, 'great count of the stable, great duke of Charsianon', really belonged to the former king of Armenia: W. Seibt, 'War Gagik II von Grossarmenien ca. 1072–3 *megas duke Charsianou?*', *To Hellenikon: studies in honour of Speros Vryonis Jr* (New Rochelle and New York, 1993), II, 159–68. Gagik was married to the daughter of David Artzrouni.
[77] The Armenian forces were under the command of Vahran Pahlawuni who perished with his son in the battle against Abu'l-Aswar: *Aristakes de Lastivert*, ed. Canard and Berberian, 56. The Armenian forces were immediately enrolled in the Roman army. On the immigration of Armenians into the empire since the tenth century but also after the fall of Ani: G. Dédéyan, 'L'immigration arménienne en Cappadoce', *B*, 45 (1975), 41–117; and N. G. Garsoian, 'The problem of Armenian integration into the Byzantine empire', *Studies on the internal diaspora of the Byzantine empire*, ed. H. Ahrweiler and A. E. Laiou (Washington, DC, 1998), 53–124.

commander if ever there was one, capable of shattering the strategies and plans of his enemies. Knowing full well that his forces were insufficient to withstand the Romans in formal battle, he shut himself up in the city and diverted the river flowing by to flood the entire plain and turn it into a quagmire of mud and puddles; then he awaited the arrival of the foe. He stationed infantrymen who were archers at random in the vineyards surrounding the city with orders to remain hidden until he should give the signal 'to arms!' with the trumpet. The Roman leaders deduced that closing himself up in the city and flooding the plain were acts of a coward who had abandoned hope, so they ran towards the city in a disorderly, sporadic fashion, some dismounted, some not, each man doing what he would, thinking they were going to take it at the first shout. When they got into the paths running through the vineyards and were approaching the city, then Aplesphares sounded the trumpet, ordering his men into action. [438] The infantrymen rose up from the undergrowth and began firing arrows and throwing stones while others damaged the Romans from the very battlements, thus preventing them from defending themselves against the adversaries. The Romans were severely defeated and an innumerable host of them was slain, for the horses were unable to flee without falling in the mud and the swamp. Iassites and Constantine were only just able to get away to safety in Ani, where they personally reported the disaster to Nicholas.

When the disaster which had befallen them was reported to the emperor, Nicholas and Iassites were relieved of their commands; Iassites being replaced by Kekaumenos,[78] duke of Iberia, Nicholas by Constantine, the commander plenipotentiary, colonel of the Great Hetaireiai. This man was a eunuch of Saracen origin who had served the emperor before his accession and never wavered in his fidelity to him. When [the new commanders] arrived on the scene they assembled their forces and addressed themselves to the task. They were hesitant to attack the city of Tivion, which was the metropolis of the entire nation, but they assaulted the rest of the fortresses, as many of them as were located in Ani, taking St Mary, the one called Ampier and St Gregory[79] – which is located on a precipice and very strongly fortified. Aplesphares tried several times to bring relief to the beleaguered garrison there but he was repelled as many times as he

---

[78] The appointment of Katacalon Kekaumenos as duke of Iberia and Greater Armenia is also mentioned by Aristaches de Lastivert, who reports that he removed the katholikos Peter from Ani (6 January 1046) and sent him to Arzn, near Karin/Theodosioupolis, 46.
[79] St Mary is Surmari; Ampier is Abert; St Gregory is Xor Virap. These fortresses, like Dvin, were located in the upper Araxes valley.

tried. The Romans came to the fortress known as Chelidonion[80] which is built on a craggy mountainside not far from Tivion. They surrounded it with trenches and palisades and tried to take it by starving it out. The people within the walls were short of the necessities of life, not having been able to build up supplies on account of the suddenness of the assault. Indeed, the Romans would have taken it if the insurrection of the patrician Leo Tornikios[81] had not suddenly broken out in the west.

This Leo Tornikios had been commander in Iberia[82] but was dismissed from his post on a charge of attempted usurpation [439] and given monastic tonsure.[83] He was brought to the city and ordered to remain at home in Adrianople.[84] Not being able easily to tolerate the misfortune which had befallen him, little by little he discreetly appropriated the support of those commanders in Adrianople who had been overlooked and were cooling their heels. By means of these men and his own relatives, he subverted all who were officers in command of the Macedonian and Thrakesion units,[85] all the unemployed soldiers[86] and all who rejoiced in pillage and rapine. When he had raised an adequate army, he was proclaimed emperor. He set out with the entire host under his command and shortly appeared beneath the walls of the capital. The emperor did not have sufficient forces to resist him,[87] nor did he trust the citizens faithfully to continue supporting him. For this reason a courier was sent to Constantine in Iberia (by the state

---

[80] Chelidonion was where Erivan now stands; the siege was in 1047.

[81] The Tornikioi have already been named by Skylitzes as partisans of Constantine IX. They had been prominent in the west since the tenth century, for, at the head of Macedonian units, they had opposed the rise of Nikephoros Phokas: Leo the Deacon, 45, trans. 95. Leo, a cousin of Monomachos on his mother's side, was on excellent terms with Euprepia, the emperor's sister: Psellos, *Chronographia*, trans. Sewter, 6.100–4.

[82] Attaleiates says Tornikios' command was at Melitene but Psellos, *Chronographia*, 6.101, trans. Sewter, 206–7, says in Iberia.

[83] Skylitzes' narrative is incomplete here; it has to be augmented by Attaleiates, *Historia*, ed. Perez Martin, 18, and by the speech to Monomachos by John Mauropous in honour of the imperial victories: Lefort, 'Rhétorique', *TM*, 6 (1976), 265–303, at 266. The Patzinaks who had invaded the empire were now established in the Balkans around Naisos. The army of the west rebelled against the order to demobilise (spring 1047), judging it to be harmful to the interests of the empire.

[84] Adrianople was where the family residence was located. The accounts of Psellos, *Chronographia*, 6, 99–100, trans Sewter, 205–6, and of Attaleiates, *Historia*, ed. Perez Martin, 22, seem more credible: on 14 September 1047 Leo was taken out of the capital by a group of officers from Macedonia who brought him to Adrianople, having killed the horses of the public relay system to prevent themselves from being pursued.

[85] The Tornikioi had been influential, at least in military circles in the west, for a century or more. Their circle of officers constituted a faction which was known as Macedonian. Psellos says that Leo himself 'reeked of Macedonian arrogance': Psellos *Chronographia*, 6, 99–100, trans Sewter, 205–6.

[86] Recently demobilised.

[87] The army which Monomachos had sent forward to Selymbria returned in haste to seek the protection of the city walls: Atteleiates, 19.

relay horses) bearing an imperial letter which ordered him to abandon the task in hand and to come with his forces as quickly as possible to the capital. Upon receiving the letter, even though the fortress was in his hands, he lifted the siege and made a treaty with Aplesphares in which he ascertained by curses and oaths that he would continue to support the emperor and would never contemplate anything deleterious to the Romans. That done, he mobilised his forces and made haste to come to the capital; and that is how Chelidonian escaped being taken. When Constantine came with all the units of the east and the entire army, he entered the capital himself but, at the emperor's command, the entire host passed over into Thrace, some at Chrysopolis opposite to the capital, some at Abydos on the Hellespont;[88] but more of that later.

Before the forces arrived, as we said, Tornikios was proclaimed emperor in the month of September, first year of the indiction,[89] and he reached the capital sooner than it takes to tell, expecting to take it at the first assault because the emperor was short of forces. He set up a palisade [440] opposite to Blachernae, close to the monastery of the Anargyroi,[90] then tried to suborn the citizens with words and promises. When nobody paid any attention to him, he went into action; but the emperor resisted him using the citizens and whatever soldiers might be found there. He stationed the citizens and the rabble on the wall. Then by way of the Blachernae gate he led out from the walls the soldiers they had been able to find and a few others whom the leaders of the Senate had armed (at the emperor's command), not more than a thousand in all. These he stationed to face the tyrant after digging a ditch in front of them to hinder their attackers. The magister Argyros the Italian[91] respectfully insisted that he should have remained within the gates in wait of the attackers, begging him to stay inside and not sally forth; certainly not to engage a raging, furious host of experienced soldiers with a small army of raw recruits. This is what he said, but he did not convince the emperor, and in fact Constantine Leichoudes[92] took the other point of view. He stood first in the emperor's favour[93] at that time and had a great deal of influence with him; it was he who formulated the plan which was followed.

---

[88] The object was to circle around behind and enclose an enemy already in difficulties.
[89] 1047.
[90] Saints Kosmas and Damian.
[91] This is the former Italian rebel, the son of Meles, now become one of the emperor's advisers since he joined the fight against Maniakes.
[92] Like John Mauropous, Leichoudes belonged to the circles of *literati* who were conducting affairs of state under Monomachos.
[93] 'Was close to the emperor', MSS ABCU.

Constantine IX Monomachos

Out they went in the late afternoon; as soon as the tyrant got wind of it he armed his forces and charged into them with great force. In less time than it takes to tell, they crossed the ditch and put to flight those inside, some of whom were taken prisoner while others fell into the moat of the city where they died a miserable death. The citizens also deserted the walls by leaping down from them while the doorkeepers of the walls at Blachernae opened wide their gates. Indeed, if fortune had not dealt Tornikios a bad turn he would have entered easily and imposed his authority. But he stopped the pursuit when they reached the moat before the wall, at which point those with the emperor took fresh heart; they secured the gates and remounted the guard on the walls.[94] At that point the emperor was all but carried off, struck by an arrow, but God intervened in a spectacular manner: the arrow [441] lodged in the pine-cone-shaped helmet of an attendant, which saved both the man wearing it and the emperor. In this way the city came close to being taken – and was saved.

The apostate remained encamped for a few more days, but when his supporters began to melt away and desert to the emperor he feared they might all abandon him and go away, or that they would take him and hand him over to the emperor; so he rose up and returned to Arkadioupolis.[95] There he encamped together with John Vatatzes,[96] and waited. He despatched Theodore Strabomytes, a man they called Polys and Marianos Vranas,[97] officers commanding units in the west, related to him by blood, to lay siege to Rhaidestos; for when the other cities of Macedonia and Thrace had come over to his side, only this city had continued to support the emperor, thanks to the determination of the bishop of that city and a local magnate named Vatatzes, a relative of Tornikios. [Theodore and Marianos] went there but some time later had still accomplished nothing, so Tornikios arose with his entire army and went there too. He used every assault and all kinds of siege-engines against the city, but he was repulsed

---

[94] The accounts agree here, including that of Psellos who was an eyewitness of the matter: Psellos, *Chronographia*, 6, 113–19, trans Sewter, 214–17. Tornikios had repulsed his adversaries; the walls were deserted, the gates abandoned; he would have encountered no resistance if he had continued the action. It is not clear why he held back. Doubtless he wanted to avoid taking the city by storm, followed by the inevitable pillage, which would have alienated those whom he sought to rule. He was probably over-confident, assuming that the Byzantines would acclaim him next day.

[95] A stronghold commanding the road from Constantinople to Adrianople.

[96] A Vatatzes of Adrianople had once offered to deliver his city to Samuel of Bulgaria (reign of Basil II, c. 26, above). The family of this name became increasingly significant under the Komnenoi and in the thirteenth century, one member attaining the throne.

[97] Member of another distinguished family from Adrianople which achieved a measure of fame under their relatives, the Komnenoi.

at all points because those within valiantly repelled the siege-engines. In the end he lifted the siege and returned to Arkadioupolis.

As soon as the troops of the east had crossed into Thrace from Chrysopolis and Abydus, the emperor sent them into action against the apostates with the magister Michael Iassites in command. He concentrated his forces in one body and encamped near the apostates but did not let battle commence. He occupied himself rather with the villages which were for the apostates; he treated the prisoners with kindness and discreetly sent a letter to [the apostates] announcing an amnesty of misdeeds and a generous distribution of benefits.[98] As winter was drawing on, the apostates themselves, the pack animals and the horses were running short [442] of the necessities of life. Unable to fight off the cold, hunger and the enemy at once, little by little they began to defect to the magister. As long as it was only the lowly who deserted and not the distinguished, [the tyrant] bided his time and was buoyed up by his hopes. But when Marianos Vranas, Polys and Theodore Strabomytes (who were of the Glabas clan) and some other persons of standing suddenly abandoned him and defected to Iassites, he fled together with John Vatatzes, second in command after him in the apostate army. And since there was no escape, they sought refuge in a church[99] and the insurrection of the apostates was dissipated. Iassites sent men to arrest them and brought them to the emperor in chains. At the emperor's orders, each member of the [rebel] army went off to his homeland. Tornikios and Vatatzes were blinded in the evening of the day of Christ's birth,[100] while those who remained faithful to the tyrant right to the end had their goods confiscated after being paraded through the Forum and were sent into exile. Such was the end of the uprising; and now begin the woes for which the Turks were responsible.

9. Taking up again from above, I will now explain who the Turks are and how they came to fight against the Romans. The Turkish people are Hunnic by race, living to the north of the Caucasus mountains, populous and autonomous, never enslaved by any nation. Once domination of the Persians had passed to the Saracens, the Saracens went on to rule over not only Persia and Medea and Babylon and Assyria, but also Egypt and

---

[98] The emperor also set an army of Bulgars on the rearguard of the rebels; John Vatatzes repulsed it victoriously in the region of Kypsela: Attaleiates, *Historia*, ed. Perez Martin, 23.
[99] This was at Bulgarophygon, a fortress to the south-west of Adrianople: Attaleiates, *Historia*, ed. Perez Martin, 23.
[100] 25 December 1047. There was some discussion among the emperor's advisers as to what punishment the two rebel chiefs should suffer; some were inclined to clemency: Lefort, 'Rhétorique', 270, 281–2.

Constantine IX Monomachos 417

Libya and a considerable part of Europe.[101] Then it came about in various circumstances that they rose up against each other and that one great empire was torn into many segments. Spain had one ruler,[102] Libya another, likewise Egypt, [443] Babylon[103] and Persia. And these neighbours did not share a common mind but rather waged war on each other. He who was the ruler of Persia, the Khorasians, the Oretanes and the Medes in the time of the emperor Basil was Mouchoumet, son of Imbrael.[104] Waging war against the Indians and Babylonians and getting the worst of it in battle, he decided that he should treat with the ruler of Turkey,[105] requesting some allied forces from that source.

So he sent ambassadors to him bearing rich gifts and they asked for allies to be sent to him, three thousand in number. [The Turk] gave the embassy a warm reception and was pleased with the gifts that were sent. He sent three thousand men under the command of Tangrolipex Moukalet, son of Mikeel, to Mouchoumet.[106] He did this in the hope that, if they succeeded in repelling the enemies of the Saracens, they would quite easily render passable the bridge on the river Araxes (which was preventing the Turks from entering Persia since it had guard-towers at either end and it was always watched by guards). After doing away with its garrison, they could subject the land of the Persians to his rule. When the mercenaries arrived Mouchoumet marched them out with his own forces, attacked Pissasirios[107] the Arab ruler and easily routed him as the Arabs could not withstand the archery. When he returned to his own land[108] he urged the Turks to join him in fighting against the Indians[109] who were

---

[101] Skylitzes defines the Umayyad caliphate at its widest extent.
[102] A reference to the caliphate of Cordova, set up after the civil war in which the Abassids triumphed over the Umayyads, when a representative of the latter took refuge in Spain.
[103] Babylon here means Baghdad.
[104] Mahmud the Ghaznavid (998–1030), Sunni sultan, master of Persia and the Khorasan, was a great conqueror who extended his realm into northern India: *EI*, under the word Mahmud b. Sebuktikin.
[105] Here meaning, not Hungary, but Turkestan in Central Asia.
[106] The beginnings of the Seljuks are obscure. Their ancestor was Seljuk of the Oghuz people who were in the service of the Samanids of Persia; that was when they converted to Islam. At the beginning of the eleventh century they were being led by the three sons of Seljuk, Musa, Mik'ail and Arslan Isra'il. Later they were led by two sons of Mik'ail, Togril Beg (Skylitzes' Tangrolipex) and Čaghri Beg: *EI*, under the word Saljukides.
[107] Skylitzes' chronology is inaccurate here; it was Togril Beg who attacked the top-ranking military commander in the service of the Buyid emir of emirs, who also was a Turk, but Shi-ite: al-Basasiri, who was driven out of Baghdad in 1055, retook it in 1059 and died fighting in January 1060.
[108] Mahmud defeated the Oghuz bands who were dispersed throughout Khorasan in 1029. It was his son, Mas'ud, who confronted Togril Beg.
[109] Mahmud the Ghaznavid conquered the entire basin of the Indus, opening up a new domain for Moslem expansion.

at war but they asked to be allowed to return to their own land, with the task of guarding the crossing of the river Araxes committed to them. As Mouchoumet insisted and was prepared to use force, they mutinied for fear some harm might befall them. They secreted themselves in the Carbonites [444] desert[110] because so few men could not confidently withstand tens of thousands, and from there they conducted raids, pillaging and ravaging Saracen lands. Mouchoumet was profoundly annoyed at these occurrences; he raised an army of about twenty thousand and sent it against the Turks under the command of ten of the most noble and wise Saracens, distinguished by their valour. These now rose up and went to war. They were of the opinion that it would not be to their advantage to enter the desert, because of the scarcity of water and food there; so they pitched camp as near as possible to where the desert begins and contemplated what ought to be done. When Tangrolipex, encamped deep in the desert, learnt of the campaign against him, he communed with those who accompanied him and came to the conclusion that it would be advantageous to launch a night attack on the Saracens and Persians. Travelling at speed for two days, he struck on the third night, [the victims] lying in their tents without a care in the world, anticipating no harm. They were routed in less time than it takes to tell while he seized carriages, horses and a great amount of money. He no longer conducted his raids surreptitiously like a refugee and a thief, but openly disputed possession of fortified positions. Some of those criminals who feared for their lives, some slaves and some of those who took pleasure in robbery with violence joined his camp; in very short time a large force of about fifty thousand congregated around him.[111] And that is what was happening to him.

Mouchoumet for his part was not quietly accepting the defeat which had taken place; deeply humiliated, he blinded the ten commanders and threatened to parade in women's clothing those soldiers who had fled from danger. [445] He began arming himself for retaliation, but when the recently defeated soldiers learned of his threat they went over to Tangrolipex. With so many additional troops of such excellent quality *he* mobilised the entire army and advanced on Mouchoumet, anxious to have the outcome decided by a full-scale battle. But Mouchoumet had also raised an army of about fifty thousand by arming Saracens, Persians, Kabirs[112] and Arabs;

[110] The Steppes between the Caspian and the Aral seas, to the north of Khorasan.
[111] This first victory allowed the Turkish chieftain to occupy the town of Persia and to acquire resources to strengthen his army.
[112] The Kabirs in the army of Mas'ud cannot be identified with those who supported Thomas the Slav (reign of Michael II, c. 6, above). These are probably Khorasians, for these had always constituted a corps d'élite in the Perso-Arab armies.

he also had a hundred elephants carrying towers. He confronted [the foe] with all these forces at the place called Aspachan,[113] where a violent battle took place in which many fell on either side. Mouchoumet himself also fell; he was riding his horse backwards and forwards in an irregular fashion, encouraging his own people, when the horse fell on him; he died of a broken neck.[114] When he fell, the host that was with him came to an agreement with the enemy, as a result of which Tangrolipex was universally declared to be king of Persia. Once he was proclaimed, he sent and eliminated the guard on the crossing of the Araxes, giving free access into Persia to any Turk who wanted it. Freed of this impediment, the entire host of them rushed in (except for those who preferred their own homeland), killing Persians and Saracens. Thus [the Turks] became masters of Persia, naming Tangrolipex Sultan; that is, absolute ruler and king of kings.[115] He relieved all the indigenous governors of their commands and transferred them to Turks, among whom he divided out the whole of Persia, entirely crushing and humiliating the people of the land.[116]

10. When everything seemed to him to be going well, his first task [446] was to wage war on the bordering potentates. He personally attacked Pissasirios, governor of Babylon, defeated him in various battles, killed him and thus became master of the Babylonian region. He sent out Koutloumous,[117] his father's brother's son, against Karbeses, chieftain of the Arabs, giving him a powerful army.[118] He marched off and engaged the Arabs, but he was defeated and fled in disgrace. On his way back from the defeat, he was about to cross Medea, also known as Vaspurakan. Now this country was being ruled at that time by the emperor's emissary, the patrician Stephen, son of Constantine Leichoudes[119] who was co-ruling with the

[113] The decisive battle took place in 1040 at Dandankan, near to Ispahan.
[114] Mas'ud survived and fled to India, abandoning Persia to the conqueror.
[115] This is a civil, not a religious, title. The caliph was maintained at Baghdad by Togril Beg, under his tutelage.
[116] Togril Beg was accompanied by undisciplined bands of Turcomans who pillaged the conquered lands.
[117] The son of Arslan Isra'il.
[118] There are difficulties with the chronology here because Qutlumus was vanquished by the chief of the Arabs, Basasiri (Pissasirios *pace* Skylitzes) much later. The campaign to which he is referring here took place in 1044. Both Aristakes de Lastivert and *Matthew of Edessa*, ed. Dostourian, 74, know of it. Matthew gives the names of the three chiefs, none of which is Qutlumus. The offensive was directed against the Uqaylid Qirwas Ibn a-Muqallad (Karbeses *pace* Skylitzes), emir of Mossul. The battle took place on 24 April 1044: Felix, *Byzanz und Islam*, 162.
[119] He was probably not the son of Leichoudes but a protege, the son of Leichoudeia, sister of Constantine (?), which would make him a nephew of the emperor's *mesazon*. Such is the understanding of N. Oikonomides, 'St George of Mangana', 244, n. 52. The *mesazon* does not occupy an official position recognised in the *Taktika*. Like the *paradynasteuon*, he assisted the emperor to govern by serving as an intermediary between the sovereign and the main offices of state.

emperor.[120] Koutloumous sent an embassy to Stephen asking permission to pass through unimpeded and promising with solemn oaths that his men would leave the country unharmed and intact. Stephen received the ambassadors and, thinking the request sprang from cowardice, he assembled the regional army and confronted the Turks in battle order. Koutloumous was profoundly dismayed at this occurrence for the people with him, returning from a defeat, were all on foot and unarmed. Nevertheless, and against his will, he was forced to fight. In the engagement which ensued Stephen's forces were routed while he himself and many others were taken prisoner. As Koutloumous was passing through Tabriz he sold Stephen to the local ruler there,[121] then made his way to the Sultan to explain the defeat. He put the blame on others and declared that if he were to campaign again, with another army, against Karbeses, he would easily subdue Arabia for the Sultan. He mentioned Vaspurakan in passing, saying that it was a highly productive region defended by women, a reference to the soldiers against whom he had fought. But the Sultan, angered by the disgrace of the defeat, was thinking of arresting him and putting him to death. He was moreover frightened off from taking up arms against the Romans merely by the report [447] of the glorious deeds of three former emperors: Nikephoros, John and Basil. Imagining that the Romans were still possessed of the same valour and might, he was in two minds, wondering what he ought to do. Koutloumous found out what the Sultan had in mind for *him* and took to flight, taking his men with him. He seized a strongly fortified city in the Khorasian country known as Pasar[122] and there he set himself up in opposition to the Sultan, who did not think it worthwhile fighting him for the time being. Instead, he assembled his own forces in their entirety and marched off himself against the Arabs. A battle ensued and, once again, he was defeated. Returning vanquished, he could not endure the disgrace nor the contempt of Koutloumous, so taking the greater part of his army he advanced on Pasar, where he spent a great deal of time waging war on his own nephew. But Koutloumous was heartened by the strength of the city. He frequently flung the gates open, charged out and did considerable harm to the forces of the Sultan. The Sultan then sent another army against the Romans, about twenty thousand men, appointing his nephew,

---

[120] *Paradynasteuon.*
[121] *Matthew of Edessa*, ed. Dostourian, 74, says the unfortunate *katepan* had been flayed and that his relatives were finally allowed to purchase his body and skin for ten thousand pieces of gold. Caution is called for.
[122] On Qutlumus: C. Cahen, 'Qutlumush et ses fils avant l'Asie mineure', *Der Islam (Zeitschrift für Geschichte und Kultur des islamischen Orients). Festschrift Taeschner*, 39, (Berlin, 1964), 14–27, rpr. in Cahen, *Turcobyzantina*, no. v.

Asan the Deaf, to command them. He ordered Asan to proceed in all haste and, if it were feasible, to occupy Medea for him. That is what was happening in Persia.

11. Pankratios,[123] the chieftain of Iberia, was a dissolute fellow; he had defiled the marriage bed of Liparites, the son of that Horace Liparites who was killed in the war against George in the time of the emperor Basil. [The son] was renowned for his wisdom and valour, a man of great power in Iberia, second to Pankratios. Deeply offended by what had taken place, he was obliged to take up arms against [the adulterer] whom he defeated in battle, driving him into Caucasia and inner Abasgia. When [Liparites] came into the royal residence he violated his own Sovereign Lady, the mother of Pankratios, and made himself master of the entire country of Iberia. [448] He sent a letter to the emperor asking to become a friend and ally of the Romans. The emperor received his embassy and entered into negotiations with him. A little while later Pankratios came to Trebizond travelling by way of the river Phasis, through the territory of the Suani and the Colchi.[124] From Trebizond he sent messengers to the emperor intimating that he would like to come into the capital and have an audience with him. This was granted; he came and entered the emperor's presence then proceeded to upbraid him severely, charging that he who was an emperor was bound by several treaties to the ruler of the important territory of Abasgia. But he had broken those treaties and transferred his support to a commoner, a slave and a rebel. Then he requested that relations between them be restored, which is what happened. On the emperor's initiative, they came to an agreement with each other that Pankratios was to be lord and ruler of all Iberia and Abasgia while Liparites was to be governor of Meschia[125] for life, but with Pankratios as his overlord and king. That is how the affair in Abasgia turned out.

12. Asan, whom the Sultan had sent against the Romans, passing through Tabriz and the place called Tiflis, came to Vaspurakan. He destroyed and burnt everything, slaughtering everybody he encountered, not even sparing those of tender age. The governor of the region was the vestes Aaron, son of [John] Vladisthlav and brother of Prousianos.[126] Knowing that he himself was unequal to the task of withstanding so great

---

[123] Bagrat IV (1027–72).
[124] The Souani were located to the south of Mount Elbrouz in the upper reaches of the Enguri; the Colchi were the Laz. Bagrat extended his domains to the eastern shore of the Black Sea.
[125] A land to the south of Bagrat's domain.
[126] This information is correct; see the genealogical table of the Bulgar royal family, *ODB*, 1, 1. Here is a further instance of a Bulgar prince in the service of the empire.

a multitude of Turks, he sent a letter to the vestes Katakalon Kekaumenos who was in command of Ani and Iberia asking the help of as many troops as he could muster.[127] Once the letter was received, quicker than it takes to tell, [Kekaumenos] mobilised the forces at his disposal, moved them out in haste and [449] joined them with Aaron's. A discussion was held: would it be better to fight by night or in broad daylight? Kekaumenos was in favour of neither; he inclined to another way, to deceiving the enemy. His plan was to abandon the camp just as it was with the tents, the pack animals and the other paraphernalia and to establish hiding places in suitable locations. Then, when the Turks arrived, discovered the stockade to be devoid of men and proceeded to pillage what lay within, the men in hiding were to come out and attack them. He was not disappointed in his scheme. At dawn Asan emerged from his own encampment on the river Stragna[128] and advanced ready to do battle. When he encountered nobody, he approached the Roman stockade. No guards could be seen, no voice was heard; it was completely devoid of forces. Thinking the Romans had taken to flight, he breached the fortification at several points and ordered the seizure of booty to begin. Towards evening, the Romans emerged from their hiding places and hurled themselves on the Turks, who were now scattered and disorganised. They were immediately routed, for they could not withstand the irresistible force of the Roman charge. Asan was the first to fall, fighting in the front line; every stout-hearted man in the army fell too. The very few who survived the fray fled unarmed through the mountains and found refuge in the cities of Persarmenia.

13. When the Sultan learnt of the calamity which had taken place from those who had escaped he fell into great tribulation and gave his mind seriously to the matter of recovering from the disaster which had befallen him. He raised an army of about one hundred thousand superior soldiers from among the Turks, Kabirs and Dilimniti,[129] which he handed over to his half-brother, Abram Aleim, [450] and sent against the Romans.[130] When this expedition became known, the army commanders mentioned above convened and held a conference to decide what ought to be done.

---

[127] Skylitzes gives a detailed account of events in Armenia 1047–8 because Katakalon Kekaumenos was a participant therein.
[128] The great Zab marking the eastern limit of the *katepanate* of Vaspurakan. Hasan was surprised, over-burdened with booty, while returning to Tabriz.
[129] The Daylamites (who originated from a province to the south of the Caspian Sea) provided warriors of reputable quality.
[130] In the summer of 1048 (*pace Aristakes de Lastivert*, ed. Canard and Berberian) Togril Beg sent his half-brother, Ibrahim Inal, against the empire, but there are difficulties with this dating: Shepard, 'Scylitzes on Armenia', 271–4; *Georgian Chronicles*, 294–5.

Kekaumenos was of the opinion that they ought to confront the Turks with the forces then available, outside the Roman frontiers, and fight them there. For many of the enemy were still without horses and what animals they had were worn out by travel because the Turks lacked the iron [shoes] which it is customary to fix on the beasts' hooves. The morale of the Romans (on the other hand) was very good; they were full of confidence after the recent victory and anxious to come to blows with the enemy. Aaron, however, opined that they should conserve their forces; he said they should fortify the cities and strongholds, withdrawing everything within their walls. They should report to the emperor and certainly not offer battle to such a multitude of barbarians, given their meagre forces, without knowing his mind. The [two] commanders gave their opinions but it was Aaron's that won the day; so they returned to Iberia with the army. They came to a plain known locally as Outrou[131] and there they remained, inactive, in open country. But first they enclosed all the rural population, the women and children and everything that was of value, within the fortifications. They also wrote to the emperor by courier reporting the approach of the enemy. When he received the letter he ordered them to refrain from action until Liparites arrived with the Iberian forces and was united with the Roman soldiery. To this man he sent a letter in all haste telling him that, if he judged himself to be an ally and friend of the Romans, he should mobilise the entire available host, go to meet with the Roman commanders and join them in doing battle against the barbarians. When the commanders received their letter, they stayed where they were as ordered, waiting the arrival of Liparites. As soon as he received the imperial order he hastily assembled and armed his own host; yet, while he was gathering up his own forces, time was passing. Abram reached Vaspurakan and learnt that, on hearing of his approach, the Romans who had been concentrated there had now returned [451] to Iberia. Not unreasonably, he thought they had retreated out of fear; so, putting aside all thought of booty and spoil, he went chasing after them, anxious to attack them as they were, prior to the addition of any other forces. When the Roman commanders learnt of this, they were afraid they might be obliged to fight before Liparites arrived (which they were reluctant to do). So they withdrew into an inaccessible position surrounded on all sides by ravines and waited there. Meanwhile they wrote to Liparites to come in all haste and not delay. Now Abram, having failed to encounter the Roman army, arrived at Artze,[132] a town of

---

[131] The plain of Orduru was in the Basean plain, not far from Theodosioupolis, the principal fortress of the area.
[132] Erzerum today.

many people and much wealth, for there are many native merchants living there [as well as] Syrians, Armenians and other nationalities.[133] Putting their trust in their own great population, the people of Artze would not agree to be enclosed by walls, even though Kekaumenos urged and insisted on this and in spite of the fact that Theodosioupolis lay close by, a great city with strong, impregnable walls. When the Turks arrived and began the assault, the people of Artze first blocked the means of access then, climbing up onto the roofs, defended themselves against the attackers with stones, staves and bows. For six whole days they continued fighting; when news of it reached the commanders, Kekaumenos pleaded most insistently with [the Romans] to go out and do battle with the Turks, now that their attention was occupied with the siege. They ought not to be sitting idle, letting time go by, waiting for Liparites' fictitious aid; they were watching an opportune moment (which it would not be easy to recapture) slip by. But as Aaron took the opposite view, saying that nothing should be done contrary to the emperor's wishes, he too kept his peace. As for Abram, since the campaign was not going according to plan (for he could not take the town by assault), disregarding its wealth and booty he ordered the roofs to be set on fire. The Turks immediately took torches, lit kindling and threw it on the roofs. Fires broke out everywhere and a great conflagration ensued. Unable to resist both the fire and the archery, the people of Artze [452] wavered and turned to flight. They say that about one hundred and fifty thousand men perished, victims of either the sword or of fire. When they realised they were vanquished, they slaughtered their wives and children then threw themselves into the flames. After Abram had taken Artze in that manner, he found a great amount of gold, arms and a quantity of serviceable ironware which had not been rendered useless by the fire. He also captured a large number of horses and draught animals; he now equipped his host in an appropriate manner and returned in search of the Roman army.[134]

14. Once Liparites arrived, the Roman army came down from the fortified position mentioned above and halted on the plain at the foot of the mountain, there where the Kapetros[135] fortress stands. When the Turks started arriving again, a few at a time, Kekaumenos advised attack while

---

[133] The market there was very lively because the town was located on roads leading into both the Caucasus and the Djezir.

[134] *Aristakes de Lastivert*, ed. Canard and Berberian, 60–8, gives a long account of the massacres perpetrated by the Turks, especially in the town of Artze, previously enriched by vigorous commercial activity.

[135] This was the main fortress of the Basean, to the east of Artze and of Theodosioupolis. On the discrepancies in the various accounts of the battle: Shepard, 'Scylitzes on Armenia', 276–9.

they were spread out and disorganised; but Liparites was reluctant because of the day. It was a Saturday, the eighteenth of September, second year of the indiction,[136] and for Liparites Saturday was reckoned among the inauspicious days, which is why he shunned it and refused to fight. While this was happening on the Roman side, Abram learnt from scouts where the Romans were located and also that they were inactive. He drew up his own forces and advanced in battle order. When the opposing forces saw this, they too had to prepare to give battle, willy-nilly. Kekaumenos had the right wing, Aaron the left, while Liparites was stationed in the centre; it was towards evening.[137] Abram was opposite to Kekaumenos, [453] Khorasantes,[138] the other [Turkish] commander to Aaron, while Liparites was facing Aspan Salarios, half-brother of Abram.

Battle was joined; Kekaumenos and Aaron routed their opposing wings and pursued them until cockcrow[139] but Liparites, desolated by the loss of his nephew, charging at full tilt, fell when his horse was wounded; then he was taken prisoner. While that was happening to him, the Romans called off their pursuit, dismounted and offered hymns of victory to God, crying out with one voice: 'What god is great like our God?'[140] They were waiting for Liparites in the hope that he too was in pursuit of the enemy; but they began to worry when he failed to appear. They were perplexed and worrying about what might have happened, when a soldier who was under Liparites' orders approached and advised the commanders of his commander's misfortune and capture; also, how Abram had returned from flight and joined up with his own brother (for Asan had fallen in the battle). Taking Liparites and the other captured Iberians with them, they had returned, travelling at speed, to the place known as Kastrokome.[141] The army commanders were flabbergasted to hear this; they kept watch all night, then at daybreak held a conference at which they all felt it would be advantageous for each [commander] to go back home. Aaron collected his own host and left for Iban, the capital of Vaspurakan, while Kekaumenos returned to Ani with his forces.[142] Gratified by the capture of Liparites,

---

[136] 18 September 1048, which was a Saturday.
[137] 'About the hour for unhitching [draught-animals].'
[138] i.e. a man from Khorasan.
[139] *Aristakes de Lastivert*, ed. Canard and Berberian, 69–70, confirms that Aaron ran off. As usual, *Matthew of Edessa*, ed. Dostourian, 79, holds the Romans responsible for the defeat. It was they (he claims) who hamstrung Liparites' horse.
[140] See Ps. 134/135:5.
[141] The fortress of Okomi, 40 km east of Theodosioupolis.
[142] The battle of Kapetrou must have been a partial reverse for the Roman commanders, but Skylitzes exonerates Kekaumenos of all blame.

Abram considered himself the most fortunate of men on account of his recent success. He attempted no further major project but, travelling at speed, reached the place called Re[143] in five days and from there made his way to the Sultan, sending his news on ahead and the report that Liparites was captured. [454] The Sultan gave the appearance of rejoicing and gladness at the capture of Liparites, but he was actually jealous of his brother for having merited such good fortune and was ever applying himself to the search for some pretext for getting rid of him.

15. When the emperor learnt of the capture of Liparites he was all for redeeming him. He sent extravagant gifts and ransom [money] to the Sultan by the hand of George Drosos,[144] the secretary of Aaron, requesting freedom [for Liparites] and a peace treaty. The Sultan received the delegation and, wishing to be a magnanimous ruler rather than a sordid tradesman, he presented the man to the emperor as a gift. He took the ransom [money] and gave it to Liparites, exhorting him ever to remember that day and never again of his own free will to take up arms against the Turks. The Sultan was served as ambassador to the emperor by one whom they call *seriphos*,[145] a word which signifies for them a man who stands in the same relationship to the caliph as that in which the synkellos used to stand to the patriarch here; when the caliph died, he was immediately installed on the vacant throne. When this *seriphos* came to the capital and was admitted to an audience with the emperor, he spoke with great arrogance and boldness, finally attempting to show that the Roman empire was a tributary state to his own Sultan. Not finding the emperor inclined to agree with him, he returned empty-handed to the one who had sent him. From that moment the emperor anticipated war with the Sultan and, to the best of his ability, he sent [agents] to fortify the regions bordering on Persia. [455] While that was happening, the disturbance of the Patzinaks occurred. Why and how must now be said.

16. The Patzinak people are Scyths pertaining to the so-called 'Royal Scyths'.[146] They are numerous and no other people of the Scyths is able to withstand them alone. They are divided into thirteen tribes all of which have the same name in common, but each tribe has its own proper name inherited from its own ancestor and chieftain. They graze their flocks on

---

[143] Rayy on the Iranian plateau, near to Tehran.
[144] The Drosoi provided the empire with several officials from the ninth century on. As secretary to Aaron, George had good experience of frontier affairs. This may explain why he was later appointed judge of Chaldia and Derxene: Staurakos, *Bleisiegel*, no. 79.
[145] A *šarif* is a descendant of the prophet.
[146] On the Patzinaks (most recently): E. Malamut, 'L'image byzantine des Petchénègues', *BZ*, 88 (1995), 105–7 and Stephenson, *Balkan Frontier*, 108–10.

the plains which extend beyond the Danube from the river Borysthenon[147] to Pannonia, for they are nomads who always prefer to live in tents. At that time, the leader of the people was Tyrach son of Bilter, highly distinguished by birth but otherwise unremarkable, a man who preferred to live in peace. But there was another person in that people whose name was Kegenes, the son of Baltzar, a nobody by birth and practically nameless, but extremely effective in battle and in the waging of war. He had on many occasions routed and repelled the Ouzes (a Hunnic people)[148] from attacking the Patzinaks, when Tyrach, lacking the courage to go out against them, took refuge in the marshes and lakes along the Danube. The Patzinaks honoured Tyrach for his family but they greatly preferred Kegenes for his outstanding bravery and his skill in war. Tyrach was stung to the core when he heard and noticed this; fearing for his position, he sought a way of getting rid of Kegenes. He set several traps for him but always in vain. When his covert schemes repeatedly went astray he realised that he could delay no longer and must act openly, whereupon he despatched a company [456] with orders to seize and destroy him. But Kegenes got wind of the plan and fled to the marshes of the Borysthenon, escaping death. From his hiding place there he sent secret messages to his relatives and fellow tribesmen, whereby he was able to divert the affections of his tribe (the Belemarnes) away from the king and also the affections of another tribe, the Pagoumanes. He raised an army and, with two tribes, confronted Tyrach who had eleven. [Kegenes] held his own for a long time, but, nevertheless, he was eventually overcome by weight of numbers. Wandering in the marshes he realised that the only way to safety for him and those with him was to take refuge with the emperor of the Romans. So he came to Dorostolon and installed himself with his followers (who numbered about twenty thousand) on a little island in the river to avoid being taken by surprise. Then he reported to the governor of the region, Michael son of Anastasios,[149] letting him know who he was, what adventures had befallen him before arriving there, and that he wished to transfer his allegiance to the emperor. He promised that, if he was accepted, he would be a great advantage to imperial affairs. Quicker than words can tell [Michael] passed this message on to the emperor and

---

[147] The Dniepr.
[148] The Ouzes or Oghuz, Hunnic (i.e. Turkic) people had established themselves in the Steppes of the present Ukraine in the tenth century. Constantine VII (*DAI*, ed. Moravcsik and Jenkins, 62) thought they could be usefully employed as a countermeasure against the Patzinaks.
[149] This is the man who was defeated by the Serbs at the beginning of the reign of Constantine IX, c. 2.

was hastily ordered to accept the man and his followers, to provide these with necessary provisions and to send him to Byzantium with every mark of respect. Michael did as he was commanded; Kegenes came to the capital where he was generously and graciously received in audience by the emperor. On promising to accept baptism himself and to persuade his followers to do likewise, [Kegenes] was raised to the dignity of patrician; he received three of the fortresses standing on the banks of the Danube and many hectares of land. [457] Finally, he was inscribed among the friends and allies of the Romans,[150] all this because he and his followers accepted baptism (as he promised). Euthymios, a devout monk, was sent to administer the sacred bath by the Danube river, giving them all holy baptism.[151]

17. Once Kegenes was safe and secured against unexpected attacks he turned his attention to warding off the enemy. He would cross the Danube now with a thousand, now with two thousand men, sometimes more, sometimes less, and spring surprise attacks, inflicting serious damage on the Patzinaks who were with Tyrach. They would slaughter the men they encountered but enslave the women and children then sell them to the Romans. Tyrach could not tolerate these clandestine incursions of Kegenes; he sent a delegation to the emperor insisting that a great emperor who had treaties with the Patzinak people absolutely ought not to receive one of their rebels. But since he had received one, he should certainly prevent that man from crossing the river to despoil allies of the empire. He should either restrain that man from such actions or risk losing allies like these. Otherwise, let the emperor make no mistake: he would be bringing down a most severe war upon himself and on his country. Such were the admonitions of Tyrach; when the emperor received them he laughed out loud at them; would he, because a Patzinak was threatening him, betray a man who had taken refuge with him? Would he prevent that man from harming those who did the emperor harm? – and he sent the ambassadors away empty-handed. He also sent out letters to Michael, the governor of the cities along the Danube, and to Kegenes in person [458] [ordering] a strict watch on the banks of the river. Should any significant force appear, they were to advise him by letter so that some of the western regular troops

---

[150] A seal of Kegenes exists. It bears the Christian name John and the title of magister. He is described as archon of Patzinakia, suggesting that he governed a territory centred on the fortresses given to him by the emperor, within the duchy of Paristrion: W. Seibt and M.-L. Zarnitz, *Das byzantinische Bleisiegel als Kunstwerke. Katalo zur Austellung* (Vienna, 1997), no. 3.2.9.
[151] The chronology of these events has yet to be established. They pre-date the great Patzinak invasion; they may belong to the period when Kekaumenos was duke of Paristrion. He did have ties with a Patzinak chieftain named Koulinos, who could be Goulinos, the son of Kegenes. This could explain why Skylitzes seems to be so much better informed that the other chroniclers.

could be sent to join with them in preventing the Patzinaks from crossing the river. He also sent a hundred ships with orders to cruise the Danube and intercept any Patzinaks attempting to traverse that river. When the ambassadors returned with nothing accomplished Tyrach was irritated and annoyed; he prayed for winter to come quickly. It was toward the end of autumn and winter about to begin, the sun being in Capricorn,[152] when a very strong wind arose from the north so that the river froze to a depth of fifteen cubits.[153] All guard duties being relaxed, Tyrach seized the opportunity for which he prayed: he crossed the Danube with all the Patzinaks, eighty thousand in number they say. They installed themselves on the other side, razing and devastating everything they came across.[154] A letter was sent to the emperor asking for aid as quickly as possible; before he had read the whole letter he wrote to the duke of Adrianople, the magister Constantine Arianites,[155] to take his forces; also to the officer commanding in Bulgaria, Basil Monachos, telling him to bring the Bulgar regiment and join forces with Michael[156] and Kegenes; with them he was to fight against the Patzinaks. They did as the imperial directives required, bringing all their forces together. Kegenes took [command of] the Roman legions, set up camp in open country and day by day made sudden sorties, which greatly harmed the Patzinaks. For, once they had crossed the river, they found a plentiful supply of beasts, of wine and of drinks prepared from honey of which they had never even heard. These they consumed without restraint and were afflicted by a flux of the bowels; many of them perished each day. When news of this reached Kegenes by the mouth of a deserter, [459] he judged that the opportune moment had arrived to attack the enemy, now distressed both by winter and by sickness. He convinced the Romans too, hesitant though they were and fearful of taking action against such a numerous host; for now they hurled themselves at the enemy. As for the Patzinaks, they were astounded by the violence of the onslaught and no longer had any stomach for the battle. Tyrach, all the leaders and the rest of that numerous host threw down their arms and gave

---

[152] Between 15 December and 13 January.
[153] About 7 m, which is most unlikely; even in the coldest winters flowing water rarely freezes to a depth of more than 1.5 m.
[154] The date of this crossing of the frozen Danube has long been discussed, but it is now fixed by an oration delivered by John Mauropous sometime in 1047: it was in the winter of 1046–7: J. Lefort, 'Rhétorique et politique: trois discours de jean mauropos en 1047', *TM*, 6 (1976), 274–5.
[155] Probably the son (or a close relative) of David Arianites whom Basil II appointed duke of Thessalonike.
[156] Just as he had done to counter the attack of the Turks in the east, the emperor again orders the forces of several major duchies to be combined: in this case, of Paristrion, Bulgaria and Thrace.

themselves up.¹⁵⁷ Kegenes advised and urged that every man capable of bearing arms be slain and he told them a proverb which, barbarian though it be, has something in it: 'One should kill the snake while it is still winter and it cannot move its tail; for once it is warmed by the sun it will give us much toil and trouble.' This advice did not commend itself to the leaders of the Romans; they thought it was a barbaric and impious act, unworthy of Roman benevolence. To them it seemed preferable to disperse the Patzinaks over the desert plains of Bulgaria, settling them here and there and imposing tax on them, for the tax accruing from such [settlers] would not be inconsiderable. And if the emperor needed an army [to fight] against the Turks or some other alien folk, he could arm some of these people. Many words were spoken and the opinion of the Romans won the day, but Kegenes slew all those *he* had captured alive (except the ones he had sold), then he returned to his home. Basil Monachos, the governor of Bulgaria, took the tens of thousands of Patzinaks and settled them on the plains of Sardike, Naissos and Eutzapolis.¹⁵⁸ They were all well spread out and completely stripped of weapons to guard against uprisings. As for Tyrach and his hundred and forty followers, these were brought to the emperor who received them benevolently, had them baptised and awarded them highest honours, entertaining them in luxury.

18. [460] The Sultan could not bear seeing his ambassadors returning with nothing accomplished, so he combined all the Persian and Babylonian forces and invaded the Roman empire.¹⁵⁹ Forewarned of this, Monomachos exerted himself to present a warlike resistance with his own forces; he also armed fifteen thousand of the Patzinaks, appointing four of the Patzinaks in Constantinople to command them: Soutzoun, Selte, Karaman and Kataleim. These he then showered them with gifts, providing them with first-rate weapons and excellent horses, then shipped them over to Chrysopolis. He gave them the patrician Constantine Hadrobalanos as a guide to lead them to Iberia. They crossed over [the Bosporos], mounted their horses and took the road leading to the east. When they had advanced a few miles they came near to a place named Damatrys¹⁶⁰ where they

---

¹⁵⁷ Skylitzes' account is endorsed by an oration of John Mauropous delivered 21 April 1047: tens of thousands of men from the far corners of the earth were in Constantinople because the Romans had won an unexpected victory over barbarians who greatly outnumbered them, some of whom were baptised: Lefort, 'Rhétorique', 267. Now the order of events in 1047 makes more sense: the Patzinaks invaded in spring, they were conquered; the western army was demobilised. This bred discontent which erupted in a brief mutiny (the prelude to the revolt of Tornikios in September) and explains why troops from the east were sent against Abul-Aswar in the summertime.
¹⁵⁸ Today Sofia, Nish and Ovchopol.
¹⁵⁹ The Turkish offensive of the year 1048, one of several.
¹⁶⁰ Thus they were still in the region of the capital.

came to a halt and, standing there in the road, held a conference which in their tongue they call a *komenton*. To some of them it seemed that they should press on and not disobey the emperor's orders in the emperor's own land. They were separated from their own people, unable to withstand the strength of Rome on their own, devoid of support for resisting any unwelcome turn of events. Others thought they should journey as far as some of the mountains of Bithynia, wait there and repulse those who attacked them; that they should under no circumstance go into Iberia, a distant and outlandish country where they would have not only the enemies of the Romans but the Romans themselves as enemies. Kataleim alone was of the opinion that they should return and be reunited with their kinsmen. 'And how are we going to cross the sea?' somebody asked, to which his only reply was a command to follow him. At that point they turned on Hadrobalanos, [461] but did not succeed in killing him for he took refuge on the upper floor of a three-storey building in the palace of Damatrys. So then they followed Kataleim and came to the sea, no doubt hoping that he had shipping ready there which was going to facilitate their crossing of the straits. Nevertheless, they were puzzled and wished to know how the crossing was going to be effected. When they arrived at the shore, the only thing Kataleim said was: 'Let everyone who wants himself and all the Patzinaks to survive follow me' – whereupon he spurred on his horse and entered the sea. Seeing this, another man did likewise and, after him, another; then, all at once, the entire multitude. They crossed over at St Tarasios[161] by swimming; some with their arms, others having first thrown away their arms. Once they were across, they continued their journey and were able to find refuge with their own people at Triaditza; nobody had dared to withstand or impede them. It was the totally unexpected nature of their journey which facilitated their passage. When they were united with the Patzinaks in Triaditza they made contact with those located in other regions, and when they were all assembled in a single company, armed with rustic axes, scythes and other iron tools taken from the fields, they reached Philippopolis, crossed the Haemos and pitched camp, the entire host of them, at the river Osmos on the Danubian plain. Selte alone remained at Lobitzos to rest.[162] As soon as Arianitzes had assembled the Macedonian forces he went in pursuit of them. He reached Selte encamped at Lobitzos

---

[161] Thus Kataleim crossed the Bosporos to the north of Constantinople, probably where the straits are narrow.
[162] Loveć today, a town north of the Balkan Mountains lying between Sofia and Tirnovo.

but could not capture him, for he escaped; he did, however, capture his entire camp and then he returned. That is what was happening in the west.

19. [462] As we said, the Sultan, affronted by the disdain his ambassadors had encountered and frustrated in his wishes, had mobilised his entire forces and marched out against the lands subject to the Romans.[163] He penetrated as far as the place called Komion[164] without achieving anything worthy of note, because the people of the land secured themselves and everything they needed in fortresses (Iberia has a wealth of very strong fortresses).[165] He dared not advance any further on learning that the Roman forces were concentrated at Caesarea so he returned, burning with anger and seeking to achieve some great thing. He came to Vaspurakan and, there too, he found everything similarly secured behind walls so he turned to siegecraft, first trying the strength of Manzikert.[166] Now Manzikert is a city lying on a plain but it is surrounded by a triple wall and has a plentiful supply of spring water. At that time it was very well supplied with the necessities of life.[167] The Sultan thought he could easily take it by siege since it was located in a position which gave advantage to the attacker; so he set up a palisaded camp as close as possible and laid siege to it. He spent thirty days relentlessly storming it, using various engines and every kind of machine. But the people inside courageously repelled the onslaughts, thanks to the experience and wisdom of the commander, the patrician Basil Apokapes.[168] When it became clear to the Sultan that he was attempting the impossible, he decided to raise the siege and go back home. But the general of the Khorasians, Alkan,[169] delayed this decision by asking for one more day and that [command] be turned over to him. The Sultan was pleased with this request and did postpone the retreat. Early next morning Alkan assembled the entire

---

[163] This offensive (whose object was Armenia) is also known from the eastern sources. It began in spring 1054.
[164] Okomi was located to the north-east of Kaputru on the road leading to Erzerum.
[165] *Aristakes de Lastivert*, ed. Canard and Berberian, 75–80, tells it differently: the countryside was ravaged. Seljouk forces dispersed and a band of them, encountering the Varangians stationed at Baïburt (in the south of theme of Chaldea) were put to flight, their prisoners and booty re-captured.
[166] A fortress to the north of lake Van, the capital of Vaspurkan, part of the territory of David the kouropalates at whose death (in 1000) it reverted to the empire
[167] According to *Aristakes de Lastivert*, ed. Canard and Berberian, 81–2, Togril Beg appeared before Manzikert once before, surprising the defenders who were short on provisions. But he only remained there for three days; by the time he returned the town was well stocked.
[168] This could be the son of Apokapes mentioned in the time of Basil II: *Matthew of Edessa*, ed. Dostourian, 51, 105–6.
[169] This is a title (Al Khan), not a name. *Matthew of Edessa*, ed. Dostourian, 87, names him Osketsam which means 'golden haired' in Armenian.

host under his command. He stationed the Sultan and such Turks as were of distinction where they could be seen, on an eminence facing the eastern gate of the city. Then he took the siege engines and came to the gate in question, [463] for there the city walls seemed to be neither so high nor as strong. And as there was rising ground there, this was an advantage for the besiegers, permitting those outside the walls to fire on those within. Now he divided his forces into two. One half he stationed on the rising ground with orders to make exclusive use of the bow. As for himself, he had constructed tents of wickerwork covered over with ox hides and equipped with wheels under the supporting substructure, machines which are called *lesai*. These he manned with people carrying two-pronged forks and other agricultural tools. His plan was to advance these tents a little at a time right up to the walls; then they could excavate the foundations without danger and at their leisure. He was counting on nobody being able to look down from the walls because of the heavy discharge of arrows. This was the way in which he imagined he was going to take the city; but Apokapes, observing all this from the walls, commanded the sentries on the walls not to move a muscle and certainly not to lean out. They were to occupy themselves with stockpiling hand-sized stones, arrows and other projectiles and wait until he gave the agreed signal (it was to be 'Christ help us!'). Once that was given, they could spring into action. He had by him some large beams, sharpened at one end. Those were his orders. As for Alkan, while the Turks outside the city were shooting their arrows like hail and were (supposedly) striking down the people within the walls, he advanced the *lesai* little by little and so approached the wall. When these tents had almost completed their approach and it seemed impossible for them to retreat, then Apokapes suddenly gave the agreed signal; those stationed by the beams cast them down on the tents while the rest hurled arrows and stones. The tent which contained Alkan was overturned by the weight of the several beams which had pierced its roof. As it turned over, the men within were exposed to arrows and stones from all directions and against which nothing could offer any protection.[170] [464] All the other men fell right there but Alkan was taken alive; he was recognisable by the splendour of his arms. Two handsome and excellent young men leapt out of the gates, seized him by the hair and dragged him into the city.

---

[170] On siege-warfare see the tenth-century treatises edited in D. Sullivan, *Siegecraft. Two tenth-century instructional manuals by 'Heron of Byzantium'*, Dumbarton Oaks Studies XXXVI, Washington, DC, 2000.

Basil instantly cut off his head and hurled it at the Turks.[171] The Sultan was deeply distressed by this reverse; he raised the siege and departed,[172] pretending that some compelling necessity obliged him to return home, but also threatening that he would return the following spring[173] and confront the Romans with even greater forces.[174]

20. Distracted by this threat and defending himself against Aplesphares, the ruler of Tivion (who had broken the treaty made under Constantine and was now making trouble for Roman lands), Monomachos assembled all the units of the east and appointed a eunuch named Nikephoros to command them. He was a former priest who had served the emperor while he was still a private citizen. He had renounced the priesthood in favour of secular prestige and glory; the emperor honoured him with the title of rector, named him *stratopedarches* and sent him to the east, not because he was effective and energetic in warfare, but because he was a loyal supporter of the emperor. He advanced with the army as far as the so-called Iron Bridge of Kantzakion without meeting any Turks. These were in fact encamped on the plain of Persarmenia with a commander named Abimelech, brother of Koutloumous, when they learnt that the Romans were advancing in force. Not daring to encounter this offensive, they went back home. The Roman army, however, enclosed Aplesphares within the walls, devastated the surrounding countryside and persuaded him against his will to renew the treaty, giving as hostage Artaseiras, the son of Phatloum, his own brother, ruler of the Kantzakenes' territory.[175] Nikephoros took the son and returned to the capital.

21. [465] As we said, the Patzinaks crossed the Haemos and explored the plain between that range and the river Danube, stretching as far as the

---

[171] Basil remained *katepan* of Vaspurakan but he was raised to the dignity of vestarch. He went on to a long career; he was promoted magister and duke of Paristrion towards 1065 and ended up sebastos and more or less independent duke of Edessa until 1083, the year of his death: M. Grünbart, 'Die Familie Apokapes im Lichte Neuer Quellen', *SBS*, 5 (1998), 35–6.

[172] On his way back, the Sultan took Arcke/Artzike, the residence of a commander, on the northern shore of Lake Van: *Aristakes de Lastivert*, ed. Canard and Berberian, 87, but the information given here is questionable; there could be confusion here with Arces/Artzesion, a town on the road to Manzikert, towards Berkri and Azerbaïdjan.

[173] The following year Togril Beg took the road to Baghdad.

[174] All the sources agree in praising the courage and resourcefulness of Apokapes. The sultan had built a huge balista. *Aristakes de Lastivert*, ed. Canard and Berberian, 83–5, credits an Armenian priest with knowing how to construct an instrument capable of intercepting the stones hurled by this balista. The Turks then brought up a huge, old catapult which had been built for Basil II, but a Roman, pretending to be a messenger from the governor, came by and burnt it down with a grenade filled with Greek fire. Attaleiates, *Historia*, ed. Perez Martin, 35, insists that this hero was a Latin.

[175] Phatloum ruled the Principality of Ganga in the Caucasus, of which the capital (Kirovobad today) was on the road from Tiflis to Barda'a.

sea. They found a place with vales and groves, variegated thickets, streams and pasture, known locally as Hundred Mountains.[176] They settled there and from there they made incursions which greatly afflicted the country subject to the Romans. The emperor summoned Kegenes to the capital for consultation; he came at once with all his own army and encamped on the grounds designated for training[177] named Maitas, with the entire army. He had not yet met with the emperor, nor even learnt why he was summoned, when three armed Patzinaks attacked him in bed at night and wounded him, not mortally. The bodyguards detected them immediately; they made some feeble resistance and ran off but they were captured when several men together with Valtzar, son of Kegenes, came running at the cries for help. In the morning Valtzar placed his father in a four-wheeled carriage, dragging the conspirators behind the carriage in chains. He dare not do any more than that to them as they were appealing to the emperor. Then he came to the emperor with the whole army on horseback, except him and his brother Goulinos who were on foot, following the carriage drawn by two horses. When they arrived at the Hippodrome they stopped the carriage there while Valtzar went in to the emperor; word of his coming had preceded him and prepared his way. When he was introduced to the presence, the emperor asked him why he had not punished his father's murderers right away. 'Because they were invoking your name,' the other replied, at which the emperor began to have some very dark suspicions. Quick as a flash he had the prisoners brought before them and put the question to them: Why had they undertaken to kill the patrician? [466] 'Because he was evilly disposed towards your reign and to the city; he was intending to enter the city at dawn, to slaughter everybody in it, pillage the city and return to the Patzinaks.' He ought to have examined these statements to find out the truth but that is not what he did; he put his faith in some irresponsible and inconsistent accusations. Under pretence of getting Kegenes healed and restored, he brought him into the capital and confined him in the Elephantine [prison], locating the man's sons each in a different place, some distance from him. The rest of the Patzinaks he entertained with food and drink under pretence of being well disposed towards them; but in fact doing everything in his power to deprive them of weapons and horses and to hold them in detention. He ordered the would-be assassins to be allowed to go wherever they wished, freely and

---

[176] This name occurs in the *Alexiad* (2:104) in connection with the wars against the Patzinaks. The precise location is not known; it was in Bulgaria, near to Preslav.
[177] Reading *paideian* for *pedian*.

unimpeded. He thought he had escaped notice in doing this but he had not deceived the Patzinak folk. They reckoned it betokened no good that he had arrested their leader and separated his sons; now they took the release of the would-be assassins as a clear sign of malevolence. So they gratefully accepted all that was sent to them [by the emperor] and sang his praises; indeed, they affirmed that everything met with their approval. But, when night fell and nobody was suspecting anything, they left the camp and travelled all night without stopping. On the third day they recrossed the Haemos and were united with the main body of the Patzinaks. When they were all together, now that they were sufficiently provided with arms, they crossed the Haemos and established a camp at Aule, a fortress lying in the foothills of the Haemos, not far from Adrianople, turning their attention to pillaging and looting.

22. When the ruler of the west, the magister Constantine Arianites, [467] learnt of this, he took the forces under his command which were ready for action and marched out of Adrianople against them. Encountering some scattered forces of the enemy on his journey he got the better of them, but when he approached the fortress of Dampolis,[178] there he encountered the main army, gave battle and was defeated. Many Macedonians and Thracians fell in the battle; Theodore Strabomytes and Polys were lost, men distinguished by birth and become famous through the treachery of Tornikios. The magister retired to Adrianople from where he announced the disaster to the emperor by letter. He advised that a new army would have to be raised, for it was impossible to resist so large a host with the present troops, they having already turned and run. The emperor (who knew something of what had happened prior to the letter) now won over Tyrach and the Patzinak chieftains who were detained in the city with gifts and favours; then he dismissed them, they having sworn that they would pacify their folk. The emperor also summoned all the eastern units by letter; when they came, crossing at Abydos and Chrysopolis, he appointed Nikephoros the rector to be commander plenipotentiary and sent him out against the Patzinaks. Together with him he sent Katakalon Kekaumenos (promoted stratelates of the east) and Hervé Frankopoulos, chieftain of his fellow countrymen at that time.[179] Their orders were to go

---

[178] Today Jambol in Bulgaria. Lying in the valley of the Tundza, this fortress controlled the road between the Balkan and the Haemos mountains. It was a key position when Alexios I was fighting the Patzinaks.

[179] This is the earliest mention by a Byzantine chronicler of the chief of the Latin contingent. Hervé had previously served under George Maniakes (the first Byzantine commander who had made extensive use of the Franks), in charge of a contingent bearing the name of Maniakates, in honour of the commander-in-chief.

along with the rector, to be of one mind with him and to carry out his orders and wishes.

The rector took his forces and advanced against the Patzinaks, crossing the Haemos through the Iron [Gates]. As he advanced he encamped at a village called Diakene, not far from the Hundred Mountains, where he erected a solid palisade. It was his intention to leave the baggage there next day plus whatever was superfluous to the needs of the army while he [468] made a rapid advance and engaged the foe, whom he fondly imagined he would overcome at the first blow. He was afraid and concerned that any might evade capture; not only he, but the whole army too was thinking along those lines. They had even brought along ropes and thongs with which to detain the captives; what gave them these ideas was the disaster which had befallen the Patzinaks at the beginning, under Kegenes.[180] The Patzinaks were of course fully aware of the approach of the Romans for, after leaving the city, Tyrach and the chieftains who accompanied him had joined up with them and were looking out for their own interests, regardless of the undertakings they had given Monomachos. As the bravest men ran forward, Kekaumenos proclaimed and urged loudest of all that now was the time for battle, now while the enemy was spread out and dispersed; that they should not wait for the entire host to assemble.[181] But the remaining portion of the Romans were not in favour of what he advocated; the rector laughed openly. 'Stop this, stratelates,' he said, 'and do not contradict my orders, for I am in command here. We ought not to attack the Patzinaks while they are dispersed for we might frighten them into taking cover in the woods. And if I were to go in pursuit of them, my man, I would have no hunting dogs capable of tracking them down by scent and dragging them from their hiding places.' That is how it was with the Romans.

The Patzinaks now began approaching the encampment of the Romans; the first arrivals withdrew a little and pitched their camp, signalling to those behind to advance in all haste. They all arrived and formed a single army; next day the rector led out the Roman forces and drew them up in battle order. The rector himself took command of the centre of the Roman formation; Kekaumenos commanded the right wing, Frankopoulos the other. When battle was joined, the Romans were repelled, the Stratelates[182]

---

[180] This no doubt refers to the defection of Kegenes and his victories against his fellow countrymen before 1046: reign of Constantine IX, cc. 16 and 17.

[181] Once again Skylitzes is using a source which records the exploits of Kekaumenos; the stratelates is rendered blameless for the disaster which is about to occur.

[182] The word is plural; it does *not* refer to Kekaumenos, but to a regiment of this name which was already active in the eleventh century.

[469] being the first to turn and flee. It is said that they were put to flight before they even heard the hoof-beats of the horses! Kekaumenos alone stood his ground with his attendants and some distant relatives; he fell together with all his retinue, fighting heroically. The Patzinaks were reluctant to pursue the Romans for fear of an ambush and, on that account, the Romans were able to reach safety unscathed. The foe despoiled the fallen and captured a great quantity of arms. They even took possession of the Roman camp together with the baggage and set up their tents against the Roman defence works.[183] There was a Patzinak, Koulinos by name, who knew who Kekaumenos was because he came from the fortresses on the Danube where the peoples mingle with each other. When he found Kekaumenos lying among the dead and was about to despoil him, as he turned him over he recognised the face. Realising that he was still breathing, the Patzinak set him on his horse, where he lay unconscious, for he had received some mortal wounds. One had laid bare his skull (his helmet having fallen off) from the peak to the eyebrow, another on the collar had cut the neck at the root of the tongue, right through to the mouth; he had lost much blood. The man took him to his own tent where, by dint of diligent care and attention, he saved his life.[184]

After having so easily disposed of the invading army the Patzinaks proceeded freely and fearlessly to plunder Roman territory. The emperor was greatly distressed (as well he might be) when he learnt of the disaster from fugitives. He raised another army, enlisted the survivors and attempted the following year to repair the former reverse. At the beginning of the third year of the indiction, AM 6558, the emperor appointed the hetaireiarch Constantine commander plenipotentiary [470] and sent him against the Patzinaks. Taking the troops which had recently been brought across from the east[185] and assembling those who were wintering in the west, he came to Adrianople. There he constructed an immense defence work and stayed there, trying to decide (together with the senior officers) in what direction to continue the advance. While he was pondering this question, suddenly, on the eighth of June, the Patzinaks crossed the Haemos and appeared before Adrianople. Constantine was advised of their invasion by scouts; a council was held to decide whether to fight them or not. The senior officers

---

[183] Samuel Boutzes was the grandson of the conqueror of Antioch: reign of Nikephorus Phokas, c. 17; Chenier and Vanier, *Études prosopographiques*, 34–5, rpr. in Cheynet, *Société*, 356–7.
[184] A seal of Kekaumenos qua duke of Antioch has been found on Ukranian soil in an area where the Patzinaks used to roam. This could indicate bonds of friendship with Koulinos/Goulinos: c. 21 above.
[185] 1049; there is a temporary lull in the Seljuk attacks.

discussed what should be done in the tent of the hetaireiarch. The patrician Samuel Bourtzes was a bold and brazen man who was then officer commanding the infantry, fully responsible for guarding the defence work. Without waiting for the commander's signal, he broke ranks, opened the defence work, sallied forth with the infantry and attacked the Patzinaks, who violently fell upon them so that the infantry began to make heavy weather of it. Hence Samuel sent several times to the hetaireiarch asking for help which, in turn, obliged *him*, against his will, to give the signal for battle. So the entire army marched out at a place called Basilike Libas and a general engagement ensued. The Patzinaks were heartened by the sudden and irregular onslaught of the previously defeated infantry; hence the Romans now suffered an appalling defeat, although they suffered no great loss of life because they shamefully enclosed themselves within the defence work. The patrician Michael Dokeianos fell; the magister Constantine Arianites suffered a mortal wound in the intestines and died two days after; there also fell a few other persons of no distinction. All the rest of the army was besieged by the Patzinaks, ignobly enclosed within the defence work. The enemy filled up the ditch with stones and branches, attempting to take the defence work by storm. They would soon have succeeded too if [471] Soultzous together with his horse had not been struck by an arrow fired from a catapult, which threw the Patzinaks who witnessed the event into great consternation. Then relief arrived when the protospatharios Niketas Glabas, acting commander of the regiment of the Scholai, marched out from Adrianople. The Patzinaks saw this, and as they were apprehensive of the arrival of Basil the synkellos with the troops of the Bulgarikon (who was indeed expected to come) they became afraid and dispersed in flight, retreating this way and that; otherwise the entire Roman army would have been lost to a man.

23. In that year there was a charge of attempted usurpation against certain high officials of the city, their leaders being Nikephoros and Michael, sons of Euthymios,[186] and other members of their family. All the others were acquitted; the only exception was Nikephoros, who was condemned to be exiled without trial and his goods were confiscated by the state.

24. Searching to stiffen his resistance to the Patzinaks, the emperor brought Kegenes out of prison and sent him to them, he having undertaken to divide them and win their support for the emperor. Then he

---

[186] It is not known what was behind this conspiracy; the sons of Euthymios both exercised the office of judge in the Thrakesion theme in due course: *Catalogue of the Byzantine seals at Dumbarton Oaks and in the Fogg Museum of Art*, I–IV, ed. J. Nesbitt and N. Oikonomides (Washington, DC, 1991–7), 3.2.18.

concentrated all the auxiliary forces, Franks and Varangians I mean. He summoned mounted archers, about twenty thousand of them, from Telouch, from the Black Mountains and from Karkaros. He committed each of the nations to men of distinction and appointed the patrician Bryennios leader of them all with the title of ethnarch;[187] he was sent out with orders to hinder and terminate the incursions of the Patzinaks. These had begun to despise the Romans altogether after the battle of Adrianople; they were pillaging and burning Macedonia and Thrace [472] with impunity, mercilessly slaughtering even babes at the breast. They were so bold that one party of them advanced as far as Katasyrtai, which is very close to the capital, but they reaped their reward in very quick time. The emperor easily got the better of them by arming a company drawn from the palace guards and some other men who happened to be available; this company was committed to the patrician John Philosopher,[188] one of the eunuchs of the empress Zoe's bedchamber. John went out by night and, finding the enemy all drunk and sleeping, slew them. He piled their heads in farm carts and delivered them to the emperor.

25. Kegenes set out and despatched a delegation to the Patzinaks who promised him with oaths to do whatever he wanted. Trusting their oaths, he went to them but he was promptly murdered and cut up into small pieces. Taking the forces entrusted to him, Bryennios came to Adrianople and gave his attention to the task of protecting the villages. The patrician Michael the *akolouthos*[189] was sent as supreme leader of the whole army, he too with orders to avoid a formal battle but to hinder and terminate the incursions. He set out and made contact with Bryennios, then they went into action. They encountered a company of Patzinaks at Goloes which they routed and eliminated. Then again at Toplitzos, a fortress on the Hebros, they found and destroyed another detached company of Patzinaks. Sobered by these initiatives, the Patzinak forces desisted from pillaging the villages in the foothills of the Haemos, directing their entire onslaught against Macedonia. They overran the villages of Macedonia with what was discerned as their superior forces, preparing

---

[187] With the appointment of Bryennios in 1050 the Romans changed their tactics; in future formal, large-scale battles were avoided. Bryennios (whose Christian name is unknown) is the first member of this illustrious family of Adrianople mentioned by our author. His son, Nikephoros, made an unsuccessful attempt to seize the throne in 1078 but his great-grandson married Anna, elder daughter of Alexios Komnenos.

[188] Philosopher is a family name by which certain other officials are known. It could be of Arab or oriental origin for a Basil Chasanes, son of Philosopher, magister and judge of Velum, is attested in the second half of the eleventh century: Staurakos, *Bleisiegel*, 409.

[189] Probably the commander of the Varangians.

to give whatever foe should come upon them a most vigorous reception. When Bryennios [473] and Michael learnt of this they took off by night in such a way that nobody would have any idea where they were going and came to Charioupolis,[190] travelling at speed. They entered that town with the whole army and waited for the right moment. When the Patzinaks had pillaged all the fields and the estates, they returned close to the town towards evening, about the time for unhitching, and set up camp there, not in the least aware that the entire army was housed in the town. They hadn't a care in the world, dancing to flutes and cymbals; but when night had fallen, the men with Bryennios and Michael went out, found them abed and snoring, and slew every one of them. This reverse put fear and caution into the Patzinaks; in the fourth and fifth years of the indiction they no longer raided with impunity as before, but sporadically.

26. It was in that year that the sudden rise to fame of Romanos Boilas[191] took place. He was enrolled in the hetaireiai, a sharp-tongued individual who, on that account, seemed very urbane and quick-witted. There was an occasion when he came to the emperor's notice and spoke with him; he seemed most pleasant [to the ruler] who became henceforth inseparable from him all the time, using him as counsellor, agent, attendant and performer of every kind of service. Gradually advancing him through the ranks, he exalted and promoted him to a high position until he occupied the chief position in the palace. He was an ingenious and complex fellow with his eye on the throne; he was always sounding out any of the senators who were at odds with the emperor and revealing his secret [desire]. He quietly and surreptitiously won over those he met who appreciated his talk of a conspiracy, assuring himself of their support with oaths. As for those who started aside at the mere whisper of [a conspiracy], he pretended to applaud [474] their reaction and to admire their support for the emperor, claiming he had only spoken in that way to try them out and swearing that he would speak up on their behalf before the emperor. In the end, after he had corrupted many of the citizens and was actually fostering a revolt, his cover was blown. All the others who had taken oaths to him first endured painful examinations. Then they were stripped of their personal possessions and sent off into exile, but Romanos suffered no unpleasant

---

[190] Hayrabolu today, to the south of Bulgarophygon/Babaeski on the road leading from Rhaidestos to Didymoticus.
[191] Scion of an old family, probably of Slavic origin, which seems to have been established in Cappadocia at that time. A Eustathios Boilas, a contemporary of Romanos, has left a will dated 1059: P. Lemerle, *Cinq études sur le XIe siècle byzantin* (Paris, 1977), 15–63. Psellos gives a lengthy account of this court intrigue: Psellos, *Chronographia*, 6.139–51, trans. Sewter, 228–35.

experiences. The emperor kept his distance from him for a short while, but then he was pardoned and resumed his former position.

27. As we said, the Sultan was ill-disposed towards his brother Abram, always plotting against his life and constantly seeking to do away with him. When Abram became aware of this, he slipped away to his nephew, Koutloumous, whereupon the two of them went to war against the Sultan. But he encountered them and put them to flight at the place called Pasar, capturing Abram, whom he slew. Koutloumous got away with six thousand men including Melech, the son of Abram. He made overtures to the emperor asking to be accepted as an ally and friend of the Romans; he came to the place called Kars[192] in Persarmenia and awaited the response to his embassy. Meanwhile he besieged Kars and took it, except for the acropolis. Then the Sultan, coming in pursuit, arrived in Iberia with his forces; when Koutloumous learnt of this he fled into Saba and Arabia Felix. While the Sultan was in Iberia he looted and burned everything that came his way, which caused the emperor to recall Michael the *akolouthos* from the west in haste and send him into Iberia.[193] When he arrived there he gathered up the Franks and Varangians who were dispersed in Chaldia and Iberia and undertook to do the best he could to prevent the incursions of the Sultan who, when he heard of Michael's precipitous arrival and mustering of a host, hastened to join battle with him. He calculated (as well he might) that neither outcome of the affair would be to his advantage: victorious, he would only have conquered a slave of the emperor while, if he were defeated, he would be put to severe disgrace. So he took his entire army and returned to Tabriz.

28. At that time Michael, son of Stephen, who had succeeded his father as chieftain of the Traballes and Serbs, made a treaty with the emperor and was inscribed among the allies and friends of the Romans; he was honoured with the title of protospatharios.[194] Beasts were sent to the emperor from Egypt by its ruler: an elephant and a giraffe.[195] The

---

[192] Kars was the capital of the small Armenian kingdom of Vanand, ruled by Gagik (the same name as the sovereign of Ani) from 1029 to 1064, when he surrendered his kingdom to the Romans. In 1053 it was taken by the Seljoukids, probably under the command of Qutlumus: Felix, *Byzanz und Islam*, 173.

[193] The narrative is confused here. It seems to have reverted to the Sultan's attack of 1054 when the Franks and the Varangians repelled bands of Turks.

[194] The date of this treaty is uncertain as it depends on Skylitzes' chronology, never very reliable. It could be dated to 1053 if it were coeval with the serious defeat of the Romans by the Patzinaks.

[195] Constantine IX maintained close relations with the Fatimids; Psellos criticises his submissiveness towards Al Mustancir: Psellos, *Chronographia*, 6.190, trans. Sewter, 253–4. The ten-year truce signed by Michael IV in 1035/6 was renewed and, in 1054, the emperor sent great quantities of grain to Egypt, then in the grip of a famine: Felix, *Byzanz und Islam*, 119–20.

Constantine IX Monomachos

emperor wished to have done once and for all with the Patzinaks, so he assembled troops from all parts, east and west, confiding them to Michael the *akolouthos*. He ordered Basil the Synkellos to take command of the Bulgar forces, then he sent them both out against the Patzinaks. When *they* heard of this, they erected a palisade adjacent to Great Preslav, fortified with a deep moat and stockades. They enclosed themselves within when the Romans arrived and withstood the ensuing siege.[196] When the Romans realized that they were wasting time to no avail, achieving nothing worthy of note, also that they were running short of the necessities of life, they held a conference to consider what they should do. Everybody was of the opinion that they should return home so, in the middle of the night, in silence (as they were ordered), they opened the gates and abandoned the camp. This did not escape the notice of Tyrach; when he learnt that they were attempting to get away, he led an enormous host out of the palisade and sent it along the routes which the Romans were going to traverse while he himself attacked them as soon as they came out. There was a terrible rout of the Romans; some were overtaken and slain by pursuers, others were captured by those who had taken up positions along the difficult routes. A large number fell, including [476] the synkellos himself, while the rest found refuge in Adrianople with Michael.[197] The emperor was distressed by this misfortune; he gathered up those who had escaped the disaster, mustered another army and enlisted some mercenaries, thinking that life would not be worth living if he could not completely destroy the Patzinak people. But when the Patzinaks learnt of this from a deserter they sent a delegation to the emperor asking for peace. He received the delegation and made a thirty-year treaty with them.[198]

---

[196] The Patzinaks were firmly entrenched to the north of the Haemos mountains; Monomachos was afraid they might constitute themselves another nomad state, as the Bulgars before them had done.

[197] Michael Attaleiates, *Historia*, ed. Perez Martin, 37–43, gives a lengthy account of this battle because involved in it was his hero, Nikephoros Botaneiates. He explains that the defeat was due to the divided command and especially due to the incompetence of the commander of Bulgaria, Basil the synkellos. When the retreat began, Nikephoros Botaneiates, probably commanding one of the regiments from the east, succeeded in getting his troops out in one piece and in perfect formation.

[198] Monomachos acquiesced in the presence of the Patzinaks in the region of Preslav and Dristra, an area in which they had settled because it was compatible with their way of life. He also granted dignities to the conspicuous inhabitants of the towns of Paristrion to ensure their loyalty: Stephenson, *Balkan Frontier*, 93.

29. In building the monastery to the holy and great martyr George, known as Mangana, the emperor lavished public money on the project,[199] now building up, now tearing down what he had constructed. He ran so short of money that he invented all kinds of commerce to increase revenue, devising unusual and exquisite taxes and appointing impious and criminal men as tax collectors through whom he amassed wealth by unjust means. He even disbanded the Iberian army numbering about fifty thousand[200] by the agency of Leo Serblios and then raised heavy taxes instead of soldiers in those regions.[201] He devised many other wicked and iniquitous taxes which it would be a disgrace to list; but there is one thing which has to be mentioned and I will say it: that it was from the time of this emperor and on account of his prodigality and pretentiousness that the fortunes of the Roman empire began to waste away.[202] From that time until now it has regressed into an all-encompassing debility. He simply sought to be open-handed yet he ended up being utterly profligate.

He was not, however, totally devoid of good works, and some of them are worthy of being recorded in history. [477] The above-mentioned monastery with its homes for the aged, its hostels and its poorhouses is deserving of praise. Nor should the services he rendered to the Great Church be denied their accolade. Until his time the holy Eucharist was only offered to God on greater feast days, Saturdays and Sundays in that place and not at all on the other days, for want of revenue. This the emperor generously augmented in such a way that the sacred liturgy could be celebrated every day, as it continues to be until our time. He also presented to that church golden vessels set with valuable pearls and precious stones, dedicated for

---

[199] The Mangana was already the centre of a *kouratorikion* (adminstered by a *kourator*) attested from the beginning of the ninth century, renovated by Basil I. Constantine Monomachos determined to build a foundation, *oikos* or *sekreton* (designed to bring in a large income for his mistress) in honour of St George – for whom he had a particular devotion and of whom he possessed a relic. Psellos says he used to visit his mistress (Skleraina, who lived near the Kynegion) under pretext of inspecting the work-in-progress there: Psellos, *Chronographia*, 6.54–5, trans. Sewter, 182. This *oikos* was provided with magnificent buildings: a hospice, a hospital, a residence for the poor, etc. The foundation was inaugurated on 21 April 1047 and was under the direction of the oikonomos of the Tropaiophore: N. Oikonomides, 'St George of Mangana', 239–47.

[200] This could not have been the number of men on active service in the Iberian army; it may be the number of families recorded in the army registers.

[201] Apparently the emperor wanted to replace the military service owed by the resident population with a tax, thus bringing Iberia into line with the model of the older Roman themes. Yet the resistance of the Iberian army against the sultan at Manzikert shows that on the eve of the death of Monomachos there is no evidence of weakening near the frontier, the first line of defence.

[202] This accusation is a little unfair from a military point of view considering what splendid generals served under him: Katakalon Kekaumenos, Basil Apokapes, Isaac Komnenos, Michael Iassites, etc.

the holy communion. These far outdistanced the other vessels in size, beauty and value. He also enhanced that church with many other treasures. Such were his deeds.[203]

30. In the seventh and eighth years of the indiction the capital was visited by plague; the living were unequal to the task of bearing away the dead. In the summer of the seventh year of the indiction there was a great hailstorm which caused many deaths, not only of animals but of men too.[204] The emperor had an attack of gout, a familiar affliction for him, and was lying in the Mangana monastery which he had recently built. A further illness followed on the first one and he was near to death; the question of whom they should establish on the imperial throne was debated by those who held the highest positions in the palace. These were John the logothete who was the emperor's partner in government since he had expelled Leichoudes,[205] Constantine the protonotary of the drome, [478] Basil the prefect of the imperial inkstand and the rest of those [eunuchs] who were close to the emperor in some way. They all thought that Nikephoros proteuon[206] was a suitable candidate so a courier was sent in haste to Bulgaria to bring him from there, for at that time he was functioning as governor of Bulgaria. When those who served the empress Theodora learnt of this (Zoe had already departed this life),[207] Niketas Xylinites,[208] Theodore and Manuel took her aboard ship, brought her to the imperial residence in the Great Palace and proclaimed her ruling emperor. The emperor died[209]

---

[203] The extent of the imperial generosity is indicated within Hagia Sophia itself by the famous mosaic portraying Monomachos (originally Romanos III) offering a purse of gold to the church: N. Oikonomides, 'The mosaic panel of Constantine IX and Zoe in Saint Sophia', *REB*, 36 (1978), 219–32.

[204] The summer of the seventh indiction means July–September 1054. Together with the other Byzantine chroniclers, Skylitzes says nothing of the event which was to make such a deep impression on religious history: the mutual excommunication of the Patriarch Michael Keroularios and the papal legates in July 1054, incorrectly known as 'the schism of 1054': M. Kaplan, 'Le "schisme" de 1054: quelques éléments de chronologie', *BS*, 56 (1995), *Mélanges V. Vavrínek*, 147–157l: J.-Cl. Cheynet, 'Le schisme de 1054: un non-événement', in *Faire l'événement au Moyen Âge*, ed. Cl. Carozzi and H. Taviani-Carozzi (Aix, 2007), 299–312.

[205] Psellos has given a portrait of this eunuch *epi tou koitonos*, president of the senate whom Monomachos sent packing: Psellos, *Chronographia*, 6.191–9, trans. Sewter, 254–8.

[206] The governor of Bulgaria was usually a duke or a *katepan* (i.e. a military officer), but Nikephoros proteuon is mentioned above as a judge and those who supported him were all ranking civil servants. On the family of this man (of which other representatives are known): Cheynet, *Pouvoir*, 65–6.

[207] Zoe died towards 1050. Psellos says she died of old age when she was seventy-two: Psellos, *Chronographia*, 6.184, trans. Sewter, 250. She was buried in a church of her founding, Christ Antiphonites: *Anonymous Sathas, MB*, VII, 163.

[208] The Xylinitai were one of the oldest families of the empire, known already in the eighth century when Niketas Xylinites participated in an abortive conspiracy against Leo III the Isaurian: *Theophanis Chronographia*, 1, ed. C. de Boor (Leipzig, 1883–5), 400.

[209] 7–8 January 1055.

in the Mangana and received a tomb like any other. They of the empress' entourage sent and arrested the proteuon in Thessalonike,[210] took him from there into the Thrakesion theme and exiled him to the monastery of Kouzenas which is there.[211]

---

[210] Attaleiates, *Historia*, ed. Perez Martin, 51, says Monomachos died before he was able to complete his project.
[211] Located near to Magnesia on the river Maeander: Janin, *Grands centres byzantins*, II, 241.

CHAPTER 22

Theodora [1055–1056]

1. [479] Once she had acquired her hereditary throne[1] Theodora[2] immediately pursued with vengeance those who had plotted to make the proteuon ruler, depriving them of their property and sending them into exile. She promoted all her eunuchs to high office,[3] appointing Theodore to be domestic of the scholai for the east and sending him to the orient to obstruct the inroads of the Turks (she had previously removed the magister Isaac Komnenos[4] from his position of stratopedarch). Monomachos had already shipped all the Macedonian forces over to the east with Macedonians exclusively in command (of whom Bryennios was one) because it was rumoured among the Turkish people that they would be overturned by a force similar to that with which Alexander the Macedonian overturned the Persians. She appointed Niketas[5] to be logothete of the drome, Manuel droungarios of the watch. She also appointed to her service the synkellos, Leo Strabospondylos,[6] who had

---

[1] Psellos relates that Theodora took shipping from her place of confinement and was immediately acclaimed by the imperial guard, on account of the 'the purple in which she was swathed': *Chronographia*, 6.202, trans. Sewter, 259–60.
[2] On Theodora (most recently): K.-P. Todt, 'Die Frau als Selbstherrscher: Kaisarin Theodora, die lezte Angehörige der Makedonischen Dynastie', *JÖB*, 50 (2000), 139–71.
[3] Psellos says the capital was surprised by the sight of an aged empress ruling by herself without choosing an emperor. This attitude was shared by the patriarch, Michael Keroularios, to the point that the empress was thinking of deposing him: Psellos, *Chronographia*, 6 (Theodora), 18, trans. Sewter, 269.
[4] This Isaac was the elder son of Manuel Komnenos-Erotikos who defended Nicaea against Bardas Skleros under Basil II. After the death of the father it fell to Basil II to educate the sons, Isaac and his brother John. The elder brother married Catherine of the Bulgar royal family while the younger was wed to Anna Dalassena. By the time Theodora came to the throne Isaac already had a long career to his credit; he had commanded a number of important themes, including Vaspurakan. He was probably stratopedarch of the east at the death of Monomachos and officer responsible for the security of the eastern frontier. The empress distanced herself from this faithful servant of Monomachos: K. Barzos, *Hê genealogia tôn Komnênôn*, Byzantina keimena kai meletai 20, Thessalonica 1984, 1, 41–7.
[5] Niketas Xylinites had been strongly in favour of her accession.
[6] Leo Strabospondylos or Paraspondylos (Psellos, *MB*, v, 104, 115ff) was a scion of the Spondylai family which provided many officials in those days: Seibt, *Bleisiegel*, 1, no. 163. While Psellos is

served under the emperor Michael, on account of his experience in the administration of public affairs.

When Leo, Archbishop of Bulgaria, died she appointed the monk Theodoulos, originally from Iconium, a city of Tetrapolis, hegoumenos of the monastery of the great and holy martyr Mokios; he was totally ignorant of secular learning but was profoundly versed in divinity, exuding the grace and virtue which sacred studies inspire.[7]

{That is how it was in the city. As for Bryennios, when he heard of the emperor's death, he set out with the Macedonian troops and came to Chrysopolis where the empress had him arrested [480] for deserting his post contrary to orders. She confiscated his property and sent him into exile, arranging for his host to be sent back.[8] The empress lived throughout the ninth year of the indiction, AM 6564, but towards the end of August she fell ill with a blockage of the bowel and died.}[9]

Even while she was still taking her last breaths, the eunuchs together with Leo synkellos elevated the patrician Michael Stratiotikos[10] to the imperial throne. He was a native of Byzantium, a simple and straightforward man who, from his youth up, had only been occupied with military matters; he knew nothing about anything else. He was already over the hill and entering old age, the age in which it is better to be retired (as the poet Archilochos declares).[11] They took this action to ensure that he would only have the appearance and the name of emperor while they themselves conducted affairs of state as they wished and became master of all. He had previously sworn never to do anything contrary to their opinion and volition.

    moderately favourable to Leo (*Chronographia*, 6.207, trans. Sewter, 263), Attaleiates (*Historia*, 39) covers him with praise, alleging that he was incorruptible. He had served under Michael IV but appears to have been somewhat in disgrace under Constantine IX: E. de Vries-van der Velden, 'Les amitiés dangereuses: Psellos et Léon Paraspondylos', *BS*, 60 (1999), 315–50.

[7] MSS ACEUV. This prelate is also known from a list of Bulgarian archbishops drawn up in the twelfth century. He had the large church above Ochrid built with financial help from John Anzas. He must have died c. 1063: P. Gautier, *Théophylacti Achridensis orationes, tractatus, carmina: introduction, traduction et notes* (CFHB, 16/1, Thessalonike, 1980), 31–2.

[8] Ever since Togril Beg entered Baghdad the east was once again under the Turkish threat and suffered several invasions. Theodora sent an embassy to Baghdad: *Aristakes de Lastivert*, ed. Canard and Berberian, 93–4. On the first Turkish invasions of Anatolia: C. Cahen, 'La première pénétration turque en Asie Mineure (seconde moitié du XIe siècle)', *B*, 18 (1948), 5–67, rpr. in Cahen, *Turcobyzantina*, no. I; S. Vryonis, *The decline of medieval hellenism in Asia Minor and the process of Islamization from the eleventh through the fifteenth century* (Los Angeles, 1971), 70–113.

[9] 21 August 1056: Schreiner, *Kleinchroniken*, no. 15, 160.

[10] Michael's surname was Bringas; he was related to Joseph Bringas the parakoimomenos who had opposed Nikephoros Phokas in 963. He was known as stratiotikos because he had been logothete of the stratiotikon: Oikonomides, *Listes*, 314. He appears to have been quite old and childless.

[11] Archilochos, Fragment 50D = 330 West.

CHAPTER 23

Michael VI the Elder/Stratiotikos [1056–1057]

1. [481] Michael was proclaimed ruling emperor on 31 August, ninth year of the indiction. When Theodosios the proedros, son of the brother of the father of the emperor Constantine Monomachos, heard of the proclamation he was deeply offended and, without stopping to think about what he was doing or counting the cost and the likelihood of it miscarrying or considering how the throw of the dice might turn out (as it were), he called up his relations, his slaves and others who served him in any way, many of his neighbours and some of his acquaintances, in fact as many as were somewhat hot-headed. Towards evening he set out with them from his house which lies in the district called Leomakellion[1] and proceeded, complaining and protesting, along the main artery [Mese], as though they were going to the palace. As one who had been utterly wronged, he called out the injustice of it to those he encountered, demanding the throne as though it were a hereditary property which ought to be his because he was more closely related by blood to the departed emperor than the others.[2] When he came to the praetorium he broke down the gates of the prison and led out the captives in the hope (I think) of accomplishing some great and noble deed with them. He did the same when he got to the Chalke. But when the uprising became known to the palace eunuchs they speedily armed the soldiers on guard duty in the palace, Romans and Varangians (the Varangians are a Celtic[3] people serving the Romans as mercenaries), and speedily alerted the crews of the imperial ships. [482] An able-bodied company was assembled and made ready to be sent against Theodosios.

---

[1] Possibly 'the meat-market of Leo' (near the Marmara, south of the forum of Theodosios): R. Janin, *Constantinople byzantine* (*AOC*, 4A, Paris, 1964), 379–80. The emperor Leo I is known as *makelles*, 'butcher'.

[2] As a first cousin of Constantine Monomachos (who had died childless), he considered himself to be the heir. His standing as proedros (which at that time was still a very high rank indeed) indicates that the emperor had granted him high distinction.

[3] Is Skylitzes giving a definition of Varangians which was still correct in his time or had the Russians been replaced by Latins at the core of the Varangian Guard since the mid-eleventh century?

When he learned of this he deviated from the route leading to the palace and fell back on the Great Church of God in the hope that when he entered that place the patriarch and clergy would receive him; that a numerous crowd would congregate and proclaim him emperor.[4] Quite the opposite happened; the patriarch and the clergy of the church closed its gates to him as he arrived[5] and of those who usually rejoice in such events and come running there was nobody at all. Even those who had accompanied him as far as this place, on hearing that a force was about to be sent against them, slipped away little by little and were scattered until, at the end, he was left devoid of all support, a miserable suppliant sitting before the church with his child. [The eunuchs] sent and dragged him from the church then exiled him to Pergamon; they did likewise to the more distinguished of those who had been involved with him. Thenceforth the proclamation of Michael as ruling emperor was uncontested.

2. Taking the reins of the empire into his hands he advanced all the illustrious members of the Senate on the scale of honours and made the people promises of many good things to come.[6] Being a man of great age who could recall many aspects of the past, he undertook to revive several ancient customs which had fallen into disuse; not that these would benefit the state or the people in any way. He ordered the place called the strategion to be cleaned out,[7] at which the citizens scoffed and said that they were shovelling out the earth in search of one of his bones he had lost while playing there. He also stipulated that the citizens' heads were to be covered, not with plain linen as now, but with striped linen [483] woven with [bands of?] Indian cotton and purple. As tax collectors he appointed not senators, but shorthand secretaries who had made their way up through various departments. There were many such things, but it would become tiresome to the reader if I were to opt for listing them one by one. He went on like this, wielding the sceptre artlessly and governing without skill. When the time came round for the imperial bounty which the emperors were accustomed to distribute to the Senate annually

---

[4] Theodosios was hoping for the support of Keroularios who was antipathetic to the faction which governed with Theodora and continued to exercise power under Michael VI.
[5] The patriarch could not support such an ill-prepared movement for it was doomed to fail.
[6] Michel Psellos, (*Chronographia* 7.2, trans. Sewter, 276–7) says Michael VI was excessive in his distribution of dignities – which only went to Constantinopolitans. Attaleiates (*Historia*, 53) accuses him of exclusively favouring those of his own faction, for which he was blamed by both the aristocracy and the lower orders.
[7] On the decay of this large space inherited from antiquity and the vain attempt of Michael VI to restore it: P. Magdalino, *Constantinople médiévale: études sur l'évolution des structures urbaines* (Paris, 1996), 51–2.

at Eastertide, all those army commanders who were distinguished by birth or valour came into his presence: the magister Isaac Komnenos,[8] the magister Katakalon Kekaumenos (formerly duke of Antioch[9] but he had been relieved of his command and was succeeded by Michael, nephew of the emperor who had given him the name of Ouranos on the occasion of his proclamation because his family supposedly derived from the ancient Ouranos. The emperor honoured him with the title magister of Antioch which that other Ouranos[10] had held – and sent him to succeed Kekaumenos) – the vestarches Michael Bourtzes,[11] Constantine and John of the eastern branch of the Doukai[12] family and the rest of those distinguished persons who held high office. They all came running to see the new emperor and to collect his bounty, for the word had gone out to all that he was open-handed, liberal on a grand scale and generous. Addressing Komnenos and Kekaumenos the emperor praised them, calling them noble and fine commanders (especially Kekaumenos, because he had attained the rank he now held not by birth nor by any favour but by his own exceptional merits), and he dealt similarly with the others. But he had no desire to fulfil the wishes of any of them, nor would he advance Komnenos and Kekaumenos to the rank of proedros[13] (as they requested). In fact he turned them all against himself by rejecting their requests. That is how he dealt with the commanders of the east.

3. [484] Bryennios, however, he recalled from exile, appointed him governor of Cappadocia, promoted him commander plenipotentiary of the Macedonian army units and sent him against the Turks. There was one Turk, Samouch by name, undistinguished by birth but a brave man of action in war. He had fought with the Sultan on the occasion of the second

---

[8] As we saw, Isaac Komnenos had been relieved of his command by Theodora; he was now reviled by Michael VI and accused of having nearly lost Antioch: Psellos, *Chronographia*, 7.3–4, trans. Sewter, 276–7.

[9] There is a seal of the duke of Antioch: most recently, with photograph, Spink's sale catalogue no. 127 (October 1998), no. 41.

[10] i.e. Nikephoros Ouranos, the famous general of Basil II. Michael could have been related to him on the female side.

[11] The grandson of Michael Bourtzes who took Antioch in 969; officer, magister, vestes, vestarches and strategos (or former strategos) of the Anatolikon theme: seal in the former Zacos collection, J.-C. Cheynet and J.-F. Vannier, *Etudes prosopographiques* (ByzSorb 5, Paris, 1986), 7–122, at 32–3, rpr. in Cheynet, *Société*, 354–5.

[12] Thus the future emperor Constantine X Doukas and his brother John were military officers and not part of the so-called civilian nobility, using the classification of Ostrogorsky which makes a sharp distinction between two aristocracies: the civil aristocracy thought to have governed after the death of Constantine VIII and the military aristocracy, excluded and in opposition, of which the Komnenoi are typical representatives: Cheynet, *Pouvoir*, 191–8.

[13] Thus while Michael VI promoted his friends by leaps and bounds, he would not advance these military men a single space.

invasion of Roman lands; on his return to Persia Samouch remained at the scene of action with three thousand men, wandering over the plateaux and lowlands of Greater Armenia. He did serious damage to Roman lands by making sudden raids and pillaging them.[14] The emperor was unequal to the task of winning over this man. He was quite inept at flattery and mollifying with smooth words those men whose pride had been hurt and who carried a secret resentment in their hearts. For when Bryennios petitioned for the money which Theodora had taken from him to be restored, the emperor would not listen. When Bryennios persisted in his complaint and continued his entreaty, the other merely replied in the words of the common and well-worn cliché 'Deeds first, then ask for a reward', with which he dismissed him. Thus humiliated, Bryennios went his way turning over terrible things in his mind and looking for an opportunity to be revenged.

4. He dealt in a similar manner with Hervé Frankopoulos who had fought with Maniakes in Sicily and gained many great victories, remaining openly a supporter of the Romans from that time until now. When he requested to be accorded the title of magister not only was he denied a reply: the emperor dismissed him with sneers and derision. That indicates just how disagreeable and unapproachable he was where petitions were concerned. But Hervé, true barbarian, was beside himself with rage, totally unable to swallow his pride. Unaware of the conspiracy that the Romans were hatching,[15] he wasted no time. His only thought was to wreak vengeance on the one who had given him offence. He asked for and received permission to proceed to his estate; [485] he made his farewell address to the emperor and promptly went out [of the city]. He crossed over to the east and continued to his estate of Dagarabe[16] in the Armeniakon theme. He spoke his mind to some Franks who were dispersed, wintering over in that region, of whom he was able to bribe three hundred. He then left [with them] and came into Media where he made common cause to fight against the Romans with Samouch who was staying there. Their agreement held for a while but then there was an altercation between the Franks and the Turks which brought the two people into conflict with each other. Samouch made a pretence of observing the terms of the agreement but

[14] *Aristakes de Lastivert* (93) emphasises the cruelty of this chieftain who committed a massacre in the canton of Okomi.
[15] The army chiefs who were planning to engineer a revolt did not take the foreign mercenaries into their confidence.
[16] The Frankish chieftains who had been in imperial service for some time had integrated themselves into society and acquired estates, just like other officers. There were Frankish contingents stationed in the Armeniakon theme. The precise location of Dagarabe is unknown.

Hervé was ever suspicious; he expected a sudden attack and warned the Franks not to sleep off guard, but with weapons to hand. He did this discreetly without alerting Samouch, waiting for the moment when the Turk would reveal his intentions under the impression that he had escaped detection. And, sure enough, the day came when he armed all the Turks he had to hand and attacked the Franks as they were dining. But they, faithful to their commander's orders, had their horses ready to go; they were in the saddle and riding to meet the Turkish onslaught as soon as they became aware of it. An intense battle ensued in which the Turks resisted for a while but were then put to flight. Many of them fell; the rest took refuge in Chleat,[17] on foot and disarmed. When Hervé returned with the Franks from pursuing them he decided to take cover in [their] encampment, but the Franks protested and obliged him to enter the city of Chleat. They had a treaty secured by oaths with the Emir there; they wanted some recreation and to take a bath to cleanse themselves of the defilement of war. Hervé entreated them most earnestly not to insist on this and certainly not to put much faith in the oaths of those of an alien faith and people, men who held it an act of piety if they could bring about the death of many Christians. But as his words won nobody's attention and all were of one mind that they should without question enter the city, he broke camp and went in with them. But first he poured out [486] many prayers to God, exhorting and admonishing his men to be constantly on their guard and to have weapons in both hands. In went the Franks, heedless of their commanders' warnings; they bathed, they drank, they made merry. But the emir, Aponasar, took counsel with Samouch and the Saracens who were in the city and ordered the innkeepers that, at a given signal, they were to seize their guests and tie them up; or, if that were impossible, to slaughter them. Then he bided his time until the Franks had had their fill of pleasure and were turning in to sleep, at which time he gave the agreed signal. Some of the Franks were slain forthwith, some were seized, others threw themselves down from the walls and were able to save their lives. Hervé was captured and kept in fetters. When the emir had accomplished this, he reported to the emperor that, being his loyal supporter, he had destroyed those who were plotting against his interests and arrested their leader. That is how the affair of Frankopoulos ended.[18]

---

[17] Ahlat today, Chliat was a fortress on the northern shore of lake Van, to the south of Manzikert, belonging to the Marwanid emir, Nasr ad-Dawla, who died in 1061: T. Ripper, *Die Marwâniden von Diyâr Bakr: eine kurdische Dynastie im islamischen Mittelalter* (Würzburg, 2000), 151–2.
[18] Herve does not seem to have taken part in the revolt of Komnenos, probably because he was not retained once the latter came to power. He did get the promotion he wanted in the end for there

5. After the eastern commanders were turned away by the emperor in the way I described above they decided to make a second attempt. They approached the protosynkellos, Leo Strabospondylos, who was administering the affairs of state at that time, to intercede with the emperor. They asked not to be treated with disdain like everyone else nor to be shamefully dismissed. They adduced various justifications [for their request], stating at the end that it was unjust for citizens who had never manned the battlements nor contended in battle to attain imperial honours while they, who from their youth up had been waging war and standing guard duty by night so that the others could sleep soundly, should be passed over and be deprived of the imperial largesse. But Leo was aloof and unapproachable. He not only failed to accept the proffered request with encouraging words, but actually sent the petitioners on their way in an arrogant fashion, in no small way making light [487] of each of the men. They lost all hope, now they had been insultingly repulsed a second time; they chafed under the wound and seethed with rage. At first, each one of them complained quietly in conversation with whoever came his way, castigating the emperor, encouraging each person not to suffer each act of drunken misconduct in silence, but to resist, in order to obtain a just redress. Subsequently they congregated in the Great Church, making and receiving oaths neither to be silent nor to abandon the cause but to see those who had offended them punished; and they sealed their conspiracy 'with links of iron',[19] as they say. Kekaumenos was of the opinion that they should take Bryennios into the plot, for as a man posted to command a large army (the Macedonian troops) he would have a large part to play in the undertaking.[20] He promptly agreed when they sounded him out about this; then, when their plan was about to be put into action, some thought was given to whom they should proclaim emperor. All the conspirators were agreed that, since Kekaumenos was superior to the others in age, bravery and experience, he was the worthy candidate.[21] But he was anxious to escape this burden and with a single word he put an end to their confabulation. He stood up and immediately declared the magister

---

is a seal on which he is described as magister, vestes and stratelates of Anatolia: G. Schlumberger, *Sigillographie de l'empire byzantin* (Paris, 1884), 659.

[19] Ps. 149:8.

[20] By winning over Bryennios the conspirators could hope to congregate the larger part of the armies of both east and west, thus to avert the disaster which befell Leo Tornikios.

[21] This version of the facts, favourable to Kekaumenos, is not reliable; the choice of Komnenos was the better one, given his social connections. Yet there is no doubt that Kekaumenos was one of the principal conspirators. Psellos, being a devotee of the Doukai, implies that the troops were in favour of (the future emperor) Constantine Doukas: Psellos, *Chronographia*, ed. Renauld, 7.83ff.

Isaac Komnenos emperor of the Romans and he contrived for the rest of them to do likewise. They bound themselves to each other, securing their project insofar as this was possible. Each of them took his leave of the emperor then went his way, ostensibly to his [country] home.

6. Once Bryennios was established in his command as the emperor wished, he set off for the east in company with the patrician John Opsaras whom the emperor had sent with gold with which he was to pay the soldiers their allowances. When they arrived at a flat and open area in the Anatolikon theme, [488] he distributed the bounty to the Cappadocians. When [Bryennios] increased the bonuses and commanded more to be given than was stipulated he encountered opposition and disobedience in Opsaras, who stated that he dare not give supplementary payments to the soldiers since the emperor had issued no orders to that effect. Bryennios told him to stay calm and to do as he was told in silence but Opsaras insolently contradicted him, which greatly angered Bryennios. Rising from his seat, he punched him, finally grabbing him by the hair and the beard and throwing him to the ground. He then put him in irons and held him under guard in his own tent. He seized the emperor's gold and personally distributed it the way he wanted to, with a supplement. Now it so happened that the patrician Lykanthes, commander of Pisidia and Lykaonia, was encamped nearby. When he heard what had happened to Opsaras, he conjectured (as well he might) that the matter denoted a usurpation attempt (he was unaware of the intentions of the eastern commanders). He armed two units of the Anatolikon theme[22] and attacked the tent of Bryennios, proclaiming Michael the ruling emperor. He arrested Bryennios and put him in irons while releasing Opsaras from his fetters. He handed Bryennios over to Opsaras just as he was, chained up, telling him to do what he wished with him. Relieved of his fetters and now the master of Bryennios so he could do with him as he wished, Opsaras promptly put out his eyes and sent him bound to the emperor with a report on the attempted uprising. As for himself, he stayed where he was, perhaps to give the rest of the troops their pay. Such were the rewards Bryennios reaped for his rashness and wilfulness, to say nothing of his mindlessness. Those commanders whose homes were in the Anatolikon theme, the proedros Romanos Skleros (even he was no stranger to the conspiracy), Bourtzes, Botaneiates, the sons of Basil Argyros and the rest of the band, these all remained quiet for the time being, [489] waiting for the uprising to break out elsewhere. But when they heard about Bryennios and

---

[22] The Lykaonians and the Pisidians.

the misfortune which he had insanely brought upon himself, they quickly realised that when he was examined he would reveal the conspiracy and that, in the end, this would do the conspirators no good whatsoever. So they all took off and came to Kastamon in Paphlagonia, an estate of the magister Isaac Komnenos. There they found him still living quietly but they mobilised him despite his reluctance and went with him to a flat and sufficiently wide place known as Gounaria. There they assembled all the soldiers of the region together with all those who wished to join the uprising when they learnt of it and, with all those men, they proclaimed [Isaac] ruling emperor of the Romans on 8 June, tenth year of the indiction.[23]

7. Newly proclaimed emperor, [Isaac] set up a fortified camp and waited there, expecting the rest of those who were partakers in the conspiracy to congregate there. What most determined him to remain there and not to ride out was the delay of Kekaumenos. While he conjectured and sought for the reason for this delay, a messenger came to him from the east announcing that, the oaths he had taken notwithstanding, Kekaumenos had changed sides and gone over to the emperor; that he was now raising an army with which to attack the insurgents. This news threw the supporters of Komnenos into severe disarray and confusion at the thought of having such an enemy at their backs, so they still remained within the palisade, desirous of knowing the truth. That is how it was with them; for his part, Kekaumenos actually remained faithful to the conspirators but he held himself in check and delayed for the following reason.

After leaving the city, as he was returning home he encountered an imperial courier when he was at Nikomedia. He told him to say to the logothete of the drome, Niketas Xylinites, in straightforward military language: 'Know, brother, that your master and emperor holds Komnenos and me to be worthless; that he has rejected our petitions with disdain and sent us home. I would have you know that we are on our way. If our withdrawal is not to your own liking, then prepare to send an army to drive us back again against our will.' He spoke these words to the courier then continued on his journey. But when he arrived home[24] and Komnenos was keeping his peace as though he had nothing to do with the conspiracy, he began to be alarmed and to be troubled by fears that Komnenos and the participants in the conspiracy had changed their minds and were trying to bury the plot in silence; in which case he alone would pay the price of apostasy because he had already shown his hand by the message [to the logothete]. He wracked his brains for some way of ensuring his safety.

[23] 8 June 1057.   [24] Meaning Koloneia in the east.

Michael VII/Stratiotikos

He did not have an army ready for action and the forces to hand were insufficient to confront the Roman emperor. Moreover, since he had made no contact with the soldiery of the region, he had no way of knowing how he would be received by them. This is why he delayed and seemed to withdraw in the eyes of those who did not really understand what a plight he was in. Now it so happened that at that time there were two units of Franks and one of Russians quartered in the area for the winter. He worried even more about them: that if word got out he would be arrested by them and sent to the emperor. Apprehensive on all these scores, he held his hand until he could devise some way of ensuring his safety. Then, when he was ready to go into action, he first revealed the plot to his own clients and neighbours, after which he raised a force of a thousand men and began to sound out those whose loyalties were uncertain. [491] He began by making contact with the leading people of the region then, little by little, with the brave and military-minded. He was eventually able to win over the notables to his side, at which point he began to sound out the troops in general. He forged an imperial letter ordering him to take the three units of allies plus the two units [from the themes] of Koloneia and Chaldia[25] and march out against Samouch. Then he ordered all five units to assemble at the plain of Nikopolis[26] and put them to the test like this. Each day he devised some pretext for holding a parade. Early in the morning he would ride out and, when he was a good distance from the others, first summon the officer commanding [a section] and declare his intentions to him. The officer would be given two choices: either to become a participant in what had been said or to suffer decapitation. He would call out one section [commander] then another and, in the same way, bind all [the officers] with oaths even against their will. First he overcame the two units of Romans, then after them, with his own troops, he approached the foreigners' units, of which he easily got the better and bound them with oaths. No longer fearful, he mustered the officers and men of Sebasteia, Melitene, Tephrike[27] and the rest of the Armenian cities and sallied forth, sending a message ahead to Komnenos to the effect that all was well with him and that he was already on his way with a large army. This news filled Komnenos with gladness and confidence; he who until now had been timid and apprehensive became bold and courageous. Nevertheless, he waited for the other to arrive. In his progress Kekaumenos brought along with him the unit

---

[25] The auxiliaries were Franks and Russians as opposed to the local units from Koloneia and Chaldia. Only professional units seem to have been involved.
[26] A town near to Koloneia, to the south-west.
[27] The former town of the Paulicians, now the capital of a theme.

of the Armeniakon theme (against its will)[28] and the officers of that unit, [492] some willingly, others against their will. He continued his journey, arrived and was united with Komnenos who, thinking in his own heart that the situation was now secure, handed over his wife {Aikaterina [Catherine], daughter of Vladisthlav, king of Bulgaria},[29] and what wealth he had to his brother John[30] and sent them to the fortress of Pemolissa,[31] a rocky point on the banks of the river Halys. As for himself, he departed with the entire army, crossed the river Sangarios, then made a leisurely advance on Nicaea,[32] accompanied by hymns and cheering. He decided to occupy this city as a base for operations against any unwelcome turn of fortune and then to advance yet further. He gave the troops and commanders who remained faithful to the emperor time to retreat, but in fact, on learning of his advance on Nicaea, they began quietly withdrawing and disbanding. The soldiers went home one by one, fearing for their wives and children or for other compelling reasons; the commanders presented themselves before the emperor, reporting the arrival of Komnenos to him. These were Lykanthes, commander of the units of the Anatolikon theme, Theophylact Maniakes,[33] Pnyemios the Iberian who commanded the army of the theme of Charsianon and many others of no great distinction.

8. The emperor was now aware of the uprising against him and that the entire forces of the east (with a few exceptions) were on the move against him. Nevertheless, he did not think he should send ambassadors to arrange for peace, since the rebellion was still in its early days and phlegmatic towards the government. He did, however, make preparations, readying himself to offer armed resistance. He recalled all the western forces and set in command of them those of the Macedonians who, by distinguished birth and excellent former accomplishments, seemed to be of good repute.[34] He showered the commanders and the soldiers with honours, gifts and extravagant grants of money; [493] he did the same for those of the eastern units who had not been carried away by

---

[28] This is odd because Kekaumenos had commanded this unit with brilliance before Messina.
[29] MSS UV only.
[30] Little is known of the career of his brother John, the father of the future emperor Alexios I Komnenos.
[31] Osmancik today, guarding the crossing of the Halys (Melikoff, *Danishmend*). Isaac was establishing a remote base on a road leading to the eastern frontier in case things went awry.
[32] The road he was taking led directly to Nikomedia but the imperial forces had got there before him, hence his plan to secure his rear by occupying the main fortress of the Opsikion theme.
[33] Could this be the son of George Maniakes? We find him – not unnaturally – among the partisans opposed to Romanos Skleros.
[34] The reverse of Bryennios permitted Michael VI to rally the soldiers of the west. Since he also had some of the troops of Asia Minor at his disposal, his situation was not without hope.

Komnenos, men of the Anatolikon[35] and Charsianon[36] themes. He promoted Theodore, domestic of the east, a eunuch of the empress Theodora, to be commander plenipotentiary of these forces,[37] giving him the magister and duke Aaron, the brother of Komnenos' wife, to be co-commander and adviser: Aaron was a well-tried veteran of many campaigns. These he then sent to oppose Komnenos. The two of them moved off with the forces already mentioned; they crossed the straits at Chrysopolis, opposite to the city, and proceeded to Nikomedia. When they got there, they sent men to dismantle the bridge over the river Sagarios[38] so that it would not be easy for Komnenos to approach them; nor, being forced to make a detour, would he be able to take them by surprise after that. They moved off and came up to Mount Sophon[39] where they set up a fortified camp and prepared for battle.

9. Komnenos sent out scouts and spies in all directions in order to be aware of everything that was happening; thus he learnt that the forces of the domestic had already occupied the heights of Mount Sophon. Travelling at speed, he reached Nicaea and made himself master of it at one blow. He deposited there whatever money he had with him and all surplus equipment but set up camp about twelve furlongs to the north of the city and made his quarters there. As they came out of each camp in search of forage, Komnenos' soldiers and those of the enemy side mingled with each other. Being fellow countrymen, relatives and friends, they argued with each other, the emperor's men encouraging the others to abandon Komnenos, a usurper and apostate, to come over to the emperor's side, and not for the ambition and desire of one man run the risk not only of being shortly driven out of the army [494] and deprived of their income, but also of losing the most sweet light of their eyes. Those on the other side urged these to abandon an emperor who had only the name of emperor, a putrid, outdated, ancient old thing, ruled by eunuchs, and come over to Komnenos, a man so noble, so illustrious, so distinguished by his former military successes that he had caused all the Roman forces to rally to him like the spokes of a wheel unanimously converge on its centre. But when all this was said, neither side was able to convince the other. This is hardly

---

[35] Meaning the soldiers who had arrested Bryennios.
[36] Psellos (*Chronographia*, 7.10, trans. Sewter, 281) claims that it was he who advised the emperor to adopt this course.
[37] Theodore combined this charge with the command of the Thrakesion theme: *DOSeals*, 3.99.9.
[38] Justinian built a bridge over the Sangarios which is no longer on the water today, because of the changing course of the river.
[39] Today Sabandja dagh, to the south of the lake of the same name. The imperial forces prevented the rebels from moving freely between Nicaea and Nikomedia.

surprising because the commanders on either side sent out men skilled in argument to talk to the soldiers on the other side and to change the minds of any [on their own side] whose loyalty was wavering. Even after they had pursued this initiative for some time, nobody's mind was changed by the arguments. Then Komnenos directed that the collecting of wood and fodder was to be conducted with greater caution, the men not straying too far from the camp. The domestics' troops, especially the Macedonians, thinking this withdrawal was a symptom of baseness and fear, decided it was time to fight. Persuaded somewhat reluctantly by the Macedonians, the forces of the domestic went and set up camp at a place called Petroes, not far from the enemy camp; only about fifteen furlongs distant. The two armies were now very close to each other and they were urging their commanders to lead them out without delay. Komnenos was convinced; he marched out his own platoons and drew them up in battle order, appointing Kekaumenos commander of the left wing, Romanos Skleros of the right, while he took up his own position in the centre. The domestic was also convinced [to fight] and so was Aaron; he led out his own host and stationed it opposite to the enemy. Basil Trachaniotes[40] was in command of the right wing; he was stratelates of the western troops at that time and the most eminent of the Macedonians, distinguished by birth, intelligence and experience. The left wing was entrusted to the magister [495] Aaron, with Lykanthes, Pnyemios and the patrician Randolf the Frank[41] as sub-commanders. When the armies were drawn up in this manner at a place known to the people of the region as Haides, at the signal for battle to commence the armies charged each other. Aaron routed the right wing and pursued it to the palisade [of the encampment], capturing Romanos Skleros alive. He would have scored a complete victory if he had not been too humane and refrained from pillaging the encampment. Komnenos was already unnerved and thinking of retreating to Nicaea. As for Kekaumenos, he had definitively put the troops opposing him to flight and did not refrain from pursuing them. He came right up to the palisade, broke it down and, once he was inside, seized the tents, slashed them with swords and threw them to the ground. This was visible to those who were at a distance because the encampment lay on an eminence; it put new heart into Komnenos' men: apprehension into Aaron's. When these saw the palisade being pillaged, some of them howled in protest; others took to their heels. Many people fell on the emperor's side, especially among the

---

[40] The Trachaniotai were one of the leading families of Adrianople.
[41] Presumably Randolf had succeeded Hervé as chief of the Franks.

Macedonians, not only soldiers but commanders too: Maurokatakalos, Pnyemios, Katzamountes and not a few others; many more were taken prisoner than were killed.

10. They say that in that battle, after the emperor's forces had been put to flight, Randolf the Frank was wandering around among the refugees and the pursuers in search of somebody of rank with whom to fight. When he heard that Nikephoros Botaneiates[42] was passing by he abandoned the others and went towards him, shouting from a distance, calling upon him to stand. He revealed his name, who he was and why he was calling to him. Botaneiates came to a halt when he knew who it was and engaged Randolf in combat when he approached. He dealt Randolf a blow with the sword on his shield and sliced it in two. [495] The Frank struck him on the helmet too but the sword glanced off and did no harm. The others rushed to Botaneiates' aid, took the Frank alive and brought him to Komnenos. Of Komnenos' army one commander fell, Leo of Antioch, and some soldiers.[43]

11. After the defeat, survivors of the reverse and of the battle came to the emperor together with the domestic and Aaron. The emperor now despaired of the situation and was already thinking of abandoning everything and seeking safety in flight, but his entourage would not allow this. They urged him to stay where he was and to die nobly for the empire, if needs must be. He thought it would be difficult and pointless to raise another army to put up a second line of resistance; maybe he would survive if he could secure the support of the citizens, so he tried to address them and to win them over with gifts and bounties.

Having crushed and dispersed the enemy armies, Komnenos left Nicaea and two days later came to Nikomedia, where ambassadors from the emperor approached him: the proedros Constantine Leichoudes,[44] the proedros Theodore Alopos[45] and Constantine Psellos,[46] the consul of the Philosophers. These three men seemed to be superior to other men of that time in wisdom and eloquence, Psellos especially; they were chosen to act as ambassadors because the emperor expected great things to be

---

[42] Attaleiates, *Historia*, ed. Perez Martin, 56, says the magister Nikephoros Botaneiates especially distinguished himself by bringing the unit he commanded back in one piece.
[43] In fact there appear to have been very severe losses. Attaleiates, *Historia*, ed. Perez Martin, 55, emphasises the ferocious violence of this fratricidal combat.
[44] The former *mesazôn* of Constantine IX.
[45] A close friend of Psellos, an eminent senator, but his position is unknown.
[46] The same Psellos (*Chronographia*, 7.15–42, trans. Sewter, 284–302) has left a long account of this embassy. He gives himself an important role in it but his lively description well portrays the reaction of the victors to the suggestions of Michael VI, which came too late.

accomplished by their eloquence and graceful conversation. The embassy promised that if Komnenos laid down his arms he would be adopted as his son by the emperor and proclaimed Caesar; there would be an amnesty of iniquities and forgiveness of their misdeeds for all his supporters.[47] [497] According to what they say, nobody paid any attention to them. They returned to the emperor, received another commission and came back again, meeting Komnenos as he advanced at the village of Rheai.[48] The embassy announced that Komnenos would be proclaimed emperor and adopted as son, while all those who had fought with him would be confirmed with imperial letters in the honours granted to them by Komnenos. When the emperor's undertaking was made known, Komnenos and all the officers with him approved of it, asking that the promises be authenticated by written chrysobulls.[49] Kekaumenos alone was not pleased with all this, insisting that the old man vacate the throne and retire; it was improper (he said) for one who had already broken and repudiated his most solemn oaths to be allowed yet again to rule the Roman people. He would provoke the wrath of God by his perjury, nor would it bring [the conspirators] any advantage to lay down their arms for, once he was adopted, Komnenos would quickly succumb to poison and die while each one who was implicated with him would have both eyes put out. It is also said that the ambassadors went against their master by each one of them coming secretly to Kekaumenos, one at a time, urging him to maintain his opposition and not to concede one jot or tittle. They are well-informed men, incapable of falsehood, who say they acted in that way and that they told Komnenos himself on their oath that the entire urban multitude was on his side; that he only need approach the city and they would expel the old man, receiving *him* with triumphal songs and hymns. And that is what is said to have been taking place in the camp.

12. The old man reinforced the citizens' support for himself with gifts, money, excessive honours [498] and whatever else flatters and artfully wins over a people, securing their support and loyalty. Wishing to render the bond of their support yet less breakable, he issued a written statement affirmed with awesome oaths and bloody curses that they would never name Komnenos emperor or sovereign or do him the honour due to an

---

[47] Isaac was prepared to accept these conditions, which guaranteed him the throne before long, given the advanced age of the emperor Michael VI. He insisted, however, on the dismissal of Leo Paraspondyles: Psellos, *Chronographia*, 7.32, trans. Sewter, 284–95.

[48] Isaac continued his advance on the capital; Rheai must have been between Nikomedia and the shore of the Bosporos.

[49] Psellos confirms that he and his colleagues reached an agreement with Isaac by which he would become the designated heir of Michael VI.

emperor; then he obliged each of the senators to subscribe to this and put his seal to the document. They all subscribed, coerced by authority, since Komnenos, though advancing, was still far away. But when he approached a village called Almeas and was going to stay the next day in the palace of Damatrys, suddenly, early in the morning, there presented themselves at the Great Church of God the magister Michael[50] (the son of Anastasios), the patrician Theodore Chryselios,[51] the patrician Christopher Pyrros,[52] all the officers of the Hetaireiai and some others of little note. They shouted up from below for the patriarch to come down to them as they had some urgent petitions which they wanted to present to him. By no means convinced to descend, he in fact closed his door and the entry to the labyrinth leading to the upper storey of the church. But he did send the brothers Nikephoros and Constantine, his own nephews,[53] to them with orders that the petitions were to be brought to him by them. To the people already congregated below was now added another numerous horde, for news of what was happening was already abroad. Hence, they came running by the hundreds, not only those who delight in some novel event, but also a good number of wiser folk and several senators whose affections the emperor had not cultivated. This whole multitude seized the patriarch's nephews and threatened to carry them off if he did not quickly come down to them. He now, either against his will (I am not sure) or willingly (as most people would have it), assumed the priestly pallium and the rest of the episcopal vestments and came down, feigning ignorance and pretending to be suffering violence; but that was all a façade, as events showed. When he arrived, those who were inciting the crowd took him, [499] brought a throne and seated him at the right hand side of the sanctuary. First of all (probably a mere formality) they asked him to be an ambassador to the emperor to retrieve the document they had signed as the emperor had already treated with Komnenos and used the word 'emperor' of him. If that document remained undestroyed, they were bound to suffer one of two evils, they said: either to perjure themselves by proclaiming Komnenos emperor or to be punished by the emperor for insulting him. At first the patriarch

---

[50] One of the principal supporters of Constantine IX Monomachos.
[51] This descendent [?] of the Chryseleios of Dyrrachion (reign of Basil II, c. 24) has left some seals: Wassiliou-Seibt, *Bleisiegel*, no. 174.
[52] A person otherwise unknown but the family is subsequently attested, notably in the reign of Alexis Komnenos: P. Gautier, 'Le synode de Blachernes (fin 1094); étude prosopographique', *REB* 29 (1971), 218.
[53] The nephews of Keroularios went on to distinguished careers under the Doukai and the Komnenoi (to whom they were related by marriage). Constantine became the first known sebastos (under Michael VII): P. Gautier, 'La curieuse ascendance de Jean Tzetzès', *REB*, 18 (1970), 212–16.

approved of what they said and declared that he would fulfil their request. But a little later, regardless of everything, they proclaimed Komnenos ruling emperor,[54] naming all those who were unwilling to do likewise enemies of the Romans and apostates whose houses should be pillaged by the rabble. The patriarch himself, by the agency of Stephen, the second-in-command of the church, who was present and the first to approve of what was happening, followed by Theodore, patriarch of Antioch.[55] The patriarch himself was the first to cry out the acclamation of approval and to permit the razing and pillaging of the houses of those high officials who were not pleased with what was happening; and he did it inside that sacred and famous church! He sent a messenger to Komnenos, others to the old man, the first telling him to make haste and not delay, also requesting a reward for his cooperation, as though the other had already attained the goal for which he longed. The message to the old man told him to begone from the palace to which he had no right whatsoever. From this it appeared abundantly evident to all that the patriarch was not only a participant in the uprising but was the instigator of it.[56] When the old emperor asked the metropolitan bishops who had been sent to him, 'What will the patriarch grant me in place of the kingdom?' they answered, 'The kingdom of heaven.' [500] On that he set aside the purple [robe] and the scarlet buskins, put on the clothing of a private citizen and went his way.

It would surely have been as he wished and as the metropolitans promised if he had left the palace as soon as the uprising broke out but he waited until there was war. He was actually prepared to countenance such a severe loss of fellow countrymen! Indeed, it was only after being bruised and shaken by the citizens that he did eventually reluctantly withdraw from the throne. I do not know whether he will receive the heavenly kingdom as a reward for losing the earthly one; let it be as God pleases. When the old man was installed in his house in the Acropolis, on Wednesday, 31 August,

[54] 30 August 1057.
[55] His name was actually Theodosios Chrysoberges, a monk at one of the Bithynian monasteries who had been chosen to succeed John IV as patriarch of Antioch: K.-P. Todt, 'Region und griechisch-orthodoxes Patriarchat von Antiocheia in mittelbyzantinischer Zeit und im Zeitalter der Kreuzzüge (969–1204)', thesis (Wiesbaden, 1998), 693–5.
[56] The role of the patriarch Keroularios was decisive; he was acting as the leader of a faction (rather than as the head of the church) in favour of Constantine Doukas, the husband of his niece, Eudokia Makrembolitissa. Psellos emphasised this in *Chronographia*, but later, when he was drawing up the charge sheet against Keroularios, he itemised that prelate's political intrigues: how he controlled senior appointments and even gave orders to the troups of the capital: *Scripta minora*, 1, 232–328. Commentary on these events: M. D. Spadaro, 'La deposizione di Michele VI: un episodio di "concordia discors" fra Chiesa e militari?' *JÖB*, 37 (1987), 153–71; and J.-C. Cheynet, 'Le patriarche "tyrannos": le cas Cérulaire', *Ordnung und Aufruhr im Mittelalter*, ed. M. T. Fögen (Frankfurt, 1995), 1–16.

tenth year of the indiction, Kekaumenos (now honoured as kouropalates) was sent by Komnenos together with several nobles, early on Friday in a ship, to enter and take possession of the palace. Komnenos himself came towards evening and, next morning, 1 September, he went in public procession to the Great Church where, on top of the ambo, he received the imperial diadem at the hands of the patriarch and was proclaimed ruling emperor of the Romans.[57]

[57] 1 September 1057. On the entry of Isaac Komnenos into Constantinople and his crowning: J. Shepard, 'Isaac Comnenos' coronation day', *BS*, 38 (1977), 22–30.

Glossary

acheiropoietos	literally 'not made by [human] hands', meaning images created without human intervention.
akolouthos	possibly the commander of the Varangian Guard.
amermoumnes	from the Arabic *amir al-mu'minim*, 'the commander (or emir) of the faithful', a title denoting the religious function of the caliph.
archon	a person holding a command (arche), meaning a degree of authority delegated by the emperor. The term was also given to some of the heads of state institutions, such as the archon of the blattion (in charge of the silk-weaving) or the archon of the Pantheon, who commanded the guard of a suite in the imperial palace. A foreign ruler was often said to be the archon of his country or people.
archon ton archonton	a title given to the chief prince in Armenia.
asekretis	from the Latin secretis, one of the secretaries of the imperial chancery, under the direction of the protoasekretis, q.v.
autokrator	one who exercises complete control of matters both civil and military. The emperor *autokrator* is distinguished from co-emperors by his effective exercise of power, power which he could delegate to a strategos on a temporary and local basis.

basileus	the official title of the emperor of the Romans after Heraclius triumphed over the Persians (629), reluctantly conceded on occasion to other sovereigns (e.g. the German emperor, the archon of the Bulgars) on condition that they not claim to be basileus 'of the Romans', that title being the exclusive prerogative of the emperor enthroned at Constantinople. Skylitzes sometimes uses the term incorrectly, e.g. of Mortagon, khan of the Bulgars.
chrysotriklinos	the 'golden hall' in the Great Palace, where ceremonial receptions were held, guarded by officials (e.g. protospathars) said to be *epi tou chrysotriklinou*.
cleisurarch	an officer commanding a region that included a pass on the borders of the Empire (*kleisoura*) which could become a theme, as did Cilicia.
count of the stable	[*komes tou stablou*] the director of the imperial stables; person responsible for the provision of horses when the emperor went on campaign.
count of the tent	[*komes tes kortes*] the chief of staff; the strategos of a theme.
dignity	a dignity is to be distinguished from a post or function (q.v.) in that it is an appointment for life conferred by diploma and only withdrawn in exceptional circumstances, e.g. for treason.[1] See and cf. function.
domestic of the scholai	officer (never a eunuch) commanding the unit (tagma) of the scholai (q.v.) who assumed command of the army in the absence of the emperor.
duke	subsequent to the reign of John Tzimiskes, the officer commanding a large frontier

---

[1] On this matter see R. Guilland, 'La collation et la perte ou la déchéance des titres nobiliaires à Byzance', *Etudes byzantines*, 4 (1946), 24–69, rpr. in R. Guilland, *Institutions*, I, 32–64.

	region comprising several themes was known as a *doux* (or *katepan*).
drakkar	(from the Scandinavian *drekei,* dragon) the square-sailed boat with oars in which the Vikings sailed: monoxylon.
drome	*see* logothete of the drome.
droungarios of the watch (or of the arithmos)	originally an officer commanding a regiment of the guard with special responsibility for the security of the palace and the emperor; but after the reign of Basil II the title denotes the presiding judge of one of the tribunals at the capital.
droungarios of the fleet	naval officer commanding the squadron based at the capital.
eidikon	the imperial treasury, directed by the eidikos or logothete of the eidikon, who was responsible for providing the specie for paying the salaries (rogai) of the officials, also the precious objects in gold and the silks which the emperors could use as gifts.
Elates	the oarsmen of the imperial fleet.
emperor	see autokrator, basileus.
encaenia	usually the consecration ceremonies of a new church but also the anniversary of some important event, e.g. the founding of a city.
eparch	the prefect of Constantinople; he governed the city in the absence of the emperor, controlled the markets (especially the silk trade), supervised foreigners resident in the capital and presided over the tribunal which exercised criminal and civil jurisdiction over the capital and its suburbs.
epeiktes	an official serving under the count of the stables responsible for maintaining the supply of horses and pack animals. This position was, however, associated with several activities, not all military.

episkepsis	a domain pertaining to the Treasury administered by an episkeptites, a curator or a pronoetes.
exkoubitors	one of the four regiments (tagmata) responsible for defending the capital, the others being the scholai, the watch and the hicanatoi, each of which was commanded by a domestic.
foederati	a unit attested from the reign of Nikephoros I to the eleventh century, usually commanded by a *tourmarch*, recruited in the Anatolikon theme, stationed in Lycaonia and Pisidia.
function	the chief civil and military posts were temporary appointments, conferred directly by the emperor by word of mouth [*dia logou*] on whom he would, and similarly withdrawn; see and cf. dignity.
genikon	the main revenue office of the empire, responsible for determining the rate of taxation and for collecting what was due to the state; directed by a logothete.
hegumen, hegoumenos	the superior of a religious community.
hentenarion	one hundred pounds of gold, 7,200 nomismata, weighing over 30 kg.
hetaireiai	certain military units (possibly as many as four, some composed of foreigners) sometimes responsible for the personal security of the sovereign.
hetaireiarch	officer commanding the Hetaireia.
hicanatoi	a regiment of the imperial guard created by Nikephoros I in 809.
judge [*krites*]	judges functioning in the provinces tended to eclipse the authority of the commanders [*strategoi*] of the themes in the first half of the eleventh century. Judges presided over the tribunals of the capital, the most important one being the imperial tribune of

	the Hippodrome, of which the first twelve were known as Judges of the Velum.
katepan	the officer commanding a military detachment sent into a theme (e.g. the *katepan* of Paphlagonia), co-existing with the strategos of that theme. From the time of John Tzimiskes the term was synonymous with duke (q.v.), even though certain areas were traditionally commanded by a *katepan* rather than by a *doux*.
katholicos	the title of the heads of certain oriental churches, notably of the Armenian church.
kleisourarch	the military commander of a unit defending a *kleisura*, a defile or pass.
koitonites, koubikoularios	a eunuch attached to the imperial bedchamber. (*cubiculum*) under the orders of the parakoimomenos.
kouropalates	[*cura palatii*] originally the caretaker of the palaces but a high honorific title from the sixth century. Until the middle of the eleventh century this was one of the highest positions in the Empire, usually occupied by a member of the imperial family. The person ruling the section of Georgia known as Iberia was traditionally designated kouropalates.
logothete of the drome	the director of the imperial post (drome) responsible for the reception of foreign ambassadors. He drew up reports on the state of mind of the people in the provinces and supervised the officials who governed them. He was both the minister of foreign affairs and the chief of espionage.
logothete of the genikon	*see* genikon.
logothete of the stratiotikon	an official in charge of the department responsible for financing the army, keeping recruitment up to strength and making sure the army lists are up to date.

Glossary

merarch	= *tourmarch*, q.v.
mesazon	name given to the chief counsellor of the emperor. The title was not official and is not found in any official documents or on seals.
mitatorion	a chamber at the Great Church in which the emperor changed his vestments.
modios	a unit of measurement both of space (1,000 m^2) and of volume (17 litres).
nomisma or solidus	(also known as bezant) the characteristic Byzantine gold coin, 4.45 g of pure gold, instituted by Diocletian and maintaining its value until the time of Constantine IX Monomachos when it began to be devalued.
novels	from *novellae constitutiones*: new laws promulgated by an emperor.
oikos	(literally, a house) the palace of an aristocrat then, by extension, the estates connected with it, which explains why the centres from which the great imperial monasteries were administered are also denominated oikoi, e.g. the oikos of Manganes. These oikoi were administered by kourators. Oikos is often used to mean a church too.
oikonomos	in the church, usually a priest responsible for the material assets of a church. See reign of Romanos III, n. 1. In a monastery, the monk who conducted the business of the institution.
papias	the custodian of the Great Palace, the jailer of Michael II.
paradynasteuon	this title has no official status and is not found in the *Taktika*. It designated a person whom the emperor had chosen to assist him in governing the empire.
parakoimomenos	usually a eunuch (although the future Basil I was not) who, by virtue of being responsible for the security of the imperial bedchamber, was one of the most influential people in the state.

praepositos *epi tou kanikleiou*	literally, the official in charge of the inkwell, i.e. he who maintained the vessel containing the purple ink with which the emperor signed the documents prepared by the protoasekrites (q.v.) but in reality the one who authenticated the imperial signature.
proasteion	usually a large estate defined by the tax collectors, independent of a rural township.
prostagma or horismos	a brief imperial directive of an administrative nature, authenticated by a menolog (the date written by the emperor's own hand in purple ink) and sealed with the imperial seal in lead or wax.
protoasekretis	chief of the asekretis (q.v.), head of the imperial chancery, responsible for producing the definitive text of imperial acts.
protospatharios	a title conferred on commanders of themes and those of similar rank; the first dignity permitting access to the senate, but the dignity went into decline from the eleventh century.
protostrator	the first of the imperial stable masters who accompanied the emperor on some ceremonial occasions. In time the term came to designate the supreme commander of the cavalry.
protothronos	within the ecclesiastical hierarchy, the senior bishop of an archbishopric or the senior archbishop of a patriarchate. The archbishop of Caesarea in Cappadocia was the protothronos of the patriarchate of Constantinople.
psychika	donations which might be offered for the salvation of the soul of a deceased person.
quaestor	a jurist who presided over a tribunal which specialised in matters of hereditary and inheritance; he was also involved in the composition of novels (new laws).
sakellarios	comptroller of the financial services of the state. He was also the officer in charge of the chrysocheion (bullion store).

scholai	a unit (tagma) of the imperial guard; a ceremonial guard which became a *corps d'élite* under the Isaurian emperors (eighth century).
sebastophoros	an ill-defined title conferred on eunuchs connected with the emperor that became a simple dignity in the eleventh century.
silention	a solemn assembly presided over by the emperor at which, having imposed *silence* on those taking part, he made his decisions known.
spatharios	(lit. 'sword-bearer') a modest dignity that gradually went out of use.
strategos	commander. Originally a military commander, but after the constitution of the themes (seventh century) the term designated the commander of one of these new areas (except for the Opsikion theme). Until the end of the tenth century, the strategos of a theme exercised complete authority (civil and military) but he was then supplanted by a judge (q.v.).
stratelates	a dignity known in Latin as *magister militum* that disappeared in the ninth century. But from the reign of John Tzimiskes the term was used of a certain senior army officer, doubtless because he was in charge of the newly formed unit (tagma) of the Stratelatai.
stratiotikon	*see* logothete of the stratiotikon.
synkellos	a cleric appointed by the emperor to assist the patriarch, often designating him to be the other's successor. From the time of Romanos Argyros (c. 1) this dignity was more widely conferred.
tagma	a unit of professional soldiers available for duty at all times, paid directly by the emperor, to be distinguished from a theme.

theme	both a body of troops and the area in which they were recruited. Thematic soldiers were remunerated with tax exemptions but they also received some cash payment when they were on active service.
toparches	an unofficial term designating the lord of a territory who was independent of the empire but willing to be associated with it.
tourmarch	the commander of the subdivision of a theme known as a tourm.
vestes	an honorific title found from the tenth century, not easily distinguishable from protovestes and vestarches, for persons (eunuchs and others) originally connected with the imperial wardrobe.

Bibliography

ABBREVIATIONS

AIPHOS: *Annuaire de l'Institut de Philologie et d'Histoire Orientale et Slave* (Brussels, 1936–)

AnalBoll: *Analecta Bollandiana* (Brussels, Paris and Geneva, 1882–)

Aristakes of Lastivert, ed. Canard and Berberian: *Aristakes de Lastivert: Récit des malheurs de la nation arménienne,* French translation and commentary by M. Canard and H. Berberian following the edition and Russian translation of K. Yuzbashian (Bibliothèque de *Byzantion*, 5, Brussels, 1973)

AOC: *Archives de l'Orient Chrétien* (Bucharest, 1948–)

Attaleiates, Historia, ed. Perez Martin: *Miguel Ataliates: Historia*, ed. I. Perez Martin (Madrid, 2002)

B: *Byzantion* (Paris and Brussels, 1924–)

BCH: *Bulletin de Correspondance Hellénique* (Paris, Athens, 1877–1967)

BHG: *Bibliotheca hagiographica graeca*, ed. F. Halkin (Brussels, 1957)

BIAB: *Bulletin de l'Institut Archéologique Bulgare. Izvestija na Bulgarskija Archeogiceski Institut* (1921–)

BMGS: *Byzantine and Modern Greek Studies* (Oxford, 1975–)

Bryennios, ed. Gautier: *Hylê historias: Nicephori Bryennii historiarum libri quattuor*, ed. P. Gautier (CFHB, 9, Brussels, 1975)

BS: *Byzantinoslavica* (Prague, 1929–)

Byzantine court culture, ed. Maguire: *Byzantine court culture from 829 to 1204*, ed. H. Maguire (Washington, DC, 1997)

Byzantium, ed. Magdalino: *Byzantium in the year 1000*, ed. P. Magdalino (The Medieval Mediterranean, 45, Leiden and Boston, 2003)

Byzantium in the ninth century, ed. Brubaker: *Byzantium in the ninth century: dead or alive: Papers from the Thirteenth Spring Symposium of Byzantine Studies*, ed. L. Brubaker (Society for the Promotion of Byzantine Studies, 5, Aldershot, 1998)

BZ: *Byzantinische Zeitschrift* (Leipzig and Munich, 1892–)

ByzSorb: Byzantina Sorbonensia (Paris, 1975–)

CBHB: Corpus Bruxellense Historiae Byzantinae (Bruxelles, 1975)

CFHB: Corpus Fontium Historiae Byzantinae (Washington, DC, 1967–; Berlin, 1967–; Vienna, 1975–; Rome, 1975–; Brussels, 1975–)

Chronicle of the Priest of Diokleia, ed. Sisi: *Letopis Popa Dukljanina*, ed. F. Sisi (Belgrade and Zagreb, 1928)
Constantine Porphyrogenitus, Expeditions, ed. Haldon: *Constantine Porphyrogenitus: three treatises on imperial military expeditions*, ed. J. F. Haldon (CFHB, 28, Vienna, 1990)
CSHB: Corpus Scriptores Historiae Byzantinae, ed. B. G. Niebuhr (Bonn, 1828–)
CSCO: Corpus Scriptorum Christianorum Orientalium (Leuven, 1996)
G. Dagron, *Histoire du christianisme*, IV: *Evêques, moines et empereurs (610–1054)*, ed. G. Dagron, P. Riché and A. Vauchez (Paris, 1993)
DAI, ed. Moravcsik and Jenkins: *Constantine Porphyrogenitus: De administrando imperio*, ed. G. Moravcsik, English tr. R. H. J. Jenkins (CFHB, 1, Washington, DC, 1967)
De cer., Vogt: *Le Livre des cérémonies*, I, Livre i: *Chapitres 1–46 (37) Constantin VII Porphyrogénète*; II, Livre i: *Chapitres 47 (38)–92 (83) Constantin VII Porphyrogénète*, edition and French translation by A. Vogt (Paris 1935, 1939)
De cerimoniis, ed. Reiske: *Constantinus Porphyrogenitus: De cerimoniis aulae byzantinae libri duo*, ed. J. J. Reiske (CSHB, Bonn, 1829–30)
DOC: *Catalogue of the Byzantine coins in the Dumbarton Oaks Collection and in the Whittemore Collection*, II–III (Washington, DC, 1968–73)
DOP: *Dumbarton Oaks Papers* (Washington, DC, 1958–)
DS: *Dictionnaire de Spiritualité*, 1–16 (Paris, 1937–1992)
DOSeals I–IV: *Catalogue of the Byzantine seals at Dumbarton Oaks and in the Fogg Museum of Art*, I–IV, ed. J. Nesbitt and N. Oikonomides (Washington, DC, 1991–7)
EHB: *The economic history of Byzantium from the seventh through the fifteenth century*, ed-in-chief, A. Laiou (Dumbarton Oaks Studies XXXIX), Washington DC, 2002
EI: *Encyclopédie de l'Islam* (Leiden, 1954–)
EO: *Échos d'Orient* (Paris, Constantinople and Bucharest, 1898–1943)
Genesios, ed. Lesmüller-Werner and Thurn: *Iosephi Genesii regum libri quattuor*, ed. A. Lesmüller-Werner and I. Thurn (CFHB, 14, Berlin, 1978)
GRBS: *Greek, Roman and Byzantine Studies* (Cambridge, MA, 1963–)
George Hamartolos: Prodolzenie chroniki Georgija Amartola po Vatikanskomu spisku no 153, ed. V. Istrin, *Knigy vremennyja i obrazniya Georgija Mnicha. Chronika georgija Amartola v drevnem slavjanorusskom perevode. tekst, izsledovanie i slovar*, 2 (Petrograd, 1922), 1–65
George Kedrenos, ed Bekker: *George Kedrenos: Compendium historiarum*, ed. I. Bekker (CSHB, Bonn, 1838)
George the Monk, Continuatus, ed. Bekker: *Theophanes Continuatus*, ed. I. Bekker (CSHB, Bonn, 1838), 761–924
IFEB: Institut Français des Études Byzantines
Iviron, I: *Actes d'Iviron*, I: *Des origines au milieu du XIe siècle*, ed. J. Lefort, N. Oikonomides, D Papachrysanthou, H. Métrévéli (Archives de l'Athos, 14, Paris, 1985)

Iviron, II: *Actes d'Iviron*, II: *Du milieu du XIe siècle à 1204*, ed. J. Lefort, N. Oikonomides, D. Papachrysanthou (Archives de l'Athos, 16, Paris, 1990)
IRAIK: *Izvestija Russkago Archeologiceskago Istituta v Konstantinopole* (Odessa and Sofia, 1896–1912)
Islamic Egypt, ed. Petry: *The Cambridge History of Egypt*, I: *Islamic Egypt, 640–1517*, ed. C. F. Petry (Cambridge, 1998)
JÖB: *Jahrbuch der Österreischischen Byzantinistik* (Vienna, 1950–)
John Mauropous, ed. de Lagarde: *Johannis Euchaitarum metropolitae quae in codice Vaticano graeco 676 supersunt*, ed. P. de Lagarde (Abhandlungen der histphilol. Klasse der Königl. Gessellschaft d. Wiss. in Göttingen, 28, 1882)
Life of Basil [I, the Macedonian]: = Book V of *Theophanes Continuatus*
Life of Stephen the Younger, ed. Auzépy: *La Vie d'Étienne le Jeune: introduction, édition, traduction*, ed. M.-F. Auzépy (Birmingham, 1997)
Leo the Deacon, ed. Hase: *Leonis Diaconi Caloënsis historiae libri decem*, ed. C. B. Hase (CSHB, Bonn, 1828)
Leo the Deacon, ed. Talbot and Dennis, *The history of Leo the Deacon: Byzantine military expansion in the tenth century: introduction, translation, and annotations*, ed. A.-M. Talbot and D. Sullivan (Washington, DC, 2006)
LXX: Septuagint
MAIET: *Materialy po Arkheologii, Istorii i Etnografii Tavriki* (Simferopol, 1990–)
Matthew of Edessa, ed. Dostourian: *Armenia and the crusades tenth to twelfth centuries: the chronicle of Matthew of Edessa*, ed. and tr. A. E. Dostourian (New York and London, 1993)
Mélanges Ahrweiler: ΕΥΨΥΧΙΑ, *Mélanges offerts à Hélène Ahrweiler*, ed. M. Balard *et al.*, (Paris, 1998)
Mélanges Dagron: *Mélanges Gilbert Dagron*, ed. V. Déroche, D. Feissel, C. Morrisson, C. Zuckerman, *TM*, 14 (2002)
Miller and Nesbitt, *Peace and war*: *Peace and war in Byzantium; essays in honour of george T. Dennis SJ*, ed. T. S. Miller and J. Nesbitt (Washington, DC, 1995)
Nicholas Mystikos, *Letters*, ed. tr. Jenkins and Westerlink: *Nicholas I, Patriarch of Constantinople: Letters*, ed. and tr. R. J. H. Jenkins and L. G. Westerink (CFHB, 6, Washington, DC, 1973)
Niketas magistros: *Nicétas magistros: lettres d'un exilé, 928–946*, ed. L. G. Westerink (Paris, 1973)
ODB: *Oxford Dictionary of Byzantium*, 3 vols., ed. A. P. Kazhdan (New York and Oxford, 1991)
PBE: *The prosopography of the Byzantine empire*, I, *641–867*, ed. J. Martindale (Aldershot, 2001) (CD-Rom)
PG: *Patrologiae cursus completus: Series graeca*, ed. J.-P. Migne, 161 vols. (Paris, 1857–66)
PLP: *Prosopographisches Lexikon der Palaiologenzeit*, ed. E. Trapp and H.-V. Beyer (Vienna, 1976–96)
PmbZ: *Prosopographie der mittel-byzantinischen Zeit*, F. Winkelmanns erstellt von R.-J. Lilie, C. Ludwig, T. Pratsch, I. Rochow unter Mitarbeit von W. Brandes, J. R. Martindale, B. Zielke (Berlin and New York, 1998–2000)

PO: *Patrologia Orientalis*, ed. R. Graffin and F. Nau (Paris, 1903)
Psellos, Chronographia, ed. Renauld: *Michel Psellos: Chronographie*, ed. É. Renauld (Paris, 1967), tr. E. R. A. Sewter (London, 1953)
Pseudo-Symeon the Logothete, ed. Bekker: *Symeon Magister*, ed. I. Bekker (Bonn, 1838), 603–760
RÉArm, n.s.: *Revue des Études Arméniennes*, nouvelle série (Paris, 1944–)
REB: *Revue des Études Byzantines* (Bucharest and Paris, 1944–)
SBS: *Studies in Byzantine Sigillography*, vols. 1–7 (Washington, DC, 1987–2002); vols. 8–10 (Munich-Leipzig, 2003–2010)
Seibt, *Bleisiegel*, 1: W. Seibt, *Die byzantinischen Bleisiegel in Österreich*, 1: *Kaiserhof* (Vienna, 1978)
Symeonis magistri: *Symeonis magistri et logothetae chronicon*, rec. St. Wahlgren (CFHB Series Berolinensis XLIV/1, Berlin–New York, 2006).
Synaxaire de Constantinople: *Synaxarium ecclesiae constantinopolitanae*, ed. H. Delehaye (Brussels, 1902)
Theodosios of Melitene: *Theodosii de Meliteni qui fertur chronographia*, ed. Th. F. Tafel (Munich, 1859)
Theophanes: *Theophanis Chronographia*, 2 vols., ed. C. de Boor (Leipzig, 1883–5)
Theophanes Continuatus: *Theophanes Continuatus*, ed. I. Bekker (CSHB, Bonn, 1838)
Theophylact of Ochrid, *Opera*: *Théophylacte d'Achrida: Discours, traités, poésies* ed. P. Gautier (CHFB 16/1, Thessalonica, 1980)
TIB: *Tabula Imperii Byzantini* (Vienna, 1976–)
TM: *Travaux et Mémoires* (Paris, 1965–)
Traité, ed. Dagron and Mihàescu: *Le traité sur la guérilla de l'empereur Nicéphore Phocas*, ed. G. Dagron and H. Mihàescu (Le monde byzantin, Paris, 1986)
Vasiliev and Canard I and II: A. A. Vasiliev, *Byzance et les Arabes*, I: *La dynastie d'Amorium, 820–867* (Brussels, 1935); II: *Les relations politiques de Byzance et des Arabes à l'époque de la dynastie macédonienne*, ed. M. Canard (CBHB 2, 1, Brussels, 1968)
VAthanA, ed. Noret: *Vitae duae antiquae sancti Athanasii Athonitae*, ed. J. Noret (Corpus Christianorum, Series Graeca, 9, Turnhout, 1982)
V. Euthymii, ed. Karlin-Hayter: *Vita Euthymii patriarchae CP: Text, translation, introduction and commentary*, ed. P. Karlin-Hayter (Bibliothèque de Byzantion, 3, Brussels, 1970)
VizVrem: *Vizantijskij Vremennik* (St Petersburg, 1894–; n.s Moscow, 1947–)
Yahya of Antioch, I, II, III: *Histoire de Yahya ibn-Said al-Antaki, Continuateur de Said ibn-Bitriq*, ed. and tr. I. Kratchovsky and A. Vasiliev, I: *PO*, 18 (1924), 700–833; II: *PO*, 23 (1932), 347–520; III: ed. I. Kratchovsky, with notes by F. Micheau and G. Troupeau, *PO*, 47, fasc. 4 (Turnhout, 1997)
Zacos, II: G. Zacos, *Byzantine lead seals*, compiled by J. W. Nesbitt (Berne, 1985)
John Zonaras III, ed. Pinder: *Ioannis Zonarae epitomae historiarum*, ed. M. Pinder (CSHB, Bonn, 1897)
ZRVI: *Zbornik Radova Vizantoloskog Institute* (Belgrade, 1958–)

PRIMARY AND SECONDARY SOURCES

N. Adontz, 'L'âge et l'origine de l'empereur Basile Ier (867–86)', *B*, 8 (1933), 475–500
H. Ahrweiler, 'Recherches sur la société byzantine au XIe siècle: nouvelles hiérarchies et nouvelles solidarités', *TM*, 6 (1976), 99–124
H. Glykatzi-Ahrweiler, 'Recherches sur l'administration de l'empire byzantin aux IXe–XIe siècles', *BCH*, 84 (1960), 1–111 = *Études sur les structures administratives et sociales de Byzance* (London, 1971), VIII
Annales Barenses: G. H. Pertz, *Monumenta Germaniae Historica. Scriptores*, V (Hanover, 1844), 52–6
Étienne Asolik de Taron, *Histoire universelle*, tr. F. Macler (Paris, 1917)
I. Bekker (ed.), Λέοντος γραμματικοῦ χρονογραφία (CSHB, Bonn, 1842)
K. Belke, mit Beiträgen von M. Restle, *Galatien und Lykaonien* (TIB, 4, Vienna, 1984)
K. Belke and N. Mersich, *Phrygien und Pisidien* (TIB, 7, Vienna, 1990)
A. Berger, *Untersuchungen zu den Patria Konstantinupoleos* (Poikila Byzantina, 8, Bonn, 1988)
W. G. Brokkaar, 'Basil Lacapenus', *Studia Byzantina et neohellenica Neerlandica*, 3 (1972), 199–234
M. Canard, *Byzance et les Musulmans du Proche-Orient* (London, 1973)
  Histoire de la dynastie des Hamdanides de Jazira et de Syrie (Paris, 1953)
J.-C. Cheynet, *The Byzantine aristocracy and its military function* (Variorum Reprints, Aldershot, 2006)
  'Du stratège de thème au duc: chronologie de l'évolution au cours du XIe siècle', *TM*, 9 (1985), 181–94 = Cheynet, *Aristocracy*, XI
  'Les Phocas', *Le traité sur la guérilla de l'empereur Nicéphore Phocas*, ed. G. Dagron and H. Mihàescu (Le monde byzantin, Paris, 1986), 289–315 = Cheynet, *Société*, 473–97
  Pouvoir et contestations à Byzance (963–1210) (Paris, 1990)
  La société byzantine. L'apport des sceaux (Bilans de recherche 3, Paris, 2008)
J.-C. Cheynet and J.-F. Vannier, *Etudes prosopographiques* (ByzSorb 5, Paris, 1986), 7–122, partly reprinted in Cheynet, *Société*, 339–471
A. Cutler and J.-M. Spieser, *Byzance médiévale 700–1204* (Paris, 1996)
J. Darrouzès, *Épistoliers byzantins du Xe siècle* (Le monde byzantin, Paris, 1960)
G. Dédéyan, *Les Arméniens entre Grecs, Musulmans et Croisés. Étude sur les pouvoirs arméniens dans le Proche-Orient méditerranéen (1060–1150)*, 2 vols. (Lisbon, 2003)
F. Dölger, *Regesten der Kaiserurkunden des oströmischen Reiches von 565–1453*. 1. Teil. *Regesten von 565–1025* (Munich and Berlin, 1924)
F. Dölger and P. Wirth, *Regesten der Kaiserurkunden des oströmischen Reiches von 565–1453:* 2. Teil. *Regesten von 1025–1204* (Munich, 1995)
V. von Falkenhausen, *La dominazione bizantina nell' Italia meridionale dal IX all' XI secolo* (Bari, 1978)

W. Felix, *Byzanz und die islamische Welt im früheren 11. Jahrhundert* (Byzantina Vindobonensia, 15, Vienna, 1981)

S. Franklin and J. Shepard, *The emergence of Rus, 750–1200* (London, 1996)

J. Gay, *L'Italie méridionale et l'empire byzantin depuis l'avènement de Basil I jusqu'à la prise de Bari par les Normands (867–1071)* (Paris, 1904)

H. Grégoire, 'Manuel et Théophobe, ou la concurrence de deux monastères', *B*, 9 (1934), 183–204.

P. Grierson, *Catalogue of the Byzantine coins in the Dumbarton Oaks Collection and in the Whittemore Collection*, II–III (Washington, DC, 1968–73)
  'The tombs and obits of the Byzantine emperors (337–1042) with an additional note by C. Mango and I. Ševčenko', *DOP*, 16 (1962), 3–63

V. Grumel, *La Chronologie* (Traité d'études Byzantines, 1, Paris, 1958)
  Les regestes des actes du patriarcat de Constantinople, I: *Les actes des patriarches*; II and III: *Les regestes de 715–1206*, 2nd edn revised and corrected by J. Darrouzès (Paris, 1989)

R. Guilland, *Recherches sur les institutions Byzantines*, I–II (Berlin and Amsterdam, 1968)
  Études de topographie de Constantinople byzantine (Amsterdam, 1969)

J. F. Haldon, 'Theory and practice in tenth-century military administration. Chs. II, 44 and 45 of the *Book of Ceremonies*', *TM*, 13 (2000), 202–352
  'Military service, military lands, and the status of soldiers: current problems and interpretations', *DOP*, 47 (1993), 1–67 = *State, army and society in Byzantium* (Aldershot, 1995), VII
  Recruitment and conscription in the Byzantine army c. 550–950: a study on the origins of the stratiotika ktemata (Vienna, 1979)

J. Herrin, *Women in purple: rulers of medieval Byzantium* (London, 2001)

F. Hild and H. Hellenkemper, *Kilikien und Isaurien* (TIB, 5, Vienna, 1990)

F. Hild and M. Restle, *Kappadokien (Kappadokia, Charsianon, Sebasteia und Lykandos)* (TIB, 2, Vienna, 1981)

C. Holmes, *Basil II and the governance of empire (976–1025)* (Oxford Studies in Byzantium, Oxford, 2005)

E. Honigmann, *Die Ostgrenze des byzantinischen Reiches von 363–1071 nach griechischen, arabischen, syrischen und armenischen Quellen* (CBHB, 3, Brussels, 1935)

R. Janin, *Constantinople byzantine* (*AOC*, 4A, Paris, 1964)
  La géographie ecclésiastique de l'empire byzantin, I: *La siège de Constantinople et le patriarcat œcuménique*; III: *Les églises et les monastères de l'empire byzantin* (Paris, 1969)
  Les églises et les monastères des grands centres byzantins (Paris, 1975)

R. H. J. Jenkins, 'The chronological accuracy of the Logothete for the years AD 867–913', *DOP*, 19 (1965), 91–112 = Jenkins, *Studies on Byzantine history*, III
  Studies on Byzantine history of the ninth and tenth centuries (London, 1970)

I. Jordanov, *Pecatite ot strategijata v Preslav* (Sofia, 1993)

I. Kalavrezou, 'Helping hands for the empire: imperial ceremonies and the cult of relics at the Byzantine court', *Byzantine court culture from 829 to 1204*, ed. H. Maguire (Washington, DC, 1997)

M. Kaplan, *Les hommes et la terre à Byzance, propriété et exploitation du sol du VIe au XIe siècle* (ByzSorb, 10, Paris, 1992)
A. P. Kazhdan, *Armjane v sostave gospodstvujuščego klassa vizantijskoj imperii v XI–XII vv.* (Erivan, 1975), 14–17
A. Kazhdan, *A history of Byzantine literature (650–850)*, in collaboration with L. F. Sherry and C. Angelidi (Athens, 1999)
E. Kisslinger, *Regionalgeschichte als Quellenproblem. Die Chronik von Monembasia und das sizilianische Demenna. Eine historisch-topographische Studie* (Vienna, 2001)
J. Koder, *Aigaion Pelagos (Die nordliche Agais)* (TIB, 10, Vienna, 1998)
J. Koder and F. Hild, *Hellas und Thessalien*, Register von P. Soustal (TIB, 1, Vienna, 1976)
A. E. Laiou, *Mariage, amour et parenté à Byzance aux XIe–XIIIe siècles* (Paris, 1992)
    'Imperial marriages and their critics in the eleventh century: the case of Skylitzes', *DOP*, 46 (1992), 165–76
V. Laurent, *Le Corpus des sceaux de l'empire byzantin*, II, *L'a inistration centrale* (Paris, 1981)
    Le Corpus des sceaux de l'empire byzantin, v, *L'Église*, 1–3 (Paris, 1963–72)
J. Lefort, 'Rhétorique et politique: trois discours de Jean Mauropous en 1047', *TM*, 6 (1976), 265–303
P. Lemerle, *Cinq études sur le XIe siècle byzantin* (Le monde byzantin, Paris, 1977)
    'L'histoire des Pauliciens d'Asie Mineure d'après les sources grecques', *TM*, 5 (1973), 1–144
    Le premier humanisme byzantin: notes et remarques sur enseignement et culture à Byzance des origines au xe siècle (Paris, 1971)
    'Thomas le slave', *TM*, 1 (1965), 255–97
G. G. Litavrin (ed.), *Sovety i rasskazy Kekavmena (Cecaumeni consilia et narrationes)* (Moscow, 1972)
G. A. Loud, *The age of Robert Guiscard: southern Italy and the Norman conquest* (London, 2000)
P. Magdalino, *Constantinople médiévale: études sur l'évolution des structures urbaines*, *TM*, 9 (Paris, 1996)
    'Observations on the Nea Ekklesia of Basil I', *JÖB*, 37 (1987), 51–64
    'Paphlagonians in Byzantine high society', *Byzantine Asia Minor (sixth–twelfth centuries)*, Athens 1998, 141–50
C. Mango, *Le développement urbain de Constantinople, IVe–VIIe siècles* (Paris, 1990)
    The homilies of Photius, patriarch of Constantinople (Dumbarton Oaks Series, 3, Cambridge, MA, 1958)
    'The legend of Leo the Wise', *ZRVI*, 6 (1960) = *Byzantium and its image* (London, 1984), XVI
    'The palace of Marina, the poet Palladas and the bath of Leo VI,' *Mélanges Chatzidakis* (Athens, 1991), 321–30
A. Markopoulos, Βίος τῆς αὐτοκράτειρας Θεοδώρας [*Life of Theodora*] (*BHG* novum auctarium 1731), Σύμμεικτα [*Symmeikta*], 5 (Athens, 1983), 249–85

B. Martin-Hisard, 'Constantinople et les archontes du monde caucasien dans le *Livre des cérémonies* II.48', *TM*, 13 (2000), 359–530
'La vie de Jean et Euthyme et le statut du monastère des Ibères sur l'Athos', *REB*, 49 (1991), 67–142
M. McCormick, *Eternal victory: triumphal rulership in late antiquity, Byzantium, and the early medieval west* (Cambridge, MA, 1986)
E. McGeer, *Sowing the dragon's teeth: Byzantine warfare in the tenth century* (DOS, 33, Washington, DC, 1995)
The land legislation of the Macedonian emperors (Toronto, 2000)
W. Müller-Wiener, *Bildlexikon zur Topographie Istanbuls* (Tubingen, 1977)
N. Oikonomides, *Fiscalité et exemption fiscale à Byzance, IXe–XIe siècles* (Athens, 1996)
Les listes de préséance byzantines des IXe et Xe siècles: introduction, text, French translation and commentary (Le monde byzantin, Paris, 1972)
D. I. Polemis, *The Doukai: a contribution to Byzantine prosopography* (University of London Historical Studies, 22, London, 1968)
T. Ripper, *Die Marwâniden von Diyâr Bakr: eine kurdische Dynastie im islamischen Mittelalter* (Würzburg, 2000)
S. Runciman, *The emperor Romanus Lecapenus and his reign: a study of tenth-century Byzantium* (Cambridge, 1922, repr. 1990)
P. Schreiner, *Die byzantinischen Kleinchroniken*, I: Enleitung und Text, II: Historicher Kommentar (CFHB, 12, Vienna, 1975–7)
Scriptor incertus, intro. by E. Pinto; text, Italian trs. and notes by F. Iadevaia (Messina, 1987)
W. Seibt, 'Ioannes Skylitzes. Zur Person des Chronisten', *JÖB*, 25 (1976), 81–5
Die Skleroi. Eine prosopographisch-sigillographische Studie (Byzantina Vindobonensia, 9, Vienna, 1976)
Ch. Settipani, *Continuité des élites à Byzance durant les siècles obscurs* (Paris, 2006)
J. Shepard, 'Scylitzes on Armenia in the 1040s, and the Role of Catacalon Cecaumenos', *RÉArm.*, n.s. 11 (1975–6), 269–311
'Symeon of Bulgaria – peacemaker', *Annuaire de l'Université Saint-Clément d'Ochride*, 83.3 (Sofia, 1989), 9–48
P. Soustal, *Thrakien (Thrake, Rodope und Haiminontos)* (TIB, 6, Vienna, 1991)
P. Stephenson, *Byzantium's Balkan frontier: a political study of the northern Balkans, 900–1204* (Cambridge, 2000).
N. Svoronos, 'Le serment de fidélité à l'empereur byzantin et sa signification constitutionelle', *REB*, 9 (1951), 106–42.
K.-P. Todt, 'Region und griechisch-orthodoxes Patriarchat von Antiocheia in mittelbyzantinischer Zeit und im Zeitalter der Kreuzzüge (969–1204)', unpublished thesis (Wiesbaden, 1998)
'Herrscher in Schatten: Konstantin VIII (960/1–1028)', *Thetis*, 7 (2000), 93–105
S. Tougher, *The reign of Leo VI (886–912): politics and people* (The Medieval Mediterranean, 15, Leiden, 1997)

C. Toumanoff, *Les dynasties de la Caucasie chrétienne de l'Antiquité jusqu'au XIXe siècle: tables généalogiques et chronologiques* (Rome, 1990)

W. Treadgold, *The Byzantine revival, 782–842* (Stanford, CA, 1988)

Byzantium and its army, 284–1081 (Stanford, CA, 1995)

D. Tsougarakis, *Byzantine Crete: from the fifth century to the Venetian conquest* (Athens, 1988)

D. Turner, 'The origins and accession of Leo V (813–20)', *JÖB*, 40, (1990), 171–203

J. F. Vannier, *Familles byzantines: les Argyroi, IXe–XIIe siècles* (ByzSorb, 1, Paris, 1975)

A.-K. Wassiliou and W. Seibt, *Die byzantinischen Bleisiegel in Österreich*, II: *Zentral- und Provincialverwaltung* (Vienna, 2004)

G. Zacos and A. Veglery, *Byzantine lead seals*, 1 (Basle, 1972)

C. Zuckerman, 'À propos du *Livre des cérémonies* II.48', *TM*, 13 (2000), 531–94

'Deux étapes de la formation de l'ancien état russe', *Les centres proto-urbains russes entre Scandinavie, Byzance et Orient*, ed. M. Kazanski, A. Nersessian and C. Zuckerman (Réalités Byzantines, 7, Paris, 2000), 95–121

'Le voyage d'Olga et la première ambassade espagnole à Constantinople en 946', *TM*, 13 (2000), 647–72

Index

Aaron, brother-in-law of Isaac I Komnenos, 459
Aaron, son of John Vladisthlav, 421
Abelbakes, 183
Aboulchare, 255
Abouzachar, 69
Abram, 422, 425, 442
Abramites, monastery of the, 61
Abu Hafs, 44, 45, 375, 380
Abydos, 36, 37, 170, 177, 279, 306, 307, 319, 320, 329, 347, 366, 414, 436
Adrian, 152, 210
Adrianople, 5, 8, 15, 42, 117, 118, 157, 196, 211, 276, 325, 328, 338, 413, 415, 416, 429, 436, 438, 440, 443, 460
Aetios, 76
Africa, 49, 81, 149, 150, 252, 253, 254, 256, 274, 365, 375, 378, 380, 381
Agros, monastery, 18
Aikaterina daughter of Vladisthlav, 458
Aleim, emir of Tarsus, 93, 422
Aleppo, 217, 233, 243, 245, 259, 260, 262, 304, 322, 328, 352, 356, 357, 358, 359, 360, 363, 366, 374, 387
Alexander, brother of Leo VI, 166, 186, 188–91
Alexios, patriarch, 348, 368, 378, 404
Alexios, son-in-law of Theophilos, 66
Alexios Mosele, 208
Alkan, 432
All Saints, church of, 330
allelengyon, xxvi, 329, 345, 354
Amara, 93
Ambron, emir of Anabarzos, 138
amermoumnes, 45
Amorion, 7, 10, 21, 24, 28, 51, 75, 76, 77, 78, 80, 95, 103, 135, 308
Amr, emir of Melitene, 77, 93, 94, 95, 99, 100, 101, 110, 113, 133, 138, 146, 216, 363, 376
Anargyroi
   church of the, 37, 390
   monastery of the, 414
Anastasios, bastard of Thomas the Slav, 37, 42

Anatolia, 35
Anatolikon, 4, 5, 7, 9, 11, 12, 28, 33, 46, 47, 67, 76, 93, 97, 167, 176, 178, 230, 247, 285, 308, 346, 402, 451, 455, 458, 459, 469
Andrew the Scyth, 140
Andrew the stratelates, 165, 167
Andronikos Doukas, 92, 181
Anemas, 240, 289, 292
Ani, 409, 410, 411, 412, 422, 425, 442
Anna, sister of Basil II, xi, xxxi, 54, 55, 60, 66, 98, 157, 175, 179, 204, 220, 245, 274, 280, 319, 347, 440, 447
Anthemios, monastery at, 67
Anthony Kauleas, patriarch, 169, 311
Anthony the Stoudite, patriarch, 295
Antigonus, domestic of the scholai, 113
Antigonos, son of Bardas, 113, 124
Anzes, 77, 100
Aplesphares, ruler of Tivion, 410
Apochaps, 45, 147, 216, 375
Apolaphar Mouchoumet, 375, 400
Apomerbanes, emir of Miepherkeim, 365
Aponasar, 453
Apostypes, 150, 151, 152, 175
Araxes, 418
Archangel, church of the, 398
Archimedes, 186
Ardouin, 400, 401
Argaion, mount, 109
Argaoun, 93, 135
Armamenton, 126
Armeniakon, 11, 34, 36, 66, 67, 70, 77, 100, 101, 136, 193, 221, 222, 243, 247, 272, 273, 293, 294, 352, 364, 382, 452, 458
Arsaber, brother of Jannes, 22, 87, 98, 99
Arsacids, 116
Artabasdos, 191
Artze, 424
Asan the deaf, 421, 425
Asekretis, monastery 250
Asotios [Ashot], 196

Index

Aspachan, 419
Athens, 344
Athinganoi, 28, 29, 33
Azizios [Hakem], 329, 365

Babek, 34, 60, 68, 72, 75, 76
Baboutzikos, 76, 77, 98
Baghdad, 34, 59, 60, 68, 70, 197, 211, 324, 339, 366, 398, 417, 419, 434, 448
Bardanios Tourkos, 9–15, 30, 33
Bardas, caesar, 83–113, 116–27, 132, 178
Bardas Phokas, xxvi, 197, 221, 227, 228, 229, 230, 232, 236, 250, 251, 272, 278, 280, 304, 307, 309, 313, 314, 317, 346, 351, 387
Bardas Skleros, xxvi, 247, 275, 280, 281, 284, 286, 292, 295, 299, 303, 304, 310, 321, 328, 387, 402, 447
Barka, 8
Basil I, 74, 113, 116–65, 252, 266
Basil II, 239, 298–349, 352, 367
Basil Apokapes, 432, 444
Basil Argyros, 330, 336, 357, 455
Basil Lekapenos, 230, 248, 271, 283, 296, 299–318
Basil the parakoimomenos, 229
Basil Peteinos, 226, 227, 228, 230, 241, 242
Basil Skleros, 366, 398
Basil Synadenos, 385
Basil the synkellos, 443
Basil Theodorakanos, 382, 388, 406
Basil Trachaniotes, 460
basileopator, 169, 172, 202
Basilikinos, 114
Basilitzes, 189, 190, 195
baths, 17, 110, 250, 316, 368, 370
Bathyrryax, 136
Belgrade, 332, 344, 345, 384
Berroia, 243, 245, 304, 326, 337, 356, 357, 358, 374
Berydes, 40
Bizyes, 42, 43
Black Mountain,, 260
Bogoris, *see* Boris
  ruler of the Bulgars
Boioannes, 401
Boris, ruler of the Bulgars, 79, 90, 91, 92, 170, 246, 266, 275, 282, 283, 294, 312, 328
Boukellarion, 210, 273, 351, 362, 375
Boukoleon, 12, 81, 180, 201, 202
Brindisi, 252, 402
Bryas palace, 60
Bryennios, xxxi, xxxii, 280, 306, 440, 447, 448, 452, 454, 455, 458, 459, 479
Bulgarophygon, 172, 416, 441
Bulgars, conversion of, 91
buskins, 7, 24, 230, 294, 464

Byrsis, monastery, 66

Caesarea, xiv, 2, 77, 109, 138, 139, 166, 178, 179, 211, 219, 228, 247, 278, 279, 301, 303, 307, 308, 309, 315, 432, 472
Cappadocia, 72, 109, 138, 139, 151, 173, 202, 203, 230, 232, 247, 257, 278, 279, 303, 307, 308, 315, 318, 322, 336, 346, 361, 364, 411, 441, 451, 472
Carthage, 142, 145, 146, 255
Chalke, 8, 63, 131, 192, 223, 294, 408, 449
Chambdan, emir of Aleppo, 240, 241
Chandax, 46, 240, 241
Charax, 45, 46
Charpete, 300
Charsianon, 70, 101, 136, 138, 166, 173, 178, 183, 278, 303, 308, 315, 388, 411, 458, 459, 480
Chazaria, 336
Chelidonion, 413
cherniboxestra, 58
Cherson, 74, 75, 108, 158, 173, 196, 265, 336
Chiliokomon, 78
Choireas, 44
Chosroes, ruler of Babylon, 310, 315
Chrysocheir, xxiii, 133, 135, 154, 347
Chrysopolis, imperial monastery at, 66
Chrysotriklinos, 8, 63, 182, 368
churches restored by Basil I, 155
Cistern of Aspar, 94
comet, 179, 189, 295, 301, 399
Constantine
  droungarios of the watch, 85, 113
  son of Basil I, 138, 160
Constantine V Kopronymos, 16, 31, 107, 251, 363
Constantine VI, 32, 33, 47
Constantine VII, 168, 179, 184, 187, 189, 191–206, 225–39, 255
Constantine VIII, 239, 305, 349–53
Constantine IX, 397–446
Constantine the Alan, 411
Constantine Arianites, 436
Constantine Artoklines, 397
Constantine Chage, 376, 404
Constantine Dalassenos, 352, 359, 370, 373, 380
Constantine Diogenes, 334, 337, 345, 355, 362, 363
Constantine Doukas, 178, 191
Constantine Gabras, 308
Constantine Gongylios, 237
Constantine Kaballourios, 407
Constantine Kabasilas, 397
Constantine Karantenos, 356, 358
Constantine Leichoudes, 414, 461
Constantine Lips, 180
Constantine Psellos, 461

Corfu, 364
Corinth, Isthmus of, 148, 324
Crete, 30, 35, 45, 46, 47, 70, 95, 108, 112, 127, 147, 149, 157, 169, 178, 185, 195, 207, 229, 236, 240, 241, 243, 245, 246, 289, 292, 483
Cross, wood of the True, 38, 136, 178, 197, 202, 371
Cyclades, 108, 352, 374, 375
Cyprus, 259, 403
Cyril, bishop of Gortyn, 47

Dagisthe, 17
Dalmatia, 50, 142, 143, 384
Dalmatos, monastery of, 193
Damian, chamberlain, eunuch, 127
Damian, count of the stables, 37, 46, 127, 173, 177, 322, 352, 390, 414
Damian, mir of Tyre, 196
Damideia, monastery, 272
Damokraneia, 398
Dandulf, 253
Danielis, 123, 124, 154
David, ruler of the Iberians, 309
David Areianites, 327, 339
Dazimon, 70, 75, 77, 82
Debeltos (Zagora), 92
Deleanos, 384, 385, 386, 388, 389
Denderis, 55, 56
Despotai, monastery, 30
Diabasis, 41, 197
Diabolis, xxx, 335, 339, 340, 341
Diakonitzes, 137
Doge of Venice, 325
Dorostolon, 171, 284, 285, 286, 287, 337, 427
Dorylaion, 76, 140, 279
Dristra, *see* Dorostolon
Dyrrachion, 323, 324, 332, 335, 338, 343, 363, 364, 366, 367, 385, 386, 399, 403, 463

Edessa, 62, 223, 224, 236, 259, 295, 322, 327, 336, 364, 365, 366, 371, 374, 377, 380, 410, 411, 419, 420, 425, 432, 434
eidikos, 98, 468
Eirene, empress, 4, 9, 14, 16, 17, 32, 47, 66, 69, 95, 98, 117, 167, 223, 398
Elaias, monastery at, 66
Elegmoi, monastery, 208, 242, 396
Elephantine prison,, 435
Elephantine gate, 24
Elijah the Tishbite, church of, 152
Ephesos, 100, 133, 240, 357, 381, 384
Ergodotes, 352, 371
Esman, emir of Tarsos, 146
ethnarch, *see* Bryennios
Eudokia, wife of Michael III, 115

Eudokia Baiane, third wife of Leo VI, 175
Euphemios, rebel in Sicily, 48
Euphrosyne, empress, 47
Euripos, 86, 146
Eustathios, droungarios of the fleet, 177
Eustathios, patriarch, 345, 348
Eustathios Argyros, 183, 197
Eustathios Daphnomeles, 325, 339, 341, 356
Eustathios Maleinos, 315
Euthymios, bishop of Sardis, 31
Euthymios, patriarch, 180, 184, 185, 188, 236
Euxine Bridge, 37
Exkoubitores, 15, 192, 197, 210, 359, 394

foderati, corps of the, 11
fire-signals, 109
Forty Martyrs, church of the, 70, 77, 104, 304, 330, 408, 409
Forty-two Martyrs, corps of the, 70, 77
Franks, 80, 144, 231, 232, 236, 400, 436, 440, 442, 452, 457, 460

Galakrenai, monastery, 180
Gastria, monastery, 52, 54, 55, 98
gates of Tarsos and of Mopsuestia, 258
Gazarenos, 44
Gazouro, lake, 10
genikon, 121, 131, 160, 239, 288, 469, 470
geometry, 103
George, logothete of the stratiotikon, 74
George, ruler of Abasgia, 346, 356
George of Abasgia, 367
George Maniakes, xxvii, 109, 360, 361, 365, 366, 374–83, 392, 397, 400–6, 410, 414, 436, 452, 458
George Probatas, 375, 384
Germanicaea, 139
Golden Gate, 8, 108, 121, 135, 194, 249, 259, 344
grain, 54, 89, 211, 233, 248, 258, 266, 267, 273, 281, 287, 307, 337, 378, 387, 442
Great Dyke, 265
Greek fire, 40, 147, 148, 221, 306, 328, 406, 434
Gregoras Iberitzes, 181
Gregory, 37, 39, 40
Gregory Taronites, 321, 324, 387
Gryllos, 111
Gylas, chieftain of the Turks, 231

Hakem, the mad Caliph, *see* Azizios
Harmonianoi, monastery, 165
Hebdomon, 135, 189, 194, 216, 249, 348
Helen Lekapena, wife of Constantine VII, 202, 227, 229, 243
Helladikon, 40, 147, 207, 218
Heraclius, 117, 155, 158, 467

Index

Herakleia, 41, 43, 146, 166, 228, 235
Hervé Frankopoulos, 436, 452, 453
Hetaireiai, 41, 96, 195, 199, 201, 208, 226, 230, 360, 406, 463
Hexakionion, 108
Hidrous, 256
Hieron, 37, 221
Hikanatoi, 77, 196, 197, 203, 222
Himerios, 97, 176, 177, 178, 181, 185, 188, 190
Hippodrome, 27, 44, 70, 74, 82, 86, 95, 96, 106, 131, 149, 176, 189, 192, 242, 243, 245, 264, 265, 269, 394, 404, 435, 470
Hodegetria, church of the, 112
Holy Apostles, church of the, 156, 392, 397
Horkosion, 36
Horologion, 214

Ibatzes, xxix, 335, 340, 386, 389
Iber, 209
Iberia, 44, 209, 309, 321, 322, 347, 349, 356, 357, 379, 409, 410, 412, 413, 421, 422, 423, 430, 432, 442, 444, 470
Iberon, monastery, 356
Iconium, 44, 181
Ignatios, patriarch, 106, 107, 111, 112, 132, 135, 137, 155
Ignatios the Great, 62
Ikmor, 289
Imbrael, Arab ruler, 67, 69, 417
impaled, 43, 44, 93, 149, 194, 231, 319, 327, 375
imperial yacht, 200, 208, 236, 395, 405
Ingerina, wife of Basil I, 127
Iovanesikes, 409
Isaac I Komnenos, 447, 450–66
Ishmael, 12, 72
Italy, xxvi, 50, 99, 137, 142–46, 150, 175, 223, 252, 253, 294, 318, 327, 330, 362, 367, 373, 378, 397, 400, 401, 481
Izeth emir of Tripoli, 240

Jannes, *see* John the Grammarian
Jerusalem, 65, 265, 267, 329, 366, 374
Jew[s], 28, 31
Job, patriarch of Antioch, 35
John I Tzimiskes, 247, 256, 268, 271–98
John the Baptist, church of at Phoberos, 62, 63
John the Baptist, relics of:
  hair of, 259
  hand of, 236
  raiment of, 245
John Chaldos, 359
John Exaboulios, 7, 27
John the Grammarian, patriarch, 61–73, 83–99, 105

John Grapson, 197
John the Hagiopolite, 165
John Hexaboulios, 22, 43
John Kourkouas, xvi, 2, 138, 163, 204, 210, 216, 222
John Lazares, 189
John Philosopher, 440
John Pilatos, 255
John the Orphanotrophos, 364, 368, 370–97, 398, 399, 404
John the syncellos, 58, 60
John Vatatzes, 415, 416
John-Vladisthslav, 339
Joseph Bringas, 239–41, 245–50, 312

Kabala, 44, 181
Kakikios [Gagic], 410
Kalokyros, 174, 215, 265, 275, 276, 282
Kalypa, monastery, 190
kapnikon, 294
Karbeas, 93, 94, 99, 133
Kassiteras, *alias* Theodotos Melissenos, 12, 19, 73
Kastoria, 312, 337, 343
Katakalon Abidelas, 172
Katakalon Kekaumenos, xxi, 382, 394, 407, 422, 436, 444, 450–66
Katakylas, 34, 36, 40, 41, 220
Kataleim, 431
Kedouktos, 41
Kegenes, 428, 435, 437, 439
keramidion, 259
Khazars, 74, 75, 108, 170, 208, 222
Khorossan, 72
Kibyrrhaiote, 47, 70, 176, 177, 303, 347, 374, 376, 404, 407
Kometopoloi, 312
Konstantios, adopted son of Thomas the Slav, 33, 35, 156
Kormates, 72
Kos, island, 48, 407
Kotyaeon, 129, 151, 304
Koulinos, 438
koumparia, 146, 147
Kourtikios, 134, 170, 193, 227, 230, 303, 306
Koutloumous, 419, 442
Kouzenas, monastery, 446
krabra, bovine disease, 242
Krakras, 329, 337, 338
Krambonitai, family of the, 25
Krateros, commander, 47
Krinites Chaldos, 254
Krum, 5, 13, 15, 40, 118, 119
Kyros, 372

Larissa, 313
Latros, mount, 100
Lazaros, iconographer, 63
learning, x, xxvi, 48, 53, 63, 71, 84, 86, 102, 105, 106, 107, 186, 229, 301, 377, 448
Leo I Makelles, 116
Leo V, 4, 15–26, 30, 33, 40, 83
Leo VI, 132, 155, 161–65
Leo Apostypes, 150
Leo Argyros, 92, 207
Leo of Attaleia, 176
Leo Chatzilakios, 177
Leo Choirosphaktes, 171, 179, 193, 359, 362
Leo the Fool, 208, 211
Leo the kouropalates, 271, 279, 288, 304
Leo the Mathematician, 102, 106, 108, 126
Leo Phokas, 197, 199, 203, 204, 225
Leo the protovestiarius, 304
Leo Strabospondylos, 447, 454
Leo Tornikios, 228, 413, 414, 416, 454
Leo of Tripoli, 211
Leomakellion, 449
Lighthouse, church at the, 9
locusts, 215, 367, 372, 376
Longobardia, 66, 143, 150, 151, 153, 168, 223, 241, 253, 325, 330, 376, 378, 383, 402
Louis II, 143
Loulon, 109, 138, 140
Lykaonia, 11

Magnaura, xix, 51, 81, 102, 109, 126, 131, 154, 159, 183, 188, 238
Maiktes, 117
Malagina, 11, 77, 95, 110, 279, 304
Mamme, monastery, 98
Mamoun, 103, 104
mandylion, 224, 377
Mangana, monastery, 444
Manichees, 92–100, 135, 138, 154, 183, 273
Mantineion, monastery, 362
Manuel, 71, 84, 89, 94, 100, 102
Manuel, bishop of Adrianople, 118
Manuel, domestic of the scholae, 82
Manuel, monastery of, 323, 355
Manuel, protospatharios, 222
Manuel, protostrator, 67
Manuel Erotikos, 306
Manzikert, 432, 434, 444, 453
Maria, grandaughter of Romanos I, 215
Maria, wife of John Vladisthlav, 343, 344
Martinakioi, family of the, 73, 127, 166
martyrs' honours for the fallen, 263
Marykatoi, 404
Megathymoi, 388
Mesembria, 152, 197, 198, 215, 218

Messina, 382
Methodios, monk, painter, 91
Methodios, patriarch, 27, 31, 71, 85, 87, 88, 106, 108, 158, 159
Metrophanes, bishop of Smyrna, 87, 169
Michael, son of Anastasios the logothete,
Michael I Rangabe, 4–14
Michael II, 6–15, 86
Michael III, 66, 82–94, 125–30, 142, 166
Michael IV, 366, 368, 370–91
Michael V, 375, 391–97
Michael VI, 448, 449–66
Michael the *akolouthos*, 440, 442, 443
Michael the archangel, church of, 60
Michael Bourtzes, 260, 268, 272, 299, 304, 307, 322, 350, 356, 451
Michael Dokeianos, 400, 401, 439
Michael Iassites, 416
Michael Keroularios, 387
  patriarch, 404
Michael Ouranos, 451
Michael Psellos
  of Andros, 105
Michael Spondyles, 356, 399
Michael, the synkellos, 65
mitatorion, 179, 184, 471
Mokios the martyr, church of St, 157
Monembasia, 153
Monobata, monastery, 391
Monokastanos, monastery, 214
Morocharzianoi, family of the, 85
Mortagon, ruler of the Bulgars, 118
Mousaraph, 358, 361
Myrelaion, monastery, 209, 219, 223, 228, 243
Mytilene, 107, 108, 186, 228, 230, 246, 398, 404

Nasar, 149, 150
Naupaktos, 351
New Church, 158, 168, 251, 398
Nicaea, 84, 117, 119, 306, 308, 392, 447, 458, 459, 461
Nikephoros Ouranos, 327
Nicholas, patriarch, 212
Nicholas Chrysoberges, patriarch, xxvi, 311, 323
Nicholas Mystikos, patriarch, 175, 179, 181, 188, 201
Nikephoros, former priest, 434, 437
Nikephoros, patriarch, 14, 18, 20, 30, 88
Nikephoros I, 4, 11
Nikephoros II Phokas, 233, 240, 243, 245–70, 295
Nikephoros Botaneiates, 461
Nikephoros Karantenos, 364, 365
Nikephoros Komnenos, 336, 349, 350

Nikephoros Ouranos, 310, 318, 322, 324, 327, 344, 451
Nikephoros Phokas the elder, 154, 171, 172, 252
Nikephoros Xiphias, 326, 327, 331, 334, 346, 355
Niketas Glabas, 439
Niketas Ooryphas, droungarios of the fleet, 48, 131, 143, 148
Niketas Pegonites, 338, 367
Niketas Skleros, 170
Niketas Xylinites, 456
Nikoulitzas, 326, 339, 343

Ochrid, 195, 331, 333, 335, 339, 341, 343, 403, 448
Olbianos, 34, 36, 40, 41
Olga, 228, 231, 239, 265, 275, 483
Ooryphas, droungarios, 48, 81
Opsaras, 455
Opsikion, 34, 129, 132, 140, 175, 204, 220, 322, 392, 401, 458, 473
Otto, 231, 236, 276, 294
Ouzer, 182
Oxeia, 67, 351
Oxylithos, 305

Palermo, 49, 252, 256, 380, 383, 402
Panion, 43
Pankaleia, 309
Pankratios, 347, 356, 421
Papias, 27, 130
Patzinaks, 426
Paul the Apostle, church of 13
Paulicians, *see* Manichees
Peganes, 129
Pentapyrgion, 51
Peribleptos, monastery, 370
Pernikos, 329
Persia[ns], 66–69, 117, 310–17, 367, 419
Peter, ruler of the Bulgars, 214–16, 246
Peter the camp commander, 286, 299, 301, 304, 305
Petrion, 117, 133, 157, 204, 250, 356, 363, 393, 395
Petronas, 74, 75, 94, 98, 100, 101, 146, 178, 188
Phatloum, 253, 255, 434
Philomelion, 9, 15, 16, 23, 29, 33
Philopation, 126
Phoenicia, 322
Photeinos, 46
Photios, patriarch, 132, 137, 165, 224
Pinzarach emir of Tripoli, 361, 366
plague, 215, 376, 445
Plateia Petra, 129, 220, 311
Polyeuktos, patriarch, 235, 238, 240, 249, 251, 272, 274
Poson, 101
Pothos Argyros, 207, 208

Poulades, 137
Preslav, 195, 275, 282, 284, 293, 294, 313, 326, 435, 443, 480
Prinkipo, monastery, 47
Prokonnesos, 18, 108, 228, 272
Prokopia, 7, 9
Prokopios, protovestiarios 150
Prokopios Krinites, 170
Prote, island, 9, 11, 27, 30, 224, 227, 230, 288
Prousianos the Bulgar, 351, 355
Pulcheria, daughter of Theophilos, 55

Ragusa, 142, 143, 364, 384
Randolf the Frank, 460
Rentakios, 207
Rhapsakion, 134
Romanos I Lekapenos, 186, 198, 201, 206–24, 230, 235, 242, 252, 254, 345
Romanos II, 228, 237, 239–45, 298
Romanos III Argyros, 354–70
Romanos Boilas, 441
Romanos Kourkouas, 138
Romanos Moseles, 242
Romanos Skleros, 351, 355, 402, 455, 458, 460
Romanos-Gabriel, 334
Russians, xxvi, 107, 108, 159, 221, 232, 265, 266, 273, 275, 276, 277, 281, 282, 284, 285, 286, 287, 289, 291, 293, 319, 330, 367, 376, 401, 404, 405, 407, 410, 449, 457

Sabbatios, 16
Saet, son of Apochaps, 147
Saktikios, 210
Salibas, 373
Samonas, 178, 180, 185
Samosata, 99, 134, 217, 271, 361, 365
Samouch, 451, 457
Samuel, ruler of the Bulgars, 246, 312, 313, 314, 321, 323, 324, 325, 326, 327, 328, 329, 330, 331, 332, 333, 334, 335, 337, 338, 339, 340, 343, 344, 357, 359, 385, 386, 387, 415, 438
Samuel Bourtzes, 439
Saniana, 44
Santabarenos, 161, 165, 166, 167, 168, 192, 206
Sardica/Traditza, 313
Sarkel, 74, 75, 178, 265
Satyros, monastery, 106
Scholae, 41
Scyths, *see* Russians
Semas, son of Tael, 138
Senate, xxvii, 47, 96, 98, 128, 130, 162, 174, 186, 283, 371, 450
Seon, 99
Sergios, 98
Sergios, brother of Photios, 98

Sergios, patriarch, 329, 344
Sergios and Bacchos,
 church of, 155
 monastery of, 85
Sibylline oracle, 23
Sigma, 395
silention, 188
Sinope, 68, 75, 100
Sisinnios, patriarch, 323
Skleraina, 402, 408, 409, 444
Skyla gate, 27, 96
Skyros, 37
Smyrna, 87, 169, 381
Soldan, 142–46
Soudales, 92
Soultzous, 439
Speirai, monastery, 184
Sphendoslav, prince of Kiev, 265
St Andrew, the Apostle, church of, 122
St Diomedes, monastery of, 121
St Euphemia, monastery of, 117, 133, 204
St John the Baptist, *see* John the Baptist
St John the Evangelist, church of, 348
St Mamas, palace, 108, 109, 114,
 130, 209, 223
St Mamas the Martyr, church of, 108, 109
St Mokios, church of, 175
 monastery of, 448
St Phokas' monastery, 87
St Tarasios' monastery of, 184, 431
St Anne, church of, 108
stammering, of Michael III, 33
stampede at the Hippodrome, 265
Staurakios, 4
Stenon, 108, 159, 209, 221, 393
Stephen, patriarch, 133, 169, 216
Stephen Leichoudes, 419
Stephen Lekapenos, 225–8, 246
Stephen Maxentios, 153
Stephen the synkellos, 301
Stephen-Boisthlav 384, 399
Stethatos, 409
Stilianos Zaoutzes, 151, 166, 169, 170, 172, 173,
 174, 175, 193
Stoudios' monastery, 8, 19, 39, 83, 161, 193, 243,
 348, 355, 362, 375, 408
Stylianos Zaoutzes, 166, 202
Stypeiotes, 141, 259
Stypes, 398
Sviatoslav, 231, 275, 276, 282, 284, 285, 286, 287,
 290, 291, 293, 312, 319, 404
Symbatios, 30
Symbatios, logothete of the drome, 113, 128
Symbatios/Constantine,
 son of Leo V, 27, 30, 113, 129, 132, 220, 311

Symeon, ruler of the Bulgars, 169, 190, 194,
 206–15
Symeon the asecretis, 177
Synades Pantaleon, 185
Syracuse, 31, 49, 152, 153, 252, 380

Ta Karianou, 58, 89, 98
Tanais, river, 74
Tangrolipex, 417, 418
Taranto, 151
Tarasios, patriarch, 16, 23
Tarsus, 76, 77, 93, 101, 138, 140, 141, 142, 146,
 183, 197, 232, 240, 243, 257, 258, 259, 260
Tephrike, 93, 133, 137, 140, 183, 457
tetarteron, 263
Thebes, 386
Theodora, daughter of Constantine VIII,
 empress, xxiv, 8, 52, 53, 54, 55, 56, 58, 63,
 67, 77, 80, 82, 84, 85, 90, 92, 96, 97, 98,
 99, 107, 115, 118, 156, 167, 169, 209, 243,
 281, 288, 353, 355, 356, 363, 393, 394, 395,
 397, 404, 408, 445, 447, 448, 450, 451, 452,
 459, 481
Theodora, empress, 53–99, 111, 126
Theodora, wife of John I, 281
Theodora, wife of Romanos I, 206
Theodore Karantenos, 306
Theodore Koupharas, xvi, xxi, xxxii, 2, 8, 14, 19,
 32, 47, 61, 65, 70, 73, 77, 83, 90, 91, 94, 106,
 107, 161, 201, 220, 236, 237, 239, 251, 273,
 292, 293, 305, 459
Theodore Krateros, 70, 76, 77, 80
Theodore the tutor, 202, 204, 225
Theodorokanos, 326, 352, 406
Theodosia, empress, 22
Theodosios Baboutzikios, 27, 30, 67, 81, 113, 153,
 220, 265, 283, 398, 449, 450, 464
Theodotos Melissenos, 17, 19, 73, 93
Theodoulos, archbishop of Bulgaria, 448
Theoktiste, mother of Theodora, 54
Theoktistos, 84, 94, 96
Theoktistos, logothete of the drome, 74, 82, 104
Theoktistos, magister, 14
Theoktistos, prefect of the ink pot, 24
Theoktistos the hetaireiarch, 366
Theophanes and Theodore, *graptoi*, 63, 89
Theophanes Confessor, 18
Theophanes the Metropolitan, of Thessalonike,
 379
Theophano, first wife of Leo VI, 166, 175
Theophano, wife of Romanos II, 4, 9, 166, 173,
 175, 216, 221, 232, 242, 243, 245, 246,
 247, 250, 251, 257, 268, 272, 273, 330,
 356
Theophilitzes, 122, 124, 125

Theophilos, emperor, xviii, xxvi, 19, 21, 30, 31, 33, 38, 40, 46, 47, 48, 51, 52, 53, 54, 55, 56, 57, 58, 60, 61, 63, 64, 66, 67, 70, 71, 75, 77, 81, 82, 83, 85, 89, 95, 100, 102, 111, 119, 122, 127, 131, 143, 208, 210, 222, 229, 247, 293, 323
Theophilos Erotikos, 403
Theophobos, 67–81
Theophylact, first son of Michael I, 9
Theophylact, patriarch, 213, 217, 220, 228, 234
Theophylact Botaneiates, 332
Thermopylae, 344
Thomaites, patriarchal library at, 64
Thomas the priest, 179
Thomas the Slav, 10–15, 30–44
Thracesian, xxxii, 94, 100, 112, 401
trade, 232, 279, 293, 404, 468
Trebizond, 421
Triaditza, 431
Triakontaphyllos, monastery, 362
Triballes, 399
Triphyllioi, 74
Tripolites, *see* John of Attaleia
Trophonios, 87
    Tryphon, patriarch, 217, 219
Turks, xxvi, xxix, xxxii, 77, 78, 79, 93, 170, 215, 220, 223, 231, 265, 276, 315, 336, 416, 417, 419, 420, 422, 424, 426, 429, 430, 434, 442, 447, 451, 452
Tyrach, 429, 436, 443
Tzykanisterion, 394

Valentinian, aqueduct of, 346
Valtzar, son of Kegenes, 435
Varangians, 107, 372, 376, 393, 432, 440, 442, 449
Vaspurakan, 336, 350, 357, 361, 374, 419, 421, 422, 423, 425, 432, 434, 447
vision, ix, 23, 112, 121, 122, 301, 348, 372, 374
Vladimir, 170, 319, 335, 336, 340, 347, 376, 405
Vladislav, 312, 334, 335, 338, 388

Xerolophos, 214

Zapetra, 134
Zilix, *asecretis*, 90
Zochar, 274
Zoe Carbonopsina, fourth wife of Leo VI, 46, 157, 168, 169, 173, 176, 179, 188, 190, 195, 197, 199, 201, 203, 204, 225, 237, 243, 298, 353, 354, 369, 370, 393, 394, 395, 399, 408, 445
Zoe Zaoutza, 173
    second wife of Leo VI, 169
Zoe, empress, 353, 354–70, 379, 391–97, 445

Printed in Great Britain
by Amazon.co.uk, Ltd.,
Marston Gate.